SO-ADP-636

WHAT CRITICS SAY ABOUT
CAMP THE U.S. FOR $5.00 OR LESS: WESTERN STATES

"No glove compartment should be without this book.

More than half of the sites listed in the guide are totally free. In most cases, the savings made by staying in one of the recommended sites more than covers the cost of buying the book. To me, that's good economics!

I find one of the aspects of this book unique and "right on." Those of us who enjoy the outdoor lifestyle recognize that because of maintenance and other costs, free campgrounds are slowly becoming as extinct as the dinosaur. The Smiths remind us all that there are ways we can each help contain costs and at the same time add to our personal enjoyment of the natural environment. Whenever appropriate, each of their listings includes the slogan, "choose a chore." I plan to incorporate their "choose a chore" suggestions each time I enjoy one of nature's beautiful camp sites."　　　　　　　　　　　　　　　—Bob Carter, *RV Today*

"Pack this guide when you travel…and finding a campsite will be easy!"
　　　　　　　　　　　　　　　　　　　　　　—*Great Expeditions*

"This is a fact-packed, no nonsense listing of bargain campgrounds…with detailed information about each campground and its facilities."
　　　　　　　　　　　　　　　　　　　　　　—*Touring America*

"Highly recommended as a good reference source for all public libraries."
　　　　　　　　　　　　　　—Thomas K. Fry, *Library Journal*

"The authors list more than 2,100 campgrounds…that charge $5 or less a night. Also included are lists of facilities, descriptions of terrain, and guides to activities such as fishing and hiking."　　—Richard P. Carpenter, *The Boston Globe*

"Looks like a good way to avoid the popular and overcrowded sites."
　　　　　　　　　　　　　　　—Mary Sarber, *El Paso Times*

"A directory to campsites…for RV users and tent campers both. Lots of detail packed into short listings for each place!"—Colman Andrews, *Los Angeles Times*

"What a great book - a fantastic compilation of valuable information. We checked out our favorite - Kalalau Trail on Na Pali Coast of Kauai, and it was just right."　　　　　　　　—Diana and Bill Gleasner, travel writers and photographers

"This guide is easy to use, and includes tried and true camping tips…. This book is dedicated to anyone looking for a positive experience in the natural environment."　　　　　　　　　　　　　　　　　—*Thriving on Thrift*

▲ ▲

WHAT READERS SAY ABOUT
CAMP THE U.S. FOR $5.00 OR LESS: WESTERN STATES

"We are writing to thank you…. Your book has been an essential part of our trip. It has kept costs down, yet has allowed us to try places we never would have known existed. The day we found your book, we now know, was the real beginning to making our trip possible."   —Elizabeth & David Armstrong

"This is the best book investment we've ever made–and we're eagerly awaiting publication of the eastern edition. *Camp the U.S.* has brought us friends for life!"   —Laurene & Amory Bradford

"Last year, my wife and I toured the West for 5 months in a pickup truck and we sure could have used your book."   —Dave Cannarelle

"We have just purchased *Camp the U.S.* in anticipation of cutting loose next May for a bit less hectic way of life."   —Debbie & John Dowler

"I took a few minutes to peruse your book and you two are to be commended for a great, great job! Not only do I hope to read it soon, I also hope to use it."   —Jane Tappan Elins

"We stayed in over 30 sites you listed and passed through a dozen more. We also shared your book with numerous other campers.
…There were perfect entries where we spent memorable days and nights. I'd like to give special thanks for the listings of Bicentennial in Golden Gate Rec Area, which gave us a way to do San Francisco inexpensively; the backcountry of Whites Sands; Andrew Molera, our base for diving in northern California; Clearwater Falls in Oregon….
I look forward to your book covering the eastern states. The volume of sites you cover is amazing. Keep up the good work."   —LoAnn Halden

"Next February, I'll be leaving to travel the U.S.….I am so excited! And that's why I was so thrilled to find your book! …Thanks for the book!"   —Sunshine Hoehn

"Not only is it easy to use, but its priorities are in the right order."   —Barbara Jones

"My camping equipment is now complete. On the tiny bookshelf rests my bible for the next 18 months - *Camp the U.S. for $5.00 or Less*."   —Frank M. McDonough

"You've done it now. I'm sitting here scratching my head, wondering why I'm sitting behind a desk."   —Kris Nye

CAMP THE U.S. FOR $5.00 OR LESS

Eastern and Midwestern States

MARY HELEN & SHUFORD
SMITH

The
Globe
Pequot
Press

P.O. Box 833, Old Saybrook, CT 06475

Produced by Sally Hill McMillan and Associates, Inc., Charlotte, North Carolina, for The Globe Pequot Press.

Library of Congress Cataloging-in-Publication Data

Smith, Mary Helen.
    Camp the U.S. for $5.00 or less. Eastern and Midwestern States / Mary Helen & Shuford Smith.
        p.   cm.
    "A voyager book."
    Includes index.
    ISBN 1-56440-287-8
    1. Camp sites, facilities, etc.—East (U.S.)—Directories.
2. Camp sites, facilities, etc.—Middle West (U.S.)—Directories.
I. Smith, Shuford. II. Title. III. Title: Camp the U.S. for five dollars or less.
GV191.42.E19S65   1994
647.947409—dc20
                                                                        93-42695
                                                                        CIP

Manufactured in the United States of America

First Edition / First Printing

Contents

Authors

At ages 39 and 43, Mary Helen and Shuford Smith embarked on an odyssey to see North America and, ultimately, the world. For over four years they journeyed with their van, tent, cameras, and computers. With hundreds of nights under the stars and hundreds of miles of trails under their boots, they've received insights into the splendors of our natural world.

They've written newspaper and magazine articles on travel, food, and computers. Soon they hope to publish their first novel as well as the cookbook they've created for any stove top.

With this book, the Smiths invite you to experience more real America. Use their western states book too, and explore what's natural in America.

Introduction

When we were asked to write this series, we did a lot of soul-searching. We realized here was an opportunity to write the guides we had wanted while we were camping the North American continent. To write the books, however, meant we would have to make a few changes in our nomadic lifestyle–including giving up travel for a couple of years. Obviously, we decided compiling America's best camping values for thousands of other campers was worth our time and effort.

This book is dedicated to **all** campers looking for **positive** experiences in the **natural** environment–whether they're adventurous RVers or tenters. That includes fishermen, hikers, backpackers, bicyclists, boaters, mountain climbers, skiers–an endless number of people with as many styles of camping.

We share tips we've observed and learned in our years of camping. These ideas are rooted in common sense and deep concern for our land and our world.

We've gathered the information on camping America's public lands from numerous sources. We've made an honest attempt to be as up-to-date and as accurate as possible.

To be included in this book, a campground must meet these criteria: cost of $5 or less; access by vehicle or short walk; and provision of at least one facility such as water spigot, pit toilet, or picnic table. Campgrounds located within national and state parks/recreation areas are listed under the park's name. All listings appear alphabetically within each state. For space reasons, we've eliminated most group camps, horse camps, long distance boat-ins and hike-ins. All the listed campgrounds are actual places to camp–not just wide spots beside the road.

We mention backcountry opportunities in each state's introduction to public lands camping as well as in appropriate campground listings. These areas offer no manmade facilities, but give the camper greater insight into the natural world.

With this first eastern and midwestern states edition of the series, we introduce a campground locator chart to help you find nearby listed campgrounds. Too, use the index of nearest towns at the back of this guide to help you discover almost 2,000 places to camp.

Look at this book as a way to get in touch with the real America. Pack it along with your adventurous spirit and go camping. Hopefully, you'll discover our information rings true to your personal experiences.

We welcome your comments and questions. If you want to be on our mailing list for future publications, write us through our mail service:

Mary Helen & Shuford Smith
36642 West Jefferson Avenue
Dade City, FL 33525

▲ ▲

HOW TO READ LISTINGS

Each state begins with a State Map and related Campground Locations Chart plus an overview of Public Lands Camping.

Alphabetical Listings follow a form:

CAMPGROUND NAME

Administrator
Information Phone Number
State Map Coordinates
Directions
Fee

Season
Sites
Facilities
Natural Description
Recreational Opportunities
Concerns
Altitude

Alongside the handy Locator Map, find the *Administrator* and *Information Phone Number* as well as official *State Map Coordinates*. In *Directions*, NEAREST TOWNS appear in all capital letters (and metric distances in parentheses). Whenever road conditions create hazards for vehicles, they're indicated. (If you're driving a RV or pulling a trailer, be sure to check for restrictions on type of sites as well as concerns). Also in directions, find nearby campground options in parentheses.

Fee is in bold type whether it's **FREE** or up to **$5**. These days free camping choices are becoming fewer because of maintenance costs. There are ways we campers can contain costs and add to our enjoyment of natural environments. When a listing includes the slogan "choose a chore," take the initiative to pick up litter, clean fire rings, etc. (See page 5.)

Season varies with location. If off-season camping is allowed, that's

indicated. If it's dry camping (no drinking water), that's stated too. Opening and closing dates are provided.

In *Sites*, find out how many and what types. They may be undesignated, a combination of tent and RV, or tent-only sites due to topography. Rangers tell if sites are scattered or close as well as open or screened.

Under *Facilities*, basics are listed first: water then toilets. Whenever possible, specifics are given (such as hand water pumps or flush toilets) to aid your decision-making. Sometimes you'll find improvements such as boat ramps, playgrounds, and pay phones. Generally, trash cans are available. If not, that's indicated in concerns.

Natural Description gives you an idea of what to expect when you get there—a creek or a lake, pine trees or no trees, mountain or prairie.

Recreational Opportunities vary with location. This information helps you decide whether you want to spend one night or longer. Fishing and hiking are available at most campgrounds. Other opportunities such as swimming, boating, and cross-country skiing are mentioned too.

Concerns list other awareness areas. If there's no drinking water, that's marked with a capital NO so you can adequately provision yourself. Rangers have indicated restrictions on length of stay and length of vehicle as well as problems with insects and noise. In almost every eastern and midwestern campground, **pets are required to be leashed at all times.**

Last, but not least, *Altitude* is noted wherever that information has been provided.

Happy camping!

▲ ▲

ABBREVIATIONS

Besides accepted abbreviations for directions (such as N), geography (Mt), measurement (ft), months (Aug), roads (Hwy), states (VT), we use these from various governmental agencies:

ATV	All Terrain Vehicle
CA	Conservation Area
CCB	County Conservation Board
COE	Corps of Engineers
CR	County Road
DEC	Department of Environmental Conservation
DNR	Department of Natural Resources
FH	Forest Highway
FM	Farm to Market Road
FR	Forest Road
FWA	Fish and Wildlife Area
I-	Interstate
NF	National Forest
NG	National Grassland
NHP	National Historic Park
NL	National Lakeshore
NP	National Park
NPS	National Park Service
NS	National Seashore
NRA	National Recreation Area
NWR	National Wildlife Refuge
RA	Recreation Area
SF	State Forest
SFL	State Fishing Lake
SHP	State Historical Park
SHS	State Historic Site
SP	State Park
SRA	State Recreation Area
TVA	Tennessee Valley Authority
WA	Wildlife Area
WMA	Wildlife Management Area

THE STATE OF
PUBLIC LANDS CAMPING

Have you noticed–
- campground fees increase dramatically?
- significant dollar differences between one campground and another with comparable facilities?
- addition of entrance fees, motor vehicle fees, and utility fees whether used or not?

In recent years, why have we Americans been asked to pay more money to visit and camp on lands already purchased with past tax dollars? What does it cost to surround ourselves with nature instead of four walls, to create a modern version of what our ancestors enjoyed free for millions of years? What does it really cost to perform the service of maintaining public campgrounds?

It's easy to complain. It's harder to define the roots of the problem and to determine solutions. From our experience traveling the continent for almost five years, we've seen a deterioration in quality at many public lands sites. In many places, campers are getting less natural beauty, facilities, or service while paying more dollars. From our experience of creating this database of public lands campgrounds in all 50 states, we see remarkable differences in land use philosophies between geographic regions. Too, we find discrepancies among federal, state, and local government agencies. While we've been working on this eastern-midwestern states camping guide, the US Congress has passed a law releasing the US Army Corps of Engineers from maintaining at least one free campground on each manmade lake. Until this summer, citizens had been guaranteed access to some recreation without regard to their economic status. It's as if we're seeing the passing of an ethic. No longer does our federal government promise recreational access to all citizens regardless of their financial abilities. It's a logical question to ask: as federal public land camp fees increase, will camp fees increase at state, county, and city levels also?

What we've figured out is that a vision for camping on public lands is missing. Recreational camping is a rather recent phenomenon. Only in the past century, has the automobile caused great inroads onto our public lands, allowing almost unlimited access. Only since World War II with aircraft technology applied to recreational vehicles, have trailers and motor homes become common sights on roads and in campgrounds. Only now is the noise emanating from hordes of people and their engines, generators, and air conditioners being considered a problem. Only now is quiet being considered a natural resource.

It's as if many overworked and underappreciated park administrators have become caught up in keeping everyone happy. These managers have been so busy applying the technological possibilities of plumbing and wiring that, as a group, they've lost sight of why parks were created. In other words, without an ethos from the top down on which to base decisions, many park personnel have fallen into reactionary rather than visionary management. It's time for public lands administrators to ask how parks can help people escape from stressful environments and "re-create" themselves.

We campers must accept responsibility for the problems too. We're the ones making the complaints about lack of paving or facilities. We have to come to

▲ ▲

terms with what we want our public lands to be. When we go camping, do we need all the modern conveniences of home or can we benefit from more primal circumstances?

What can we campers do to control costs? One idea is to carry out the "choose a chore" concept to help maintain free campgrounds. Another idea is to volunteer time as campground hosts at developed campgrounds. Other volunteer categories include assistance in campground and trail maintenance, forest and wildlife management, computers and office work, photography and design, as well as interpretation and education.

How can we citizens guarantee access to public lands to everybody? As individuals, we can exert pressure on government agencies to keep fees and passes affordable. We must call attention to instances of price ratcheting and of competing with private campground resorts. We must demand designations of distinctly different areas for various types of campers. In other words, within each park, distinct areas must be set aside—wilderness opportunities for backpackers seeking solitude, a natural area with auto access for tent/small RV campers, and, perhaps, one area with hookups for recreational vehicles. Then, each user's camping fee can reflect the cost of the addition and maintenance of manmade facilities.

As one of many campers enjoying America's greatest recreational pastime, make your wishes known. Call or write your representatives on the federal, state, and local levels. Let these legislators know that you feel our governments' guaranteeing the citizens' right to recreation is important. Encourage legislators to distinguish between user fees for ranchers, miners, and loggers who are engaged in exploiting our public lands for personal profit and user fees for citizens simply enjoying the land for recreation. Remember the bumper sticker, "When the people lead, the leaders will follow."

▲ ▲

CHOOSE A CHORE

Here are some ideas on how to keep free campgrounds free:

▲ Pick up litter ▲
▲ Clean fire rings ▲
▲ Untie ropes from trees ▲
▲ Remove wax from tables ▲
▲ Tighten loose screws ▲
▲ Tidy toilets ▲
▲ Leave a roll of toilet paper ▲
▲ Ask if ranger needs any assistance ▲

6

▲ ▲

ACKNOWLEDGMENTS

This book series is extracted from a database we've constructed of campgrounds–the first comprehensive public lands camping database. We've scoured every state's tourist information, we've ordered hundreds of maps and other materials, and we've mailed thousands of questionnaires then compiled the returns. To assemble this eastern and midwestern states edition, we sent out 4,000 questionnaires and received back 68%. Then, if we had incomplete information, we called the campground administrators.

We thank all the public servants who helped us gather the information for our database. We thank readers of our western states book who asked questions and communicated their excitement. Too, we thank family and friends who encouraged us:

Karen & Henry Alexander
Al Armstrong
Elizabeth & David Armstrong
Dr David Bang & Staff
Betty Bertrand
Virginia & David Bint
Dr Rebecca Borders & Staff
Laurene & Amory Bradford
Shirley Bragg
Carol & Frank Bremer
Fan Brooke
Marge & Lenny Bruss
Julie Bryant
Dave Cannarella
Betty & Russ Carpenter
Karen Carter
Sandy McAvoy & Alan Christensen
Bob Cowan
Dottie Aldrich & Carolyn Cypher
Paula & Bob Deyoe
Connie & Steve Dieleman
Debbie & John Dowler
Jane Tappan Elins
Jane Faircloth
Charles Fertig
Ellen & Bill Fiero
Amy Gill
Diana & Bill Gleasner
Triona Gogarty
Al Gore
Joyce & Nelson Graves
Pat Grediagin
Barbara & Marvin Greenberg
David Gressette & Old Post Office Staff
Dominique Guillet de la Brosse
LoAnn Halden
Janet & Gordon Hildebrant
David Hirsch
Sunshine Hoehn

Olive & Manuel Holland
Charlotte & Robert Hope
Sherry Browne & Buck Howland
Danny Hoyt
Island Video Crew
Deborah & Victoria Joy
Sandy Katz
Karen Lindsay
Evelyn & Frank Lloyd
John & Norma Long
Frank McDonough
Marsha & Charles Milford
Nathalie & Charles Neal
Rolfe Neill
Kris Nye & Eureka! Tents
James Page Brewery Crew
Jim Parkhurst
Nancy Parks
Ima Dale & Arvil Reynolds
Suzanne & Dustan Rine
Carolyn Bovaird & Matt Ross
Gloria & Hub Schleicher
Vicky & Jay Semple
Deborah & Robert Sesco
Barbara & Jim Shanks
Gene Sloan
Pat Soares
Mary Jackson & Bill Staton
Deborah & Jack Streich
Russ Stuttle
Lucia Summers
Kay & Lewis Tanno
Connie Toops
Frances & Jim Tupper
Nancy Urbanski
Libby Ward
Sarah Wicker
Debi & Bill Winski
Sandy & Herb Wright

ABC's of Camping

911: This emergency telephone number works across most of United States.

Animals: Bears, rodents, and other furry creatures are attracted to campsites by food. Keep food stored in tamper-proof containers out of sight (car trunk) or out of reach (two balanced bags hanging from tree limb).

Attitude: Keep an "Are we having fun yet?" frame-of-mind. Whatever the situation, try not to panic.

Backpacking: Get away from it all. Learn how little is necessary to survive and how much is just "nice." High on the essentials list are water, waterproof matches, food, map, and compass.

Bathing: If showers are unavailable, hang waterbag in sunny place to absorb rays and heat water. Rinse off with plain water or, for spot cleanup, use baby wipes. You'll sleep better; your sleeping bag/linens will stay fresher.

Birds: Observe birds and other animals. Never feed them as you may become their executioner. Research has proved feeding birds and other animals interferes not only with their instinct but also with their ability to survive. Animals accustomed to eating human junk foods are less likely to live through winter. They absorb their insulating layer of body fat before winter is over and natural foods become available.

Blanket, Space: This lightweight, coated-on-one-side piece of Mylar is an example of beneficial spinoffs from space technology. Take along space blanket when hiking. In case of sudden hypothermia, wrap individual in blanket (reflective side in) to conserve body heat. If day gets too hot, rig space blanket as reflective tarp. Keep one in your tent nightsack. If weather turns cold during night, spread it (reflective side down) over sleeping bag to trap body heat.

Books: Guidebooks add to your understanding and enjoyment of the world around you. Select one or two well-recommended books so you're not overburdened with information or weight. Well-paced novels can also add to your "great escape."

Budget: Whether trip is weekend jaunt or extended tour, it pays to plan your finances. Allocate money for necessities such as food and any camp fees before niceties such as that raft trip or hot air balloon ride.

Bug Zapper: Leave this disruptive item at home.

Choose a chore: See page 5.

Clothing: Learn art of layering. It allows garments to perform more than one duty to keep you comfortable. Dressing in layers has other benefits: you buy less and you pack less. Always prepare for the worst-case weather scenario.

COE Projects: Until 1993, federal law required one free campground per project. Ask, if you don't see it on project map. It may still be available.

▲ ▲

Compass: Carry one (and use it) when you're hiking.

Cooking Pots & Pans: Pots that nest inside one another take up less space (that valuable commodity when camping or traveling). If you're concerned about weights and oxides, purchase lightweight stainless steel. A pressure cooker makes sense while camping (as long as you're not backpacking). It can turn out an entire meal in a half-hour whether bean pot or three-course chicken dinner.

Dishes: Carry reusable cups, dishes, and flatware. Think twice about buying paper plates, plastic forks, and spoons. These items really aren't "disposable." They're extravagant wastes of world's resources. When washing dishes outdoors, use that indispensable waterbag to rinse dishes. After drying, place utensils out of animals' reach.

Documents: While traveling in US, Americans need only their driver's licenses. Travelers from other countries also need visas or passports.

Ethics: Here is where golden rule applies. If you take care of plants, animals, objects, and structures as you wish you or your property were treated, there would be no need for any other rules or regulations.

Exercise: Make exercise a natural part of your day. Take a walk, bike ride, paddle, or swim. If it's raining, perform stretches and isometrics in your tent or RV.

Fires: If you must have a campfire, build a small one. Burn fiber egg cartons, cereal boxes—any paper or wood product. Never burn plastics, styrofoam, glass, metal, or batteries. Make certain your fire is totally out before you leave it.

First-Aid (Basic Kit): In alphabetical order, pack aloe cream for sun or wind burn; antibiotic (such as penicillin or erythromycin) to treat infections; antihistamine (such as *Benadryl*) for respiratory problems; aspirin to lower fever; band-aids/bandages; DEET (diethylmeta-toluamide) to prevent mosquito bites; hydrocortisone cream (such as *Cortaid*) to relieve skin irritations; rubbing alcohol to clean cuts; and *Sting-eze* (if ice is unavailable) to treat insect bites.

Fishing: What a rewarding way to let your mind wander! While you solve world's problems or simply get lost in wonders of nature, you might catch dinner!

Flashlight: To prevent accidental draining of batteries, rubber-band flashlight switch "off."

Focus: Choose interest area if you're planning extended trip–bird sightings, battlefields, emigration trails, Native American petroglyphs....

Foods: Buy fresh, locally-grown foods whenever possible. Not only do they taste better and have more food value, but also they're less expensive. Store all food items carefully against pests as well as spoilage.

Footwear & Footcare: Sandals, shoes, and boots that fit can make or break you. It's important to choose comfortable as well as appropriate footwear. For example, in camp change from hiking boots to moccasins or sandals to avoid unnecessary trampling of vegetation. If you're sweating or blistering, take off your socks and shoes, and bathe your feet in rubbing alcohol. Another way to avoid blisters is to wear two pairs of socks: a thin pair next to your feet with a thicker pair on top.

▲ ▲

Guns: Statistics indicate—carry no guns.

Hiking: Your feet set the best pace for your mind to absorb the wonders of nature.

Hunting: Over America's last three hundred years, hunting has evolved from survival to sport. Now as population centers encroach on country's last wild places, hunting must be carefully regulated.

Insects: Ants, bees, chiggers, flies, hornets, mosquitos, no-see-ems, scorpions, ticks, and wasps can make you miserable no matter where you are. Practice avoidance: shun scented soaps and lotions; camp in breezy locations; wash dishes and pack away food after eating; check shoes, clothes, and linens before using; dress appropriately (for example, to avoid mosquitos or ticks, wear light-colored long sleeves and pants); use DEET sparingly. If bitten, remove insect. Wash area with soap and water; then cool with ice, if available. In case of swelling or itching, take antihistamine (such as *Benadryl*).

Itineraries: Let someone (friend, family member, or ranger) know your plans, including arrival place and time.

Kids: #1 rule is keep your sense of humor. #2 rule is pack plenty of snacks that can become pleasurable distractions as well as energizers. #3 rule is dress children in bright colors so they're easy to spot outdoors. Child carriers allow babies who can hold up their heads to accompany you on walks and hikes. Carry baby gently. Plan on stops for diaper changes, feedings, and stretches. Check baby's body temperature and adjust clothing frequently. If child is toddling, expect any foot travel to take about one hour per half-mile. Plan accordingly and carry as little as possible, in case you have to pick up child. Older children love to bring along friends on day trips or overnight excursions. For overnights, pack separate tent for them. They'll love "responsibility"; you'll love relative peace.

Knots: Take time to learn basic knots. They'll save you much frustration in rainstorms or windstorms.

Lantern, Makeshift: Place candle in empty tuna can to catch melting wax.

Litter: Carry litter bag to pick up trash marring natural beauty of landscape.

Mail: When you're out for extended time, arrange for family member or friend to forward your mail. Ask individual to number each piece (for example, 1 of 10) then forward all "General Delivery" to appointed place. Specify when to forward. Allow one week for all items to arrive.

Maps: These necessary items help take frustration out of travel. You can figure out where you want to go and how to get there. Carry official state maps in your vehicle and US Geological Survey (USGS) topographical maps in your backpack.

Medical Information: Wear any medical identification bracelets/tags and know yourself (for example, when you last had tetanus shot).

Messages: At least one no-fee *Gold MasterCard* offers free telephone message service.

Money: This commodity is relatively easy to obtain this day and time. Automatic teller machine networks crisscross the country; advances on charge cards are available at most banks; many auto club members can purchase free travelers checks.

▲ ▲

Nature: Take only pictures; leave only footprints. Show consideration to all living things you see. Picking wildflowers and feeding or capturing wild creatures for pets is forbidden–it's hard to improve on Mother Nature's schemes. (Too, never buy souvenirs made from endangered animals.)

Moon & Stars: In our electric world, we've lost familiarity with these stellar objects. Buy star chart to get reacquainted. Learn phases of moon.

Nightsack: Pack books, flashlight and batteries, tissues, baby wipes and powder, space blanket–all those little necessities–into one carryall.

Nocturnal Animals: Meet wide range of animals that come out at night.

Observation: Try to use all your senses to identify all that surrounds you.

Options: Keep your eyes open to more efficient ways of doing anything and everything. Remember that goal of camping is to enjoy it–not to work at it.

Organization: Develop systems for loading your backpack, your automobile, your RV.... For example, carry heavy items in backpack near your pelvis and back for balance. Many campers have adapted almost-indestructible milk crates to their needs. Each crate serves a different purpose such as pantry, his or her clothes.... Designate specific places for water bottles, maps, first-aid kit, raingear.... Always put any item back in place so you can find it when you need it.

Passes: Purchasable Golden Eagle Pass allows you into unlimited number of national park service locations. Golden Age Pass qualifies anyone over age 62 to camping and entrance discounts. Golden Access Pass guarantees disabled individuals to free entrance to national park sites. Check out state and local passes too.

Pets: Pets can create problems when traveling. If you must bring one, be prepared to make allowances for needs of other people and animals as well as your pet. **Keep pet leashed.**

Photography: Here is another focus that allows you to enjoy your trip again and again.

Poisonous Plants: Know how poison ivy, oak, and sumac look to avoid them. Pack cortisone cream in case you have a close encounter.

Quiet: Now recognized as a resource in need of protection in many parks, rules have been made to restrain generators and other noise during specific hours. If fellow camper is noisy, approach immediately and courteously request quiet.

Recreational Equipment: Keep it simple. How about a frisbee?

Rules & Regulations: Take responsibility to determine if there are any specifics beyond golden rule.

RV Ethics: Use generator sparingly–never at night. Discharge gray/black water at dump stations–never at campsite.

Safety: Always consider safety of others as well as self.

Sanitation: If toilets are unavailable, walk as far away from camp or trail as feasible. Dig small hole at least four inches deep. Afterward, fill hole with soil and tamp down. Cover with large rock or branch to keep animals from digging. Carry plastic bags for toilet paper, sanitary napkins, and tampons.

Shelters (Tents, Screenhouses, RVs): Select best option according to your needs–not salesperson's.

▲ ▲

Site Selection: In campgrounds, choose inside curves along roads to avoid headlights. Look around. Avoid low places for water drainage and never trench area. Look overhead to avoid dead tree limbs. To hold your place, leave large but inexpensive item–for example, a lawn chair. In backcountry, select site 200 ft or more from trails, lakes, and streams and hide your camp from view.

Sleeping Gear (Pads, Bags, Liners, Pillows): Make yourself comfortable. A washable liner acts as a sheet and protects your sleeping bag.

Smoking: If you must, dispose of matches, ashes, and cigarette butts in responsible manner–they're litter as well as fire hazards.

Snakes: Remember that snakes tend to shy away from humans.

Solar Cell Panel: When stopped, use this environmentally sound way to power appliances–operates without gas or oil and creates no noise.

Stoves: To lessen site impact, use campstove instead of fire. Select reliable model and take care of it for dependable service.

Styrofoam: Avoid purchasing Styrofoam containers whenever possible. These containers cannot be recycled, creating hazards to our environment.

Sun Protection: As world's ozone layer depletes and allows ultraviolet rays to harm skin, you must take steps to protect yourself and, especially, your children. When sun is bright, wear hats or sunscreen or both. Pay special attention to noses.

Telephone Cards: These pieces of plastic come in handy at pay phones. Make sure you have long-distance carrier's customer service number for any assistance.

Time: Take your time, but know when to go. Be aware of time zones and daylight savings time changes.

Tools & Spare Parts: Keep it simple–for example, a hubcap works as a shovel.

Trails: Stay on trails. Avoid trampling fragile undergrowth or causing erosion by taking switchbacks.

Transportation: Choose your wheels–bicycle, motorcycle, car, RV–and maintain for reliable service. Consider options of boat, plane....

Trash: Purchase recyclable or refillable containers. Avoid butane cylinders, sterno cans, disposable lighters, and razors. Also, avoid individually packaged items such as cereal and juice boxes, cheese singles, or fruit and pudding cups. Use wax paper instead of plastic for food-wrap. Wax paper burns cleanly–plastic doesn't. Make sure your garbage doesn't end up in ocean, lake, creek, gully, or side of road. Pack it in; pack it out.

Volunteer: Get involved in special places and projects. Often, you receive as much as you give.

Water: Importance of water cannot be underestimated. Carry and drink plenty. A multi-gallon container allows freedom to camp where water is unavailable–often saving you a camp fee. If backpacking and collecting water from streams and lakes, carry water filter or purifying tablets.

Weather: Watch the weather so you can decide when to pack up, tie down, or bring extra gear inside tent or RV.

▲ ▲

ALABAMA
CAMPGROUND LOCATIONS

▶ ▶ Find location on facing page map grid. ▶ ▶
▼ ▼ Locate area campgrounds on these page numbers. ▼ ▼

Alabama

Grid conforms to official state map. For your copy, call (800) 252-2262
or write Bureau of Tourism & Travel, 401 Adams Ave, Montgomery, AL 36104.

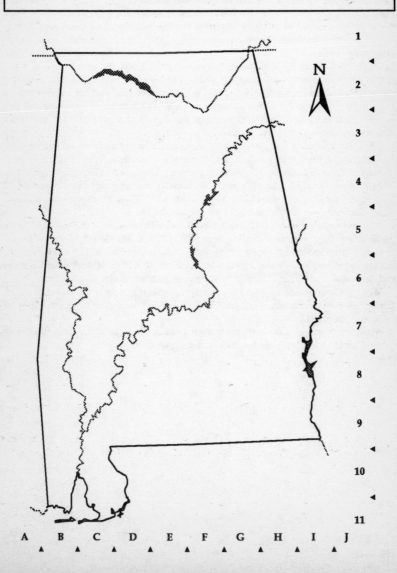

N

1 2 3 4 5 6 7 8 9 10 11

A B C D E F G H I J

▲ ▲

PUBLIC LANDS CAMPING

Alabama, the state of surprises, boasts everything from mountain splendors to seashore delights. Indeed, most of the naturally beautiful recreation areas on public lands are in the Appalachian foothills, along rivers winding their way to Mobile Bay and the Gulf of Mexico, or on the white-sand coast.

The **US Forest Service** has four national forests in Alabama: Bankhead, Talladega, Tuskegee, and Conecuh. Both the 180,000-acre Bankhead and the 377,000-acre Talladega national forests extend across the highlands of the state. Tiny 11,000-acre Tuskegee National Forest (NF) exists in the piedmont or "Plantation Country." The 83,000-acre Conecuh NF lies in the swampy wiregrass approaching the Gulf Coast and Florida border. Two wildernesses preserve special places in Alabama's national forests: Sipsey within Bankhead NF protects scattered patches of virgin hardwoods; Cheaha in Talladega NF offers Appalachian peak experiences. Look for endangered wildlife making homes in these areas: red-cockaded woodpecker, bald eagle, and flattened musk turtle. In the Bankhead NF, float along the national wild and scenic river, Sipsey Fork. In the Talladega NF, motor along the 23-mile Talladega Scenic Drive that follows Horse Black Mountain. While camping at developed campgrounds in Alabama's national forests, expect to pay between $3.00–$10.00.

US Army Corps of Engineers (COE) maintains campgrounds on lakes along the Alabama River, Black Warrior River, and Tennessee–Tombigbee Waterway. Enjoy such manmade lakes as Claiborne, Coffeeville, Dannelly, Demopolis, George and Andrews, Holt, Warrior, West Point, and Woodruff. COE camp fees can range from free to $16.00 with electricity. Too, the **Tennessee Valley Authority** (TVA) offers six campgrounds along the Tennessee River. Basic TVA campsites cost $8.00.

Improved campsites at 18 **Alabama State Parks** (SP) range from $8.00–$12.00. State parks advertising primitive camping from $3.00 to $8.00 include Blue Springs, Buck's Pocket, Chattahoochee, Cheaha, Chewacla, Chickasaw, Claude D Kelley, DeSoto, Florala, Joe Wheeler, Lake Guntersville, Monte Sano, Paul M Grist, Rickwood Caverns, and Roland Cooper. Frank Johnson has camping facilities under construction.

Mobile County offers a $5.00 primitive experience in the bottomlands of Chickasabogue. Find swamps and creeks with sandbars amid pine trees, moss-draped oaks, and magnolias.

Wherever you decide to camp, bring your camera. From delicate spring flowers to colorful autumn leaves, Alabama puts on a surprising show.

ABBIE CREEK PARK

COE (912) 768-2516
State map: H9
From COLUMBIA, head N on
AL 95. Bear Right (N) on
CR 97.
FREE so choose a chore.
Open All Year.
Undesignated scattered, open sites.
Central faucet, pit toilets, tables, fire
rings, boat ramp.
Next to Lake George W Andrews.
Boat or fish.
14-day limit.
125 ft (38 m)

BELLS LANDING PARK

COE (205) 682-4244
State map: D8
From CAMDEN, drive S on
AL 41 for 16 miles (25.6 k).
Turn Right (W) at sign.
(Nearby East Bank costs $12.)
FREE so choose a chore.
Open All Year.
11 close, open sites. Chemical toilets,
tables, fire rings, boat ramp.
In woods adjacent to backwaters of
Alabama River.
Walk nature trail. Fish. Do nothing.
NO water. High water possible. Hunting
in season.
40 ft (12 m)

BELMONT PARK

COE (205) 289-3540
State map: C7
From DEMOPOLIS, travel W
on US 80 about 15 miles
(24 k). Turn Right (N) on
AL 28 for 2 miles (3.2 k). Turn Right (E)
on CR 23 and drive 15 miles (24 k).
FREE so choose a chore.
Open All Year.
Undesignated close, open sites.
Central faucet, chemical toilets, tables,
fire rings, grills, boat ramp.
On gentle, wooded slope next to
Tombigbee River.
Boat, fish, or just enjoy seclusion.
14-day limit. Hunting in season.

BLUE CREEK

COE (205) 553-9373
State map: C5
From TUSCALOOSA, head N
on AL 69 about 20 miles
(32 k). Turn Right (E) on
CR 38 and follow signs to end of road.
(Nearby Deerlick Creek costs $10.)
FREE so choose a chore. Open All Year.
25 scattered, open, tent sites.
Pit toilets, tables, grills, boat ramp.
On top of ridge overlooking Holt Lake.
Boat or fish. Relax.
NO water.

BLUE SPRINGS SP

(205) 397-4875
State map: G8
From CLIO, drive SE on
AL 10 for 7 miles (11.2 k).
Turn Right (S).
$5; $11 improved. Open All Year.
70 (20 tent-only) scattered, open sites.
Central faucet, flush toilets, showers,
dump station, electric hookups, tables,
grills, pool.
In pine thicket on hill.
Swim. Hike.
14-day limit.

BRUSHY LAKE

Bankhead NF (205) 489-5111
State map: D3
From MOULTON, head S on
AL 33 for 15 miles (24 k). Bear
Left (SE) on CR 63 for .5 mile
(800 m). Again, bear Left (E) on FR 245
(Mt Olive Rd). Continue 5 miles (8 k).
$3. Open All Year.
13 close, open sites. Central faucet, pit
toilets, tables, fire rings, boat ramp.
In forest next to lake.
Hike. Fish or boat (no gas motors).
14-day limit.

CHEAHA SP

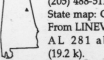

(205) 488-5111
State map: G3
From LINEVILLE, travel N on
AL 281 about 12 miles
(19.2 k).

$5; $11 improved. Open All Year.
Undesignated or 73 developed sites.
Central faucet, flush toilets, showers,
dump station, electric hookups, tables,
fire rings.
In wooded region atop mountain.
Hike to appreciate scenery. Swim or fish.
14-day limit.
2400 ft (720 m)

CHICKASABOGUE PARK
(205) 452-8496
State map: B10
In MOBILE, take I-65 N to
Exit 13 W (Industrial
Blvd/AL 158). Go to Shelton
Beach Rd S and turn Left (signed). Drive
about 4 miles (6.4 k) to blinking light
and turn Left (E) on Whistler St. Go to
Aldock Rd and turn Left. (Nearby
Dauphin Island costs $11.)
$5; $8 electric; $10 full; winter rate;
reservations accepted at (205) 452-8496
for an additional $5.
Open All Year.
61 (10 tent-only) close, open sites.
Water at every site, flush toilets,
showers, dump station, electric hookups,
tables, fire rings, grills, boat ramp,
laundry, store, rentals, pay phone.
In dense wood with some privacy.
Hike and bike to enjoy natural areas.
Swim, canoe, or fish. Play frisbee golf.
14-day limit.
25 ft (8 m)

CHICKASAW SP
(205) 295-8230
State map: C7
From LINDEN, drive N on
US 43 for 4 miles (6.4 k).
$3; $8 improved.
Open All Year.
Undesignated or 3 developed sites.
Central faucet, flush toilets, dump
station, electric hookups, tables, grills.
In rolling woodland.
Find threatened red-cockaded wood-
pecker. Walk nature trails. Hike. Relax.
14-day limit.

COLEMAN LAKE
Talladega NF (205) 463-2272
State map: G4
From HEFLIN, take US 78 N
for 6 miles (9.6 k). Turn Left
(NW) on FR 553 and go
8.5 miles (13.6 k). Turn Right (NE) on
FR 500 and travel 1.5 miles (2.4 k). (Also
see Pine Glen).
$5. Open Apr 30–Nov 30.
39 close, open, tent sites.
Central faucet, flush toilets, showers,
tables, grills, fire rings, boat ramp.
In hardwood and pine next to 20-acre
lake in Choccolocco Wildlife Area.
Enjoy spring and fall weather. Hike to
view wildlife and take photos. Swim,
boat, or fish.
14-day limit.
1200 ft (360 m)

CORINTH
Bankhead NF (205) 489-5111
State map: D3
From DOUBLE SPRINGS,
drive E on US 278 for 4 miles
(6.4 k). Turn Right (S) on
FR 113 and travel 3 miles (4.8 k).
$5, may increase after renovation.
Open Apr 1–Oct 31.
70 close, open sites.
Central faucet, flush toilets, dump
station, tables, fire rings, boat ramp.
Next to Lewis Smith Lake.
Swim, boat, ski, or fish. Hike or
mountain bike.
14-day/22-ft limits.

DAMSITE PARK

COE (205) 289-3540
State map: C6
From EUTAW, take AL 14 E
for 1 mile (1.6 k). Turn Right
(S) on CR 39 and go 4 miles
(6.4 k). (Also see Lock 7 East).
FREE so choose a chore. Open All Year.
6 scattered, open sites.
Pit toilets, tables, fire rings, boat ramp.
In open grassy spot with few large trees.
Fish or boat.
NO water. 14-day limit.

▲ ▲

HARDRIDGE CREEK PARK

COE (912) 768-2516
State map: H8
From FORT GAINES, GA,
drive W across river then bear
Right on CR 97 (Old River
Rd). Continue 2 miles (3.2 k).
FREE so choose a chore. Open All Year.
Undesignated scattered, open sites.
Central faucet, pit toilets, tables, fire
rings, boat ramp, shelter.
Next to Walter F George Lake.
Boat or fish.
14-day limit.
200 ft (60 m)

JENNINGS FERRY

COE (205) 289-3540
State map: C6
From EUTAW, travel 5 miles
(8 k) E on AL 14. Pass bridge.
Turn Right (S) on paved road
and go 1 mile (1.6 k).
$4. Open Apr 15–Sep 15; dry camping
allowed off-season.
19 scattered, open sites. Central faucet,
pit toilets, tables, fire rings, boat ramp.
In woods with excellent creek access.
Boat, fish, or do nothing.
14-day limit. Occasional day-use noise.

LAKE CHINNABEE

Talladega NF (205) 362-2909
State map: G5
From MUNFORD, drive S on
CR 47 for 2.3 miles (3.7 k).
Turn Left (E) on CR 42 and
continue 11 miles (17.6 k). (Nearby
Cheaha SP costs $12.)
$4. Open May 1–Nov 30.
8 (6 tent-only) close, open sites.
Central faucet, chemical toilets, tables,
grills, boat ramp.
Next to 17-acre, manmade lake.
Hike to water falls (.5 mile, 800 m).
Explore area including nearby Cheaha
Wilderness. Fish or boat (electric or
paddle only).
Hunting in season. Crowded holiday
weekends.
800 ft (240 m)

LENOIR LANDING

COE (205) 289-3540
State map: B8
From BARRYTOWN, go N on
CR 14 for 4 miles (6.4 k). Turn
Right (E). Go 2 miles (3.2 k).
FREE so choose a chore.
Open All Year.
Undesignated close, open sites.
Central faucet, pit toilets, boat ramp.
In woods near Tombigbee River.
Fish or boat.
14-day limit.

LOCK 2 PARK

COE (205) 289-3540
State map: B7
From PENNINGTON, take
CR 33 S to end – dirt last
2 miles (3.2 k).
FREE so choose a chore.
Open All Year.
Undesignated close, open sites. Central
faucet, pit toilets, tables, boat ramp.
In open and wooded areas near
Tombigbee River.
Boat and fish.
14-day limit. Occasional day-use noise.

LOCK 3 PARK

COE (205) 289-3540
State map: B7
From YORK, take AL 17 S for
12 miles (19.2 k). Turn Left (E)
on CR 42 and drive 13 miles
(20.8 k). Turn Left (N) on dirt road and
go 3 miles (4.8 k).
FREE so choose a chore. Open All Year.
6 close, open sites.
Central faucet, pit toilets, tables.
On mainly open bluff overlooking
Tombigbee River.
Fish. Enjoy seclusion.
14-day limit.

LOCK 5 PARK

COE (205) 289-3540
State map: C6
From GREENSBORO, travel
SW on AL 69 for 8 miles
(12.8 k). Turn Right (W) on

CR 16 and go 7 miles (11.2 k).
FREE so choose a chore. Open All Year.
Undesignated scattered, open sites.
Central faucet, pit toilets, tables, fire
rings, grills, boat ramp.
In light woods on overlook of Black
Warrior River near Big Prairie Creek.
Boat or fish.
14-day limit. Occasional day-use noise.

LOCK 7 EAST PARK

COE (205) 289-3540
State map: C6
Head N on AL 14 for 4 miles
(6.4 k) from SAWYERVILLE.
Turn Left (SW) on CR 38. Go
4 miles (6.4 k). Take dirt road 1 mile
(1.6 k). (Also see Damsite Park.)
FREE so choose a chore. Open All Year.
Undesignated scattered, open sites.
Central faucet, pit toilets, tables, grills,
boat ramp.
In woods and grassy field.
Fish and boat Black Warrior River.
14-day limit. Occasional day-use noise.

LOCK 8 PARK

COE (205) 289-3540
State map: C6
From AKRON, take CR 36 W
about 2 miles (3.2 k) to end.
FREE so choose a chore.
Open All Year.
Undesignated close, open sites.
Central faucet, pit toilets, tables, fire
rings, grills, boat ramp.
In woods next to Black Warrior River.
Fish and boat.
14-day limit. Occasional day-use noise.

MCCARTY FERRY LANDING

COE (205) 289-3540
State map: B8
From BUTLER, take AL 17 S
for 2.5 miles (4 k). Turn Left
(SE) on CR 23 and go 10 miles
(16 k). Turn Left on dirt road and drive
2 miles (3.2 k).
FREE so choose a chore.
Open All Year.
Undesignated scattered, open sites.

Pit toilets, tables.
Next to Tombigbee River.
Fish or boat.
NO water. 14-day limit.

OLD LOCK 16

COE (205) 553-9373
State map: C5
E of BROOKWOOD, drive N
on CR 59 about 20 miles
(32 k). Watch for sign to bear
Left. (Nearby Deerlick Creek costs $10.)
$4.
Open All Year.
16 scattered, open sites.
Central faucet, flush/pit toilets, tables,
fire rings, boat ramp.
Near shore of Holt Lake, below
Bankhead Dam.
Swim, boat, or fish.
Sometimes crowded.

OPEN POND

Conecuh NF (205) 222-3516
State map: E9
From ANDALUSIA, travel S
on US 29 for 9 miles (14.4 k).
Bear Left (S) on AL 137 and
go 7 miles (11.2 k).
$4. Open All Year.
44 scattered, open sites. Central faucet,
flush toilets, showers, dump station,
tables, fire rings, boat ramp.
In live oak, dogwood, and longleaf pine.
Relax in quiet spot. Fish in pond.
14-day/35-ft limits. Hunting in season.
No horses. Crowded holidays.
300 ft (90 m)

PAUL M GRIST SP

(205) 872-5846
State map: D6
From SELMA, travel NE on
AL 22 for 17 miles (27.2 k).
Turn Left (W) at sign.
$5; $10 hookups. Open All Year.
12 close, open sites. Water at 6 sites,
flush toilets, showers, electric hookups,
tables, grills, boat ramp.
In primitive woodland setting with some
sites near lake.

▲ ▲

Walk to enjoy natural features. Swim, boat, or fish lake.
Crowded weekends.

PAYNE LAKE

Talladega NF (205) 926-9765
State map: D6
From CENTERVILLE, drive W on US 82 for 2 miles (3.2 k). Turn Left (S) on AL 5 and go 6 miles (9.6 k). Turn Left (W) on AL 25 and continue 15 miles (24 k).
$4. Open All Year.
77 scattered, open sites.
Central faucet, flush toilets, showers, dump station, tables, grills, boat ramp.
In three sections (East, West, and Spillway) around lake.
Swim, fish, or boat (no motors). Walk nature trail.
14-day/22-ft limits.

PINE GLEN

Talladega NF (205) 463-2272
State map: G4
From HEFLIN, travel W on US 78 for 2 miles (3.2 k). Turn Right (N) on FR 500 and go 8 miles (12.8 k). (See Coleman Lake).
$3. Open All Year.
35 scattered, open, tent sites. Hand pump, pit toilets, tables, grills, fire rings.
In pine/hardwood next to Shoal Creek.
Hike the Pinhoti Trail System to spot wildlife or take photos. Fish. Enjoy relaxed setting.
14-day limit.
950 ft (285 m)

RUNAWAY II PARK

COE (205) 289-3540
State map: C6
From DEMOPOLIS, head N on US 43 for 3 miles (4.8 k). Turn Left (W) on CR 73 and drive .5 mile (800 m). Turn Left (S) on dirt road. Go .5 mile (800 m). (Nearby Foscue and Forkland parks cost $10.)
$4. Open Apr 15–Sep 15; dry camping allowed off-season.
Undesignated close, open sites.

Central faucet, pit toilets, tables, fire rings, grills, boat ramp.
In wooded/grassy spot near Lake Demopolis.
Boat and fish.
14-day limit. Occasional day-use noise.

SILVER CREEK PARK

COE (205) 682-4244
State map: C8
From CLAIBORNE, head NW on US 84 about 5 miles (8 k). Turn Right (N) and go about 6 miles (9.6 k). Turn Right (E). Continue 1 mile (1.6 k). (Also see West Bank).
FREE so choose a chore. Open All Year.
8 scattered, open sites.
Pit toilets, tables, fire rings, boat ramp.
On Claiborne Lake.
Boat or fish.
NO water. 14-day limit.

STEELES LANDING

COE (205) 269-1053
State map: E7
From PRATTVILLE, head W on AL 14 about 10 miles (16 k) to Statesville and CR 1. Turn Left (S) on CR 1 and follow signs.
FREE so choose a chore. Open All Year.
5 scattered, open sites.
Chemical toilets, tables.
In secluded woods on Woodruff Lake.
Boat and fish. Enjoy peaceful setting.
NO water. No trash arrangements (pack it out). 14-day limit. No generators in quiet hours.

WEST BANK-DAM SITE

COE (205) 682-4244
State map: C8
From CLAIBORNE, head NW on US 84 about 5 miles (8 k). Turn Right (N) and drive 3 miles (4.8 k). (Also see Silver Creek).
FREE so choose a chore. Open All Year.
Undesignated scattered, open sites.
Pit toilets, tables, fire rings.
Next to Claiborne Lock & Dam.
Fish or boat.
NO water. 14-day limit.

▲ ▲

ARKANSAS
CAMPGROUND LOCATIONS

► ► Find location on facing page map grid. ► ►
▼ ▼ Locate area campgrounds on these page numbers. ▼ ▼

GRID	PAGE
A2	41
A5	29, 30, 37, 38, 42, 43
A6	38
B3	29, 33, 35, 41
B4	26, 28, 30, 36, 43
B5	24, 25, 30, 35, 40
B6	29, 32
C2	26, 39, 43
C3	30, 31, 36, 38, 43
C4	24, 25, 34, 38
C5	40
C6	26, 31
C8	27
D2	32, 33, 42
D3	23, 25, 26, 27, 28, 31, 34, 36, 41
D4	29, 36, 37, 38, 39
D5	28

GRID	PAGE
E2	24, 34, 35, 40
E3	24, 25, 28, 29, 30, 32, 38, 40, 42
E4	32, 33, 41
E6	28
E8	34
E9	42
F1	27, 34
F2	23, 25, 31, 37, 39, 41
F3	24, 27, 33, 34, 36, 37
F6	42
F7	32
F8	32
G1	37
G2	23, 39, 40, 42
G5	35
G7	35

Arkansas

▲ ▲

Grid conforms to official state map. For your copy, call (800) NATURAL
or write Dept of Parks & Tourism, 1 Capitol Mall, Little Rock, AR 72201.

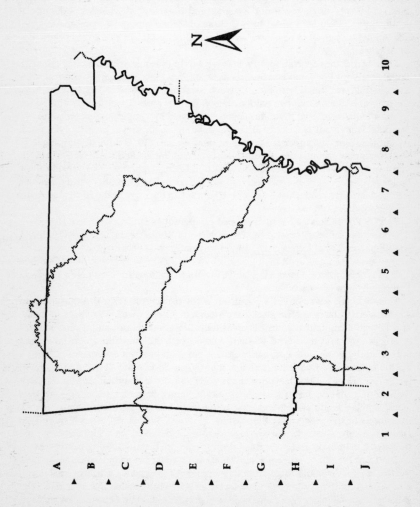

PUBLIC LANDS CAMPING

Arkansas, the natural state, makes camping easy. The Arkansas Department of Parks and Tourism publishes a Camper's Guide that lists all the public lands camping opportunities within the state. Here is a quick overview of camping among the 48 state parks, 5 units of the national park system, 500,000 acres of lakes, 9,700 miles of streams and 18 million acres of forests including 3 national forests.

In the **Arkansas State Parks** (SP), individual campsites cost $6.00 to $14.00 per day depending on the level of available services at 27 locations. In addition, there are Rent-A-Camp spaces at three parks ($21.00 per day) and hike-in, tent-only spots on Mount Nebo ($4.00 per day). You'll find geographical diversity in Arkansas parks: scenic mountaintops, secluded valleys, lush Mississippi Delta plains, quiet rivers and streams. Too, immerse yourself in history or adventure. Most sports can be enjoyed year-round in Arkansas.

Only two of the five **National Park Service** (NPS) sites in Arkansas offer camping: Buffalo National River and Hot Springs National Park (NP). The Buffalo National River is a 138-mile river lined with limestone and sandstone bluffs as tall as 450 feet. Float the river or backpack into two wildernesses within the park: Lower Buffalo and Ponca. At most Buffalo National River developed sites (listed by campground name), find free camping. From April 1–October 31, however, pay $7.00 for sites at popular Tyler Bend. At Buffalo Point, encounter $5.00 walk-in camping and $10.00 drive-in camping. Off-season camping remains free at both Tyler Bend and Buffalo Point. At Hot Springs NP, you can enjoy what is left of the natural by visiting Bathhouse Row. Inside these buildings, thermal springs have been capped and controlled for profit over the past one hundred and fifty years. Soak in a hot tub then spend the night at the $6.00 manicured campground at Gulpha Gorge.

The **US Forest Service** offers developed campgrounds ranging from free to $8.00 in the Ouachita National Forest (NF), Ozark NF, and Saint Francis NF. (The Ozark and Saint Francis national forests are now jointly administered.) Other manmade attractions to the forests include the following scenic byways: Arkansas Highway 7 (in Ouachita NF), Mount Magazine, Ozark Highlands, Pig Trail, Sylamore (in Ozark NF), and Saint Francis (in Saint Francis NF).

Ouachita NF covers over 1.5 million acres from west-central Arkansas into southeastern Oklahoma. The Black Fork Mountain, Caney Creek, Dry Creek, Flatside, and Poteau Mountain wilderness areas help preserve where eastern and western ecologies meet and mix. Find western wildlife such as armadillo, roadrunner, and scissortail flycatcher in the primarily eastern pine and hardwood forest.

One-million-acre Ozark NF contains the rugged Boston and Ozark mountains in northwest Arkansas. Also here, find the recently discovered Blanchard Springs Caverns with six miles of cave formations—flowstones, columns, stalactites, stalagmites, crystals —plus sightless wildlife. Above ground, find natural bridges and other interesting rock formations in the predominantly oak-hickory forest. Wilderness areas include East Fork, Hurricane Creek, Leatherwood, Richland Creek, and Upper Buffalo. Here, the threatened bald eagle and peregrine falcon species are making soaring comebacks.

The Saint Francis NF covers about 21,000 acres along the Saint Francis River near the Mississippi River and Mississippi state border. Although it's a small national forest, it contains geologically interesting Crowley's Ridge rising above the river flats. The ridge's composition of clay, orange sand, and gravel erodes into fantastic carvings and sculptures and supports plant life found nowhere else in the area.

▲ ▲

US Army Corps of Engineers (COE) maintains recreation areas along the McClellan-Kerr-Arkansas River Navigation System. Find campgrounds around the following lakes: Beaver, Blue Mountain, Bull Shoals, Dardanelle, DeGray, DeQueen, Dierks, Gillham, Greers Ferry, Greeson, Millwood, Nimrod, Norfolk, Ouachita, Ozark, Table Rock, and Toad Suck Ferry. COE camp fees range from free to $11.00. In addition, the engineers have created the Felsenthal Pool for navigation and flood control along the Ouachita River. The Saline River also flows through this vast basin of sloughs, bayous, and lakes. Additional public lands camping is administered by Union County and the Crossett Port Authority.

Too, a few **towns**, such as Jonesboro, offer camping in their parks.

Arkansas asks campers to cooperate in its antilitter campaign–"Fight Dirty. Keep Arkansas Clean."

▲ ▲

ARROWHEAD POINT

COE (501) 285-2151
State map: F2
From DAISY, drive W on US 70 for 4 miles (6.4 k). (Also see Star of the West. Nearby Self Creek costs $7.)
$3.
Open Mar 15–Nov 15.
23 scattered, open sites.
Central faucet, flush toilets, tables, fire rings, grills, boat ramp.
Near water on flat to steep terrain.
Enjoy swimming, boating, skiing, or fishing on Lake Greeson.
14-day/30-ft limits. No generators in quiet hours. Crowded holidays.
563 ft (169 m)

ASHLEY CREEK

COE (501) 947-2372
State map: D3
Head S from BLUE MOUNTAIN on marked CR for 2 miles (3.2 k). (Also see Cameron Bluff, Hise Hill, and Outlet Area.)
FREE so choose a chore.
Open All Year.
10 close, open sites.
Central faucet, pit toilets, dump station, tables, fire rings, grills, boat ramp.
Near Blue Mountain Lake.
Boat or fish. View wildlife and take photos.

ASHLEY'S CAMP

COE (501) 898-3343
State map: G2
From ASHDOWN, head N on US 71 for 10 miles (16 k). (Also see White Cliffs. Nearby Paraloma costs $8.)
FREE so choose a chore.
Open All Year.
4 close, open sites.
Pit toilets, tables.
On banks of Little River.
Fish and boat.
NO water. 14-day limit.

BARD SPRINGS

Ouachita NF (501) 356-4186
State map: F2
From ATHENS, take AR 246 NW for 8 miles (12.8 k). Turn Right (NW) on rough FR 38 and go 9 miles (14.4 k). Turn Right on FR 106. Continue .5 mile (800 m). (Also see Crystal. Nearby Albert Pike and Shady Lake cost $7.)
$4. Open All Year.
17 close, open sites.
Central faucet, flush & chemical toilets, tables, grills, fire rings.
Under hardwood and pine trees next to pretty Blaylock Creek.
Hike several trails (Athens Big Fork and Little Missouri). Explore Caney Creek Wilderness. Swim or relax.
14-day limit. Hunting in season. No

generators in quiet hours.
1300 ft (390 m)

BARKSHED

Ozark-St Francis NF
(501) 269-3228
State map: B5
From MOUNTAIN VIEW,
take AR 14 N for 24 miles (38.4 k). Turn
Right on gravel FR 1112 and go 8 miles
(12.8 k). (Also see Gunner Pool. Nearby
Blanchard Springs costs $8.)
FREE so choose a chore.
Open All Year.
6 (5 tent-only) scattered, open sites.
Chemical toilets, tables, fire rings.
Among high bluffs near North Sylamore
Scenic River.
Hike Sylamore Trail or explore nearby
Leatherwood Wilderness.
NO water. Hunting in season. Observe
quiet hours. Crowded holidays and
summer weekends.
990 ft (297 m)

BAYOU BLUFF

Ozark-St Francis NF
(501) 284-3150
State map: C4
From HECTOR, head N on
AR 27 for 6 miles (9.6 k).
$4.
Open Apr 2 – Nov 1; dry camping
allowed off-season.
7 close, open sites.
Hand pump, chemical toilets, tables, fire
rings, shelter.
Near scenic bluffs next to Illinois Bayou.
Splash in water. Fish. Take photos.
14-day limit.

BEAR CREEK

COE (501) 285-2151
State map: F3
From KIRBY, drive S on
AR 27 for 1.5 miles (4 k).
Turn Right (W) on paved road and
travel to end. (Also see Laurel Creek.
Nearby Kirby Landing costs $10 and Self
Creek costs $7.)
FREE so choose a chore.

Open All Year.
19 scattered, open sites.
Hand pump, pit toilets, tables, grills, fire
rings, boat ramp.
Under trees near Lake Greeson shoreline.
Use mountain bike trail or take
advantage of lake with boating, skiing,
or fishing.
14-day/35-ft limits. Hunting in season.
No generators in quiet hours. Crowded
holidays.
563 ft (169 m)

BIG BRUSHY

Ouachita NF (501) 356-4186
State map: E2
From PENCIL BLUFF, head
NW on US 270 for 7 miles
(11.2 k). Turn Left (S) on gravel FR 6 and
go 200 ft (61 m). (Also see Mill Creek
and Shirley Creek.)
FREE so choose a chore.
Open All Year.
11 close, open sites.
Hand pump, chemical toilets, tables,
grills, fire rings.
In forest with creek and grassy area.
Hike part of trail complex. Observe
wildlife. Fish. Visit nearby Blowout
Mountain Scenic Area.
14-day limit. Crowded hunting season.
970 ft (291 m)

BIG FIR

COE (501) 767-2101
State map: E3
From MOUNT IDA, take
AR 27 N for 5 miles (8 k).
Turn Right (E) on AR 188. Drive 9 miles
(14.4 k). Continue on gravel Housley/Big
Fir Road for 4 miles (6.4 k). (Nearby
Highway 27 and Little Fir cost $7.)
FREE so choose a chore.
Open All Year.
17 scattered, open sites.
Hand pump, pit toilets, tables, fire rings,
grills, boat ramp.
In pine forest with view of Lake
Ouachita.
Fish, boat, or waterski. Relax and view
wildlife.

▲ ▲

14-day limit. Hunting in season. No generators in quiet hours.
592 ft (178 m)

BROCK CREEK

Ozark-St Francis NF
(501) 284-3150
State map: C4
From JERUSALEM, drive N on gravel FR 1305 for 5 miles (8 k). Turn Right (E) on FR 1309 for .1 mile (160 m) then jog Left (NE) on FR 1331 for 1 mile (1.6 k).
FREE so choose a chore.
Open Apr 2–Nov 30; camping allowed off-season.
6 close, open sites.
Pit toilets, tables, fire rings.
Next to 35-acre lake.
Fish. Enjoy solitude.
NO water. 14-day limit.

BUCKHORN

COE (501) 285-2151
State map: F2
From MURFREESBORO, drive N on AR 19 for 7 miles (11.2 k) to dam. Turn Left (W) on gravel road and go 8 miles (12.8 k). (Also see Pikeville. Nearby Parker Creek costs $7.)
FREE so choose a chore.
Open Mar 15–Nov 15.
9 scattered, open sites.
Chemical toilets, tables, grills, fire rings.
In remote, hilly, wooded setting next to Lake Greeson.
Fish, take photographs, or relax.
NO water. 14-day/40-ft limits. No generators in quiet hours. Crowded holidays.
563 ft (169 m)

BUCKVILLE

COE (501) 767-2101
State map: E3
Drive S from AVANT community for 3.6 miles (5.8 k). (Also see Iron Fork. Nearby Lena Landing costs $6.)
FREE so choose a chore.

Open All Year.
9 scattered, open sites.
Hand pump, pit toilets, tables, fire rings, grills, boat ramp.
In remote setting on Lake Ouachita.
Swim, boat, ski, or fish. Enjoy locale.
14-day limit. Hunting in season. No generators in quiet hours.
592 ft (178 m)

BUFFALO POINT WALK-IN

Buffalo National River
(501) 741-5443
State map: B5
From HARRIET, take AR 14 NW for 10 miles (16 k). Turn Right (E) on AR 268 and go 3 miles. (Also see Highway 14.)
$5; $10 drive-in; reservations accepted at (501) 741-5443 for an additional $10.
Open Apr 1–Oct 31; dry camping allowed off-season.
109 (22 tent-only) close, open sites. ♿
Central faucet, flush toilets, showers, dump station, electric hookups, tables, grills, boat ramp, pay phone.
Mainly in shade next to river.
Canoe, boat, swim, or fish. Hike scenic area. Attend ranger programs.
14-day limit. Pests (snakes, ticks, chiggers). Crowded summer.
500 ft (150 m)

CABIN CREEK

COE (501) 968-5008
State map: D3
From KNOXVILLE, drive 2 miles (3.2 k) W. (Also see Flat Rock and Piney Bay.)
FREE so choose a chore.
Open All Year.
9 scattered, open sites.
Central faucet, pit toilets, tables, fire rings, boat ramp, group pavilion.
Under heavy shade on Lake Dardanelle. Enjoy boating or fishing. View wildlife and take photos.
14-day limit. Hunting in season.

▲ ▲

CAMERON BLUFF

Ozark-St Francis NF
(501) 963-3076
State map: D3
From HAVANA, travel N
on AR 309 for 12 miles (19.2 k). (Also see
Ashley Creek, Cove Lake, and Spring
Lake.)
FREE so choose a chore.
Open All Year.
16 close, screened sites.
Central faucet, chemical toilets, tables,
grills, fire rings.
Near spectacular high rock cliffs and
bluffs at highest point in Arkansas.
Hike and explore. Drive scenic loop.
14-day limit. No generators in quiet
hours. Crowded holidays.
2600 ft (780 m)

CANE CREEK

COE (501) 968-5008
State map: D3
From SCRANTON, drive E
for 3 miles (4.8 k) on
AR 197. (Also see Dublin and
Horsehead. Nearby Shoal Bay costs $10.)
$4.
Open All Year.
14 scattered, open sites.
Central faucet, pit toilets, tables, fire
rings, boat ramp, group picnic pavilion.
Next to Cane Creek and Lake
Dardanelle.
Enjoy seclusion. Boat and fish on lake.
14-day limit. Hunting in season.

CARDEN POINT

COE (501) 272-4324
State map: D3
From PLAINVIEW, take
AR 60 E for 5.5 miles
(8.8 k). Turn Right (S) on access road.
(Nearby Carter Cove costs $8 and
County Line costs $10.)
FREE so choose a chore.
Open All Year.
9 scattered, open sites.
Central faucet, pit toilets, tables, fire
rings, grills, boat ramp.
In one free area on Nimrod Lake, nestled

between Ouachita and Ozark Mountains.
Boat, ski, or fish.
14-day limit. Hunting in season.
375 ft (113 m)

CARVER

Buffalo National River
(501) 741-5443
State map: B4
From HASTY, drive S on
AR 123 for 4 miles (6.4 k). (Also see
Mount Hersey.)
FREE so choose a chore.
Open All Year.
Undesignated scattered, open sites.
Central faucet, pit toilets, grills.
In open field next to river.
Boat and fish.
14-day limit. Occasional crawling pests
(chiggers, ticks, snakes). No generators
in quiet hours. Crowded late spring.
800 ft (240 m)

CHEROKEE

COE (501) 362-2416
State map: C6
From DRASCO, travel W
on AR 92 for 7.5 miles
(12 k). Turn Left (S) on access road.
Continue 4.5 miles (7.2 k). (Also see Hill
Creek. Nearby Shiloh costs $7.)
$5; $8 electric.
Open Mar 31–Nov 1; dry camping
allowed off-season.
33 close, screened sites.
Central faucet, pit toilets, dump station,
electric hookups, tables, fire rings, grills,
boat ramp.
Among pine/hardwood trees on banks
of Greers Ferry Lake in southern Ozarks.
Swim, boat, ski, or fish.
14-day limit. No generators in quiet
hours. Crowded holiday weekends.
480 ft (144 m)

CITADEL BLUFF

COE (800) 844-2129
State map: C2
From CECIL, drive N on
AR 41 for 1.2 miles (1.9 k).
(Also see River Ridge.)

▲ ▲

$4.
Open All Year.
36 scattered, screened sites.
Hand pump, pit toilets, tables, fire rings, grills, boat ramp.
In heavily wooded bluff section of Arkansas River.
Walk to enjoy scenery and wildlife.
Enjoy boating or fishing.
14-day/35-ft limits. Hunting in season. Crowded holiday weekends.

COON CREEK

COE (501) 386-2141
State map: F1
From GRANNIS, head S and turn Right (E) on CR 3 (Frachiseur/Holly Grove) and go about 4 miles (6.4 k). (Also see Little Coon Creek. Nearby Cossatot Reefs costs $7.)
$5; $8 electric.
Open All Year.
31 scattered, open sites.
Central faucet, pit toilets, dump station, electric hookups, tables, fire rings, grills, boat ramp, playground.
Amid hills on beautiful Cossatot River.
Walk to enjoy wildflowers, wildlife, and clear streams. Swim, fish, or boat.
14-day limit. Floods possible. Hunting in season. No generators in quiet hours. No pets on beach.
900 ft (270 m)

COVE LAKE

Ozark-St Francis NF
(501) 963-3076
State map: D3
From PARIS, drive 1 mile (1.6 k) S on AR 109. Turn Left (SE) on AR 309. Continue 9 miles (14.4 k). (Also see Cameron Bluff and Spring Lake.)
$5; reservations accepted at (501) 963-3076 for an additional $6.
Open All Year.
29 close, screened sites. &
Central faucet, flush toilets, showers, tables, fire rings, grills, boat ramp.
On beautiful 160-acre lake near Mt Magazine.
Swim, boat, fish, and ski (weekdays

only). Hike Magazine Trail. Play volleyball or horseshoes. Attend ranger programs.
14-day limit. No generators in quiet hours. No pets on beach. Crowded holidays.
1000 ft (300 m)

CRAIGHEAD FOREST PARK

Jonesboro City Parks
(501) 932-8719
State map: C8
From JONESBORO, head S on AR 141 (South Culberhouse). (Nearby Crowley's Ridge SP costs $12.)
$5; $10 hookups.
Open All Year.
26 close, open sites.
Water at every site, flush toilets, showers, dump station, electric hookups, tables, grills, fire rings, boat ramp, group pavilions, playground, ballfields, pay phone.
Among rolling hills near small lake.
Swim, paddleboat, or fish. Walk and relax.
14-day limit. Crowded Jul 4. Summer mosquitos.
1200 ft (360 m)

CRYSTAL

Ouachita NF (501) 356-4186
State map: F3
From NORMAN, drive N on AR 27 for 1 mile (1.6 k).
Turn Right (E) on FR 177 and go 3 miles (4.8 k). (Also see Bard Springs.)
$4.
Open All Year.
9 scattered, open sites.
Hand pump, chemical toilets, tables, grills, fire rings.
On small stream (with spring) beneath hardwood-pine canopy.
Hike or swim.
14-day limit. Hunting in season. No generators in quiet hours.
1000 ft (300 m)

▲ ▲

CYPRESS CREEK

COE (501) 329-2986
State map: D5
From HOUSTON, head N
on AR 113 about 2 miles
(3.2 k). Watch for sign. (Nearby Sequoia
and Toad Suck cost $11.)
FREE so choose a chore.
Open Mar 1–Oct 31.
9 close, open sites.
Hand pump, pit toilets, tables, fire rings,
grills, boat ramp.
In hardwoods with view of Arkansas
River.
Boat, fish, or relax.
14-day limit.
267 ft (80 m)

D D TERRY DAM SITE WEST

COE (501) 534-0451
State map: E6
From LITTLE ROCK Port
(Exit 5 on I-440), drive S for
3.2 miles (5.1 k).
FREE so choose a chore.
Open All Year.
6 close, open, tent sites.
Central faucet, pit toilets, tables, fire
rings, boat ramp.
Next to lock & dam on Arkansas River.
Enjoy boating or fishing.
14-day limit.

DELAWARE

COE (501) 968-5008
State map: D3
From DELAWARE, travel
2 miles (3.2 k) N On
AR 393. (Nearby Lake Dardanelle SP
costs $12 and Shoal Bay costs $10.)
$4.
Open All Year.
13 scattered, open sites.
Central faucet, pit toilets, tables, fire
rings, boat ramp.
On wooded peninsula in Lake
Dardanelle's Delaware Bay.
Boat and fish.
14-day limit.

DRAGOVER FLOAT CAMP

Ouachita NF (501) 356-4186
State map: E3
From PENCIL BLUFF, take
AR 88 E for 7 miles
(11.2 k). Turn Right (S) on gravel
FR D82A. Go 1 mile (1.6 k).
FREE so choose a chore.
Open All Year.
7 (1 tent-only) close, open sites.
Hand pump, pit toilets, tables, fire rings,
grills, boat ramp (canoe or flat-bottom).
In forest alongside Ouachita River.
Canoe, float, or paddle. Fish. Hike to
observe wildlife.
14-day/20-ft limits. Crowded spring and
summer weekends.
680 ft (204 m)

DUBLIN

COE (501) 968-5008
State map: D3
From SCRANTON, head E
8 miles (12.8 k) on AR 197.
(Also see Cane Creek. Nearby Shoal Bay
costs $10.)
$4. Open All Year.
16 scattered, open sites. ♿
Central faucet, pit toilets, tables, fire
rings, boat ramp, group picnic pavilion.
On wooded slope next to Lake
Dardanelle.
Swimming, boating, skiing, and fishing.
14-day limit. Hunting in season.

ERBIE

Buffalo National River
(501) 741-5443
State map: B4
From JASPER, head N on
AR 7 for 4 miles (6.4 k). Turn Left (W)
on gravel road. Drive 7 miles (11.2 k).
(Also see Ozark.)
FREE so choose a chore.
Open All Year.
30 scattered, open sites. ♿
Central faucet, pit toilets, tables, fire
rings, grills, boat ramp.
In old-field bottomland next to river.
Swim, boat, and fish. Hike isolated area.
Enjoy peaceful surroundings.

▲ ▲

14-day limit. Occasional crawling pests (chiggers, snakes, ticks). No generators after 8pm. Crowded Memorial Day. 900 ft (270 m)

FAIRVIEW

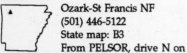

Ozark-St Francis NF (501) 446-5122 State map: B3 From PELSOR, drive N on AR 7 for 2 miles (3.2 k). $4. Open All Year. 12 scattered, open sites. Central faucet, chemical toilets, tables, fire rings. In hardwood and pine trees with excellent spring and fall color. Walk. Take photos. Relax. 14-day limit. 2000 ft (600 m)

FLAT ROCK

COE (501) 968-5008 State map: D4 From LONDON, drive 4 miles (6.4 k) E on US 64. Turn Left (N) on AR 359 and go 1 mile (1.6 k). (See Cabin Creek and Piney Bay.) $4. Open All Year. 15 scattered, screened sites. Central faucet, pit toilets, tables, fire rings, boat ramp, group picnic pavilion. In heavy woods on Lake Dardanelle surrounded by scenic bluffs. Boat, ski, swim, or fish. Walk, take photos, or relax. 14-day limit.

FOURCHE MOUNTAIN PICNIC AREA

Ouachita NF (501) 495-2844 State map: E3 From ROVER, travel S on AR 27 for 5 miles (8 k). FREE so choose a chore. Open All Year. 8 close, open, tent sites. Pit toilets, tables, grills, fire rings. In undeveloped pine-hardwood forest. Relax or seek out photos.

NO water. Hunting in season. 1100 ft (330 m)

FULTON BRANCH

Ouachita NF (501) 867-2101 State map: E3 From MOUNT IDA, take US 270 NW for .5 mile (800 m). Turn Right (N) on AR 27 and go 1 mile (1.6 k). Turn Left (NW) on gravel CR 59 and drive 5 miles (8 k). (Also see River Bluff and Rocky Shoals.) FREE so choose a chore. Open All Year. 7 scattered, open sites. Hand pump, pit toilets, tables, grills, fire rings. In forest next to Ouachita River. Hike or bike Womble Trail. Canoe, kayak, raft, or fish. No trash arrangements (pack it out). 14-day limit. Hunting in season. No generators in quiet hours. 600 ft (180 m)

GEORGE'S COVE

COE (501) 425-2700 State map: A5 Drive S on AR 5 from MOUNTAIN HOME for 6.5 miles (10.4 k). Turn Left (E) on AR 342 and go 2.5 miles (4 k). (Also see Jordan and Tracy. Nearby Quarry Cove costs $6 and Robinson Point costs $10.) FREE so choose a chore. Open All Year. 12 close, open sites. Central faucet, pit toilets, dump station, tables, fire rings, grills, boat ramp. On banks of Norfolk Lake's southern section. Swim, fish, or boat. 14-day limit. No littering or gray-water dumping. No noise after 10pm. Crowded weekends and holidays.

GUNNER POOL

Ozark-St Francis NF (501) 269-3228 State map: B6 Go N for 15 miles (24 k) on

AR 14 from MOUNTAIN VIEW. Turn Right on gravel FR 1102 and continue 3 miles (4.8 k). (Also see Barkshed. Nearby Blanchard Springs costs $8.) **$5.**
Open All Year.
26 (6 tent-only) scattered, screened sites. Central faucet, chemical toilets, tables, grills, fire rings.
On beautiful North Sylamore Creek beneath towering sandstone and limestone bluffs.
Hike or visit nearby Blanchard Springs Caverns. Swim or fish.
Hunting in season. Observe quiet hours. Crowded summer and holidays.
550 ft (165 m)

HAND COVE

COE (501) 425-2700
State map: A5
From MOUNTAIN HOME, take US 62 E for 16 miles (25.6 k). Turn Right (S) on CR 91 and go 9 miles (14.4 k). (Also see Woods Point. Nearby Henderson costs $8.)
FREE so choose a chore.
Open All Year.
7 close, open sites.
Pit toilets, tables, fire rings, grills, boat ramp.
On Big Creek Arm of Norfolk Lake. Enjoy seclusion. Boat or fish.
NO water. 14-day limit. Crowded weekends.

HASTY

Buffalo National River
(501) 741-5443
State map: B4
From JASPER, take AR 123 E for 5 miles (8 k). Turn Left (E) on AR 74 and go to Hasty Low Water Bridge sign. Turn Left then continue 2 miles (3.2 k). (Also see Ozark.)
FREE so choose a chore.
Open All Year.
4 close, open, tent sites.
Pit toilets, grills.
In small open area next to river.
Swim and fish. Relax.

NO water. 14-day limit. Occasional crawling pests (chiggers, ticks, snakes). No generators in quiet hours. Crowded spring weekends and holidays.
800 ft (240 m)

HAW CREEK FALLS

Ozark-St Francis NF
(501) 284-3150
State map: C3
From HAGARVILLE, travel N on AR 123 for 12 miles (19.2 k).
$4.
Open Apr 2–Nov 30.
8 close, open sites.
Central faucet, pit toilets, tables, fire rings.
Next to scenic falls among rocks and bluffs.
Take photos. Hike to Hurricane Creek Natural Bridge Scenic Area. Fish.
14-day limit.

HICKORY NUT

Ouachita NF (501) 867-2101
State map: E3
From MOUNT IDA, take US 270 E for 15 miles (24 k). Turn Left (N) at sign on FR W47 and go 3.5 miles (5.6 k). (Nearby Charlton costs $6.)
FREE so choose a chore.
Open All Year.
8 scattered, screened sites.
Hand pump, chemical toilets, tables, grills, fire rings.
On forested mountain with nearby vista of Lake Ouachita.
Relax, walk, or take photos.
14-day limit. Hunting in season. No generators in quiet hours.
1100 ft (330 m)

HIGHWAY 14 (DILLARDS FERRY)

Buffalo National River
(501) 741-5443
State map: B5
From HARRIET, go N on AR 14 for 6.5 miles (10.4 k). (Also see Buffalo Point and Rush.)
FREE so choose a chore.

▲ ▲

Open All Year.
38 (10 tent-only) close, open sites. &
Central faucet, pit toilets, boat ramp.
In open field beside bridge.
Swim, canoe, or fish. Walk nearby trails
to explore scenic, rugged country. Take
photos. Attend ranger programs.
14-day limit. Occasional crawling pests
(chiggers, ticks, snakes). Often crowded.
500 ft (150 m)

HILL CREEK

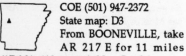

COE (501) 362-2416
State map: C6
From DRASCO, drive W
on US 92 for 12 miles
(19.2 k). Turn Right (N) on AR 225 and
go 3 miles (4.8 k). Turn Left (S) on access
road for 2 miles (3.2 k). (Also see
Cherokee. Nearby Shiloh costs $7.)
$5; $8 electric.
Open Mar 31–Nov 1; dry camping
allowed off-season.
41 scattered, screened sites.
Central faucet, pit toilets, dump station,
electric hookups, tables, fire rings, grills,
boat ramp.
In pine and hardwood trees on banks of
Greers Ferry Lake.
Swimming, boating, skiing, fishing.
14-day limit. No generators in quiet
hours. Crowded holiday weekends.
480 ft (144 m)

HISE HILL

COE (501) 947-2372
State map: D3
From BOONEVILLE, take
AR 217 E for 11 miles
(17.6 k). (Also see Ashley Creek.)
FREE so choose a chore.
Open All Year.
11 close, open sites.
Central faucet, pit toilets, tables, fire
rings, grills, boat ramp.
On Blue Mountain Lake in mountainous
terrain.
Relax in quiet setting. View wildlife. Fish
or boat.

HORSEHEAD

COE (501) 968-5008
State map: D3
From CLARKSVILLE, take
AR 194 W for 6 miles
(9.6 k). Turn Left (S) on AR 194 Spur and
go 1 mile (1.6 k). (Also see Cane Creek.
Nearby Spadra costs $7.)
FREE so choose a chore.
Open All Year.
5 scattered, open sites. Central faucet, pit
toilets, tables, fire rings, boat ramp.
In woods on Horsehead Creek near Lake
Dardanelle.
Enjoy seclusion. Boat or fish.
14-day limit. Hunting in season.

HORSEHEAD LAKE

Ozark-St Francis NF
(501) 754-2864
State map: C3
From CLARKSVILLE, head
NW on AR 103 for 8 miles (12.8 k). Turn
Left (W) on AR 164 for 4 miles (6.4 k).
Turn Right (N) on gravel FR 1408 and
travel 3 miles (4.8 k).
$5. Open Apr–Dec 15; dry camping
allowed off-season.
10 scattered, screened sites. &
Central faucet, flush toilets, cold
showers, tables, fire rings, grills, boat
ramp.
Under trees near mountain lake.
Swim or boat (10 hp limit). Hike to
explore area.
14-day limit. No generators in quiet
hours.

HORSESHOE BEND

COE (501) 286-2346
State map: F2
From DIERKS, travel W on
US 70 for 2 miles (3.2 k).
Turn Right (NW) on access road and go
4 miles (6.4 k). (Nearby Blue Ridge costs
$8 and Jefferson Ridge costs $10.)
FREE so choose a chore.
Open All Year.
11 close, open sites.
Central faucet, pit toilets, dump station,
tables, grills, fire rings.

Below Dierks Lake on wooded Saline
River banks.
Swim or float river. Fish. Wander natural
area.
14-day limit. Hunting in season.
500 ft (150 m)

HUFF ISLAND

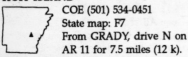

COE (501) 534-0451
State map: F7
From GRADY, drive N on
AR 11 for 7.5 miles (12 k).
FREE so choose a chore.
Open Mar 1–Oct 31.
4 close, open sites. Central faucet, pit
toilets, tables, fire rings.
Next to Arkansas River, so fish.
14-day limit.

IRON FORK

COE (501) 767-2101
State map: E3
From STORY, take AR 298
E for 8 miles (12.8 k). Turn
Right at sign and drive 1.3 miles (2.1 k)
on gravel road. (Also see Buckville.)
FREE so choose a chore.
Open All Year.
9 scattered, open sites.
Hand pump, pit toilets, tables, fire rings,
grills, boat ramp.
On Lake Ouachita in isolated setting.
Swim, boat, ski, or fish. Enjoy quiet.
14-day limit. Hunting in season. No
generators after dark.
592 ft (178 m)

IRON SPRINGS

Ouachita NF (501) 984-5313
State map: E4
From JESSIEVILLE, head N
on AR 7 (Scenic Byway) for
5 miles (8 k). (Also see South Fourche.)
FREE so choose a chore.
Open All Year.
13 scattered, open sites.
Hand pump, pit toilets, tables, fire rings.
Near headwaters of Saline River in
shortleaf pine/hardwood forest.
Walk 3-hour Hunt's Loop Trail. Explore
nearby Flatside Wilderness. Swim or

wade.
14-day limit. Small vehicles only.
Hunting in season. No generators in
quiet hours.
870 ft (261 m)

JACK CREEK

Ouachita NF (501) 675-3233
State map: D2
From BOONEVILLE, take
AR 23 S for 2 miles (3.2 k).
Turn Left (E) on AR 116 and go .8 mile
(1.3 k). Turn Right (S) on CR 19 and go
5.5 miles (8.8 k). Continue S on gravel
FR 19 for 1.1 miles (1.8 k). Turn Left (E)
on FR 141 for last 1.1 miles (1.8 k). (Also
see Knoppers Ford.)
FREE so choose a chore.
Open May 15–Sep 15.
5 close, open, tent sites. Central faucet,
pit toilets, tables, fire rings.
Among rugged rock bluffs and pine/oak
forests near natural pool in Sugar Creek.
Walk Jack Creek Overlook Trail or hike
Hole In The Ground Mountain Trail.
Swim or fish. Enjoy beauty of nearby
Dry Creek Wilderness.
14-day limit.
600 ft (180 m)

JACK'S BAY

White River NWR
(501) 946-1468
State map: F8
From TICHNOR, travel E
on gravel road for 8 miles (12.8 k). (Also
see Moores Bayou.)
FREE so choose a chore.
Open Mar 1–Oct 31.
Undesignated scattered, open sites.
Central faucet, flush toilets, boat ramp.
On banks of White River, so boat or fish.
No trash arrangements (pack it out).
Flooding possible. Hunting in season.
151 ft (45 m)

JORDAN

COE (501) 425-2700
State map: B6
Drive 11 miles (17.6 k) S
from MOUNTAIN HOME

on AR 5. Turn Left (E) on AR 177 to cross dam and travel 8 miles (12.8 k). Turn Left (N) on Baxter 64 and go 3 miles (4.8 k). (Also see George's Cove and Woods Point. Nearby Quarry Cove costs $6.)

$5; $8 electric. Open Apr 1–Oct 31; dry camping allowed off-season.

40 (7 tent-only) close, open sites.

Central faucet, pit toilets, dump station, electric hookups, tables, fire rings, grills, boat ramp, marina.

On Big Creek portion of Norfolk Lake. Swim, boat, or fish.

14-day limit. No gray-water dumping. Quiet hours. Crowded weekends.

KNOPPERS FORD

Ouachita NF (501) 675-3233
State map: D2
From BOONEVILLE, take AR 23 S for 2 miles (3.2 k). Turn Left (E) on AR 116 and go .8 mile (1.3 k). Turn Right (S) on CR 19 and go 5.5 miles (8.8 k). Drive S on gravel FR 19 for 2.5 miles (4 k). (Also see Jack Creek.)

FREE so choose a chore.

Open All Year.

6 close, screened tent sites.

Hand pump, pit toilets, tables, fire rings. Among unique geologic formations in woods near natural pool in Sugar Creek. Walk new Sugar Creek Trail. Swim or fish. Spot wildlife and take photos.

14-day limit.

620 ft (186 m)

KYLES LANDING

Buffalo National River (501) 741-5443
State map: B3
From JASPER, drive W on AR 73 for 7 miles (11.2 k). Turn Right (N) on rough, steep, winding gravel road for 3 miles (4.8 k). (Also see Steel Creek.)

FREE so choose a chore. Open All Year.

Undesignated close, open sites.

Central faucet, pit toilets, fire rings.

Next to river.

Hike to Hemmed-In-Hollow or Indian Creek. Explore wilderness. Take photos.

Swim or canoe.

14-day limit. No RVs. Hunting in season. Occasional pests (chiggers, ticks, snakes). Crowded late spring.

1000 ft (300 m)

LAKE SYLVIA

Ouachita NF (501) 889-5176
State map: E4
From PERRYVILLE, travel S on AR 9 for 9 miles (14.4 k). Bear Right (S) on AR 324 and go 4 miles (6.4 k).

$4; $8 hookups. Open May–Oct.

33 (14 tent-only) close, open sites. &

Water at 19 sites, flush toilets, showers, dump station, electric hookups, tables, fire rings, grills, boat ramp, pier, pay phone.

In pine/oak forest beside 14-acre mountain lake. (Tent area near Narrow Creek.)

Walk interpretive and hiking trails. Mountain bike. Swim, boat, or fish. Play volleyball. Attend ranger programs.

14-day/22-ft limits. Hunting in season. No ATVs. Crowded holiday weekends

640 ft (192 m)

LAUREL CREEK

COE (501) 285-2151
State map: F3
From MURFREESBORO, go N on AR 27 for 8 miles (12.8 k). Turn Left (W) on unimproved access road and drive 5 miles (8 k). (Also see Bear Creek. Nearby Cowhide Cove costs $7.)

FREE so choose a chore.

Open Mar 15–Nov 15.

24 scattered, open sites.

Central faucet, pit toilets, tables, fire rings, grills, boat ramp.

In rolling, tree-covered hills with some sites close to Lake Greeson shoreline.

Hike, bike, or take photographs. Swim, boat, ski, or fish.

14-day/40-ft limits. Hunting in season. No generators in quiet hours. Crowded holidays.

563 ft (169 m)

LENOX MARCUS

COE (501) 246-5501
State map: F3
From BISMARK, go W on
AR 84 for 2 miles (3.2 k).
At Lambert, turn Left (SW) on access
road, then Left (S) again for total of
3 miles (4.8 k). (Also see Point Cedar.
Nearby Shouse Ford and Arlie Moore
cost $10.)
FREE so choose a chore.
Open All Year.
Undesignated scattered, open sites.
Central faucet, flush toilets, tables, grills,
boat ramp.
In large, wooded area with views of
DeGray Lake.
Swim, boat, ski, or fish. Explore. Relax.
14-day limit. Hunting in season.
Crowded major holiday weekends.

LICK CREEK

COE (501) 947-2372
State map: D3
From WAVELAND, head S
on AR 309 for 4 miles
(6.4 k). (Also see Outlet Area.)
FREE so choose a chore.
Open All Year.
7 close, open sites.
Hand pump, pit toilets, tables, fire rings,
grills, boat ramp.
On Blue Mountain Lake in mountainous
setting.
Enjoy fishing and boating.

LITTLE COON CREEK

COE (501) 386-2141
State map: F1
From GRANNIS, head S
then turn Right (E) on
CR 3 (Frachiseur/Holly Grove) and go
about 4 miles (6.4 k). (Also see Coon
Creek. Nearby Cossatot Reefs costs $7.)
FREE so choose a chore.
Open All Year.
10 scattered, open sites.
Central faucet, pit toilets, tables, fire
rings, grills, boat ramp.
On beautiful Cossatot River's Gilliam
Lake.

Waterski, boat, swim, or fish. Walk to
experience surroundings.
Drinking water may be off. 14-day limit.
Hunting in season. No generators in
quiet hours.
900 ft (270 m)

LITTLE PINES

Ouachita NF (501) 637-4174
State map: E2
From WALDRON on US 71
Bypass, take AR 248 W for
12 miles (19.2 k). Turn Left (S). (Also see
Mill Creek.)
$5; $7 electric; reservations accepted at
(501) 637-4174 for an additional $6.
Open Mar 31–Nov 1.
18 scattered, open sites.
Central faucet, flush toilets, showers,
dump station, electric hookups, tables,
grills, boat launch, store, pay phone.
In woods within 300 yards of 1000-acre
Hinkle Lake.
Hike to view wildlife and take photos.
Swim, boat, or fish.
14-day limit. Hunting in season.
Crowded holidays.
800 ft (240 m)

LONE PINE

Ozark-St Francis NF
(501) 295-5278
State map: E8
From MARIANNA, head
SE on AR 44 for 7 miles (11.2 k). Turn
Left (NE) on FR 1913 and continue
1 mile (1.6 k). (Nearby Beech Point on
west side of Bear Creek Lake costs $6.)
$4. Open Apr 1–Dec 31.
10 close, open sites.
Central faucet, pit toilets, tables, fire
rings, boat ramp.
On eastern shore of 635-acre lake.
Swim, boat, or fish. Hike.
14-day/22-ft limits.

LONG POOL

Ozark-St Francis NF
(501) 284-3150
State map: C4
From HAGARVILLE, take

▲ ▲

AR 164 E for 11 miles (17.6 k). Turn Left
(N) on gravel FR 1801 and go 3 miles
(4.8 k). Bear Left (NW) on FR 1804 and
continue 2 miles (3.2 k).
$5. Open Apr 2–Nov 1; dry camping
allowed off-season.
14 close, open sites.
Central faucet, chemical toilets, tables,
fire rings, canoe launch.
In high, scenic bluff area next to large
natural pools in Big Piney Creek.
Splash in pools. Canoe. Fish. Hike to
Waldo Mountain Special Interest Area.
14-day limit. Hunting in season.

LOST VALLEY

Buffalo National River
(501) 741-5443
State map: B3
From PONCA, head W on
AR 43 for 2 miles (3.2 k). Watch for sign.
(Also see Steel Creek.)
FREE so choose a chore.
Open All Year.
15 close, screened tent sites.
Central faucet, pit toilets, tables, grills,
fire rings.
In flat but wooded area.
Walk to Eden Falls and Cob Cave. Snap
a few photos.
14-day/15-ft limits. Hunting in season.
Occasional snakes. No generators in
quiet hours. Crowded spring and fall.
1100 ft (330 m)

MAUMEE SOUTH

Buffalo National River
(501) 741-5443
State map: B5
At MORNING STAR,
follow signs N to camp.
FREE so choose a chore.
Open All Year.
Undesignated close, open sites.
Pit toilets, tables, fire rings.
In remote spot next to river.
Swim, boat, or fish.
NO water. 14-day limit. Occasional
crawling pests (chiggers, ticks, snakes).
No generators in quiet hours.
600 ft (180 m)

MILL CREEK

Ouachita NF (501) 637-4174
State map: E2
From BEE BRANCH, travel
14 miles (22.4 k) NW on
AR 92. Turn Left (N) on access road and
go 3 miles (4.8 k). (Also see Big Brushy
and Little Pines.)
$5. Open Mar 31–Oct 15.
27 scattered, open sites.
Central faucet, flush toilets, tables, grills.
Among pine and hardwood trees on
banks of Greers Ferry Lake.
Enjoy water activities on lake.
14-day limit. Crowded holiday
weekends. No generators in quiet hours.
870 ft (261 m)

MILL CREEK

COE (501) 362-2416
State map: G5
From BEE BRANCH, travel
14 miles (22.4 k) NW on
AR 92. Turn Left (N) on access road and
go 3 miles (4.8 k). (Nearby Narrows and
Sugar Loaf cost $7.)
FREE so choose a chore.
Open All Year.
39 scattered, screened sites.
Central faucet, pit toilets, tables, fire
rings, grills, boat ramp.
On banks of Greers Ferry Lake among
pine and hardwood.
Swim, boat, waterski, and fish.
14-day limit. Crowded holiday
weekends. No generators in quiet hours.
480 ft (144 m)

MOORES BAYOU

COE (501) 548-2291
State map: G7
From DEWITT, take
AR 165 S for 19 miles
(30.4 k). Turn Left (E) on AR 169 and go
2 miles (3.2 k). (Also see Jack's Bay.)
FREE so choose a chore.
Open All Year.
7 close, open sites.
Hand pump, pit toilets, tables, fire rings,
grills, boat ramp.
On bayou with access to Arkansas River.

▲ ▲

Boat and fish. Watch wildlife.
14-day limit. Hunting in season.
Crowded holidays.

MOUNT HERSEY

Buffalo National River
(501) 741-5443
State map: B4
Just W of PINDALL on
US 65, turn Left (S) on dirt road. Drive
6 miles (9.6 k). (Also see Carver and
Woolum.)
FREE so choose a chore. Open All Year.
Undesignated scattered, open sites.
Pit toilets.
Next to river.
Swim and fish. Enjoy seclusion.
NO water. 14-day limit. Occasional
crawling pests (chiggers, ticks, snakes).
No generators in quiet hours.
700 ft (210 m)

MOUNT NEBO SP-WALK-IN

(501) 229-3655
State map: D4
From DARDANELLE, head
NW on AR 22 for .5 mile
(800 m). Turn Left (W) on AR 155. Drive
to end. Walk in from .25 mile (400 m) to
3 miles (4.8 k). (Also see River View.)
$4; $10 drive-in. Open All Year.
35 (10 tent-only) scattered, open sites.
Water, flush toilets, showers, electric
hookups, tables, grills, fire rings, pool,
tennis courts.
On wooded mountain with river views.
Hike to enjoy overlooks. Mountain bike.
Play tennis or volleyball. Hang glide.
Attend ranger programs.
15-ft limit. Crowded holidays.
1800 ft (540 m)

OUTLET AREA

COE (501) 947-2372
State map: D3
From WAVELAND, drive S
on AR 309 for 2 miles
(3.2 k). (Also see Ashley Creek and Lick
Creek. Nearby Waveland Park costs $7.)
$5; $8 electric. Open All Year.
29 close, open sites. Central faucet, pit

toilets, dump station, electric hookups,
tables, grills, fire rings, pay phone.
On Blue Mountain Lake in Ozarks.
Walk nature trail. Fish. Attend ranger
programs.

OZAN POINT

COE (501) 246-5501
State map: F3
From ALPINE, take Finley
Rd E for 8 miles (12.8 k).
(Nearby Alpine Ridge and Iron
Mountain cost $10.)
FREE so choose a chore.
Open All Year.
50 close, open, tent sites.
Central faucet, flush toilets, tables, fire
rings, grills, boat ramp.
On shore of DeGray Lake.
Enjoy remote feeling and scenic views.
Swim, boat, waterski, or fish.
14-day limit. Hunting in season.
Crowded major holiday weekends.

OZARK

Buffalo National River
(501) 741-5443
State map: B4
From JASPER, head N on
AR 7 for 4 miles (6.4 k). Turn Left (W) at
sign and go 1.5 miles (2.4 k). (Also see
Erbie and Hasty.)
FREE so choose a chore. Open All Year.
Undesignated scattered, screened sites.
Central faucet, flush toilets, tables, fire
rings.
In shade among river bluffs.
Swim or fish. Attend ranger programs.
Walk nature trail. Enjoy scenery.
14-day limit. Occasional crawling pests
(chiggers, ticks, snakes). No generators
in quiet hours. Crowded spring
weekends.
800 ft (240 m)

OZONE

Ozark-St Francis NF
(501) 754-2864
State map: C3
Take scenic byway AR 21
N from CLARKSVILLE for 18 miles

(28.8 k).
FREE so choose a chore.
Open Apr 6–Dec 1.
8 scattered, screened sites.
Hand pump, chemical toilets, tables, grills, fire rings, shelter.
In tall pine trees at site of CCC camp. Hike Ozark Highlands Trail to appreciate ecology. Enjoy water activities on Lake Ludwig, 10 miles (16 k) S.
14-day limit. No generators in quiet hours.

PANTHER BAY

COE (501) 425-2700
State map: A5
From MOUNTAIN HOME, drive 9 miles (14.4 k) E on US 62. Turn Left (N) on AR 101 and go 1 mile (1.6 k). (Nearby Bidwell costs $9 and Henderson costs $8.)
$5; $8 electric. Open Apr 1–Oct 31.
28 scattered, open sites.
Central faucet, pit toilets, dump station, electric hookups, tables, fire rings, grills, boat ramp, marina.
On banks of Norfolk Lake.
Swim, boat, or fish.
14-day limit. No littering or gray water dumping. No noise after 10pm. Crowded weekends.

PIKEVILLE

COE (501) 285-2151
State map: F2
From MURFREESBORO, drive N on AR 19 for 7 miles (11.2 k) to dam. Turn Left (W) on gravel road and continue 6.5 miles (10.4 k). (Also see Buckhorn. Nearby Parker Creek costs $7.)
FREE so choose a chore.
Open Mar 15–Nov 15.
12 scattered, open sites. Hand pump, pit toilets, tables, grills, fire rings.
Under trees near shore of Lake Greeson. Enjoy boating, skiing, or fishing. Hike and take photographs.
14-day/35-ft limits. No generators in quiet hours. Crowded holidays.
563 ft (169 m)

PINE RIDGE PARK

COE (501) 584-4161
State map: G1
From DEQUEEN, take US 71 N for 3 miles (4.8 k). Turn Left (W) on access road and go 5 miles (8 k). Turn Right (N) on CR and continue 2 miles (3.2 k). (Nearby Bellah Mine costs $8 and Oak Grove costs $10.)
FREE; $7 developed; $10 electric.
Open Mar 1–Oct 31; dry camping allowed off-season.
54 close, open sites.
Central faucet, flush toilets, showers, dump station, electric hookups, tables, fire rings, grills, boat ramp.
Near shore of DeQueen Lake in foothills of Ouachita Mountains.
Swim or fish.
14-day limit. Hunting in season. Observe quiet hours.

PINEY BAY

COE (501) 968-5008
State map: D4
From LONDON, take US 64 E for 4 miles (6.4 k). Turn Left (N) on AR 359. Go 4 miles (6.4 k). (Also see Cabin Creek and Flat Rock.)
$5; $8 electric.
Open All Year.
91 scattered, open sites. &
Central faucet, pit toilets, dump station, electric hookups, tables, fire rings, boat ramp, group picnic pavilion, pay phone.
On scenic Piney Bay Arm of Lake Dardanelle.
Boat, waterski, swim, or fish. Attend ranger programs.
14-day limit. Crowded holidays.

POINT CEDAR

COE (501) 246-5501
State map: F3
From POINT CEDAR, head SE on access road for 2 miles (3.2 k). (Also see Lenox Marcus. Nearby Shouse Ford costs $10.)
$3.
Open Mar 1–Dec 1.

▲ ▲

62 (4 tent-only) close, open sites.
Central faucet, flush toilets, tables, fire rings, grills, boat ramp.
With scenic view of DeGray Lake.
Enjoy water activities on lake.
14-day limit. Hunting in season.
Crowded major holidays.

POINT REMOVE

COE (501) 329-2986
State map: D4
From MORRILTON, drive S on South Division Street for 2 miles (3.2 k). (Nearby Cherokee and Sequoia cost $11.)
FREE so choose a chore.
Open Mar 1–Oct 31.
20 scattered, open sites.
Central faucet, flush toilets, tables, fire rings, grills, boat ramp.
Next to creek under hardwoods.
View wildlife. Take photos. Fish or boat.
14-day limit.
271 ft (81 m)

POINT RETURN

COE (501) 425-2700
State map: A5
Go E of BULL SHOALS on AR 178 toward dam. (Nearby Dam Site and Bull Shoals cost $7.)
$5. Open Mar 1–Nov 30; dry camping allowed off-season.
35 close, open sites. Central faucet, flush toilets, showers, dump station, tables, fire rings, boat ramp.
In shade with water view.
Enjoy quiet. Swim, fish, boat, or ski.
14-day limit.
750 ft (225 m)

RED BANK

COE (501) 425-2700
State map: A6
From MOUNTAIN HOME, drive 9 miles (14.4 k) E on US 62. Turn Left (N) on AR 101 and go 5 miles (8 k). Turn Right (E) on CR 41 and travel 3 miles (4.8 k). (Also see Udall in MO. Nearby Gamaliel costs $10.)
$4. Open All Year.

12 close, open sites.
Central faucet, pit toilets, tables, fire rings, grills, boat ramp.
On northern arm of Norfolk Lake.
Swim, boat, and fish.
14-day limit. No littering or gray-water dumping. No noise after 10pm. Crowded weekends.

REDDING

Ozark-St Francis NF
(501) 754-2864
State map: C3
From just N of CASS on AR 23, take gravel FR 1003 E for 3 miles (4.8 k). (Also see Wolf Pen.)
$5. Open All Year.
25 scattered, screened sites.
Hand pump, flush toilets, showers, tables, grills, fire rings, canoe ramp.
Next to Mulberry River.
Hike loop trail to Ozark Highlands Trail.
Fish or canoe.
14-day limit. No generators in quiet hours.

RICHLAND CREEK

Ozark-St Francis NF
(501) 446-5122
State map: C4
From BEN HUR, head S on AR 16 for 1 mile (1.6 k). Turn Left (E) on FR 1205 and go 1 mile (1.6 k). Turn Left (N) on rough, gravel FR 1205 and continue 8 miles (12.8 k).
FREE so choose a chore.
Open All Year.
4 close, open sites.
Central faucet, chemical toilets, tables, fire rings.
Beside pretty mountain stream with waterfalls, rocks, and bluffs.
Hike. Relax. Take photos.
14-day limit. No trailers.

RIVER BLUFF

Ouachita NF (501) 867-2101
State map: E3
From MOUNT IDA, take US 270 NW for .5 mile (800 m). Turn Right (N) on AR 27. Go

▲ ▲

1 mile (1.6 k). Turn Left (NW) on gravel CR 59. Go 4 miles (6.4 k). Turn Left on FR 138. Drive 2.5 miles (4 k). (Also see Fulton Branch and Rocky Shoals.)
FREE so choose a chore.
Open All Year.
7 scattered, screened sites.
Hand pump, pit toilets, tables, grills, fire rings.
In forest along Ouachita River.
Explore area on Womble Trail. Canoe river. Swim or fish.
No trash arrangements (pack it out).
14-day limit. Hunting in season. No generators in quiet hours.
600 ft (180 m)

RIVER RIDGE

COE (800) 844-2129
State map: C2
From CECIL, take AR 96 W for 12 miles (19.2 k). Turn Right (N) on unimproved CR. Go 1.5 miles (2.4 k). (Also see Citadel Bluff.)
FREE so choose a chore.
Open All Year.
25 scattered, open sites.
Central faucet, pit toilets, tables, fire rings, grills, boat ramp.
Among cottonwood on shore of Arkansas River.
Boat or fish.
14-day/35-ft limits. Hunting in season.

RIVER RUN EAST

COE (501) 898-3343
State map: G2
From ASHDOWN, drive E on AR 32 for 12 miles (19.2 k). (Nearby Beard's Bluff and Beard's Lake cost $10.)
FREE so choose a chore.
Open All Year.
7 close, open sites. Pit toilets, tables, fire rings, grills, boat ramp.
Below dam along winding stretch of Little River.
Fish or boat.
NO water. 14-day limit.

RIVER RUN WEST

COE (501) 898-3343
State map: G2
From ASHDOWN, drive E on AR 32 for 10 miles (19.2 k).
FREE so choose a chore.
Open All Year.
5 close, open sites. Pit toilets, tables, fire rings, grills, boat ramp.
Along Little River below Millwood Dam.
Enjoy boating and fishing.
NO water. 14-day limit.

RIVER VIEW

COE (501) 968-5008
State map: D4
From DARDANELLE, head N toward dam. (Also see Mount Nebo SP Walk-In. Nearby Old Post Road costs $9 and Lake Dardanelle SP costs $12.)
$5; $8 electric.
Open All Year.
32 (14 tent-only) close, open sites.
Central faucet, pit toilets, electric hookups, tables, fire rings, group picnic pavilion.
Below Lake Dardanelle Dam overlooking Arkansas River.
Fish.
14-day limit.

ROCK CREEK

COE (501) 285-2151
State map: F2
From NEWHOPE, take US 70 E for 5 miles (8 k). Turn Right (SE) on unimproved road and go 7 miles (11.2 k). (Also see Buckhorn and Star of the West.)
FREE so choose a chore.
Open Mar 15–Nov 15.
Undesignated scattered, open sites.
Pit toilets.
On tree-covered, flat terrain next to Lake Greeson.
Fish or relax.
NO water. 14-day/40-ft limits. Hunting in season. No generators in quiet hours. Crowded holidays.

▲ ▲

ROCKY SHOALS

Ouachita NF (501) 867-2101
State map: E3
From MOUNT IDA, take
US 270 NW for 6 miles
(9.6 k). Turn Right before Ouachita River
Bridge. (Also see Fulton Branch and
River Bluff.)
FREE so choose a chore.
Open All Year.
6 scattered, screened sites.
Hand pump, pit toilets, tables, grills, fire
rings.
In forest along Ouachita River.
Swim or fish.
No trash arrangements (pack it out).
14-day limit. Hunting in season. No
generators in quiet hours.
600 ft (180 m)

RUSH

Buffalo National River
(501) 741-5443
State map: B5
From YELLVILLE, go S on
AR 14 for 11 miles (17.6 k). Turn Left (E)
on access road and continue 8 miles
(12.8 k). (Also see Highway 14. Nearby
Buffalo Point costs $7.)
FREE so choose a chore.
Open All Year.
Undesignated scattered, open sites.
Central faucet, pit toilets, grills.
At site of old mining town near river.
Swim, boat, or fish. Explore. Hike into
Lower Buffalo Wilderness Area.
14-day limit. Occasional crawling pests
(chiggers, ticks, snakes). No generators
in quiet hours. Crowded summer.
520 ft (156 m)

SARATOGA LANDING

COE (501) 898-3343
State map: G2
From SARATOGA, head S
for 1 mile (1.6 k) on AR 32.
Turn Right (W) on AR 234 and go 1 mile
(1.6 k). (Nearby Cottonshed costs $10.)
FREE so choose a chore.
Open All Year.
21 close, open sites.

Central faucet, pit toilets, tables, fire
rings, grills, boat ramp, playground.
On flat next to Millwood Lake among
rolling hills.
Boat or fish. Enjoy waterfowl,
wildflowers, and other natural beauty.
14-day limit.

SHIRLEY CREEK FLOAT CAMP

Ouachita NF (501) 356-4186
State map: E2
From PENCIL BLUFF,
drive W on AR 88 for
6 miles (9.6 k). Turn Right (S) on gravel
FR 7991. Go .5 mile (800 m). (Also see
Big Brushy.)
FREE so choose a chore.
Open All Year.
4 close, open sites.
Hand pump, pit toilets, tables, fire rings,
grills, boat ramp (canoe or flat-bottom).
In shade along Ouachita River.
Canoe, kayak, or float. Fish. Watch
wildlife.
14-day limit. Crowded hunting season.
880 ft (264 m)

SOUTH FORK

COE (501) 362-2416
State map: C5
From CLINTON, go
2 miles (3.2 k) E on AR 16.
Turn Right (SE) on gravel access road
and drive 7 miles (11.2 k). (Nearby
Choctaw and Van Buren cost $7.)
FREE so choose a chore.
Open All Year.
13 scattered, screened sites.
Central faucet, pit toilets, tables, fire
rings, grills, boat ramp.
On Greers Ferry Lake amid pine and
hardwood.
Enjoy swimming, boating, skiing, and
fishing. Walk to enjoy solitude.
14-day limit. No generators in quiet
hours. Crowded holiday weekends.
480 ft (144 m)

▲ ▲

SOUTH FOURCHE

Ouachita NF (501) 984-5313
State map: E4
From HOLLIS, head S on
AR 7 (Scenic Byway)
.25 mile (400 m). (Also see Iron Springs.)
FREE so choose a chore.
Open All Year.
7 scattered, open sites.
Hand pump, pit toilets, tables, fire rings.
Next to picturesque South Fourche
LaFave River in shortleaf
pine/hardwood forest.
Fish. Explore. Enjoy fall color.
14-day limit. Small vehicles only. No
generators in quiet hours. Crowded
holidays.
500 ft (150 m)

SPRING LAKE

Ozark-St Francis NF
(501) 963-3076
State map: D3
From BELLEVILLE, take
AR 307 N for 4 miles (6.4 k). Turn Right
(E) on gravel FR 1602 and go 3 miles
(4.8 k). (Also see Cameron Bluff and
Cove Lake. Nearby Shoal Bay costs $10.)
$5; reservations accepted at (501)
963-3076 for an additional $6.
Open May 25–Sep 5.
13 close, screened sites.
Central faucet, chemical toilets, tables,
fire rings, grills, boat ramp, bathhouse
with cold showers.
On scenic, 82-acre mountain lake.
Swim or fish. Hike. Play volleyball or
horseshoes. Attend ranger programs.
14-day limit. No pets on beach. No
generators in quiet hours. Crowded
holidays.
700 ft (210 m)

STAR OF THE WEST

COE (501) 285-2151
State map: F2
From DAISY, drive W on
US 70 for 5 miles (8 k).
(Also see Arrowhead Point and Rock
Creek. Nearby Self Creek costs $7.)
FREE so choose a chore.

Open All Year.
21 scattered, open sites. Hand pump, pit
toilets, tables, grills, fire rings.
Next to Little Missouri River on flat,
wooded terrain.
Fish, take photos, or do nothing.
14-day/18-ft limits. No generators in
quiet hours. Crowded holidays.
563 ft (169 m)

STARKEY

COE (501) 636-1210
State map: A2
From EUREKA SPRINGS,
head W on US 62 for
4 miles (6.4 k). Turn Left (SW) on
AR 187 and access road. Drive 7 miles
(11.2 k). (Nearby Dam Site costs $9.)
FREE so choose a chore.
Open All Year.
31 close, open sites. ❧
Central faucet, pit toilets, tables, fire
rings, grills, boat ramp, playground,
group pavilion.
At only free area on Beaver Lake.
Swim, boat, ski, or fish. Hike. Attend
ranger programs.
14-day limit.
1120 ft (336 m)

STEEL CREEK

Buffalo National River
(501) 741-5443
State map: B3
From PONCA, take AR 74
NE for 2.5 miles (4 k). Turn Left (N) on
steep gravel road and go 3 miles (4.8 k).
(Also see Kyles Landing and Lost
Valley.)
FREE so choose a chore.
Open All Year.
Undesignated scattered, open sites.
Central faucet, pit toilets, fire rings.
On river flat beneath towering bluffs.
Canoe, fish, or swim. Hike to
Hemmed-In-Hollow. Take photos.
14-day limit. No RVs. Occasional
crawling pests (chiggers, ticks, snakes).
Observe quiet hours. Crowded spring
weekends.
1000 ft (300 m)

STORM CREEK LAKE

Ozark-St Francis NF
(501) 295-5278
State map: E9
From WEST HELENA, take
AR 242 N for 4 miles (6.4 k). Turn Right
(E) on FR 1900 and travel 3 miles (4.8 k).
$3. Open Apr 1–Sep 14; dry camping
allowed off-season.
18 close, open sites.
Central faucet, flush toilets, showers,
tables, fire rings, boat ramp.
On Crowley's Ridge next to 420-acre
lake.
Swim, fish, or boat (10 hp limit).
14-day limit.

TRACY

COE (501) 425-2700
State map: A5
From MOUNTAIN HOME,
go 6.5 miles (10.4 k) S on
AR 5. Turn Left (E) on AR 3411 and
drive 3 miles (4.8 k). (Also see George's
Cove. Nearby Robinson Point costs $9.)
FREE so choose a chore.
Open All Year.
7 close, open sites.
Hand pump, pit toilets, tables, fire rings,
grills, boat ramp, marina.
On banks of Norfolk Lake.
Boat or fish.
14-day limit. No littering or gray-water
dumping. No noise after 10pm. Crowded
weekends and holidays.

TRULOCK

COE (501) 534-0451
State map: F6
From NOBLE LAKE, head
N on access road for
3 miles (4.8 k).
FREE so choose a chore.
Open Mar 1–Oct 31.
15 close, open sites.
Central faucet, flush toilets, tables, fire
rings, boat ramp, playground.
On Arkansas River.
Fish and boat.
14-day limit.

TWIN CREEK

COE (501) 767-2101
State map: E3
From MOUNT IDA, drive
7.5 miles (12 k) on US 270.
Turn Left (NW) and take signed access
road 1 mile (1.6 k). (Nearby Denby Point
costs $7.)
FREE so choose a chore.
Open All Year.
15 scattered, open sites. Central faucet,
flush toilets, dump station, tables, fire
rings, grills, boat ramp.
On Lake Ouachita.
Boat, ski, swim, or fish.
14-day limit. Hunting in season. No
generators in quiet hours.
592 ft (178 m)

VACHE GRASSE

COE (800) 844-2129
State map: D2
From LAVACA, take
AR 255 W for 2.5 miles
(4 k). Turn Right (N) on CR and go
1.2 miles (1.9 k).
FREE so choose a chore.
Open All Year.
20 scattered, screened sites.
Central faucet, flush toilets, tables, fire
rings, grills, boat ramp.
In heavy woods along creek near
Arkansas River.
Enjoy fishing or boating. Relax.
14-day/35-ft limits.

WHITE CLIFFS

COE (501) 898-3343
State map: G2
Head S on AR 317 from
BROWNSTOWN–watch
signs. (Also see Ashley's Camp.)
FREE so choose a chore.
Open All Year.
18 close, open sites. Pit toilets, tables, fire
rings, grills, boat ramp.
Next to Millwood Lake among cedar
trees and limestone outcroppings.
Boat or fish. Take photos of scenic
surroundings. Relax.
NO water. 14-day limit.

▲ ▲

WHITE ROCK MOUNTAIN

Ozark-St Francis NF
(501) 667-1248
State map: C2
From MULBERRY, head N
on AR 215 for 15 miles (24 k). Drive
twisting, paved/gravel FR 1505 for
5 miles (8 k). (Nearby Shores Lake costs
$7.)
$3; reservations accepted at
(501) 667-2191.
Open All Year.
8 close, open, tent sites. Central faucet,
chemical toilets, tables, grills.
On mountain with spectacular bluffs and
scenic views.
Hike rim trail or venture onto Ozark
Highlands Trail. Take photographs.
14-day limit. Small vehicles only. 50-80
foot bluffs–NOT for small children!
2250 ft (675 m)

WOLF PEN

Ozark-St Francis NF
(501) 754-2864
State map: C3
From CLARKSVILLE, head
NW on AR 103 for 22 miles (35.2 k).
Turn Left (W) on gravel FR 1003 and go
2 miles (3.2 k). (Also see Redding.)
FREE so choose a chore.
Open All Year.
6 scattered, screened sites.
Hand pump, chemical toilets, tables,
grills, fire rings, canoe ramp.
Along Mulberry River with scenic bluffs.
Canoe, swim, or fish.
14-day limit. Hunting in season. No
generators in quiet hours.

WOODS POINT

COE (501) 425-2700
State map: A5
From MOUNTAIN HOME,
go 16 miles (25.6 k) E on
US 62. Turn Right (S) on CR 91 and
drive 5 miles (8 k). Continue S on CR 93.
(Also see Hand Cove and Jordan.)
$5.
Open Apr 1–Oct 31; dry camping
allowed off-season.
11 close, open sites.
Central faucet, pit toilets, dump station,
tables, fire rings, grills, boat ramp.
On banks of Norfolk Lake.
Boat and fish.
14-day limit. No littering or gray-water
dumping. No noise after 10pm. Crowded
weekends.

WOOLUM

Buffalo National River
(501) 741-5443
State map: B4
From ST JOE, take access
road SW for 7 miles (11.2 k). (Also see
Mt Hersey. Nearby Tyler Bend costs $7.)
FREE so choose a chore.
Open All Year.
Undesignated scattered, open sites.
Pit toilets.
On flat field and gravel bar near river.
Swim or fish. Hike to Ozark Highlands
Trail.
NO water. 14-day limit. Hunting in
season. Occasional crawling pests
(chiggers, ticks, snakes). No generators
in quiet hours.
700 ft (210 m)

▲ ▲

CONNECTICUT
PUBLIC LANDS CAMPING

Connecticut considers itself classic. To quote the Connecticut Tourism Office, "In every season of the year, Connecticut's ageless beauty and essential New England qualities shape its leisure time pleasures in a classic mold. It's where history and tradition blend with today's creative spirit, where old and new produce enjoyment that is, at once, exciting, familiar and rewarding."

In this New England state known for its people's hard-earned sense of values, there are no public lands camp fees of $5.00 or less—unless you're trail-riding in the Natchaug State Forest or backpacking the Appalachian Trail. The Appalachian National Scenic Trail passes through the northwest corner of the state. There are, however, no national parks or national forests in Connecticut. The **US Army Corps of Engineers** (COE) does offer camping at West Thompson Lake for $8.00–$14.00.

From $9.00 to $12.00, the following **Connecticut State Parks** (SP) and **State Forests** (SF) offer camping:

American Legion SF
Black Rock SP
Burr Pond SP
Devil's Hopyard SP
Hammonasset Beach SP
Hopeville Pond SP
Housatonic Meadows SP
Kettletown SP
Lake Waramaug SP
Macedonia Brook SP
Mashamoquet Brook SP
Pachaug SF
Rocky Neck SP

Horse camping is available at Natchaug SF and Pachaug SF. Canoe camping on the Connecticut River is permitted at Hurd, Gillette Castle, and Selden Island state parks.

On the positive side for nature enthusiasts, nearly two-thirds of Connecticut is open land, making it ideal for hikers, birdwatchers, wildlife photographers, and, by permit, fishermen and hunters. Woodland, wetland, farmland, and coastal habitats allow hundreds of different species of wildlife to flourish in Connecticut—from wintering bald eagles and breeding bluebirds to roving bobcats and visiting black bears.

Season changes offer additional variety in the public recreation areas: in autumn, view fall color; in winter, cross-country ski and ice skate; in spring, see wildflowers bloom; in summer, enjoy swimming, boating, and other water sports.

Connecticut

Grid conforms to official state map. For your copy, call (800) CTBOUND
or write CT Tourism Office, 865 Brook St, Rocky Hill, CT 06067.

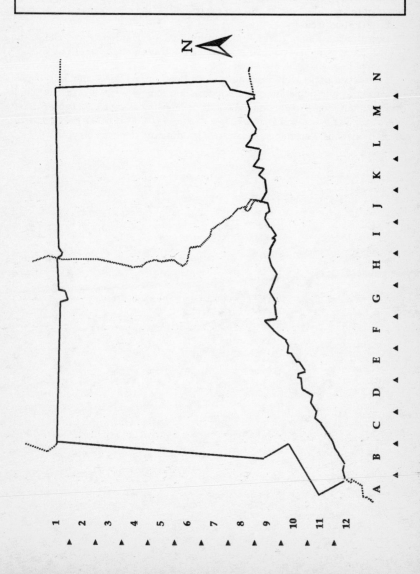

▲ ▲

DELAWARE
PUBLIC LANDS CAMPING

The "Small Wonder," Delaware, has no public lands campgrounds that cost $5.00 or less per night. In this small state, there are no national parks or forests.

Delaware Division of Parks and Recreation maintains campgrounds at five **State Parks** (SP). Depending on manmade facilities, these parks charge $13.00–$19.00 per site at the seashore and $10.00–$12.00 per site at inland areas. Senior citizens can qualify for a $1.00–$2.00 discount depending on the season, the park location, and the desired facilities.

Atlantic Coast state parks with camping (Cape Henlopen and Delaware Seashore) are extremely popular from Memorial Day through Labor Day though the beaches are enjoyable year-round.

Inland state parks with camping (Killens Pond, Lums Pond, and Trap Pond) offer insights into human history and interesting ecologies as well as recreational opportunities. Enjoy rowing on the ponds or canoeing along a bald cypress trail.

Numerous state wildlife areas are managed and offer no camping accommodations. Remember: Delaware's good nature depends on you!

Delaware

Grid conforms to official state map. For your copy, call (800) 441-8846 or write Delaware Tourism Office, 99 Kings Hwy, Dover, DE 19903.

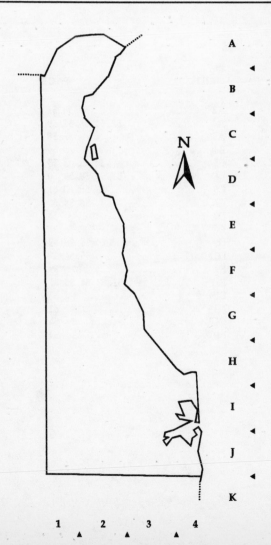

N

A B C D E F G H I J K

1 2 3 4

FLORIDA
CAMPGROUND LOCATIONS

► ► Find location on facing page map grid. ► ►
▼ ▼ Locate area campgrounds on these page numbers. ▼ ▼

Florida

Grid conforms to official state map. For your copy, call (904) 487-1462
or write Dept of Commerce, Collins Building, Tallahassee, FL 32399-2000.

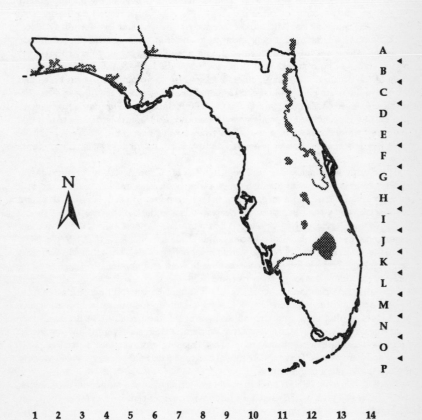

▲▲▲▲▲▲▲▲▲▲▲▲▲▲▲▲▲▲▲▲▲▲▲▲▲▲▲▲▲▲▲▲▲▲▲▲▲

PUBLIC LANDS CAMPING

Natural wonders such as miles of beaches, keys, colorful coral reefs, a river of grass called the Everglades, countless inland lakes and springs, manatees, and pink flamingos beckon campers from great distances to Florida the year-round. In winter, the Sunshine State becomes an extremely popular destination because of its relatively comfortable temperatures.

Camping is available in the following **National Park Service** (NPS) areas: Big Cypress National Preserve, Biscayne National Park (NP), Canaveral National Seashore (NS), Dry Tortugas NP (formerly Fort Jefferson), Everglades NP, and Gulf Islands NS. Along the Tamiami Trail and Loop Road in Big Cypress National Preserve, recreational vehicle boondocking has become so popular that NPS is developing a campground. While here study subtropical plant and animal life. Also, show respect for the ancestral home of the Seminole and Miccosukee Indians. At Biscayne and Dry Tortugas national parks, you must arrange boat transportation to and from these Florida Key subtropical locations. There are free developed campgrounds at Biscayne Bay and backcountry opportunities at both parks. At both places, enjoy the birds of the sky and the coral reefs of the ocean. Canaveral NS offers backcountry camping on its north beach and islands in the north end of Mosquito Lagoon. Here enjoy beach activities and wildlife studies. In Everglades NP, camp at $4.00–$8.00 Flamingo on Florida Bay or various free canoe-in locations. View alligators and crocodiles, tropical birds and plants that live in and around this expansive, shallow river of water and grass. At Gulf Islands NS there is a $10.00 campground near 19th-century Fort Pickens on barrier island, Santa Rosa.

The Florida National Scenic Trail begins in the Big Cypress National Preserve with cypress trees draped with Spanish moss, bromeliads, and orchids. Follow the trail through central Florida's pines, oaks, and palm hammocks. In north Florida, hikers and backpackers enjoy the serenity of the deep woods and dark rivers.

US Forest Service offers developed campgrounds as well as primitive camping experiences in the Apalachicola, Osceola, and Ocala national forests. While camping, enjoy the great outdoors by hiking, swimming, boating, waterskiing, horseback riding, berry picking, birdwatching, photographing flowers and animals. In these national forest areas, camp fees range from free to $15.50.

In the Florida panhandle, Apalachicola National Forest (NF) encompasses over 500,000 acres of primarily pine forest. Claims to fame include unusual limestone sink holes, lots of alligators, and two wilderness areas: the usually wet Bradwell Bay Wilderness and Mud Swamp/New River Wilderness. In these swampy environments, find insect-eating plants, titi bushes, azaleas, creeping ground pines as well as pond pines and hardwoods. Drive the 31-mile Apalachee Savannahs Scenic Byway to view these unusual plant communities.

Osceola NF, over 150,000 acres in northern Florida, features numerous depressions such as Ocean Pond, a 1,760-acre lake filled with magnificent bald cypress. Big Gum Swamp Wilderness area preserves over 13,000 acres of cypress-gum swamps with pine perimeters. Part of the Florida National Scenic Trail passes through the forest as well as a canoe trail along the Middle Prong to the Saint Mary's River.

300,000-acre Ocala NF in central Florida offers the only entirely subtropical forest in the US. There are four wilderness areas: Alexander Springs Creek, Billies Bay, Juniper Prairie, and Little Lake George. At least a thousand lakes, springs, and sink holes dot the Ocala NF, an ecology made famous in Marjorie Kinnan Rawlings' Pulitzer Prize-winning novel, *The Yearling*. Too, the area is familiar to archeologists, Civil War history

▲ ▲

buffs, and birdwatchers. Canoeing is popular (along Get Out Creek, Juniper Creek, and the Oklawaha River) as well as walking the Ocala Trail section of the Florida National Scenic Trail.

US Army Corps of Engineers (COE) has turned out to be a mixed blessing in Florida, creating navigable waterways for commerce but, in the process, changing fragile ecosystems. In recent years, much time and money have been spent on how to save the Everglades. The engineers offer campgrounds on nearby Lake Okeechobee and Okeechobee Waterway plus waterfront camping along the Lake Seminole Project. COE camp fees range from $6.00–$12.00. The state of Florida is in the process of taking over COE facilities along Oklawaha and Saint Johns rivers.

One administrator's vision for **Florida State Parks** (SP) was to return parklands to the pristine level found when Hernando de Soto set foot on the peninsula. Camp the "Real Florida" at 44 of the 110 parks. Try coastal camping at Anastasia, Bahia Honda, Big Lagoon, Cayo Costa, Collier-Seminole, Flagler Beach, Fort Clinch, Grayton Beach, John Pennekamp, Jonathan Dickinson (on Loxahatchee National Wild and Scenic River), Koreshan, Little Talbot Island, Long Key, Oscar Scherer, Saint Andrews, Saint George Island, Saint Joseph, Sebastian Inlet, and Tomoka. Additional camping via boat is available at Bahia Honda, Cape Florida, Caladesi Island, and John Pennekamp. Find interesting inland ecologies while camping at Blackwater River, Blue Spring, Dead Lakes, Falling Waters, Faver-Dykes, Florida Caverns, Gold Head Branch, Highlands Hammock, Hontoon Island (boat camping too), Lake Griffin, Lake Kissimmee, Lake Manatee, Little Manatee River, Manatee Springs, Myakka River, Ochlockonee River, O'Leno, Paynes Prairie, Rocky Bayou, Suwannee River, Three Rivers, Torreya, and Wekiwa Springs.

Fees for camping in the state parks vary with location and season–anywhere from $8.00 to $19.00. The state park fee schedule also denotes primitive camping along nature and equestrian trails for $3.00 per person. Check out the primitive camping possibilities at Florida Caverns, Gold Head Branch, Jonathan Dickinson, Lake Kissimmee, Little Manatee River, Myakka River, O'Leno, Prairie River, Saint George Island, Saint Joseph Peninsula, Torreya, and Wekiwa Springs.

Florida Division of Forestry offers camping opportunities too–at Blackwater River and Pine Log state forests in the panhandle area as well as the Withlacoochee State Forest (SF) above Tampa Bay. There are free backpacking opportunities at Blackwater River and Withlacoochee state forests. More backpacking is available at three state preserves perfect for communing with nature: Fakahatchee Strand (near Copeland), Prairie Lakes (out of Kenansville), and Tosohatchee (between Orlando and Titusville). Check with rangers before venturing into these pristine areas. The **Florida Game and Freshwater Fish Commission** allows camping in many wildlife management areas. Practice careful safety and sanitation procedures in these areas used by hunters and fishermen.

In addition to national and state public lands, many **cities** and **counties** offer campgrounds. Those that qualify for this price-conscious guide are Dixie County, Gadsden County, Leon County, Levy County, and Washington County.

There's a lot of natural beauty left in Florida. Enjoy and protect these unique ecologies of plants and animals–the real Florida.

▲ ▲

BEAR LAKE

Blackwater River SF
(904) 957-4201
State map: A2
From MUNSON, drive
W on FL 4 for 2.5 miles
(4 k). Turn Left (N). (Also see Hurricane
Lake and Krul RA.)
$4; $10 developed.
Open All Year.
45 (5 tent-only) close, open sites.
Water at every site, flush toilets,
showers, dump station, electric hookups,
tables, fire rings, boat ramp.
In shade on sloping, grassy banks of
107-acre lake.
Fish or boat (paddle or electric motor
only). Hike Jackson Trail.
14-day limit. Hunting in season. No
generators in quiet hours. Crowded
spring and fall weekends.

BIG BASS LAKE

Ocala NF
(904) 669-7495
State map: E11
From ALTOONA, go W
on CR 42 for 9 miles
(14.4 k). Turn Right (N) on gravel FR 588
and go .25 mile (400 m). (Nearby Lake
Dorr and Clearwater Lake cost $7.)
$4.
Open Oct 1–Apr 30.
34 scattered, open sites.
Central faucet, chemical toilets, dump
station, tables, grills, fire rings.
In live oak/longleaf pine hammock on
Big Bass Prairie (shallow lake).
Spot wildlife.
14-day/32-ft limits. Hunting in season.
50 ft (15 m)

BIG SCRUB

Ocala NF
(904) 669-7495
State map: E11
From UMATILLA, drive
N on FL 19 for 8 miles
(12.8 k). Turn Left (W) on FR 573 and go
7 miles (11.2 k). (Nearby Alexander
Springs costs $9 and Lake Dorr costs $7.)

FREE so choose a chore.
Open All Year.
100 close, open sites.
Central faucet, flush toilets.
In open stand of sand pine near old
dunes.
Relax.
14-day limit. Hunting in season.
Crowded winters.
75 ft (23 m)

BISCAYNE NP

(305) 247-7275
State map: N14
FREE.
Open All Year.
NO water. No trash
arrangements (pack it out). 14-day limit.
Mosquitos most of year.
6 ft (2 m)

▲ **Boca Chita Key Boat-In**
From Convoy Point (E of
HOMESTEAD), boat 10 miles (16 k)
ENE. (Open when Hurricane Andrew
damage is repaired.)
Undesignated scattered, open sites.
Flush toilets, tables, grills.
On coral rock island.
Fish, observe birds, and take photos.

▲ **Elliott Key Boat-In**
From Convoy Point (E of
HOMESTEAD), boat 8 miles (12.8 k) E.
Undesignated close, open sites.
Central faucet, flush toilets, showers,
tables, grills.
On subtropical, coral island.
Swim and boat. Snorkel reef. Explore
island. Take photos.

BLUE POND PARK

Washington County
(904) 638-6200
State map: A4
Locate park near CROW,
just off FL 77.
FREE so choose a chore.
Open All Year.
Undesignated scattered, open sites.
Tables, grills, boat ramp, playground.
Next to pond in county park.
Swim, boat, ski, or fish.

▲ ▲

NO water. No toilet facilities. 21-day limit.

BUCK LAKE

Ocala NF (904) 669-7495
State map: E11
From UMATILLA, travel
N on FL 19 for 11 miles
(17.6 k). Turn Left (W)
on gravel FR 595 and drive 2 miles
(3.2 k). Turn Left (S) on FR 514 and go
1 mile (1.6 k). (Also see Farles Lake.)
FREE so choose a chore.
Open All Year.
25 close, screened sites.
Hand pump, chemical toilets, tables, boat ramp.
Beneath sand pine next to 40-acre natural lake.
Relax in peaceful setting. Hike or fish. Canoe.
14-day limit. Hunting in season. Crowded winters.
100 ft (30 m)

CAMEL LAKE

Apalachicola NF
(904) 926-3561
State map: B5
From BRISTOL, travel S
on CR 12 for 12 miles
(19.2 k). Turn Left (E) on FR 105 and go
2 miles (3.2 k). (Also see Cotton Landing,
Silver Lake, and White Oak Landing.)
FREE so choose a chore.
Open All Year.
10 close, open sites.
Central faucet, flush toilets, tables, grills, boat ramp.
Under pine next to quiet, natural lake on Florida National Scenic Trail.
Hike to explore area. Spot wildlife.
Swim, boat (small motors), or fish.
14-day limit.

CANAVERAL NS-Backcountry

(407) 267-1110
State map: E13
From Turtle Mound
Archaeological Site (SE
of NEW SMYRNA
BEACH), go .25 mile (400 m) S on
US A1A to Information Center. Get free
permit and map. Boat or hike-in.
FREE.
Open Nov 1–Apr 30.
9 scattered, open, tent sites.
On several boat-accessible islands in
Mosquito Lagoon plus 1 hike-in site
(Klondike) on beach.
Observe wildlife and wetlands ecology.
NO water. No toilet facilities. No trash
arrangements (pack it out). 14-day limit.
Closed during space launches and
May 1–Oct 31 turtle-nesting season.
5 ft (2 m)

COE LANDING

Leon County Parks
(904) 487-3070
State map: B6
From TALLAHASSEE,
drive W on FL 20 for
9 miles (14.4 k). (Also see Halls Landing
and Williams Landing.)
FREE so choose a chore; reservations
accepted at (904) 487-3070.
Open All Year.
12 (8 tent-only) scattered, open sites.
Central faucet, flush toilets, showers,
tables, fire rings, grills, boat ramp.
Next to Lake Talquin.
Boat or fish. Watch wildlife.
10-day limit.
100 ft (30 m)

COTTON LANDING

Apalachicola NF
(904) 926-3561
State map: C5
From SUMATRA, head
NW on CR 379 for
3.2 miles (5.1 k). Turn Left (W) on
FR 123 and drive 2.8 miles (4.5 k). Turn
Left (SW) on FR 123-B and go .7 mile
(1.1 k). (Also see Camel Lake, Hickory
Landing, White Oak Landing, and
Wright Lake.)
FREE so choose a chore.
Open All Year.
4 close, open sites.
Hand pump, pit toilets, tables, boat

ramp.
In woods along Kennedy Creek.
Canoe or fish.
14-day limit. Hunting in season
(Oct–Jan).

DRY TORTUGAS NP-Boat-In

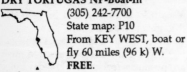

(305) 242-7700
State map: P10
From KEY WEST, boat or
fly 60 miles (96 k) W.
FREE.
Open All Year.
10 close, open, tent sites.
Flush toilets, tables, grills.
On sandy beach outside Fort Jefferson.
Snorkel, swim, boat, or fish. Explore fort.
Attend ranger programs. Take photos.
Watch birds.
NO water. No trash arrangements (pack
it out).
5 ft (2 m)

EVERGLADES NP-Flamingo Walk-In

(305) 247-6211
State map: O13
From FLORIDA CITY,
take FL 9336 SW about
45 miles (72 k). Also, **free**
backcountry permits (boat-in) available
at Visitor Center.
$4; $8 drive-in; $5 entrance fee.
Open All Year.
290 (60 tent-only) scattered, open sites.
Central faucet, flush toilets, cold
showers, dump station, tables, grills,
boat ramp, store, rentals (at lodge).
On edge of Florida Bay in grassy field.
Hike and bike to view incredible display
of wildlife. Take photos (spectacular
sunsets). Canoe. Attend ranger
programs.
14-day limit. Mosquitos.

FARLES LAKE

Ocala NF
(904) 669-7495
State map: E11
From UMATILLA, travel
N on FL 19 for 11 miles

(17.6 k). Turn Left (W) on gravel FR 595
and drive 4 miles (6.4 k). (Also see Buck
Lake.)
FREE so choose a chore.
Open All Year.
40 close, open sites.
Hand pump, chemical toilets, boat ramp.
In open, piney area next to natural lake.
Hike. Fish.
14-day limit. Hunting in season.
Crowded winters.
75 ft (23 m)

GAP/GIN LAKES

Washington County
(904) 638-6200
State map: A4
From WAUSAU, drive E
on FL 278 about .5 mile
(800 m) then bear Right (S) on unpaved
road and go about 5 miles (8 k). Turn
Right (W) for Gap Lake or Left (E) for
Gin Lake. (Also see Porter Lake.)
FREE so choose a chore.
Open All Year.
Undesignated scattered, open sites.
Tables, fire rings, boat ramp.
Next to 2 lakes in primitive settings.
Swim, boat, ski, or fish.
NO water. No toilet facilities. 30-day
limit.

GORNTO SPRINGS

Dixie County Parks
(904) 498-5806
State map: C9
From OLD TOWN, drive
NE on FL 349 for
11 miles (17.6 k). Turn Right (E) and go
2 miles (3.2 k).
FREE; $2 electric.
Open All Year.
Undesignated close, open sites.
Central faucet, flush toilets, electric
hookups, tables, grills, boat ramp.
At spring and Suwannee River.
Swim, scuba, boat, or fish.
14-day limit.

▲ ▲

GRASSY POND

Ocala NF
(904) 625-7470
State map: D11
From OCALA, travel E
on FL 40 for 12 miles
(19.2 k). Turn Left (N) on CR 314 and go
15 miles (24 k). Continue N on gravel
FR 88 for 6 miles (9.6 k). Turn Right (E)
on FR 88-C and drive 1 mile (1.6 k).
(Also see Lake Delancy. Nearby Salt
Springs costs $12.)
FREE so choose a chore.
Open All Year.
Undesignated scattered, open sites.
Hand pump, chemical toilets, tables.
In pines next to grassy wetlands.
Hike.
No trash arrangements (pack it out).
14-day limit. Noisy clearcut logging
nearby.
200 ft (60 m)

HALFMOON LAKE

Ocala NF
(904) 669-7495
State map: E11
From OCALA, head E on
FL 40 for 20 miles (32 k).
Turn Right (S) on gravel FR 579 and go
1 mile (1.6 k). Turn Right (W) on
FR 579-D and drive 1 mile (1.6 k).
(Nearby Juniper Springs costs $10.75.)
FREE so choose a chore.
Open All Year.
10 close, open, tent sites.
Hand pump, boat ramp.
On live oak hammock next to natural
lake in remote, unsecured area.
Fish.
No toilet facilities. 14-day limit. Hunting
in season.
100 ft (30 m)

HALL'S LANDING

Leon County Parks
(904) 487-3070
State map: B6
From TALLAHASSEE,
drive W on FL 20 for
15 miles (24 k). (Also see Coe Landing

and Williams Landing.)
FREE so choose a chore; reservations
accepted at (904) 487-3070.
Open All Year.
10 scattered, open, tent sites.
Central faucet, flush toilets, showers,
tables, grills, fire rings.
Next to Lake Talquin.
Boat or fish. Spot wildlife.
10-day limit.
100 ft (30 m)

HICKORY LANDING

Apalachicola NF
(904) 926-3561
State map: C5
From SUMATRA, take
FL 65 S for 2 miles
(3.2 k). Turn Right (W) on FR 101 and
drive 1.5 miles (2.4 k). Turn Left (SW) on
FR 101-B and go 1 mile (1.6 k). (Also see
Cotton Landing and Wright Lake.)
FREE so choose a chore.
Open All Year.
10 close, open sites.
Hand pump, pit toilets, electric hookups,
tables, boat ramp.
On Owl Creek (with spring) among oak
and hickory plus access to Apalachicola
River.
Canoe or fish.
14-day/22-ft limits. Crowded hunting
season (Oct–Jan).

HINTON LANDING

Dixie County Parks
(904) 498-5806
State map: D9
From OLD TOWN, head
SW on FL 349 for 5 miles
(8 k). Turn Left (SE) on CR 346A. (Also
see New Pine Landing and Purvis
Landing.)
FREE; $2 electric.
Open All Year.
Undesignated close, open sites.
Central faucet, flush toilets, electric
hookups, tables, boat ramp.
On Suwannee River.
Swim, scuba, waterski, boat, or fish.
14-day limit.

HITCHCOCK LAKE

Apalachicola NF
(904) 926-3561
State map: C6
From TELOGIA, drive S
on CR 67 for 22.8 miles
(36.5 k). Turn Left (E) on FR 184 and go
1.5 miles (2.4 k). (Also see Porter Lake
and Whitehead Lake.)
FREE so choose a chore.
Open All Year.
10 close, open sites.
Pit toilets, tables, boat ramp.
On lake near Ochlockonee River.
Canoe or fish.
NO water. 14-day/32-ft limits. Hunting
in season (Oct–Jan).

HOLMES CREEK

Washington County
(904) 638-6200
State map: A4
Find area just E of RED
HEAD.
FREE so choose a chore.
Open All Year.
7 scattered, screened sites.
Tables, fire rings, boat ramp.
Along several miles of Holmes Creek.
Canoe. Swim, boat, or fish.
NO water. No toilet facilities. No trash
arrangements (pack it out).

HOPKINS PRAIRIE

Ocala NF
(904) 625-7470
State map: D11
From OCALA, travel E
on FL 40 for 33 miles
(52.8 k). Turn Left (N) on FL 19 and go
8 miles (12.8 k). Turn Left (W) on gravel
FR 86 for 3 miles (4.8 k). Turn Right (N)
on FR 86-F for 1 mile (1.6 k). (Nearby
Salt Springs costs $12 and Juniper
Springs costs $10.75.)
FREE so choose a chore.
Open All Year.
Undesignated scattered, screened sites.
Hand pump, pit toilets.
Next to prairie.
Hike and view wildlife. Boat and fish.

No trash arrangements (pack it out).
14-day limit.
200 ft (60 m)

HORSESHOE BEACH

Dixie County Parks
(904) 498-5806
State map: D8
From CROSS CITY, drive
SW on FL 351 for
20 miles (32 k).
FREE; $2 electric.
Open All Year.
Undesignated close, open sites.
Central faucet, flush toilets, electric
hookups, tables, grills, boat ramp.
In open area on Gulf of Mexico.
Enjoy quiet. Swim, scuba, boat, or fish.
Gather oysters.
14-day limit.

HURRICANE LAKE

Blackwater River SF
(904) 957-4201
State map: A2
From MUNSON, travel
W on FL 4 for 3.5 miles
(5.6 k). Turn Left (N) and drive 6.5 miles
(10.4 k). Turn Right (NE) on clay
Kennedy Bridge Rd and go 2.5 miles
(4 k). (Also see Bear Lake.)
FREE so choose a chore.
Open All Year.
20 close, open sites.
Central faucet, flush toilets, showers,
tables, fire rings, boat ramp.
In shade on banks of 350-acre lake with
two camping areas..
Fish or boat (paddle or electric motor).
Hike area trails. Mountain bike.
14-day limit. Hunting in season. No
generators in quiet hours. Crowded
spring and fall weekends.

KARICK LAKE

Blackwater River SF
(904) 957-4201
State map: A2
From BAKER, head N on
FL 189 for 7.5 miles
(12 k). Turn Right (E) and continue

▲ ▲

.5 mile (800 m).
FREE so choose a chore.
Open All Year.
20 close, open sites.
Water at every site, flush toilets,
showers, dump station, tables, fire rings.
In shade on lakeshore.
Fish or boat (paddle or electric motor).
Hike Jackson Trail.
14-day limit. Hunting in season. No
generators in quiet hours. Crowded
spring and fall weekends.

KRUL RA

 Blackwater River SF
(904) 957-4201
State map: A2
From MUNSON, drive
W on FL 4 for 1.25 miles
(2 k). Turn Left (N). (Also see Bear
Lake.)
$4; $10 developed.
Open All Year.
55 (5 tent-only) close, open sites.
Water at every site, flush toilets,
showers, dump station, electric hookups,
tables, grills, fire rings.
In shade next to small (6.5-acre), manmade lake with swimming area.
Swim. Walk trail to Bear Lake.
14-day limit. No generators in quiet
hours. Crowded all summer.

LAKE DELANCY

 Ocala NF
(904) 625-7470
State map: D11
From OCALA, travel E
on FL 40 for 12 miles
(19.2 k). Turn Left (N) on CR 314 and go
15 miles (24 k). Continue N on gravel
FR 88 for 9 miles (14.4 k). Turn Right (E)
on FR 75 and drive 2 miles (3.2 k). (Also
see Grassy Pond. Nearby Salt Springs
costs $12.)
FREE so choose a chore.
Open All Year.
Undesignated scattered, open sites.

Hand pump, pit toilets, tables.
In longleaf pine and scrub near wetlands
and shallow lake–more private,
primitive sites to Right (W).
Hike or relax.
No trash arrangements (pack it out).
14-day limit. Noisy clearcut logging
nearby. Possible bug swarms.
200 ft (60 m)

LAKE EATON

 Ocala NF
(904) 625-7470
State map: E11
From OCALA, travel E
on FL 40 for 17 miles
(27.2 k). Turn Left (N) on CR 314A and
go 5 miles (8 k). Turn Right (E) on gravel
FR 96 and drive .5 mile (800 m). Turn
Left (N) on FR 96A and continue 1 mile
(1.6 k). (Nearby Fore Lake costs $7.50
and Salt Springs costs $12.)
$4.25.
Open All Year.
15 close, screened sites.
Hand pump, pit toilets, tables, fire rings,
grills, boat ramp.
Next to lake.
Boat or fish.
No trash arrangements (pack it out).
14-day limit.
200 ft (60 m)

LUCAS LAKE

 Washington County
(904) 638-6200
State map: A4
From GREENHEAD,
head NW on FL 279
about 4 miles (6.4 k). Turn Left (W).
FREE so choose a chore.
Open All Year.
Undesignated scattered, open sites.
Tables, fire rings, boat ramp.
Beside lake in primitive setting.
Swim, boat, ski, or fish.
NO water. No toilet facilities. No trash
arrangements (pack it out).

MACK LANDING

Apalachicola NF
(904) 926-3561
State map: C6
From SOPCHOPPY,
travel W on CR 375 for
10 miles (16 k). Turn Left (W) on FR 336.
(Also see Porter Lake and Wood Lake.)
FREE so choose a chore.
Open All Year.
Undesignated close, open sites.
Hand pump, pit toilets, tables, boat
ramp.
On creek feeding Ochlockonee River.
Canoe or fish.
14-day limit. Crowded hunting season
(Oct–Jan).

NEAL'S LANDING

COE (912) 662-2001
State map: A5
From MALONE, drive E
on FL 2 for 9 miles
(14.4 k). Turn Right (S)
just before bridge.
$5.
Open All Year.
22 close, open sites.
Central faucet, flush toilets, showers,
dump station, tables, fire rings, grills,
boat ramp.
On shady bluffs next to Chattahoochee
River.
Boat, ski, or fish. Watch birds. Explore
area.
14-day limit.
80 ft (24 m)

NEW PINE LANDING

Dixie County Parks
(904) 498-5806
State map: D9
From OLD TOWN, head
SW on FL 349 for 8 miles
(12.8 k). Turn Left (SE) on Rock Rd.
(Also see Hinton Landing.)
FREE; $2 electric.
Open All Year.
30 close, open sites.

Central faucet, flush toilets, electric
hookups, tables, grills, boat ramp.
On Suwannee River.
Swim, scuba, waterski, boat, or fish.
14-day limit.

PAT THOMPSON PARK AT HOPKINS LANDING

Gadsden County Parks
(904) 875-4544
State map: B6
From QUINCY, head S
for 10 miles (16 k) on
US 267. Turn Left (E) on Hopkins
Landing Rd and proceed 1 mile (1.6 k).
**$5; $10 electric; reservations accepted at
(904) 875-4544.**
Open All Year.
30 scattered, open sites.
Water at every site, flush toilets,
showers, dump station, electric hookups,
boat ramp, shelter.
Under large trees on peninsula in Lake
Talquin.
Boat or fish. Bike. Hike. Enjoy quiet.
10-day limit. No generators in quiet
hours. Crowded holidays.
81 ft (24 m)

PORTER LAKE

Apalachicola NF
(904) 643-2282
State map: B6
From TELOGIA, head S
on CR 67 about 16 miles
(25.6 k). Turn Left (E) on FR 13 and
drive 3 miles (4.8 k). (Also see Hitchcock
Lake, Mack Landing, Silver Lake,
Whitehead Lake.)
FREE so choose a chore.
Open All Year.
Undesignated close, open sites.
Central faucet, pit toilets, tables.
Next to Ochlockonee River and Florida
National Scenic Trail.
Hike. Canoe or fish.
14-day limit. Crowded hunting season
(Oct–Jan).

▲ ▲

PORTER LAKE

Washington County
(904) 638-6200
State map: A4
From GRANTHAM,
drive SE on unpaved
road about 1 mile (1.6 k). (Also see
Gap/Gin Lakes and Rattlesnake Lake.)
$5.
Open All Year.
Undesignated scattered, open sites.
Tables, fire rings, grills, boat ramp.
Around lake in 3 locations (Charley
John's Landing, Retreat II, and Sweet
Gum Landing at White Oak).
Swim, boat, ski, or fish.
NO water. No toilet facilities. No trash
arrangements (pack it out). 30-day limit.

PURVIS LANDING

Dixie County Parks
(904) 498-5806
State map: D9
From OLD TOWN, head
N on FL 349 for 6 miles
(9.6 k). Turn Right (E) and proceed
2 miles (3.2 k). (Also see Hinton
Landing.)
FREE so choose a chore.
Open All Year.
Undesignated close, open sites.
Central faucet, flush toilets, tables, boat
ramp.
On Suwannee River.
Swim, scuba, waterski, boat, or fish.
14-day limit.

RATTLESNAKE LAKE

Washington County
(904) 638-6200
State map: B4
From GRANTHAM,
drive SE on unpaved
road about 5 miles (8 k). (Also see Porter
Lake.)
$5.
Open All Year.
Undesignated scattered, open sites.
Tables, fire rings, boat ramp.
Next to lake in primitive setting.
Swim, boat, ski, or fish.

NO water. No toilet facilities. No trash
arrangements (pack it out).

SHELLMOUND PARK

Levy County Parks
(904) 543-6153
State map: E9
From SUMNER, drive
SW on FL 24 about
4 miles (6.4 k). Turn Right (NE) on
CR 347 and go 1 mile (1.6 k). Turn Left
(W) on CR 326 and travel 3 miles (4.8 k).
$3.50; $5 electric.
Open All Year.
15 close, open sites.
Central faucet, flush toilets, showers,
dump station, electric hookups, tables,
grills, boat ramp.
Among fantastic-shaped oaks on Gulf of
Mexico.
Hike in nearby Lower Suwannee NWR.
Watch wildlife. Boat or fish.
7-day limit. Hunting in season.

SHIRED ISLAND

Dixie County Parks
(904) 498-5806
State map: D8
From CROSS CITY, drive
SW on FL 351 for 9 miles
(14.4 k). Turn Left (S) on FL 357 and go
11 miles (17.6 k).
FREE; $2 electric.
Open All Year.
Undesignated close, open sites.
Central faucet, flush toilets, electric
hookups, tables, grills, boat ramp.
In trees on long mud beach next to Gulf
of Mexico.
Enjoy quiet. Swim, scuba, boat, or fish.
Gather oysters.
14-day limit. Crowded in summer.

SILVER LAKE

Apalachicola NF
(904) 926-3561
State map: B6
From TALLAHASSEE,
take FL 20 W for 9 miles
(14.4 k). Turn Left (S) on CR 260 and
drive 4 miles (6.4 k). (Also see Camel

▲ ▲

Lake and Porter Lake.)
$5.
Open All Year.
25 close, open sites.
Central faucet, flush toilets, cold
showers, dump station, tables, grills,
boat ramp.
Next to cypress-bordered, spring-fed
23-acre lake.
Swim, fish, or boat (no motors). Walk to
view wildlife and take photos.
14-day/32-ft limits.

WHITE OAK LANDING

Apalachicola NF
(904) 926-3561
State map: C5
From BRISTOL, travel S
on CR 12 for 12.8 miles
(20.5 k). Bear Right (SW) on CR 379 and
drive 9 miles (14.4 k). Turn Right (W) on
FR 115 and continue 3 miles (4.8 k).
(Also see Camel Lake, Cotton Landing,
and Wright Lake.)
FREE so choose a chore.
Open All Year.
Undesignated close, open sites.
Pit toilets, tables, boat ramp.
In quiet wooded setting along River Styx
with access to Apalachicola River.
Canoe or fish.
NO water. 14-day limit. Crowded
hunting season (Oct–Jan).

WHITEHEAD LAKE

Apalachicola NF
(904) 643-2282
State map: B6
From TELOGIA, head S
on CR 67 about 16 miles
(25.6 k). Turn Left (E) on FR 13 and
drive 1.5 miles (2.4 k). Turn Right (S) on
FR 186 and go another 1.5 miles (2.4 k).
(Also see Hitchcock Lake and Porter
Lake.)
FREE so choose a chore.
Open All Year.
6 close, open sites.

Central faucet, pit toilets, tables, boat
ramp.
Next to lake leading to Ochlockonee
River.
Canoe or fish.
14-day/22-ft limits. Crowded hunting
season (Oct–Jan).

WILLIAMS LANDING

Leon County Parks
(904) 487-3070
State map: B6
From TALLAHASSEE,
drive W on FL 20 for
12 miles (19.2 k). (Also see Coe Landing
and Hall's Landing.)
FREE so choose a chore; reservations
accepted at (904) 487-3070.
Open All Year.
18 scattered, open sites.
Central faucet, flush toilets, showers,
tables, fire rings, grills, boat ramp.
Next to Lake Talquin.
Boat or fish. Watch wildlife.
10-day limit.
100 ft (30 m)

WOOD LAKE

Apalachicola NF
(904) 926-3561
State map: C6
From SOPCHOPPY,
head W on CR 375 for
.5 mile (800 m). Bear Left (W) on FL 22
and drive 1 mile (1.6 k). Turn Left (SW)
on FL 399 and go 4 miles (6.4 k). Turn
Right (W) on FR 338 and continue
2 miles (3.2 k). (Also see Mack Landing
and Porter Lake.)
FREE so choose a chore.
Open All Year.
Undesignated close, open sites.
Hand pump, pit toilets, tables, boat
ramp.
On small oxbow lake plus creek feeding
Ocholockonee River.
Canoe or fish.
14-day limit. Crowded hunting season
(Oct–Jan).

▲ ▲

WRIGHT LAKE

Apalachicola NF
(904) 926-3561
State map: C5
From SUMATRA, travel
S on FL 65 for 2 miles
(3.2 k). Turn Right (W) on FR 101 and
continue 2 miles (3.2 k). (Also see Cotton
Landing, Hickory Landing, and White
Oak Landing.)
FREE so choose a chore.
Open All Year.
21 close, open sites.
Central faucet, pit toilets, dump station,
tables, grills.
In woods next to peaceful lake.
Swim, canoe, or fish. Hike.
14-day/22-ft limits.

▲ ▲

GEORGIA
CAMPGROUND LOCATIONS

▶ ▶ Find location on facing page map grid. ▶ ▶
▼ ▼ Locate area campgrounds on these page numbers. ▼ ▼

Georgia

Grid conforms to official state map. For your copy, call (800) VISIT GA
or write Tourism Division, PO Box 1776, Atlanta, GA 30301-1776.

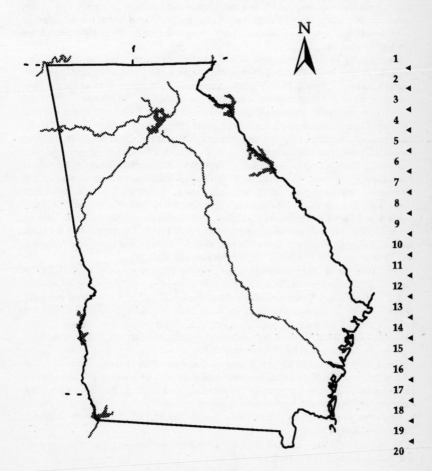

PUBLIC LANDS CAMPING

The sounds of "Georgia, Georgia...Georgia on my mind" seem to reverberate through this state's great getaways: Appalachian mountains, pristine lakes and rivers, and sunny coastal beaches. Seemingly eternal trees (live oaks with Spanish moss), spring flowers (dogwoods and azaleas), and fall colors (maples and gums) add to the year-round natural beauty and vivid visual memories of this largest state east of the Mississippi River.

The **National Park Service** (NPS) administers the Cumberland Island National Seashore on an approximately twenty-mile-long island of magnificent beaches with dunes, tidal marshes, maritime forests with freshwater ponds, wild horses, armadillos, alligators, and many types of shorebirds. Catch the ferry (and watch the dolphins) to camp free at Sea Camp or to backpack with permit into the live oak wilderness of this Georgia Golden Isle.

Each spring backpackers begin a 5–6 month foot journey up the Appalachian National Scenic Trail. This trail begins in Georgia and extends through Tennessee, North Carolina, Virginia, West Virginia, Maryland, Pennsylvania, New Jersey, New York, Connecticut, Massachusetts, Vermont, New Hampshire, to Maine.

Two national forests encompass large areas of Georgia: Chattahoochee and Oconee. Developed campsites in both national forests range in price from free to $10.00. Dispersed or primitive campsites are, of course, without fee. **Chattahoochee National Forest** (NF) contains 750,000 acres in north Georgia that include the Chattooga Wild and Scenic River, Cohutta Wilderness, Ellicott Rock Wilderness, Southern Nantahala Wilderness, numerous waterfalls, plus the Russell-Brasstown Scenic Byway. In the **Oconee NF**, discover over 100,000 wooded acres in the rolling Piedmont of middle Georgia showcasing the Oconee River and three lakes (Hillsboro, Oconee, and Sinclair).

US Army Corps of Engineers (COE) has constructed recreational opportunities on the following lakes: Allatoona, Carters, Hartwell, J Strom Thurmond (Clarks Hill), Richard B Russell, Seminole, Sidney Lanier, Walter F George and George W Andrews, and West Point. COE camp fees range from free to $14.00.

In 58 state parks and historic sites, discover the highest waterfall this side of the Rockies (Amicalola Falls at 729 feet), the "Little Grand Canyon" (Providence Canyon), and the Okefenokee Swamp. **Georgia State Parks** (SP) offer a variety of camping experiences at 39 locations. Fees range from $6.00 for walk-in sites to $10.00 for tent/RV sites. In addition, primitive camping at $3.00 per person is permitted at Black Mountain, Cloudland Canyon, Fort Mountain, Providence Canyon, Unicoi, and Vogel state parks. Contact each park about availability.

Georgia Department of Natural Resources Game and Fish Division allows camping in designated Wildlife Management Areas unless otherwise posted. These campgrounds are used primarily for hunting and fishing. Be sure to practice recommended safety and sanitation procedures.

Rounding out Georgia's public lands camping, find Holiday Park in northeast Georgia's **Wilkes County**.

Savor the peach state and find out there's a whole lot more to it—including peanuts and peanut farmers who become presidents.

▲ ▲

ANDREWS COVE

Chattahoochee NF
(404) 754-6221
State map: G2
From HELEN, drive
5 miles (8 k) N on GA 75.
(Also see Lake Chatuge. Nearby Unicoi SP costs $10.)
$5. Open May 7–Nov 15.
11 scattered, open sites. Hand pump, chemical toilets, tables, fire rings.
In mountain cove next to clear stream.
Hike and explore nearby Anna Falls or High Shoals Scenic Area.
14-day limit. Crowded weekends.
2000 ft (600 m)

BUSSEY POINT WALK-IN

COE (803) 333-2476
State map: M6
From LINCOLNTON, head SE on GA 47 about 6 miles (9.6 k). Bear Left (SE) on GA 220 Spur and drive 4 miles (6.4 k) to end of road. Walk (or boat) about .25 mile (400 m).
FREE so choose a chore.
Open All Year.
20 scattered, screened, tent sites.
Hand pump, pit toilets, tables.
On wooded peninsula in Strom Thurmond Lake.
Boat or fish. Hike. Observe wildlife.
No trash arrangements (pack it out).
14-day limit.

COHEELEE CREEK PARK

COE (912) 768-2516
State map: C16
From Hilton (SW of BLAKELY), head NW about 3 miles (4.8 k).
FREE so choose a chore.
Open All Year.
Undesignated scattered, open sites.
Central faucet, pit toilets, tables, fire rings, boat ramp.
Fish and boat Lake George F Andrews.
14-day limit.
125 ft (38 m)

COOPER CREEK

Chattahoochee NF
(404) 632-3031
State map: F2
From DAHLONEGA, drive NW on GA 60 for 26 miles (41.6 k). Turn Right (NE) on FR 4 and continue 6 miles (9.6 k). (Also see Deep Hole and Mulky.)
$5.
Open Mar 23–Oct 31.
17 close, open sites.
Central faucet, flush toilets, tables, fire rings.
Next to trout-stocked mountain stream in 1240-acre scenic area.
Hike to savor mountain beauty. Fish.
14-day/22-ft limits.

CUMBERLAND ISLAND NS
Sea Camp

(912) 882-4335
State map: P19
From ST MARYS, take ferry or boat to Sea Camp Dock. Load cart and push .5 mile (800 m) E to assigned site. Also, free backcountry permits available on quota basis. (Nearby Crooked River SP costs $10.)
FREE; reservations required at (912) 882-4335. Open All Year.
16 close, screened, tent sites.
Central faucet, flush toilets, showers, tables, grills, fire rings, food cages (persistent raccoons).
Behind dunes, in spectacular setting with massive live oak canopy and palmetto undergrowth.
Hike up to 17 miles (27.2 k) N into wilderness. Enjoy barrier island at its best. Swim, fish, and hunt for shells.
Take photos of plants and animals, including wild horses. View Carnegie estate ruins. Attend ranger programs.
No trash arrangements (pack it out).
7-day limit. Crowded Mar–May.
10 ft (3 m)

▲ ▲

DEEP HOLE

Chattahoochee NF
(404) 632-3031
State map: F2
From DAHLONEGA, drive
NW on GA 60 for 27 miles
(43.2 k). (Also see Cooper Creek, Frank
Gross, and Mulky.)
$5.
Open Mar–Oct.
8 close, open sites. Central faucet, flush
toilets, tables, fire rings.
Next to Toccoa River in pretty,
mountainous spot.
Fish. Hike.
14-day limit.

DOCKERY LAKE

Chattahoochee NF
(404) 864-6173
State map: F2
From DAHLONEGA, head
N on GA 60 for 12 miles
(19.2 k). Turn Right (E) on FR 654 and
continue 1 mile (1.6 k). (Also see Deep
Hole.)
$5.
Open May 1–Sep 30.
11 close, open sites.
Central faucet, flush toilets, tables, fire
rings.
In wood next to 6-acre trout lake.
Hike to observe wildlife. Fish.
14-day/22-ft limits. Occasionally
crowded.

FORT MOUNTAIN SP-Primitive

(706) 695-2621
State map: D2
From CHATSWORTH,
drive 8 miles E on GA 52.
(Also see Lake Conasauga.)
$3 per person; $5–$12 developed; $2
entrance fee.
Open All Year.
88 (18 tent-only) open sites. &
Water, flush toilets, showers, dump
station, electric hookups, tables, grills,
fire rings.
Atop wooded Fort Mountain–named
after ancient stone wall.

Hike and take photos of Native
American site. View wildlife. Swim,
pedal-boat, or fish. Play mini-golf.
Attend ranger programs.
14-day limit.
2854 ft (856 m)

FRANK GROSS

Chattahoochee NF
(404) 632-3031
State map: F2
From DAHLONEGA, drive
NW on GA 60 for
27.5 miles (43.8 k). Turn Left (S) on
FR 69 and continue 5 miles (8 k). (Also
see Deep Hole.)
$5.
Open Mar 23–Oct 31.
9 close, open sites.
Central faucet, flush toilets, tables, fire
rings.
Along beautiful Rock Creek near
Chattahoochee National Fish Hatchery.
Fish, of course.
14-day/22-ft limits.

HALE'S LANDING

COE (912) 662-2001
State map: D19
From BAINBRIDGE, take
US 27 NW across bridge.
Turn Left (SW) on
Ten Mile Still Rd and drive 4.5 miles
(7.2 k). Turn Left (S).
$5. Open All Year.
17 close, open sites.
Central faucet, flush toilets, showers,
tables, fire rings, grills, boat ramp.
In shade on shores of Lake Seminole.
Boat or fish. Watch wildlife.
14-day limit.
80 ft (24 m)

HIDDEN CREEK

Chattahoochee NF
(404) 638-1085
State map: C3
From CALHOUN, take
GA 156 SW for 7.5 miles
(12 k). Turn Right (NW) on Everett
Springs CR and drive 2 miles (3.2 k).

▲ ▲

Turn Right (N) on Rock Creek CR and go 3 miles (4.8 k). Turn Right (N) on FR 955 and continue to end of road.
FREE so choose a chore.
Open Apr 1–Oct 31.
16 close, screened sites.
Hand pump, pit toilets, tables, fire rings.
In old-growth native hardwood forest (dogwood, sourwood, hickory, and oak) next to Dry Branch Creek (often disappears).
Enjoy natural setting and take photos.
14-day limit. Hunting in season. No generators.
900 ft (270 m)

HOLIDAY PARK

Wilkes County Park
(706) 678-1454
State map: K6
From WASHINGTON, take US 378 E toward
Lincolnton about 20 miles (32 k). Turn Right (SE) at park sign.
FREE so choose a chore.
Open All Year.
Undesignated scattered, open sites.
Pit toilets, dump station, tables, fire rings, boat ramp.
Swim, boat, ski, or fish remote area of Strom Thurmond Lake.
NO water.

LAKE BLUE RIDGE

Chattahoochee NF
(404) 632-3031
State map: E1
From BLUE RIDGE, head E on Old US 76 for 1.5 miles
(2.4 k). Turn Right (S) on Dry Branch Rd and drive 3 miles (4.8 k). (Nearby Morganton Point costs $6.)
$5.
Open May 8–Oct 31.
55 close, open sites.
Central faucet, flush toilets, tables, fire rings, boat ramp.
In mountains next to 3290-acre reservoir.
Boat, ski, or fish. Hike.
14-day/28-ft limits.

LAKE CHATUGE

Chattahoochee NF
(404) 745-6928
State map: G1
From HIAWASSEE, take US 76 NW for 2 miles
(3.2 k). Turn Left (S) on GA 288 and continue 1 mile (1.6 k). (Also see Andrews Cove.)
$5.
Open May 11–Oct 22.
32 close, open sites.
Central faucet, flush toilets, tables, fire rings, boat ramp.
On pine peninsula in Lake Chatuge.
Swim, boat, ski, or fish. Walk loop trail.
14-day/22-ft limits.

LAKE CONASAUGA

Chattahoochee NF
(404) 695-6736
State map: D1
From ETON, head E, following signs, on gravel
FR 18 and drive 10 miles (16 k). Turn Left (N) on FR 68 and continue 4 miles (6.4 k). (Also see Fort Mountain SP.)
$5.
Open Apr 15–Oct 15.
35 scattered, open sites. &
Central faucet, flush toilets, tables, fire rings, boat ramp.
In woods on Grassy Mountain next to 19-acre lake (highest in GA).
Take nature trail or hike extensively.
Mountain bike. Swim, fish, or boat (paddle or electric motor). Take photos.
14-day/22-ft limits. Crowded holidays and some weekends.
3100 ft (930 m)

LAKE SINCLAIR

Oconee NF (404) 468-2244
State map: I8
From EATONTON, travel S on US 129 for 10 miles
(16 k). Turn Left (E) on GA 212. Drive 1 mile (1.6 k). Bear Left (E) on FR 1062. Proceed 2 miles (3.2 k).
$5. Open May 27–Sep 3.
44 close, open sites.

Central faucet, flush toilets, dump station, tables, fire rings, boat ramp.
Next to large lake.
Swim, boat, ski, or fish. Walk Twin Bridges Trail.
14-day/22-ft limits.

MACEDONIA

COE (404) 382-4700
State map: D4
From Exit 125 of I-75N (N of CARTERSVILLE), take GA 20 E for 7.5 miles (12 k). Turn Right (S) on dirt Macedonia Rd and drive 5 miles (8 k), bearing Right at fork. (Also see Upper Stamp Creek. Nearby Red Top Mountain SP costs $10.)
FREE so choose a chore.
Open Apr 1–Sep 30.
26 close, open sites.
Hand pump, pit toilets, tables, fire rings, boat ramp.
In woods next to Allatoona Lake.
Boat, ski, and fish.
14-day/30-ft limits. No generators in quiet hours. Crowded weekends and holidays.
863 ft (259 m)

MULKY

Chattahoochee NF (404) 632-3031
State map: F2
From DAHLONEGA, drive NW on GA 60 for 26 miles (41.6 k). Turn Right (NE) on FR 4 and go 5 miles (8 k). (Also see Cooper Creek and Deep Hole.)
$5. Open Mar 28–Oct 31.
10 close, open sites. Central faucet, flush toilets, tables, fire rings.
On banks of Cooper Creek.
Fish. Hike to explore area.
14-day/22-ft limits.

OCONEE RIVER

Oconee NF (404) 468-2244
State map: I7
From GREENSBORO, drive NW on GA 15 for 12 miles (19.2 k).

FREE so choose a chore.
Open All Year.
7 close, open sites. Hand pump, pit toilets, tables, fire rings.
In rolling hills next to river.
Boat or fish. Walk to Scull Shoals Historical Area. Take photos.
14-day limit.

RIDGEWAY PARK

COE (404) 334-2248
State map: D2
From ELLIJAY, travel W on US 76/GA 282 about 7 miles (11.2 k). Turn Left (S) on dirt road and go about 3 miles (4.8 k). (Also see Woodring Branch-Old. Nearby Woodring Branch-New costs $8.)
FREE so choose a chore.
Open All Year.
22 scattered, screened, tent sites.
Hand pump, pit toilets, tables, grills, fire rings, boat ramp.
In woods beside clear Carters Lake.
Swim, boat, or fish. Walk nature trail or take longer hikes.
1072 ft (322 m)

RINGER ACCESS

COE (706) 645-2937
State map: C9
From LAGRANGE, drive N on US 27 about 5 miles (8 k). Turn Left (W) on access road.
FREE so choose a chore. Open All Year.
37 close, open, tent sites.
Hand pump, pit toilets, tables, fire rings, grills, boat ramp.
In pine/hardwood mix next to West Point Lake (only free choice).
Swim or fish. Boat or ski. Hike or bike.
14-day limit. Crowded holidays.
635 ft (191 m)

ROOD CREEK PARK

COE (912) 768-2516
State map: C14
From FLORENCE, head S on GA 39 about 4 miles (6.4 k).

FREE so choose a chore.
Open All Year.
Undesignated scattered, open sites.
Central faucet, pit toilets, tables, fire rings, boat ramp.
Next to Walter F George in Eufaula NWR.
Boat and fish. Observe wildlife.
14-day limit.
200 ft (60 m)

TOTO CREEK

COE (404) 945-9531
State map: G3
At intersection of GA 53 and US 19/GA 400, head N on GA 400 about 3 miles (4.8 k). Turn Right (E) on Henry Grady Highway and drive to end. (Nearby Bolding Mill and Duckett Mill cost $8.)
FREE so choose a chore.
Open Mar 6–Oct 23.
10 close, open sites.
Central faucet, flush toilets, tables, fire rings, grills, boat ramp.
In woods on Lake Sidney Lanier (only free spot).
Boat, ski, swim, or fish. Take nature trail to view wildlife.
14-day limit.
1100 ft (330 m)

UPPER STAMP CREEK

COE (404) 382-4700
State map: D4
From Exit 125 of I-75N (N of CARTERSVILLE), take GA 20 E for 4 miles (6.4 k).
Turn Right (S) on Wilderness Camp Rd and drive 2 miles (3.2 k), bearing Left at sign. (Also see Macedonia. Nearby Red Top Mountain SP costs $10.)
FREE so choose a chore.
Open Apr 1–Oct 31.
Undesignated close, open sites.

Central faucet, flush toilets, tables, boat ramp.
Open All Year.
Undesignated scattered, open sites.
On pine-covered slope next to Allatoona Lake.
Boat or fish.
14-day/30-ft limits. No generators in quiet hours. Crowded weekends and holidays.
863 ft (259 m)

WATERS CREEK

Chattahoochee NF
(404) 864-6173
State map: G2
From DAHLONEGA, take US 19 N for 12 miles (19.2 k). Turn Left (NW) on FR 34 and drive 1 mile (1.6 k).
$5.
Open All Year.
8 close, open sites.
Central faucet, flush toilets, tables, fire rings.
Along scenic mountain stream.
Hike to enjoy area. Fish. Relax.
14-day limit.

WOODRING BRANCH-OLD

COE (404) 334-2248
State map: D2
From ELLIJAY, head W on US 76/GA 282 about 11 miles (17.6 k). Turn Left (S) on access road. Go 6 miles (9.6 k).
(Also see Ridgeway. Nearby Woodring Branch-New costs $8.)
$5.
Open All Year.
16 close, screened sites.
Central faucet, pit toilets, tables, fire rings.
At old camp on wooded shores of Carters Lake.
Swim, boat, or fish. Hike.
14-day limit.
1072 ft (322 m)

▲ ▲

ILLINOIS
CAMPGROUND LOCATIONS

▶ ▶ Find location on facing page map grid. ▶ ▶
▼ ▼ Locate area campgrounds on these page numbers. ▼ ▼

Illinois

Grid conforms to official state map. For your copy, call (800) 223-0121
or write Bureau of Tourism, 100 W Randolph St, 3-400, Chicago, IL 60601.

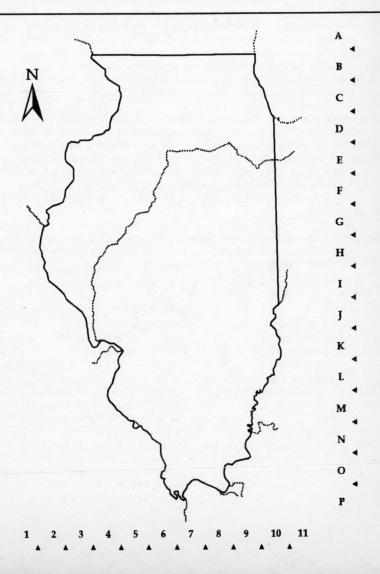

▲ ▲

PUBLIC LANDS CAMPING

Illinois, the Land of Lincoln, reflects its past in its public lands camping opportunities.

Named in honor of the great Shawnee Indian nation, the **Shawnee National Forest** (NF) covers over 250,000 acres in southern Illinois. There are still remnants of Indian and other past occupations, exceptional animal and plant varieties, and unusual rock formations. In the LaRu-Pine Hills, an extension of the Ozark Mountains, botanists have recorded over a thousand different flowering plants from prickly pear cacti at sandstone canyon edges to delicate Dutchman's Breeches on canyon floors. The most popular area is the Garden of the Gods where sandstone blocks have eroded, primarily from glaciation, into fantastic shapes such as Camel, Anvil, and Devil's Smokestack. While camping in the Shawnee, you can rough it or enjoy the conveniences of sixteen developed areas. Camp fees range from free to $6.00 for single sites.

US Army Corps of Engineers (COE) provides campgrounds along the Mississippi River, Carlyle Lake, Lake Shelbyville, and Rend Lake. COE camp fees range from free to $12.00.

Illinois State Parks (SP), **Fish and Wildlife Areas** (FWA), **Conservation Areas** (CA), and **State Forests** (SF) offer camping at various rates: $7.00 for vehicular access, $8.00 for vehicular access plus showers, $10.00 for vehicular access plus electricity, $11.00 for vehicular access, showers, plus electricity. Walk-in, tent sites are available at $6.00 per night. Along Illinois' only national wild and scenic river, the Middle Fork of the Vermilion River, camp at Middle Fork State Fish and Wildlife Area.

Towns and **counties** providing camping facilities include the Village of Oblong and Vermilion County.

Too, several national historic trails begin or pass through Illinois: Lewis & Clark, Mormon Pioneer, and Trail of Tears. Following one of these historic trails can add a new understanding of times and places as well as an interesting focus to a trip.

Illinois, "Don't Miss It!"

▲ ▲

ANDALUSIA SLOUGH

COE (319) 263-7913
State map: D4
From ANDALUSIA, drive 3 miles (4.8 k) W on IL 92. (Also see Blanchard Island.)

FREE so choose a chore.
Open All Year.
15 close, open sites.
Central faucet, pit toilets, tables, fire rings, grills, boat ramp, shelter.
Along Mississippi River.
Fish or boat. View wildlife. Watch river traffic.
14-day limit.

BEAR CREEK

COE (217) 228-0890
State map: H2
From URSA, drive W on CR 2150N. Turn Right (N) on CR 500E and go to CR 2400N.
Turn Left. Follow signs to Park Crossing Levee. (Also see Fenway Landing.)

FREE so choose a chore.
Open All Year.
30 scattered, open sites.
Hand pump, pit toilets, dump station, tables, fire rings, boat ramp.
In natural setting on backwaters of Mississippi River.
Boat and fish. Hike to view wildlife.
14-day limit. Hunting in season.
Occasional flooding.

BLANCHARD ISLAND

COE (319) 263-7913
State map: D3
From ILLINOIS CITY, travel W
on IL 92 about 6 miles (9.6 k).
Turn Left (S) on CR 11 (New
Boston Rd). Follow signs 9 more miles
(14.4 k). (Also see Andalusia Slough.)
FREE so choose a chore.
Open All Year.
30 close, open sites.
Central faucet, pit toilets, dump station,
tables, fire rings, boat ramp.
Along Mississippi River.
View wildlife. Boat or fish. Watch river
traffic.
14-day limit. Hunting in season.

BUCK RIDGE

Shawnee NF (618) 658-2111
State map: N8
From CREAL SPRINGS, travel
S for 3 miles (4.8 k) on IL 2.
Turn Right (W) on gravel
FR 870 and drive 1.75 miles (2.8 k). Turn
Right (NW) on FR 871 and go .5 mile
(800 m). Turn Left (W) on FR 871A and
continue 1.75 miles (2.8 k).
$5. Open Mar 15–Oct 31.
41 close, screened sites. ♿
Hand pump, pit toilets, tables, fire rings,
grills, boat ramp.
On wooded ridge near Lake of Egypt.
View wildlife and take photos. Fish or
boat.
14-day/32-ft limits. Hunting in season.
Sometimes dusty.
600 ft (180 m)

CAMP CADIZ

Shawnee NF (618) 287-2201
State map: N9
From KARBERS RIDGE, drive
E for 1 mile (1.6 k). Turn Right
at sign on gravel road. Go
3 miles (4.8 k). (Also see Garden of the
Gods and Pounds Hollow.)
$4. Open All Year.
11 scattered, open sites.
Hand pump, pit toilets, tables, grills, fire
rings.

Within gently rolling hills plus
River-To-River Trail access.
Hike to explore area.
Crowded in deer hunting season.
600 ft (180 m)

FOREST GLEN PRESERVE

Vermilion County
Conservation District
(217) 662-2142
State map: H11
From WESTVILLE, take CR 5 E
for 7 miles (11.2 k). Turn Left.
$3; $7 electric.
Open All Year.
84 (14 tent-only) scattered, open sites.
Central faucet, pit toilets, dump station,
electric hookups, tables, fire rings, grills,
boat ramp, pay phone.
In preserve with small lake, arboretum,
and nature area.
Backpack 11-mile trail or hike 25-mile
system. Climb 72-ft observation tower.
Visit tree research area, arboretum,
homestead, prairie, and other natural
areas. Fish, too.
Crowded major holidays.
700 ft (210 m)

FRANCIS PARK

Kewanee City Parks
(309) 852-0511
State map: E5
From KEWANEE, drive NE on
US 34 for 4 miles (6.4 k).
$3; $6 electric.
Open Mar 15–Oct 15.
75 (15 tent-only) close, open sites.
Central faucet, flush toilets, electric
hookups, tables, fire rings.
In mix of walnut, oak, and hickory trees.
Visit Woodland Palace to marvel at
inventiveness. Bike. Relax.

GARDEN OF THE GODS RA- Pharoah

Shawnee NF (618) 287-2201
State map: N9
From KARBERS RIDGE, drive
W to signed entrance road.
Turn Right (N). (Also see
Camp Cadiz or Pounds Hollow.)

$5. Open All Year.
12 close, open sites. Hand pump, pit toilets, tables, fire rings, grills.
On high ridge overlooking Garden of the Gods region, adjacent to wilderness.
Walk interpretive trail. Hike to explore fascinating geologic area. Take photos.
14-day limit. Often crowded. Steep bluffs near sites (watch children).
840 ft (252 m)

GRAPEVINE TRAIL
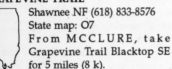
Shawnee NF (618) 833-8576
State map: O7
From MCCLURE, take Grapevine Trail Blacktop SE for 5 miles (8 k).
FREE so choose a chore.
Open All Year.
6 scattered, open sites.
Central faucet, pit toilets, tables, fire rings.
Next to road in scattered pine.
Relax.
Hunting in season.

GUN CREEK
COE (618) 724-2493
State map: M8
Take IL 154 Exit W off I-57 (W of WHITTINGTON). Turn Left (S) at Southern Illinois Marketplace. Follow signs.
FREE at 10 sites; **$6** at 90 sites; reservations accepted at (618) 724-2493 for an additional $2.
Open Apr 1–Oct 31.
100 close, open sites.
Central faucet, pit toilets, dump station, tables, grills, boat ramp, pay phone.
In woods next to Rend Lake.
Swim, boat, ski, or fish. Bike. Attend ranger programs.
14-day limit.

JOHNSON CREEK
Shawnee NF (618) 687-1731
State map: N6
From MURPHYSBORO, take IL 149 W for 8 miles (12.8 k). Turn Right (NW) on IL 3 and

drive 4 miles (6.4 k). Turn Right (NE) IL 151 and go another 4 miles (6.4 k). (Also see Turkey Bayou.)
$4.
Open All Year.
77 (12 tent-only) close, open sites. &
Central faucet, pit toilets, dump station, tables, fire rings, boat ramp.
In woods near Kincaid Lake with nearby old-growth timber plus unusual rock formations.
Enjoy good hiking and photo opportunities. Swim, boat, or fish.
Hunting in season.
520 ft (156 m)

LOCK & DAM 13

COE (815) 589-3229
State map: C5
From FULTON, drive N on IL 84 for 5 miles (8 k). Turn Left (W) at sign and go 1.5 miles (2.4 k). (Nearby Thomson Causeway costs $6.)
FREE so choose a chore.
Open All Year.
6 close, screened sites.
Water 1 mile (1.6 k) away, pit toilets, tables, fire rings, boat ramp.
In beautiful setting on Mississippi River backwaters.
View beaver, muskrat, blue heron, and, in winter, breeding eagle. Watch river traffic. Boat, canoe, or fish. Bike too.
14-day limit. Hunting in season.
Occasional flooding.

MCNAIR/DAM EAST

COE (618) 594-2484
State map: L7
From CARLYLE, head E on US 50 to E side of dam. Turn Left (N). (Nearby Dam West costs $6.)
$5 (available if not reserved for group).
Open May 1–Sep 30.
25 scattered, open sites.
Central faucet, flush toilets, showers, dump station, tables, grills, pay phone.
In shady and open spots next to Lake Carlyle.

▲ ▲

Swim, boat, ski, or fish. Walk nature trail. Attend ranger programs.
14-day limit. Crowded holidays and weekends.
450 ft (135 m)

ONE HORSE GAP

Shawnee NF (618) 287-2201
State map: O9
From ELIZABETHTOWN, head W on IL 146 for 7 miles (11.2 k). Turn Right (N) on signed gravel road and drive 6 miles (9.6 k). (Also see Tecumseh Lake.)
$4.
Open Apr 1–Dec 15.
3 close, open sites.
Pit toilets, boat ramp.
In quiet, rustic setting with wonderful view of lake.
Hike to explore area. Swim, boat, or fish. Enjoy fall color (mid-Oct).
NO water. No trash arrangements (pack it out). 14-day limit. Small vehicles only. Hunting in season. Crowded holiday weekends.
480 ft (144 m)

PARK-N-FISH

COE (217) 228-0890
State map: I2
From HULL, take IL 106 W. Turn Left (S) at sign and follow to park–total distance about 7 miles (11.2 k).
FREE so choose a chore.
Open All Year.
6 scattered, open sites.
Hand pump, pit toilets, tables, grills, fire rings, shelter.
Near Mississippi River with gravel parking and no shade.
Fish (high water can prevent access).
14-day limit.

PINE HILLS

Shawnee NF (618) 833-8576
State map: O7
From WOLF LAKE, go E on state forest blacktop for .5 mile (800 m). Turn Left (N) on

gravel FR 236 and continue another .5 mile (800 m).
$4.
Open Apr 1–Dec 15; dry camping allowed off-season.
12 scattered, open sites.
Hand pump, pit toilets, tables, fire rings.
In wooded valley.
Hike. Take photos. Fish.
Hunting in season.
400 ft (120 m)

POUNDS HOLLOW RA-Pine Ridge

Shawnee NF (618) 287-2201
State map: N9
From KARBERS RIDGE, drive E, bearing Left at fork to signed entrance. (Also see Camp Cadiz and Garden of the Gods.)
$5.
Open Apr 1–Dec 15.
76 close, screened sites.
Hand pump, pit toilets, tables, grills, fire rings, rentals, pay phone.
In shortleaf pine forest next to 25-acre lake.
Swim ($2), boat, or fish. Walk Rim Rock Trail. Mountain bike.
Crowded holiday weekends.
600 ft (180 m)

REDBUD

Shawnee NF (618) 658-2111
State map: O9
From EDDYVILLE, travel N on IL 145 for 2.5 miles (4 k). Turn Left (W) on FR 447 and drive 3.5 miles (5.6 k). Turn Left (SW) on gravel FR 848 and go 1.75 miles (2.8 k). (Also see Teal Pond.)
$5.
Open Mar 15–Dec 31.
21 close, screened sites.
Hand pump, pit toilets, tables, grills, fire rings.
In woods.
Hike trails. View wildlife. Fish.
14-day/32-ft limits. Hunting in season. Occasionally dusty.
600 ft (180 m)

▲ ▲

STEAMBOAT HILL

Shawnee NF (618) 658-2111
State map: O9
From GOLCONDA, take IL 146
N for 1 mile (1.6 k). Turn Right
(E) on FR 411 and go .5 mile
(800 m).
$4.
Open Apr 1–Dec 31.
17 close, screened sites.
Hand pump, pit toilets, tables, grills, fire rings.
Among trees with view of Ohio River.
View wildlife. Fish or boat nearby.
14-day/32-ft limits.
600 ft (180 m)

TEAL POND

Shawnee NF (618) 658-2111
State map: O9
From EDDYVILLE, travel N on
IL 145 for 2.5 miles (4 k). Turn
Left (W) on gravel FR 447 and
drive 3.5 miles (5.6 k). (Also see Redbud.)
$5.
Open All Year.
10 close, screened sites.
Hand pump, pit toilets, tables, grills, fire rings.
In woods.
Fish. View wildlife and take photos.
14-day/32-ft limits. Hunting in season.
Sometimes dusty.
700 ft (210 m)

TECUMSEH LAKE

Shawnee NF (618) 287-2201
State map: O9
From ELIZABETHTOWN,
head W on IL 146 to ranger
station and Basset blacktop.
Turn Right (N) and go 2 miles (3.2 k) to
sign. Turn Left (W) on gravel road for
2 miles (3.2 k). (Also see One Horse Gap
and Tower Rock.)
FREE so choose a chore.
Open Apr 1–Dec 15.
3 close, screened sites.
Pit toilets, boat ramp.
In quiet, secluded spot next to lake.

Hike to explore area. Swim, boat, or fish.
Enjoy fall color (mid-Oct).
NO water. No trash arrangements (pack
it out). 14-day limit. Small vehicles only.
Hunting in season. Crowded holiday
weekends.
420 ft (126 m)

TOWER ROCK

Shawnee NF (618) 287-2201
State map: O9
From ELIZABETHTOWN,
head NE on IL 146 for 1 mile
(1.6 k). Turn Right (S) on
signed gravel road and go 4 miles
(6.4 k). (Also see Tecumseh Lake.)
$4.
Open Apr 1–Dec 15.
35 close, open sites.
Hand pump, pit toilets, tables, fire rings,
grills, boat ramp, playground.
In grassy, park-like setting next to
beautiful Ohio River.
Walk nature trail. Take photos. Boat or
fish.
14-day limit. Crowded holiday
weekends.
350 ft (105 m)

TURKEY BAYOU

Shawnee NF (618) 687-1731
State map: N7
From MURPHYSBORO, go W
on IL 149 for 8 miles (12.8 k).
Turn Left (SW) on IL 3 and
drive 6 miles (9.6 k). Turn Left (E) on
FR 786 (John Spur) and continue 4 miles
(6.4 k). (Also see Johnson Creek.)
$4.
Open Apr 1–Dec 15; dry camping
allowed off-season.
17 close, open sites. &
Hand pump, pit toilets, tables, fire rings,
boat ramp.
On bayou near Big Muddy River near
Little Grand Canyon National Recreation
Trail.
Hike. View wildlife. Boat or fish.
Hunting in season.
350 ft (105 m)

▲ ▲

VILLAGE OF OBLONG PARK

(618) 592-3122
State map: K10
Locate park in OBLONG on
IL 33 (Legion Parkway).
$5.

Open Apr 15 – Oct 15; dry camping
allowed off-season.
25 close, open sites.
Water at every site, flush toilets,
showers, dump station, electric hookups,
tables, pay phone.
In shade next to 4.5-acre lake.
Enjoy quiet. Fish (no boats). Visit oil
museum.
Crowded last week in Jul (county fair),
2nd week in Aug (tractor show), last
weekend in Oct (follies).

WHITLEY CREEK

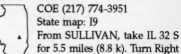

COE (217) 774-3951
State map: I9
From SULLIVAN, take IL 32 S
for 5.5 miles (8.8 k). Turn Right
(W) on Findlay Rd for 1 mile
(1.6 k). Turn Right (N) and go 1.5 miles
(2.4 k). (Nearby Bo Wood RA costs $10.)
FREE at 26 sites; $6 at other 61 sites;
reservations accepted at (217) 774-3951
for an additional $2.
Open May 5 – Sep 6; dry camping
allowed off-season.
87 (9 tent-only) screened sites. &
Central faucet, flush toilets, showers,
dump station, tables, fire rings, grills,
boat ramp, playground, pay phone.
In heavy woods on Lake Shelbyville.
Boat or fish. View wildlife. Attend
ranger programs.
14-day limit.
627 ft (188 m)

▲ ▲

INDIANA
CAMPGROUND LOCATIONS

▸ ▸ Find location on facing page map grid. ▸ ▸
▾ ▾ Locate area campgrounds on these page numbers. ▾ ▾

Indiana

Grid conforms to official state map. For your copy, call (800) 289-6646
or write Tourism Division, 1 N Capitol, Indianapolis, IN 46204-2288.

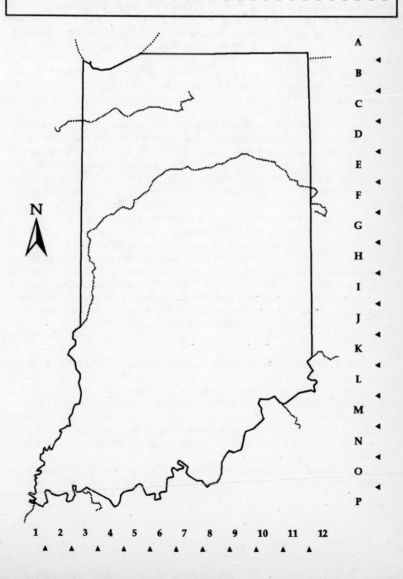

▲ ▲

PUBLIC LANDS CAMPING

The state of Indiana is committed to preserving its dwindling natural areas. The state has issued the country's first environmental license plate, featuring a bald eagle soaring across the sun. Too, the state has created the Indiana Heritage Trust to secure more lands for conservation, preservation, and recreation.

Indiana Department of Natural Resources (DNR) has become the primary steward of the state's natural areas and offers a host of outdoor possibilities. The department publishes a free annual recreation guide to Indiana's state parks, forests, reservoirs, fish and wildlife areas, plus state museum and historic sites. You'll find the department promotes a wide range of recreational opportunities: camping, swimming, waterskiing, boating, fishing, hunting, bicycling, horseback riding, cross-country skiing, tobogganing, and cave-touring as well as wildlife viewing. State parks with campgrounds are located near two popular National Park Service (NPS) sites: Indiana Dunes National Lakeshore and Lincoln Boyhood National Memorial. In addition, the department has erected hundreds of brown signs with binocular symbols to alert you to wildlife viewing areas.

State DNR camping fees range from $5.00 to $14.00 per site during warm weather. Class C sites (primitive) cost $5.00; class B sites (modern restrooms and showers) cost $7.00; class A sites (electrical hookups) cost $11.00; class AA sites (all hookups) cost $13.00. Prime locations cost an additional $1.00. Rates are half-price during winter. Find campgrounds at twenty state parks, nine reservoirs, nine fish and wildlife areas, and fourteen state forests. Two state parks (Lincoln and Tippecanoe) offer Rent-A-Tent facilities at $15.00 per night plus tax and damage deposit. There are special rates for rallies (five or more family units), canoeists, horsemen, and youth groups.

Wayne-Hoosier National Forest (NF) encompasses approximately 200,000 acres interspersed among over 400,000 acres located in the rolling hills of southern Indiana. These areas stretch north from the Ohio River Valley. Within the forest, discover the twelve-mile Two Lakes Loop Hiking Trail (a National Recreation Trail connecting Lake Celina and Indian Lake), the fifteen-mile Wildcat Hollow Backpack Trail, and the Charles C Deam Wilderness. You'll find wooded bluffs (including an 88-acre tract of virgin hardwoods showcasing wildflowers), and an incredible number of sandstone caves (exhibiting prehistoric occupation). Dispersed camping locations and developed campgrounds are found throughout the Hoosier NF. Camp fees range from free to $8.00 for a single site.

US Army Corps of Engineers (COE) has built and the Indiana DNR maintains campgrounds on the following manmade lakes: Brookville, Cagles Mill, Cecil M Harden, Hardy, Huntington, Mississinewa, Monroe, Patoka, and Salamonie. Again, DNR camp fees range from $5.00 to $13.00 depending on the desired level of facilities.

Other administrators of Indiana public lands campgrounds include **water conservancies** and **counties** such as Big Blue River Conservancy District and Vigo County Parks and Recreation Department. Their camp fees, however, are higher than the cutoff level for this book.

Discover why Indiana considers itself a natural. Explore this state's caves, canyons, waterfalls, lakes, sand dunes, and fossil beds. Enjoy its wildlife. Wander Indiana.

▲ ▲

CECIL M HARDIN LAKE
Raccoon SRA

(317) 344-1412
State map: H4
From ROCKVILLE, take US 36
E for 10 miles (16 k). (Nearby
Turkey Run SP costs $7.)

$5 class C; $7 class B; $11 class A; $2
entrance fee; reservations accepted at
(317) 344-1412 for an additional $2.
Open All Year.
342 close, open sites. &
Central faucet, flush toilets, showers,
dump station, electric hookups, tables,
fire rings, playground, ball courts, store,
rentals, pay phone.
In woods near lake.
Swim, boat, ski, or fish. Hike trail
system. Explore county's covered
bridges.
14-day limit. Hunting in season.
670 ft (201 m)

CELINA LAKE

Wayne-Hoosier NF
(812) 547-7051
State map: N5
From TELL CITY, go N on
IN 37 for 18 miles (28.8 k).
Turn Left (W) on FR 501. (Also see
Tipsaw Lake.)

$5; $14 prime; reservations accepted at
(812) 547-7051.
Open Apr 1–Dec 15.
63 close, screened sites.
Central faucet, flush toilets, showers,
tables, fire rings, grills, boat ramp.
Near lake among pine and mixed
hardwood trees.
Boat or fish. Walk nature trail. Hike to
view wildlife.
14-day limit. Hunting in season.
Crowded holidays.

CHAIN O' LAKES SP

(219) 636-2654
State map: C9
From ALBION, head S on
IN 9 for 4 miles (6.4 k).
$5 class C; $7 class B; $11
class A; $2 entrance fee.

Open Apr 1–Nov 1; dry camping
allowed off-season.
419 close, open sites. &
Central faucet, flush toilets, showers,
dump station, electric hookups, tables,
fire rings, boat ramp, store, rentals, pay
phone.
In scattered woods.
Hike trail system. Swim, canoe, or fish in
several lakes. Take photos.
14-day limit. Occasionally
crowded/noisy on weekends and
holidays.

CLARK SF

(812) 294-4306
State map: M8
From SALEM, drive E on
IN 160 about 20 miles (32 k)
to HENRYVILLE. Turn Left
(N) on US 31 and go to entrance on Left.
(Nearby Deam Lake SRA costs $11.)
$5.
Open All Year.
70 scattered, screened sites.
Central faucet, pit toilets, dump station,
tables, fire rings, pay phone.
Adjacent to I-65, in woods near several
small lakes and open field for sports.
Hike Clark Trail to view wildlife and
take photos. Fish or boat (paddle and
electric motors).
14-day limit. Traffic noise.

CLIFTY FALLS SP

(812) 265-1331
State map: L9
From MADISON, drive W on
IN 56 for 3 miles (4.8 k).
$5 class C; $11.00 class A; $2
entrance fee.
Open All Year.
165 close, open sites.
Central faucet, flush toilets, showers,
dump station, electric hookups, tables,
fire rings, pool.
Near deep-bouldered canyons and
waterfalls.
Hike to enjoy scenery. Swim.
14-day limit.

FERDINAND SF

(812) 367-1524
State map: M5
From FERDINAND, drive E
on IN 264 for 6 miles (9.6 k).
(Also see Lincoln SP and
Patoka Lake.)
$5; $2 entrance fee.
Open All Year.
69 close, open sites.
Central faucet, pit toilets, dump station,
tables, fire rings, boat ramp, rentals.
With shaded and open areas among
pine/hardwood trees.
Hike to view wildlife. Swim, fish, or boat
(paddle or electric motors).
14-day limit. Hunting in season.
Crowded Memorial Day.

GERMAN RIDGE

Wayne-Hoosier NF
(812) 547-7051
State map: N6
From TELL CITY, drive E on
IN 66 about 10 miles (16 k).
Turn Left (N) on CR 1002.
$4.
Open Apr 1–Dec 15; dry camping
allowed off-season.
20 close, screened sites.
Hand pump, pit toilets, tables, fire rings.
In pine and mixed hardwood ecology.
Hike. Swim or fish nearby.
14-day limit. Hunting in season.
Sometimes used as horse camp.

GREENE-SULLIVAN SF

(812) 648-2810
State map: K3
From DUGGER, drive S on
IN 139. (Also see Shakamak
SP.)
$5.
Open All Year.
130 close, open sites.
Central faucet, pit toilets, dump station,
tables, fire rings.
In reclaimed strip-mine area.
Hike. Observe wildlife. Relax.
14-day limit. Hunting in season.

HARDY LAKE

(812) 794-3800
State map: L9
From AUSTIN, drive E on
IN 256 for 6 miles (9.6 k) to
caution light. Turn Left (N) on
CR 400 and go 4 miles (6.4 k).
$5 class C; $11 class A; $2 entrance fee.
Open All Year.
166 close, open sites. ♿
Central faucet, flush toilets, showers,
dump station, electric hookups, tables,
fire rings, boat ramp, playground, pay
phone.
Next to 741-acre lake.
Swim, boat, ski, or fish. Hike or walk
nature trails. Attend ranger programs.
14-day limit. Hunting in season.
Occasionally crowded.

HARRISON-CRAWFORD SF
Stage Stop

(812) 738-8232
State map: M7
From CORYDON, take IN 62
W for 8 miles (12.8 k). Turn
Left (S) and proceed .5 mile
(800 m). (Nearby Wyandotte Woods SRA
costs $11.)
$5.
Open Apr 15–Nov 1.
22 (20 tent-only) close, open sites.
Central faucet, pit toilets, tables, grills,
fire rings, canoe ramp.
Along Blue River with some shade.
Canoe. Fish. Watch wildlife. Tour
Wyandotte Caves.
14-day limit.
450 ft (135 m)

HOVEY LAKE FWA

(812) 838-2927
State map: P1
From MOUNT VERNON, go
W on IN 62 for 2 miles (3.2 k).
Turn Left (S) on IN 69 and
drive 9 miles (14.4 k).
$5.
Open All Year.
48 close, open sites.
Central faucet, pit toilets, tables, fire

▲ ▲

rings, grills, boat ramp, pay phone.
On bluff overlooking 1400-acre lake.
Fish or boat. Spot wildlife.
14-day limit. Hunting in season.
Crowded holiday weekends.

HUNTINGTON RESERVOIR

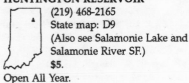

(219) 468-2165
State map: D9
(Also see Salamonie Lake and
Salamonie River SF.)
$5.

Open All Year.
806 ft (242 m)
▲ Kil-So-Quah
From HUNTINGTON, head 2 miles
(3.2 k) E on US 224.
100 close, open sites.
Central faucet, pit toilets, tables, fire
rings.
In woods overlooking lake.
Walk nature trail or hike. Take photos.
Fish.
14-day limit. Occasionally floods.
Crowded major holidays.
▲ Little Turtle
From HUNTINGTON, drive S on IN 5
for 2 miles (3.2 k).
30 close, open sites.
Central faucet, pit toilets, tables, fire
rings.
In woods with spring wildflowers.
Walk nature trails or hike to view
wildlife. Swim, boat, ski, or fish.
14-day limit. Crowded major holidays.

JACKSON-WASHINGTON SF

(812) 358-2160
State map: K7
From BROWNSTOWN, travel
E on IN 250 for 2.5 miles
(4 k). (Nearby Starve Hollow
SRA costs $7.)
$5.
Open All Year.
60 scattered, open sites.
Central faucet, pit toilets, tables, grills,
fire rings, pay phone.
In peaceful forest near lake.
Fish or boat (paddle and electric motors).
Walk nature trails. Hike. Practice

archery.
14-day limit. Hunting in season.
Crowded holidays.
500 ft (150 m)

JASPER-PULASKI FWA

(219) 843-4841
State map: D4
From MEDARYVILLE, head
N on US 421 about 4 miles
(6.4 k). Turn Left (W).
$5.
Open All Year.
51 close, open sites.
Central faucet, pit toilets, tables, fire
rings.
Near small fishing ponds.
Observe sandhill cranes (spring & fall).
Fish.
14-day limit. Hunting in season.

KINGSBURY FWA

(219) 393-3612
State map: B5
From LA PORTE, drive SE on
IN 4. Continue SE on IN 104.
$5.
Open All Year.
18 close, open sites.
Central faucet, pit toilets, tables, fire
rings.
Near Kankakee River.
Fish. Observe wildlife.
14-day limit. Hunting in season.

LINCOLN SP

(812) 937-4710
State map: N4
Locate park just S of
LINCOLN CITY on IN 162.
(Also see Ferdinand SF.)
$5 class C; $11.00 class A; $2 entrance
fee.
Open All Year.
270 close, open sites.
Central faucet, flush toilets, showers,
dump station, electric hookups, tables,
fire rings, boat ramp.
In rolling shady hills next to Lincoln
Boyhood National Memorial with
working farm.

Swim. Canoe. Fish. Hike. Explore
historical exhibits.
14-day limit.

LYNNVILLE CITY PARK

(812) 922-5144
State map: N3
Find park in LYNNVILLE, on
IN 68.
$5; $10 hook-ups.
Open All Year.
56 (30 tent-only) close, open sites.
Central faucet, flush toilets, showers,
dump station, electric hookups, tables,
fire rings, boat ramp.
Next to 275-acre lake.
Boat or fish. Hike. Observe wildlife
(perhaps spot albino deer).
Crowded holiday weekends.

MARTIN SF

(812) 247-3491
State map: L5
From SHOALS, go E on US 50
for 4 miles (6.4 k).
$5.
Open All Year.
26 close, open sites. &
Central faucet, pit toilets, tables, grills,
fire rings.
In open woods at end of road.
Walk nature trail or take longer hikes.
Fish.
14-day/30-ft limits. Hunting in season.
700 ft (210 m)

MCCORMICK'S CREEK SP

(812) 829-2235
State map: J5
From SPENCER, drive E on
IN 46 about 4 miles (6.4 k).
(Also see Morgan-Monroe SF
and Owen-Putnam SF.)
$5 class C; $11.00 class A; $2 entrance
fee.
Open All Year.
324 close, open sites.
Central faucet, flush toilets, showers,
dump station, electric hookups, tables,
fire rings, pool, tennis courts.
In woods among high limestone cliffs

plus scenic waterfalls.
Hike and take photos. Swim.
14-day limit.

MISSISSINEWA LAKE-Miami SRA

(317) 473-6528
State map: E8
From PERU, take IN 19 SE to
CR 500 S. Turn Left (E) and
drive 3 miles (4.8 k). Turn Left
on CR 625 E.
$5 class C; $7 class B; $11 class A; $13
class AA; $2 entrance fee.
Open All Year.
630 close, open sites.
Water at 39 sites, flush toilets, showers,
electric hookups, tables, fire rings, boat
ramp, pay phone.
Next to 3200-acre lake.
Swim, boat, or fish. Walk Blue Heron
Trail. Hike Frances Slocum Trail on E
side of dam. Bike. Attend ranger
programs.
14-day limit. Hunting in season.
Crowded holidays.
750 ft (225 m)

MONROE LAKE

(812) 837-9546
State map: K6
From BLOOMINGTON, head
S on IN 37 about 10 miles
(16 k).
$5 class C; $7.00 class B; $11.00 class A.
Open All Year.
412 close, open sites.
Central faucet, flush toilets, showers,
dump station, electric hookups, tables,
fire rings, boat ramps, volleyball courts.
In 6 SRAs next to 10750-acre lake.
Swim, boat, ski, or fish. Hike.
14-day limit. Hunting in season.

MORGAN-MONROE SF

(317) 342-4026
State map: J6
From BLOOMINGTON, drive
NE on IN 37 for 16 miles
(25.6 k). Turn Right (E) at
sign. (Also see McCormick's Creek SP
and Yellowwood SF.)

$5.
Open All Year.
30 close, open sites.
Central faucet, pit toilets, dump station, tables, grills.
In woods.
Walk nature trail. Hike to take photos or view wildlife. Fish or boat.
14-day limit. Hunting in season. No generators in quiet hours.
968 ft (290 m)

OWEN-PUTNAM SF

(812) 829-2462
State map: J5
From SPENCER, take IN 46 W for 5 miles (8 k). Turn Right (N) at sign on gravel road and continue .5 mile (800 m). (Also see McCormick's Creek SP.)
$5.
Open All Year.
33 close, screened sites.
Central faucet, pit toilets, dump station, tables, fire rings.
In hardwood setting (or drive 10 miles (16 k) farther to more remote Rattlesnake Camp).
Walk Fish Creek or Poplar Top trails.
Fish. View wildlife. Enjoy quiet.
14-day limit. Hunting in season.
800 ft (240 m)

PATOKA LAKE

(812) 685-2464
State map: M6
From FRENCH LICK, go S on IN 145 about 10 miles (16 k). (Also see Ferdinand SF.)
$5 class C; $11 class A.
Open All Year.
546 scattered, open sites.
Central faucet, flush toilets, showers, dump station, electric hookups, tables, fire rings, boat ramps.
In 7 SRAs around 8800-acre lake.
Swim, boat, ski, or fish. Hike or bike.
Play frisbee golf. Cross-country ski in winter.
14-day limit.

PIGEON RIVER FWA

(219) 367-2164
State map: B10
From LAGRANGE, drive 7 miles (11.2 k) E on US 20. Turn Left on IN 3 and travel 3 miles (4.8 k) to village of Mongo. Turn Right (E) on CR 300N and go .5 mile (800 m). (Also see Pokagon SP.)
$5.
Open All Year.
44 close, open sites.
Central faucet, pit toilets, tables, fire rings.
In woods on banks of Pigeon River millpond.
Fish. Canoe. Watch wildlife.
14-day limit. Hunting in season.

PIKE SF

(812) 789-5251
State map: M3
From WINSLOW, head E about 4 miles (6.4 k).
$5.
Open All Year.
11 close, open sites.
Central faucet, pit toilets, tables, fire rings.
In bottomland and hilly uplands.
Fish (ice fish in winter). Hike to observe ecologies.
14-day limit. Hunting in season.

POKAGON SP

(219) 833-2012
State map: B10
From ANGOLA, drive N on US 27. (Also see Pigeon River FWA.)
$5 class C; $7.00 class B; $11.00 class A; $2 entrance fee.
Open All Year.
310 close, open sites.
Central faucet, flush toilets, showers, dump station, electric hookups, tables, fire rings, boat ramp, rentals.
Next to Lake James and Snow Lake.
Hike. Swim, boat, ski, or fish. In winter, cross-country ski, toboggan, and ice fish.
14-day limit.

▲ ▲

SADDLE LAKE

Wayne-Hoosier NF
(812) 547-7051
State map: N5
From TELL CITY, head NE on IN 37 about 9 miles (14.4 k). Turn Left (NW) on FR 443 and travel 1 mile (1.6 k). (Also see Tipsaw Lake.)
$4.
Open May 15–Dec 15; camping allowed off-season.
25 close, screened sites.
Pit toilets, tables, fire rings, boat ramp.
Among pine/mixed hardwood trees near lake.
Swim or fish. Hike.
NO water. 14-day limit. Hunting in season.

SALAMONIE LAKE-Lost Bridge SRA

(219) 468-2125
State map: E8
From MOUNT ETNA, drive W on IN 124 to IN 105. Turn Right (N) and go 1.5 miles (2.4 k). Turn Left (W). (Also see Huntington Reservoir and Salamonie River SF.)
$5 class C; **$11** class A; **$2** entrance fee; reservations accepted at (219) 468-2125 for an additional $2.
Open All Year.
246 close, open sites.
Central faucet, flush toilets, showers, dump station, electric hookups, tables, fire rings, grills, boat ramp, playground, ball fields, rentals, pay phone.
Near lake with some trees.
Swim, boat, ski, or fish. Walk nature trails. Visit nature center. Attend ranger programs.
14-day limit. Hunting in season. No generators. Crowded weekends and holidays.

SALAMONIE RIVER SF

(219) 782-2349
State map: D8
From LAGRO, take IN 524 S for 3.5 miles (5.4 k). (Also see Huntington Reservoir and

Salamonie Lake.)
$5.
Open All Year.
34 scattered, open sites.
Central faucet, pit toilets, tables, fire rings.
At site of old CCC camp with trees, manmade lake, and trails.
Hike to view wildlife and take photos. Fish.
14-day limit. Hunting in season.
Crowded major holidays.
755 ft (227 m)

SHAKAMAK SP

(812) 665-2158
State map: K3
From JASONVILLE, take IN 48 W for 2 miles (3.2 k). Turn Left (S). (Also see Green-Sullivan SF.)
$5 class C; **$11.00** class A; **$2** entrance fee; reservations accepted at (812) 665-2158 for an additional $2.
Open All Year.
180 (60 tent-only) close, screened sites.
Central faucet, flush toilets, showers, dump station, electric hookups, tables, fire rings, boat ramp, tennis courts, pool, rentals, pay phone.
In woods near lake.
Walk trails. Swim, boat, or fish. Attend ranger programs.
14-day limit. Occasionally noisy.

SPRING MILL SP

(812) 849-4129
State map: L6
From MITCHELL, drive E on IN 60 for 3 miles (4.8 k).
$5 class C; **$11** class A; **$2** entrance fee; reservations accepted at (812) 849-4129 for an additional $2.
Open All Year.
238 close, open sites.
Central faucet, flush toilets, showers, dump station, electric hookups, tables, fire rings, boat ramp, pool, tennis courts.
In rolling terrain with heavy woods.
Visit pioneer village. Walk nature trail. Hike. Canoe. Swim or fish. Attend

ranger programs.
14-day limit.

TIPSAW LAKE

Wayne-Hoosier NF
(812) 843-9402
State map: N5
From TELL CITY, go N on
IN 37 about 15 miles (24 k).
Turn Left (SW) on FR 503 and drive
2.5 miles (4 k). (Also see Celina Lake and
Saddle Lake.)
$5; $14 prime.
Open May 15–Sep 30.
39 close, screened sites.
Central faucet, flush toilets, showers,
tables, fire rings, grills, boat ramp, pay
phone.
Near lake in pine/mixed hardwood
trees.
Swim, boat, or fish. Walk nature trails.
Hike.
14-day limit. Hunting in season.

YELLOWWOOD SF

(812) 988-7945
State map: J6
From NASHVILLE, head SW
on IN 46 about 5 miles (8 k).
(Also see Morgan-Monroe SF.)
$5.
Open All Year.
80 close, open sites.
Central faucet, pit toilets, tables, fire
rings, boat ramp, shelter, rentals.
Near 133-acre lake.
Fish or boat (no gas motors). Hike.
14-day limit.

IOWA
CAMPGROUND LOCATIONS

▶ ▶ Find location on facing page map grid. ▶ ▶

▼ ▼ Locate area campgrounds on these page numbers. ▼ ▼

GRID	PAGE
A7	110
B3	134
B4	98, 107, 118
B5	97, 116, 121, 127
B6	109, 128
B7	100, 108, 122, 133
C1	124
C2	105, 113, 117, 119, 120
C3	93, 96, 101
C4	113, 134
C5	96, 105, 112, 122
C6	93, 99, 109, 110, 114, 126
D2	110, 134
D3	95, 111, 116
D4	99, 106, 107, 115, 117, 122, 127
D5	97, 101, 104, 109, 112, 121, 131
D6	115
D7	103, 112, 130, 135
E1	102, 112, 120, 126
E2	103
E3	99, 119, 132
E4	99, 127, 128
E5	93, 94, 98, 109
E6	103, 108, 113, 126
E7	107
F1	92
F2	128
F3	106, 114, 119, 122
F5	98, 100, 108, 111, 112, 128

GRID	PAGE
F6	113, 121, 123, 134
F7	98, 118, 125, 126, 129
G1	111, 125, 133
G2	100, 119
G3	99, 101, 104, 117, 121, 123, 132
G4	94, 118, 122, 129, 130
G5	91, 97, 104, 130, 131, 135
G6	90, 94, 96, 104, 106
G7	97, 105, 107, 109, 118, 127, 133
H1	121
H2	93, 108, 113, 115, 120, 123
H3	92, 98, 105, 135
H4	92, 105, 106, 116, 123
H5	102, 111, 125, 133
H6	91, 95, 100, 104, 117, 124, 125, 127, 131, 132
H7	109, 110, 111
I1	95, 98, 107, 121, 125, 134
I2	93, 97, 103, 113, 118, 131, 132
I3	97, 101, 107, 111, 114, 115, 126, 128, 129
I4	95, 101, 106, 110, 115, 119, 122, 124, 126, 132
I5	91, 92, 93, 96, 103, 108, 120, 130
I6	92, 100, 103, 108, 118
I7	135
J2	90, 102
J3	94, 102, 124, 133
J4	92, 94, 95, 101, 114, 124, 125, 132, 133
J5	91, 102, 114, 116, 117, 128
K4	94, 123
K5	120

Iowa

Grid conforms to official state map. For your copy, call (800) 345-IOWA
or write Division of Tourism, 200 East Grand, Des Moines, IA 50309.

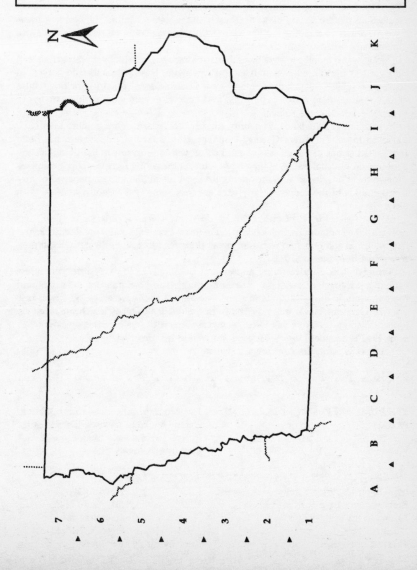

▲ ▲

PUBLIC LANDS CAMPING

Iowa is the rolling land between the mighty Mississippi and the wide Missouri, the scene of the Great Flood of 1993. Although the topography is mainly flat with gentle hills, the people who settled here brought variety. Find it in their history, celebrations, festivals, fairs, and genuine hospitality.

The state of Iowa offers 58 campgrounds with over 5,700 sites in its state parks, recreation areas, and forests. **Iowa Department of Natural Resources** (DNR) permits camping in designated sites only on a first-come, first-serve basis. At Iowa State Parks (SP), basic areas cost $5.00 and modern areas, $7.00. Electric hookups and water/sewer connections require an additional $2.00 each. In the state's Wildlife Management Areas (WMA), primitive camping is allowed in public hunting fields. Be sure to practice safe and sanitary procedures in these tracts.

During warm months in state areas, harvest asparagus, mushrooms, edible fruits and nuts (unless prohibited). Of course, you can swim, boat, fish, and ride horses. In winter, ice skate, cross-county ski, and sled. Other seasonal activities include nature center visits, interpretive programs, and special events such as historic event reenactments and crafts festivals.

In addition to state lands, 99 county conservation boards manage more than 1,100 parks in Iowa. The **Iowa County Conservation Board** (CCB) system has been recognized as one of the most successful conservation programs in the US, educating about environmental issues, managing wildlife, and creating recreation opportunities. Indeed, these developed sites are among the most plentiful and best managed county campgrounds in the country. Many sites are free; some cost as much as $9.00 with electricity.

On the federal level of public lands, **US Army Corps of Engineers** (COE) has constructed campgrounds on lakes created in Iowa: Coralville, Rathbun, Red Rock, and Saylorville. In addition, find recreation areas along the Mississippi River. COE camping fees range from free to $10.00.

National Park Service (NPS) administers two areas in Iowa. Neither one offers camping, but together they offer interesting insights and comparisons to ancient and modern culture. Effigy Mounds National Monument (NM) preserves 191 prehistoric Native American burial mounds, many in the shapes of birds and bears. Herbert Hoover National Historic Site (NHS) showcases the cottage where this president was born, his Presidential Library–Museum, as well as his gravesite.

The time is right. Discover Iowa treasures.

▲ ▲

4TH PUMPING PLANT RECREATION PARK

Des Moines CCB
(319) 753-8260
State map: J2
From KINGSTON, head N on IA 99 for 5 miles (8 k). Turn Right (E) and drive 5 miles (8 k).
$3; $6 electric.
Open All Year.
40 close, open sites.

Hand pump, pit toilets, dump station, electric hookups, tables, grills, fire rings. In wooded area near Mississippi River. Boat or fish. Spot wildlife.

ACKLEY CREEK

Floyd CCB
(515) 257-6214
State map: G6
From MARBLE ROCK, drive W on B60 for 1 mile (1.6 k). Turn

Left (S) on gravel road and continue
.5 mile (800 m).
$3. Open May–Oct.
56 (40 tent-only) scattered, open sites.
Hand pump, pit toilets, electric hookups,
tables, grills.
In rural setting along creek.
Walk to spot wildlife. Relax.
1000 ft (300 m)

AIRPORT LAKE

Chickasaw CCB
(515) 394-4714
State map: H6
Travel W on IA 18 for
1 mile (1.6 k) from NEW HAMPTON.
Turn Right (N) on gravel road and go
1 mile (1.6 k) then W for .5 mile (800 m).
(Also see Chickasaw, Saude Park, Split
Rock, and Twin Ponds.)
$3; $4 electric. Open All Year.
Undesignated close, open sites.
Central faucet, pit toilets, electric
hookups, tables, grills.
Among young oak, with evergreen
windbreak, next to 10-acre lake.
Swim, boat, or fish. Watch birds.

ALCOCK

Bremer CCB
(319) 882-4742
State map: H6
From FREDERIKA,
take C16 W for 1 mile (1.6 k). (Also see
Cedar Bend, North Cedar Park, and
Northwoods.)
$4; $5 electric.
Open May 1–Oct 31.
Undesignated scattered, open sites.
Central faucet, pit toilets, electric
hookups, tables, fire rings, grills, boat
ramp.
In woods next to Wapsipinicon River.
Fish and boat.

BAILEY'S FORD

Delaware CCB
(319) 927-3410
State map: I5
Drive SE on CR D5X

for 3 miles (4.8 k) from MANCHESTER.
(Also see Coffins Grove, Pin Oak, and
Turtle Creek.)
$4; $6 electric.
Open May 1–Oct 31.
30 scattered, open sites.
Hand pump, chemical toilets, dump
station, electric hookups, tables, fire
rings, grills, boat ramp, shelter,
playground, ball fields.
Near South Fork Maquoketa River.
Walk to view wildlife. Play any of
several sports. Fish for trout. Visit nature
center.
14-day limit. Hunting in season.

BANKSTON

Dubuque CCB
(319) 556-6745
State map: J5
From BANKSTON,
travel W on Bankston Park Rd about
3 miles (4.8 k). (Also see New Wine and
Swiss Valley.)
$5.
Open Apr 15–Oct 31; dry camping
allowed off-season.
50 scattered, open sites.
Central faucet, pit toilets, tables, grills.
In valley with wooded bluffs and trout
stream.
Relax. Fish.
14-day/24-ft limits. Not recommended
for RVs larger than pop-ups. Hunting in
season.
800 ft (240 m)

BEAVER MEADOWS

Butler CCB
(319) 278-4237
State map: G5
Find park on N side of
PARKERSBURG.
$4; $5 electric.
Open All Year.
Undesignated scattered, open sites.
Central faucet, pit toilets, electric
hookups, tables, fire rings.
Next to stream.
Canoe. Fish. Play golf nearby.

▲ ▲

BELVA DEER RA

Keokuk CCB
(515) 622-3757
State map: H3
From SIGOURNEY,
drive E on IA 92 for 2 miles (3.2 k). Turn
Left (N) on CR and go 2 miles (3.2 k).
(Also see Yenruogis.)
$2; $5 at 25 electric sites. Open All Year.
35 close, open sites.
Central faucet, pit toilets, dump station,
electric hookups, tables, fire rings, boat
ramp, shelter, playground.
In rolling hills, woodlands, and
grasslands with 5 ponds.
Fish or boat (no gas motors). Hike trails
to observe wildlife. Visit restored
one-room schoolhouse.

BENNETT PARK

Cedar CCB
(319) 886-6930
State map: J4
From BENNETT, drive
2 miles (3.2 k) NE on IA 130. (Also see
Cedar Valley and Massillon.)
FREE so choose a chore.
Open May–Oct.
Undesignated close, open sites.
Central faucet, pit toilets, tables, grills,
fire rings.
Among open rolling hills with
reconstructed prairie, butterfly garden,
and small pond.
Hike to enjoy surroundings. Bike. Take
macro photos. Fish.
14-day limit.

BENTON CITY-FRY

Benton CCB
(319) 472-4942
State map: H4
From VINTON, head E
on CR E24 about 6 miles (9.6 k). Turn
Left (N) on gravel road. (Also see
Hoefle-Dulin.)
$4; $5 weekends; +$2 electric.
Open May 1–Sep 15.
12 scattered, open sites.
Hand pump, chemical toilets, electric

hookups, tables, fire rings, boat ramp.
On level spot with some shade next to
Cedar River.
Boat or fish.
14-day limit. Hunting in season.
800 ft (240 m)

BLOODY RUN

Clayton CCB
(319) 245-1516
State map: I6
From MARQUETTE,
travel W on US 18 for 2 miles (3.2 k).
FREE so choose a chore.
Open All Year.
Undesignated scattered, open sites.
Central faucet, pit toilets, tables, fire
rings.
Along creek.
Fish. Relax.

BOBWHITE SP

(515) 873-4670
State map: F1
From ALLERTON,
head W on CR J46 for
1 mile (1.6 k).
$5; $7 electric.
Open All Year.
32 close, open sites.
Central faucet, flush toilets, electric
hookups, tables.
Next to 89-acre lake.
Swim, boat, or fish. Walk nature trail or
hike farther.

BOIES BEND AREA

Buchanan CCB
(319) 636-2617
State map: I5
Drive W for 1 mile
(1.6 k) from QUASQUETON. (Also see
Buffalo Creek.)
FREE so choose a chore.
Open All Year.
Undesignated scattered, open sites.
Pit toilets, tables, fire rings.
Next to Cranes Creek.
Fish. View native prairie.
NO water.

BOND HILL

Keokuk CCB
(515) 622-3757
State map: H2
From RICHLAND,
head N on CR W15 about 3 miles (4.8 k).
(Also see Manhattan Bridge.)
FREE so choose a chore.
Open All Year.
Undesignated scattered, open sites.
Pit toilets, tables, playground.
In rural setting.
Relax. Enjoy overnight stop.
NO water. No trash arrangements.

BOTNA BEND

Pottawattamie CCB
(712) 741-5465
State map: C3
Locate campground on
W side of HANCOCK.
$5; $7 electric. Open All Year.
80 scattered, open sites.
Central faucet, flush toilets, showers,
dump station, electric hookups, tables,
grills, fire rings.
With nearby herd of buffalo and elk in
woods near Nishnabotna River.
Take photos. Canoe or fish.
14-day limit.

BRIGHTON RIVER ACCESS

Washington CCB
(319) 657-3457
State map: I2
From BRIGHTON,
head N on CR I for 1.5 miles (2.4 k).
(Also see Brinton Timber.)
FREE so choose a chore.
Open All Year.
Undesignated scattered, open sites.
Pit toilets, tables, fire rings, boat ramp.
Along Skunk River.
Boat or fish.
NO water. No trash arrangements.

BRINTON TIMBER

Washington CCB
(319) 657-3457
State map: I2
From BRIGHTON,

drive W on IA 78 for 3 miles (4.8 k).
Turn Right (N) on CR W21 (Elm). Travel
2 miles (3.2 k). (Also see Brighton River
Access and McKain River Access.)
FREE so choose a chore.
Open All Year.
Undesignated scattered, open sites.
Pit toilets, tables.
In large timber tract along Skunk River
in wildlife refuge.
Hike over 6 miles (9.6) of trails. Observe
wildlife.
NO water. No trash arrangements.

BRUSHY CREEK SRA

(515) 359-2501
State map: E5
From LEHIGH, head E
on CR D46 for 4 miles
(6.4 k). (Also see Carlson RA and
Kennedy Park.)
$5; $7 electric.
Open All Year.
125 close, open sites.
Central faucet, flush toilets, electric
hookups, tables.
Next to creek.
Fish. Hike.
Hunting in season.

BUENA VISTA COUNTY PARK

Buena Vista CCB
(712) 295-7985
State map: C6
From LINN GROVE,
drive E on CR C13 for 6 miles (9.6 k).
(Also see Linn Grove Dam Area.)
$2; $4 electric. Open Apr–Oct 15.
19 scattered, open sites.
Central faucet, flush toilets, showers,
dump station, electric hookups, tables,
grills, fire rings, pay phone.
In woods on level terrain.
Hike trails. Spot wildlife. Relax.

BUFFALO CREEK AREA

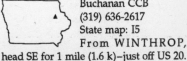

Buchanan CCB
(319) 636-2617
State map: I5
From WINTHROP,
head SE for 1 mile (1.6 k)–just off US 20.

(Also see Boies Bend.)
FREE so choose a chore.
Open All Year.
Undesignated scattered, open sites.
Pit toilets, tables, fire rings, shelter.
Along Buffalo Creek.
Fish. Observe wildlife.
NO water.

BUFFALO SHORES

Scott CCB
(319) 381-2900
State map: J3
Find park on IA 22
near BUFFALO. (Also see West Lake.)
$5; $9 electric. Open Apr 1–Oct 15.
65 scattered, open sites.
Central faucet, flush toilets, showers,
dump station, electric hookups, tables,
fire rings, grills, boat ramp.
On Mississippi River.
Hike to watch wildlife, especially birds.
Swim, boat, or fish.
14-day limit. Often crowded.

BULGERS HOLLOW

COE (815) 589-3229
State map: K4
From CLINTON, take
IA 67 N about 6 miles
(9.6 k). Turn Right (E) on gravel road at
Bulgers Hollow sign.
FREE so choose a chore.
Open All Year.
31 (6 tent-only) close, screened sites.
Central faucet, pit toilets, dump station,
tables, fire rings, boat ramp, playground,
pay phone.
On shore of Mississippi River.
Watch wildlife (deer, beaver, muskrat,
even eagles in winter). Watch river
traffic. Bike. Canoe, boat, or fish. Attend
ranger programs.
14-day limit. Occasional floods.
Crowded holiday weekends.

BUZZARD RIDGE WA

Jackson CCB
(319) 652-3783
State map: J4
From CANTON, travel

CR E17 E for 2 miles (3.2 k). Turn on
30th Ave. (Also see Central Park.)
FREE so choose a chore.
Open All Year.
Undesignated scattered, screened sites.
Pit toilets, tables, fire rings.
Along North Fork Maquoketa River.
Hike to view wildlife and take photos.
Canoe or fish.
NO water. No trash arrangements (pack
it out). 14-day limit. Hunting in season.

C D COPPOCK COUNTY PARK

Marshall CCB
(515) 754-6303
State map: G4
From LE GRAND, head
W on US 30 about 3 miles (4.8 k). Turn
Left (S). (Also see Three Bridges.)
FREE so choose a chore.
Open All Year.
Undesignated scattered, open sites. &
Central faucet, pit toilets, tables, grills,
shelter.
In small park.
Make overnight stop.

CAMP COMFORT

Butler CCB
(319) 278-4237
State map: G6
From GREENE, travel
SE on CR for 4 miles (6.4 k). (Also see
Greene Recreational Park.)
$4; $5 electric. Open All Year.
40 close, open sites.
Central faucet, pit toilets, electric
hookups, tables, fire rings, boat ramp.
Near Shell Rock River.
Boat or fish.

CARLSON RA

Webster CCB
(515) 576-4258
State map: E5
From DAYTON, take
IA 175 E for 5 miles (8 k). Turn Right (S)
on gravel road and go 1.5 miles (2.4 k)
(Also see Brushy Creek SRA.)
FREE so choose a chore.
Open All Year.

▲ ▲

Undesignated close, open sites.
Hand pump, pit toilets, tables, grills.
In scenic Des Moines River valley with
large stands of oak and hickory.
Fish, canoe, or just relax. Take photos.
Hunting in season.

CASEY CITY PARK

Casey City Park
(515) 746-3315
State map: D3
Locate park in CASEY.

$4. Open May–Sep.
50 close, open sites.
Central faucet, flush toilets, dump
station, electric hookups, tables,
playground.
In town park.
Enjoy overnight stop.

CEDAR BEND

Bremer CCB
(319) 882-4742
State map: H6
From WAVERLY, take
12th St NW. (Also see Alcock, North
Cedar Park, and Seven Bridges.)
$4; $5 electric. Open May 1–Oct 31.
52 scattered, open sites.
Central faucet, pit toilets, dump station,
electric hookups, tables, grills, fire rings.
On timbered ridge overlooking Cedar
River.
Hike trail system. Spot wildlife,
especially birds. Take photos. Fish.
Hunting in season.

CEDAR BLUFF ACCESS

Cedar CCB
(319) 886-6930
State map: I4
From TIPTON, drive
CR F28 (N Fairgrounds Rd) W for
9 miles (14.4 k).
FREE so choose a chore.
Open All Year.
Undesignated close, open sites.
Pit toilets, tables, boat ramp.
In wooded bottomland next to Cedar
River.
Canoe or kayak river. Fish.

NO water. 14-day limit. No RVs.
Occasional floods. Road not plowed for
snow.

CEDAR VALLEY

Cedar CCB
(319) 886-6930
State map: J4
From TIPTON, take
CR F36 (South St) SW. Bear Left (S) on
CR X40 (Garfield Ave). Turn Left (E) at
first road. (Also see Bennett Park and
Massillon.)
$3; $5 electric. Open All Year.
Undesignated close, open sites.
Central faucet, pit toilets, electric
hookups, tables, fire rings, grills, boat
ramp.
Along Cedar River with two abandoned
quarries (one stocked with trout).
Hike and take photos. Canoe or fish.
Attend ranger programs. In winter,
cross-country ski.
14-day limit. Occasional floods.
Crowded weekends.

CENTRAL PARK

Jones CCB
(319) 487-3541
State map: J4
From AMBER, go
4 miles (6.4 k) E on CR E29. (Also see
Buzzard Ridge WA.)
$4; $6 electric; $8 full hookups.
Open May 1–Oct 15.
100 close, open sites. Water at 10 sites,
flush toilets, showers, electric hookups,
tables, fire rings, grills, boat ramp.
Under mature oak overlooking 25-acre
lake.
Hike to view wildlife and find photo
opportunities. Swim, boat, or fish.
Attend ranger programs.
14-day limit.
876 ft (263 m)

CHATFIELD

Lee CCB (319) 463-7673
State map: I1
From KEOKUK, travel
NW on CR W62 for

3 miles (4.8 k).
$4; $5 electric. Open All Year.
Undesignated scattered, open sites.
Central faucet, pit toilets, electric hookups, tables, fire rings, boat ramp.
Next to 10-acre lake.
Canoe, fish, or boat (no gas motors). Hike. Cross-country ski, skate, or sled in winter.
No trash arrangements (pack it out).

CHAUTAUQUA PARK

Sac City Park
(712) 662-4295
State map: C5
Locate park in SAC CITY at 104 Park Ave. (Also see Hagge Park.)
FREE; $5 after 3 nights; reservations accepted at (712) 662-4295.
Open May 1–Oct 1.
14 (6 tent-only) close, open sites.
Water at every site, flush toilets, showers, dump station, electric hookups, tables, grills.
In trees with view of Raccoon River.
Canoe or fish. Watch birds.
Crowded Jul 4.

CHICKASAW

Chickasaw CCB
(515) 394-4714
State map: G6
From IONIA, drive W for 2.5 miles (4 k) on 220th St. (Also see Airport Lake, Howards Woods, and Twin Ponds.)
FREE so choose a chore.
Open All Year.
Undesignated close, open sites.
Hand pump, pit toilets, tables, grills.
In woods along Little Cedar River.
Fish. View wildlife. Take photos.
14-day limit. Small vehicles only.
Occasional ATV traffic.

COCKLIN FISH FARM

Cass CCB
(712) 778-2408
State map: C3
From GRISWOLD,

head N on IA 48 for 2 miles (3.2 k). (Also see Cold Springs.)
$4; $6 electric. Open Apr–Oct.
70 close, open sites.
Central faucet, pit toilets, dump station, electric hookups, tables, grills, fire rings.
On level, wooded terrain.
Fish.
14-day limit. Crowded on long weekends. Occasionally noisy.

COFFINS GROVE

Delaware CCB
(319) 927-3410
State map: I5
Take CR D22 W for 2.5 miles (4 k) from MANCHESTER. Turn Right (N) on CR W69. Turn Left (W) on second gravel road. Go .5 mile (800 m). (Also see Bailey's Ford and Pin Oak.)
$4; $6 electric.
Open May 1–Nov 30.
25 scattered, open sites.
Hand pump, chemical toilets, dump station, electric hookups, tables, grills, fire rings, playground, ball fields.
In park setting.
Fish. Play one of several sports. Spot birds.
14-day limit.

COLD SPRINGS

Cass CCB
(712) 769-2372
State map: C3
From LEWIS, travel S on CR M56 for 1 mile (1.6 k). (Also see Cocklin Fish Farm.)
$4; $6 electric. Open Apr–Oct.
160 close, open sites.
Central faucet, pit toilets, dump station, electric hookups, tables, fire rings, grills, boat ramp, pay phone.
Among oak and hickory trees.
Hike trail system. Swim, fish, or boat (paddle or electric motors). Attend ranger programs.
14-day limit. Crowded on long weekends. Occasionally noisy.

COLWELL

Floyd CCB
(515) 257-6214
State map: G7
From COLWELL, drive
W on B28 for 2 miles (3.2 k). Continue W
on gravel road for .25 mile (400 m).
(Also see West Idlewild.)
FREE so choose a chore.
Open May–Oct.
80 (40 tent-only) scattered, open sites.
Hand pump, pit toilets, tables, grills.
In woods near Little Cedar River.
Fish.
1000 ft (300 m)

CONSIDINE LAKE

Butler CCB
(319) 278-4237
State map: G5
From BRISTOW, drive
S on CR T24 for 3 miles (4.8 k). Turn
Left (W) and go 1 mile (1.6 k).
FREE so choose a chore. Open All Year.
Undesignated scattered, open sites.
Pit toilets, tables, boat ramp.
Next to 20-acre lake.
Canoe, boat, or fish.
NO water. No trash arrangements.

COOPERS COVE

Pocahontas CCB
(712) 335-4395
State map: D5
From PALMER,
proceed E on CR C56 for 7 miles (11.2 k).
Turn Right (S) at arrowhead sign and go
.5 mile (800 m).
$4. Open May 1–Oct 31.
12 close, screened sites.
Central faucet, pit toilets, electric
hookups, tables, grills, fire rings.
Within 300 ft (90 m) of natural pond.
Hike. Enjoy quiet.
14-day limit.

COPPOCK ACCESS

Washington CCB
(319) 657-3457
State map: I2
Find area on SW side

of COPPOCK. (Also see Sockum Ridge.)
FREE so choose a chore.
Open All Year.
Undesignated scattered, open sites.
Tables, boat ramp, shelter.
On Skunk River.
Boat or fish.
NO water. No toilet facilities. No trash
arrangements (pack it out).

COTTONWOOD

COE (319) 338-3543
State map: I3
In IOWA CITY off I-80,
take Dubuque St Exit
(W66) N for 4 miles (6.4 k). Turn Right
(E) on West Overlook Rd. Go 1.5 miles
(2.4 k). (Also see Linder Point and
Tailwater West. Nearby West Overlook
costs $8.)
$4. Open Apr 15–Oct 15; dry camping
allowed off-season.
25 (19 tent-only) scattered, open sites.
Central faucet, flush toilets, showers,
dump station, tables, fire rings, boat
ramp, pay phone.
Below dam near Coralville Lake and
Iowa River.
Swim or fish. Hike.
14-day limit. Crowded holiday
weekends.
710 ft (213 m)

CRAWFORD CREEK

Ida CCB (712) 364-3300
State map: B5
From BATTLE CREEK,
go S for 2 miles (3.2 k)
on CR L51. (Also see Moorehead Park.)
$4; $6 electric.
Open May–Oct.
36 close, open sites.
Central faucet, flush toilets, showers,
dump station, electric hookups, tables,
fire rings, boat ramp, pay phone.
On hilltop with view of 62-acre lake.
Enjoy quiet. Swim, fish, or boat. Hike to
take photos or spot wildlife. Attend
ranger programs.
14-day/40-ft limits. Crowded holidays.
1200 ft (360 m)

CROSS FORD AREA

Hardin CCB
(515) 648-3825
State map: F5
From IOWA FALLS,
head SE for 6 miles (9.6 k). (Also see
Eagle City Access.)
FREE so choose a chore.
Open All Year.
Undesignated scattered, open sites.
Pit toilets, tables, boat ramp.
Near Iowa River.
Boat or fish.
NO water. No trash arrangements.

CROTON CIVIL WAR PARK

Lee CCB (319) 463-7673
State map: I1
In CROTON. (Also see
Shimek SF.)
$4. Open All Year.
Undesignated scattered, open sites.
Central faucet, pit toilets, tables, fire
rings, boat ramp, shelter, playground.
At historic site near Des Moines River
and state forest.
Fish and boat.
No trash arrangements (pack it out).

DAHLE PARK

Winnebago CCB
(515) 565-3390
State map: F7
From LAKE MILLS,
drive NE on US 69 for 2 miles (3.2 k).
Turn Left (W) on CR A16 and go 4 miles
(6.4 k). (Also see Thorpe Park.)
FREE so choose a chore.
Open All Year.
6 close, open sites.
Hand pump, pit toilets, electric hookups,
tables, grills, fire rings.
On oak savannah near Winnebago River.
Boat or fish. Watch wildlife.
No trash arrangements. 10-day limit.

DAVID BATES MEMORIAL PARK

Hardin CCB
(515) 648-3825
State map: F5
From UNION, go NE

on CR for 3 miles (4.8 k). (See Lepley
and Long Memorial.)
FREE so choose a chore.
Open All Year.
Undesignated scattered, open sites.
Central faucet, pit toilets, tables, fire
rings.
In forest near stream.
Hike. Fish.
No trash arrangements (pack it out).

DAYTON OAK MUNICIPAL PARK

(515) 547-2711
State map: E5
Find park on S edge of
DAYTON, off IA 175 at
golf course. (See Don Williams Park.)
$5. Open May 1–Nov 1.
40 close, open sites. &
Central faucet, flush toilets, dump
station, electric hookups, tables, grills.
In trees on top of hill overlooking
natural amphitheater (for rodeo).
Relax. Watch wildlife. Play golf.
Crowded Labor Day weekend.

DECATUR BEND ACCESS

Monona CCB
(712) 423-2400
State map: B4
From ONAWA, head
W on IA 175 for 4 miles (6.4 k). Turn
Left (S) and go 1 mile (1.6 k).
FREE so choose a chore.
Open All Year.
Undesignated scattered, open sites.
Central faucet, pit toilets, tables, fire
rings, boat ramp.
Next to 30-acre lake.
Boat or fish.
No trash arrangements (pack it out).

DELTA COVERED BRIDGE

Keokuk CCB
(515) 622-3757
State map: H3
From DELTA, drive S
on IA 21 to CR G48. Turn Left (E) then
Left (N) again. (Also see Griffin Park.)
FREE so choose a chore.
Open All Year.

▲ ▲

Undesignated scattered, open sites.
Pit toilets, tables, grills, shelter, playground.
Next to oldest covered bridge W of Mississippi River.
Relax. Take photos.
NO water.

DEXTER CITY PARK

(515) 789-4210
State map: E3
In DEXTER, at Del Rio Rd and State St. (Also see Nation's Bridge.)
$5. Open All Year.
10 scattered, open sites.
Central faucet, flush toilets, electric hookups, tables, grills, fire rings, playground.
In small park surrounded by farm land.
Relax. Bike. Visit nearby Beaver Lake (.75 mile N).
Occasionally noisy.
1200 ft (360 m)

DIAMOND LAKE RA

Poweshiek CCB
(515) 623-3191
State map: G3
From MONTEZUMA, travel 1 mile (1.6 k) N on US 63. (Nearby Rock Creek SP costs $7.)
$5; $8 electric.
Open May 1–Oct 10; dry camping allowed off-season.
40 scattered, open sites.
Central faucet, flush toilets, showers, dump station, electric hookups, tables, fire rings, grills, boat ramp.
With 100-acre lake surrounded by timber, prairie, and grassland.
Fish or boat (paddle or electric motors).
Hike trails. Spot wildlife.
14-day limit.

DICKSON TIMBER

Carroll CCB
(712) 792-4614
State map: D4
From GLIDDEN, drive E on US 30 for 2 miles (3.2 k). Turn Left

(N). Go 3.5 miles (5.6 k). (Also see Hyde Park, Merritt Access, and Richey Access. Nearby Swan Lake SP costs $7.)
$3; $4 electric.
Open May 1–Nov 1; dry camping allowed off-season.
28 scattered, open sites.
Central faucet, pit toilets, electric hookups, tables, grills, fire rings.
In woods next to creek.
Hike trails. Take photos. Attend ranger programs.
14-day/32-ft limits. Hunting in season.

DOG CREEK PARK

O'Brien CCB
(712) 448-2254
State map: C6
From SUTHERLAND, proceed SE on IA 10 for 3 miles (4.8 k). Turn Right (S) on CR M12 and go .5 mile (800 m). (Nearby Mill Creek SP costs $8.)
$5. Open May 1–Sep 30.
30 close, open sites.
Water at every site, pit toilets, dump station, electric hookups, tables, fire rings, boat ramp.
In prairie hills with some trees next to small lake.
Swim or fish. Observe wildlife.
14-day limit.

DON WILLIAMS PARK

Boone CCB
(515) 353-4237
State map: E4
From OGDEN, drive N on CR P70 for 5.5 miles (8.8 k). (Also see Dayton Oak Municipal Park and Swede Point.)
$5; $7 electric. Open Apr 15–Oct 30.
100 close, open sites.
Central faucet, flush toilets, showers, dump station, electric hookups, tables, boat ramp, pay phone.
Next to 160-acre lake and 9-hole golf course.
Hike area and spot birds. Bike. Swim, canoe, or fish. Play golf.
Crowded major holidays.
1100 ft (330 m)

DOUMA PARK

O'Brien CCB
(712) 448-2254
State map: B7
From SANBORN, head
W on US 18 for 2 miles (3.2 k). Turn Left
(S) on Polk Ave for 2 miles (3.2 k).
$3. Open May 1–Sep 30.
10 close, open sites.
Water at every site, pit toilets, electric
hookups, tables, fire rings.
On shaded flat next to small pond.
Fish. Relax.
14-day limit.

DOWNING PARK

Fayette CCB
(319) 425-3613
State map: H6
From FAIRBANK,
travel 7.5 miles (12 k) N on CR U68.
(Also see Twin Bridges.)
$3. Open Apr 1–Oct 31; dry camping
allowed off-season.
40 close, open sites.
Central faucet, pit toilets, tables, grills,
fire rings.
In burr oak stand with creek.
Enjoy quiet. Walk nature trail. Spot
wildlife.
14-day limit.

DRAKESVILLE CITY PARK

State map: G2
In DRAKESVILLE at
square, go 2 blocks N
and 1 block E.

FREE; donations requested.
Open All Year.
40 scattered, open sites.
Central faucet, chemical toilets, electric
hookups, tables, grills, playground.
Relax in shaded city park.
Crowded Jul 4 and Sep. No generators in
quiet hours.

DUTTON'S CAVE

Fayette CCB
(319) 425-3613
State map: I6
From WEST UNION,
go NE on US 18 for 3 miles (4.8 k). Turn
Left (N) on Ironwood Rd. Go 1.25 miles
(2 k). (Also see Echo Valley SP and
Goeken.)
$3; $5 electric.
Open Apr 1–Oct 31; dry camping
allowed off-season.
14 scattered, open sites.
Central faucet, pit toilets, electric
hookups, tables, grills, fire rings.
In deep ravine with oak and maple and
50-ft vertical limestone wall.
Enjoy spring wildflowers. Walk nature
trail. Spot wildlife.
14-day/36-ft limits.

EAGLE CITY ACCESS

Hardin CCB
(515) 648-3825
State map: F5
From IOWA FALLS,
drive SE for 7 miles (11.2 k). (Also see
Cross Ford Area.)
FREE so choose a chore.
Open All Year.
Undesignated scattered, open sites.
Central faucet, pit toilets, tables, fire
rings, boat ramp.
Along Iowa River.
Fish or boat. Hike to observe wildlife.
No trash arrangements (pack it out).

ECHO VALLEY SP

Fayette CCB
(319) 425-3613
State map: H6
From WEST UNION,
drive 1.5 miles (2.4 k) SE on Echo Valley
Rd. (Also see Dutton's Cave,
Gilbertson's Park, and Gouldsburg.)
$3.
Open Apr 1–Oct 31; camping allowed
off-season.
Undesignated scattered, open sites.
Pit toilets, tables, grills, fire rings.
In open grassy areas spotted throughout
park.
Explore CCC-built structures: lime kiln
and keystone archway. Fish.
NO water. 14-day/36-ft limits. No RVs.

▲ ▲

EDEN VALLEY REFUGE

Clinton CCB
(319) 847-7202
State map: J4
From BALDWIN, take
50th Ave S for 1.5 miles (2.4 k).
$4.
Open All Year.
29 (4 tent-only) scattered, open sites.
Hand pump, pit toilets, tables, grills, fire rings.
In valley with wooded limestone bluffs.
Hike trails to spot wildlife and take photos. Visit nature center.
Cross-country ski in winter.
14-day limit. No generators in evening.

ELK HORN CREEK RA

Shelby CCB
(712) 755-2628
State map: C3
From ELK HORN,
drive SW on CR for 2.5 miles (4 k).
FREE so choose a chore.
Open All Year.
Undesignated scattered, open sites.
Central faucet, pit toilets, tables, fire rings.
In trees next to 5-acre lake.
Hike. Fish. Relax.
No trash arrangements (pack it out).
14-day limit.

EVELAND ACCESS

Mahaska CCB
(515) 673-9327
State map: G3
From BEACON, take
CR T39 SW for 4 miles (6.4 k). (Also see Quercus Wilderness Area.)
$3; $5 electric.
Open Apr 15–Oct 25.
26 close, open sites.
Central faucet, pit toilets, electric hookups, tables, fire rings, grills, boat ramp, playground.
In manicured setting along Des Moines River.
Boat or fish.
10-day limit.

F W KENT PARK

Johnson CCB
(319) 645-2315
State map: I4
From TIFFIN, drive W
on IA 6 for 3 miles (4.8 k). (Also see Hills Access.)
$4; $8 electric. Open May 1–Oct 31.
86 close, screened sites.
Central faucet, pit toilets, dump station, electric hookups, tables, fire rings, grills, boat ramp, pay phone.
In pleasant, shady setting.
Hike trail system. Swim, boat, or fish.
Take photos.
14-day limit.

FEATHERSTONE MEMORIAL PARK

Calhoun CCB
(712) 297-8323
State map: D5
From ROCKWELL
CITY, travel N on CR N57 for 5 miles (8 k). Turn Left (W). Go .25 mile (400 m). Turn Right (N). Follow lake road for 3 miles (4.8 k). (Also see Hagge Park and Kelly Access.)
$5; $8 electric.
Open Mar–Oct; dry camping allowed off-season.
69 (20 tent-only) close, open sites.
Water at every site, flush toilets, showers, dump station, electric hookups, tables, fire rings, boat ramp.
On flat next to 600-acre lake.
Swim, boat, and fish.
Crowded major holidays.

FERN CLIFF

Washington CCB
(319) 657-3457
State map: I3
Drive S on CR W55 for
6 miles (9.6 k) from WASHINGTON.
Turn Left (E) on 320th St and continue 3 miles (4.8 k). (Also see Sockum Ridge.)
FREE so choose a chore.
Open All Year.
Undesignated scattered, open sites.
Hand pump, pit toilets, tables, fire rings, shelter.

▲ ▲

Along Crooked Creek.
Fish. Hike. Relax.
No trash arrangements (pack it out).

FERRY LANDING

COE (319) 263-7913
State map: J2
From OAKVILLE, take
X61 N, following signs.
FREE so choose a chore.
Open All Year.
20 scattered, open sites.
Central faucet, pit toilets, dump station,
tables, fire rings, boat ramp.
Along Mississippi River.
Explore Mark Twain NWR. Spot birds.
Fish and boat.
No trash arrangements (pack it out).
14-day limit. Hunting in season.

FIFE'S GROVE

Ringgold CCB
(515) 464-2787
State map: E1
Head N from MOUNT
AYR for 1 mile (1.6 k). (Also see Poe
Hollow.)
FREE so choose a chore.
Open All Year.
Undesignated scattered, open sites.
Hand pump, pit toilets, tables, fire rings.
Next to small pond.
Fish. Relax.
No trash arrangements (pack it out).
14-day limit.

FILLMORE RA

Dubuque CCB
(319) 556-6745
State map: J5
From CASCADE, drive
NW on US 151 for 6 miles (9.6 k). Turn
Left (N) on Fairway Rd. (Also see Swiss
Valley.)
$5; $7 electric.
Open Apr 15–Oct 31; dry camping
allowed off-season.
16 close, open sites.
Central faucet, flush toilets, electric
hookups, tables, grills, fire rings, pay
phone.

In rural setting next to 9-hole golf
course.
Play golf.
14-day limit. Nearby highway noise.
800 ft (240 m)

FINLEY'S LANDING

Dubuque CCB
(319) 552-1017
State map: J5
From SHERRILL, take
Great River Rd N about .5 mile (800 m).
Turn Right (E) on Finley's Landing Rd.
Go 3 miles (4.8 k). (Also see Mud Lake.)
$5; $7 electric.
Open Apr 15–Oct 31; dry camping
allowed off-season.
30 close, open sites.
Central faucet, pit toilets, electric
hookups, tables, fire rings, grills, boat
ramp, pay phone.
At juncture of Basswood Creek and
Mississippi River surrounded by high,
wooded river bluffs.
Walk area to observe abundant wildlife.
Fish or boat.
14-day/25-ft limits. Hunting in season.
Crowded holidays.
800 ft (240 m)

FLAMING PRAIRIE

Louisa CCB
(319) 523-8381
State map: J3
From GRANDVIEW,
travel E for 5 miles (8 k).
$3; $4 electric.
Open All Year.
Undesignated scattered, open sites.
Central faucet, pit toilets, electric
hookups, tables, fire rings, boat ramp.
On river.
Boat or fish.
No trash arrangements (pack it out).

FONTANA PARK

Buchanan CCB
(319) 636-2617
State map: H5
From HAZLETON,
drive S for 1 mile (1.6 k). (Also see

▲ ▲

Jakway Forest.)
$5; $7 electric. Open All Year.
75 close, open sites.
Central faucet, pit toilets, electric
hookups, tables, grills, fire rings, shelter,
playground.
With woods and lake at site of old mill.
Walk nature trail or hike farther. Fish or
boat (no gas motors). Cross-country ski
in winter.

FORT DEFIANCE SP

(712) 337-3211
State map: D7
From ESTHERVILLE,
drive S for 1 mile
(1.6 k) on CR N26.
$5; $7 electric. Open All Year.
32 close, open sites.
Central faucet, pit toilets, electric
hookups, tables, grills, fire rings, pay
phone.
Among oak trees surrounded by rolling
farmland.
Walk nature trail. Hike to observe
wildlife and take photos. Cross-country
ski in winter.

FOUNTAIN SPRINGS

Delaware CCB
(319) 927-3410
State map: I5
From GREELEY, head
NW on signed gravel road for 3 miles
(4.8 k)–signs also off IA 3. (Also see
Twin Bridges.)
$4; $6 electric. Open May 1–Oct 30.
25 scattered, open sites.
Hand pump, chemical toilets, electric
hookups, tables, grills, fire rings.
In beautiful rugged area along mile of
Elk Grove trout stream.
Hike to enjoy scenery. Fish.
14-day limit. Hunting in season.

FRANK A GOTCH PARK

Humboldt CCB
(515) 332-4087
State map: E6
From HUMBOLDT,
head S on IA 169 for 4 miles (6.4 k).

Turn Left (E) on CR C49. Drive 1 mile
(1.6 k). Turn Left (N) on CR P56. Go
2 miles (3.2 k). (Also see Joe Sheldon.)
$5; $7 electric.
Open May 1–Oct 31; dry camping
allowed off-season.
20 scattered, open sites. &
Central faucet, flush toilets, showers,
dump station, electric hookups, tables,
fire rings, grills, boat ramp, shelter.
Among variety of trees overlooking Des
Moines River.
Walk trail system. Canoe or fish. Bike.
Cross-country ski in winter.
14-day limit. Crowded Jul 4.

GARFIELD

Union CCB
(515) 782-7111
State map: E2
From AFTON, head W
for 1 mile (1.6 k) on US 34.
$4. Open All Year.
Undesignated scattered, open sites.
Central faucet, pit toilets, electric
hookups, tables.
Enjoy stop in small county park.

GIBSON RA

Henry CCB
(319) 986-5067
State map: I2
From SALEM, travel N
on Franklin Ave to 260th St. Turn Left
(W). (Also see Oakland Mills.)
FREE so choose a chore. Open All Year.
20 close, open, tent sites.
Hand pump, pit toilets, tables, fire rings.
In upland hardwoods with nearby
ponds, prairie, and marsh.
Hike trails to spot wildlife and take
photos. Fish.
14-day limit. Hunting in season.
870 ft (261 m)

GILBERTSON'S PARK

Fayette CCB
(319) 425-3613
State map: I6
From ELGIN, head E
on Agate Rd. (Also see Echo Valley SP.)

▲ ▲

$5; $7 electric.
Open Apr 1–Nov 1; dry camping allowed off-season.
28 close, screened sites.
Central faucet, flush toilets, showers, dump station, electric hookups, tables, grills, fire rings, canoe ramp.
Near Turkey River with palisading limestone bluffs.
Canoe. Walk miles of trails. Swim or fish. Visit petting zoo, nature center, Dummermuth Historical Building.
Attend ranger programs. Cross-country ski in winter.
14-day/36-ft limits. Hunting in season.

GLENDALE ACCESS

Mahaska CCB
(515) 673-9327
State map: G3
From OSKALOOSA, drive 4 miles (6.4 k) NE on CR T65.
FREE so choose a chore. Open All Year.
Undesignated close, open sites.
Tables, fire rings, grills, boat ramp.
Next to majestic Skunk River.
Boat or fish.
NO water. No toilet facilities.

GOEKEN

Fayette CCB
(319) 425-3613
State map: H6
From ELDORADO, drive S on IA 150 for .5 mile (800 m).
(Also see Dutton's Cave.)
$3; $5 electric. Open Apr 1–Nov 1.
4 scattered, open sites.
Central faucet, pit toilets, electric hookups, tables, grills, fire rings.
At scenic overlook with panoramic view of Turkey River and seven towns.
Relax. Take photos.
14-day/36-ft limits.

GOULDSBURG

Fayette CCB
(319) 425-3613
State map: H6
From HAWKEYE, travel N on CR W14 for 4 miles (6.4 k).

Turn Left (W) on Sunset Rd. Go .5 mile (800 m). (Also see Echo Valley SP.)
$3; $5 electric. Open Apr 1–Oct 31.
26 scattered, open sites.
Central faucet, pit toilets, electric hookups, tables, grills, fire rings.
In open area near confluence of Crane Creek and Little Turkey River.
Swim or fish. Hike trails. Attend ranger programs.
14-day/36-ft limits.

GRAMMER GROVE WA

Marshall CCB
(515) 754-6303
State map: G5
From LISCOMB, head W on CR E18 about .5 mile (800 m).
Turn Left (S) on access road and drive 1.2 miles (1.9 k). Turn Left (W). (Also see Timmons Grove.)
$5. Open All Year.
Undesignated scattered, open sites. &
Central faucet, pit toilets, electric hookups, tables, fire rings, shelter.
In woods near Iowa River.
Walk interpretive trail or hike farther to observe wildlife. Canoe. Cross-country ski or sled in winter.

GRANT PARK

Sac CCB (712) 662-4530
State map: D5
From AUBURN, travel .25 mile (400 m) W on US 71. Turn Right (N). Go 1 mile (1.6 k).
Turn Left (W) on gravel road. Continue .25 mile (400 m). (Also see Hagge Park.)
$5; $7 electric. Open May 1–Oct 31.
15 close, open sites.
Water at every site, flush toilets, showers, dump station, electric hookups, tables, grills, fire rings.
In woods overlooking Raccoon River.
Fish a little and relax.

GREENE RECREATIONAL PARK

Butler CCB
(319) 278-4237
State map: G6
Find park in GREENE.

(Also see Camp Comfort.)
$4; $5 electric.
Open All Year.
50 close, open sites.
Central faucet, flush toilets, electric hookups, tables, fire rings, boat ramp.
On Shell Rock River.
Boat or fish.

GRIFFIN PARK

Keokuk CCB
(515) 622-3757
State map: H3
Find park on SW edge of WHAT CHEER. (Also see Delta Covered Bridge.)
FREE so choose a chore.
Open All Year.
Undesignated scattered, open sites.
Pit toilets, tables, grills, shelter, playground.
Next to 3 ponds at site of old coal mine.
Fish. Relax.
NO water.

HACKLEBARNEY WOODS

Montgomery CCB
(712) 623-4753
State map: C2
From VILLISCA, take US 71 N for 4 miles (6.4 k). Turn Right (E) on US 34 and go .5 mile (800 m). (Also see Pilot Grove Park.)
$4. Open Mar–Oct.
15 scattered, open sites.
Central faucet, pit toilets, electric hookups, tables, fire rings.
Next to 10-acre pond and 120-acre woodland.
Walk trail system to view wildlife. Boat or fish.
Hunting in season.

HAGGE PARK

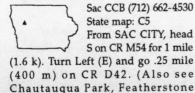

Sac CCB (712) 662-4530
State map: C5
From SAC CITY, head S on CR M54 for 1 mile (1.6 k). Turn Left (E) and go .25 mile (400 m) on CR D42. (Also see Chautauqua Park, Featherstone

Memorial Park, and Grant Park.)
$5; $7 modern. Open May 1–Oct 31; dry camping allowed off-season.
15 close, open sites.
Water at every site, flush toilets, showers, dump station, electric hookups, tables, grills, fire rings.
On wooded flat above Raccoon River.
Fish. Walk trails and take photos. Attend ranger programs.

HALVORSON

Mitchell CCB
(515) 736-4946
State map: G7
From ST ANSGAR, drive S on CR T26 for 2 miles (3.2 k). (Also see Interstate Park, Otranto, and Spring Park.)
$5; $8 electric.
Open May 31–Oct 31.
50 scattered, open sites. &
Central faucet, flush toilets, showers, dump station, electric hookups, tables, fire rings, grills, boat ramp, store, canoe rentals.
On shaded slope above Cedar River with excellent views.
Canoe or boat. Swim or fish.
14-day limit.

HANNEN

Benton CCB
(319) 454-6382
State map: H4
From BLAIRSTOWN, follow signs SW for 4.5 miles (7.2 k). (Also see Rodgers Park.)
$4; $5 weekends; +$2 electric.
Open All Year.
55 (5 tent-only) scattered, open sites.
Central faucet, flush toilets, showers, dump station, electric hookups, tables, fire rings, grills, boat ramp, store, rentals, pay phone.
On both sides of 50-acre lake surrounded by upland timber.
Walk trail system. View wildlife. Swim, boat or fish. Cross-country ski or sled in winter.
14-day limit. Crowded holidays.

HENDERSON

Greene CCB
(515) 386-4629
State map: D4
Head S on IA 4 about
1 mile (1.6 k) from JEFFERSON. Turn
Left (E). (Also see Oak Hill and Squirrel
Hollow.)
$2; $3 electric. Open All Year.
Undesignated scattered, open sites.
Central faucet, pit toilets, tables, fire
rings, boat ramp.
On North Raccoon River.
Canoe. Fish or boat.

HENRY WOODS SP

Butler CCB
(319) 278-4237
State map: G6
Find park on S edge of
CLARKSVILLE.
$5; $7 electric. Open All Year.
Undesignated scattered, open sites.
Central faucet, flush toilets, electric
hookups, tables, fire rings, boat ramp.
Next to Shell Rock River.
Boat or fish. Hike. Visit nature center.
Cross-country ski in winter.

HICKORY HILLS PARK

Warren CCB
(515) 961-6169
State map: F3
From INDIANOLA,
drive S on US 69 for 13 miles (20.8 k).
(Also see Otter Creek Park.)
FREE so choose a chore. Open All Year.
Undesignated scattered, open sites.
Central faucet, pit toilets, electric
hookups, tables, grills, fire rings.
Among wooded and open ridges near
Squaw Creek.
Hike to view wildlife and explore Native
American mound. Picnic at 1900's
farmstead. Fish.

HILLS ACCESS

Johnson CCB
(319) 645-2315
State map: I4
From HILLS, drive E

on 520th St for .25 mile (400 m). (Also
see F W Kent and River Junction.)
FREE so choose a chore.
Open All Year.
15 close, open sites.
Hand pump, pit toilets, tables, fire rings,
grills, boat ramp.
In open area next to Iowa River.
Boat or fish.
14-day limit.

HOBBS ACCESS

Carroll CCB
(712) 792-4614
State map: D4
From GLIDDEN, take
IA 286 N for 7 miles (11.2 k). Turn Right
(E) and go 1 mile (1.6 k). (Also see
Merritt Access.)
FREE so choose a chore. Open May
1–Nov 1; camping allowed off-season.
25 close, open sites. Pit toilets, electric
hookups, tables, grills, fire rings.
On banks of North Raccoon River.
Fish. Canoe. Walk nature trail.
NO water. 14-day/24-ft limits.

HOEFLE-DULIN

Benton CCB
(319) 472-4942
State map: H4
From VINTON, drive
W on CR E24 for 2 miles (3.2 k). Turn
Right (N) on 24th Ave and proceed
1.5 miles (2.4 k). (Also see Benton City-
Fry, Minne-Estema, and Rodgers Park.)
$4; $5 weekends; +$2 electric.
Open All Year.
12 scattered, open sites.
Hand pump, pit toilets, electric hookups,
tables, fire rings, boat ramp.
In dense shade on banks of Cedar River.
Canoe or fish. Take photos.
14-day limit. Hunting in season.
800 ft (240 m)

HOWARDS WOODS

Chickasaw CCB
(515) 394-4714
State map: G6
From NASHUA, head

▲ ▲

1 mile (1.6 k) N on Asherton Ave. Turn
Left (W) on 260th St. Go 1 mile (1.6 k).
(Also see Chickasaw and Twin Ponds.)
FREE so choose a chore.
Open All Year.
Undesignated close, open sites.
Hand pump, pit toilets, tables, fire rings,
grills, boat ramp.
In woods along Cedar River with access
to Cedar Lake.
Canoe or fish. Walk nature trail. Spot
birds.
Small vehicles only. Some ATVs.
Occasionally crowded.

HUFF-WARNER ACCESS

Monona CCB
(712) 423-2400
State map: B4
From BLENCOE, head
SW on CR for 2.5 miles (4 k).
$4; $5 electric. Open All Year.
Undesignated scattered, open sites. ♿
Central faucet, pit toilets, tables, fire
rings, boat ramp.
Next to Missouri River.
Boat or fish.
No trash arrangements (pack it out).

HYDE PARK

Greene CCB
(515) 386-4629
State map: D4
From CHURDAN,
drive W on CR E19 for 5 miles (8 k).
Turn Left (S) on CR N65 and go 2 miles
(3.2 k). (Also see Dickson Timber.)
$2; $3 electric. Open All Year.
30 close, open sites.
Central faucet, pit toilets, dump station,
electric hookups, tables, fire rings, boat
ramp, shelter.
Along North Raccoon River.
Canoe, boat, or fish. Hike to observe
wildlife.

INDIAN PATH

Lee CCB (319) 463-7673
State map: I1
From WEVER, drive
NE on US 61.

$4; $5 electric.
Open All Year.
25 close, open sites.
Central faucet, pit toilets, electric
hookups, tables, fire rings, boat ramp,
shelter, playground.
Next to Skunk River.
Boat or fish.
14-day limit.

INTERSTATE PARK

Mitchell CCB
(515) 736-4946
State map: G7
Locate park on SW
edge of MITCHELL on CR A43. (Also
see Halvorson and Spring Park.)
$5; $8 electric.
Open May 31–Oct 31.
25 scattered, open sites.
Central faucet, flush toilets, showers,
dump station, electric hookups, tables,
fire rings, grills, boat ramp.
On Cedar River next to historical dam
and powerhouse.
Walk nature trail. Canoe, boat, or fish.
14-day limit. Some noise from dam.

IOWA LAKE

Osceola CCB
(712) 754-4107
State map: E7
From HARRIS, drive N
on CR M20 for 4 miles (6.4 k). Turn Left
(W) and go .5 mile (800 m).
FREE so choose a chore.
Open All Year.
Undesignated scattered, open sites.
Central faucet, pit toilets, tables, fire
rings, boat ramp.
In small park next to 114-acre lake.
Boat or fish. Hike.
No trash arrangements (pack it out).

IOWA TOWNSHIP PARK

Washington CCB
(319) 657-3457
State map: I3
Find park on Tulip in
RIVERSIDE. (Also see Marr Park.)
FREE so choose a chore.

▲ ▲

Open All Year.
Undesignated scattered, open sites.
Hand pump, pit toilets, tables, shelter.
In town park with pond.
Hike. Fish.
No trash arrangements (pack it out).

ISLAND PARK

Rock Rapids Municipal
Parks (712) 472-2511
State map: B7
Locate park in ROCK
RAPIDS at North Marshall and North
2nd. (Also see West Side Park.)
$5; $6 electric.
Open Apr–Oct.
10 scattered, open sites.
Central faucet, flush toilets, dump
station, electric hookups, tables, grills,
fire rings, swimming pool.
Next to Rock River.
Fish or swim.
5-day limit.

J L REECE MEMORIAL PARK

Hardin CCB
(515) 648-3825
State map: F5
Head SW on CR from
NEW PROVIDENCE for 2.5 miles (4 k)..
FREE so choose a chore.
Open All Year.
Undesignated scattered, open sites. &
Hand pump, pit toilets, tables.
In wooded setting.
Hike. Practice archery.
No trash arrangements (pack it out).

JAKWAY FOREST

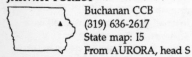

Buchanan CCB
(319) 636-2617
State map: I5
From AURORA, head S
on CR W45 for 1 mile (1.6 k). Turn Left
(W) on 136th St. (Also see Fontana Park.)
$5; $7 electric.
Open All Year.
40 close, open sites.
Hand pump, pit toilets, electric hookups,
tables, fire rings, shelter, playground.
In tall woods near stream.

Fish. Hike trails and view wildlife.
Cross-country ski in winter.

JEFFERSON COUNTY PARK

Jefferson CCB
(515) 472-4421
State map: H2
From FAIRFIELD,
drive SW on CR H43 for 1 mile (1.6 k).
(Also see Mac Coon Access.)
$5; $7 electric. Open May 1–Oct 31.
25 scattered, open sites.
Central faucet, flush toilets, showers,
dump station, electric hookups, tables,
grills, fire rings, pay phone.
In timbered valley with small creek.
Walk trails. Take photos. Fish.
14-day limit.
200 ft (60 m)

JOE SHELDON PARK

Humboldt CCB
(515) 332-4087
State map: E6
From HUMBOLDT,
travel W on IA 3 for 1.75 miles (2.8 k).
(Also see Frank Gotch Park and Lotts
Creek.)
$5; $7 electric.
Open May 1–Oct 31; dry camping
allowed off-season.
28 scattered, open sites.
Central faucet, flush toilets, showers,
electric hookups, tables, fire rings, grills,
boat ramp, shelter.
On wooded hill overlooking Des Moines
River.
Hike trails to observe wildlife. Bike. Boat
or fish. Cross-country ski in winter.
14-day limit. Crowded Jul 4.

JOY SPRINGS

Clayton CCB
(319) 245-1516
State map: I6
From STRAWBERRY
POINT, drive W on IA 3 for 3 miles
(4.8 k). Turn Left (S) and travel 1 more
mile (1.6 k).
$3. Open All Year.
Undesignated scattered, open sites.

Central faucet, pit toilets, tables, fire rings.
On stream.
Fish. Relax.

KELLY ACCESS

Calhoun CCB
(712) 297-8323
State map: D5
From POMEROY, drive
S on IA 4 for 2 miles (3.2 k). Turn Left (W) on CR D15 and go 5 miles (8 k) to village of KNOKE. Continue W another 5 miles (8 k). (Also see Featherstone Memorial Park.)
FREE so choose a chore.
Open All Year.
Undesignated scattered, open sites.
Pit toilets, tables, grills.
Next to Big Cedar Creek.
Fish. Relax.
NO water. No trash arrangements (pack it out). Hunting in season.

KENDALLVILLE

Winneshiek CCB
(319) 534-7145
State map: H7
Find campground in
KENDALLVILLE. (Also see Lake Meyer and Lidtke Park.)
$4; $6 electric. Open May–Oct.
26 (10 tent-only) scattered, open sites.
Central faucet, flush toilets, showers, electric hookups, tables, fire rings, grills, canoe ramp.
Next to scenic Upper Iowa River.
Canoe. View wildlife. Fish.
800 ft (240 m)

KENNEDY PARK

Webster CCB
(515) 576-4258
State map: E5
From FORT DODGE,
drive N on 15th St for 5 miles (8 k).
(Also see Brushy Creek SRA.)
$5; $7 electric; $9 full hookups.
Open May 1–Oct 15.
101 (22 tent-only) close, open sites.
Water at 29 sites, flush toilets, showers,

electric hookups, tables, fire rings, grills, boat ramp, rentals, pay phone.
Next to 60-acre lake with golf course nearby.
Hike trails through wildlife area. Swim, fish, or boat (no gas motors). Visit nature center. Attend ranger programs.
14-day limit. No generators. Occasional ATV noise. Crowded holidays.

KINDLESPIRE LITTLE SIOUX ACCESS

Clay CCB
(712) 262-2187
State map: C6
From SIOUX RAPIDS,
drive 2 miles (N). Turn Right (E) and go 2 miles (3.2 k).
FREE so choose a chore.
Open All Year.
10 close, open, tent sites.
Pit toilets, tables, fire rings, grills, boat ramp.
In riparian setting with burr oak next to Little Sioux River.
Hike to view wildlife. Fish.
NO water. Hunting in season.

KOSER SPRING LAKE PARK

Cherokee City Parks
(712) 225-2715
State map: B6
Turn W off US 59 on S
edge of CHEROKEE.
FREE; $6 RV electric.
Open May–Oct; dry camping allowed off-season.
35 close, open sites. Water at every site, flush toilets, showers, dump station, electric hookups, tables, grills, fire rings, playground, pay phone.
With 18-acre lake near Little Sioux River.
Canoe or boat (electric motors only).
Walk paths. Fish.
1200 ft (360 m)

LAKE HENDRICKS

Howard CCB
(319) 547-3634
State map: G7
From RICEVILLE,

travel 1 mile (1.6 k) N on IA 9.
$3; $5 electric.
Open May–Oct; dry camping allowed
off-season.
150 scattered, open sites.
Central faucet, flush toilets, showers,
dump station, electric hookups, tables,
fire rings, grills, boat ramp, ball fields,
archery range.
In two loops outlined by pine and oak
around a 54-acre lake.
Walk trail system. Bike. Swim, boat
(paddle or electric motors), or fish. Take
photos. Cross-country ski in winter.
14-day limit.

LAKE MACBRIDE SP-South

(319) 644-2200
State map: I4
From SOLON, drive
SW on CR F28 for
5 miles (8 k). (Nearby Lake MacBride
SP-North costs $7.)
$5. Open All Year.
60 scattered, open sites.
Central faucet, pit toilets, tables, fire
rings, boat ramp, pay phone.
In woods near part of Coralville Lake.
Walk trails. Spot birds. Boat or fish.
14-day limit.

LAKE MEYER

Winneshiek CCB
(319) 534-7145
State map: H7
From CALMAR, head
SW on IA 24. Watch for signed gravel
road. Turn Right (W) and go 1 mile
(1.6 k). (Also see Kendallville.)
$5; $6 electric.
Open Apr–Oct.
24 close, open sites.
Central faucet, flush toilets, showers,
dump station, electric hookups, tables,
fire rings, grills, boat ramp.
In woods near 40-acre lake.
Walk nature trails. Visit nature center.
Attend ranger programs. Boat or fish.
Cross-country ski in winter.
1200 ft (360 m)

LAKE ORIENT RA

Adair CCB
(515) 743-6450
State map: D2
From ORIENT, drive W
on IA 25 for 1 mile (1.6 k). (Also see
Mormon Trail Park.)
$3; $6 electric.
Open May 1–Oct 30; dry camping
allowed off-season.
21 close, open sites.
Central faucet, pit toilets, electric
hookups, tables, fire rings, boat ramp.
Amid gentle rolling hills with scattered
small trees next to 24-acre lake.
Fish. Hike to observe wildlife.
14-day limit. Occasionally crowded.

LAKE PAHOJA RA

Lyon CCB
(712) 472-2217
State map: A7
From INWOOD, travel
S on IA 182 for 4 miles (6.4 k). Turn
Right (W) on CR A26 for 2 miles (3.2 k).
$4; $8 electric; $2 entrance fee.
Open All Year.
72 (10 tent-only) close, open sites.
Central faucet, flush toilets, showers,
dump station, electric hookups, tables,
fire rings, grills, boat ramp, ball courts,
rentals, pay phone.
In woods next to 70-acre lake among
rolling hills.
Swim, fish, or boat (no motors). Walk
nature trail or hike to spot wildlife.
Attend ranger programs.
14-day limit.

LARSON LAKE

Cherokee CCB
(712) 225-5959
State map: C6
From AURELIA, go W
on IA 70 about 1 mile (1.6 k) to sign.
Turn Left (N) and drive 1 mile (1.6 k).
(Also see Martin Area.)
FREE so choose a chore.
Open All Year.
Undesignated sites.
Hand pump, pit toilets, tables, grills,

▲ ▲

playground, shelter.
In wildlife refuge next to 5-acre lake.
Hike to view wildlife and take photos.
Fish.
14-day limit.

LELAH BRADLEY PARK & PRESERVE

Appanoose CCB
(515) 856-8528
State map: G1
Locate park on SW
edge of CENTERVILLE. (Also see Sharon
Bluffs SP.)
$5; $7 electric.
Open All Year.
Undesignated scattered, open sites.
Central faucet, pit toilets, electric
hookups, tables, fire rings, boat ramp.
In wooded area with 140-acre lake.
Hike. Observe wildlife. Fish or boat.
14-day limit.

LENON MILL

Guthrie CCB
(515) 755-3061
State map: D3
Locate campground at
SW edge of PANORA on South St W.
(Also see Nation's Bridge.)
$5.
Open All Year.
14 (8 tent-only) scattered, open sites.
Central faucet, pit toilets, dump station,
electric hookups, tables, fire rings, grills,
boat ramp.
On Middle Raccoon River at site of old
wool mill.
Canoe. Bike. Fish for smallmouth bass.
14-day limit.

LEPLEY

Hardin CCB
(515) 648-3825
State map: F5
From UNION, travel N
on IA 215 for 1.5 miles (2.4 k). (Also see
David Bates Memorial Park and Long
Memorial.)
FREE so choose a chore.
Open All Year.
Undesignated scattered, open sites.

Central faucet, pit toilets, electric
hookups, tables, fire rings.
In quiet setting.
Relax. Enjoy overnight stop.
No trash arrangements (pack it out).

LIDTKE PARK

Howard CCB
(319) 547-3634
State map: H7
Find park just N of
LIME SPRINGS. (Also see Kendallville.)
$3; $5 electric. Open May–Oct.
50 scattered, open sites.
Hand pump, pit toilets, electric hookups,
tables, fire rings, grills, boat ramp.
On Upper Iowa River next to Lidtke Mill
and dam.
Canoe or fish. Bike. Watch birds. Take
photos.
14-day limit.

LIME CREEK

Buchanan CCB
(319) 636-2617
State map: H5
From BRANDON, head
NE on Diagonal Blvd for 1 mile (1.6 k).
$5; $7 electric.
Open All Year.
30 close, open sites.
Hand pump, pit toilets, electric hookups,
tables, fire rings, shelter, playground.
Along creek.
Fish. Relax.

LINDER POINT

COE (319) 338-3543
State map: I3
In IOWA CITY off I-80,
take Dubuque St Exit
(W66) N for 4 miles (6.4 k). Turn Right
(E) on West Overlook Rd and go
1.5 miles (2.4 k). (Also see Cottonwood
and Sugar Bottom.)
$4; $8 electric. Open Apr 15–Oct 15.
25 (7 tent-only) close, open sites with
some screening.
Central faucet, flush toilets, showers,
dump station, electric hookups, tables,
fire rings, playground, pay phone.

In walking distance of Coralville Lake.
Boat, ski, or fish. Walk Woodpecker
Nature Trail.
14-day limit. Crowded holiday
weekends.
770 ft (231 m)

LINN GROVE DAM AREA

Buena Vista CCB
(712) 295-7985
State map: C5
Locate area beside river
in LINN GROVE. (Also see Buena Vista
County Park.)
FREE so choose a chore. Open Apr–Oct.
Undesignated scattered, open sites.
Central faucet, pit toilets, tables, fire
rings, grills, boat ramp.
On both sides of Little Sioux River.
Canoe or boat. Fish.

LITTLE RIVER RA

Decatur CCB
(515) 446-7307
State map: E1
From LEON, head W
on IA 2 for .5 mile (800 m). Turn Right
(N). (Also see Skip Bluff.)
$5; $7 electric. Open All Year.
Undesignated scattered, open sites.
Central faucet, pit toilets, electric
hookups, tables, fire rings, boat ramp.
Next to 787-acre lake.
Swim, boat, or fish. Hike.
14-day limit.

LIZARD LAKE ACCESS

Pocahontas CCB
(712) 335-4395
State map: D5
From PALMER, head E
on CR C56 for 6 miles (9.6 k). Turn Left
(N) on gravel road. Go 2.5 miles (4 k).
FREE so choose a chore.
Open All Year.
6 close, open, tent sites.
Tables, fire rings, grills, boat ramp.
Next to lake.
Fish. Observe wildlife.
NO water. No toilet facilities. Hunting in
season.

LOGSDON

Hardin CCB
(515) 648-3825
State map: F5
From IOWA FALLS,
travel S on US 65 for 9 miles (14.4 k).
FREE so choose a chore.
Open All Year.
Undesignated scattered, open sites.
Central faucet, pit toilets, tables, fire
rings.
In woods near stream.
Fish. Hike.
No trash arrangements (pack it out).

LONG MEMORIAL

Hardin CCB
(515) 648-3825
State map: F5
From UNION, head E
on CR for 1 mile (1.6 k). (Also see David
Bates Memorial Park and Lepley.)
$3. Open All Year.
10 close, open sites. ♿
Central faucet, pit toilets, electric
hookups, tables, fire rings, boat ramp.
Along Iowa River.
Boat or fish. Canoe.
14-day limit.

LOST ISLAND-HUSTON PARK

Palo Alto CCB
(712) 837-4866
State map: D7
From RUTHVEN, drive
2 miles (3.2 k) N. Turn Right (E) and go
.5 mile (800 m). Turn Left (N) and go
2 miles (3.2 k). Turn Left (W) and
continue .75 mile (1.2 k). Turn Left (S)
and proceed .5 mile (800 m).
$5; $8 electric. Open Apr 15–Oct 15.
38 close, open sites.
Central faucet, flush toilets, showers,
dump station, electric hookups, tables,
fire rings, boat ramp, pay phone.
In woods with marsh and 1200-acre lake.
Swim, boat, or fish. Walk nature trails.
Take photos. Cross-country ski in winter.
14-day limit. Hunting in season. No
generators. Crowded holidays.

▲ ▲

LOTTS CREEK

Humboldt CCB
(515) 332-4087
State map: E6
From LIVERMORE,
drive W for .5 mile (800 m) on 130th St.
(Also see Joe Sheldon Park.)
$5; $7 electric. Open May 1–Oct 31.
16 scattered, open sites.
Central faucet, flush toilets, electric
hookups, tables, grills, fire rings, shelter.
On wooded flat.
Hike to watch wildlife or take photos.
Bike.
No trash arrangements. 14-day limit.

LOWER AUGUSTA ACCESS

Des Moines CCB
(319) 753-8260
State map: I2
From AUGUSTA, go E
for .5 mile (800 m). (See Upper Augusta
Access and Welter Recreation Park.)
$3; $6 electric. Open All Year.
48 close, open sites.
Hand pump, pit toilets, dump station,
electric hookups, tables, grills, fire rings.
In woods along Skunk River.
Fish and boat. Walk nature trail.

MAC COON ACCESS

Jefferson CCB
(515) 472-4421
State map: I2
From LOCKRIDGE, go
4 miles (6.4 k) N on gravel road. (Also
see Jefferson County Park.)
$3; $5 electric. Open Apr 1–Oct 31.
40 scattered, open sites.
Central faucet, pit toilets, electric
hookups, tables, fire rings, boat ramp.
In beautiful spot next to Skunk River.
Hike trails to spot wildlife. Boat or fish.
Hunting in season.
200 ft (60 m)

MALLORY MEMORIAL PARK

Franklin CCB
(515) 456-4375
State map: F6
From HAMPTON,

drive S for 6 miles (9.6 k) on US 65. Turn
Right (W) on gravel road and go 2 miles
(3.2 k). (Also see Robinson Park.)
$3. Open Apr 1–Nov 30.
40 scattered, open sites. &
Hand pump, pit toilets, electric hookups,
tables, grills, fire rings.
In scattered oak next to Maynes Creek.
Walk nature trail. Fish.
14-day limit. Occasional floods.

MANHATTAN BRIDGE

Keokuk CCB
(515) 622-3757
State map: H2
From OLLIE, travel N
on CR V5G for 4 miles (6.4 k). (Also see
Bond Hill.)
FREE so choose a chore.
Open All Year.
Undesignated scattered, open sites.
Pit toilets, table, boat ramp, playground.
Next to South Skunk River.
Boat or fish.
NO water.

MANTENO PARK

Shelby CCB
(712) 755-2628
State map: C4
From DEFIANCE, head
NW on CR for 8 miles (12.8 k).
$4; $5 electric.
Open All Year.
Undesignated scattered, open sites. &
Central faucet, flush toilets, showers,
electric hookups, tables, fire rings, boat
ramp.
Next to 11-acre lake.
Boat or fish. Hike.

MANTI

Page CCB
(712) 542-3864
State map: C2
From intersection of
IA 2 and US 59 (S of SHENANDOAH),
head W on IA 2 for 1 mile (1.6 k). Turn
Left (S) on M16 and go 1 mile (1.6 k).
Turn Left (E) on J40. (Also see Pierce
Creek and Pioneer Park.)

FREE so choose a chore.
Open Apr 15–Oct 15.
20 scattered, open, tent sites.
Hand pump, pit toilets, tables, fire rings, shelter.
In woods next to Fisher Creek at site of early Mormon settlement.
Explore historic area including old cemetery. Watch songbirds. Find green dragon plant and other wildflowers.

MARION COUNTY PARK

Marion CCB
(515) 828-2214
State map: F3
Locate park on Willets Dr on W side of KNOXVILLE. (Also see Roberts Creek.)
$5; $6 electric.
Open Apr 1–Nov 15.
170 (30 tent-only) close, open sites.
Hand pump, flush toilets, showers, dump station, electric hookups, tables, fire rings, pay phone.
In gentle rolling hills with 7-acre lake.
Fish.
800 ft (240 m)

MARIPOSA RA

Jasper CCB
(515) 792-9780
State map: F3
From NEWTON, drive E on US 6 for 2 miles (3.2 k). Turn Left (N) on CR T12 and go 5 miles (8 k).
FREE so choose a chore.
Open All Year.
Undesignated scattered, open sites.
Central faucet, pit toilets, tables, fire rings.
Next to 19-acre lake.
Fish. Hike. Skate in winter.

MARR PARK

Washington CCB
(319) 657-3457
State map: I3
From AINSWORTH, travel W on IA 92 for 1 mile (1.6 k). (Also see Iowa Township Park.)
$5; $7 electric. Open All Year.

48 (20 tent-only) scattered, open sites.
Central faucet, flush toilets, electric hookups, tables, fire rings, shelter, playground.
With 20-acre prairie and small pond.
Hike. Fish. Cross-country ski in winter.

MARTIN AREA

Cherokee CCB
(712) 225-5959
State map: C6
Travel E on CR C16 for 4 miles (6.4 k) from LARRABEE. Turn Right (S) on Martin Access Rd and go 1 mile (1.6 k). (Also see Larson Lake.)
FREE so choose a chore.
Open All Year.
44 sites. Hand pump, pit toilets, tables, grills, fire rings.
With forest, prairie remnants, and picturesque overlooks.
Hike trail system. Take photos. Fish or boat. Cross-country ski in winter.
14-day limit. Hunting in season.

MASSEY MARINA

Dubuque CCB
(319) 556-4703
State map: J5
From DUBUQUE, take US 52 S to Massey Station Rd. Turn Left (E). Go 3 miles (4.8 k). (Also see Swiss Valley. Nearby Spruce Creek costs $7.)
$5; $7 electric. Open Apr 15–Oct 31; dry camping allowed off-season.
40 scattered, open sites.
Central faucet, flush toilets, showers, dump station, electric hookups, tables, fire rings, grills, boat ramp.
Next to Mississippi River on level plain with some trees.
Boat and fish.
14-day limit. Often noisy and crowded.
800 ft (240 m)

MASSILLON

Cedar CCB
(319) 886-6930
State map: J4
Find campground on N edge of MASSILLON. (Also see Cedar

▲▲▲▲▲▲▲▲▲▲▲▲▲▲▲▲▲▲▲▲▲▲▲▲▲▲▲▲

Valley and Bennett.)
FREE so choose a chore. Open All Year.
25 close, open sites.
Central faucet, pit toilets, tables, fire
rings, grills, boat ramp.
Along Wapsipinicon River.
Hike to spot wildlife. Bike. Canoe or fish.
14-day limit.

MATSELL BRIDGE & MOUNT HOPE NATURAL AREA

Linn CCB
(319) 398-3505
State map: I4
From VIOLA, head N
on gravel road. Turn Left (W) at Matsell
Bridge sign. Go 2 miles (3.2 k). Turn
Right (N) at Mount Hope sign. Go
2 miles (3.2 k).
$4. Open Apr 15–Oct 1; dry camping
allowed off-season.
Undesignated scattered, open sites.
Hand pump, pit toilets, tables, fire rings,
grills, boat ramp.
Under hardwood trees on banks of
Wapsipinicon River.
Hike to view wildlife and take photos.
Boat or fish. Cross-country ski in winter.
Hunting in season. Rifle range noise.

MCKAIN RIVER ACCESS

Washington CCB
(319) 657-3457
State map: I3
From BRIGHTON,
drive W on IA 78 for 3 miles (4.8 k).
Turn Right (N) on CR W21 (Elm) and go
5 miles (8 k). (Also see Brinton Timber.)
FREE so choose a chore. Open All Year.
Undesignated scattered, open sites.
Hand pump, pit toilets, tables, fire rings,
boat ramp.
With access to Skunk River.
Boat or fish.
No trash arrangements (pack it out).

MERIDITH PARK

Pocahontas CCB
(712) 335-4395
State map: D6
From PLOVER, drive N

on CR N57 for 1.5 miles (2.4 k).
$4; reservations accepted at
(712) 335-4395.
Open May 1–Oct 31.
12 close, screened sites.
Central faucet, pit toilets, electric
hookups, tables, grills, fire rings.
In small park surrounding pond.
Fish. Hike trails to spot wildlife,
especially birds.

MERRITT ACCESS

Carroll CCB
(712) 792-4614
State map: D4
From GLIDDEN, take
IA 286 N for 4 miles (6.4 k). Turn Right
(E) and go 2 miles (3.2 k). (Also see
Dickson Timber and Hobbs Access.)
FREE so choose a chore.
Open May 1–Nov 1; dry camping
allowed off-season.
40 (20 tent-only) close, open sites.
Hand pump, pit toilets, tables, fire rings,
boat ramp.
Along banks of North Raccoon River.
Fish. Hike. Canoe.
14-day/24-ft limits. Hunting in season.

MIAMI PARK

Monroe CCB
(515) 946-8112
State map: H2
From LOVILIA, head E
about 5 miles (8 k).
$5; $9 electric. Open May 1–Sep 30; dry
camping allowed off-season.
65 (15 tent-only) close, open sites. &
Central faucet, flush toilets, showers,
dump station, electric hookups, tables,
fire rings, grills, boat ramp.
In game preserve next to state fishing
lake.
Watch wildlife. Boat or fish.
14-day limit.

MID RIVER

COE (319) 338-3543
State map: I4
From IOWA CITY,
head N on US 965

about 7 miles (11.2 k). Turn Right (E) at
Mid River sign. (Also see Sandy Beach
and Sugar Bottom.)
FREE so choose a chore.
Open All Year.
20 scattered, open sites.
Pit toilets, tables, fire rings.
Overlooking Coralville Lake.
Fish.
NO water. 14-day limit. Crowded
holiday weekends.
750 ft (225 m)

MINNE-ESTEMA

Benton CCB
(319) 472-4942
State map: H4
From VINTON, go N
on IA 150 for 3.5 miles (5.6 k). Turn Left
(W) on gravel 24th Ave and drive
3.25 miles (5.2 k). Turn Left. (Also see
Hoefle-Dulin and Rodgers Park.)
$4; $5 weekends; +$2 electric.
Open All Year.
15 scattered, open sites.
Hand pump, pit toilets, electric hookups,
tables, fire rings, boat ramp.
In shade next to Cedar River among
wooded hills.
Boat or fish. Watch birds.
14-day limit. Hunting in season.
800 ft (240 m)

MOOREHEAD PARK

Ida CCB (712) 364-3300
State map: B5
From IDA GROVE,
drive W on US 59 for
1 mile (1.6 k). (Also see Crawford
Creek.)
$4. Open All Year.
Undesignated scattered, open sites.
Central faucet, pit toilets, tables, grills,
fire rings.
In native Iowa woodland.
Hike numerous trails and observe
abundant wildlife. Fish or boat (no
motors). Attend ranger programs.
Cross-country ski in winter.
14-day limit.
1200 ft (360 m)

MORMAN TRAIL PARK

Adair CCB
(515) 743-6450
State map: D3
Go about 1.5 miles
(2.4 k) E from BRIDGEWATER. (Also see
Lake Orient RA and Nodaway Valley.)
$3; $6 electric.
Open May 1–Oct 31; dry camping
allowed off-season.
25 (10 tent-only) close, open sites.
Central faucet, pit toilets, electric
hookups, tables, fire rings, grills, boat
ramp.
In rolling hills next to 35-acre lake.
Swim, fish, or boat (no gas motors).
Watch birds.
14-day limit.

MUD LAKE

Dubuque CCB
(319) 552-2746
State map: J5
From center of
DUBUQUE, go 5 miles (8 k) NW on
US 52. Turn Right (E) on Mud Lake Rd.
Follow signs. (See Finley's Landing.)
$5; $7 electric.
Open Apr 15–Oct 31; dry camping
allowed off-season.
50 scattered, open sites.
Central faucet, flush toilets, showers,
dump station, electric hookups, tables,
fire rings, grills, boat ramp, pay phone.
On level river plain and marsh next to
Mississippi with some shade.
Boat and fish. View wildlife.
14-day/40-ft limits. Crowded weekends
and holidays.
800 ft (240 m)

NATION'S BRIDGE

Guthrie CCB
(515) 755-3061
State map: D3
From STUART, drive
6 miles (9.6 k) N on CR P28. (Also see
Dexter City Park and Lenon Mill.)
$5; $7 electric. Open All Year.
50 scattered, open sites.
Central faucet, flush toilets, showers,

▲ ▲

dump station, electric hookups, tables, grills, fire rings.

On bottomland next to South Raccoon River.

Hike trail system. View wildlife. Fish. Enjoy quiet.

14-day limit.

NEW WINE

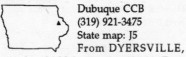

Dubuque CCB
(319) 921-3475
State map: J5
From DYERSVILLE,
take IA 136 N for 4 miles (6.4 k). Turn Left (W) on Vashe Rd and go .5 mile (800 m). Turn Left on New Wine Park Rd. (Also see Bankston or Swiss Valley.)

$5; $7 electric. Open Apr 15–Oct 31; dry camping allowed off-season.

24 (6 tent-only) close, open sites.

Central faucet, flush toilets, showers, dump station, electric hookups, tables, grills, fire rings, pay phone.

In wooded valley next to North Fork Maquoketa River.

Hike. Fish.

14-day/40-ft limits. Crowded holidays and weekends.

800 ft (240 m)

NICHOLSON PARK

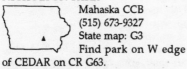

Mahaska CCB
(515) 673-9327
State map: G3
Find park on W edge
of CEDAR on CR G63.

FREE so choose a chore. Open All Year.

Undesignated scattered, open sites.

Pit toilets, tables, grills, fire rings, playground, ball field, shelter.

On site of old high school.

Make overnight stop.

NO water. 2-day limit.

NODAWAY VALLEY

Page CCB
(712) 542-3864
State map: C2
From CLARINDA,
travel N on US 71 for 2 miles (3.2 k). (See Morman Trail Park, Pierce Creek,

Pioneer, Ross Park, and Windmill Lake.)

$4. Open Apr 15–Oct 15; dry camping allowed off-season.

10 close, open sites.

Water at every site, pit toilets, dump station, electric hookups, tables, fire rings, grills, playground.

In upland timber, overlooking town of Clarinda.

Walk extensive trail system. Spot wildlife and take photos.

14-day limit.

1100 ft (330 m)

NORTH CEDAR PARK

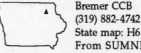

Bremer CCB
(319) 882-4742
State map: H6
From PLAINFIELD,
head E on IA 188 for 1 mile (1.6 k). (Also see Alcock and Cedar Bend.)

$4; $5 electric. Open May 1–Oct 31.

40 scattered, open sites.

Central faucet, pit toilets, dump station, electric hookups, tables, grills, fire rings, boat ramp.

In grassy spot with some trees along Cedar River.

Hike. Fish or boat.

Hunting in season.

NORTHWOODS

Bremer CCB
(319) 882-4742
State map: H6
From SUMNER, take
V 62 N for 1 mile (1.6 k). (Also see Alcock and Seven Bridges.)

$4; $5 electric. Open May 1–Oct 31.

40 scattered, open sites.

Central faucet, pit toilets, electric hookups, tables, grills, fire rings.

In woods along creek.

Enjoy solitude. Hike. Fish.

Hunting in season.

OAK HILL

Greene CCB
(515) 386-4629
State map: D4
From JEFFERSON,

drive W on US 30 for 3 miles (4.8 k).
(Also see Henderson.)
$2; $3 electric.
Open All Year.
Undesignated scattered, open sites.
Central faucet, pit toilets, electric
hookups, tables, fire rings.
In quiet setting.
Enjoy overnight stop.

OAKLAND MILLS

Henry CCB
(319) 986-5067
State map: I2
Drive SW on CR W55
for 3.5 miles (5.6 k) from MOUNT
PLEASANT. (Also see Gibson RA.)
FREE; $5 electric.
Open All Year.
70 (10 tent-only) close, open sites. &
Central faucet, pit toilets, electric
hookups, tables, grills, fire rings,
shelters.
In bottomland with view of Skunk River.
Hike trails. Take photos. Fish or boat.
14-day limit.
900 ft (270 m)

OCHEE YAHOLA

Worth CCB
(515) 324-1524
State map: F7
From NORTHWOOD,
drive W on IA 105 for 1 mile (1.6 k).
Turn Right (N) on CR and go 2.5 miles
(4 k). (Also see Silver Lake.)
$4.
Open All Year.
Undesignated scattered, open sites.
Pit toilets, electric hookups, tables, fire
rings, shelter.
In upland timber with marsh and
prairie.
Hike. Cross-country ski in winter.
NO water. No trash arrangements.

OLDHAM RA

Monona CCB
(712) 423-2400
State map: B4
From SOLDIER, travel

NW for 1.5 miles (2.4 k).
$4; $5 electric.
Open All Year.
Undesignated scattered, open sites. &
Central faucet, pit toilets, electric
hookups, tables, fire rings, boat ramp.
Next to 12-acre lake.
Swim, boat, or fish.

OSBORNE VISITOR WELCOME & NATURE CENTER

Clayton CCB
(319) 245-1516
State map: I6
From ELKADER, travel
S for 5 miles (8 k) on IA 13.
$3. Open All Year.
50 close, open sites. &
Central faucet, flush toilets, tables, fire
rings, shelter, playground.
Along Volga River among scenic hills
and large pond.
Visit Nature Center. Walk trail system.
Fish. Skate or sled in winter.

OTRANTO

Mitchell CCB
(515) 736-4946
State map: G7
From OTRANTO, drive
.5 mile (800 m) E on CR A19. (Also see
Halvorson.)
$5. Open May 31–Oct 31.
25 scattered, open sites.
Central faucet, chemical toilets, tables,
fire rings, grills, boat ramp, playground,
shelter.
Under oak on Cedar River.
Canoe, boat, or fish.
14-day limit.

OTTER CREEK LAKE & PARK

Tama CCB
(515) 484-2231
State map: G4
From TOLEDO, head N
on US 63 for 1.5 miles (2.4 k). Turn Right
(E) on CR E43 and go 4 miles (6.4 k).
After S-curve, turn Left (N) on gravel
road and continue 1.5 miles (2.4 k).
$5; $8 full hookups.

▲ ▲

Open May 15–Nov.
97 scattered, open sites.
Central faucet, pit toilets, dump station, electric hookups, tables, fire rings, boat ramp, playground, pay phone.
In pleasant setting with mix of oak-hickory trees and grass next to 65-acre lake.
Hike to view wildlife. Take photographs. Swim, boat, or fish.
14-day limit. No generators. Crowded holidays and weekends.

OTTER CREEK PARK

Warren CCB
(515) 961-6169
State map: F3
From INDIANOLA, head S on US 65 for 10 miles (16 k). Turn Left (W) on Quebec St. Go 1 mile (1.6 k). (Also see Hickory Hills Park.)
FREE so choose a chore.
Open All Year.
Undesignated scattered, open sites.
Pit toilets, tables, grills, fire rings, shelter.
With secluded wood, tallgrass prairie, and frog pond.
Relax. Enjoy ecology.
NO water.

OUTLET

COE (515) 647-2464
State map: G2
From CENTERVILLE, travel N on IA 5 for 2.8 miles (4.5 k). Turn Left (NW) on CR J29 and drive 2.8 miles (4.5 k). Turn Right (N) on CR J5T and go .25 mile (400 m). (Nearby Buck Creek and Island View cost $8.)
FREE so choose a chore.
Open All Year.
11 close, open sites.
Central faucet, pit toilets, tables, fire rings, boat ramp, shelter.
In flat, wooded spot below Rathbun Lake.
View wildlife. Fish or boat. Ice skate in winter.
14-day limit.

PALISADES ACCESS

Linn CCB
(319) 398-3505
State map: I4
Drive S on IA 1 for 3 miles (4.8 k) from MOUNT VERNON. After bridge, turn Right (W). Go 4 miles (6.4 k). Turn Right (N) on Palisades Access Rd. (Also see South Cedar Natural Area.)
$4. Open All Year.
Undesignated scattered, open sites.
Pit toilets, tables, fire rings, boat ramp.
On Cedar River.
Boat or fish.
NO water.

PAMMEL

Madison CCB
(515) 462-3536
State map: E3
From WINTERSET, go W on IA 92 for 2 miles (3.2 k). Turn Left (SW) on IA 322 for 3 miles (4.8 k).
$5. Open Apr–Nov; dry camping allowed off-season.
32 close, open sites. &
Central faucet, chemical toilets, tables.
Next to Middle River.
Canoe or fish. Hike. Cross-country ski in winter.
14-day limit.

PIERCE CREEK

Page CCB
(712) 542-3864
State map: C2
From SHENANDOAH, go 5 miles (8 k) N on US 59. Turn Right (E). Go 1.5 miles (2.4 k). (Also see Manti, Nodaway Valley, and Pioneer Park.)
$2; $4 electric.
Open Apr 15–Oct 15; dry camping allowed off-season.
20 (8 tent-only) close, open sites.
Water at every site, pit toilets, electric hookups, tables, fire rings, boat ramp, shelter.
In wooded area near prairie grassland with 38-acre lake.
Fish and boat (no gas motors). Walk

▲ ▲

nature trail and view wildlife.
14-day limit. Hunting in season.
1100 ft (330 m)

PILOT GROVE PARK

Montgomery CCB
(712) 623-4753
State map: C2
From GRANT, drive W
on CR H14 for 4 miles (6.4 k). (Also see
Hacklebarney Woods.)
$4. Open Mar–Oct.
17 (2 tent-only) scattered, open sites.
Central faucet, pit toilets, dump station,
electric hookups, tables, grills, fire rings.
Among oak next to small pond.
Fish. Relax.

PIN OAK

Delaware CCB
(319) 927-3410
State map: I5
Head SE on CR D5X
from MANCHESTER for 1 mile (1.6 k).
Turn Right (S) and go 1 mile (1.6 k).
(Also see Bailey's Ford, Coffins Grove,
and Turtle Creek.)
$4; $6 electric.
Open May 1–Oct 30.
25 scattered, open sites.
Hand pump, chemical toilets, electric
hookups, tables, grills, fire rings, shelter,
playground.
At old pioneer rivercrossing with
shallow rocky bottom.
Watch birds. Fish.
14-day limit.

PIONEER PARK

Page CCB
(712) 542-3864
State map: C2
From CLARINDA, go
10 miles (16 k) W on IA 2. (See Manti,
Pierce Creek, and Nodaway Valley.)
$5. Open Apr 15–Oct 15; dry camping
allowed off-season.
10 close, open sites.
Water at every site, pit toilets, electric
hookups, tables, fire rings, shelter,
playground.

Near 2-acre pond.
Fish or boat (no gas motors).
14-day limit.
1100 ft (330 m)

PIONEER RIDGE NATURE AREA

Wapello CCB
(515) 682-3091
State map: H2
From OTTUMWA, take
US 63 S for 6 miles (9.6 k). Watch for
signs on E side. (Also see Rock Bluff.)
$4; reservations accepted at
(515) 682-3091.
Open All Year.
Undesignated scattered, screened sites.
Chemical toilets, tables, fire rings.
In 737-acre preserve.
Hike trails to view wildlife and take
photos. Attend ranger programs. Fish.
NO water. No trash arrangements (pack
it out). 14-day limit.

PLEASANT CROOK

COE (319) 582-0881
State map: K5
From BELLEVUE, take
IA 52 S for 3 miles
(4.8 k). Turn Left (E) at sign.
$5. Open May 14–Oct 10; dry camping
allowed off-season.
70 scattered, screened sites.
Central faucet, pit toilets, dump station,
tables, fire rings, boat ramp.
On main channel of Mississippi River.
Boat or fish. Watch birds. Attend ranger
programs.
14-day limit.
600 ft (180 m)

POE HOLLOW

Ringgold CCB
(515) 464-2787
State map: E1
From MOUNT AYR,
head E for 1.5 miles (2.4 k). (Also see
Fife's Grove.)
FREE so choose a chore.
Open All Year.
Undesignated scattered, open sites.
Hand pump, pit toilets, tables, fire rings.

▲ ▲

Next to 1-acre pond.
Fish. Hike.
No trash arrangements. 14-day limit.

POLLMILLER

Lee CCB (319) 463-7673
State map: I1
Find campground just
E of WEST POINT off
IA 103.
$4; $5 electric.
Open All Year.
Undesignated scattered, open sites.
Central faucet, flush toilets, showers,
dump station, electric hookups, tables,
fire rings, boat ramp, shelter,
playground.
Next to 16-acre lake.
Swim, fish, or boat (no gas motors). Bike.
Skate in winter.

POPEJOY CONSERVATION PARK

Franklin CCB
(515) 456-4375
State map: F6
From POPEJOY, go
.5 mile (800 m) S.
$3. Open Apr 1–Nov 30.
Undesignated close, open sites.
Hand pump, pit toilets, electric hookups,
tables, fire rings, playground.
Next to Iowa River.
Fish. Sled in winter.
14-day limit. Occasional floods.

PULASKI CITY PARK

Davis CCB
(515) 664-1664
State map: H1
Locate park in
PULASKI. (Also see West Grove.)
FREE so choose a chore.
Open Apr–Oct; dry camping allowed
off-season.
Undesignated close, open sites.
Central faucet, flush toilets, tables, grills,
ball field.
In park with overnight area for RVs.
Relax.
7-day limit.
600 ft (180 m)

QUERCUS WILDERNESS AREA

Mahaska CCB
(515) 673-9327
State map: G3
From OSKALOOSA,
take IA 137 S for 7 miles (11.2 k). Turn
Right (W) on CR G71. (Also see Eveland
Access.)
FREE so choose a chore.
Open All Year.
5 scattered, screened, tent sites.
Tables, fire rings.
Under oak and other hardwood trees in
sandy soil similar to Loess Hills.
Hike trails to view wildlife.
NO water. No toilet facilities. Hunting in
season.

RAINBOW BEND

Calhoun CCB
(712) 297-8323
State map: D5
From LAKE CITY,
head W for 1.5 miles (2.4 k). Turn Left
(S) and drive 2.5 miles (4 k).
FREE so choose a chore.
Open All Year.
Undesignated scattered, open sites.
Hand pump, pit toilets, tables, canoe
ramp.
Along Raccoon River with 3-arch historic
bridge.
Canoe or fish.
No trash arrangements (pack it out).

RANNEY KNOB AREA

Cherokee CCB
(712) 225-5959
State map: B5
From WASHTA, drive
1 mile (1.6 k) W on CR C66. (Also see
Stieneke Area.)
FREE so choose a chore.
Open All Year.
15 scattered, open sites.
Hand pump, pit toilets, tables, grills,
playground, shelter.
With access to Little Sioux River.
Fish. View wildlife.
14-day limit. Hunting in season.

▲▲▲▲▲▲▲▲▲▲▲▲▲▲▲▲▲▲▲▲▲▲▲▲▲▲▲▲▲▲▲▲

REIFF PARK

Sac CCB (712) 662-4530
State map: C5
From EARLY, travel S
on US 71 for 1.5 miles
(2.4 k).
$5; $7 electric. Open May 1–Oct 31.
25 close, open sites.
Water at every site, flush toilets, dump
station, electric hookups, tables, grills.
With stream and lake, offering wetlands
and wooded uplands environments.
Fish. Canoe. Hike. Relax.

RICHEY ACCESS

Carroll CCB
(712) 792-4614
State map: D4
From RALSTON, go
3 miles (4.8 k) N. (See Dickson Timber.)
FREE so choose a chore.
Open May 1–Nov 1; dry camping
allowed off-season.
Undesignated close, open sites.
Central faucet, pit toilets, electric
hookups, tables, grills, fire rings.
On banks on North Raccoon River.
Canoe. Fish. Watch wildlife.
14-day/32-ft limits.

RIVER JUNCTION

Johnson CCB
(319) 645-2315
State map: I4
From RIVERSIDE, head
E on IA 22 about 3 miles (4.8 k). Turn
Right (S) on Sand Rd and go .25 mile
(400 m). (Also see Hills Access.)
FREE so choose a chore. Open All Year.
15 close, open sites.
Hand pump, pit toilets, tables, fire rings,
grills, boat ramp.
In bottomland next to Iowa River.
Fish or boat.
14-day limit.

RIVER OF RED ROCK PARK

Lyon CCB
(712) 472-2217
State map: B7
Find park on S edge of

LITTLE ROCK.
$4. Open All Year.
4 close, screened sites.
Central faucet, pit toilets, dump station,
electric hookups, tables, grills, fire rings.
In wooded park.
Relax. Enjoy natural surroundings.
14-day limit.

RIVERSIDE

Carroll CCB
(712) 792-4614
State map: D4
Find campground on
NE edge of COON RAPIDS.
FREE so choose a chore.
Open May 1–Nov 1; dry camping
allowed off-season.
30 (10 tent-only) scattered, open sites.
Central faucet, flush toilets, tables, fire
rings.
Along bluffs of Middle Raccoon River.
Walk nature trail. Watch wildlife. Fish.
14-day/24-ft limits.

RIVERVIEW MUNICIPAL PARK

(515) 754-5715
State map: G4
Locate park at IA 14
and Woodland St in
MARSHALLTOWN.
$4.50; $6.50 electric.
Open May 1–Oct 1.
40 close, open sites.
Central faucet, flush toilets, showers,
dump station, electric hookups, tables,
fire rings, grills, boat ramp, pool.
Under shade trees.
Swim. Bike or hike trails.
14-day limit. No generators.

ROBERTS CREEK

Marion CCB
(515) 627-5507
State map: F3
From KNOXVILLE,
drive N on IA 14 for 9 miles (14.4 k).
Turn Right (E) on CR G28. Go 3 miles
(4.8 k). (Also see Marion County Park
and Wallashuck.)
$5; $6 electric.

▲ ▲

Open Apr 1–Nov 10.
210 (30 tent-only) close, open sites. &
Hand pump, flush toilets, showers,
dump station, electric hookups, tables,
fire rings, grills, boat ramp.
In two areas–one in heavy woods, other
on hill overlooking lake.
Walk nature trail. Fish.
14-day limit. Hunting in season.
830 ft (249 m)

ROBINSON LAKE ACCESS

Mahaska CCB
(515) 673-9327
State map: G3
Go N on IA 146 from
NEW SHARON for 3 miles (4.8 k).
FREE so choose a chore.
Open All Year.
47 close, open sites.
Pit toilets, tables, fire rings.
Among native timber next to beautiful
Skunk River.
Boat or fish. Walk nature trail.
NO water.

ROBINSON PARK

Franklin CCB
(515) 456-4375
State map: F6
From HAMPTON,
drive N on US 65 for 2 miles (3.2 k).
Turn Right (E) and go 1 mile (1.6 k).
(Also see Mallory Memorial Park and
WKW Conservation Park.)
$3. Open Apr 1–Nov 30.
30 scattered, open sites. &
Hand pump, pit toilets, electric hookups,
tables, grills, fire rings.
With scattered oak trees along Otter
Creek.
Fish. Walk nature trail.
14-day limit. Occasional floods.

ROCK BLUFF

Wapello CCB
(515) 682-3091
State map: H2
From OTTUMWA,
head W on IA 34. Turn Right (N) on
CR H21 and go about 4 miles (6.4 k).

(Also see Pioneer Ridge Nature Area.)
$4. Open May 25–Sep 5.
Undesignated close, open sites.
Chemical toilets, tables, fire rings.
At base of bluff next to Des Moines
River.
Boat or fish. Watch wildlife.
NO water. No trash arrangements (pack
it out). 14-day limit.

ROCK CREEK PARK

Clinton CCB
(319) 847-7202
State map: K4
From CAMANCHE,
travel SW on US 67 for 3 miles (4.8 k).
Turn Left (E) at Shafton Quarries and
follow signs.
$4. Open May–Nov.
39 (10 tent-only) scattered, open sites.
Hand pump, pit toilets, tables, fire rings,
grills, boat ramp.
Along backwaters of Mississippi River.
Fish.
14-day limit. Occasional floods. No
generators in evening.

RODGERS PARK

Benton CCB
(319) 472-4942
State map: H4
From VINTON, take
US 218 NE. Turn Right (N) on 20th Ave.
Drive to 57th St Trail. Continue .5 mile
(800 m). (Also see Hannen, Hoefle-Dulin,
Minne-Estema, and Wildcat Bluff.)
$4; $5 weekends; +$2 electric.
Open All Year.
41 (3 tent-only) close, open sites.
Central faucet, flush toilets, showers,
dump station, electric hookups, tables,
fire rings, grills, boat ramp, rentals,
phone.
In gently rolling hills with 21-acre lake.
Hike or walk nature trail. Swim or fish
(handicapped-accessible pier). Attend
ranger programs. Cross-country ski in
winter.
14-day limit. Sometimes noisy.
860 ft (258 m)

▲ ▲

ROSS PARK

Page CCB
(712) 542-3864
State map: C1
Take J55 E for 3 miles
(4.8 k) from BRADDYVILLE. Turn Left
(N) and go 1 mile (1.6 k). Turn Right (E)
and proceed .25 mile (400 m). (Also see
Nodaway Valley.)
FREE so choose a chore.
Open Apr 15–Oct 15; camping allowed
off-season.
Undesignated scattered, open sites.
Pit toilets, tables, fire rings.
In reclaimed quarry managed for
wildlife with two 6-acre ponds.
Fish and boat (no gas motors).
NO water. Hunting in season.
1100 ft (330 m)

SANDY BEACH

COE (319) 338-3543
State map: I4
From SHUEYVILLE, go
SW on signed CR about
2.5 miles (4 k). (Also see Mid River and
Sugar Bottom.)
$4; $10 electric.
Open May 1–Sep 30.
60 (10 tent-only) close, open sites.
Central faucet, flush toilets, showers,
dump station, electric hookups, tables,
fire rings, boat ramp, pay phone.
With view of Coralville Lake.
Enjoy somewhat remote location. Swim,
boat, or fish.
14-day limit. Nearby ATV area noise.
750 ft (225 m)

SAUDE PARK

Chickasaw CCB
(515) 394-4714
State map: H6
From PROTIVIN, head
W on CR B16 for 3 miles (4.8 k). Turn
Left (S) on CR V56 and drive 2 miles
(3.2 k). Turn Right (W) on CR B22 and
go 1 mile (1.6 k). Turn Right (N) on
gravel Stevens Ave and continue .5 mile
(800 m). (Also see Airport Lake.)

FREE so choose a chore.
Open All Year.
Undesignated close, open sites.
Hand pump, pit toilets, tables, grills, fire
rings, ball field.
In woods along Little Turkey River.
Fish. Relax. Watch birds.
14-day limit. Small vehicles only.
Hunting in season.

SAULSBURY BRIDGE RA

Muscatine CCB
(319) 649-3379
State map: J3
From MUSCATINE,
drive NE on US 61 for 8 miles (12.8 k).
Turn Left (N) on Mulberry Ave. (Also
see Wildcat Den SP.)
$3; $5 river; $7 main.
Open Apr 1–Nov 1; dry camping
allowed off-season.
33 scattered, open sites.
Central faucet, pit toilets, showers, dump
station, electric hookups, tables, fire
rings, grills, boat ramp.
On bottomland next to Cedar River with
trees, marsh, and open areas.
Walk trails and view wildlife. Fish or
boat. Take photos. Attend ranger
programs. Cross-country ski in winter.
14-day limit. Occasional floods.

SCOTT COUNTY PARK

Scott CCB
(319) 285-9656
State map: J4
Locate park outside
LONG GROVE at 19251 290th St. (Also
see West Lake Park.)
$5; $9 electric.
Open All Year.
135 scattered, open sites.
Central faucet, flush toilets, showers,
dump station, electric hookups, tables,
grills, fire rings, pool, pay phone.
Among rolling hills with deer and
18-hole golf course.
Walk nature trail. Swim. Cross-country
ski in winter.
14-day limit. Often crowded.

SEVEN BRIDGES

Bremer CCB
(319) 882-4742
State map: H6
Near READLYN, at intersection of IA 3 and V49, head S on V49 for 4 miles (6.4 k). Turn Left (E) on gravel road and go 3 miles (4.8 k). (Also see Cedar Bend and Northwoods.)
FREE so choose a chore.
Open May 1–Oct 31.
Undesignated scattered, open sites.
Hand pump, pit toilets, tables, fire rings.
In woods next to Wapsipinicon River.
Fish or just relax.
Hunting in season.

SHARON BLUFFS SP

Appanoose CCB
(515) 856-8528
State map: G1
From CENTERVILLE, drive E on IA 2 for 3 miles (4.8 k). Turn Right (S). (Also see Lelah Bradley Park.)
$5; $7 electric.
Open All Year.
Undesignated scattered, open sites.
Central faucet, pit toilets, electric hookups, tables, fire rings, boat ramp.
On bluffs next to Chariton River.
Canoe or boat. Fish. Hike.
14-day limit.

SHELLROCK PRESERVE

Cerro Gordo CCB
(515) 423-5309
State map: F7
From MASON CITY, drive IA 18 E to gravel Yarrow Ave. Turn Left (N) and go 1 mile (1.6 k). Turn Right (E) on 277th St and continue .5 mile (800 m). Turn Left (N) on Yucca Ave. Proceed .75 mile (1.2 k). (Nearby Rockfalls' Pioneer Park costs $6.)
FREE so choose a chore.
Open May 1–Oct 1.
12 scattered, open sites.
Hand pump, pit toilets, tables, fire rings.
On forested hill near Shellrock River.
Hike to view wildlife. Canoe. Fish. Ride horses.

No horse trailers in camp.
1150 ft (345 m)

SHERMAN PARK

Clinton CCB
(319) 847-7202
State map: J4
From CALAMUS, head W on IA 30 for 1.5 miles 92.4 k). Turn Right (S) and follow signs. (Also see Walnut Grove.)
$4. Open May–Nov.
25 scattered, open sites.
Hand pump, pit toilets, tables, fire rings, grills, boat ramp.
In woods on banks of Wapsipinicon River.
Hike trail system. Take photos. Canoe or fish. Cross-country ski in winter.
14-day limit. Occasional floods. No generators in evening.

SHIMEK SF

(319) 878-3811
State map: I1
From FARMINGTON, go E on IA 2 for 1 mile (1.6 k). (Also see Croton Civil War Park.)
$5. Open All Year.
38 close, open sites.
Central faucet, flush toilets, tables.
In forest near 20-acre lake.
Fish. Hike.
Hunting in season.

SIGGELKOV

Black Hawk CCB
(319) 266-6813
State map: H5
From DUNKERTON, drive N for 5 miles (8 k) on IA 281. (Also see Thunder Woman Park. Nearby Black Hawk costs $7.)
$4; $6 electric. Open All Year.
50 scattered, open sites.
Hand pump, pit toilets, electric hookups, tables, grills, fire rings, shelter.
In wooded greenbelt along Wapsipinicon River.
Fish or canoe. Take photos.
14-day limit.

SILVER LAKE RA

Worth CCB
(515) 324-1524
State map: F7
Go W on IA 105 from NORTHWOOD about 8 miles (12.8 k). Turn Right (N) on CR S22. Go 3 miles (4.8 k). (Also see Ochee Yahola.)
$4. Open All Year.
Undesignated scattered, open sites.
Pit toilets, electric hookups, tables, fire rings, boat ramp, shelter.
Next to lake.
Boat or fish.
NO water.

SILVER SIOUX RA

Cherokee CCB
(712) 225-5959
State map: C6
From CHEROKEE, take IA 59 S for 7 miles (11.2 k). Turn Right (W) on access road for 1 mile (1.6 k). (Also see Stieneke Area.)
FREE basic; $7 electric.
Open All Year.
29 scattered, open sites.
Central faucet, pit toilets, dump station, electric hookups, tables, fire rings, grills, boat ramp.
Among wooded hills and reestablished prairie next to Little Sioux River.
Walk miles of trails. Fish or boat river.
Snowtube in winter.
14-day limit. Hunting in season.

SLIP BLUFF

Decatur CCB
(515) 446-7307
State map: E1
From DAVIS CITY, go W on CR J52 for 4 miles (6.4 k). Turn Right (N). (Also see Little River RA.)
$3; $5 electric.
Open All Year.
20 close, open sites.
Central faucet, pit toilets, electric hookups, tables, fire rings, shelter, playground.
With 100 acres of hardwood and 10 acres of native prairie plus 16-acre lake.

Fish or boat (no gas motors). Hike. Cross-country ski in winter.
14-day limit.

SMITH LAKE

Kossuth CCB
(515) 295-2138
State map: E6
From ALGONA, drive 3.25 miles (5.2 k) N on IA 169.
$5; $6 electric.
Open Apr 1–Oct 31.
48 (15 tent-only) close, open sites.
Hand pump, flush toilets, showers, dump station, electric hookups, tables, fire rings, grills, boat ramp, pay phone.
In peaceful setting near 50-acre lake.
Walk nature trail. Swim, fish, or boat (paddle or electric motors).
14-day limit.

SOCKUM RIDGE

Washington CCB
(319) 657-3457
State map: I3
Drive S on CR W55 from WASHINGTON for 4.5 miles (7.2 k). Turn Left (E) and go .25 mile (400 m). (Also see Fern Cliff and Coppock Access.)
FREE so choose a chore.
Open All Year.
Undesignated scattered, open sites.
Hand pump, pit toilets, tables, archery range.
In woods with small pond.
Hike. Fish. Cross-country ski in winter.
No trash arrangements (pack it out).

SOUTH CEDAR NATURAL AREA

Linn CCB
(319) 398-3505
State map: I4
Head S on IA 1 from MOUNT VERNON. Turn Right (W) after bridge onto Ivanhoe Rd. Turn Right (N) at South Cedar Post and Arm sign. (Also see Palisades Access.)
$4.
Open All Year.
Undesignated scattered, open sites.

▲ ▲

Hand pump, pit toilets, tables, fire rings, grills, boat ramp.
In woods along Cedar River.
Fish and boat. Spot birds.
Hunting in season.

SOUTHEAST WILDWOOD PARK

Plymouth CCB
(712) 947-4270
State map: B5
From KINGSLEY, drive
NW on CR C66 about 3 miles (4.8 k).
FREE so choose a chore.
Open All Year.
Undesignated scattered, open sites.
Pit toilets, tables, grills, shelter, playground.
Near Little Sioux River.
Fish. Relax.
NO water. No trash arrangements (pack it out).

SPLIT ROCK

Chickasaw CCB
(515) 394-4714
State map: H6
Take CR V48 S from
FREDERICKSBURG for 4 miles (6.4 k).
Turn Left (W) on gravel 310th St and go
1.5 miles (2.4 k). (Also see Airport Lake.)
$3; $4 electric.
Open All Year.
Undesignated close, open sites.
Central faucet, pit toilets, electric hookups, tables, grills, fire rings.
With some woods, some open areas next to 10-acre lake.
Swim, boat, or fish.
14-day limit. Hunting in season.

SPORTSMAN PARK

Dallas CCB
(515) 465-3577
State map: E4
From DAWSON, take
gravel 130th St NW about 1 mile (1.6 k).
$2; $4 electric.
Open May 1–Oct 31.
18 (6 tent-only) scattered, open sites.
Central faucet, flush toilets, electric hookups, tables, grills, fire rings.

On wooded high bluff overlooking North Raccoon River.
Observe wildlife. Relax.
No trash arrangements (pack it out).
980 ft (294 m)

SPRING LAKE

Greene CCB
(515) 386-4629
State map: D4
Drive E on US 30 from
JEFFERSON about 5 miles (8 k). Turn
Left (N) on CR P33. Go 3 miles (4.8 k).
$4; $5 electric.
Open All Year.
44 close, open sites.
Central faucet, chemical toilets, electric hookups, tables, fire rings, boat ramp, shelter.
At forest edge on shore of 50-acre lake.
Swim, canoe, boat, or fish. Hike. Skate in winter.
14-day limit.

SPRING PARK

(515) 732-3709
State map: G7
From OSAGE, go W on
IA 9 for 2 miles (3.2 k).
Turn Left (S) on gravel road and drive
1 mile (1.6 k). (Also see Halvorson and Interstate Park.)
FREE so choose a chore.
Open May 1–Nov 30.
26 (20 tent-only) scattered, open sites.
Spring, pit toilets, tables, grills, fire rings, shelter.
On scenic Cedar River.
Walk trails and spot wildlife. Bike.
Canoe and fish. Cross-country ski in winter.
1200 ft (360 m)

SQUIRREL HOLLOW

Greene CCB
(515) 386-4629
State map: D4
From JEFFERSON,
head E on CR E53 then S on CR P30
about 5 miles (8 k). Turn Right (SE) at sign. (Also see Henderson.)

$2; $3 electric.
Open All Year.
Undesignated scattered, open sites.
Central faucet, pit toilets, electric hookups, tables, fire rings, boat ramp.
Near North Raccoon River and 147-acre wildlife area.
Canoe. Boat or fish. Hike.
No trash arrangements (pack it out).

STEAMBOAT ROCK (TOWER ROCK)

Hardin CCB
(515) 648-3825
State map: F5
Find area on S edge of STEAMBOAT ROCK.
FREE so choose a chore.
Open All Year.
Undesignated scattered, open sites.
Hand pump, pit toilets, tables, fire rings, boat ramp.
Next to Iowa River.
Boat or fish.
No trash arrangements. 14-day limit.

STEPHENS SF

(515) 774-5632
State map: F2
From CHARITON, head E on CR H32.
$5. Open All Year.
60 close, open sites.
Central faucet, flush toilets, tables.
Near 10-acre lake.
Fish. Walk nature trail. Hike.
Hunting in season.

STIENEKE AREA

Cherokee CCB
(712) 225-5959
State map: B6
From QUIMBY, go SW on IA 31 for 2 miles (3.2 k). Turn Right (W) on 628th St. Go 1 mile (1.6 k). (Also see Ranney Knob and Silver Sioux RA.)
FREE so choose a chore.
Open All Year.
3 close, open sites.
Hand pump, pit toilets, tables, grills, playground.
Next to Little Sioux River.

Enjoy quiet. Fish.
14-day limit. Hunting in season.

SUGAR BOTTOM

COE (319) 338-3543
State map: I3
In IOWA CITY off I-80, take Dubuque St Exit (W66) N for 7 miles (11.2 k). Turn Right (NE) on CR F28 and go 3 miles (4.8 k), making hard Right after crossing lake. (Also see Linder Point, Mid River, and Sandy Beach.)
$4; $10 electric. Open May 1–Sep 30.
250 (17 tent-only) close, screened sites.
Central faucet, flush toilets, showers, dump station, electric hookups, tables, fire rings, boat ramp, playground, pay phone.
Surrounded by heavy timber with view of Coralville Lake.
Swim, boat, ski, or fish. Walk trail system. Mountain bike. Watch birds.
Attend ranger programs.
14-day limit. Crowded most weekends.
750 ft (225 m)

SWEDE POINT

Boone CCB
(515) 353-4237
State map: E4
From MADRID, drive 1 mile (1.6 k) W on IA 210. Turn Right (N). Go 1 mile (1.6 k). (See Don Williams Park. Nearby Ledges SP costs $7.)
$5; $7 electric.
Open Apr 15–Oct 30.
40 close, open sites.
Central faucet, flush toilets, showers, dump station, electric hookups, tables, grills.
In beautiful, pastoral setting.
Walk trails. View wildlife. Relax.
Wet in early spring.
1100 ft (330 m)

SWISS VALLEY

Dubuque CCB
(319) 556-6745
State map: J5
From DUBUQUE city

limits, drive 4.5 miles (7.2 k) W on US 20. Turn Left (S) on Swiss Valley Rd and go to White Top Rd. Turn Left and proceed .5 mile (800 m). (Also see Bankston, Fillmore RA Massey Marina, and New Wine.)
$5; $7 electric.
Open Apr 15–Oct 31; dry camping allowed off-season.
52 (15 tent-only) open sites. &
Central faucet, flush toilets, showers, dump station, electric hookups, tables, grills, fire rings.
In wooded valley with trout stream. Hike 400-acre nature preserve. Visit nature center. Attend ranger programs. Fish. Cross-country ski in winter.
14-day limit. Crowded holidays and weekends.
800 ft (240 m)

T F CLARK PARK

Tama CCB
(515) 484-2231
State map: G4
From TRAER, drive 2 miles (3.2 k) N on US 63. Turn Right (E) on gravel 150th St. Go 2.5 miles (4 k).
FREE so choose a chore.
Open May 14–Oct 31.
9 scattered, screened sites.
Central faucet, pit toilets, electric hookups, tables, fire rings.
In open setting with large trees and small creek.
Fish. Observe wildlife. Do nothing.
14-day limit.

TAILWATER EAST

COE (319) 338-3543
State map: I3
In IOWA CITY off I-80, take Dubuque St Exit (W66) N for 4 miles (6.4 k). Turn Right (E) on W Overlook Rd and go 2 miles (3.2 k). (Also see Tailwater West.)
$4; $8 electric.
Open Apr 15–Oct 15.
33 (5 tent-only) close, open sites.
Central faucet, flush toilets, showers, dump station, electric hookups, tables,

fire rings, boat ramp, playground, pay phone.
On Iowa River below Coralville Lake dam.
Boat or fish.
14-day limit. Crowded most weekends.
660 ft (198 m)

TAILWATER WEST

COE (319) 338-3543
State map: I3
In IOWA CITY off I-80, take Dubuque St Exit (W66) N for 4 miles (6.4 k). Turn Right (E) on W Overlook Rd and go 2 miles (3.2 k). (Also see Cottonwood and Tailwater East. Nearby West Overlook costs $8.)
$4.
Open Apr 15–Oct 15.
30 (10 tent-only) close, open sites.
Central faucet, flush toilets, dump station, tables, fire rings, pay phone.
Below Coralville Lake dam on west bank of Iowa River.
Fish.
14-day limit. Crowded holiday weekends.
660 ft (198 m)

THORPE PARK

Winnebago CCB
(515) 565-3390
State map: F7
From FOREST CITY, head W on CR B14 for 5 miles (8 k). Turn Right (N) on gravel road. Drive 1.5 miles (2.4 k). At stop sign, turn Left (W). Go 1 mile (1.6 k). (Also see Dahle Park.)
FREE so choose a chore.
Open All Year.
12 scattered, open sites.
Central faucet, pit toilets, tables, fire rings, grills, boat ramp, shelter.
On oak savannah in prairie-wetland setting.
Hike and walk nature trail to observe wildlife. Boat or fish. Attend ranger programs. Cross-country ski in winter.
14-day limit. Hunting in season.

▲ ▲

THREE BRIDGES

Marshall CCB
(515) 754-6303
State map: G4
From LE GRAND, head
W on US 30 about 1 mile (1.6 k). Turn
Right (N). Continue about 1 mile (1.6 k).
(Also see C D Coppock County Park.)
FREE so choose a chore.
Open All Year.
Undesignated scattered, open sites.
Pit toilets, tables, fire rings, boat ramp.
Next to Iowa River at old mill site.
Walk interpretive trail or hike farther.
Canoe. Fish.
NO water.

THUNDER WOMAN PARK

Black Hawk CCB
(319) 266-6813
State map: G5
From FINCHFORD, go
.25 mile (400 m) N on Finchford Rd.
(Also see Siggelkov.)
$2; $4 electric.
Open All Year.
50 scattered, open sites.
Hand pump, pit toilets, electric hookups,
tables, grills, fire rings.
In pine greenbelt on West Fork River.
Hike. Fish.
14-day limit.

TIMMONS GROVE

Marshall CCB
(515) 754-6303
State map: G4
From ALBION, drive S
on CR S75 about 1 mile (1.6 k). (Also see
Grammer Grove WA.)
$5.
Open All Year.
Undesignated scattered, open sites. &
Central faucet, pit toilets, electric
hookups, tables, fire rings, boat ramp,
shelter.
In wooded area with 2 oxbow lakes and
Iowa River.
Hike to observe wildlife. Canoe and fish.
Cross-country ski in winter.

TURTLE CREEK

Delaware CCB
(319) 927-3410
State map: I5
Drive SE on CR D5X
from MANCHESTER for 4 miles (6.4 k).
Turn Right on CR X21 and go 4 miles
(6.4 k) to first gravel road. Turn Left and
continue 3 miles (4.8 k). (Also see
Bailey's Ford and Pin Oak.)
$4; $6 electric.
Open May 1–Oct 30.
29 scattered, open sites.
Hand pump, chemical toilets, electric
hookups, tables, fire rings, grills, boat
ramp, shelter.
On Maquoketa River above Delhi Dam.
Fish, boat, or ski lake. Spot wildlife.
14-day limit.

TUTTLE LAKE

Emmet CCB
(712) 362-2510
State map: D7
From DOLLIVER, drive
2 miles (3.2 k) N. (Also see Wolden RA.)
$5.
Open Apr 1–Nov 1.
60 sites.
Central faucet, pit toilets, electric
hookups, tables, fire rings, grills, boat
ramp, pay phone.
On lakeshore.
Swim, boat, or fish. Take photos.
Hunting in season. No generators in
quiet hours. Occasionally crowded.
1250 ft (375 m)

TWIN BRIDGES

Delaware CCB
(319) 927-3410
State map: I5
From COLESBURG,
travel 5 miles (8 k) W on IA 3. (Also see
Fountain Springs.)
$4; $6 electric.
Open May 1–Oct 30.
20 scattered, open sites.
Hand pump, chemical toilets, electric
hookups, tables, grills, fire rings, shelter,
playground.

In park setting.
Fish or hike.
14-day limit. Hunting in season.

TWIN BRIDGES

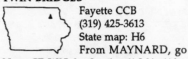

Fayette CCB
(319) 425-3613
State map: H6
From MAYNARD, go
N on CR W25 for 3 miles (4.8 k). (Also
see Downing Park.)
$3.
Open Apr 1–Oct 31.
15 scattered, open sites.
Hand pump, pit toilets, tables, grills, fire
rings.
In walnut-butternut woods with flowing
stream.
Canoe, swim, or fish. Watch wildlife.
14-day/36-ft limits.

TWIN PONDS

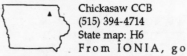

Chickasaw CCB
(515) 394-4714
State map: H6
From IONIA, go
2 miles (3.2 k) S on CR V14. Turn Left
(E) on gravel 240th St. Drive 3 miles
(4.8 k). (Also see Airport Lake,
Chickasaw, and Howards Woods.)
FREE so choose a chore.
Open All Year.
Undesignated close, open sites.
Hand pump, pit toilets, tables, grills, fire
rings.
In woods along Wapsipinicon River near
prairie.
Walk trail system to view wildlife and
take photos. Fish.
14-day limit. Small vehicles only.
Hunting in season.

UNION GROVE SP

(515) 473-2556
State map: G5
From GLADBROOK,
drive S on CR T47 for
4 miles (6.4 k).
$5; $7 electric.
Open All Year.
32 close, open sites.

Central faucet, flush toilets, electric
hookups, tables.
Next to 110-acre lake.
Swim, boat, and fish. Hike.

UNIVERSITY 40

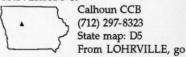

Calhoun CCB
(712) 297-8323
State map: D5
From LOHRVILLE, go
S for 1 mile (1.6 k).
FREE so choose a chore.
Open All Year.
Undesignated scattered, open sites.
Central faucet, pit toilets, tables, fire
rings, shelter.
Among trees and shrubs (formerly
owned by University of Iowa).
Observe wildlife especially raptors and
songbirds.
No trash arrangements (pack it out).

UPPER AUGUSTA ACCESS

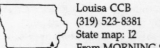

Des Moines CCB
(319) 753-8260
State map: I2
From AUGUSTA, drive
NW for 1 mile (1.6 k). (Also see Lower
Augusta Access and Welter Recreation
Park.)
$3. Open Apr–Oct.
18 close, open sites.
Pit toilets, tables, fire rings, grills, boat
ramp.
In woods along Skunk River.
Boat or fish.
NO water.

VIRGINIA GROVE

Louisa CCB
(319) 523-8381
State map: I2
From MORNING SUN,
drive NW on CR X37 for 5 miles (8 k).
$2. Open All Year.
Undesignated scattered, open sites. &
Central faucet, pit toilets, electric
hookups, tables, fire rings.
In trees next to 5-acre lake.
Canoe. Fish. Hike.
No trash arrangements (pack it out).

VOLGA RIVER RA

(319) 425-4161
State map: H6
From FAYETTE, head
N on IA 150 for 3 miles
(4.8 k). Turn Right (E). Go 1 mile (1.6 k).
$5.
Open All Year.
42 scattered, open sites.
Pit toilets, tables, fire rings.
On river among rolling hills with trees
and meadows.
Walk trail system. Observe wildlife.
Canoe and fish. Cross-country ski in
winter.
NO water. Hunting in season.

WAKPICADA NATURAL AREA

Linn CCB
(319) 398-3505
State map: I4
At S edge of CENTRAL
CITY, take signed gravel road.
$4.
Open Apr 15–Oct 15.
Undesignated scattered, open sites.
Hand pump, pit toilets, tables, fire rings.
In woods next to river.
Swim, canoe, or fish. View wildlife.
14-day limit. Hunting in season. Possible
bugs. No generators in quiet hours.
800 ft (240 m)

WALLASHUCK

COE (515) 828-7522
State map: G3
From PELLA, take G28
W for 2 miles (3.2 k).
Locate free sites on outer boundary of
campground. (Also see Roberts Creek.
Nearby North Overlook costs $6.)
FREE at 11 sites. $8 at 80 developed
sites; $10 electric.
Open Apr 29–Sep 7; dry camping
allowed off-season.
91 scattered, open sites.
Central faucet, flush toilets, showers,
dump station, electric hookups, tables,
fire rings, grills, boat ramp.
With some oak and hickory trees on Red
Rock Lake.

Swim, boat, ski, or fish Iowa's largest
lake. Bike or hike.
14-day limit. Occasionally crowded and
noisy.

WALNUT GROVE

Clinton CCB
(319) 847-7202
State map: J4
Locate campground on
N edge of TORONTO. (Also see
Sherman Park.)
FREE so choose a chore.
Open May–Nov.
25 scattered, open sites.
Hand pump, pit toilets, tables, fire rings,
grills, boat ramp.
On wooded banks of Wapsipinicon
River.
Canoe or fish.
14-day limit. Occasional floods. No
generators in evening.

WALNUT WOODS SP

(515) 285-4502
State map: E3
On SW side of DES
MOINES on I-35, take
Exit 68 (IA 5) E. Turn Left (N) at sign.
$5; $7 electric.
Open All Year.
28 close, open sites.
Central faucet, flush toilets, electric
hookups, tables, shelter.
Along Raccoon River.
Fish. Hike.

WELTER RECREATION PARK

Des Moines CCB
(319) 753-8260
State map: I2
Find park on E edge of
AUGUSTA. (Also see Lower Augusta
Access and Upper Augusta Access.)
$3.
Open Apr–Nov.
24 close, open sites.
Hand pump, pit toilets, tables, fire rings,
grills.
In woods along Skunk River.
Fish.

▲ ▲

WEST GROVE

Davis CCB
(515) 664-1664
State map: G1
Locate area in WEST
GROVE on IA 2. (Also see Pulaski City Park.)
FREE so choose a chore.
Open Apr-Sep; dry camping allowed off-season.
Undesignated scattered, open sites.
Central faucet, pit toilets, tables, grills.
In small, wooded park.
Relax overnight.
600 ft (180 m)

WEST IDLEWILD

Floyd CCB
(515) 257-6214
State map: G7
From FLOYD, head
NW on blacktop. Turn Right at sign on gravel road and drive 1 mile (1.6 k). (Also see Colwell.)
FREE so choose a chore.
Open All Year.
60 scattered, open sites.
Hand pump, pit toilets, tables, grills.
In woods along Cedar River.
Canoe or kayak. Fish. Walk to spot wildlife, especially birds.
Hunting in season.
1000 ft (300 m)

WEST LAKE PARK

Scott CCB
(319) 381-3589
State map: J4
Find park on W side of
DAVENPORT at 14910 110th Ave. (Also see Buffalo Shores and Scott County Park.)
$5; $7 electric; $9 full.
Open Apr 1-Oct 15.
119 scattered, open sites.
Central faucet, flush toilets, electric hookups, tables, fire rings, grills, boat ramp, rentals, pay phone.
Near lakes.
Swim, boat, or fish. Hike.
14-day limit. Often crowded.

WEST SIDE PARK

Rock Rapids Municipal
Parks (712) 472-2511
State map: B7
Locate park in ROCK
RAPIDS at IA 9 and US 75. (Also see Island Park.)
$5; $6 electric.
Open Apr-Oct.
20 scattered, open sites.
Central faucet, flush toilets, dump station, electric hookups, tables, grills, playground.
Among trees.
View wildlife. Relax.
5-day limit.

WILDCAT BLUFF

Benton CCB
(319) 472-4942
State map: H5
From URBANA, take
CR W26 S about 2.5 miles (4 k). (Also see Rodgers Park.)
$4; $5 weekends.
Open All Year.
25 scattered, open sites.
Hand pump, pit toilets, tables, grills, fire rings.
In heavy woods next to Cedar River.
Hike to spot wildlife. Fish or boat. Enjoy quiet.
14-day limit. Occasional floods.
800 ft (240 m)

WILDCAT DEN SP

(319) 263-4337
State map: J3
From MUSCATINE, go
10 miles (16 k) E on
IA 22. Turn Left (N) at sign. Go 1 mile (1.6 k). (Also see Saulsbury Bridge RA.)
$5.
Open All Year.
28 close, open sites.
Central faucet, pit toilets, tables, fire rings.
In forested area.
Walk trails to view wildlife.
14-day limit. Crowded holidays.
650 ft (195 m)

WILLOW CREEK

Carroll CCB
(712) 792-4614
State map: C4
Locate campground on
E side of MANNING of IA 141.
FREE so choose a chore.
Open May 1–Nov 1; dry camping
allowed off-season.
30 (10 tent-only) scattered, open sites.
Central faucet, flush toilets, electric
hookups, tables, grills, fire rings.
In small patch of woods.
Relax.
14-day limit.

WILSON ISLAND SRA

(712) 642-2069
State map: B3
From MISSOURI
VALLEY, take US 30 W
for 3 miles (4.8 k). Turn Left (S) at sign.
Go 6 miles (9.6 k) on gravel road.
$5; $7 modern; $9 electric.
Open All Year.
140 scattered, open sites.
Central faucet, flush toilets, showers,
dump station, electric hookups, tables,
fire rings, boat ramp.
In dense cottonwood trees along
Missouri River.
Walk trail system. Bike. Boat or fish.
Spot birds. Attend ranger programs.
14-day limit. Hunting in season.
Crowded holidays.

WILSON LAKE

Lee CCB (319) 463-7673
State map: I1
Drive E on CR from
DONNELLSON for
4 miles (6.4 k).
$4; $5 electric. Open All Year.
Undesignated scattered, open sites.
Central faucet, pit toilets, dump station,
electric hookups, tables, fire rings, boat
ramp. shelter, playground.
Next to 6-acre lake.
Fish or boat (no gas motors). Hike.
Cross-country ski or skate in winter.
No trash arrangements (pack it out).

WILSON LAKE

Taylor CCB
(712) 542-3864
State map: D2
From LENOX, drive
3 miles (4.8 k) SE. (Also see Windmill
Lake.)
FREE so choose a chore.
Open All Year.
Undesignated scattered, open sites.
Central faucet, pit toilets, tables, fire
rings, boat ramp.
On 35 acres of manicured parkland next
to 16.5-acre lake.
Fish and boat (no gas motors).
14-day limit.

WINDMILL LAKE

Taylor CCB
(712) 542-3864
State map: D2
Drive E for 6 miles
(9.6 k) from NEW MARKET. (Also see
Wilson Lake and Nodaway Valley.)
FREE so choose a chore.
Open All Year.
Undesignated scattered, open sites.
Pit toilets, tables, fire rings, boat ramp.
On hill with fish ponds and parklands.
Fish and boat (no gas motors).
NO water. 14-day limit.

WKW CONSERVATION PARK

Franklin CCB
(515) 456-4375
State map: F6
From HAMPTON,
drive N on US 65 for 2 miles (3.2 k).
Turn Right (E) and go 1 mile (1.6 k).
(Also see Robinson Park.)
$3.
Open Apr 1–Nov 30.
6 scattered, open sites.
Hand pump, pit toilets, electric hookups,
tables, grills, fire rings, playground,
shelter.
Among oak trees.
Walk trails. Cross-country ski in winter.
14-day limit.

▲ ▲

WOLDEN RA

Emmet CCB
(712) 362-2510
State map: D7
Drive 6 miles (9.6 k) E
from WALLINGFORD. (Also see Tuttle
Lake.)
$5. Open Apr 10–Nov 1.
120 sites.
Central faucet, flush toilets, showers,
dump station, electric hookups, tables,
fire rings, grills, boat ramp.
Between High Lake and Ingram Lake.
Swim, boat, or fish. Walk trails. Spot
wildlife. Attend ranger programs.
Hunting in season. No generators in
quiet hours. Occasionally crowded.
1300 ft (390 m)

WOLF CREEK RA

Grundy CCB
(319) 345-2688
State map: G5
Go S for 11 miles
(17.6 k) on CR T29 from GRUNDY
CENTER.
$3; $6 electric.
Open All Year.
21 (4 tent-only) scattered, open sites.
Central faucet, pit toilets, electric
hookups, tables, grills, fire rings.
In peaceful burr oak grove.
Hike or walk nature trail. Observe
wildlife and take photos. Fish.
21-day limit. Hunting in season.

YELLOW RIVER SF

(319) 586-2548
State map: I7
From HARPERS
FERRY, drive 6 miles
(9.6 k) SW on CR B25.
$5. Open All Year.
225 (50 tent-only) scattered, open sites.
Central faucet, pit toilets, tables, grills,
fire rings, pay phone.
In deep valley with trout springs,
surrounded by 300-ft bluffs covered with
hardwood trees.
Hike to take photos and view wildlife.
Fish. Cross-country ski in winter.
Hunting in season.

YENRUOGIS

Keokuk CCB
(515) 622-3757
State map: H3
From SIGOURNEY,
travel N for 2 miles (3.2 k) on CR. (Also
see Belva Deer RA.)
$2. Open All Year.
30 scattered, open sites.
Hand pump, pit toilets, tables, grills.
In reclaimed rock quarry with 10-acre
lake (Sigourney spelled backwards).
Swim or fish.
14-day limit.

KANSAS
CAMPGROUND LOCATIONS

▸ ▸ Find location on facing page map grid. ▸ ▸

▾ ▾ Locate area campgrounds on these page numbers. ▾ ▾

Kansas

Grid conforms to official state map. For your copy, call (800) 2-KANSAS or write Travel & Tourism Division, 400 SW 8th, 5th Floor, Topeka, KS 66603.

▲ ▲

PUBLIC LANDS CAMPING

Kansas means endless grass and grain on sweeping prairies, rolling hills, abundant fish and deer, migrating birds, the quintessential buffalo, a colorful heritage from the Great Plains Indian tribal migrations to the United States' westward expansion, and diverse outdoor opportunities that include watching unimpeded views of clouds and sunsets.

Twenty-two **Kansas State Parks** (SP) offer developed camping. Camping fees begin at $3.00 per unit. There are also $3.00 vehicle and $5.00 utility fees. To encourage the enjoyment of camping, the state provides equipment rentals and 30-day/annual permits. Most of these state parks furnish beaches, boat docks and ramps, as well as hiking trails. Canoeists paddle and camp along ten state-maintained "trails." Find free camping at **State Fishing Lakes** (such as Leavenworth SFL) and **Wildlife Areas** (such as Mined Land WA). If fishing, be sure to have your current license.

On the federal level of public lands, there are two **National Park Service** (NPS) historic sites: Fort Larned and Fort Scott. Neither site provides camping facilities. **US Forest Service** administers the Cimarron National Grassland in the southwest corner of Kansas through Colorado's Pike and San Isabel national forests. Near Elkhart, the grassland offers a $7.00 developed campground, aptly named Cimarron. **US Fish & Wildlife Service** allows free camping at Kirwin National Wildlife Refuge (NWR). **US Army Corps of Engineers** (COE) maintains campgrounds at Big Hill Lake, Clinton Lake, Council Grove Lake, Elk City Lake, Fall River Lake, John Redmond Reservoir, Kanapolis Lake, Marion Lake, Melvern Lake, Milford Lake, Perry Lake, Pomona Lake, Tuttle Creek Lake, and Wilson Lake. COE camp fees range from free to $12.00.

Towns offering $5.00-or-less camping include Anthony City, Arkansas City, Atchison, Chanute, Concordia, Ellis, Horton, La Crosse, Lyons., and Oswego. **Counties** involve Linn, Pottawatomie, and Sedgwick.

Cruise the vast prairies of Kansas. Get into a rut—one left by the wagons along the Santa Fe Trail. Ponder the past of Native Americans and pioneers. Get lost in the wonder of the wildlife and of the sky.

▲ ▲

110 MILE PARK

COE (913) 453-2201
State map: D11
From LYNDON, drive 8 miles (12.8 k) N on US 75. Turn Right (E) on CR and go 4 miles (6.4 k). Turn Right (S) on CR and follow signs for 5 miles (8 k). (Also see Cedar Park. Nearby Wolf Creek costs $8.)
FREE so choose a chore.
Open All Year.
Undesignated scattered, open sites.
Central faucet, pit toilets, tables, fire rings, grills, boat ramp, shelter.
In wooded and open grassy areas within walking distance of Pomona Lake.
Swim, boat, or fish. Walk nature trail.
14-day limit. Hunting in season. No generators in quiet hours.
1000 ft (300 m)

AIRPORT PARK

Concordia Parks
(913) 243-7600
State map: B8
Locate park off US 81 on S side of CONCORDIA.
FREE; donations requested.
Open All Year.
10 close, open, RV sites.
Water at every site, flush toilets, dump station, electric hookups, tables, grills.
In trees overlooking pond.
Observe wildlife. Relax.

▲ ▲

3-day limit. Permission needed for longer stays. Crowded weekends and holidays.
1486 ft (446 m)

ANTHONY CITY LAKE

(316) 842-5434
State map: G7
From ANTHONY, go N on KS 2 for 1 mile (1.6 k). Turn Left (W).
$3; $5 electric.
Open All Year.
20 close, open sites.
Central faucet, flush toilets, electric hookups, tables, grills, boat ramp.
In two loops next to lake near 9-hole golf course.
Swim, boat, ski, and fish.
14-day limit.

ATCHISON SFL

(913) 367-7811
State map: B12
From ATCHISON, take KS 7 N for 3 miles (4.8 k). Turn Left (W) and go 2 miles (3.2 k). Turn Right (N) on gravel road and continue .5 mile (800 m).
FREE so choose a chore.
Open All Year.
Undesignated scattered, open sites.
Central faucet, pit toilets, tables, boat ramp.
Next to lake among oak-hickory hills.
Fish and boat. Watch wildlife.
No trash arrangements (pack it out).
14-day limit. Hunting in season.
Crowded holidays.

BARBER SFL

(316) 227-8609
State map: F7
Locate park just N of MEDICINE LODGE.
FREE so choose a chore.
Open All Year.
20 scattered, open sites.
Hand pump, pit toilets, tables, fire rings, boat ramp.
Next to 77-acre lake.
Fish or boat. Hike to spot wildlife.
14-day limit.

BOURBON SFL

(316) 362-3671
State map: E12
From ELSMORE, go E on CR for 5 miles (8 k).
FREE so choose a chore. Open All Year.
10 scattered, open sites.
Central faucet, pit toilets, tables, boat ramp.
Surrounded by oak-hickory woodland next to lake built on Wolf Pen Creek.
Fish. View wildlife.
No trash arrangements (pack it out).
14-day limit. Hunting in season.

BROWN SFL

(913) 367-7811
State map: B11
From HIAWATHA, take US 36 E for 8 miles (12.8 k).
FREE so choose a chore.
Open All Year.
Undesignated scattered, open sites.
Pit toilets, tables, boat ramp.
In heart of corn country among rolling hills next to lake.
Boat and fish. Watch wildlife.
NO water. No trash arrangements (pack it out). 14-day limit. Hunting in season.
Crowded holidays.
1000 ft (300 m)

BUTLER SFL

(316) 628-4592
State map: F10
From LATHAM, drive W on CR about 3 miles (4.8 k). Turn Right (N) and continue 1 mile (1.6 k).
FREE so choose a chore.
Open All Year.
20 scattered, open sites.
Hand pump, pit toilets, tables, fire rings, boat ramp.
Next to 124-acre lake.
Fish or boat.
14-day limit.

CAMP SIESTA

Oswego City Parks
(316) 795-4433
State map: F12

▲ ▲

Find park in OSWEGO, N of fairgrounds.
$5.
Open Mar 15–Oct 15; dry camping allowed off-season.
25 close, open sites.
Central faucet, flush toilets, showers, dump station, electric hookups, tables, grills.
Among trees and grassy areas on bluff overlooking Neosho River.
Enjoy overnight stop.
Crowded last week in Jul.

CARNAHAN

Pottawatomie County
(913) 457-3551
State map: C10
From MANHATTAN, head N for 3 miles (4.8 k) on US 24. Continue N for 5 miles (8 k) on KS 13. Turn Left (W) on CR 43 and go 5 miles (8 k). Turn Left (S) and drive 1 mile (1.6 k). (Also see Tuttle Creek Cove.)
FREE so choose a chore.
Open All Year.
6 scattered, open sites.
Pit toilets, tables, fire rings, grills, boat ramp.
Next to Tuttle Creek Lake.
Swim, fish, or boat. Hike.
NO water. No trash arrangements (pack it out). 14-day limit.

CEDAR BLUFF SP

(913) 726-3212
State map: C5
From OGALLAH (Exit 135 off I-70), travel S on KS 147 for 13 miles (20.8 k).
$3; $5 electric; $3 entrance fee; reservations accepted at (913) 726-3212 for an additional $5.
Open Apr 15–Oct 15; dry camping allowed off-season.
123 (7 tent-only) close, open sites. &
Central faucet, flush toilets, showers, dump station, electric hookups, tables, fire rings, grills, boat ramp, store, pay phone.
Among native grasses and woods near

reservoir.
Walk nature trail or hike farther to view wildlife. Swim, boat, ski, or fish. Take photos. Attend ranger programs.
14-day limit. Hunting in season.
Crowded holiday weekends.
2144 ft (643 m)

CEDAR PARK

COE (913) 453-2201
State map: D11
From LYNDON, drive 8 miles (12.8 k) N on US 75. Turn Right (E) on CR and go 4 miles (6.4 k). Turn Right (S) on CR and follow signs for 4 miles (6.4 k). (Also see 110 Mile Park.)
FREE so choose a chore.
Open All Year.
Undesignated scattered, open sites.
Pit toilets, tables, fire rings, grills, boat ramp, shelter.
In woods and grassy areas next to Pomona Lake.
Swim, boat, or fish. Observe wildlife.
NO water. 14-day limit. Hunting in season. No generators in quiet hours.
1000 ft (300 m)

CHASE SFL

(316) 767-5900
State map: D10
From COTTONWOOD FALLS, go W for 2 miles (3.2 k) on CR.
FREE so choose a chore.
Open All Year.
Undesignated scattered, open sites.
Water needs treating, pit toilets, tables, grills, fire rings.
In Flint Hills tallgrass prairie next to lake.
Fish. Watch birds.
No trash arrangements (pack it out).
14-day limit. Hunting in season.
1200 ft (360 m)

CHENEY SP

(316) 542-3664
State map: F8
From CHENEY, drive N on KS 251 for 6 miles (9.6 k). (Also see Lake Afton Park.)

$3; $5 electric; **$3** entrance fee; reservations accepted at (316) 542-3664 for an additional $5.
Open Apr 15–Oct 15; dry camping allowed off-season.
185 scattered, open sites.
Central faucet, flush toilets, showers, dump station, electric hookups, tables, fire rings, grills, boat ramp, rentals, pay phone.
In woods and open areas near lake.
Walk nature trail. Swim, boat, ski, or fish. Bike. Spot birds.
14-day limit. Occasionally crowded.

CLARK SFL

(316) 873-2572
State map: F5
From KINGSDOWN, take KS 94 S for 11 miles (17.6 k).
FREE so choose a chore. Open All Year.
Undesignated scattered, open sites.
Pit toilets, tables, fire rings, grills, boat ramp, pay phone.
At bottom of canyon next to lake.
Fish. Observe wildlife.
NO water. No trash arrangements (pack it out). 14-day limit. Hunting in season.

CLINTON SP

(913) 842-8562
State map: C12
From LAWRENCE, travel W on KS K-10 for 4 miles (6.4 k). (Also see Douglas SFL.)
$3; $5 electric; **$3** entrance fee; reservations accepted at (913) 842-8562 for an additional $5.
Open All Year.
460 close, open sites. &
Central faucet, flush toilets, showers, dump station, electric hookups, tables, fire rings, grills, boat ramp, store, rentals, laundry, pay phone.
On high bluff next to reservoir with woods and open fields.
Walk nature trail or take extensive hike. Bike. Windsurf and swim. Boat, waterski, or fish. Attend ranger programs.
14-day limit. Crowded summer holidays.
900 ft (270 m)

COWLEY SFL

(316) 628-4592
State map: G9
Travel E on US 166 for 13 miles (20.8 k) from ARKANSAS CITY.
FREE so choose a chore.
Open All Year.
10 scattered, open sites.
Hand pump, pit toilets, tables, boat ramp.
Next to 84-acre lake.
Fish or boat.
14-day limit.

CRAWFORD SP

(316) 362-3671
State map: F12
From GIRARD, drive N for 9 miles (14.4 k) on KS 7.
$3; $5 electric; **$3** entrance fee.
Open All Year.
263 close, open sites.
Water at every site, flush toilets, showers, dump station, electric hookups, tables, fire rings, grills, boat ramp, store, rentals, pay phone.
Among oak and hickory along Drywood Creek next to tranquil lake.
Enjoy quiet. Swim, boat, or fish. Walk nature trail. Hike to view wildlife. Attend ranger programs. Take fish hatchery tour.
14-day limit.
900 ft (270 m)

CUSTER PARK

COE (316) 767-5195
State map: D10
Drive N from COUNCIL GROVE on KS 57/177 for 3.2 miles (5.1 k). Turn Left (W). (Also see Kit Carson Cove.)
$4.
Open Apr 1–Oct 31.
11 close, open, tent sites.
Central faucet, pit toilets, tables, fire rings, grills, boat ramp.
On Council Grove Lake with some trees.
Swim, boat, ski, or fish.
14-day limit. No generators in quiet hours. No bug zappers. Crowded

▲ ▲

holidays.
1274 ft (382 m)

DAM SITE

COE (316) 658-4445
State map: F10
From FALL RIVER, drive
4.5 miles (7.2 k) NW to spot below dam.
(Also see Whitehall Bay.)
$5; $8 electric.
Open Apr 1–Oct 31; dry camping
allowed off-season.
33 scattered, open sites.
Central faucet, pit toilets, dump station,
electric hookups, tables, grills, fire rings.
In shade along Fall River.
Walk nature trail. Fish. Watch wildlife.
Attend ranger programs.
14-day limit. Hunting in season.
Crowded holidays.
900 ft (270 m)

DOUGLAS SFL

(913) 842-8562
State map: D12
From BALDWIN CITY,
drive N on CR 1055 for 1 mile (1.6 k).
Turn Right (E) on CR 12 and go 3 miles
(4.8 k). (Also see Clinton SP.)
FREE so choose a chore.
Open All Year.
20 scattered, open sites.
Central faucet, pit toilets, tables, grills,
boat ramp, rentals.
On rolling plains with limestone
outcroppings.
Boat and fish. Spot wildlife.
14-day limit. Hunting in season.
1000 ft (300 m)

DOWNSTREAM POINT

COE (316) 336-2741
State map: F11
From CHERRYVALE,
travel E on Main St to Olive. Turn Right
(S) and go 2 blocks. Turn Left (E) on
access road and drive 4 miles (6.4 k).
(Also see Mound Valley.)
FREE so choose a chore.
Open All Year.
10 close, screened sites.

Central faucet, pit toilets, tables, grills,
fire rings.
In "Little Ozarks" near Big Hill Lake.
Fish. View wildlife.
14-day limit. Crowded major holidays.
858 ft (257 m)

EISENHOWER SP

(913) 528-4102
State map: D11
From LYNDON, travel S
on US 75 for 5 miles (8 k). Turn Right
(W) on KS 278 and continue 3 miles
(4.8 k). (Also see Lyon SFL, Pomona SP,
and Sun Dance.)
$3; $5 electric; $3 entrance fee.
Open All Year.
195 close, open sites. &
Central faucet, flush toilets, showers,
dump station, electric hookups, tables,
fire rings, grills, boat ramp, pay phone.
In native tallgrass prairie with wooded
draws next to 7000-acre Melvern Lake.
Swim, boat, or fish. Walk nature trail for
photos and wildlife. Attend ranger
programs.
14-day limit.
1040 ft (312 m)

EL DORADO SP

(316) 321-7180
State map: E9
From EL DORADO, take
US 54 E for 3 miles (4.8 k). Turn Left (N)
on Prospect Rd and go 2 miles (3.2 k).
$3; $5 electric (352 sites); $3 entrance fee;
reservations accepted at (316) 321-7180
for an additional $5.
Open All Year.
1100 scattered, open sites.
Central faucet, flush toilets, showers,
dump station, electric hookups, tables,
grills, boat ramp, pay phone.
In four areas on edge of Flint Hills next
to 8000-acre El Dorado Lake.
Swim, boat, ski, or fish. Walk trail
system to view wildlife. Bike. Attend
ranger programs.
14-day limit. NO water in basic sites.
Hunting in season. Horses on trails.
1350 ft (405 m)

ELK CITY SP

(316) 331-6295
State map: F11
Drive W on US 160 about 2 miles (3.2 k) from INDEPENDENCE. Turn Right (N) and go 2 miles (3.2 k). (Also see Montgomery SFL and Outlet Area.)
$3; $6 electric; $3 entrance fee.
Open Apr–Oct.
160 close, open sites.
Central faucet, flush toilets, showers, dump station, electric hookups, tables, fire rings, boat ramp.
Next to Elk City Lake.
Swim, boat, waterski, or fish. Walk nature trail.
14-day limit.
800 ft (240 m)

ELLIS LAKESIDE CAMPGROUND

(913) 726-4812
State map: C5
Locate park in ELLIS at 300 E 8th.
$5; $7 electric.
Open May 1–Oct 1; dry camping allowed off-season.
25 close, open sites.
Central faucet, flush toilets, showers, dump station, electric hookups, tables, grills, boat ramp, pay phone.
Under large shade trees on banks of Big Creek.
Enjoy quiet. Swim, fish, or boat (5 mph limit). Bike. Visit local museums.

FALL RIVER SP

(316) 637-2213
State map: F10
$3; $5 electric;
$3 entrance fee.
Open All Year.
14-day limit. Crowded summer holidays.
1000 ft (300 m)
▲ Fredonia Bay
From FALL RIVER, drive W on KS 96 for .5 mile (800 m). Turn Right (N) on CR and go 1.5 miles (2.4 k). (Also see Toronto SP and Woodson SFL.)
100 scattered, open sites.

Central faucet, flush toilets, showers, dump station, electric hookups, tables, fire rings, grills, boat ramp, pay phone. Among oak woodlands and tallgrass prairies next to 2450-acre lake.
Boat, ski, or fish. Walk nature trail. Take photos. Attend ranger programs.
▲ Quarry Bay
From FALL RIVER, drive W on KS 96 for .5 mile (800 m). Turn Right (N) on CR and go 2.5 miles (4 k).
25 scattered, open sites.
Central faucet, flush toilets, showers, tables, fire rings, boat ramp, pay phone.
In native grasslands and oak savannahs next to 2450-acre lake.
Swim, boat, ski, or fish. Walk nature trail or hike farther. View wildlife. Attend ranger programs.

FRENCH CREEK COVE

COE (316) 382-2101
State map: D9
From HILLSBORO, drive E on US 56 for 2 miles (3.2 k). Turn Right (N) on CR 839 and go 1 mile (1.6 k). Turn Right (E) on gravel CR and continue 1 mile (1.6 k). Turn Left (N). (Also see Marion Cove. Nearby Hillsboro Cove costs $10.)
$4.
Open All Year.
12 close, open sites.
Central faucet, pit toilets, tables, fire rings, grills, boat ramp.
In farm and ranchland next to 6000-acre Marion Lake.
Boat, ski, or fish. Spot wildlife.
14-day limit. Nearby hunting in season.
1350 ft (405 m)

GEARY SFL

(913) 238-3014
State map: C9
From JUNCTION CITY, travel 10 miles (16 k) S on US 77.
FREE so choose a chore.
Open All Year.
50 scattered, open sites.
Hand pump (treat water), pit toilets, tables, fire rings, grills, boat ramp.

▲ ▲

With native grasses, red cedars, and limestone bluffs next to pristine lake. Boat or fish. Observe wildlife.
14-day limit. Hunting in season.
1150 ft (345 m)

GLEN ELDER SP

(913) 545-3345
State map: B7
From GLEN ELDER, travel W on US 24 for 12 miles (19.2 k).
$3; $5 electric; $3 entrance fee; reservations accepted at (913) 545-3345 for an additional $5.
Open All Year.
350 (10 tent-only) close, open sites. &
Central faucet, flush toilets, showers, dump station, electric hookups, tables, fire rings, grills, boat ramp, store, rentals, pay phone.
In rural setting next to Waconda Lake. Swim, boat, or fish. Walk trails to view wildlife. Attend ranger programs.
14-day limit. Hunting in season.
1450 ft (435 m)

HAIN SFL

(316) 873-2572
State map: E5
From SPEARVILLE, travel SW on US 56 for 1 mile (1.6 k) then turn Right (W) on CR and continue 5 miles (8 k).
FREE so choose a chore.
Open All Year.
Undesignated scattered, open sites.
Tables, fire rings.
Next to open lake in prairie pasture. Fish. Watch birds.
NO water. No toilet facilities. No trash arrangements (pack it out). Hunting in season.

HAMILTON SFL

(316) 276-8886
State map: E2
From SYRACUSE, head W on KS 50 for 3 miles (4.8 k). Turn Right (N) on CR. Drive 2 miles (3.2 k).
FREE so choose a chore.
Open All Year.

Undesignated scattered, open sites.
Pit toilets, tables, grills.
In shortgrass prairie next to small manmade lake.
Fish. Observe wildlife.
NO water. No trash arrangements (pack it out). 14-day limit. Hunting in season.

HARTFORD

COE (316) 364-8614
State map: D11
From HARTFORD, head SE about 3 miles (4.8 k).
FREE so choose a chore.
Open All Year.
12 close, open sites.
Central faucet, pit toilets, tables, fire rings, boat ramp.
On Neosho River near upper end of John Redmond Reservoir.
Fish. Relax.
14-day limit.

HILLSDALE SP

(913) 783-4507
State map: D12
From HILLSDALE, drive W on 255th St for 3 miles (4.8 k) to park office. Continue on gravel another 6 miles (9.6 k).
$3; $5 electric; $3 entrance fee.
Open All Year.
128 (15 tent-only) close, open sites.
Water at every site, flush toilets, showers, dump station, electric hookups, tables, fire rings, boat ramp.
In mix of mature hardwood and tallgrass prairie ecologies next to Hillsdale Lake. Fish or boat. Hike to view wildlife.
14-day limit. Hunting in season.
931 ft (279 m)

HODGEMAN SFL

(316) 276-8886
State map: E5
From JETMORE, go S on US 283 for 1.5 miles (2.4 k). Turn Right (W) on CR and continue 4 miles (6.4 k).
FREE so choose a chore.
Open All Year.
Undesignated scattered, open sites.

Pit toilets.
Next to small lake in mixed-grass prairie.
Fish. Spot wildlife.
NO water. No trash arrangements (pack
it out). 14-day limit. Hunting in season.

JEWEL SFL

(913) 753-4971
State map: B7
From MANKATO, head
S on CR for 6 miles (9.6 k). Turn Right
(W) and go 2 miles (3.2 k).
FREE so choose a chore.
Open All Year.
10 scattered, open sites.
Pit toilets, tables, fire rings, grills, boat
ramp.
In trees next to small lake.
Boat and fish. View wildlife.
NO water. No trash arrangements (pack
it out). 14-day limit. Hunting in season.
1500 ft (450 m)

KANOPOLIS SP

(913) 546-2565
State map: D8
From BROOKVILLE,
head W on KS 140 for 6 miles (9.6 k).
Turn Left (S) on KS 141 and go about
9 miles (14.4 k). (Also see Riverside.)
$3; $5 electric; $3 entrance fee.
Open All Year.
418 close, open sites.
Central faucet, flush toilets, showers,
dump station, electric hookups, tables,
fire rings, grills, boat ramp, store, pay
phone.
On mixed prairie with sandstone
outcroppings next to Kanopolis Lake.
Swim, boat, waterski, or fish. Take
advantage of 13-mile multi-purpose trail
system. Attend ranger programs.
14-day limit. Hunting in season.
1463 ft (439 m)

KANSA VIEW

COE (316) 767-5195
State map: D10
Drive N from COUNCIL
GROVE on KS 57/177 for 2 miles (3.2 k).
Turn Left (W) on dam road. Go .2 mile

(300 m). (Also see Kit Carson Cove.)
FREE so choose a chore.
Open All Year.
4 (3 tent-only) scattered, open sites.
Central faucet, pit toilets, tables, grills,
fire rings.
On Council Grove Lake with some trees.
Fish, of course.
No generators in quiet hours. No bug
zappers. Crowded holidays.
1274 ft (382 m)

KINGMAN SFL

(316) 532-3242
State map: F7
From KINGMAN, head
W on US 54 for 7 miles (11.2 k).
FREE so choose a chore.
Open All Year.
60 scattered, open sites.
Pit toilets, tables, fire rings, boat ramp.
In Ninnescah River valley with mature
cottonwoods and rolling grasslands.
Fish and boat. Walk 3 miles (4.8 k) of
trails. View wildlife and take photos.
NO water. No trash arrangements (pack
it out). 14-day limit. Hunting in season.

KIOWA SFL

(316) 227-8609
State map: F6
Locate lake on N edge
on GREENSBURG.
FREE so choose a chore.
Open All Year.
10 scattered, open sites.
Hand pump, pit toilets, tables, fire rings,
boat ramp.
Next to 21-acre lake.
Fish or boat.
14-day limit.

KIRWIN NWR

(913) 543-6673
State map: B6
Locate refuge SE of
KIRWIN.
FREE so choose a chore.
Open All Year.
150 scattered, open sites.
Central faucet, pit toilets, tables, grills.

Around Kirwin Reservoir.
Observe wildlife. Fish.
No trash arrangements (pack it out).
7-day limit.
1700 ft (510 m)

KIT CARSON COVE

COE (316) 767-5195
State map: D10
Drive N from COUNCIL
GROVE on KS 57/177 for 2.4 miles
(3.8 k). Turn Left (W). (Also see Custer
Park and Kansa View. Nearby Richey
Cove costs $7.)
$4; $8 electric.
Open Apr 1–Oct 31.
13 close, open sites.
Central faucet, pit toilets, electric
hookups, tables, fire rings, grills, boat
ramp.
On Council Grove Lake with shady and
open areas.
Swim, boat, ski, or fish. Walk nature
trail.
14-day limit. No generators in quiet
hours. No bug zappers. Crowded
holidays.
1274 ft (382 m)

LA CROSSE CITY PARK

(913) 222-2511
State map: D6
Find park in LA CROSSE
on US 183 S.
FREE; $5 electric.
Open All Year.
25 close, open sites.
Central faucet, flush toilets, electric
hookups, tables, pay phone.
In city park.
Enjoy overnight stop.
3-day limit.

LA CYGNE LAKE & WA

(913) 352-8941
State map: D12
From LA CYGNE, head
E on KS 152 for 6 miles (9.6 k). (Also see
Miami SFL.)
FREE so choose a chore.

Open All Year.
6 close, open sites.
Pit toilets.
Near popular fishing lake.
Fish. Watch wildlife.
NO water. No trash arrangements.
14-day limit. Hunting in season.
700 ft (210 m)

LAKE AFTON PARK

Sedgwick County Parks
(316) 794-2774
State map: F8
From WICHITA, travel W on US 54 for
14 miles (22.4 k). Turn Left (S) on 199th
W (Goddard Rd) and drive 2 miles
(3.2 k). Turn Left (W) on 39th St S
(MacArthur Rd) and go 4 miles (6.4 k).
(Also see Cheney SP.)
$4; $7.50 electric.
Open All Year.
474 (300 tent-only) close, open sites.
Central faucet, flush toilets, showers,
dump station, electric hookups, tables,
fire rings, grills, boat ramp, store, pay
phone.
Next to 258-acre lake.
Swim, boat, ski, or fish. Walk nature
trail. Visit observatory.
No generators.

LEAVENWORTH SFL

(913) 842-8562
State map: C12
From TONGANOXIE,
head NW on KS 16 for 2 miles (3.2 k).
Turn Left (W) on KS 90 and go about
3 miles (4.8 k).
FREE so choose a chore.
Open All Year.
20 scattered, open sites.
Central faucet, pit toilets, dump station,
tables, grills, boat ramp, shelter.
With glaciated round hills and broad
valleys.
Boat and fish. Take photos. Watch
wildlife.
No trash arrangements (pack it out).
14-day limit. Hunting in season.
1000 ft (300 m)

▲ ▲

LINN COUNTY PARK

(913) 757-6633
State map: D12
Locate park in LA
CYGNE, N of power plant.
$5; $7 electric; $8 water & electric;
$2 entrance fee. Open All Year.
101 close, open sites. &
Water at 50 sites, flush toilets, showers,
electric hookups, tables, fire rings, boat
ramp, shelter, pool, playground.
In shade near lake.
Swim, boat, or fish. Hike.

LOGAN WA

(913) 628-8614
State map: C3
From WINONA, travel
NE on US 40 for 3 miles (4.8 k). Turn
Right (S) on KS 25 and drive 9 miles
(14.4 k). Turn Left (E) on signed dirt
road and continue 2 miles (3.2 k).
FREE so choose a chore.
Open All Year.
Undesignated scattered, open sites.
Pit toilets, tables, boat ramp.
On rangeland with scattered trees.
Boat or fish. Observe wildlife.
NO water. No trash arrangements (pack
it out). Hunting in season.

LOUISBURG MIDDLE CREEK SFL

(913) 783-4507
State map: D12
From LOUISBURG, go S
on Metcalf Rd for 7 miles (11.2 k). (Also
see Miami SFL.)
FREE so choose a chore. Open All Year.
5 close, open sites.
Pit toilets, tables, fire rings, boat ramp.
In mixed wood and grassland next to
281-acre lake.
Fish and boat. View wildlife.
NO water. No trash arrangements (pack
it out). 14-day limit. Hunting in season.
900 ft (270 m)

LOVEWELL SP

(913) 753-4971
State map: B7
From MANKATO, drive

N on KS 14 about 18 miles (28.8 k). Turn
Right (E).
$3; $5 electric; reservations accepted at
(913) 753-4971 for an additional $5.
Open All Year.
120 scattered, open sites.
Central faucet, flush toilets, showers,
dump station, electric hookups, tables,
fire rings, grills, boat ramp, store, pay
phone.
In native grasses with various trees next
to 3200-acre reservoir.
Swim, boat, ski, or fish. Walk nature
trail. Watch wildlife.
14-day limit. Hunting in season.
Crowded major holidays.
1500 ft (450 m)

LUCAS

COE (913) 658-2551
State map: C7
From WILSON, drive N
on KS 232 for 10 miles (16 k). (Also see
Sylvan Park. Nearby Minoka costs $8.)
$4; $10 electric; less $2 weekdays.
Open All Year.
50 close, open sites.
Central faucet, flush toilets, showers,
dump station, electric hookups, tables,
fire rings, grills, boat ramp.
On shore of Wilson Lake with Dakota
sandstone cliffs and grassy banks.
Windsurf. Swim, boat, waterski, or fish.
Walk nature trail. Attend ranger
programs.
14-day limit.
1516 ft (455 m)

LYON SFL

(316) 699-3372
State map: D10
From READING, travel
W on KS 170 for 5 miles (8 k). Turn
Right (N) on gravel road and drive
1 mile (1.6 k). (Also see Eisenhower SP.)
FREE so choose a chore.
Open All Year.
100 scattered, open sites.
Pit toilets, tables, fire rings, grills, boat
ramp.
With native grasses and trees next to

140-acre lake.
Swim or fish. View wildlife.
NO water. No trash arrangements (pack it out). 14-day limit. Hunting in season.
1100 ft (330 m)

LYONS OVERNIGHT PARK

(316) 257-3741
State map: D7
Find park in LYONS at 600 W Taylor.
FREE so choose a chore.
Open All Year.
20 scattered, open sites. &
Central faucet, flush toilets, showers, dump station, electric hookups, tables.
In shade on edge of town.
Tour city museum. See Ralph's Ruts.

MARINA COVE

COE (316) 767-5195
State map: D10
In COUNCIL GROVE at intersection of KS 57S and US 56W, go 1 block W on US 56. Turn Right (NW) on Mission St. Drive 2.3 miles (3.7 k). (Also see Neosho Park and Santa Fe Trail.)
$4; $8 electric.
Open Apr 1 – Oct 31; dry camping allowed off-season.
7 close, open sites.
Central faucet, pit toilets, electric hookups, tables, fire rings, grills, boat ramp, store, rentals.
On Council Grove Lake with open and wooded areas.
Swim, boat, ski, or fish.
14-day limit. No generators in quiet hours. No bug zappers. Crowded holidays.
1274 ft (382 m)

MARION COVE

COE (316) 382-2101
State map: D9
From MARION, travel W on US 56 for 4 miles (6.4 k). Turn Right (N) on CR 847 and drive 1.5 miles (2.4 k). Turn Left (W). (Also see French Creek Cove.)
$4. Open All Year.

6 (4 tent-only) close, open sites.
Central faucet, pit toilets, tables, fire rings, grills, boat ramp, pay phone.
In agricultural setting next to Marion Lake.
Swim, boat, ski, or fish. Take photos.
14-day limit. Nearby hunting in season.
1350 ft (405 m)

MCPHERSON SFL

(316) 628-4592
State map: D8
From CANTON, go N on CR 304 for 6 miles (9.6 k). Turn Left (W) on gravel CR 1771. Drive 2.5 miles (4 k).
FREE so choose a chore.
Open All Year.
20 scattered, open sites.
Pit toilets, tables, fire rings, grills, boat ramp.
Under shade trees on banks of 46-acre lake next to Maxwell Wildlife Preserve with bison and elk.
Walk nature trail. View wildlife. Fish.
NO water. 14-day limit. Fires in grills only and no fireworks. Crowded holiday weekends.
1300 ft (390 m)

MEADE SP

(316) 873-2572
State map: F4
From MEADE, head SW on KS 23 for 13 miles (20.8 k).
$3; $6 electric; $3 entrance fee.
Open All Year.
137 close, open sites.
Central faucet, flush toilets, showers, dump station, electric hookups, tables, fire rings, boat ramp.
Next to lake.
Swim, canoe, boat, or fish. Hike.
14-day limit.

MIAMI SFL

(913) 783-4507
State map: D12
From FONTANA, drive N then E on CR for 2 miles (3.2 k). (Also see La Cygne Lake & WA and Louisburg Middle Creek SFL.)

▲ ▲ ▲ ▲ ▲ ▲ ▲ ▲ ▲ ▲ ▲ ▲ ▲ ▲ ▲ ▲ ▲ ● ▲ ▲ ▲ ▲ ▲ ▲ ▲ ▲ ▲ ▲

FREE so choose a chore.
Open All Year.
16 scattered, open sites.
Pit toilets, tables, fire rings.
In mature hardwood and scrub next to
118-acre lake formed from Marais des
Cygnes River.
Boat and fish. Spot wildlife.
NO water. No trash arrangements (pack
it out). 14-day limit. Hunting in season.
900 ft (270 m)

MILFORD SP

(913) 238-3014
State map: C9
From JUNCTION CITY,
head N on US 77 for 5 miles (8 k). Turn
Left (W) on KS 57 for 2 miles (3.2 k).
Find park on N side of dam.
$3; $8 electric; **$3** entrance fee.
Open All Year.
325 close, screened sites.
Central faucet, flush toilets, showers,
dump station, electric hookups, tables,
fire rings, grills, boat ramp, marina,
rentals.
With hardwood, cedar, pine, and native
grass environments on state's largest
reservoir.
Swim, boat, waterski, or fish. Walk
nature trail. Hike to observe abundant
wildlife. Attend ranger programs.
14-day limit.
1165 ft (350 m)

MINED LAND WA

(316) 231-3173
State map: F12
From COLUMBUS, drive
9 miles (14.4 k) W on KS 96. Turn Right
(N) on CR and go 1.25 miles (2.4 k).
FREE so choose a chore.
Open All Year.
Undesignated scattered, open sites.
Pit toilets, boat ramps.
Over 14000 acres of reclaimed land in
three sections with several hundred
water-filled pits and lakes plus wetlands,
grasslands, native shrub and oak-hickory
stands.
Fish. Canoe Deer Trace Trail. Walk trail

system for viewing wildlife.
NO water. No trash arrangements (pack
it out). Hunting in season.

MISSION LAKE

(913) 486-2390
State map: B11
From HORTON, go
1 mile (1.6 k) N on US 73. (Tenters can
also stay at Little Mission Lake by the
light plant off US 73.)
$2; $4 electric.
Open Apr 1 – Oct 31; dry camping
allowed off-season.
130 (60 tent-only) close, open sites.
Central faucet, pit toilets, dump station,
electric hookups, tables, grills, boat
ramp, shelter, volleyball court, pay
phone.
In quiet country setting on lakeshore.
Canoe. Boat and ski. Fish. Swim at pool
near Little Mission Lake.

MONTGOMERY SFL

(316) 331-6820
State map: F11
Head S on CR from
INDEPENDENCE for 4 miles (6.4 k).
Turn Left (E) and go 1 mile (1.6 k). (Also
see Elk City SP.)
FREE so choose a chore.
Open All Year.
60 scattered, open sites.
Pit toilets, tables, fire rings, boat ramp.
With sandstone bluffs on secluded, clear
lake.
Hike to view wildlife and take photos.
Fish, too.
NO water. No trash arrangements (pack
it out). 14-day limit.

MOUND VALLEY

COE (316) 336-2741
State map: F11
From CHERRYVALE,
travel E on Main St to Olive. Turn Right
(S). Go 2 blocks. Turn Left (E) on access
road. Drive 4.75 miles (7.6 k). (Also see
Downstream Point and Timber Hill.)
$5; $10 electric; reservations accepted at
(316) 336-2741.

Open Mar 26–Nov 1.
88 close, screened sites.
Central faucet, flush toilets, showers, dump station, electric hookups, tables, fire rings, grills, boat ramp, pay phone.
In "Little Ozarks" setting next to Big Hill Lake.
Swim, boat, or fish. Watch wildlife. Attend ranger programs.
14-day limit. Crowded major holidays.
858 ft (257 m)

MOUND VALLEY WALK-IN

COE (316) 336-2741
State map: F11
From CHERRYVALE, travel E on Main St to Olive. Turn Right (S) and go 2 blocks. Turn Left (E) on access road and drive 4.75 miles (7.6 k). Walk in about .25 mile (400 m). (Also see Downstream Point.)
FREE so choose a chore. Open All Year.
20 scattered, screened, tent sites.
Central faucet, pit toilets, fire rings.
In private "Little Ozarks" setting on Big Hill Lake.
Canoe. Fish. Observe wildlife.
No trash arrangements. 14-day limit.
858 ft (257 m)

NEBO SFL

(913) 367-7811
State map: B11
From HOLTON, go E on KS 116 for 8 miles (12.8 k). Turn Right (S). Drive 1 mile (1.6 k). Turn Right (W) on gravel road. Continue .5 mile (800 m).
FREE so choose a chore.
Open All Year.
Undesignated scattered, open sites.
Pit toilets, boat ramp.
In small area near lake.
Fish or boat. Watch wildlife.
NO water. No trash arrangements (pack it out). 14-day limit. Hunting in season.
1000 ft (300 m)

NEMAHA

(913) 226-7509
State map: B10
From SENECA, travel S

on KS 63 for 7 miles (11.2 k).
FREE so choose a chore.
Open All Year.
Undesignated scattered, open sites.
Pit toilets, tables.
On upper section of Nemaha River in woodlands.
View wildlife. Relax.
NO water. No trash arrangements (pack it out). 14-day limit. Hunting in season.
960 ft (288 m)

NEOSHO PARK

COE (316) 767-5195
State map: D10
In COUNCIL GROVE at intersection of KS 57S and US 56W, go 1 block W on US 56. Turn Right (NW) on Mission St and drive 1.7 miles (2.7 k). (Also see Marina Cove.)
$4; $8 electric.
Open Apr 1–Oct 31; dry camping allowed off-season.
17 close, screened sites.
Central faucet, pit toilets, electric hookups, tables, fire rings, grills, boat ramp.
On wooded section of Council Grove Lake.
Swim, boat, ski, or fish.
14-day limit. No generators in quiet hours. No bug zappers. Crowded holidays.
1274 ft (382 m)

NEOSHO SFL

(316) 362-3671
State map: F12
From PARSONS, drive 6 miles (9.6 k) N on US 59. Turn Right (E) on CR and go 3.5 miles (5.6 k).
FREE so choose a chore.
Open All Year.
30 scattered, open sites.
Central faucet, flush toilets, dump station, tables, fire rings, boat ramp.
Next to first state lake in Kansas.
Fish. Walk nature trail. Watch wildlife.
14-day limit.

NEOSHO WA
(316) 362-3671
State map: F12
From ST PAUL, go
1 mile (1.6 k) E on KS 57.
FREE so choose a chore.
Open All Year.
5 scattered, open sites.
Central faucet, pit toilets, boat ramp.
On edge of 3242-acre wildlife preserve.
Fish. Take photos. View birds and other
wildlife.
No trash arrangements (pack it out).
14-day limit. Hunting in season.

NEWMAN PARK
Arkansas City Parks
(316) 442-2340
State map: G9
Locate park in ARKANSAS CITY at
Summit & Lincoln (N of Arkansas
River). (Also see Walnut Park.)
FREE so choose a chore.
Open All Year.
7 scattered, open sites.
Central faucet, chemical toilets, dump
station, electric hookups, tables, grills.
In open area along Arkansas River.
Canoe. Fish. Relax.
3-day limit. Some city noise.

NORTH ROCK RIDGE
COE (316) 658-4445
State map: F10
From FALL RIVER, drive
W on KS 96 for 4 miles (6.4 k). Turn
Right (N) on Cummings Rd and go
2 miles (3.2 k). (Also see Whitehall Bay.)
$5; $8 electric.
Open Apr 1–Oct 31; dry camping
allowed off-season.
44 scattered, open sites.
Central faucet, pit toilets, dump station,
electric hookups, tables, fire rings, grills,
boat ramp.
Next to Fall River Lake.
Boat or fish. Walk nature trail. Spot
wildlife.
14-day limit. Hunting in season.
Crowded holidays.
950 ft (285 m)

OSAGE SFL
(913) 828-4933
State map: C11
From CARBONDALE,
take US 75 S for 3 miles (4.8 k). Turn
Left (E) on gravel road and go 1 mile
(1.6 k). (Also see Pomona SP.)
FREE so choose a chore.
Open All Year.
120 scattered, open sites.
Pit toilets, fire rings, grills, boat ramp.
In native prairie and woodland next to
140-acre lake.
Fish. Observe wildlife.
NO water. No trash arrangements (pack
it out). 14-day limit. Hunting in season.
1000 ft (300 m)

OTTAWA SFL
(913) 546-2565
State map: C8
From MINNEAPOLIS,
drive about 7 miles (11.2 k) E on KS 93.
FREE; $5 electric.
Open All Year.
121 close, open sites.
Central faucet, pit toilets, electric
hookups, tables, fire rings, grills, boat
ramp, store, pay phone.
In mixed grass prairie next to 111-acre
lake.
Boat and fish. Watch wildlife.
14-day limit. Hunting in season.
1300 ft (390 m)

OTTER CREEK
COE (316) 364-8614
State map: E11
From BURLINGTON,
head W on CR to Embankment Road.
Turn Right. (Also see West Wingwall.)
FREE so choose a chore.
Open All Year.
10 close, open sites.
Central faucet, pit toilets, tables, fire
rings, boat ramp.
Next to John Redmond Reservoir.
Boat or fish.
14-day limit.

▲ ▲

OUTLET

COE (913) 843-7665
State map: C11
From LAWRENCE, take
Clinton Parkway W to CR 13. Turn Left
(S) and continue .5 mile (800 m). (Also
see Rockhaven and Woodridge Walk-In.)
FREE so choose a chore.
Open May 15–Sep 30.
30 close, open sites.
Hand pump, pit toilets, tables, grills.
Below dam for Clinton Lake.
Fish. Relax.
14-day limit.

OUTLET

COE (913) 597-5144
State map: C11
From PERRY, drive
3 miles (4.8 k) N on CR 1029. Turn Left
(W) on Outlet Rd.
FREE so choose a chore.
Open All Year.
Undesignated close, open sites.
Water needs treating, pit toilets, tables,
fire rings.
Under tall trees near outlet channel
below dam for Perry Lake.
Fish. Relax, of course.
14-day limit.

OUTLET AREA

COE (316) 331-0315
State map: F11
Drive W on US 160
about 1 mile (1.6 k) from
INDEPENDENCE. Turn Right (N) on
access road and follow signs to dam
about 5 miles (8 k). (Also see Elk City
SP. Nearby Card Creek costs $8.)
$5.
Open Mar 26–Nov 1; dry camping
allowed off-season.
16 close, open sites.
Central faucet, pit toilets, tables, fire
rings, boat ramp.
Below Elk City Lake dam.
Fish or boat.
14-day limit.

PERRY SP

(913) 289-3449
State map: C11
From TOPEKA, take
US 24 E about 11 miles (17.6 k). Turn
Left (N) on KS 237. Go 4 miles (6.4 k).
$3; $6 electric; $3 entrance fee.
Open Apr 15–Oct 15; dry camping
allowed off-season.
400 scattered, open sites. ♿
Central faucet, flush toilets, showers,
dump station, electric hookups, tables,
grills, boat ramp, store.
In native grasses next to lake.
Watch abundant wildlife. Swim, boat, or
fish. Attend ranger programs.
14-day limit.

POMONA SP

(913) 828-4933
State map: D11
From OTTAWA, take
KS 68 W for 15 miles (24 k). Bear Right
(NW) on KS 268 and drive 5 miles (8 k).
Turn Right (N) on KS 368 and continue
1 mile (1.6 k). (Also see Eisenhower SP
and Osage SFL.)
$3; $5 electric; $3 entrance fee;
reservations accepted at (913) 828-4933
for an additional $5.
Open All Year; dry camping allowed off-
season.
446 (100 tent-only) close, open sites.
Central faucet, flush toilets, showers,
dump station, electric hookups, tables,
fire rings, grills, boat ramp, store, rentals,
pay phone.
In prairie and woodland environments
next to 4000-acre reservoir.
Swim, boat, or fish. Walk nature trail.
Attend ranger programs.
14-day limit. Crowded holiday
weekends.
1000 ft (300 m)

POTTAWATOMIE SFL #1

(913) 537-9804
State map: B10
Drive N on KS 99 for
5 miles (8 k) from WESTMORELAND.
(Also see Tuttle Creek SP.)

▲ ▲

FREE so choose a chore.
Open All Year.
Undesignated scattered, open sites.
Hand pump, pit toilets, tables, boat ramp.
On edge of Flint Hills in native woodlands next to lake.
Fish. Watch wildlife.
No trash arrangements (pack it out).
14-day limit.
1080 ft (324 m)

POTTAWATOMIE SFL #2
(913) 537-9804
State map: C10
From MANHATTAN, take US 24 E. Turn Left (N) on signed CR to lake—total of 6 miles (9.6 k). (Also see Tuttle Creek SP.)
FREE so choose a chore.
Open All Year.
Undesignated scattered, open sites.
Hand pump, pit toilets, tables, boat ramp.
In Flint Hills mature oak forest next to small lake.
Fish. Walk trail system. View wildlife.
No trash arrangements (pack it out).
14-day limit.
1030 ft (309 m)

PRAIRIE CENTER
(913) 884-8832
State map: C12
Locate park near OLATHE at 26325 W 135th St. Register at limestone house.
$1 per person; reservations accepted at (913) 884-8832.
Open All Year.
1 site.
Water at house, chemical toilets, tables.
In trees next to 5-acre lake.
Relax a night or two.
Only 1 camper (individual, family unit, or group) per night.

PRAIRIE DOG SP
(913) 877-2953
State map: B5
From NORTON, drive W

on US 36 for 4 miles (6.4 k). Turn Left (S) on KS 261 and continue 1 mile (1.6 k).
$3; $5 electric; reservations accepted at (913) 877-2953 for an additional $5.
Open Apr 15–Oct 15; dry camping allowed off-season.
190 (150 tent-only) scattered, open sites.
Central faucet, flush toilets, showers, dump station, electric hookups, tables, fire rings, grills, boat ramp, pay phone.
Next to lake in native mixed-grass prairie.
Swim, boat, ski, or fish. Canoe. Take photos. Attend ranger programs.
14-day limit.
2260 ft (678 m)

RIVERSIDE
COE (913) 546-2294
State map: D8
From BROOKVILLE, head W on KS 140 for 6 miles (9.6 k). Turn Left (S) on KS 141 and go about 10 miles (16 k). (Also see Kanopolis SP.)
FREE so choose a chore.
Open All Year.
40 close, open sites.
Central faucet, flush toilets, showers, dump station, tables, grills, fire rings.
In heavy shade next to Smoky Hill River below Kanopolis Lake dam.
Fish. Watch wildlife.
14-day limit. Crowded holidays.
1420 ft (426 m)

ROCKHAVEN
COE (913) 843-7665
State map: C11
Drive SW on CR 458 for 10 miles (16 k) from LAWRENCE. (See Outlet. Nearby Bloomington costs $8.)
$4.
Open Apr 1–Oct 15; dry camping allowed off-season.
50 close, open sites.
Hand pump, pit toilets, tables, grills, fire rings.
On shores of Clinton Lake.
Walk trail system. Fish.
14-day limit. Crowded holidays.
Occasional use as horse camp.

▲ ▲

ROOKS SFL

(913) 425-6775
State map: B6
From STOCKTON, go
1 mile (1.6 k) S on US 183. Turn Right
(W) on CR and drive 2 miles (3.2 k).
Turn Left (S) on gravel road and proceed
.5 mile (800 m). (Also see Webster SP.)
FREE so choose a chore.
Open All Year.
15 scattered, open sites.
Pit toilets, tables, fire rings, grills, boat
ramp.
Under oak and cottonwood next to lake
formed from Boxelder Creek.
Boat and fish. View wildlife.
NO water. No trash arrangements (pack
it out). 14-day limit. Hunting in season.
1860 ft (558 m)

SALINE SFL

(913) 628-8614
State map: C3
From SALINA, head W
on State St (Exit 93 off I-135) about
1 mile (1.6 k). Turn Right (N) on CR and
continue 5 miles (8 k).
FREE so choose a chore.
Open All Year.
Undesignated scattered, open sites.
Pit toilets, tables, boat ramp.
Next to 38-acre lake.
Fish or boat.
NO water. No trash arrangements (pack
it out). 14-day limit.

SANTA FE

Chanute Municipal Parks
(316) 431-4199
State map: F11
Locate park on S end of CHANUTE at
35th & Santa Fe.
FREE; $3 after 48 hours.
Open All Year.
26 close, open, RV sites.
Water at every site, flush toilets,
showers, dump station, electric hookups,
boat ramp, golf course, pay phone.
Between two lanes of trees near golf
course and lake.
Play golf. Boat, waterski, or fish. Watch

wildlife.
10-day limit.

SANTA FE TRAIL

COE (316) 767-5195
State map: D10
In COUNCIL GROVE at
intersection of KS 57S and US 56W, go 1
block W on US 56. Turn Right (NW) on
Mission St and drive 2.6 miles (4.2 k).
(Also see Marina Cove. Nearby Canning
Creek Cove costs $7.)
$4; $8 electric.
Open Apr 1–Oct 31; dry camping
allowed off-season.
37 close, screened sites.
Central faucet, pit toilets, electric
hookups, tables, fire rings, grills, boat
ramp, playground.
On Council Grove Lake with open and
wooded areas.
Swim, boat, ski, or fish.
14-day limit. No generators in quiet
hours. No bug zappers. Crowded
holidays.
1274 ft (382 m)

SCHOOL CREEK

COE (913) 238-5714
State map: C9
From WAKEFIELD, take
KS 82 W for 2 miles (3.2 k). Turn Left (S)
on CR 837. Go 8.7 miles (13.9 k). Drive
2 miles (3.2 k) on unpaved Luttman Rd.
(Also see South Timber Creek.)
$4.
Open Apr 15–Sep 30; dry camping
allowed off-season.
44 close, open sites.
Hand pump, pit toilets, tables, grills, fire
rings.
In rugged, wooded area next to Milford
Lake.
Boat and fish, of course.
14-day limit. Occasionally noisy with
ATVs.

SCOTT SP

(316) 872-2061
State map: D3
From SCOTT CITY,

travel N on US 83 for 10 miles (16 k).
Continue N on KS 95 for 3 miles (4.8 k).
$3; $6 electric; $3 entrance fee.
Open All Year.
220 close, open sites. &
Water at 20 sites, flush toilets, showers,
dump station, electric hookups, tables,
fire rings, boat ramp.
Next to lake and El Cuartelejo
(northernmost pueblo in US).
Swim, canoe, boat, or fish. Hike.
14-day limit.

SHAWNEE SFL

(913) 273-6740
State map: C11
From TOPEKA, drive N
on US 75. Turn Left (W) on 62nd. Turn
Right (N) on Landen Rd. Turn Left (W)
on 86th and follow signs.
FREE so choose a chore.
Open All Year.
50 scattered, open sites.
Pit toilets, tables, fire rings, grills, boat
ramp.
Next to 135-acre lake surrounded by
tallgrass prairie.
Fish or boat. Observe wildlife. Take
photos.
NO water. No trash arrangements (pack
it out). 14-day limit. Hunting in season.
1070 ft (321 m)

SHERIDAN SFL

(913) 726-3212
State map: B4
From HOXIE, go W on
US 24 for 12 miles (19.2 k).
FREE so choose a chore. Open All Year.
12 close, open sites.
Pit toilets, tables, fire rings.
In native grass with some woods next to
lake.
Swim. Boat and fish. Watch birds.
NO water. No trash arrangements (pack
it out). 14-day limit.

SHERMAN SFL

(913) 628-8614
State map: C2
From GOODLAND, head

S on KS 27 for 9 miles (14.4 k). Turn
Right (W) at sign. Drive 2 miles (3.2 k).
FREE so choose a chore.
Open All Year.
Undesignated scattered, open sites.
Pit toilets, tables, boat ramp.
In rangeland with scattered trees.
Fish. View wildlife.
NO water. No trash arrangements (pack
it out). 14-day limit. Hunting in season.

SOUTH TIMBER CREEK

COE (913) 238-5714
State map: C9
From WAKEFIELD, go E
on KS 82 for 1 mile (1.6 k). (Also see
School Creek and West Rolling Hills.)
$4. Open Apr 15-Sep 30; dry camping
allowed off-season.
45 close, open sites.
Central faucet, pit toilets, tables, fire
rings, grills, boat ramp.
In woods next to Milford Lake.
Boat or fish. Observe wildlife.
14-day limit.

STOCKDALE

COE (913) 539-8511
State map: C10
From MANHATTAN,
drive NW on US 24 for 8 miles (12.8 k).
Turn Right (N) on CR 895 and go
1.5 miles (2.4 k). Turn Right (E) on
CR 396 and continue 2 miles (3.2 k).
(Also see Tuttle Creek Cove.)
FREE so choose a chore.
Open All Year.
13 close, screened sites.
Central faucet, flush toilets, showers,
dump station, tables, fire rings, grills,
boat ramp.
On shores of Tuttle Creek Lake.
Swim, boat, or fish. Walk trail system
and view wildlife. Attend ranger
programs.
14-day limit.

SUN DANCE

COE (913) 549-3318
State map: D11
From LEBO, drive N on

CR for 8 miles (12.8 k). (Also see
Eisenhower SP. Nearby Arrow Rock
costs $8.)
FREE so choose a chore.
Open All Year.
30 scattered, open sites.
Central faucet, pit toilets, tables, fire
rings, grills, boat ramp, shelter.
Next to manmade Melvern Lake on
eastern edge of Flint Hills prairie.
Swim, boat, or fish. Watch wildlife.
14-day limit. Hunting in season.
Crowded holiday weekends.
1036 ft (311 m)

SYLVAN PARK

COE (913) 658-2551
State map: C7
From WILSON, drive N
on KS 232 for 9 miles (14.4 k). (Also see
Lucas.)
FREE so choose a chore.
Open All Year.
19 close, open sites.
Central faucet, pit toilets, tables, grills,
fire rings.
Under shade trees next to Saline River
below Wilson Lake dam.
Enjoy quiet. Walk nature trail. View
wildlife.
14-day limit.
1516 ft (455 m)

TIMBER HILL

COE (316) 336-2741
State map: F11
From DENNIS, drive S
on CR for 3.5 miles (5.2 k). Turn Right
(W) and go 2 miles (3.2 k). (Also see
Mound Valley.)
$5.
Open Mar 26–Nov 1; dry camping
allowed off-season.
20 close, screened sites.
Central faucet, pit toilets, dump station,
tables, fire rings, grills, boat ramp, pay
phone.
In "Little Ozarks" next to Big Hill Lake.
Boat, ski, or fish. Spot wildlife.
14-day limit. Crowded major holidays.
Horse trailhead.

TORONTO SP

(316) 637-2213
State map: E11
Open All Year.
Around 2800-acre Toronto Lake on
prairie terraces and oak-covered hills.
Walk nature trail or hike farther to view
wildlife. Swim, boat, waterski, or fish.
Attend ranger programs.
14-day limit. Hunting in season.
Crowded summer holidays.
950 ft (285 m)
▲ **Holiday Hill**
From TORONTO, drive 6 miles (9.6 k) S
on KS 105 to W end of dam. (Also see
Fall River SP and Woodson SFL.)
$3; $5 electric; $3 entrance fee.
30 scattered, open sites.
Central faucet, flush toilets, showers,
dump station, electric hookups, tables,
fire rings, grills, boat ramp, store.
▲ **Mann's Cove**
From TORONTO, drive 2.5 miles (4 k) S
on KS 105. (Also see Fall River SP and
Woodson SFL.)
$3; $3 entrance fee.
15 scattered, screened sites.
Central faucet, pit toilets, tables, fire
rings, grills, boat ramp.
▲ **Toronto Point**
From TORONTO, drive 2 miles (3.2 k) S
on CR. (Also see Fall River SP and
Woodson SFL.)
$3; $5 electric; $3 entrance fee;
reservations accepted at (316) 637-2213
for an additional $5.
200 scattered, screened sites.
Water at 20 sites, flush toilets, showers,
electric hookups, tables, fire rings, grills,
boat ramp, pay phone.

TUTTLE CREEK COVE

COE (913) 539-8511
State map: C10
From MANHATTAN,
drive NW on US 24 for 3 miles (4.8 k).
Turn Right (N) on KS 13 and go 1 block.
Continue N on Tuttle Creek Rd. (Also
see Carnahan, Stockdale, and Tuttle
Creek SP.)
FREE so choose a chore.

Open All Year.
24 scattered, screened sites.
Central faucet, flush toilets, tables, fire rings, grills, boat ramp, pay phone.
With scattered trees in Flint Hills next to Tuttle Creek Lake.
Swim, boat, and fish. Canoe. Photograph wildlife. Attend ranger programs.
14-day limit.

TUTTLE CREEK SP

(913) 539-7941
State map: B9–C10
(See Pottawatomie SFL.)
$3; $5 electric; $3 entrance fee; reservations accepted at (913) 539-7941 for an additional $5.
Open Apr 1–Oct 31; dry camping allowed off-season.

▲ **Fancy Creek**
N of RANDOLPH, take KS 16 E for .5 mile (800 m).
170 close, open sites.
Water at every site, flush toilets, showers, dump station, electric hookups, tables, fire rings, grills, boat ramp.
On grassy hills along western shore of Tuttle Creek Reservoir.
Boat or fish. Walk trails. Take photos.
14-day limit. Hunting in season.
1080 ft (324 m)

▲ **River Pond**
From MANHATTAN, take US 24 NW for 5 miles (8 k). Watch for signs.
254 scattered, open sites.
Water at every site, flush toilets, showers, dump station, electric hookups, tables, fire rings, grills, boat ramp, pay phone.
Under mature trees in flat below Tuttle Creek Reservoir dam.
Canoe, swim, or fish. View wildlife.
Attend ranger programs.
14-day limit.
1025 ft (308 m)

WALNUT PARK

Arkansas City Parks
(316) 442-2340
State map: G9
In ARKANSAS CITY, take US 166 E to

Walnut River. (Also see Newman Park.)
FREE so choose a chore.
Open All Year.
6 sites.
Central faucet, chemical/pit toilets, electric hookups, tables, grills.
With shade trees next to Walnut River.
Fish. Canoe. Bike. Swim at city pool (5th & 6th).
3-day limit. Occasional flooding.

WARNOCK LAKE

Atchison City Parks
(913) 367-0134
State map: B12
From ATCHISON, drive 2 miles (3.2 k) SW on signed road.
$2.
Open All Year.
17 close, open sites.
Central faucet, pit toilets, dump station, electric hookups, tables, grills, boat ramp.
On lake near International Forest of Friendship.
Walk nature trail. Swim, fish, or boat (no gas motors).
3-day limit.

WASHINGTON SFL

(913) 238-3014
State map: A9
Drive N on CR for 5 miles (8 k) from WASHINGTON. Turn Left (W) on gravel road and go 2 miles (3.2 k). Turn Right (N) and travel another 2 miles (3.2 k).
FREE so choose a chore.
Open All Year.
20 scattered, open sites.
Pit toilets, tables, fire rings, boat ramp.
With native grass and some shade next to small, isolated lake.
Fish or boat. View wildlife.
NO water. 14-day limit. Hunting in season.
1320 ft (396 m)

▲ ▲

WEBSTER SP

(913) 425-6775
State map: B5
From STOCKTON, drive
W on US 24 for 8.5 miles (13.6 k). (Also
see Rooks SFL and Webster WA.)
$3; $5 electric; $3 entrance fee;
reservations accepted at (913) 425-6775
for an additional $5.
Open Apr 15-Oct 15; dry camping
allowed off-season.
136 scattered, open sites.
Water at every site, flush toilets,
showers, dump station, electric hookups,
tables, fire rings, boat ramp, shelter,
store, pay phone.
In five separate areas among cottonwood
trees along South Fork Solomon River.
Swim, boat, ski, or fish. Windsurf. Walk
nature trail. Attend ranger programs.
14-day limit.
1870 ft (561 m)

WEBSTER WA

(913) 425-6775
State map: B5
From STOCKTON, drive
W on US 24 for 10 miles (16 k). Watch
for brown & white signs on Left. (Also
see Webster SP.)
FREE so choose a chore. Open All Year.
40 scattered, open sites.
Pit toilets, tables, grills.
Under old cottonwoods along both sides
of South Fork Solomon River.
Swim, boat, or fish. Spot wildlife.
NO water. No trash arrangements (pack
it out). 14-day limit. Hunting in season.
1970 ft (591 m)

WEST ROLLING HILLS

COE (913) 238-5714
State map: C9
From JUNCTION CITY,
go 2 miles (3.2 k) NW on KS 57. Turn
Left (W) and drive 4 miles (6.4 k) on
KS 244. (Also see South Timber Creek.)
FREE so choose a chore.for 40 basic sites;
$8 water; $10 water & electric.
Open Apr 15 – Oct 31; dry camping
allowed off-season.

98 close, open sites.
Water at 36 sites, flush toilets, showers,
dump station, electric hookups, tables,
fire rings, grills, boat ramp.
Among gentle rolling hills with open
and wooded areas next to Milford Lake.
Swim, boat, and fish.
14-day limit.

WEST WINGWALL

COE (316) 364-8614
State map: E11
Head N on US 75 about
2 miles (3.2 k) from BURLINGTON.
Turn Left (W) then Right (N) on access
road. Travel 2 miles (3.2 k) to Riverside
West Campground. (See Otter Creek.)
$4.
Open All Year.
6 close, open sites.
Central faucet, pit toilets, tables, fire
rings.
Next to John Redmond Reservoir.
Fish or boat, of course.
14-day limit.

WHITEHALL BAY

COE (316) 658-4445
State map: F10
From FALL RIVER, take
access road NW about 5 miles (8 k),
following signs. (Also see Dam Site and
North Rock Ridge.)
$5; $8 electric.
Open May 1 – Oct 1; dry camping
allowed off-season.
25 scattered, open sites.
Central faucet, pit toilets, dump station,
electric hookups, tables, fire rings, grills,
boat ramp.
In shade next to Fall River Lake.
Swim, boat, waterski, or fish.
14-day limit.
950 ft (285 m)

WILSON SFL

(316) 637-2213
State map: E11
From YATES CENTER,
drive 14 miles (22.4 k) S on US 75.
FREE so choose a chore.

▲ ▲

Open All Year.
Undesignated scattered, screened sites.
Pit toilets, tables, grills, boat ramp.
In upland prairie with limestone
outcroppings next to 119-acre lake.
Fish. Observe wildlife.
NO water. No trash arrangements (pack
it out). 14-day limit.
850 ft (255 m)

WILSON SP

(913) 658-2465
State map: C7
From WILSON, travel
8 miles (12.8 k) N on KS 232.
$3; $5 electric; $3 entrance fee;
reservations accepted at (913) 658-2465
for an additional $5.
Open All Year.
1516 ft (455 m)
▲ **Hell Creek**
400 close, open sites.
Central faucet, flush toilets, showers,
dump station, electric hookups, tables,
fire rings, grills, boat ramp, rentals, pay
phone.
With native grasses and rock
outcroppings next to 4000-acre clear lake.
Swim, boat, ski, or fish. Walk nature
trail. View wildlife. Attend ranger
programs.
14-day limit. Crowded holidays.
▲ **Otoe**
200 close, open sites.
Water at every site, flush toilets,
showers, dump station, electric hookups,
tables, fire rings, grills, boat ramp, pay
phone.
Under shade trees with native grasses
next to water.
Swim, boat, or fish. Attend ranger
programs.
14-day limit.

WOODRIDGE WALK-IN

COE (913) 843-7665
State map: C11
From LAWRENCE, drive
W on US 40 about 4 miles (6.4 k).
Continue W on CR 442 for 8 miles
(12.8 k). Turn Left (S) on CR 1023 and go
2 miles (3.2 k) to Woodridge turnoff. Set
up tent at least 100 feet (30 m) from trail.
(Also see Outlet.)
FREE so choose a chore.
Open All Year.
Undesignated scattered, open sites.
Hand pump, pit toilets.
On shores of Clinton Lake.
Hike trails to view wildlife. Fish.
14-day limit. No alcohol.

WOODSON SFL

(316) 637-2213
State map: E11
From TORONTO, take
KS 105 S for 1.25 miles (2 k). Turn Left
(E) on gravel road and go 4.5 miles
(7.2 k). (Also see Fall River SP and
Toronto SP.)
FREE so choose a chore.
Open All Year.
50 scattered, screened sites.
Central faucet, pit toilets, dump station,
tables, fire rings, grills, boat ramp.
Next to 180-acre lake surrounded by
native tallgrass prairie and oak
savannahs.
Fish. Spot wildlife.
No trash arrangements (pack it out).
14-day limit. Hunting in season.
850 ft (255 m)

▲ ▲

KENTUCKY
CAMPGROUND LOCATIONS

▸ ▸ Find location on facing page map grid. ▸ ▸
▼ ▼ Locate area campgrounds on these page numbers. ▼ ▼

Kentucky

Grid conforms to official state map. For your copy, call (800) 225-TRIP
or write Travel, PO Box 2011, Frankfort, KY 40602.

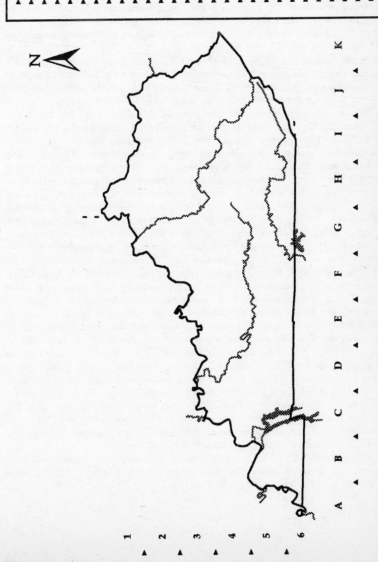

▲ ▲

PUBLIC LANDS CAMPING

Because of the grassy region between the majestic mountains of east Kentucky and the large lakes of west Kentucky, this commonwealth is called the Bluegrass State. The native grass is as green as any other, except when it blooms in the spring. Then, blue-purple buds give the grass its renowned blue hue.

This state has more miles of running water than any other state but Alaska. There are fourteen major river systems feeding many lakes and lush forests. There are numerous public lands opportunities to fish, boat, swim, hike and bike as well as camp. Bicyclists spin along 600-plus miles of the TransAmerica Trail. Hikers tread on 1,400 miles of marked paths, including the national forest's Sheltowee Trace and the state's Jenny Wiley national recreation trails.

Enjoy the outside and inside of 52,000-acre Mammoth Cave National Park (NP). Camp free in the backcountry and more isolated developed campgrounds. Pay $6.00 at popular Headquarters Campground. More **National Park Service** (NPS) backcountry sites are in the magnificent 104,000-acre Big South Fork National River and Recreation Area (RA)–see Tennessee for detailed listing. Shared with Virginia, discover the 20,000-acre Cumberland Gap National Historical Park (NHP). **US Forest Service** administers the 526,000-acre Daniel Boone National Forest (NF), including the Clifty and Beaver Creek wilderness areas, in eastern Kentucky. Popular recreation areas are found around Cave Run, Cumberland, and Laurel River lakes. In the various seasons, enjoy hiking on the Red River Gorge, Sheltowee, and Redbird Fitness national recreation trails. Also, ride horses, fish, canoe, whitewater raft, and cross-country ski. View the fascinating Red River Geological Area. Drive the Zilpo Road, a 9-mile scenic byway, popular for observing wildlife as well as fall foliage. Dispersed camping in the forest is free. Developed campground fees range from free to $12.00 for single sites. **Tennessee Valley Authority** (TVA) manages Land Between The Lakes, the peninsula between Kentucky Lake and Lake Barkley. TVA lake access areas qualify for this book with prices from free to $5.00 while TVA family campgrounds cost more. **US Army Corps of Engineers** (COE) maintains campgrounds in Kentucky on the following lakes: Barkley, Barren River, Buckhorn, Carr Fork, Cumberland, Dewey, Fishtrap, Green River, Nolin, and Rough River. COE camp fees range from free to $15.00.

The **Kentucky State Park** (SP) system calls itself the finest in the nation. With 17 resort parks out of its 47 recreational and historic sites, Kentucky has developed its scenic spots. Many people say the state has over-developed these once-natural places with airstrips, golf courses, lodges, paved campgrounds.... Of the 27 state parks offering camping, some are open year-round; others are seasonal. Camping fees range from $8.50 per couple for a primitive site to $10.50 for a developed site (15% off for senior citizens). **Kentucky State Forests** (SF) have no developed campgrounds but allow primitive camping on its entire acreage. In **Kentucky Public Wildlife Areas** (WA), remember the primary purposes: hunting and fishing. Camp only in designated areas and practice careful safety and sanitation procedures.

Sample Kentucky. Try on its music (bluegrass), legends (Daniel Boone), traditions (horse racing), spirits (bourbon), and foods (burgoo stew). Kentucky may be "What You've Been Looking For."

▲ ▲

ATV AREA

COE (502) 465-4463
State map: G5
Drive E on KY 70
about 3 miles (4.8 k) from CAMP-
BELLSVILLE. Turn Right (SE) on KY 76
and go about 2 miles (3.2 k). Turn Right
(W) at sign. (Also see Pike Ridge.
Nearby Smith Ridge costs $8.)
FREE so choose a chore.
Open All Year.
5 scattered, open sites.
Pit toilets, tables, fire rings.
In rugged terrain (open for ATVs) near
NW shore of Green River Lake.
Fish. Watch wildlife.
NO water. 14-day limit. Hunting in
season. Often noisy. Crowded holidays.
685 ft (206 m)

BACON CREEK

TVA (502) 924-5602
State map: C6
From AURORA, drive
W on US 68 about 6 miles (9.6 k) to The
Trace. Turn Right (S) for 100 yds
(100 m). Take KY 165 E for 7 miles
(11.2 k). Continue on KY 166 for 3 miles
(4.8 k).
FREE so choose a chore.
Open All Year.
11 scattered, open sites.
Central faucet, chemical toilets, tables,
grills, boat ramp.
In woods on Lake Barkley.
Boat or fish. View wildlife.
21-day limit. Hunting in season.
365 ft (110 m)

BEAVER CREEK

COE (502) 646-2055
State map: F6
From HAYWOOD, go
W on KY 252. Turn Left (S) on Beaver
Creek Rd. (Also see Tailwater.)
FREE so choose a chore.
Open Apr 1–Oct 31.
12 close, open sites.
Central faucet, pit toilets, tables, fire
rings, grills, boat ramp.
In shade about 100 yds (100 m) from

Barren River Lake.
Swim, boat, or fish. Imagine area with
buffalo herds (not long ago).
14-day limit.
560 ft (168 m)

BEE ROCK

Daniel Boone NF
(606) 679-2018
State map: H5
From SOMERSET, travel SE on KY 192
about 19 miles (30.4 k) to Rockcastle
River Bridge. Turn Right (S).
FREE so choose a chore.
Open Apr 15–Oct 1.
15 close, open sites.
Pit toilets, tables, fire rings, boat ramp.
In scenic setting with stream and large
boulders.
Hike to Clifftop Overlook and along
river. Fish or boat.
NO water. 14-day limit.

BIG SOUTH FORK NRA (See TN)

BIRMINGHAM FERRY/SMITH BAY

TVA (502) 924-5602
State map: C6
From AURORA, drive
W on US 68 about 6 miles (9.6 k). Turn
Left (N) onto The Trace and go 14 miles
(22.4 k). Turn Left (W) on KY 114 (Old
Ferry Rd) and continue 3.5 miles (5.4 k).
(Also see Kuttawa Landing.)
$5.
Open All Year.
45 scattered, open sites.
Central faucet, chemical toilets, tables,
grills, boat ramp.
In forest environment on Kentucky Lake.
Boat or fish. Watch wildlife.
21-day limit. Hunting in season.
365 ft (110 m)

BOSWELL LANDING

TVA (502) 924-5602
State map: C6
From AURORA, drive
W on US 68 about 6 miles (9.6 k) to The
Trace. Turn Right (S) and go 23 miles
(36.8 k). Turn Right (W) on KY 230 (Fort

▲ ▲

Henry Rd) and travel 7 miles (11.2 k).
Turn Right (N) on KY 233 and continue
2 miles (3.2 k). (Also see Gatlin Point.
Nearby Piney costs $10.)
$5.
Open All Year.
23 scattered, open sites.
Central faucet, chemical toilets, tables,
grills, boat ramp.
On Kentucky Lake in woods.
Fish or boat.
21-day limit.
365 ft (110 m)

BRIER CREEK

COE (502) 286-4511
State map: E5
From BEE SPRING,
drive S on KY 259 to KY 728. Turn Left
(E) and cross dam. Go about 4 miles
(6.4 k). Turn Left (N) on CR 1827 and
follow signs another 4 miles (6.4 k).
(Nearby Dog Creek costs $8.)
FREE so choose a chore.
Open All Year.
30 close, screened sites.
Central faucet, pit toilets, tables, fire
rings, boat ramp.
In forested area next to Nolin Lake.
Boat, swim, ski, or fish. Watch wildlife.
14-day limit.
560 ft (168 m)

CAVE CREEK

COE (502) 257-2061
State map: E4
From SHORT CREEK,
travel N on KY 79 about 5 miles (8 k).
Turn Right (E) on CR 736 and drive
1 mile (1.6 k).
FREE so choose a chore.
Open All Year.
86 close, open sites.
Central faucet, pit toilets, tables, fire
rings, boat ramp.
In woods next to backwaters of Rough
River Lake.
Boat or fish.
14-day limit.
530 ft (159 m)

CLAYLICK BOAT-IN

Daniel Boone NF
(606) 784-6428
State map: I3
From FARMERS, take KY 801 SE for
10 miles (16 k). Turn Right (S) on
KY 1274. Drive 1.5 miles (2.4 k). Turn
Right (W) on Claylick Rd. Go 1.5 miles
(2.4 k) to ramp. Boat 400 ft (122 m) W.
(Also see Clear Creek. Nearby Twin
Knobs and Zilpo cost $6-12.)
FREE so choose a chore.
Open All Year.
20 scattered, screened, tent sites.
Chemical toilets, tables, grills, fire rings.
On remote, wooded hillside on Cave
Run Lake.
Swim, boat, waterski, or fish. View
wildlife.
NO water. 14-day limit.
800 ft (240 m)

CLEAR CREEK

Daniel Boone NF
(606) 784-6428
State map: I3
From SALT LICK, travel S on KY 211 for
4 miles (6.4 k). Turn Left (E) on FR 129
and continue 2 miles (3.2 k). (Also see
Claylick Boat-In.)
$5.
Open Apr–Oct.
21 scattered, screened, tent sites.
Central faucet, chemical toilets, tables,
fire rings, grills, boat ramp.
Under trees next to stream. Near small
lake and ruins of old iron furnace.
Hike parts of Sheltowee National
Recreation Trail. Enjoy scenic area. Bike.
Swim or boat.
14-day limit. Hunting in season.
800 ft (240 m)

CRAVENS BAY

TVA (502) 924-5602
State map: C6
From AURORA, drive
W on US 68 about 6 miles (9.6 k). Turn
Left (N) on The Trace and go about
16 miles (25.6 k). Turn Right (E) on
KY 117 and drive 2 miles (3.2 k).

▲ ▲

Continue on KY 118 for 3 miles (4.8 k).
(Nearby Hillman Ferry costs $10.)
$5.
Open All Year.
26 scattered, open sites.
Central faucet, flush toilets, showers,
tables, grills, boat ramp.
In woods next to Lake Barkley.
Boat or fish. View wildlife.
21-day limit. Hunting in season.
365 ft (110 m)

CUMBERLAND GAP NHP
Backcountry

(606) 258-2817
State map: I6
Reach park by taking
US 25 E from Kentucky and Tennessee
or US 58 from Virginia. The Visitor
Center is .25 mile (.4 k) S of
MIDDLESBORO, KY on US 25 E.
Obtain **FREE** backcountry permit.
Undesignated open sites.
Near mountain pass in wilderness that
became continental gateway to West.
Explore forested area as did Daniel
Boone.
Snakes. Poison ivy and poison oak.

DENUMBERS BAY

TVA (502) 924-5602
State map: C5
From GRAND
RIVERS, drive 3.5 miles (5.4 k) S on The
Trace. Turn Left (E) on KY 108 and
proceed 2 miles (3.2 k). (Also see Pisgah
Point and Star Camp.)
FREE so choose a chore.
Open All Year.
Undesignated scattered, open sites.
Chemical toilets, tables, boat ramp.
In woods on Lake Barkley.
Fish or boat. Watch wildlife.
NO water. 21-day limit. Hunting in
season.
365 ft (110 m)

DEVIL'S ELBOW

TVA (502) 924-5602
State map: C6
From AURORA, drive

W on US 68 about 10 miles (16 k). Turn
Right (S) at sign.
FREE so choose a chore.
Open All Year.
Undesignated scattered, open sites.
Chemical toilets, boat ramp, fishing pier.
In forest on Lake Barkley.
Fish, boat, or waterski.
NO water. 21-day limit.
365 ft (110 m)

EDDY CREEK

COE (502) 362-4236
State map: C5
From EDDYVILLE,
take KY 93 S for 5 miles (8 k) to marina.
Find campground behind marina.
(Nearby Hurricane Creek coats $9.)
FREE so choose a chore.
Open All Year.
15 close, screened sites.
Central faucet, flush toilets, showers,
tables, fire rings, grills, boat ramp.
In heavy woods on shore of Lake
Barkley.
Swim, boat, ski, or fish.
14-day limit. Crowded holiday
weekends.
425 ft (128 m)

FALL CREEK

COE (606) 348-6042
State map: G5
Take KY 1275 N for
12 miles (19.2 k) from MONTICELLO.
Turn Left on Fall Creek Rd and follow
signs. (Nearby Cumberland Point costs
$12.)
FREE so choose a chore. reservations
accepted at (606) 679-6337 for an
additional $5.
Open May 14–Sep 30.
10 close, screened sites. ♿
Central faucet, flush toilets, showers,
dump station, tables, grills, boat ramp.
Under trees beside Lake Cumberland.
Boat, ski, or fish. Enjoy pleasant
surroundings.
14-day limit.

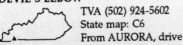

▲ ▲

FENTON

TVA (502) 924-5602
State map: C6
From AURORA, drive
W on US 68 about 2 miles (3.2 k)–just
past the Kentucky Lake bridge.
$5. Open All Year.
28 scattered, open sites.
Central faucet, chemical toilets, electric
hookups, tables, grills, boat ramp.
In forested area next to Kentucky Lake.
Fish or boat. View wildlife.
21-day limit. Hunting in season.
365 ft (110 m)

GATLIN POINT

TVA (502) 924-5602
State map: C6
From AURORA, drive
W on US 68 about 6 miles (9.6 k) to The
Trace. Turn Right (S) and go 22 miles
(35.2 k). Turn Left (E) on 277 and
continue 4 miles (6.4 k). (Also see
Birmingham Ferry/Smith Bay.)
$5.
Open All Year.
19 scattered, open sites.
Central faucet, chemical toilets, tables,
grills, boat ramp.
In woods on Lake Barkley.
Fish or boat. Watch wildlife.
21-day limit. Hunting in season.
365 ft (110 m)

GERMAN BRIDGE

COE (606) 847-9121
State map: J4
Take KY 1428 E from
PRESTONSBURG to KY 194. Turn Left
(N) and drive to bridge.
FREE so choose a chore.
Open All Year.
44 close, open sites. ♿
Central faucet, flush toilets, showers,
dump station, tables, fire rings, grills,
boat ramp, playground, laundry.
In remote, wooded setting along Dewey
Lake.
Swim, boat, or fish. Hike.
14-day limit.
655 ft (197 m)

GINGER BAY

TVA (502) 924-5602
State map: C6
From S tip of The
Trace at US 79, head N for 11 miles
(17.6 k). Turn Left (W) on KY 211 and go
4.5 miles (7.2 k). (Also see Neville Bay.)
FREE so choose a chore.
Open All Year.
13 scattered, open sites.
Chemical toilets, tables, grills, boat ramp.
In forest on Kentucky Lake.
Boat or fish. Spot wildlife.
NO water. 21-day limit. Hunting in
season.
365 ft (110 m)

GREAT MEADOWS

Daniel Boone NF
(606) 376-5323
State map: H6
From STEARNS, head W on KY 92 for
6 miles (9.6 k). Turn Left (S) on KY 1363
and drive 12 miles (19.2 k). Turn Left on
gravel FR 137 and proceed 5 miles (8 k).
FREE so choose a chore.
Open Mar 15–Nov 30; dry camping
allowed off-season.
20 close, open, tent sites.
Central faucet, pit toilets, tables, grills,
fire rings.
In remote woods with large field plus
trout stream.
Hike to view wildlife. Access Sheltowee
Trace National Recreation Trail. Swim or
fish. Take photos.
No trash arrangements (pack it out).
14-day limit.
1000 ft (300 m)

GROVE BOAT-IN

Daniel Boone NF
(606) 864-4163
State map: H5
From CORBIN interchange on I-75,
travel W on US 25W for 5 miles (8 k).
Turn Right (NW) on KY 1193 and drive
2 miles (3.2 k). Turn Right (NE) on
FR 558 and go 4 miles 96.4 k) to ramp.
Boat .5 mile (800 m). (Also see
Rockcastle. Nearby Grove costs $7.)

▲ ▲

$5.
Open All Year.
31 scattered, screened, tent sites.
Central faucet, chemical toilets, tables,
fire rings.
Under trees with all sites next to
6000-acre Laurel River Lake.
Swim, boat, waterski, or fish.
14-day limit.
1040 ft (312 m)

KINGDOM COME SP

(606) 589-2479
State map: J5
Locate park off US 119
near CUMBERLAND.
$5.
Open Apr 1–Oct 31; dry camping
allowed off-season.
4 close, open, tent sites.
Central faucet, flush toilets, tables, grills,
shelter, playground, miniature golf.
In beautiful, wooded park.
Hike to enjoy vistas of Kentucky's
highest park. Take photos of Log Rock
and Raven Rock. Fish or paddleboat.
Cars only.
2700 ft (810 m)

KOOMER RIDGE

Daniel Boone NF
(606) 663-2852
State map: I4
From SLADE, drive SE on KY 15 for
5 miles (8 k).
$5.
Open May 25–Oct 10; dry camping
allowed off-season.
57 (38 tent-only) close, open sites. ♿
Central faucet, pit toilets, tables, fire
rings.
Next to Red River Gorge Geological
Area with its fantastic sandstone
formations (arches, lighthouses, and
shelters) plus forest, streams, and
waterfalls.
Hike Koomer Ridge, Silvermine Arch,
and Hidden Arch trails to join 36-mile
(57.6-k) network. Attend ranger
programs.
14-day limit.

KUTTAWA LANDING

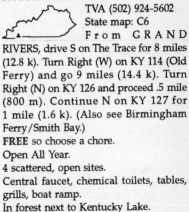

TVA (502) 924-5602
State map: C6
From GRAND
RIVERS, drive S on The Trace for 8 miles
(12.8 k). Turn Right (W) on KY 114 (Old
Ferry) and go 9 miles (14.4 k). Turn
Right (N) on KY 126 and proceed .5 mile
(800 m). Continue N on KY 127 for
1 mile (1.6 k). (Also see Birmingham
Ferry/Smith Bay.)
FREE so choose a chore.
Open All Year.
4 scattered, open sites.
Central faucet, chemical toilets, tables,
grills, boat ramp.
In forest next to Kentucky Lake.
Fish or boat. Spot wildlife.
21-day limit. Hunting in season.
365 ft (110 m)

LITTCARR

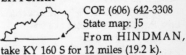

COE (606) 642-3308
State map: J5
From HINDMAN,
take KY 160 S for 12 miles (19.2 k).
FREE at 6 only; others $8 developed; $10
electric; reservations accepted at (606)
642-3308 for an additional $2.
Open May 14–Sep 13.
34 (6 tent-only) close, open sites. ♿
Water, flush toilets, showers, dump
station, electric hookups, tables, fire
rings.
In woods next to Carr Fork Lake.
Swim, boat, or fish.
14-day limit.
1010 ft (303 m)

MAMMOTH CAVE NP

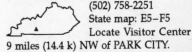

(502) 758-2251
State map: E5–F5
Locate Visitor Center
9 miles (14.4 k) NW of PARK CITY.
FREE.
On top of second-longest known cave
system in world, find limestone
landscape covered with oak-hickory
forests.
Take cave tours from Visitor Center
($3.50–8.00).

▲ ▲

▲ Backcountry

At MAMMOTH CAVE Visitor Center, obtain permit and map. Walk to various sites or stop along floodplains at least .5 mile (800 m) from developed campgrounds.

Open All Year.

12 scattered, screened, tent sites.

No trash arrangements (pack it out).

▲ Dennison Ferry

From MAMMOTH CAVE Visitor Center, take Flint Ridge Rd E about 7 miles (11.2 k).

Open Mar–Nov.

4 close, open sites.

Chemical toilets, tables, grills.

On remote S bank of Green River where ferry used to run.

Hike. Observe wildlife.

NO water. 14-day limit. No large vehicles.

▲ Houchins Ferry

From BROWNSVILLE, take Houchins Ferry Rd N about 3 miles (4.8 k).

.pen Mar–Nov.

12 close, open sites.

Central faucet, flush toilets, tables, fire rings, boat ramp, shelter.

On Green River next to operating ferry. Hike.

14-day limit. No large vehicles.

NEVILLE BAY

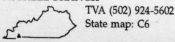

TVA (502) 924-5602
State map: C6
From S tip of The Trace at US 79, head N about 10 miles (16 k). Turn Right (E) on KY 214. Drive 2 miles (3.2 k). (Also see Ginger Bay.)

FREE so choose a chore.

Open All Year.

Undesignated scattered, open sites.

Chemical toilets, tables, boat ramp.

In forest next to Lake Barkley.

Boat, ski, or fish.

NO water. 21-day limit.

365 ft (110 m)

NICKELL BRANCH

TVA (502) 924-5602
State map: C6

From AURORA, drive W on US 68 about 6 miles (9.6 k) to The Trace. Turn Left (N) and go 24.5 miles (39.2 k). Turn Right (E) on KY 102 and proceed 2 miles (3.2 k). (Also see Twin Lakes.)

$5.

Open All Year.

13 scattered, open sites.

Central faucet, chemical toilets, tables, grills, boat ramp.

In woods on Lake Barkley.

Fish or boat. Watch wildlife.

21-day limit. Hunting in season.

365 ft (110 m)

PIKE RIDGE

COE (502) 465-4463
State map: G5
Head E on KY 70 about 3 miles (4.8 k) from CAMPBELLSVILLE. Turn Right (SE) on KY 76 and drive about 2.5 miles (4 k). Turn Right (SW) at sign on Pike Ridge Rd and go about 5 miles (8 k) to end of road. (Also see ATV Area.)

FREE so choose a chore.

Open All Year.

28 scattered, open sites.

Central faucet, pit toilets, tables, fire rings, boat ramp.

In meadow along shore of Green River Lake.

Hike to view wildlife. Swim, boat, or fish.

14-day limit. Hunting in season. Crowded holidays.

685 ft (206 m)

PISGAH POINT

TVA (502) 924-5602
State map: C5
From GRAND RIVERS, drive 5 miles (8 k) S on The Trace. Turn on KY 111 and go 1.5 miles (2.4 k). (Also see Denumbers Bay and Star Camp.)

FREE so choose a chore.

Open All Year.

Undesignated scattered, open sites.

Chemical toilets, tables, grills, boat ramp.

In woods on lake.

▲ ▲

Boat, ski, or fish. Observe wildlife.
NO water. 21-day limit.
365 ft (110 m)

REDD HOLLOW

 TVA (502) 924-5602
State map: C6
From AURORA, drive
W on US 68 about 6 miles (9.6 k). Turn
Right (S) on The Trace and go 6 miles
(9.6 k). Turn Right (W) on KY 171 and
continue 3 miles (4.8 k).
$5.
Open All Year.
39 scattered, open sites.
Central faucet, chemical toilets, tables,
grills, boat ramp.
In forest next to Kentucky Lake.
Fish or boat. Watch wildlife.
21-day limit.
365 ft (110 m)

ROCKCASTLE

 Daniel Boone NF
(606) 864-4163
State map: H5
From LONDON interchange on I-75, go
SW on KY 192 for 14 miles (22.4 k). Turn
Left (S) on KY 1193 and drive 1 mile
(1.6 k). Continue on KY 3497 for 6 miles
(9.6 k). (Also see Grove Boat-In and
Whiteoak Boat-In.)
$5.
Open Apr 15–Oct 31.
16 scattered, screened, tent sites.
Central faucet, pit toilets, tables, fire
rings, boat ramp, marina, rentals.
In woods at mouth of Rockcastle River
and Lake Cumberland.
Walk to scenic overlooks. Swim, boat,
ski, or fish.
14-day limit.
850 ft (255 m)

RODBURN HOLLOW

Daniel Boone NF
(606) 784-6428
State map: I3
From MOREHEAD, drive NE on US 60
for 2 miles (3.2 k). Turn Left (N) on
Rodburn Hollow Rd.

$5. Open Apr–Oct.
12 close, screened sites.
Central faucet, flush toilets, tables, grills,
fire rings.
In narrow, wooded valley with stream.
Enjoy quiet. Walk nature trail. Hike
nearby Sheltowee National Recreation
Trail.
14-day limit.
800 ft (240 m)

S-TREE

 Daniel Boone NF
(606) 986-8431
State map: I4
From MCKEE, take US 421 W about
1 mile (1.6 k). Turn Left (S) on KY 89
and go 3 miles (4.8 k). Turn Right (W)
on dirt FR 43 for 1 mile (1.6 k). Turn Left
(S) on FR 20 and follow signs. (Also see
Turkey Foot.)
FREE so choose a chore.
Open Mar 15–Nov 15; camping allowed
off-season.
20 close, screened sites.
Pit toilets, tables, grills, fire rings.
In remote forest setting on top of hill at
old fire tower site.
Hike to view wildlife. Walk Sheltowee
National Recreation Trail. Mountain
bike.
NO water. No trash arrangements (pack
it out). 14-day limit. Small vehicles only.
Hunting in season.
1440 ft (432 m)

SAWYER

Daniel Boone NF
(606) 679-2018
State map: H6
From PARKERS LAKE, drive NE on
KY 896 about 12 miles (19.2 k).
FREE so choose a chore.
Open All Year.
6 close, open sites.
Central faucet, pit toilets, tables, fire
rings, boat ramp.
On backwaters of Lake Cumberland with
lake and cliff views.
Boat or fish.
14-day limit.

▲ ▲

STAR CAMP

TVA (502) 924-5602
State map: C5
From GRAND
RIVERS, drive 4 miles (6.4 k) S on The
Trace. (Also see Denumbers Bay and
Pisgah Point.)
FREE so choose a chore.
Open All Year.
10 scattered, open sites.
Chemical toilets, tables, grills.
In woods at picnic area.
Relax.
NO water. 21-day limit.
365 ft (110 m)

SUGAR BAY

TVA (502) 924-5602
State map: C6
From AURORA, drive
W on US 68 about 6 miles (9.6 k) to The
Trace. Turn Left (N) and go 5 miles (8 k).
Turn Left (E) on KY 140 and travel
3 miles (4.8 k).
$5.
Open All Year.
18 scattered, open sites.
Central faucet, chemical toilets, tables,
grills, boat ramp.
In woods on Kentucky Lake.
Boat or fish. Watch wildlife.
21-day limit. Hunting in season.
365 ft (110 m)

TAILWATER

COE (502) 646-2055
State map: C6
From HAYWOOD, go
W on KY 252 about 10 miles (16 k) and
cross dam. Turn Right. (Also see Beaver
Creek. Nearby Bailey's Point costs $6.)
$5; reservations accepted at (502)
646-2055.
Open All Year.
48 close, open sites.
Central faucet, pit toilets, tables, fire
rings, grills, boat ramp.
With some shade below dam on Barren
River.
Canoe. Swim, boat, or fish. Attend
ranger programs.

14-day limit.
520 ft (156 m)

TAYLOR BAY

TVA (502) 924-5602
State map: C6
From AURORA, drive
W on US 68 about 6 miles (9.6 k) to The
Trace. Turn Left (N) and go 10 miles
(16 k). Turn Right (E) on Mulberry Flat
Rd and continue 8 miles (12.8 k).
$5.
Open All Year.
35 scattered, open sites.
Central faucet, chemical toilets, tables,
grills, boat ramp.
In woods next to Lake Barkley.
Fish or boat. Watch wildlife.
21-day limit. Hunting in season.
365 ft (110 m)

TRACE BRANCH

COE (606) 398-7251
State map: J5
From CHAVIES, drive
S on KY 451 about 5 miles (8 k). Turn
Right (SW) on Campbell Creek Rd and
go 3 miles (4.8 k).
FREE so choose a chore.
Open All Year.
15 scattered, open sites. ♿
Central faucet, chemical toilets, tables,
fire rings, grills, boat ramp.
Next to backwater of Buckhorn Lake.
Boat or fish.
14-day/21-ft limits.
850 ft (255 m)

TURKEY FOOT

Daniel Boone NF
(606) 986-8431
State map: I4
From MCKEE, travel N on KY 89 for
3 miles (4.8 k). Turn Right (E) on FR 4
and go 3 miles (4.8 k). (Also see S-Tree.)
FREE so choose a chore.
Open Mar 15–Nov 15; camping allowed
off-season.
15 close, screened sites.
Pit toilets, tables, grills, fire rings.
Under oak trees along stream that

▲ ▲

disappears into sinkhole in dry season. Hike Sheltowee National Recreation Trail. Mountain bike. Relax.

NO water. No trash arrangements (pack it out). 14-day limit. Occasional ATV and day-use noise.

875 ft (263 m)

TWIN LAKES

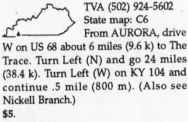

TVA (502) 924-5602
State map: C6
From AURORA, drive W on US 68 about 6 miles (9.6 k) to The Trace. Turn Left (N) and go 24 miles (38.4 k). Turn Left (W) on KY 104 and continue .5 mile (800 m). (Also see Nickell Branch.)

$5.

Open All Year.

17 scattered, open sites.

Central faucet, chemical toilets, tables, grills, boat ramp.

In woods next to Kentucky Lake.

Boat or fish. View wildlife.

21-day limit. Hunting in season.

365 ft (110 m)

WHITEOAK BOAT-IN

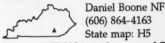

Daniel Boone NF
(606) 864-4163
State map: H5
From LONDON interchange on I-75, go SW on KY 192 for 12 miles (19.2 k). Turn Left (S) on FR 774 and go 2 miles (3.2 k) to Marsh Branch ramp. Boat .5 mile (800 m). (Also see Rockcastle. Nearby Holly Bay costs $7.)

$5.

Open All Year.

51 scattered, screened, tent sites.

Central faucet, chemical toilets, tables, fire rings.

In remote wooded setting with all sites next to Laurel River Lake.

Enjoy quiet. Swim, boat, ski, or fish. Hike.

14-day limit.

1040 ft (312 m)

▲ ▲

LOUISIANA
CAMPGROUND LOCATIONS

▸ ▸ Find location on facing page map grid. ▸ ▸
▼ ▼ Locate area campgrounds on these page numbers. ▼ ▼

GRID	PAGE
B1	175
B2	175, 178
B3	175
C1	177
C3	175, 176
D2	175
D3	176, 177
D4	178
E3	176
E4	176, 178
F3	176, 178, 179
F5	178
F7	177
G2	177
G8	177

Louisiana

Grid conforms to official state map. For your copy, call (800) 33-GUMBO
or write Office of Tourism, PO Box 94291, Baton Rouge, LA 70804-9291.

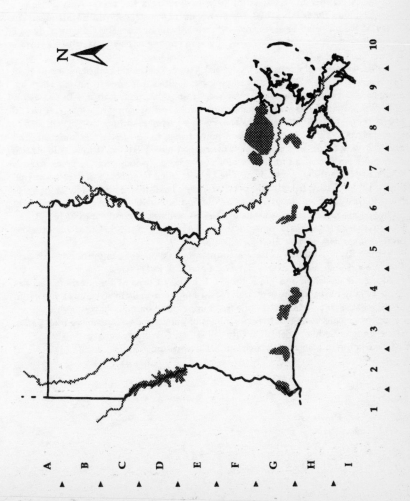

PUBLIC LANDS CAMPING

Louisiana is really cookin'! Of course, you think of New Orleans with its smoking jazz bars and its soul-searing creole restaurants. There's more, however, to what's cookin' in Louisiana. To enjoy Louisiana's true nature, there's fishing, tubing, canoeing, hunting, hiking, backpacking and, of course, camping.

Thirteen **Louisiana State Parks** (SP) offer camping: Bayou Segnette, Chemin-A-Haut, Chicot, Fairview Riverside, Fontainebleau, Grand Isle, Lake Bistineau, Lake Bruin, Lake Claiborne, Lake Fausse Pointe, North Toledo Bend, Sam Houston Jones, and Saint Bernard. Most of these sites cost $12.00 whether you use the utilities or not. During April through September, state parks stay open from 7am–10pm to make camping easy. October through March, the parks open at 8am and close at 7pm.

In the **Alexander State Forest** (SF), the Indian Creek Recreation Area (RA)offers developed sites for $6.00–$11.00. Facilities vary in the state's **Wildlife Management Areas** (WMA). These free areas are used primarily by hunters and fishermen. Be sure to follow safe and sanitary procedures. If you're hunting or fishing, purchase a current license.

Kisatchie National Forest (NF), over 500,000 acres in central Louisiana, lies in eight patches near the Red River with camping possibilities from free to $10.00. There are swamps and bayous, pine and hardwood forests. A surprising area is the Kisatchie Hills Wilderness, 8,700 acres of sandstone bluffs and outcroppings that you would expect to see out West, not in Louisiana. Further surprises include the vegetation: sun dew, colicroot (a lily), indigo, yaupon holly, fringe tree.... Drive the Longleaf Trail Scenic Byway, a 17-mile road through the rugged hills. Hike the 31-mile Wild Azalea National Recreation Trail for views of snow-white dogwoods and wild pink azaleas from mid-March through mid-April. The 7.6-mile Sugar Cane National Recreation Trail circles Upper Caney Lake in the popular Caney Lakes Recreation Area. 19 miles of Saline Bayou has been designated as a Wild and Scenic River, though it is a peaceful setting popular with canoeists for its mysterious qualities. Around the Kisatchie's lakes, look up to bald eagles; in its pines, listen for the threatened red-cockaded woodpecker; on its calm waters, look around for alligators.

Sabine River Authority offers a couple of $5.00-or-less campgrounds. Around Toledo Bend, seek out Converse Bay Site 4 and Oak Ridge Site 2.

Along the Ouachita and Black Rivers, **US Army Corps of Engineers** (COE) has created many recreation areas though most campgrounds lie in Arkansas territory. In Louisiana, the corps administers one free campground on quiet Bayou Bodcau.

Too, when considering all the possibilities of public lands, remember **parish parks**. There's one in Caddo Parish's Oil City called Earl G Williamson.

Go camping in Louisiana. Search out her true nature.

▲ ▲

CANEY LAKES

Kisatchie NF (318) 927-2061
State map: B2
From MINDEN, take
LA 159 N to Parish Road
111. Turn Left (W). Drive 2 miles (3.2 k).
$5; $10 electric.
Open Apr 15–Sep 30; dry camping
allowed off-season.
48 scattered, open sites.
Central faucet, flush toilets, showers,
dump station, electric hookups, tables,
grills, boat ramp, pay phone.
In wooded hills with access to 125-acre
upper lake and 250-acre lower lake.
Swim, boat, ski, or fish. Walk Sugar
Cane National Recreation Trail.
14-day limit.

CLOUD CROSSING

Kisatchie NF (318) 628-4664
State map: C3
From GOLDONNA, take
LA 156 SE for 2.5 miles
(4 k). Turn Left (N) on LA 1233. Go to
FR 513. Turn Left (W) and follow signs.
FREE so choose a chore.
Open All Year.
13 scattered, open sites.
Hand pump, pit toilets, tables, fire rings,
grills, boat ramp.
In large-timbered bottomland next to
Saline Bayou National Wild and Scenic
River.
Canoe (check water level first). Fish.
Hike.
Hunting in season.
120 ft (36 m)

CONVERSE BAY-SITE 4

Sabine River Authority
(318) 645-6748
State map: D2
From CONVERSE, drive W
on LA 174 about 5 miles (8 k). Follow
signs. (Also see Oak Ridge.)
FREE so choose a chore.
Open All Year.
Undesignated scattered, open sites.
Central faucet, flush toilets, showers,
tables, grills, boat ramp, playground.

In woods at north end of Toledo Bend
Reservoir.
Enjoy scenic surroundings. Swim, fish,
and boat. Observe wildlife.

CORNEY LAKE

Kisatchie NF (318) 927-2061
State map: B3
From HOMER, travel NE
on LA 9 for 18 miles
(28.8 k). Turn Right (SE) at signs.
FREE so choose a chore.
Open All Year.
8 scattered, open sites.
Central faucet, pit toilets, tables, grills,
boat ramp.
Next to beautiful 2300-acre lake with
bald cypress-tupelo bottomland and
pine-covered hills.
Boat or fish. Relax.
14-day limit. Hunting in season.

DOGWOOD

Kisatchie NF (318) 352-2568
State map: D2
From HAGEWOOD, drive S
on LA 117 for 16 miles
(25.6 k). (Also see Kisatchie Bayou and
Lotus.)
FREE so choose a chore.
Open All Year.
20 close, open sites.
Central faucet, flush toilets, tables, fire
rings.
Under large pine with dogwood and
other hardwood.
Hike. Observe wildlife. Relax.
14-day limit.

EARL G WILLIAMSON PARK

Caddo Parish Parks
(318) 995-7139
State map: B1
On S side of OIL CITY, find
park at 11425 LA 1.
$4; $8 RV.
Open All Year.
18 close, open sites.
Water at 10 sites, flush toilets, showers,
dump station, electric hookups, tables,
fire rings, grills, boat ramp, pier, pay

phone.
Along Caddo Lake with beautiful
sunsets.
Swim, boat, or fish. View wildlife. Bike.
14-day limit.
200 ft (60 m)

EVANGELINE WALK-IN

Kisatchie NF (318) 445-9396
State map: E4
From ALEXANDRIA, drive
W on LA 28 for 8 miles
(12.8 k). Turn Left (SW) on FR 273 and
go 4 miles (6.4 k). Park at Wild Azalea
trailhead and walk about 200 yds
(200 m) to select site. (Also see Valentine
Lake. Nearby Kincaid RA costs $10.)
FREE so choose a chore.
Open All Year.
Undesignated scattered, screened sites.
Hand pump, pit toilets.
Along 31-mile (49.6 k) Wild Azalea
National Recreation Trail with dogwood,
azalea, pine, and hardwood.
Hike. Observe wildlife. Take photos.
No trash arrangements (pack it out).

FULLERTON LAKE RA

Kisatchie NF (318) 239-6576
State map: E3
From PICKERING, drive E
on LA 10 for 16 miles
(25.6 k). Turn Left (N) on LA 399 and
continue 3 miles (4.8 k). Turn Left (W)
on FR 427 at post office.
FREE so choose a chore.
Open All Year.
9 close, screened sites.
Central faucet, flush/pit toilets, tables,
grills, fire rings.
At site of old logging town in remote
setting.
Enjoy quiet. Hike around lake to view
logging remains. Fish.
14-day limit. Hunting in season.

GUM SPRINGS

Kisatchie NF (318) 628-4664
State map: C3
From WINNFIELD, drive W
on US 84 for 8 miles

(12.8 k). Turn Left (S) at signs.
FREE so choose a chore.
Open All Year.
13 close, open sites.
Central faucet, pit toilets, tables, fire
rings.
In pine-hardwood hills.
Use as getaway.
14-day limit. Hunting in season.

HIGHWAY 26 CAMPSITE

LA Wildlife & Fisheries
(318) 491-2575
State map: F3
From OBERLIN, drive W on
LA 26 for 5 miles (8 k). Turn Right (N).
FREE so choose a chore.
Open All Year.
30 scattered, open sites.
Hand pump.
In pine forest.
Walk nature trail or hike farther.
Observe wildlife.
No toilet facilities. No trash
arrangements (pack it out). Hunting in
season.
150 ft (45 m)

KISATCHIE BAYOU

Kisatchie NF (318) 352-2568
State map: D3
From HAGEWOOD, drive S
on LA 117 for 16 miles
(25.6 k). Turn Left (E) on FH 59
(Longleaf Trail) and travel 7 miles
(11.2 k). Turn Right (S) on FR 321 and
continue 4 miles (6.4 k). Turn Right (W)
on FR 366 and go to end of road. (Also
see Dogwood and Lotus.)
FREE so choose a chore.
Open All Year.
18 (17 tent-only) close, open sites.
Central faucet, pit toilets, tables, fire
rings.
In mixed hardwood-pine ecology next to
Kisatchie Bayou with bluffs, white sand
beaches, and rocky rapids.
Canoe. Fish. Hike. Do nothing.
14-day limit.

▲ ▲

LOTUS

Kisatchie NF (318) 352-2568
State map: D3
From HAGEWOOD, drive S
on LA 117 for 16 miles
(25.6 k). Turn Left (E) on FH 59
(Longleaf Trail). Proceed 4 miles (6.4 k).
Turn Right (S) at sign. (Also see
Dogwood, Kisatchie Bayou, and Red
Bluff Walk-In.)
FREE so choose a chore.
Open All Year.
Undesignated scattered, open sites.
Central faucet, chemical toilets, tables,
fire rings.
In upland hardwoods near National Red
Dirt Wildlife Management Preserve.
Observe wildlife.
14-day limit. Hunting in season.

NIBLETT'S BLUFF PARK

(318) 589-7117
State map: G2
From TOOMEY, drive N on
LA 109 for 3 miles (4.8 k).
Turn Left (W) on Niblett's Bluff Park
and go another 3 miles (4.8 k).
$5; $10 electric.
Open All Year.
48 close, open sites.
Central faucet, flush toilets, showers,
dump station, electric hookups, tables,
grills, playground, shelter, laundry, pay
phone.
Under tall pine trees at site of Civil War
fort on Sabine River.
Tour historical ruins. Relax.

OAK RIDGE-SITE 2

Sabine River Authority
(318) 872-1177
State map: C1
From STANLEY, drive S on
LA 191 to Sportsmans Corner. Turn
Right (W) and follow signs. (Also see
Converse Bay-Site 4.)
FREE so choose a chore.
Open All Year.
Undesignated scattered, open sites.
Central faucet, flush toilets, showers,
tables, grills, boat ramp, playground.

In beautiful, wooded setting on Toledo
Bend Reservoir.
Swim, boat, and fish. Take photos.

PEARL RIVER WMA

LA Wildlife & Fisheries
(504) 765-2360
State map: G8
From SLIDELL, drive N on
US 11 to just pass I-12. Turn Right (E) on
Brownswitch Rd and go 3 miles (4.8 k).
Turn Right on Military Hwy and drive
to I-10 frontage road. Turn Left and go
to end.
FREE so choose a chore.
Open All Year.
Undesignated scattered, open sites.
Chemical toilets, boat ramp.
In open area under large oak next to
river.
Boat or fish. Walk nature trail. View
wildlife.
NO water. No trash arrangements (pack
it out). Hunting in season.
10 ft (3 m)

RED BLUFF WALK-IN

Kisatchie NF (318) 352-2568
State map: D3
From HAGEWOOD, drive S
on LA 117 for 16 miles
(25.6 k). Turn Left (E) on FH 59
(Longleaf Trail) and travel 4.5 miles
(7.2 k). Turn Left (N) on FR 345 and
continue 2.5 miles (4 k). Walk-in about
.25 mile (400 m). (Also see Lotus.)
FREE so choose a chore.
Open All Year.
Undesignated scattered, open sites.
Pit toilets, tables, fire rings.
On lower stretch of Kisatchie Bayou.
Fish. Observe wildlife.
NO water. No trash arrangements (pack
it out). 14-day limit.

SANDY HOLLOW WMA

LA Wildlife & Fisheries
(504) 765-2360
State map: F7
From ARCOLA, take LA 10
E for 6 miles (9.6 k). Turn Left (N) on

gravel road with sign and drive to end.
Turn Left into headquarters and camp
on Left.
FREE so choose a chore.
Open All Year.
10 scattered, open sites.
Central faucet, flush toilets.
In open area under oak.
Relax. Hike.
No trash arrangements (pack it out).
Hunting in season. Crowded Nov (quail
day field trials).
150 ft (45 m)

SHERBURNE WMA

LA Wildlife & Fisheries
(318) 948-0255
State map: F5
From KROTZ SPRINGS,
head E on US 190 crossing Atchafalaya
River. Turn Right (S) on gravel CR 975
and drive 2 miles (3.2 k).
FREE so choose a chore.
Open All Year.
Undesignated scattered, open sites.
Central faucet.
On bank of bayou.
Boat or fish. Hike. View wildlife.
No toilet facilities. No trash
arrangements (pack it out). 16-day limit.
Hunting in season. Occasional ATVs.

SPIKES

LA Wildlife & Fisheries
(318) 491-2575
State map: F3
From OAKDALE, travel W
for 3 miles (4.8 k) on LA 10. Turn Left
(S) on gravel River Rd and proceed
7 miles (11.2 k).
FREE so choose a chore.
Open All Year.
40 scattered, open sites.
Hand pump.
In pine forest.
Walk nature trail or hike farther.
Observe wildlife.
No toilet facilities. No trash
arrangements (pack it out). Hunting in
season.
150 ft (45 m)

STUART LAKE

Kisatchie NF (318) 765-3554
State map: D4
From POLLOCK, take LA 8
SW for 1.75 miles (2.8 k).
Head SW on FR 144 for 1.25 miles (2 k).
$5.
Open All Year.
8 close, screened sites.
Central faucet, flush toilets, tables, fire
rings.
In rolling hills with mixed pine and
hardwood next to lake.
Enjoy peaceful setting. Walk nature trail.
Swim and fish.
14-day limit. Hunting in season. No
generators in quiet hours.

TOM MERRILL RA

COE (318) 226-5365
State map: B2
From BELLEVUE, take
Bodcau Dam Rd NE for
3 miles (4.8 k).
FREE so choose a chore.
Open All Year.
20 close, open sites.
Hand pump, flush toilets, tables, grills,
fire rings.
In pine trees next to cypress swamps
and Bayou Bodcau.
Enjoy peaceful setting. Walk nature trail.
Boat or fish. Watch wildlife.
14-day limit. Hunting in season.
200 ft (60 m)

VALENTINE LAKE

Kisatchie NF (318) 445-9396
State map: E4
From GARDNER, head SW
on LA 121 for .25 mile
(400 m). Turn Left (S) on FR 279 and go
1.5 miles (2.4 k). Turn Right (S) on
FR 282. (Also see Evangeline Walk-In.
Nearby Kincaid RA costs $10.)
$5.
Open Apr–Oct.
32 (10 tent-only) scattered, open sites.
Central faucet, flush toilets, showers,
dump station, tables, grills, fire rings.
In pine-hardwood next to 46-acre lake.

▲ ▲

Walk Valentine Loop Trail or hike Wild
Azalea National Recreation Trail. Bike.
Canoe. Swim or fish.
14-day limit.

WOLF BAY

LA Wildlife & Fisheries
(318) 491-2575
State map: F3
From ELIZABETH, drive
SW on LA 112 for 4 miles (6.4 k).
FREE so choose a chore.
Open All Year.
50 scattered, open sites.
Hand pump.
In pine forest.
Hike. Observe wildlife.
No toilet facilities. No trash
arrangements (pack it out). Hunting in
season.
150 ft (45 m)

▲ ▲

MAINE
CAMPGROUND LOCATIONS

▶ ▶ Find location on facing page map grid. ▶ ▶
▼ ▼ Locate area campgrounds on these page numbers. ▼ ▼

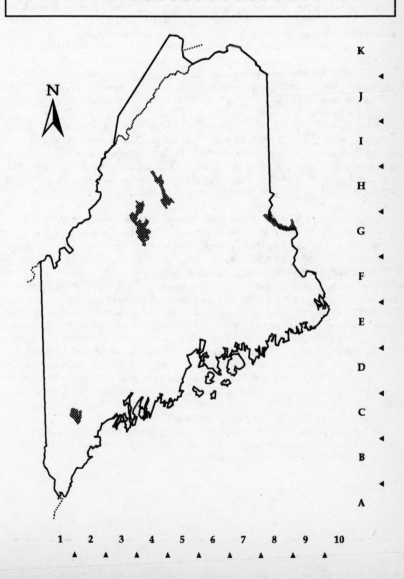

Maine

Grid conforms to official state map. For your copy, call (207) 582-9300
or write Maine Publicity Bureau, PO Box 2300, Hallowell, ME 04347-2300.

PUBLIC LANDS CAMPING

Maine means miles of picturesque coastline, rugged mountains, pure lakes and rivers, and dense woods. Courtesy of Freeport, Maine's L L Bean mail-order catalog, the idea of camping on Maine public lands conjures up many images of ultimate camping experiences.

As one of the few states to offer reduced camping rates to residents in its state parks, Maine charges residents $10.50–$12.00. Non-residents pay $14.00–$16.00. Everyone chips in an additional 7% lodging tax. If you want reservations, they're available for another $2.00 per night fee. Enjoy camping at **Maine State Parks** (SP): Aroostook, Bradbury Mountain, Camden Hills, Cobscook Bay, Lake Saint George, Lamoine, Lily Bay, Mount Blue, Peaks-Kenny, Rangeley Lake, Sebago Lake, and Warren Island.

On the Penobscot River Corridor, Maine residents spend $3.00 per person per night and non-residents $4.00 per person per night. On the 92-mile Allagash Wilderness Waterway, a National Wild and Scenic River, residents pay $4.00 per person per night and non-residents $5.00 per person per night. Groups need reservations. All others can camp on a first-come, first-serve basis.

Self-administered Baxter SP is a 200,000-acre wilderness with "mile-high" Mount Katahdin. Hike over 175 miles of trails. (280 miles of the Appalachian Trail pass through Maine and end at Mount Katahdin in Baxter SP.) Canoe on the many streams, ponds, and lakes within the park or two branches of the Penobscot River creating the east and southwest borders of the park. Camp in developed tent sites or lean-tos at $12.00 per couple. If you bring your vehicle into the park, there's an additional $8.00 daily fee.

White Mountain National Forest (NF) offers spectacular mountain scenery in all seasons. In winter, enjoy 35 miles of trails groomed for snow sports. Camp in developed sites at $8.00 per family. Backpack into more pristine areas such as the Caribou–Speckled Mountain Wilderness.

Acadia National Park (NP), the second most-visited park in the nation, encompasses 35,000 scenic acres, including portions of Mount Desert Island, the Schoodic Peninsula, and Isle au Haut. There are miles of hiking and carriage trails (suitable for cycling) plus scenic drives with lookouts on ocean panoramas. Blackwoods Campground near Otter Creek on Mount Desert Island is open year-round. Rates vary with the seasons. May 15–June 14, pay $10.00; June 15–September 15, pay $12.00; September 16–October 15, pay $10.00. Camping is free here October 16–May 14. At Seawall Campground below Manset and near Bass Harbor, walk-in sites are $7.00 and drive-in sites are $10.00. Seawall is open Memorial Day weekend–September 30. To camp for $5.00 or less involves reservations and ferries. There are five "free" lean-tos ($5.00 reservation fee plus round trip on ferry) at Duck Harbor on Isle au Haut. These popular lean-tos are available from May 15–October 15 each year.

Get lost in the Maine woods–their craggy coastal beauty; their deep, dark interior; their dramatic fall foliage; their winter cross-country skiing and snowshoeing; their spring wildflowers; their summer bounty.

▲ ▲

ACADIA NP–Duck Harbor
(207) 288-3338
State map: C6
From STONINGTON, take
ferry to Isle au Haut.
FREE; reservations advised at
(207) 288-3338 for an additional $5.
Open May 15–Oct 15.
5 scattered, screened tent sites.
Hand pump, pit toilets, fire rings.
On wooded, southern tip of island.
Walk trails to explore ecology. Take lots
of photos.
No trash arrangements (pack it out).
14-day limit. Plan ahead–popular sites!

▲ ▲

MARYLAND
CAMPGROUND LOCATIONS

▶ ▶ Find location on facing page map grid. ▶ ▶
▼ ▼ Locate area campgrounds on these page numbers. ▼ ▼

GRID	PAGE
A2	188
A3	189
A6	187
A7	188
A8	187
A10	187, 188
A13	187
B2	188
B21	187
C3	189
C11	187
L26	187

Maryland

Grid conforms to official state map. For your copy, call (800) 543-1036
or write Office of Tourism, 217 E Redwood St, Baltimore, MD 21202.

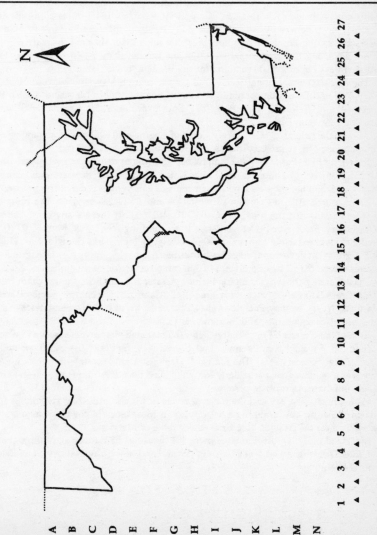

▲ ▲

PUBLIC LANDS CAMPING

More than you can imagine awaits you in Maryland. Find forested mountains, rolling farmland, tidal marshes and surprising cliffs along gigantic Chesapeake Bay, plus white-sand beaches on the Atlantic Ocean.

National Park Service (NPS) administers several sites: Assateague Island National Seashore (NS), Catoctin Mountain Park, Chesapeake and Ohio Canal National Historical Park (NHP), and Greenbelt Park. At Assateague, there are drive-in and walk-in campsites at $8.00 per night plus park entrance fee. Free backcountry permits are also available. At Catoctin Mountain Park, there's a $6.00 campground plus two free Adirondack shelters. On the C&O Canal that stretches 184.5 miles alongside the Potomac River between Washington, DC and Maryland, there are four free first-come, first-serve campgrounds. In addition, there are hiker-biker sites approximately every five miles along the former tow path. Off the Capital Beltway, Greenbelt Park is a wooded park offering $8.00 camping for the Washington, DC area.

The Appalachian National Scenic Trail passes through Maryland between Harpers Ferry, WV and Blue Ridge Summit, PA. Alongside the trail in Maryland, stretch the greenways of Gathland State Park (SP), South Mountain SP, Greenbrier SP, and Catoctin Mountain Park.

Also on the federal level, **US Army Corps of Engineers** (COE) offers camping on the Youghiogheny River project. There's a $4.50 primitive area at Mill Run.

Maryland State Parks (SP)offer "improved" and "unimproved" camping experiences. Although it's hard to improve on Mother Nature, "improved" campgrounds indicate flush toilets and hot showers while "unimproved" campgrounds denote pit toilets and a water source. All sites contain picnic tables and fireplaces or grills. The camping season varies with the weather. Call (301) 461-0052 if there's any doubt about accessibility. From April–October, state park camping fees range from $5.00 (Fort Frederick) and $6.00 (Big Run) to $18.00 (Assateague). Most parks charge at least $10.00 per night with additional fees for hookups. All parks, except Assateague and Susquehanna, charge an additional $4.00 to camp on weekends. In alphabetical order, Maryland state parks with camping include Assateague, Big Run, Cunningham Falls, Deep Creek Lake, Elk Neck, Fort Frederick, Gambrill, Greenbrier, James Island, Martinak, New Germany, Patapsco Valley, Pocomoke River, Point Lookout, Rocky Gap, Smallwood, Susquehanna, and Swallow Falls.

In the **State Forests** (SF), "primitive" sites (no manmade improvements) are available year-round. Savage River, Potomac, and Garrett state forests charge $2.00 per night; Green Ridge SF costs $4.00. The Elk Neck Demonstration Forest, with free camping, serves as a wildlife area, particularly for whitetailed deer. If hunting or using shooting range, purchase appropriate permits.

With Chesapeake Bay and the miles of rivers flowing into the bay, swimming and boating, fishing and crabbing are popular in Maryland. Savor the seasons and seasonings for the Atlantic Blue Crab–the symbol of Maryland.

Maryland proudly posts its state flower, the Black-eyed Susan, on signs throughout the state. These signs alert you to areas of cultural and historic interest as well as scenic natural beauty.

▲ ▲

ASSATEAGUE ISLAND NS
Backcountry

(410) 641-3030
State map: L26
From BERLIN, take
MD 376 SE for 5 miles (8 k). Turn Right
(S) on MD 611 for 3 miles (4.8 k).
Walk-in from 2–12 miles (3.2–19.2 k).
(Nearby Bayside and Oceanside cost $8.)
FREE.
Open All Year.
6 scattered, screened, tent sites.
Pit toilets, tables, fire rings.
With little vegetation among dunes of
Atlantic Ocean barrier island bordered
by Sinepuxent Bay.
Swim. Canoe or boat. Dig for clams or
catch crabs. Hike to explore area. View
wildlife.
NO water. No trash arrangements (pack
it out). 7-day limit. Mosquitos. Crowded
Apr–Oct.
10 ft (3 m)

CATOCTIN MOUNTAIN PARK
Backcountry

NPS (301) 663-9330
State map: A13
From THURMONT, head
W on MD 77 for 3 miles (4.8 k). Obtain
permit at Visitor Center. (Owen's Creek
costs $8.)
FREE.
Open All Year.
2 Adirondack shelters.
In heavily wooded, mountainous park.
Hike. Fish. View wildlife.
NO water. No trash arrangements (pack
it out). 7-day limit. Crowded weekends.

CHESAPEAKE & OHIO CANAL NHP
(301) 739-4200
FREE.
Open All Year.
▲ Backcountry
Find sites about every 5 miles (8 k) along
165-mile (264 k) stretch of canal between
CUMBERLAND and GREAT FALLS.
Undesignated sites.
Hand pump, pit toilets, tables.
Fish. Hike or bike.

No trash arrangements (pack it out).
1-day limit per site.
▲ 15-Mile Creek

State map: A8
From HANCOCK, take
I-68 W for 22 miles
(35.2 k). Exit S on Orleans Rd and travel
6 miles (9.6 k). Turn Right (W).
10 sites.
Central faucet, pit toilets, tables, fire
rings, boat ramp.
Walk or bike tow path. Canoe. Fish.
14-day/20-ft limits.
▲ Antietam Creek

State map: C11
From SHARPSBURG,
drive S on Harpers Ferry
Rd for 3.5 miles (5.6 k). Turn Right (W)
on Canal Rd and go 1 mile (1.6 k). Walk
across bridge to sites.
20 close, open, tent sites.
Hand pump, pit toilets, tables, grills.
Bike or walk tow path. Fish. Watch
wildlife. Visit Civil War battlefield.
14-day limit.
▲ McCoy's Ferry

State map: A10
From BIG SPRING, head
W on MD 56 to McCoy's
Ferry Rd. Turn Left. (Also see Fort
Frederick SP.)
14 close, open sites.
Pit toilets, tables, fire rings, boat ramp.
Hike or bike tow path. Fish.
NO water. 14-day/20-ft limits.
▲ Spring Gap

State map: A6
From CUMBERLAND,
drive S on MD 51 for
8 miles (12.8 k).
19 sites.
Pit toilets, tables, fire rings, boat ramp.
Hike or bike tow path. Fish.
NO water. 14-day/20-ft limits.

ELK NECK DEMONSTRATION FOREST

(410) 287-5675
State map: B21
From NORTH EAST,
take Irishtown Rd E for 1.5 miles (2.4 k)

▲ ▲

to entrance on Left. (Nearby Elk Neck SP costs $10.)
FREE so choose a chore.
Open All Year.
20 scattered, open sites.
Central faucet, pay phone.
In wooded area.
Hike to view wildlife and take photos.
No toilet facilities. No trash arrangements (pack it out). 14-day limit. Hunting in season. Crowded major holidays.
50 ft (15 m)

FORT FREDERICK SP

(301) 842-2155
State map: A10
From HAGERSTOWN, drive W on I-70 for 20 miles (32 k). Take Exit 12 (MD 56) S and continue 1 mile (1.6 k). (Also see Chesapeake & Ohio Canal NHP-McCoy's Ferry.)
$5; $9 weekends.
Open Apr 15–Oct 31.
28 close, open sites. ♿
Hand pump, pit toilets, tables, grills, fire rings, boat ramp, store, rentals, pay phone.
In woods next to Potomac River.
Walk nature trail. Visit 19th century fort. Bike. Canoe or fish. Attend ranger programs.

GARRETT SF

(301) 334-2038
State map: B2
From OAKLAND, take Herrington Manor Rd NW for 7 miles (11.2 k). Turn Left on Cranesville Rd and drive 4 miles (6.4 k). Turn Left on dirt Snaggy Mountain Rd and find sites along road. (Also see Potomac SF.)
$2.
Open All Year.
Undesignated scattered, screened sites.
Water needs treating, tables, fire rings.
In mountainous, wooded setting with streams and wildflowers.
Hike to enjoy scenery and spot wildlife. Mountain bike. Swim or fish. Attend

ranger programs. Cross-country ski in winter.
No toilet facilities. No trash arrangements (pack it out). Hunting in season.
2400 ft (720 m)

GREEN RIDGE SF

(301) 777-2345
State map: A7
From HANCOCK, head W on I-68 for 18 miles (28.8 k) to Exit 64. Take M V Smith Rd S to office. Sites are dispersed through forest.
$4.
Open All Year.
120 scattered, open sites.
Water at office, fire rings, boat ramp.
In rolling, forested hills with views of Potomac River, mountains, and two states.
Hike to observe wildlife and take photos. Mountain bike. Canoe. Fish. Attend ranger programs.
No toilet facilities. No trash arrangements (pack it out). Hunting in season.
2100 ft (630 m)

MILL RUN

COE (814) 395-3242
State map: A2
From FRIENDSVILLE, head NE on MD 53 or 4 miles (6.4 k). Turn Left (W) on dirt Mill Run Rd for 1 mile (1.6 k).
$4.50.
Open Apr–Oct; dry camping allowed off-season.
30 close, screened sites.
Central faucet, flush toilets, dump station, tables, fire rings, boat ramp, pay phone.
Next to Youghiogheny River Lake.
Boat. Canoe or kayak white water. Swim or fish. View wildlife. Attend ranger programs.
14-day limit.
1450 ft (435 m)

▲ ▲

POTOMAC SF

 (301) 334-2038
State map: C3
From OAKLAND, drive
E on MD 135 for 1 mile (1.6 k). Continue
SE on MD 560 for 2.5 miles (4 k). Turn
Left (E) on Bethlehem Rd and go for
3.75 miles (6 k). Turn on Potomac Camp
Rd for 1.25 miles (2 k). Camp along dirt
road on Left. (Also see Garrett SF.)
$2.
Open All Year.
Undesignated scattered, screened sites.
Water needs treating, tables, fire rings.
In forest setting with streams, waterfalls,
and cliffs.
Walk to observe ecology and take
photos. Bike. Swim or fish. Attend
ranger programs.
No toilet facilities. No trash
arrangements (pack it out). Hunting in
season.
2450 ft (735 m)

SAVAGE RIVER SF

 (301) 895-5759
State map: A3
In NEW GERMANY, stop
by office on New Germany Rd.
$2.
Open All Year.
42 scattered, open, tent sites.
Tables, fire rings, store.
Throughout forest with wooded and
streamside settings.
Canoe or fish 360-acre reservoir. Swim.
Hike to observe scenery and take photos.
Mountain bike. Cross-country ski in
winter. Attend ranger programs.
NO water. No toilet facilities. No trash
arrangements (pack it out). Hunting in
season. Occasionally crowded.
2500 ft (750 m)

▲ ▲

MASSACHUSETTS
CAMPGROUND LOCATIONS

▶ ▶ Find location on facing page map grid. ▶ ▶
▼ ▼ Locate area campgrounds on these page numbers. ▼ ▼

Massachusetts

Grid conforms to official state map. For your copy, call (617) 727-3201
or write Travel & Tourism, 100 Cambridge St, 13th Floor, Boston, MA 02202

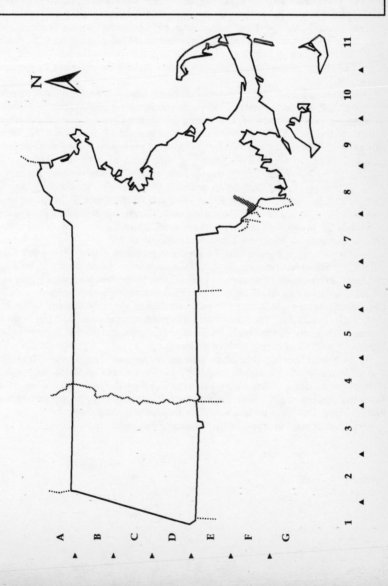

PUBLIC LANDS CAMPING

A compact state, Massachusetts can be driven easily from one side to the other in a few hours. From the Berkshires to Buzzards Bay and from Cape Ann to Cape Cod, Massachusetts is packed, however, with celebrations of history and family.

With its many rivers, such as the Merrimack and Connecticut, plus its great harbor at Boston, Massachusetts led the industrial revolution. Thank goodness, with Harvard University, Massachusetts has had the benefit of many free thinkers. In 1893, one of these idealists, Charles Eliot, created the Metropolitan District Commission to shoulder the responsibility of preserving, maintaining, and enhancing what was left of the natural, scenic, historic, and aesthetic qualities of metropolitan Boston. In conjunction with the Massachusetts Department of Environmental Management, the Commission offers $5.00 camping on Lovells and Peddocks islands in Boston Harbor. City of Salem offers camping at Winter Island Park, though fees make it too expensive for listing in this guide.

In addition to Boston Harbor, the state of Massachusetts offers camping at 32 other **State Park** (SP) and **State Forest** (SF) locations encompassing 250,000 acres. In Berkshire County, camp at Beartown SF, Clarksburg SP, Mount Greylock State Reservation, Mount Washington SF, October Mountain SF, Pittsfield SF, Sandisfield, SF, Savoy Mountain SF, Tolland SF, and Windsor SF. In the Connecticut River Valley, discover Chester–Blandford SF, DAR SF, Erving SF, Granville, SF, Mohawk Trail SF, and Monroe SF. In Worcester County, there's Federation SF, Lake Dennison Recreation Area, Otter River SF, and Wells SP. In northeast Massachusetts, try Harold Parker SF, Pearl Hill SP, Salisbury Beach State Reservation, and Willard Brook SF. In the southeast part of the state, look for Boston Harbor Islands SP, Horseneck Beach State Reservation, Massasoit SP, Myles Standish SF, Nickerson SP, Scusset Beach State Reservation, Shawme-Crowell SF, Washburn Island, and Wompatuck SP.

Basic state camping fees are $8.00 for sites with pit toilets, $10.00 for sites with flush toilets, and $12.00 for sites with flush toilets and showers. Where available, hookups cost extra. To encourage off-season camping on state lands, there's a special winter rate for self-contained RVs ($5.00). A spring and fall camping incentive program reduces basic fees $2.00 per night Sunday–Thursday (excluding Memorial Day and Labor Day weekends). In addition, the state offers wilderness camping for $5.00 per night at Mount Washington SF, Sandisfield SF, Monroe SF, Federation SF, and Boston Harbor Islands SP (additional charge for boat to island).

On the federal level of public lands, there are no **National Park Service** (NPS) sites that offer camping in Massachusetts. Most park service units in Massachusetts deal with contributions to American history. The Appalachian Trail does cross Massachusetts, entering the state near the town of Mount Washington and exiting near Williamstown. One-night backpacking sites are available along the trail.

Stop a while and steep yourself in Massachusetts' traditions.

▲ ▲

BOSTON HARBOR ISLANDS SP

(617) 740-1605
State map: C8
In BOSTON, take private ferry from Longs Wharf (near the Aquarium) to Georges Island. From there, board free water taxi available for camping on Lovells and Peddocks islands.

$5; $6 ferry; reservations accepted at (617) 740-1605.

Open Jul 1–Sep 5; camping allowed off-season.

25 scattered, screened, tent sites.

Pit toilets, tables.

On wilderness islands with beautiful vistas and historical points of interest.

Walk nature trails. Explore Fort Standish or Fort Andrews structures. Take photos. Swim, boat, or fish. Attend ranger programs.

NO water. No trash arrangements (pack it out).

50 ft (15 m)

FEDERATION SF

(508) 939-8962
State map: B4
From PETERSHAM, drive W on MA 122. Turn Left (SW) on Fever Brook Rd.

$5.

Open Apr–Oct.

20 close, open sites.

Pit toilets, tables, fire rings.

In woods within walking distance of Quabben Reservoir.

Walk trail system. Observe flora and fauna. Fish.

NO water. 14-day limit. Hunting in season.

MOUNT WASHINGTON SF

(413) 528-0330
State map: D1
Find headquarters and information on East St in MOUNT WASHINGTON.

$5.

Open Apr–Sep.

15 close, open sites.

Pit toilets, tables.

In 4169-acre forest.

Hike or fish. Canoe.

NO water. No trash arrangements (pack it out).

▲ ▲

MICHIGAN
CAMPGROUND LOCATIONS

▶ ▶ Find location on facing page map grid. ▶ ▶
▼ ▼ Locate area campgrounds on these page numbers. ▼ ▼

Michigan

Grid conforms to official state map. For your copy, call (800) 5432-YES
or write Michigan Travel Bureau, PO Box 30226, Lansing, MI 48909.

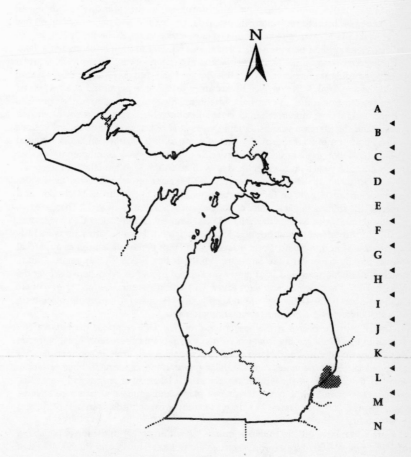

PUBLIC LANDS CAMPING

Out of the five Great Lakes, Michigan rises from four–Superior, Michigan, Huron, and Erie–in two magnificent peninsulas. To distinguish between the two land masses, residents affectionately refer to the upper peninsula as the "UP."

With 3,200 miles of Great Lakes shoreline; the world's largest assemblage of freshwater coastal dunes; more than 11,000 inland lakes; scenic rivers, streams, and waterfalls; wilderness peaks; and 6.5 million acres of forests, Michigan offers incredible natural beauty and camping opportunities on its public lands.

The **National Park Service** (NPS) provides camping at Isle Royale National Park (NP), Pictured Rocks National Lakeshore (NL), and Sleeping Bear Dunes NL. In Lake Superior, Isle Royale is returning to wilderness. On the island, you can see an environmental equilibrium among moose, wolf, beaver, fox, and hare. To camp on this jewel of an island, arrange boat or float plane service to Rock Harbor or Windigo to pick up free camping permit. At Pictured Rocks NL on Lake Superior, enjoy the lake, cliffs, beaches, sand dunes, white birches, and evergreen forests. There are $8.00 drive-in campgrounds at Hurricane River, Little Beaver Lake, and Twelvemile Beach. Along the Lakeshore Trail, however, free backcountry camping is permitted at sites spaced every two to five miles. Along Lake Michigan, Sleeping Bear Dunes NL protects massive sand dunes; numerous small, clear lakes; birch-lined streams; dense hardwood forests; and the Manitou Islands. Camping fees at D H Day and Platte River locations cost a minimum of $8.00 per night. Use of campground facilities on South Manitou Island is free though there's a $17.00 ferry ride to get there. Ask about permits to other free backcountry sites on the mainland as well as on the Manitou Islands.

Hiawatha National Forest (NF) covers 860,000 acres stretching across the eastern segment of the "UP." The forest opens onto Great Lakes Huron, Michigan, and Superior, the shining Big-Sea-Water of Longfellow's "Song of Hiawatha." There are two islands administered by the Hiawatha NF: Government Island (below Cedarville) and scenic Round Island below popular Mackinac Island. Historic attractions include lighthouses at Round Island, Point Iroquois, and Point Peninsula as well as a charcoal kiln at Bay Furnace. On Lake Superior, Whitefish Bay Scenic Byway reveals sandy beaches, hardwood-covered sand dunes, and glacial moraines. Also, here discover the National Wild and Scenic Sturgeon River. Of natural note in the forest, are climax balsam fir and white cedar. Be sure to keep your eyes open for porcupine, black bear, plus the endangered peregrine falcon and bald eagle.

Almost a million acres at the western end of the "UP" comprise the **Ottawa NF**. Special to this forest are the Sylvania Wilderness, Sylvania Recreation Area, Sturgeon River Gorge Wilderness, and North Country National Scenic Trail. In summer, you can enjoy outstanding experiences camping, hiking, swimming, canoeing, fishing, or simply enjoying the solitude of the wilderness. See glacial lakes, river gorges and waterfalls, record-size red and white pines, threatened plants and animals such as rare orchids, loons, osprey, and bald eagles. In winter, enjoy the great solitude of snowshoeing and cross-country skiing.

Huron–Manistee NF lies in two segments "down under" or in the lower peninsula of Michigan. 415,000-acre Huron stretches along Lake Huron and the 500,000-acre Manistee extends east from Lake Michigan. Three Wild and Scenic Rivers flow through the forest: Au Sable, Manistee, and Pere Marquette. Both rivers are popular with canoeists and fishermen. River Road, a 22-mile scenic byway, runs along the Au Sable. In the forest, find the nesting place of the endangered blue-gray, pale-yellow Kirtland's Warbler as well as peregrine falcon and bald eagle. Other attractions include the

▲ ▲

waterfowl in Tuttle Marsh, the wildflowers around Loda Lake, the springs of Iargo, and the wilderness of Nordhouse Dunes.

Throughout the Hiawatha, Huron–Manistee, and Ottawa national forests, most camping fees range from free to $8.00. Developed fee areas are available on a first-come, first-serve basis. Undeveloped free areas require a permit available at ranger offices. Too, the North Country National Scenic Trail covers a lot of ground in Michigan's forests as the trail winds its way from New York to North Dakota.

In **Michigan State Forests** (SF), there are 150 campgrounds (ranging from $3.00–$6.00) and unlimited primitive camping opportunities (often free). Compared to Michigan state park sites, state forest campgrounds are more remote, more spacious, and have fewer people during the busy summer season. Also, they're more reasonable in price.

Michigan State Parks (SP)offer camping at 71 state parks and recreation areas. Camping fees begin with $6.00 rustic areas then increase to $8.00 semi-modern sites and $8.00–$14.00 modern facilities, depending upon the popularity of the location. Michigan state parks charge an additional motor vehicle permit. It costs $3.50 per day or $18.00 per year. If you plan to be in Michigan state parks for six days or more, invest in an annual permit.

Additional $5.00-or-less public lands camping opportunities are available through **city**, **county**, and **township parks**. Check out Bates, Deerfield Walk-In, Drummond, Fox, North Canal, Silver Creek, and Woodland parks.

Because of Michigan's close relationship to water, there are nearly 600 public water-access sites on lakes and streams. Most access areas offer parking areas for vehicles and boat trailers, boat launching ramps, and trash barrels. In summer enjoy swimming, fishing, and boating (especially canoeing). In winter, try ice fishing.

To make the state's natural beauties enjoyable to all, Michigan approaches litter with the positive bottle deposit as well as the usual punitive angle (up to $400.00 fine and up to 90 days imprisonment). The side effect of paying a 10¢ deposit per beverage container is that not only do people return their own bottles and cans for deposit return, but people find it worthwhile to pick up other items for recycling. This process builds exponentially. While picking up beverage containers, many people pick up loose trash and, in the process, keep Michigan one of the most beautiful states in the union.

▲ ▲

AU TRAIN LAKE

Hiawatha NF
(906) 387-2512
State map: C7
From AU TRAIN, drive S
on CR H03 for 4.5 miles
(7.2 k). Turn Left (E) on FR 2276 and go
.5 mile (800 m). Turn Left (N) on
FR 2596 and continue 1.5 miles (2.4 k).
$5. Open May 15–Sep 15.
37 close, open sites. Hand pump, pit
toilets, tables, fire rings, boat ramp.
In scenic forest setting next to lake.
Swim, boat, and fish.
14-day/22-ft limits.

BATES PARK

(906) 265-9372
State map: D4
From IRON RIVER, travel
E on US 2 to Sunset Lake
Rd. Turn Left (N) and
drive to gravel West Park Dr. Turn and
follow signs.
$5.
Open May 25–Oct 31.
14 close, open sites.
Central faucet, pit toilets, tables, fire
rings, boat ramp.
In beautiful hardwoods next to lake.
Swim, boat, or fish. Bike.

▲ ▲

BEAR TRACK

Huron-Manistee NF
(616) 723-2211
State map: I8
From WELLSTON, take
CR 669 (Bosschem) SW
for 4 miles (6.4 k). Turn on 12 mile Rd
and go .5 mile (800 m). Turn Left (S) on
Bass Lake Rd. Drive 1 mile (1.6 k). Turn
Right (W) onto 11-Mile Rd for 2 miles
(3.2 k) then onto 10 ½-Mile Rd for
.5 mile (800 m). (Also see Driftwood
Valley and Pine Lake.)
$5.
Open May 25 – Sep 5; dry camping
allowed off-season.
20 close, open sites.
Hand pump, pit toilets, tables, fire rings.
On hill overlooking Little Manistee
River.
Canoe. Fish. Observe wildlife.
14-day limit. No generators in quiet
hours.

BEAUFORT LAKE

Copper Country SF
(906) 353-6651
State map: C4
From THREE LAKES,
take US 41 E for .5 mile
(800 m). Turn Right (S) on Beaufort Lake
Rd. Go 1 mile (1.6 k). (See King Lake.)
$4.
Open May–Nov.
16 close, open sites. &
Hand pump, pit toilets, tables, fire rings,
boat ramp.
In open area on north side of lake.
Swim, boat, or fish.
Hunting in season.

BIG LAKE

Copper Country SF
(906) 353-6651
State map: B4
From COVINGTON,
drive W on MI 28 for
2 miles (3.2 k). Turn Right (N) on Plains
Rd. Go 5 miles (8 k). Turn Right (E) on
rough, gravel Big Lake Rd and continue
3 miles (4.8 k). (Also see King Lake.)

$4.
Open May–Nov.
9 scattered, screened sites.
Hand pump, pit toilets, tables, fire rings.
In woods on shallow lake with sandy
beach.
Swim and fish. Observe wildlife.

BLACK RIVER HARBOR

Ottawa NF (906) 667-0261
State map: B1
From BESSEMER, drive N
on CR 513 for 15 miles
(24 k).
$5; reservations accepted at
(906) 667-0261.
Open May 22 – Oct 15; dry camping
allowed off-season.
39 close, screened sites.
Central faucet, flush toilets, dump
station, tables, fire rings, grills, boat
ramp, store, pay phone.
On Lake Superior in hardwood forest
with virgin pine and hemlock along edge
of lake.
Walk nature trail or hike farther to find
5 waterfalls. Take photos. Swim and fish.
Canoe and boat. Mountain bike.
14-day/32-ft limits. Crowded Labor Day.
600 ft (180 m)

BLOCKHOUSE

Ottawa NF (906) 265-5139
State map: C3
From IRON RIVER, drive
W on US 2 for 2 miles
(3.2 k). Turn Right (N) on
CR 657 and go 8 miles (12.8 k) to Gibbs
City. Continue N on Ponozzo Rd for
4 miles (6.4 k). Turn Right (SE) on gravel
Blockhouse Rd and proceed 4 miles
(6.4 k). (Also see Paint River Forks.)
FREE so choose a chore.
Open All Year.
2 close, open sites.
Pit toilets, tables, fire rings.
In remote, wooded setting.
Fish. View wildlife. Canoe.
NO water. Small vehicles only.
Frequently full.
1450 ft (435 m)

▲ ▲

BOB LAKE

 Ottawa NF (906) 884-2411
State map: B3
From MASS CITY, go NE
on MI 26 for 1.2 miles
(2 k). Turn Right (E) on
MI 38 for 9 miles (14.4 k). Turn Right (S)
on FH 16 for 6 miles (9.6 k) then Right
(W) on Pori Rd for 2.5 miles (4 k). Turn
Left (S) on FR 1770 for 1 mile (1.6 k)
then Left on FR 1478. (Also see Courtney
Lake.)
$4.
Open May 20–Sep 10; dry camping
allowed off-season.
17 scattered, screened sites.
Hand pump, pit toilets, tables, fire rings,
boat ramp.
In woods next to 130-acre lake.
Walk nature trail. Hike nearby North
Country Trail. Swim or fish.
14-day limit.
1100 ft (330 m)

BOBCAT LAKE

 Ottawa NF (906) 667-0261
State map: C2
From MARENISCO, go E
on MI 64 for .5 mile
(800 m). Turn Right (SE)
on gravel FR 8500 and proceed 2 miles
(3.2 k). (Also see Henry Lake.)
$4.
Open May 15–Oct 15; dry camping
allowed off-season.
12 close, screened sites.
Hand pump, pit toilets, tables, fire rings,
grills, boat ramp.
In hardwood trees with view of lake.
Canoe and boat. Swim or fish. Mountain
bike.
14-day/22-ft limits. No generators in
quiet hours.
1600 ft (480 m)

BURNED DAM

 Ottawa NF (906) 358-4551
State map: C3
From WATERSMEET,
travel E on Old US 2 for
7 miles (11.2 k). Bear Left

(N) on FR 1603 and drive 2 miles (3.2 k).
(Also see Marion Lake and Taylor Lake.)
FREE so choose a chore.
Open All Year.
6 scattered, screened sites.
Hand pump, pit toilets, tables, fire rings.
Among northern hardwood along
Middle Branch Ontonagon River.
Canoe or fish. Hike to enjoy ecology.
Observe wildlife.
14-day/22-ft limits. No generators in
quiet hours. Crowded Jul–Aug.
1603 ft (481 m)

CAMP 7 LAKE

 Hiawatha NF
(906) 341-5666
State map: D7
From MANISTIQUE,
head W on CR 442 for
9.6 miles (15.4 k). Turn Right (N) on
CR 437. Drive 7.4 miles (11.8 k). Turn
Left (W) on CR 443. Go 3.9 miles (6.2 k).
(Also see Camp Cook, Chicago Lake,
and Lyman Lake.)
$4. Open May 15–Nov 30.
41 close, screened sites. &
Central faucet, pit toilets, tables, fire
rings, grills, boat ramp, pier.
With white birch, maple, white and red
pine next to lake.
Swim, boat, or fish. Walk nature trail.
View wildlife. Attend ranger programs.
14-day limit.
800 ft (240 m)

CAMP COOK

 Hiawatha NF
(906) 341-5666
State map: D7
From MANISTIQUE,
drive 10.6 miles (17 k) W
on CR 442. Continue W on gravel
FR 2222 for 7.8 miles (12.5 k). Turn Right
(N) on CR L3 and go 3.7 miles (5.9 k).
Turn Right (NE) on CR 442 and proceed
3.1 miles (5 k). (Also see Camp 7 Lake
and Chicago Lake.)
FREE with $6/week permit; reservations
accepted at (906) 341-5666.
Open All Year.

▲ ▲

4 scattered, screened sites.
Hand pump, pit toilets.
At site of old CCC camp next to
Fishdam River.
Fish. Observe wildlife.
No trash arrangements. 14-day limit. No
large vehicles. Hunting in season.
800 ft (240 m)

CARNEY LAKE

Copper Country SF
(906) 353-6651
State map: D5
Head N on MI 95 for
9 miles (14.4 k) from
IRON MOUNTAIN. Turn Right (E) on
Merriman Truck Rd. Go 7 miles (11.2 k).
$5. Open Apr–Nov; dry camping
allowed off-season.
15 scattered, screened sites.
Hand pump, pit toilets, tables, fire rings,
boat ramp.
Next to lake.
Fish or boat. Spot wildlife.
Hunting in season.
1107 ft (332 m)

CARP RIVER

Hiawatha NF
(906) 643-7900
State map: D10
From ST IGNACE, drive
N on I-75 for 8 miles
(12.8 k). Continue N on CR 412
(Mackinac Trail) for 5 miles (8 k). (Also
see Foley Creek.)
$5. Open Apr 26–Nov 30.
44 close, open sites.
Hand pump, pit toilets, tables, fire rings,
boat ramp.
Along river.
Fish and boat. Walk nature trail.
Mountain bike.
14-day/32-ft limits.

CHICAGO LAKE

Hiawatha NF
(906) 341-5666
State map: D7
From MANISTIQUE,
drive 10.6 miles (17 k) W

on CR 442. Continue W on gravel
FR 2222 for 7.8 miles (12.5 k). Turn Right
(N) on CR L3 and go 3.7 miles (5.9 k).
Turn Right (NE) on CR 442 and travel
3.1 miles (5 k). (Also see Camp 7 Lake
and Camp Cook.)
FREE with $6/week permit; reservations
accepted at (906) 341-5666.
Open All Year.
4 (1 tent-only) scattered, screened sites.
Pit toilets, boat ramp.
In dense woods next to 188-acre lake.
Swim, canoe, or fish. Watch wildlife.
NO water. No trash arrangements (pack
it out). 14-day limit. No large vehicles.
Hunting in season. Occasional ATVs.
800 ft (240 m)

COURTNEY LAKE

Ottawa NF (906) 884-2411
State map: B3
From MASS CITY, go NE
on MI 26 for 1.2 miles
(2 k). Turn Right (E) on
MI 38 and drive 6.5 miles (10.4 k). Turn
Right (S) on FR 1960 and proceed 1 mile
(1.6 k). (Also see Bob Lake.)
$5.
Open May 20–Sep 10; dry camping
allowed off-season.
21 (2 tent-only) scattered, screened sites.
Central faucet, pit toilets, tables, fire
rings, boat ramp.
With large, wooded sites beside 30-acre
lake.
Swim or fish. Explore area, including
nearby Sturgeon River Gorge. Enjoy
quiet.
14-day/22-ft limits.
1100 ft (330 m)

DEER LAKE

Copper Country SF
(906) 353-6651
State map: C4
From CRYSTAL FALLS,
drive N on US 141 to old
US 141 and signs. Follow road to
site–about 13 miles (20.8 k) of gravel.
$4.
Open Apr 1–Oct 1; dry camping allowed

off-season.
17 scattered, screened sites.
Hand pump, pit toilets, tables, fire rings,
boat ramp.
Next to lake.
Swim, boat, and fish.
14-day limit. No generators in quiet
hours.

DEERFIELD WALK-IN

Isabella County Parks
(517) 772-0911
State map: J10
Take MI 20 W from
MOUNT PLEASANT for
6.5 miles (10.4 k). Walk in about .25 mile
(400 m). (Nearby Coldwater Lake costs
$10 and Herrick County Park costs $8.)
**$5; $4 entrance fee; reservations accepted
at (517) 772-0911 for an additional $5.**
Open All Year.
10 close, screened, tent sites.
Hand pump, pit toilets, fire rings, pay
phone.
On high, forested bank overlooking
Chippewa River.
Walk nature trail. Hike to observe
wildlife. Swim. Canoe or kayak. Fish.
950 ft (285 m)

DORNER LAKE

Huron-Manistee NF
(616) 723-2211
State map: I8
From WELLSTON, drive
S on Seaman Rd for
6.5 miles (10.4 k). Turn Left (E) on
Snyder Rd. Go about 1.5 miles (2.4 k).
(See Driftwood Valley and Sand Lake.)
$5.
Open May 25–Sep 5; dry camping
allowed off-season.
8 scattered, screened sites.
Hand pump, pit toilets, tables, fire rings,
boat ramp.
On flat terrain next to 49-acre inland
lake.
Boat or fish. View wildlife.
No trash arrangements (pack it out).
14-day limit.

DRIFTWOOD VALLEY

Huron-Manistee NF
(616) 723-2211
State map: I8
From IRONS, head W on
10 1/2 mile Rd to Bass
Lake Rd. Turn Left (S) and drive 1 mile
(1.6 k). Turn Right (W) on FR 5357 and
go 1 mile (1.6 k). (Also see Bear Track,
Dorner Lake, and Sard Lake.)
$5.
Open May 25–Sep 5; dry camping
allowed off-season.
19 close, open sites.
Hand pump, pit toilets, tables, fire rings.
On steep banks of Little Manistee River.
Hike. Fish.
14-day limit. No generators in quiet
hours.

DRUMMOND TOWNSHIP PARK

(906) 493-5473
State map: D12
From ferry terminal on
DRUMMOND ISLAND,
drive about 5 miles (8 k)
E on MI 134.
$5; $6.25 electric; $25/week.
Open Apr 15–Nov 30.
43 scattered, open sites.
Central faucet, pit toilets, dump station,
electric hookups, tables, fire rings, boat
ramp.
In woods next to water.
Swim. Fish. Bike. Take photos.
Hunting in season.

EMILY LAKE

Copper Country SF
(906) 353-6651
State map: B3
From TWIN LAKES, head
SW on MI 26 for 2 miles
(3.2 k). Turn Left (E) on gravel Pipe Lake
Rd and drive 2 miles (3.2 k). Jog Left for
.25 mile (400 m), then Right for final
.25 mile (400 m). (Nearby Twin Lakes SP
costs $10.)
$4.
Open May–Nov.
9 scattered, screened sites.

Hand pump, pit toilets, tables, fire rings, boat ramp.
Among trees overlooking lake.
Swim, boat, or fish.
Insects in Jun.

FLOWING WELL

Hiawatha NF
(906) 474-6442
State map: D7
From RAPID RIVER, take US 2 E for 14 miles (22.4 k). Turn Left (N) on FH 13 and drive 2 miles (3.2 k).
$4; reservations accepted at (906) 474-6442 for an additional $7.50.
Open Apr 15–Dec 1.
10 scattered, screened sites.
Hand pump, pit toilets, tables, grills, fire rings.
Next to Sturgeon National Wild and Scenic River.
Canoe. Fish. Observe wildlife in scenic area.
14-day limit. Often crowded-spring anglers and fall hunters.
700 ft (210 m)

FOLEY CREEK

Hiawatha NF
(906) 643-7900
State map: D10
From ST IGNACE, go N on I-75 for 4 miles (6.4 k). Continue N on CR 412 (Mackinac Trail) for 2 miles (3.2 k). (Also see Carp River.)
$5.
Open May 26–Sep 30.
54 close, open sites.
Hand pump, pit toilets, tables, fire rings.
Next to creek near Lake Huron.
Hike (good staging area). Mountain bike. Fish.
14-day/32-ft limits.

FOX PARK

Menominee County Parks
(906) 753-4582
State map: E6
From CEDAR RIVER, drive N on MI 35 for 7 miles (11.2 k).
$5.
Open Apr–Oct.
20 close, open sites.
Hand pump, pit toilets, tables, fire rings.
On shores of Green Bay.
Swim, boat, or fish.

GENE'S POND

Copper Country SF
(906) 353-6651
State map: D5
From THEODORE, head NE on CR 581 for 4.5 miles (7.2 k). Turn at sign on gravel Gene's Rd and go 2 miles (3.2 k). (Also see West Branch.)
$4.
Open Apr–Nov; dry camping allowed off-season.
14 scattered, screened sites.
Hand pump, pit toilets, tables, fire rings, boat ramp.
Beside pond with flood area that attracts wildlife.
Hike to observe ecology. Take photos.
Canoe or fish.
Hunting in season.
1147 ft (344 m)

GLIDDEN LAKE

Copper Country SF
(906) 353-6651
State map: D4
From CRYSTAL FALLS, head E on MI 69 for 5 miles (8 k). Turn Right (S) on Lake Mary Rd and drive 1.5 miles (2.4 k).
$4.
Open Apr 1–Oct 1; dry camping allowed off-season.
22 scattered, screened sites.
Hand pump, pit toilets, tables, fire rings, boat ramp.
Next to lake.
Swim, boat, ski, or fish. Walk nature trail. Hike farther to spot wildlife.
14-day limit. Hunting in season. No generators in quiet hours. Crowded holidays.

GOLDEN LAKE

Ottawa NF (906) 265-5139
State map: C3
From IRON RIVER, drive
W on US 2 about 15 miles
(24 k). Turn Right (N) on
FH 16 and proceed 1 mile (1.6 k).
$4.
Open Apr 25–Dec 1.
22 close, screened sites.
Hand pump, pit toilets, tables, fire rings,
boat ramp.
Next to lake in wooded area.
Boat or fish. Watch wildlife.
Smaller vehicles only. No generators in
quiet hours.
1600 ft (480 m)

HAYMEADOW CREEK

Hiawatha NF
(906) 474-6442
State map: D6
From RAPID RIVER,
travel E on US 2 for
2 miles (3.2 k). Turn Left (N) on gravel
CR 509 and continue 8 miles (12.8 k).
FREE so choose a chore.
Open All Year.
10 scattered, screened sites.
Hand pump, pit toilets, tables, fire rings.
In beautiful forest near creek.
Walk to Haymeadow Falls. Hike part of
Bay de Noc-Grand Island Trail. Fish for
trout. Observe wildlife. Relax in remote
spot.
No trash arrangements (pack it out).
14-day limit. Hunting in season.
700 ft (210 m)

HEMLOCK

Huron-Manistee NF
(616) 775-8539
State map: H9
From CADILLAC, head
W on MI 55 for 1 mile
(1.6 k). Turn Right (N) on South Lake
Mitchell Dr and go 1 mile (1.6 k). (Also
see Ravine.)
$5; $8 lakefront.

Open May 25–Sep 5; dry camping
allowed off-season.
19 scattered, screened sites.
Hand pump, pit toilets, tables, fire rings,
grills, boat ramp.
In dense forest on SW shore of 2580-acre
Lake Mitchell.
Boat or fish.
14-day limit. Crowded weekends.

HENRY LAKE

Ottawa NF (906) 667-0261
State map: C2
From MARENISCO, go S
on MI 64 for 5 miles (8 k).
Turn Left (W) on gravel
FR 8100 and drive 5 miles (8 k). (Also
see Bobcat Lake.)
$4.
Open May 15–Oct 15; dry camping
allowed off-season.
11 close, screened sites. &
Hand pump, pit toilets, tables, fire rings,
grills, boat ramp.
In hardwood trees overlooking lake.
Canoe or boat. Swim or fish. Observe
wildlife.
14-day/22-ft limits. No generators in
quiet hours.
1600 ft (480 m)

HORSESHOE LAKE

Huron-Manistee NF
(517) 724-6471
State map: G12
From GLENNIE, drive N
on MI 65 for 4 miles
(6.4 k). Turn Left (W) on gravel FR 4124.
(Also see Pine River and Jewell Lake.)
$4.
Open Apr 15–Nov 30.
9 scattered, open sites.
Hand pump, pit toilets, tables, fire rings,
grills, boat ramp.
In open stand of oak on ridge
overlooking 16-acre trout lake.
Fish. Walk lake trail. View wildlife.
Hunting in season.
900 ft (270 m)

▲ ▲

IMP LAKE

Ottawa NF (906) 358-4551
State map: C3
From WATERSMEET, head E on US 2 for 5 miles (8 k). Turn at sign onto FR 3978 and continue 2 miles (3.2 k). (Also see Taylor Lake.)
$4.
Open All Year.
22 close, open sites.
Hand pump, pit toilets, tables, fire rings, boat ramp.
Near lake under red pine or uphill in northern hardwood.
Swim, boat, or fish. Walk nature trail. Hike to view wildlife and find photo opportunities.
14-day/22-ft limits. Hunting in season. No generators in quiet hours. Crowded Jul–Aug.
1718 ft (515 m)

INDIAN RIVER

Hiawatha NF
(906) 341-5666
State map: D7
From SHINGLETON, drive S on MI 94 for 14.5 miles (23.2 k). (Also see Little Bass Lake. Nearby Colwell Lake costs $6.)
$4.
Open May 15–Nov 30.
11 close, screened sites.
Hand pump, pit toilets, tables, fire rings. In pretty stand of large white and red pine between highway and river.
Fish. Canoe. Observe wildlife.
14-day limit.
700 ft (210 m)

ISLAND LAKE

Huron-Manistee NF
(517) 826-3252
State map: H11
From ROSE CITY, drive N on MI 33 about 6 miles (9.6 k). Turn Left (W) on CR 486. (Also see Mack Lake and Wagner Lake.)
$5.
Open May 15–Sep 13.

17 close, open sites. ♿
Hand pump, pit toilets, tables, grills, fire rings.
Next to lake.
Swim, fish, or boat (no motors). Walk trail to Loon Lake.

ISLE ROYALE NP

(906) 482-0984
State map: A2
Arrange float plane or boat service. From HOUGHTON, boat over on Ranger III (906) 482-0984; from COPPER HARBOR, board Royale Queen (906) 289-4437; or from GRAND PORTAGE, MN, take GP-IR ferry (715) 392-2100. Obtain permit at any ranger station.
FREE. Open May 1–Oct 10.
253 scattered, open sites.
Water needs treating, chemical toilets, tables, boat ramp, lean-to structures.
In 36 locations scattered about 45-mile (72-k) long, unspoiled Lake Superior island with forests, lakes, and rocky shores.
View moose, wolf, fox, beaver, and many bird types. Hike over 166 miles (265.6 k) of trails. Fish.
No trash arrangements (pack it out).
3-day limit. Buggy in summer.

JACKPINE LAKE

Hiawatha NF
(906) 341-5666
State map: D7
From MANISTIQUE, head 9.6 miles (15.4 k) W on CR 442. Turn Right (N) on CR 437. Go 8.7 miles (13.9 k). Turn Left (NW) on gravel FR 2217. Drive 4.2 miles (6.7 k). Turn Right (NE) on FR 2715. Go .6 mile (1 k). (Also see Manistique Lakes.)
FREE with $6/week permit; reservations accepted at (906) 341-5666.
Open All Year.
2 scattered, screened sites.
Pit toilets, boat ramp.
In red and jack pines next to lake.
Swim or fish. View wildlife.

▲ ▲

NO water. No trash arrangements (pack it out). 14-day limit. No large vehicles. Hunting in season.

800 ft (240 m)

JEWELL LAKE

Huron-Manistee NF
(517) 724-6471
State map: G12
From HARRISVILLE, head W on MI 72 for 13.5 miles (21.6 k). Turn RIGHT (N) on Sanborn Rd and drive 2 miles (3.2 k). Turn Left (W) on Trask Lake Rd and go 1 mile (1.6 k). (Also see Horseshoe Lake and Pine River.)

$5.

Open May 25–Sep 8.

32 scattered, screened sites.

Hand pump, pit toilets, tables, fire rings, boat ramp.

In deep woods by 193-acre lake.

Swim, boat, or fish. Hike trail.

Hunting in season. Crowded holiday weekends.

900 ft (270 m)

KING LAKE

Copper Country SF
(906) 353-6651
State map: C4
From MICHIGAMME, travel W on MI 28 for 13 miles (20.8 k). Turn Left (S) on gravel King Lake Rd and go 5 miles (8 k). (Also see Beaufort Lake and Big Lake.)

$5.

Open May–Nov.

6 scattered, screened sites.

Hand pump, pit toilets, tables, fire rings, boat ramp.

On wooded knob at north end of lake. Boat and fish. Watch wildlife.

Hunting in season.

KNEFF LAKE

Huron-Manistee NF
(517) 826-3252
State map: G11
From GRAYLING, take MI 72 E about 8 miles

(12.8 k). Turn Right (S) on Down River Rd.

$5.

Open May 1–Sep 30.

26 scattered, open sites.

Central faucet, flush toilets, tables, grills, fire rings.

Next to 14-acre trout lake.

Swim, boat, or fish. Observe wildlife.

LAKE OTTAWA

Ottawa NF (906) 265-5139
State map: D3
From IRON RIVER, head W on US 2. Bear Left (SW) on MI 73 and travel about 4 miles (6.4 k). Turn Left (W) on Ottawa Lake Rd and go 4 miles (6.4 k). (Also see Brule River, WI.)

$5; $10 prime.

Open May 15–Sep 30.

32 close, screened sites.

Central faucet, flush toilets, dump station, tables, fire rings, boat ramp.

In woods beside lake.

Swim, boat, or fish. Walk interpretive trail or hike farther. View wildlife. Study archeological dig.

14-day limit. No generators in quiet hours. Occasionally crowded.

1600 ft (480 m)

LAKE STE KATHRYN

Ottawa NF (906) 852-3500
State map: C3
From SIDNAW, drive S on Sidnaw Rd for 8 miles (12.8 k). (Also see Norway Lake and Perch Lake.)

$4; reservations accepted at (906) 852-3500 for an additional $6.

Open May 14–Sep 19; dry camping allowed off-season.

25 close, open sites.

Hand pump, pit toilets, tables, fire rings, boat ramp.

Next to lake.

Swim, fish, or boat.

14-day/22-ft limits.

▲ ▲

LANGFORD LAKE

Ottawa NF (906) 667-0261
State map: C2
From MARENISCO, take
US 2 SE for 10 miles
(16 k). Turn Right (S) on
gravel FR 7100 and drive 6 miles (9.6 k).
Turn Right (W) on CR 527 and continue
2.5 miles (4 k). (Also see Pomeroy Lake
and Moosehead Lake.)
$4. Open May 15–Oct 15; dry camping
allowed off-season.
11 close, screened sites.
Hand pump, pit toilets, tables, fire rings,
grills, boat ramp.
In hardwood with view of lake.
Canoe or boat. Swim or fish. Watch
wildlife. Mountain bike.
14-day/22-ft limits. No generators in
quiet hours.
1600 ft (480 m)

LEG LAKE

Hiawatha NF
(906) 341-5666
State map: D7
From MANISTIQUE,
drive 9.6 miles (15.4 k) W
on CR 442. Turn Right (N) on CR 437.
Go 13.5 miles (21.6 k). Turn Left (NW)
on gravel FR 2438. Continue .7 mile
(1.1 k). (Also see Little Bass Lake and
Manistique Lakes.)
FREE with $6/week permit; reservations
accepted at (906) 341-5666.
Open All Year.
2 scattered, screened sites. Pit toilets.
In open grass surrounded by pine and
hardwood next to 40-acre lake.
Swim or fish. Explore to spot wildlife.
NO water. No trash arrangements (pack
it out). No large vehicles. Hunting in
season. Occasional ATVs.
700 ft (210 m)

LITTLE BASS LAKE

Hiawatha NF
(906) 341-5666
State map: C7
Drive S on MI 94 for
11.8 miles (18.9 k) from

SHINGLETON. Turn Right (W) on
gravel CR 437. Travel 1.7 miles (2.7 k).
Turn Left (SE) on FR 2213. Go 1.5 miles
(2.4 k). Continue S on FR 2639 for
1.1 miles (1.8 k). (Also see Indian River
and Leg Lake.)
$5.
Open May 15–Nov 30.
12 close, screened sites.
Hand pump, pit toilets, tables, fire rings.
Among hills and large pine trees near
lake.
Canoe. Swim or fish. Watch wildlife.
14-day limit.
700 ft (210 m)

LITTLE BAY DE NOC

Hiawatha NF
(906) 474-6442
State map: D6
From RAPID RIVER, take
US 2 E for 3 miles (4.8 k).
Turn Right (S) and drive 6 miles (9.6 k).
$5; $6 for two loops; reservations
accepted at (906) 474-6442 for an
additional $7.50.
Open May 15–Oct 15.
38 close, screened sites. ♿
Hand pump, pit toilets, tables, fire rings,
grills, boat ramp.
In woods along shore of Little Bay de
Noc (Lake Michigan).
Swim, boat, ski, or fish. Hike all three
trails. View wildlife. Attend
environmental programs.
14-day limit. No generators in quiet
hours. Crowded weekends and holidays.
700 ft (210 m)

LOWER DAM

Ottawa NF (906) 852-3500
State map: C3
From KENTON, head S
on FH 16 about .5 mile
(800 m). Turn Left (E) on
CR and drive 5 miles (8 k). Turn Right
(S) on FR 3500 and go 1 mile (1.6 k).
$4.
Open Apr 23–Sep 19; dry camping
allowed off-season.
7 close, open sites.

▲ ▲

Hand pump, pit toilets, tables, fire rings, boat ramp.
Next to lake.
Swim, boat, or fish.
14-day/22-ft limits.

LUMBERMEN'S MONUMENT

Huron-Manistee NF
(517) 362-4477
State map: H12
From OSCODA, take River Road Scenic Byway
W about 15 miles (24 k). (Also see Rollways.)
$5; reservations accepted at (517) 362-4477.
Open May 15–Sep 30.
20 close, screened sites.
Central faucet, pit toilets, tables, fire rings.
In 60-year red pine stand planted by CCC.
Visit nearby Monument Visitor Center.
Walk nature trail. Observe wildlife.
Attend ranger programs.
14-day limit. No generators in quiet hours.
600 ft (180 m)

LUZERNE TRAIL CAMP

Huron-Manistee NF
(517) 826-3252
State map: G11
From LUZERNE, drive SE on CR for 2 miles (3.2 k).
FREE so choose a chore.
Open All Year.
10 close, open sites.
Pit toilets, tables, fire rings.
In woods.
Hike. Relax.
NO water. No trash arrangements (pack it out). 14-day/32-ft limits.

LYMAN LAKE

Hiawatha NF
(906) 341-5666
State map: D7
From MANISTIQUE, drive 9.6 miles (15.4 k) W
on CR 442. Turn Right (N) on CR 437

and travel 7.4 miles (11.8 k). Turn Left (W) on CR 443 and go 3.9 miles (6.3 k). Turn Right (N) on FR 2218 and continue 1.4 miles (2.2 k). (Also see Camp 7 Lake.)
FREE with $6/week permit; reservations accepted at (906) 341-5666.
Open All Year.
10 scattered, screened sites.
Pit toilets, boat ramp.
In semi-open setting with hardwood and pine around 67-acre lake.
Swim or fish. Observe wildlife.
NO water. No trash arrangements (pack it out). 14-day limit. No large vehicles.
Hunting in season. Occasional ATVs.
800 ft (240 m)

MACK LAKE

Huron-Manistee NF
(517) 826-3252
State map: G11
From MIO, head S on MI 33 about 7 miles
(11.2 k). Turn Left (E) on gravel CR 489 and follow signs. (Also see Island Lake and Wagner Lake.)
$5.
Open May 15–Sep 13; dry camping allowed off-season.
42 close, open sites. &
Hand pump, pit toilets, tables, fire rings.
Next to 174-acre, shallow lake.
Fish. Observe wildlife (Kirtland Warbler here).
14-day limit. Occasional ATVs. Crowded weekends.

MANISTIQUE LAKES-Primitive

Hiawatha NF
(906) 341-5666
State map: D8
Obtain permit and map from Manistique Ranger
Station at 449 E Lakeshore Dr in MANISTIQUE. (Also see Jackpine Lake, Leg Lake, and Triangle Lake.)
FREE with $6/week permit; reservations accepted at (906) 341-5666.
Open All Year.
Undesignated scattered, open sites.
Among Bear Lake, Bass Lake, Carr Lake,

▲ ▲

Crooked Lake, East Lake, Gooseneck Lake, Ironjaw/Lake 19, Minerva Lake, and Steuben Lake.
Swim or fish. View wildlife.
NO water. No toilet facilities. No trash arrangements (pack it out). 7-day limit. No large vehicles. Hunting in season.
800 ft (240 m)

MARION LAKE

Ottawa NF (906) 358-4551
State map: C3
From WATERSMEET, head E on US 2 for 4 miles (6.4 k). Turn Left (N) on FR 3980 and travel 2 miles (3.2 k). (Also see Burned Dam and Taylor Lake.)
$4.
Open All Year.
39 scattered, screened sites.
Hand pump, pit toilets, tables, fire rings, boat ramp.
In northern hardwood next to lake.
Swim, boat, or fish. Observe wildlife.
14-day/22-ft limits. Hunting in season. No generators in quiet hours. Crowded Jul-Aug.
1718 ft (515 m)

MATCHWOOD TOWER

Ottawa NF (906) 575-3441
State map: B2
From BERGLAND, take MI 28 E to Big Bear Rd. Turn Right (S) and go to gravel Tower Rd.
FREE so choose a chore.
Open All Year.
5 close, screened sites.
Hand pump, pit toilets, tables, fire rings. In woods with open areas on two sides. Spot wildlife. Relax.
No trash arrangements (pack it out). Crowded in fall hunting season.

MOOSEHEAD LAKE

Ottawa NF (906) 667-0261
State map: C2
From MARENISCO, drive S on MI 64 for 4.5 miles (7.2 k). Turn Left (SE) on

gravel FR 8220 and proceed 5 miles (8 k). Turn Left (E) on FR 6860 and travel 3 miles (4.8 k). Turn Right (S) on FR 6862 and go 2 miles (3.2 k). (Also see Langford Lake and Pomeroy Lake.)
$3.
Open May 15–Oct 15; dry camping allowed off-season.
13 close, screened sites.
Hand pump, pit toilets, tables, fire rings, grills, boat ramp.
In pine and aspen with view of lake.
Canoe or boat. Swim or fish. See wildlife.
14-day/22-ft limits. No generators in quiet hours.
1600 ft (480 m)

MOWE LAKE

Hiawatha NF (906) 341-5666
State map: D7
From SHINGLETON, travel S on MI 94 for 11.8 miles (18.9 k). Turn Right (SW) on gravel CR 437 and drive 5.1 miles (8.2 k). Turn Right (W) on CR 440 and continue 4.4 miles (7 k). Turn Left (SW) on FR 2692 and proceed 1 mile (1.6 k). (Also see Swan Lake. Nearby Corner Lake costs $6.)
FREE with $6/week permit; reservations accepted at (906) 341-5666.
Open All Year.
2 scattered, screened sites.
Pit toilets.
In semi-open hardwood setting next to 25-acre lake.
Swim or fish. Hike some of nearby Pine Marten 26-mile (41.6 k) Trail system.
NO water. No trash arrangements (pack it out). 14-day limit. No large vehicles. Hunting in season. Occasional ATVs.
800 ft (240 m)

NORTH CANAL TOWNSHIP PARK

(906) 482-5188
State map: A4
From HOUGHTON, take North Canal Rd NW about 10 miles (16 k).

▲ ▲

$2.50.
Open May–Oct
Undesignated close, open sites.
Hand pump, pit toilets, tables, boat ramp.
Beside canal.
Swim, boat, or fish. Hike or bike.
Occasionally noisy.

NORWAY LAKE

Ottawa NF (906) 852-3500
State map: C3
From SIDNAW, drive S on Sidnaw Rd for 6 miles (9.6 k). Turn Left (E) on FR 2400 and go 2 miles (3.2 k). (Also see Lake Ste Kathryn and Perch Lake.)
$4; reservations accepted at (906) 852-3500 for an additional $6.
Open May 14–Sep 19; dry camping allowed off-season.
28 close, open sites.
Hand pump, pit toilets, tables, fire rings, boat ramp.
Next to lake.
Swim, boat, and fish. Walk nature trail.
14-day/22-ft limits.

PAINT RIVER FORKS

Ottawa NF (906) 265-5139
State map: C3
From IRON RIVER, drive W on US 2 for 2 miles (3.2 k). Turn Right (N) on CR 657 and go 8 miles (12.8 k) to Gibbs City. Bear Left (NW) on gravel CR 657 and continue 1 mile (1.6 k). (Also see Blockhouse.)
FREE so choose a chore.
Open All Year.
4 close, open sites.
Water needs treating, pit toilets, tables, fire rings.
In wooded setting on South Branch Paint River.
Canoe. Fish. Enjoy natural surroundings.
14-day limit.
1480 ft (444 m)

PAULDING POND

Ottawa NF (906) 358-4551
State map: C3
From WATERSMEET, drive N on US 45 for 9 miles (14.4 k).
$3. Open All Year.
4 scattered, screened sites.
Hand pump, pit toilets, tables, fire rings.
Next to trout pond under pine and some hardwood.
Fish. See wildlife. Relax a night or two.
14-day/22-ft limits. No generators in quiet hours.
1335 ft (401 m)

PERCH LAKE

Ottawa NF (906) 852-3500
State map: C3
From SIDNAW, drive S on Sidnaw Rd for 10.5 miles (16.8 k). Bear Left (E) on CR and proceed 1.5 miles (2.4 k). (Also see Lake Ste Kathryn and Norway Lake.)
$4; reservations accepted at (906) 852-3500 for an additional $6.
Open May 14–Sep 11; dry camping allowed off-season.
20 close, open sites.
Hand pump, pit toilets, tables, fire rings, boat ramp.
Along lake.
Swim, boat, or fish.
14-day/22-ft limits.

PETE'S LAKE

Hiawatha NF
(906) 387-2512
State map: C7
From MUNISING, head SE on MI 28 for 2 miles (3.2 k). Turn Right on FH 13 and drive 12 miles (19.2 k). Turn Right (E). (Also see Widewaters.)
$5.
Open May 15–Sep 15.
41 close, open sites. &
Hand pump, pit toilets, tables, fire rings, boat ramp.
Beside lake.

▲ ▲

Fish and swim. Boat and ski. Walk nature trail.

14-day/22-ft limits.

PETERSON BRIDGE

Huron-Manistee NF
(616) 775-8539
State map: H8
From CADILLAC, take MI 55 W for 20 miles (32 k). Turn Left (S) on MI 37 and drive 1.5 miles (2.4 k). Turn Left (E).

$5.

Open Apr 15–Sep 30.

30 scattered, screened sites.

Central faucet, flush toilets, tables, grills, fire rings.

In heavy forest with 10 walk-in sites next to Pine River.

Hike to observe wildlife and enjoy area. Canoe. Fish.

14-day limit. No generators in quiet hours. Crowded weekends.

PICTURED ROCKS NL-Backcountry

NPS (906) 387-3700
State map: C7
Obtain permit at Visitor Center in MUNISING at MI 28 & CR H58.

FREE. Open May 1–Oct 31; camping allowed off-season.

Undesignated scattered, screened sites.

Pit toilets at Mosquito River and Chapel Beach.

Along Lake Superior Lakeshore Trail about 2–5 miles (3.2–8 k) apart in 13 locations.

Enjoy beautiful coastal area. Observe wildlife.

NO water. No trash arrangements (pack it out). 14-day limit.

700 ft (210 m)

PINE LAKE

Huron-Manistee NF
(616) 723-2211
State map: H8
From WELLSTON, take Bosschem Rd SW for 1 mile (1.6 k). Turn Right (E) on Pine Lake Rd and proceed 3 miles (4.8 k). (Also see Bear Track and Udell Rollways.)

$5.

Open May 25–Sep 5; dry camping allowed off-season.

12 close, open sites.

Hand pump, pit toilets, tables, fire rings, grills, boat ramp.

Next to scenic 156-acre lake.

Canoe, boat, or fish. Take photos.

14-day limit. No generators in quiet hours.

PINE RIVER

Huron-Manistee NF
(517) 724-6471
State map: G12
From MIKADO, travel W on CR F30 for 8.25 miles (13.2 k). Turn Left (S) on gravel FR 4121 (Rearing Pond). Drive 2 miles (3.2 k). (Also see Horseshoe Lake and Jewell Lake.)

$4.

Open Apr 15–Nov 30.

11 scattered, screened sites.

Hand pump, pit toilets, tables, fire rings.

In wooded, private setting next to South Branch Pine River.

Fish. Enjoy lovely surroundings.

14-day limit. Hunting in season.

900 ft (270 m)

POMEROY LAKE

Ottawa NF (906) 667-0261
State map: C2
From MARENISCO, take US 2 SE for 10 miles (16 k). Turn Right (S) on gravel FR 7100 and drive 6 miles (9.6 k). Turn Right (W) on CR 527 and travel 2 miles (3.2 k). Turn Left (S) at sign for final .5 mile (800 m). (Also see Langford Lake and Moosehead Lake.)

$3.

Open May 15-Oct 15; dry camping allowed off-season.

16 close, screened sites.

Hand pump, pit toilets, tables, fire rings, grills, boat ramp.

In hardwood trees with lake view.
Swim, boat, or fish. Observe wildlife.
14-day/22-ft limits. No generators in
quiet hours.
1600 ft (480 m)

RAVINE

Huron-Manistee NF
(616) 775-8539
State map: H9
From CADILLAC, take
MI 55 W for 9 miles
(14.4 k). Turn Left (S) on 21-Mile Rd and
drive 1 mile (1.6 k). Turn Right (E) on
46-Mile Rd and go 2 miles (3.2 k). Turn
Left (N) on 17-Mile Rd and continue
1 mile (1.6 k). (Also see Hemlock.)
FREE so choose a chore.
Open May 25–Sep 5; dry camping
allowed off-season.
6 scattered, open sites.
Hand pump, pit toilets, tables, grills, fire
rings.
In wooded setting near Poplar Creek.
Fish. View wildlife. Enjoy seclusion.
No trash arrangements (pack it out).
14-day limit. Hunting in season.

ROBBINS POND

Ottawa NF (906) 358-4551
State map: C2
From WATERSMEET,
head N on US 45 for
5 miles (8 k). Bear Left on
gravel Old US 45 and drive 1 mile
(1.6 k). Turn Left (NW) on gravel
FR 5230 and go 4 miles (6.4 k). Turn on
FR 6964 and proceed .5 mile (800 m).
FREE so choose a chore.
Open All Year.
3 scattered, screened sites.
Hand pump, pit toilets, tables, fire rings.
In jack pine and aspen near trout pond.
Fish. Explore scenic area.
14-day/22-ft limits. Hunting in season.
No generators in quiet hours.
1609 ft (483 m)

ROLLWAYS

Huron-Manistee NF
(517) 362-4477
State map: H12
From HALE, take MI 65
N for 7 miles (11.2 k).
Turn on Rollways Rd and proceed
.1 mile (160 m). (See Lumbermen's
Monument and South Branch Trail
Camp. Nearby Round Lake costs $8.)
$5; reservations accepted at
(517) 362-4477.
Open May 15–Sep 30.
19 close, screened sites.
Central faucet, pit toilets, tables, fire
rings.
In mixed jack pine/oak near AuSable
River and River Road Scenic Byway.
Hike to observe wildlife and attractive
scenery. Explore.
14-day limit. No generators in quiet
hours.
600 ft (180 m)

SAND LAKE

Huron-Manistee NF
(616) 723-2211
State map: H8
From WELLSTON, drive
S on Seaman Rd for
4.5 miles (7.2 k). Turn Right (W) on
FR 5728. (Also see Driftwood Valley and
Dorner Lake.)
$5 per adult.
Open May 25–Sep 5.
45 close, screened sites.
Central faucet, flush toilets, showers,
tables, grills, fire rings.
In open and wooded areas near small
lake.
Swim, boat, or fish.
14-day limit. No generators in quiet
hours. Often crowded.

SEATON CREEK

Huron-Manistee NF
(616) 775-8539
State map: H8
From MESICK, drive S on
MI 37 for 6 miles (9.6 k).
Turn Right (W) on 26 Rd and go 2 miles

▲ ▲

(3.2 k). Turn Right (N) on Hodenpyle Rd and continue 1.5 miles (2.4 k). Turn Right (E) on FR 5993 for last .5 mile (800 m).

$4.

Open May 25 – Sep 5; dry camping allowed off-season.

17 scattered, screened sites.

Hand pump, pit toilets, tables, grills, fire rings.

In dense, red pine forest on Seaton Creek near Manistee River.

Hike Manistee River Trail. View wildlife. Fish.

14-day limit. Hunting in season.

SILVER CREEK COUNTY PARK

Allegan County Parks
(616) 673-8471
State map: L8
From HAMILTON, head S on MI 40 for .25 mile (400 m). Turn Left (E) on 134th Ave and go 4 miles (6.4 k).

FREE so choose a chore.

Open All Year.

25 scattered, open sites.

Hand pump, pit toilets, tables, grills.

With oak and fir plus trout stream.

Hike to take photos. Fish. Relax.

15-day limit.

SLEEPING BEAR DUNES NL

NPS (616) 326-5134
State map: F8–G8
FREE so choose a chore.
Open May–Oct.
180 ft (54 m)

▲ **Backcountry**

Obtain **free** permit and map at Visitor Center in EMPIRE. (Nearby D H Day and Platte River cost $8.)

At two hike-in locations on mainland or in wilderness area on North Manitou Island.

Enjoy special lakeshore ecology.

NO water. No toilet facilities. No trash arrangements (pack it out).

▲ **South Manitou Island**

From LELAND, take commercial ferry (616) 256-9061 (up to $17). Walk to sites,

distance varying .5 mile (800 m) to 3.5 miles (5.4 k).

50 scattered, screened, tent sites.

Central faucet, pit toilets, fire rings.

In three, mixed-hardwood settings on 5260-acre island in Lake Michigan.

Hike to view wildlife and take photos. Explore–from ruins to virgin cedar. Swim or fish.

14-day limit. Ferry may cancel in bad weather (be prepared).

SOLDIER LAKE

Hiawatha NF
(906) 635-5311
State map: C10
From SAULT STE MARIE, head S on I-75 for 6 miles (9.6 k). Exit on MI 28 W and go 24 miles (38.4 k). Turn Left (S). (Also see Three Lakes.)

$4.

Open May 25–Sep 5.

44 scattered, open sites.

Hand pump, pit toilets, tables, grills, fire rings.

In open area with red and jack pine next to North Country Hiking Trail (and highway).

Walk to observe wildlife or take photos. Bike.

14-day limit. Occasionally crowded.

SOUTH BRANCH TRAIL CAMP

Huron-Manistee NF
(517) 362-4477
State map: H12
From HALE, take MI 65 N for 7 miles (11.2 k). Turn on Rollways Rd and drive 2.5 miles (4 k). (Also see Rollways.)

$4.

Open Apr 15–Dec 31.

16 close, screened sites.

Hand pump, pit toilets, tables, fire rings.

In pine/oak setting along Michigan Shore-To-Shore Horse Trail.

Walk trail system to see ecology.

14-day limit. Horses often in area.

600 ft (180 m)

▲ ▲

SPARROW RAPIDS

Ottawa NF (906) 852-3500
State map: C3
From KENTON, drive
NW on FR 1100 for
2 miles (3.2 k).

$4.
Open Apr 23–Sep 19; dry camping allowed off-season.
6 close, open sites.
Hand pump, pit toilets, tables, fire rings.
Next to Ontonagon River.
Fish. Explore area.
14-day/22-ft limits.

STURGEON RIVER

Ottawa NF (906) 852-3500
State map: C3
On E side of SIDNAW, take FR 2200 N for 4.5 miles (7.2 k).

$4.
Open Apr 23–Sep 19; dry camping allowed off-season.
9 close, open sites.
Hand pump, pit toilets, tables, fire rings.
On edge of Sturgeon River Gorge Wilderness.
Walk North Country Trail through scenic area. Fish.
14-day/22-ft limits.

SWAN LAKE

Hiawatha NF
(906) 341-5666
State map: D7
From SHINGLETON, travel S on MI 94 for 11.8 miles (18.9 k). Turn Right (SW) on gravel CR 437 and drive 5.1 miles (8.2 k). Turn Right (W) on CR 440 and continue 5.3 miles (8.5 k). Turn Right (N) on FR 2258. Proceed .2 mile (320 m). (Also see Mowe Lake.)
FREE with $6/week permit; reservations accepted at (906) 341-5666.
Open All Year.
4 scattered, screened sites.
Pit toilets, boat ramp.
In quiet, woods beside 52-acre lake.
Hike or bike Pine Marten Trail. Swim.

Fish.
NO water. No trash facilities. 14-day limit. No large vehicles. Hunting in season.
800 ft (240 m)

SYLVANIA RA

Ottawa NF (906) 358-4551
State map: C2
From WATERSMEET, drive W on US 2 for 4 miles (6.4 k). Turn Left (S) on CR 535 and continue 5 miles (8 k).
$5.
Open May 15–Sep 15.
48 close, open sites.
Central faucet, flush toilets, showers, tables, fire rings, boat ramp.
In virgin northern hardwood next to 18327-acre wilderness.
Swim, boat, or fish. Hike over 30 miles (48 k) of trails to appreciate special character of region. Observe wildlife.
14-day/22-ft limits. Hunting in season. No generators in quiet hours. Crowded Jul–Aug.
1700 ft (510 m)

SYLVANIA WILDERNESS
BOAT/WALK-IN

Ottawa NF (906) 358-4551
State map: C2
From WATERSMEET, drive W on US 2 for 4 miles (6.4 k). Turn Left (S) on CR 535 and go 5 miles (8 k). Walk or boat .25–4 miles (400 m–6.4 k).
FREE so choose a chore; reservations accepted at (906) 358-4551 for an additional $5.
Open May 15–Sep 30; dry camping allowed off-season.
77 scattered, screened, tent sites.
Hand pump access, wilderness latrines, fire rings, grills, boat ramp.
In huge wilderness with virgin hardwood/pine plus 36 pristine lakes.
View rare orchids, bald eagles, loons, osprey. Swim, canoe, or fish. Take photos. Cross-country ski in winter.
No trash arrangements. 14-day limit.

Crowded weekends and Jul-Aug.
1700 ft (510 m)

TAYLOR LAKE

Ottawa NF (906) 358-4551
State map: C3
From WATERSMEET,
head E on US 2 for
6 miles (9.6 k). Turn Left
(N) on FR 3960 and drive 2 miles (3.2 k).
(Also see Burned Dam, Imp Lake, and
Marion Lake.)
$4.
Open All Year.
10 scattered, screened sites.
Hand pump, pit toilets, tables, fire rings,
grills, boat ramp.
Under large northern hardwood trees
near lake.
Fish or boat. View wildlife.
14-day/22-ft limits. No generators in
quiet hours. Crowded Jul–Aug.
1850 ft (555 m)

TEEPEE LAKE

Ottawa NF (906) 852-3500
State map: C3
From KENTON, go S on
FH 16 for 8 miles (12.8 k).
$5.
Open May 14–Sep 19; dry camping
allowed off-season.
17 close, open sites.
Hand pump, pit toilets, tables, fire rings,
boat ramp.
Next to lake.
Swim, boat, and fish. Walk nature trail.
14-day/22-ft limits.

THREE LAKES

Hiawatha NF
(906) 635-5311
State map: C10
From STRONGS, drive S
on FR 3142 for 3 miles
(4.8 k). (Also see Soldier Lake.)
$4.
Open May 25–Sep 5.
28 scattered, screened sites.
Hand pump, pit toilets, tables, fire rings.
Among pine trees near three lakes.

Canoe. Fish. Bike. Relax.
14-day limit.

TIMBER CREEK

Huron-Manistee NF
(616) 745-4631
State map: I8
From BRANCH, drive
2 miles (3.2 k) E.
FREE so choose a chore.
Open All Year.
9 close, open sites.
Hand pump, pit toilets, tables, fire rings.
In woods next to stream.
Fish. Walk part of North Country Trail.
14-day limit.

TRIANGLE LAKE

Hiawatha NF
(906) 341-5666
State map: D7
From SHINGLETON,
travel S on MI 94 for
11.8 miles (18.9 k). Turn Right (SW) on
gravel CR 437. Drive 4.5 miles (7.2 k).
Turn Right (W) on FR 2735. Go .4 mile
(600 m). (Also see Manistique Lakes.)
FREE with $6/week permit; reservations
accepted at (906) 341-5666.
Open All Year.
2 scattered, screened sites.
Pit toilets.
In sand or dense woods next to 160-acre
lake and small pond.
Swim, canoe, or fish. Hike or bike Pine
Marten Trail.
NO water. No trash arrangements (pack
it out). 14-day limit. No large vehicles.
Hunting in season.
800 ft (240 m)

UDELL ROLLWAYS

Huron-Manistee NF
(616) 723-2211
State map: H7
From US 31/MI 55
intersection near
MANISTEE, head E on MI 55 for
12 miles (19.2 k). Turn Left (N) on gravel
Horsehoe Bend Rd and continue 2 miles
(3.2 k). (Also see Pine Lake.)

▲ ▲

$5.

Open May 25–Sep 5; dry camping allowed off-season.

23 close, open sites.

Central faucet, flush toilets, tables, fire rings.

Next to Manistee Wild and Scenic River with steep banks and breathtaking views.

Take photos. Fish.

14-day limit. No generators in quiet hours.

WAGNER LAKE

Huron-Manistee NF
(517) 826-3252
State map: G11
From MIO, drive S on MI 33 about 8 miles
(12.8 k). Turn Right (W) on West Wagner Lake Rd and follow signs. (Also see Island Lake and Mack Lake.)

$5.

Open May 20–Sep 13.

12 scattered, open sites.

Hand pump, pit toilets, tables, fire rings.

Beside 26-acre lake.

Swim, boat, or fish.

WEST BRANCH

Copper Country SF
(906) 353-6651
State map: D5
From RALPH, head N on gravel CR 581 for 7 miles
(11.2 k). (Also see Gene's Pond.)

$4.

Open Apr–Nov; dry camping allowed off-season.

18 scattered, screened sites.

Hand pump, pit toilets, tables, fire rings.

Near stream.

Hike to view wildlife. Fish.

Hunting in season.

1200 ft (360 m)

WIDEWATERS

Hiawatha NF
(906) 387-2512
State map: C7
From MUNISING, head SE on MI 28 for 2 miles
(3.2 k). Turn Right on FH 13 and go 12 miles (19.2 k). Turn Left (W). (Also see Pete's Lake.)

$5.

Open May 26–Oct 1.

34 close, open sites.

Hand pump, pit toilets, tables, fire rings, boat ramp.

Next to lake.

Boat or fish.

14-day/22-ft limits.

WOODLAND PARK

(517) 875-3200
State map: K10
Locate park in ITHACA at 530 W Center St.
FREE so choose a chore.

Open All Year.

2 close, open sites.

Central faucet, flush toilets, electric hookups.

Relax at overnight stop.

▲ ▲

MINNESOTA
CAMPGROUND LOCATIONS

▶ ▶ Find location on facing page map grid. ▶ ▶
▼ ▼ Locate area campgrounds on these page numbers. ▼ ▼

Minnesota

Grid conforms to official state map. For your copy, call (800) 657-3700
or write Office of Tourism, 121 7th Place E, #100, St Paul, MN 55101-2112.

N

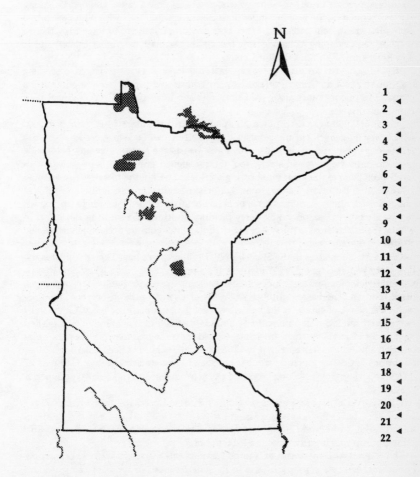

1 ◄
2 ◄
3 ◄
4 ◄
5 ◄
6 ◄
7 ◄
8 ◄
9 ◄
10 ◄
11 ◄
12 ◄
13 ◄
14 ◄
15 ◄
16 ◄
17 ◄
18 ◄
19 ◄
20 ◄
21 ◄
22

A B C D E F G H I J K L M N O P Q R S T

▲ ▲

PUBLIC LANDS CAMPING

Minnesota is known as the land of 10,000 lakes. Also, there are 93,000 miles of waterways, almost 17 million acres of forests, and 12,000 miles of recreational trails stretching across the prairies and forests of this state. For public lands camping, there's Voyageurs National Park (NP), Grand Portage National Monument (NM) backcountry, Chippewa National Forest (NF), Superior NF, US Army Corps of Engineers (COE) lakes, Minnesota State Parks (SP), Minnesota State Forests (SF), and several county and town parks.

On Minnesota's border between the United States and Canada, find Voyageurs NP. To truly appreciate these boundary waters, you must grab a canoe and paddle. Along the shores of lakes, the boater-camper finds free designated sites with pit toilets, picnic tables, fire grates, tent pads, and, often, bear-proof food lockers. To stage trips, there's $7.00 drive-in camping at Woodenfrog (near Kabetogama Lake Visitor Center) and at Ash River (near Ash River Visitor Center).

If you're up for an 8.5 mile hike, **National Park Service** (NPS) also offers a backcountry site at Grand Portage NM. In addition, the park service administers recreational opportunities along the Saint Croix and Lower Saint Croix National Wild and Scenic Rivers.

In the 660,000-acre **Chippewa NF**, pack your binoculars plus your bird and wildflower guidebooks to enjoy outstanding nature viewing. Two special delights are orchid bogs and bald eagle nests. This forest boasts the largest breeding bald eagle population in the lower 48 states. Too, the threatened gray wolf is present though rarely seen. Due to the great number of glacial lakes within the forest, water-oriented recreation is popular. Canoe, boat, water ski, swim, or fish while camping at undeveloped, remote locations (free) or at one of 26 developed lakeside campgrounds (up to $10.00). In season, enjoy berry picking, hunting, and viewing fall color. In winter, ice fish or cross-country ski. Many of these delights are accessible via Avenue of Pines, a 39-mile Scenic Byway.

Of the 3 million acres in the **Superior NF**, 1 million acres have been designated the Boundary Waters Canoe Area Wilderness. It's a pristine area full of lakes, pine forests, volcanic rock outcroppings, and wildlife. The forest provides habitat for bald eagle, black bear, and the Eastern Timber Wolf (one of twenty-four subspecies of the gray wolf). Canoeing, of course, is the best way to get the Superior experience. Canoe trails range from the 235-mile International Boundary Route to the 23-mile Sea Gull-Red Rocks Loop. For hikers, there are 47 maintained trails ranging from .5 mile to 55 miles in length. To expend less energy, drive The Gunflint Trail or the Echo Lake Trail. Other Superior experiences include trout fishing, and cross-country skiing. Camp at 27 developed campgrounds along lakes and rivers (from free to $11.00) or savor Superior solitude (for free).

US Army Corps of Engineers (COE) has developed the Mississippi River Headwaters Lakes Project encompassing Cross Lake, Gull Lake, Lake Winnibigoshish, Leech Lake, Pokegama Lake, and Sandy Lake. Around these six lakes, find campgrounds ranging from free to $13.00 per night.

The **Minnesota Department of Natural Resources** (DNR) offers a variety of camping opportunities in its state parks and in its state forests. All types of campsites are provided in 60 state parks—from cart-in areas to secluded canoe stops to horse camps to RV pads with all the amenities. Winter camping areas with pit toilets and electrical hookups are available at some parks. **Minnesota State Park** (SP) nightly camping fees include tax as follows: remote (backpack, bike-in, and boat-in)–$7.00 per site (or $1.00

▲ ▲

per person–whichever is greater), rustic–$8.00 per site, semi-modern (showers)–$10.00 per site. Modern sites with electric hookups are an additional $2.50 per night whether used or not. With innovative campgrounds (such as cart-in sites at Split Rock Lighthouse) and recreational opportunities (such as paved bike paths at 12 parks) plus strong environmental programs in all of Minnesota's state parks, "expect nature's best."

In 30 **Minnesota State Forests** (SF) locations, there are $7.00 developed sites as well as free primitive ones. All campsites consist of a cleared area, fireplace, and table. Developed sites add drinking water, pit toilets, garbage containers, and level parking spurs. Many forests provide miles of trails for canoeing, hiking, horseback riding, and cross-country skiing. Also, enjoy picking berries, hunting mushrooms, identifying wildflowers, and photographing nature.

Several **counties** have also constructed campgrounds: Aitkin, Anoka, Becker, Beltrami, Carlton, Carver, Clearwater, Cook, Crow Wing, Hennepin, Hubbard, Itasca, Koochiching, Polk, and Washington. **Towns** include Benson, Butterfield, Canby, Crookston, Fosston, Granite Falls, Hallock, Henderson, Karlstad, Lancaster, Lanesboro, McIntosh, Madelia, Melrose, Pelican Rapids, Sebeka, Thief River Falls, and Warroad. If county and town campgrounds cost $5.00 or less, find them in the following listings.

Open your senses to various, superior camping experiences in Minnesota. Try the innovative state park sites (hike-in, cart-in, bike-in, horse-in, boat-in as well as drive-in). Canoe the boundary waters. Sample the bounty and beauty of the land. Savor the solitude of vast grasslands, boreal forests, and glacial lakes.

▲ ▲

ALLANSON'S PARK

Henderson City Parks
(612) 248-3236
State map: 18I
Find park on South St in HENDERSON.

$5; $7 electric.
Open Apr 1–Dec 1.
20 (12 tent-only) close, screened sites.
Central faucet, flush toilets, showers, dump station, electric hookups, tables, fire rings, boat ramp.
In woods on scenic overlook of Minnesota River.
Walk nature trail. Observe wildlife.
Enjoy quiet.
800 ft (240 m)

AMBUSH PARK

(612) 843-3362
State map: 15D
Locate park just W of BENSON on MN 9.
$5. Open Apr–Oct; dry camping allowed off-season.
10 (3 tent-only) close, open sites.

Central faucet, flush toilets, showers, dump station, electric hookups, tables, fire rings, shelter.
Next to Chippewa River with adjacent pool and golf course.
Swim ($), boat, or fish. Walk nature trail.

ARROW POINT

Minnesota SF
(218) 935-5951
State map: 9D
From WAUBUN, drive E on MN 113 for 20 miles (32 k). Turn Left (N) on Height of Land Rd and go 4.5 miles (7.2 k).
FREE so choose a chore.
Open May 30–Nov 1; camping allowed off-season.
6 (4 tent-only) screened sites.
Pit toilets, tables, fire rings, boat ramp.
In climax hardwood forest next to lake.
Swim, boat, and fish. Watch wildlife.
NO water. No trash arrangements (pack it out). 14-day limit. Crowded weekends.
Camp lightly (overuse problem).
1813 ft (544 m)

▲ ▲

BAKER LAKE

Superior NF (218) 663-7981
State map: 6P
From TOFTE, drive N on CR 2 (Sawbill Trace) for 16.5 miles (26.4 k). Turn Right (NE) on FR 165 and continue 4.5 miles (7.2 k). (Also see Poplar River. Nearby Crescent Lake and Sawmill Lake cost $7.50.)
FREE so choose a chore.
Open May 15–Sep 15; dry camping allowed off-season.
5 close, open sites.
Central faucet, pit toilets, tables, fire rings, boat ramp.
In woods next to lake at edge of Boundary Waters Canoe Area Wilderness.
Canoe. Fish. Walk nature trail.
14-day limit.

BEMIS HILL

Minnesota SF
(218) 386-1304
State map: 3E
From WARROAD, head S on CR 5 for 12 miles (19.2 k). Turn Right (W) on Thompson FR and go 6 miles (9.6 k).
FREE so choose a chore.
Open All Year.
4 close, open, tent sites.
Hand pump, pit toilets, tables, fire rings, shelter.
In boreal forest setting.
Hike to enjoy ecology. View wildlife. Relax.
14-day limit. Hunting in season. No generators in quiet hours. Snowmobiles in winter.

BIG BEND CANOE-IN

Minnesota SF
(218) 472-3262
State map: 10F
On Crow Wing River at HUNTERSVILLE, paddle 2 miles (3.2 k) SW. (Nearby Shell City costs $7.)
FREE so choose a chore.

Open All Year.
5 close, open, tent sites.
Pit toilets, tables, fire rings.
In oak trees on beautiful river.
Canoe. Hike. Relax.
NO water. No trash arrangements (pack it out).

BIRCHDALE ACCESS (NELSON PARK)

Koochiching County
(218) 283-6296
State map: 4H
From BIRCHDALE, drive N for 1 mile (1.6 k) on gravel road. (Also see Frontier Access and Upper Sioux Access. Nearby Franz Jevne SP costs $7.)
FREE so choose a chore.
Open All Year.
10 scattered, open sites.
Hand pump, pit toilets, tables, fire rings, grills, boat ramp, shelter.
In ash tree setting on Rainy River.
Fish or boat. Relax. Explore.
14-day limit. Crowded spring and fall.

BLUEBERRY HILL

Minnesota SF
(218) 634-2172
State map: 3F
From WILLIAMS, head W on MN 11 for 5 miles (8 k).
FREE so choose a chore.
Open All Year.
14 close, open sites. Hand pump, pit toilets, tables, grills, fire rings.
Among mature jack pine.
Hike to view wildlife. Pick berries. Cross-country ski in winter.
No trash arrangements. 14-day limit. Hunting in season. No generators in quiet hours. Snowmobiles in winter.

CANBY MUNICIPAL PARK

(507) 223-7295
State map: 17C
In CANBY, drive about .5 mile (800 m) S of US 75 & MN 68. (Also see Triangle.)

▲ ▲

$5.
Open May–Oct.
10 close, open sites.
Central faucet, flush toilets, dump station, electric hookups, tables, pool, tennis court, playground.
Next to swimming pool.
Play sports. Swim ($). Enjoy overnight stop.

CASCADE RIVER

Superior NF (218) 387-1750
State map: 6P
From GRAND MARAIS, drive N on CR 12 (Gunflint Trail) for 3.7 miles (5.9 k).
Bear Left (NW) on CR 8. Travel 6 miles (9.6 k). Continue W on CR 57 for 6 miles (9.6 k). Turn Right (N) on FR 158.
FREE so choose a chore.
Open May 15–Sep 15; camping allowed off-season.
3 close, open sites.
Pit toilets, tables, fire rings.
Beside river.
Fish. Watch wildlife.
NO water. No trash arrangements (pack it out). 14-day limit.

CENTRAL PARK

(218) 281-1232
State map: 7B
Locate park in CROOKSTON.
$4; $7 electric.
Open May 15–Oct 31.
20 close, open sites.
Central faucet, flush toilets, showers, dump station, electric hookups, tables, fire rings, boat ramp, indoor pool.
Next to Red Lake River.
Swim. Boat or fish.

COTTONWOOD LAKE

Minnesota SF
(218) 246-8343
State map: 8I
From DEER RIVER, drive N on MN 6 for 4 miles (6.4 k). Turn Right (E) on CR 19 and go 3 miles (4.8 k). Turn Left (N) on CR 48

and proceed 1 mile (1.6 k). Turn Right (E) at sign and continue 1 mile (1.6 k). (Nearby Moose Lake costs $7.)
$4.
Open May 1–Sep 30.
15 (5 tent-only) close, open sites.
Hand pump, pit toilets, tables, fire rings, grills, boat ramp.
In woods next to lake.
Boat and fish. Explore. Relax.
No trash arrangements (pack it out). 14-day limit.

ESTHER LAKE

Minnesota SF
(218) 387-1075
State map: 6R
From HOVLAND, travel N on CR 16 for 12 miles (19.2 k). Turn Left (W) on Beaver Dam Rd and drive 2 miles (3.2 k). Turn on Esther Lake Rd and proceed 3.5 miles (5.4 k). (Also see McFarland Lake.)
FREE so choose a chore.
Open May 15–Sep 15.
4 close, open sites.
Pit toilets, tables, grills, fire rings.
In old-growth white pine next to lake.
Fish and boat. View wildlife. Take photos.
NO water. 14-day/22-ft limits. Hunting in season. Crowded holidays.

FAUNCE

Minnesota SF
(218) 386-1304
State map: 4F
From WILLIAMS, go S on CR 2 for 11 miles (19.2 k).
FREE so choose a chore.
Open All Year.
4 close, open sites.
Hand pump, pit toilets, tables, grills, fire rings.
Among mature jack pine.
Relax. Hike. Pick berries. Cross-country ski in winter.
No trash arrangements (pack it out). 14-day limit. Hunting in season. No generators in quiet hours. Snowmobiles in winter.

▲ ▲

FOSSTON CAMPGROUND

(218) 435-1959
State map: 7D
Find campground in
FOSSTON at fairgrounds.
$5; $7 electric.
Open May 1–Sep 30.
10 close, open sites. Central faucet, flush
toilets, showers, dump station, electric
hookups, tables, shelter.
With shade trees.
Enjoy overnight stop.

FRONTIER ACCESS

Koochiching County
(218) 283-6296
State map: 4H
From BIRCHDALE, drive
W on MN 11 for 6 miles
(9.6 k). (Also see Birchdale Access.)
FREE so choose a chore.
Open All Year.
6 scattered, open, tent sites.
Hand pump, pit toilets, tables, fire rings,
grills, boat ramp.
In open setting with small Norway pine
trees along Rainy River.
Boat or fish.
14-day limit. Crowded spring and fall.

GILBERT OLSON PARK

Hallock Municipal Parks
(218) 843-2737
State map: 3B
Locate park at 800 7th St
SE in HALLOCK.
$5. Open May 15–Sep 30.
48 scattered, open sites. &
Central faucet, flush toilets, showers,
dump station, electric hookups, tables,
fire rings, pool.
Next to river and 9-hole golf course.
Walk nature trail. Swim. Play golf. Fish.
815 ft (245 m)

GRANITE FALLS MEMORIAL PARK

(612) 564-3011
State map: 17E
From GRANITE FALLS,
head SE on MN 67 about
.25 mile (400 m).

$3; $5 electric.
Open Apr–Oct.
Undesignated plus 12 close, open sites.
Water at 12 sites, pit toilets, dump
station, electric hookups, tables, fire
rings, grills, boat ramp.
In 100-acres of wilderness along
Minnesota River.
Use fitness trail. Boat or fish.
34-ft limit.

GULCH LAKES RA

Minnesota SF
(218) 224-2424
State map: 9F
From LAPORTE, drive W
on MN 200 for 2 miles
(3.2 k). Turn Left (S) on MN 64 and go
4 miles (6.4 k). Turn Right (W) on Gulch
Forest Rd.
FREE so choose a chore.
Open Jun 1–Oct 1; camping allowed off-
season.
10 scattered, screened sites.
Pit toilets, tables, fire rings.
On 5 lakes: Bass, Halvorsen, Lake 21,
McCarty, and Nelson among hardwood-
covered rolling hills in Paul Bunyon SF.
Canoe. Fish. Hike area to view wildlife
and find photo opportunities.
NO water. No trash arrangements (pack
it out). 14-day limit. Small vehicles only.
Hunting in season. Crowded weekends.
1400 ft (420 m)

HOLE-IN-THE-MOUNTAIN

Lincoln County Parks
(507) 368-9350
State map: 19C
From LAKE BENTON,
travel E on US 14 about
1 mile (1.6 k). (Nearby are Norwegian
and Picnic Resort.)
$5; $7 hookups. Open Apr–Dec.
70 (20 tent-only) close, open sites.
Water at 18 sites, flush toilets, showers,
dump station, electric hookups, tables,
fire rings, boat ramp, playground.
Next to lake.
Swim, boat, ski, or fish. Walk nature
trail. Cross-country ski in winter.

▲ ▲

KARLSTAD MOOSE PARK

(218) 436-2178
State map: 4C
Locate park in KARLSTAD.
$3.
Open Apr–Sep 30; dry camping allowed off-season.
8 close, open sites.
Central faucet, flush toilets, dump station, electric hookups, tables, fire rings, shelter, tennis court.
Among poplar and oak trees.
Enjoy overnight stay.

KAWISHIWI LAKE

Superior NF (218) 663-7981
State map: 6O
From TOFTE, drive N on CR 2 (Sawbill Trace) for 17 miles (27.2 k). Turn Left (W) on CR 3/7 and go 7.8 miles (12.5 k). Turn Right (N) on FR 354 and continue 4.4 miles (7 k).
FREE so choose a chore.
Open May 15–Sep 15; camping allowed off-season.
5 close, open sites.
Pit toilets, tables, fire rings, boat ramp.
Next to lake at edge of Boundary Waters Canoe Area Wilderness.
Canoe. Fish. Explore.
NO water. 14-day limit.

KNEFFNER'S LANDING

Koochiching County
(218) 283-6296
State map: 4I
From LITTLEFORK, take MN 71 SW to CR 77. Turn Right (W) and go to end. Turn Left (S) on CR 13.
FREE so choose a chore.
Open All Year.
2 scattered, open, tent sites.
Pit toilets, tables, fire rings.
In open feeling of white pine on Big Fork River.
Canoe. Fish.
NO water. 14-day limit. Small vehicles only. Hunting in season. Crowded fishing season opening.

LANCASTER CITY PARK

(218) 762-4090
State map: 3B
Find park in LANCASTER.
FREE; $5 electric.
Open All Year.
18 close, open sites. &
Central faucet, flush toilets, showers, dump station, electric hookups, tables, fire rings, shelter.
In small, town park.
Enjoy overnight stay.

LEECH LAKE DAM

COE (218) 654-3145
State map: 8H
From BENA, head S on CR 8 for 8 miles (12.8 k) to Federal Dam.
FREE at 14 sites; $10 at 60 sites.
Open May 1–Nov 15.
74 scattered, screened sites. &
Central faucet, flush toilets, showers, dump station, electric hookups, tables, fire rings, grills, boat ramp, store, rentals, pay phone.
In mixed hardwood/pine with wetlands next to channel for Leech Lake.
Boat, ski, or fish. Hike area to view wildlife. Attend ranger programs.
14-day limit.
1298 ft (389 m)

LITTLE AMERICAN FALLS

Koochiching County
(218) 283-6296
State map: 6I
From EFFIE, head N for 10 miles (16 k) on gravel CR 5.
FREE so choose a chore.
Open All Year.
4 scattered, screened, tent sites.
Pit toilets, tables, grills, fire rings.
On hill near Bigfork River.
Fish. Hike. Take photos.
NO water. No trash arrangements (pack it out). 14-day limit. Hunting in season.

▲ ▲

LONG LAKE

Minnesota SF
(218) 246-8343
State map: 7I
From TALMOON, head N
on MN 6 for 6 miles (9.6 k).
$4.
Open May 1–Sep 5.
6 close, screened sites.
Hand pump, pit toilets, tables, fire rings,
grills, boat ramp.
On wooded lakeshore.
Fish or boat. Relax. Explore.
No trash arrangements. 14-day limit.

LOON LAKE

Jackson County Parks
(507) 847-2240
State map: 21F
From JACKSON, drive S
on US 71 for 6 miles
(9.6 k). Turn Right (W) on CR 4 and
proceed 4 miles (6.4 k).
$2.50; $6 RV; $7 electric.
Open Apr 1–Oct 31; dry camping
allowed off-season.
100 (25 tent-only) screened sites.
Central faucet, pit toilets, showers, dump
station, electric hookups, tables, grills,
boat ramp.
In both wooded and open settings next
to lake.
Walk nature trail. Hike trails to view
wildlife and take photos. Swim, boat, ski,
and fish.
7-day limit.
1340 ft (402 m)

MCFARLAND LAKE

Minnesota SF
(218) 387-1075
State map: 6R
From HOVLAND, travel N
on CR 16 for 18 miles
(28.8 k). (Also see Esther Lake.)
FREE so choose a chore.
Open May 15–Sep 15.
5 close, open sites.
Pit toilets, tables, fire rings, boat ramp.
In boreal forest next to lake at eastern
entry into Boundary Waters Canoe Area.

Hike to observe flora and fauna. Canoe.
Fish. Swim nearby. Take photos.
NO water. No trash arrangements (pack
it out). 14-day/22-ft limits. Hunting in
season. Crowded holidays.
1480 ft (444 m)

MIDDLE PIGEON

Chippewa NF
(218) 246-2123
State map: 8I
From DEER RIVER, drive
N on MN 46 about
24 miles (38.4 k). Turn Left (W) on
gravel CR 156 and go 3 miles (4.8 k).
Turn Left (S) for final .25 mile (400 m).
FREE so choose a chore.
Open May–Nov; dry camping allowed
off-season.
4 close, open sites.
Hand pump, pit toilets, tables, fire rings,
boat ramp.
In remote setting with lake pine.
Swim, boat, or fish. Observe wildlife.
Enjoy seclusion.
14-day limit. Crowded fishing season
opening.
1350 ft (405 m)

NINEMILE LAKE

Superior NF (218) 663-7981
State map: 7O
From FINLAND, drive NE
on CR 7 for 15 miles (24 k).
$5.
Open May 15–Sep 15; dry camping
allowed off-season.
24 close, open sites. ♿
Central faucet, pit toilets, tables, fire
rings, boat ramp.
Next to lake.
Canoe. Fish. Walk nature trail. View
wildlife.
14-day limit.

POLK COUNTY PARK

(218) 281-3952
State map: 7C
From MENTOR, travel SW
on CR 12 for 4 miles
(6.4 k). (Also see Roholt

Park and Tilberg Park.)
$5; $6 RV; $8 electric.
Open May 15–Sep 15.
30 close, open sites.
Central faucet, flush toilets, dump station, tables, fire rings.
In light woods on slope down to lake.
Swim, boat, and fish.
Crowded holidays and some weekends.

POPLAR RIVER

Superior NF (218) 663-7981
State map: 7P
From TOFTE, drive N on CR 2 (Sawbill Trace) for 11 miles (17.6 k). Turn Right (E) on FR 164 and travel 6 miles (9.6 k). (Also see Baker Lake. Nearby Crescent Lake costs $7.50.)
FREE so choose a chore.
Open May 15–Sep 15; camping allowed off-season.
4 close, open sites.
Pit toilets, tables, fire rings.
Next to river.
Fish. Observe wildlife.
NO water. 14-day limit.

RENO

Minnesota SF
(507) 523-2183
State map: 21O
From RENO, head W then N on township road for .25 mile (400 m).
FREE so choose a chore.
Open May 15–Sep 15; dry camping allowed off-season.
5 close, open sites.
Hand pump, pit toilets, tables, fire rings.
In forest.
Hike series of trails. Relax. View wildlife.
No trash arrangements. 14-day limit.

ROHOLT PARK

City of McIntosh Parks
(218) 563-3043
State map: 7D
Locate park on E side of MCINTOSH on US 2. (Also see Polk County Park and Tilberg Park.)

$5. Open May 15–Oct 15.
10 scattered, open sites.
Central faucet, flush toilets, showers, dump station, electric hookups, tables, grills, fire rings.
Among trees and flowers.
Relax for night or two.

SAMUELSON

Koochiching County
(218) 283-6296
State map: 6J
From RAUCH, take gravel CR 75 E for 3 miles (4.8 k).
FREE so choose a chore.
Open Apr 1–Dec 1.
2 scattered, open, tent sites.
Hand pump, tables.
On banks of Littlefork River.
Fish. Relax. Take photos.
No toilet facilities. No trash arrangements (pack it out). 14-day limit.

SAUK RIVER CITY PARK

(612) 256-4278
State map: 14F
Find park in MELROSE on N Fifth Ave E.
$3; $5 RV.
Open May 1–Oct 1.
28 close, open sites.
Central faucet, flush toilets, dump station, electric hookups, tables, grills.
In wooded setting along Sauk River.
Fish. Take photos.
14-day limit.

SEBEKA MUNICIPAL PARK

(218) 837-5773
State map: 11F
Locate park in SEBEKA on US 71 S.
$4; $6 electric.
Open May–Oct.
62 close, open sites.
Central faucet, flush toilets, showers, dump station, electric hookups, tables, grills, playground.
Along Red Eye River with walkbridge to business district.
Visit museum. Relax.

SERETHA LAKE

Koochiching County
(218) 283-6296
State map: 6H
From NORTHOME, head
NW on MN 71 for 12 miles
(19.2 k). Turn Left (N).
FREE so choose a chore. Open All Year.
2 scattered, open, tent sites.
Pit toilets, tables, grills, fire rings.
Next to small lake surrounded by timber
and open field.
Fish. Take photos.
NO water. No trash arrangements (pack
it out). Hunting in season.

SHERWIN PARK CAMPGROUND

(218) 863-6571
State map: 11C
Find park in PELICAN
RAPIDS on MN 108 E.
$4; $6 electric.
Open May–Sep.
26 (20 tent-only) scattered, open sites.
Central faucet, flush toilets, showers,
dump station, electric hookups, tables,
fire rings, pool.
In wooded setting on Pelican River.
Swim. Fish. Hike trails.
1300 ft (390 m)

STAR ISLAND BOAT-IN

Chippewa NF
(218) 335-2283
State map: 8G
From CASS LAKE, drive
4 miles (6.4 k) E on US 2.
Turn Left (N) on Norway Beach Rd and
follow signs to Cass Lake Visitor Center.
Boat in about 2 miles (3.2 k). (Nearby
Cass Lake and Norway Beach cost $10.)
FREE so choose a chore.
Open All Year.
Undesignated scattered, open sites.
Pit toilets, fire rings.
On Cass Lake island with sites on north
and south shores with sandy beaches.
Swim, boat, ski, or fish. Hike area to
observe wildlife and take photos.
NO water. Crowded summer weekends.
1320 ft (396 m)

SYLVAN PARK

Lanesboro Parks
(507) 467-3722
State map: 21N
Locate park in
LANESBORO on MN 250.
$5; $9 electric.
Open Apr–Nov.
30 close, open sites.
Central faucet, flush toilets, showers,
dump station, electric hookups, tables,
fire rings, playground, tennis court.
In town park with fishing ponds.
Fish. Canoe. Explore town.

THIEF RIVER FALLS TOURIST PARK

(218) 681-2519
State map: 5C
Find park in THIEF RIVER
FALLS at MN 32 and
Oakland Park Rd.
$5; $8 electric; $12 full hookups.
Open May 15–Oct 1.
51 scattered, open sites.
Central faucet, flush toilets, showers,
electric hookups, tables, grills, fire rings,
shelter, pay phone.
With groomed grass and shrubs (plus
beautiful flower beds) overlooking river.
Hike to view area and take photos. Bike.
Canoe. Fish.
10-day limit.

TILBERG PARK

Polk County Parks
(218) 281-3952
State map: 7D
From FOSSTON, head N
on CR 6 for 3 miles (4.8 k).
Turn Right (NE) on CR 3 and drive
4.5 miles (7.2 k). Turn Right (E) on CR 29
for final .5 mile (800 m). (Also see Polk
County Park and Roholt Park.)
$5; $6 RV; $8 electric.
Open May 15–Sep 15.
30 close, open sites.
Central faucet, pit toilets, dump station,
electric hookups, tables, fire rings.
In dense woods on hill overlooking
Cross Lake.
Swim, boat, or fish.

▲ ▲

TRIANGLE

Canby Municipal Parks
(507) 223-7295
State map: 17C
Find campground just NE
of CANBY at US 75 &
CR 3. (Also see Canby Municipal Park.)
$5. Open May–Oct.
10 close, open sites.
Central faucet, flush toilets, dump
station, electric hookups, tables.
In town park.
Relax. Enjoy overnight stop.

UPPER SIOUX ACCESS

Koochiching County
(218) 283-6296
State map: 4H
From BIRCHDALE, drive
2 miles (3.2 k) E on MN 11.
Turn Left (N) on gravel road. (Also see
Birchdale Access. Nearby Franz Jevne SP
cost $7.)
FREE so choose a chore. Open All Year.
2 scattered, open sites. Pit toilets, tables,
fire rings, grills, boat ramp.
On Rainy River.
Fish or boat. Observe wildlife.
NO water. Crowded spring and fall.

VOSS PARK

(507) 956-2241
State map: 20F
Locate park just W of
BUTTERFIELD on CR 2.
$5; $6 electric.
Open May–Oct.
110 close, open sites. Water at 10 sites,
chemical toilets, dump station, electric
hookups, tables, playground.
In town park. Enjoy overnight stop.

VOYAGEURS NP-Backcountry

(218) 283-9821
State map: 4K
From INTERNATIONAL
FALLS, drive about
12 miles (19.2 k) E on
MN 11 to Rainy Lake Visitor Center.
Obtain permit. Alternative canoe put-in
points include Kabetogama Lake and

Ash River visitor centers (E of RAY).
FREE. Open All Year.
120 scattered, tent sites. Water needs
treating, pit toilets, tables, fire rings.
About 120 separate boat-in camps among
30 glacier-carved lakes with rocky knobs,
bogs, marshes, and beaver ponds–
adjoining Boundary Waters Canoe Area
and Ontario's Quetico Provincial Park.
Canoe. Swim or fish. Hike. View
wildlife. Take photos. Attend ranger
programs. Cross-country ski in winter.
No trash arrangements (pack it out).
14-day limit. Biting insects in summer.
Snowmobiles in winter.
1100 ft (330 m)

WARROAD CAMPGROUND

(218) 386-1454
State map: 3E
From WARROAD, go NE
1 mile (1.6 k) on Lake St.
$5; $8 developed; $10
electric; $12 full hookups.
Open May 15–Sep 15.
180 (40 tent-only) close, open sites.
Central faucet, flush toilets, showers,
dump station, electric hookups, tables,
fire rings, boat ramp, pool, pay phone.
In trees next to Lake of the Woods on
edge of town.
Swim. Boat. Fish.
Hunting in season. Occasionally
crowded.
1075 ft (323 m)

WATONA PARK

(507) 642-3245
State map: 20G
Locate park on old Hwy
60/15 in MADELIA.
FREE so choose a chore.
Open Apr 15–Oct 15.
15 scattered, open sites. &
Water at all sites, flush toilets, showers,
dump station, electric hookups, tables,
fire rings, pool, playground, ball field.
Near river in D-loop with trees along
back next to golf course.
Fish or boat river. Swim. Walk nature
trail. Play golf.

▲ ▲

MISSISSIPPI
CAMPGROUND LOCATIONS

▸ ▸ Find location on facing page map grid. ▸ ▸
▾ ▾ Locate area campgrounds on these page numbers. ▾ ▾

▲▲▲▲▲▲▲▲▲▲▲▲▲▲▲▲▲▲▲▲▲▲▲▲▲▲▲▲

Mississippi

Grid conforms to official state map. For your copy, call (800) 647-2290
or write Division of Tourism, PO Box 22825, Jackson, MS 39205.

▲▲▲▲▲▲▲▲▲▲▲▲▲▲▲▲▲▲▲▲▲▲▲▲▲▲▲▲

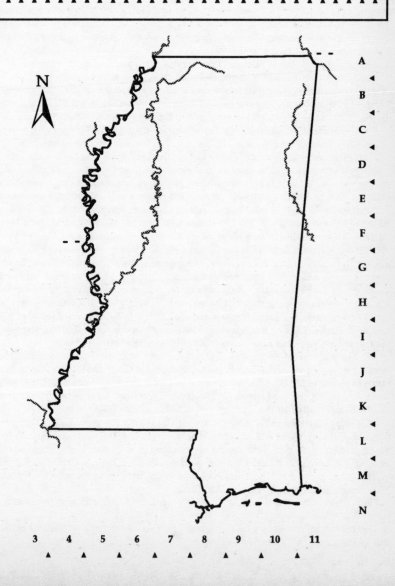

N

A B C D E F G H I J K L M N

3 4 5 6 7 8 9 10 11

PUBLIC LANDS CAMPING

The word *Mississippi* derives from the Choctaw language and means *father of waters*. The Mississippi River forms the western boundary of Mississippi and bears great impact on the state–in agriculture, commerce, tourism, literature, and music.

Beauty is diverse in Mississippi. Find deep forests and rolling hills where the Appalachian Mountains begin in the northeastern corner of the state. Discover a wide plain along the mighty river and white-sand beaches on the Gulf of Mexico. See diversity in the state's history–mysterious Indian mounds, antebellum mansions, and Civil Rights commemorations. Too, the mild climate makes the state a popular year-round camping destination. Winter's average low dips to 50 degrees; summer's average high reaches just above the 90-degree mark.

For federal public lands, **National Park Service** (NPS) administers the Natchez Trace Parkway and Gulf Islands National Seashore (NS). As you retrace the footsteps of Native Americans then early settlers along the Mississippi section of the Natchez Trace, camp at two free campgrounds. At Gulf Islands NS, camping costs $12.00 at Davis Bayou, but it's free if you boat to unimproved East Ship, Horn, or Petit Bois islands.

US Department of Agriculture's Forest Service manages Holly Springs National Forest (NF), Tombigbee NF, Delta NF, Bienville NF, De Soto NF, and Homochitto NF. The 147,000-acre Holly Springs NF lies just south of the Tennessee border and offers many recreational opportunities in and around its lakes. In the thick pines and hardwoods of the 66,000-acre Tombigbee NF, enjoy camping, hiking, horseback riding.... The 59,000-acre Delta NF protects the nation's only bottomland hardwood national forest. It's rich in wildlife, particularly migratory waterfowl. The 178,000-acre Bienville NF was named after the Frenchman who founded Mobile, Natchez, and New Orleans. This centrally located forest offers a variety of sporting activities. At over 500,000 acres, the De Soto NF is the largest national forest in Mississippi. It's mostly "piney" woods on gentle hills with winding streams. Most famous is Black Creek, popular for its wilderness area, hiking trail, and float trip on the national wild and scenic river. The Homochitto NF takes its name from the Indian word for the *big red river* flowing through the forest. This subtropical forest is a 189,000-acre tract in southwest Mississippi. Together, the 6 national forests in Mississippi offer over 230 camps, 276 miles of hiking trails, 8 swimming beaches, and innumerable lake and river access points. Camp fees range from free to $10.00 with electricity.

US Army Corps of Engineers (COE) maintains recreation areas at manmade Arkabutla Lake, Enid Lake, Grenada Lake, Okatibbee Lake, and Sardis Lake. Camp fees range from free to $12.00. Also, camping can be found along the Tennessee-Tombigbee Waterway (COE), the Pat Harrison Waterway, and the Pearl River Basin. In addition, the **Tennessee Valley Authority** (TVA) provides a facility at Goat Island.

Mississippi State Parks (SP) charge $6.00–$8.00 to tent in designated areas. Campers needing electricity, water and sewage pay an additional $4.00. There are discounts for senior citizens. Camp at Buccaneer, Clarkco, George P Cossar, Great River Road, Homes County, Hugh White, J P Coleman, John W Kyle, Lake Lowndes, LeFleur's Bluff, Legion, Leroy Percy, Natchez, Paul B Johnson, Percy Quin, Roosevelt, Shepard, Tishomingo, Tombigbee, Trace, and Wall Doxey.

Find an interesting **local park** with camping at Grand Gulf Military Park outside pretty Port Gibson.

Take time to enjoy Mississippi–its sweeping hills, its deep forests, its textured fields, and its soft sands. It's all in Mississippi.

▲ ▲

AIREY LAKE

De Soto NF (601) 928-5291
State map: M9
From MCHENRY, drive E for
5 miles (8 k) on E McHenry
Rd. Turn Right (S) on CR 412
(Airey Tower) and go 2 miles (3.2 k).
(Also see Big Biloxi.)
FREE so choose a chore. Open All Year.
Undesignated scattered, open sites.
Central faucet, chemical toilets, tables,
fire rings.
Next to remote, 3-acre lake.
Hike Tuxachanie National Recreation
Trail. Observe wildlife. Fish.
14-day limit. Hunting in season.
100 ft (30 m)

ASHE LAKE

De Soto NF (601) 928-4423
State map: L9
From BROOKLYN, head SE on
CR 318 about 2 miles (3.2 k).
Turn Right (SW) on CR 308
(Ashe Nursery) for .25 mile (400 m).
(Also see Big Creek Landing and
Moody's Landing.)
FREE so choose a chore. Open All Year.
8 scattered, open, tent sites.
Pit toilets, tables, boat ramp.
In longleaf pine next to 4-acre lake.
Fish, boat (small only), or take float trip.
Hike nearby Black Creek Trail.
NO water. 14-day limit.

ATWOOD WATER PARK

Pearl River Basin
(601) 587-7732
State map: J7
Locate park on E side of
MONTICELLO at US 84
bridge over Pearl River.
$3.50; $7 developed; reservations
accepted at (601) 354-6301.
Open All Year.
44 close, open sites.
Water at every site, flush toilets,
showers, dump station, electric hookups,
tables, grills, boat ramp, pay phone.
With large trees along Pearl River.
Boat and fish.

Occasional floods. Crowded during
Bluegrass Festival.

BEACH POINT

COE (601) 563-4531
State map: C7
From SARDIS, drive E on
MS 315 for 8 miles (12.8 k),
just SW of John Kyle SP. (Also
see Elmers Hill and Sleepy Bend.)
FREE so choose a chore. Open All Year.
14 scattered, tent sites. Central faucet,
flush toilets, tables, grills, fire rings.
In shade overlooking Sardis Lake.
Boat, waterski, or fish.
14-day limit.
290 ft (87 m)

BIG BILOXI

De Soto NF (601) 928-5291
State map: M9
From LYMAN, go N on US 49
for 5 miles (8 k). Turn Left (W)
on De Soto Park Rd for .5 mile
(800 m). (Also see Airey Lake.)
$5; $10 RV; reservations accepted at
(601) 928-5291 for an additional $6.
Open All Year.
25 (8 tent-only) close, screened sites. &
Water at every site, flush toilets,
showers, dump station, electric hookups,
tables, grills, fire rings, shelter, sports
field, pay phone.
In CCC-built setting with natural
vegetation on banks of Big Biloxi River.
Walk nature trail. Fish.
14-day limit. Often crowded.
100 ft (30 m)

BIG CREEK LANDING

De Soto NF (601) 928-4423
State map: L9
From BROOKLYN, exit on
US 49, drive S 1 mile (1.6 k).
Turn Right (W) on CR 334 and
go .5 mile (800 m). Continue W on
CR 335 for 2.5 miles (4 k). Turn Right
(N) on FR 335E. (Also see Ashe Lake.)
FREE so choose a chore. Open All Year.
1 tent site. Table, boat ramp.
On bank of Black Creek in mixed pine

and hardwood at end of Black Creek Float Trip and Hiking Trail.
Canoe. Hike. View wildlife.
NO water. No toilet facilities. 14-day limit.

BLUE LAKE

Delta NF (601) 873-6256
State map: G5
From ROLLING FORK, head E on MS 16 for 7.5 miles (12 k). Turn Right (SW) on FR 715 and proceed 3.5 miles (5.4 k).
FREE so choose a chore. Open All Year.
Undesignated close, open sites.
Chemical toilets, tables, grills.
In bottomland hardwood next to series of sloughs and small lakes (over 80 individual, primitive sites scattered through district).
Fish or boat. Watch wildlife.
NO water. Occasional floods. Hunting in season. Mosquitos and flies.
100 ft (30 m)

BURNSIDE LAKE PARK

Pearl River Basin
(601) 656-7621
State map: G9
From PHILADELPHIA, head N on MS 15 for 2 miles (3.2 k).
$3; $7 developed. Open All Year.
22 close, open sites. Water at every developed site, flush toilets, showers, dump station, electric hookups, tables, grills, boat ramp, ball fields.
On cypress-lined oxbow, Burnside Lake.
Fish. Walk nature trail.
Crowded during Neshoba County Fair.

BYNUM CREEK

COE (601) 563-4571
State map: C7
From Exit 237 of I-55 (near POPE), take US 51 S for 1 mile (1.6 k). Turn Left (E). Drive 14.5 miles (23.2 k). Turn Right (S) on gravel road. Go 2.4 miles (3.8 k). (Also see Plum Point. Nearby Chickasaw Hill costs $10.)
FREE so choose a chore. Open All Year.

10 scattered, open, tent sites. Pit toilets, tables, fire rings, grills, boat ramp.
Next to creek and backwaters of Enid Lake in peaceful setting.
Swim, boat, ski, and fish. Spot wildlife.
NO water. 14-day/35-ft limits. Hunting in season. Crowded holidays.
290 ft (87 m)

CHOCTAW

COE (601) 226-1679
State map: D8
From GRENADA, take MS 8 E about 10 miles (16 k) to Gore Springs. Turn Left (N). Go 8 miles (12.8 k). Turn Left (SW). Travel 3 miles (4.8 k). (Also see Gums Crossing, Old Fort, and Skuna-Turkey.)
FREE so choose a chore. Open All Year.
3 scattered, open, tent sites.
Central faucet, pit toilets, tables, fire rings, grills, boat ramp.
On shore of Grenada Lake.
Boat, ski, or fish. Watch wildlife.
14-day limit. Crowded summer weekends.
219 ft (66 m)

COONTOWN

COE (601) 563-4531
State map: C7
From OXFORD, take MS 314 NE about 2 miles (3.2 k). Bear Right (NE) on CR 102 and drive to end of road.
FREE so choose a chore. Open All Year.
3 scattered, open, tent sites.
Chemical toilets, tables, fire rings.
In open area near Sardis Lake.
Boat or fish. View wildlife and take photos in nearby Sardis Wildlife Refuge.
NO water. 14-day limit.
270 ft (81 m)

CYPRESS CREEK LANDING

De Soto NF (601) 928-4423
State map: L9
From BROOKLYN, head E on CR 301 about 10 miles (16 k). Continue E on MS 29 about 2 miles (3.2 k). Turn Right (S) on FR 305

▲ ▲

and go 3 miles (4.8 k). Bear Right (SW) on FR 305B. (Also see Janice Landing and Fairley Bridge Landing.)
FREE so choose a chore. Open All Year.
15 close, open, tent sites.
Central faucet, flush toilets, tables, fire rings, grills, boat ramp.
On high bluff overlooking Black Creek National Wild and Scenic River.
Canoe or float creek. Hike and explore Black Creek Wilderness via Black Creek National Recreation Trail.
14-day/22-ft limits. Hunting in season.

D'LO WATER PARK

Pearl River Basin
(601) 847-4310
State map: I7
Take MS 19/43 SW for 2 miles (3.2 k) from MENDENHALL.
$3; $8 RV; reservations accepted at (601) 354-6301.
Open All Year. 12 close, open sites.
Water at every site, flush toilets, showers, dump station, electric hookups, tables, grills, rentals, pay phone.
In grassy area near Pearl River with flat-rock beach.
Canoe. Swim. Fish.

DEWAYNE HAYES WALK-IN

COE (601) 494-4885
State map: E10
From WEST POINT, take MS 50 E about 14 miles (22.4 k). Turn Left (N) on MS 373 and go 1 mile (1.6 k). Turn Left (W) on Stenson Creek Rd and drive 2 miles (3.2 k). Turn Left (SW) on Barton's Ferry Rd and go .5 mile (800 m). Walk-in about 400 yds (400 m). (Also see Town Creek Walk-In.)
$4. Open All Year.
10 close, screened, tent sites.
Tables, fire rings.
In secluded section near Tennessee-Tombigbee Waterway.
Swim, boat, ski, or fish. Hike. Attend ranger programs.
NO water. No trash arrangements (pack it out). 14-day limit.

ELMERS HILL

COE (601) 563-4531
State map: C7
From SARDIS, go E on MS 315 for 8 miles (12.8 k). (Also see Beach Point, Oak Grove, and Sleepy Bend.)
FREE so choose a chore. Open All Year.
6 scattered, open, tent sites.
Central faucet, chemical toilets, tables, grills, fire rings.
Among oak and pine overlooking dam for Sardis Lake.
View wildlife. Relax. Enjoy nearby lake and river.
14-day limit.
300 ft (90 m)

FAIRLEY BRIDGE LANDING

De Soto NF (601) 928-4423
State map: L9
From WIGGINS, travel NE on MS 29 for 6 miles (9.6 k). Turn Right (E) on FR 374. Go 7 miles (11.2 k). Turn Right (S) on FR 374A. (See Cypress Creek Landing. Nearby Flint Creek Park costs $10.50.)
FREE so choose a chore. Open All Year.
3 close, open, tent sites. Flush toilets, tables, fire rings, grills, boat ramp.
On hardwood bluff overlooking Black Creek (with float trip take-out spot).
Hike Black Creek Trail. Canoe or float. Fish. Wade or swim.
NO water. 14-day limit. Hunting in season.

GIN CREEK

COE (601) 626-8431
State map: H10
From MERIDIAN, head NW on MS 19 for 10 miles (16 k) to Collinsville. Turn Right (NE) on W Lauderdale School Rd. Go 2 miles (3.2 k). Turn Right (E) on Martin Rd. Drive 1 mile (1.6 k). (Also see Tailrace. Nearby Twitley Branch costs $8.)
FREE so choose a chore. Open All Year.
7 close, open sites.
Central faucet, chemical toilets, tables, fire rings, boat ramp.

In partial shade under pine canopy around Okatibbee Lake.
Boat, ski, or fish. Watch wildlife.
14-day/20-ft limits. No generators in quiet hours.
348 ft (104 m)

GRAHAM LAKE

COE (601) 563-4531
State map: B8
From ABBEVILLE, travel NE on signed, paved/gravel road about 4 miles (6.4 k). (Also see Hurricane Landing.)
FREE so choose a chore. Open All Year.
6 scattered, open, tent sites.
Chemical toilets, tables, grills, fire rings.
In mixed hardwood near Tallahutchie River and Graham Lake Wildlife Refuge.
Fish. Observe wildlife.
NO water. 14-day limit. Hunting in season.
260 ft (78 m)

GRAND GULF MILITARY PARK

(601) 437-5911
State map: I5
From PORT GIBSON, take Walnut St NW 8 miles (12.8 k).
$5; $9 RV; reservations accepted at (601) 437-5911.
Open All Year.
72 (20 tent-only) scattered sites. &
Water at every site, flush toilets, showers, dump station, electric hookups, tables, grills, boat ramp, pay phone.
Near Mississippi River with Civil War fortifications and historic buildings.
Tour museum. Climb observation tower.
Walk grounds. Hike nature trail to explore river ecology. Bike. Fish.
Crowded when tour group (call ahead).

GULF ISLANDS NS-Boat-In

(601) 875-9057
State Map: N10
From OCEAN SPRINGS, drive E on US 90 for 3 miles (4.8 k).
Turn Right (S) into park headquarters. Obtain permit and boat from 9–12 miles (14.4–19.2 k) S to

islands.
FREE. Open All Year.
On three barrier islands: East Ship, Horn, and Petit Bois.
Swim, boat, or fish. Enjoy beach.
NO water. No toilet facilities. No trash arrangements (pack it out) .

GUMS CROSSING

COE (601) 226-1679
State map: D8
From GRENADA, take MS 8 E about 10 miles (16 k) to Gore Springs. Turn Left (N) and go about 11 miles (17.6 k). (Also see Choctaw, Old Fort, and Skuna-Turkey.)
FREE so choose a chore. Open All Year.
15 scattered, open, tent sites.
Central faucet, pit toilets, tables, fire rings, grills, boat ramp.
In wood next to Skuna River on backwaters of Grenada Lake.
Enjoy getaway. Boat or fish. Observe wildlife.
14-day limit.
231 ft (69 m)

HAYS CROSSING

COE (601) 563-4531
State map: C7
From COMO, drive E on MS 310 about 5 miles (8 k).
Turn Right (S) at sign on gravel road about 3 miles (4.8 k).
FREE so choose a chore. Open All Year.
5 scattered, open, tent sites.
Chemical toilets, tables, grills, fire rings.
On wooded point with Sardis Lake view.
Boat, waterski, and fish.
NO water. 14-day limit.
250 ft (75 m)

HURRICANE LANDING

COE (601) 563-4531
State map: B8
From ABBEVILLE, head W on signed road about 5 miles (8 k). (Also see Graham Lake.)
FREE so choose a chore. Open All Year.
16 scattered, open sites.
Central faucet, chemical toilets, tables,

fire rings, grills, boat ramp.
In scattered trees adjoining Sardis Lake.
Boat, ski, or fish. View wildlife in nearby
Sardis Wildlife Refuge.
14-day limit. Hunting in season.
290 ft (87 m)

ISLAND BOAT-IN

COE (601) 454-3481
State map: B11
From BOONEVILLE, take
MS 30 E for 15 miles (24 k).
Turn Right (S) on CR 3501. Go
3 miles (4.8 k) to Piney Grove Boat
Ramp. Boat E and N about 1 mile (1.6 k).
(Nearby Piney Grove RA costs $10.)
FREE so choose a chore. Open All Year.
10 scattered, screened, tent sites.
Pit toilets, tables, grills, fire rings.
In secluded, mixed hardwood/pine
forest on Bay Springs Lake.
Boat or fish. Observe wildlife.
NO water. 14-day limit.
418 ft (125 m)

JANICE LANDING

De Soto NF (601) 928-4423
State map: L9
From BROOKLYN, head E on
CR 301 about 10 miles (16 k).
Turn Right (S) on MS 29 and
go to Black Creek. (Also see Cypress
Creek Landing and Moody's Landing.)
FREE so choose a chore. Open All Year.
5 close, open, tent sites.
Central faucet, flush toilets, tables, fire
rings, grills, boat ramp.
On sand bluff above Black Creek with
large pine and hardwood.
Float or canoe creek. Fish. Hike nearby
Black Creek Trail and explore adjacent
Black Creek Wilderness.
14-day limit. Hunting in season.

KELLEY'S CROSSING

COE (601) 562-6261
State map: B7
From COLDWATER, take Tate
Rd W for 9 miles (14.4 k).
Turn Right (N) on Kelley's
Crossing Rd and continue 4.5 miles

(7.2 k). (Also see Outlet Channel.)
FREE so choose a chore. Open All Year.
Undesignated scattered, open sites.
Chemical toilets, tables, grills, boat ramp.
Among rolling hills and hardwood trees
next to Arkabutla Lake.
Boat or fish. View wildlife.
NO water. 14-day limit.
260 ft (78 m)

LONG BRANCH

COE (601) 563-4571
State map: C7
From Exit 227 of I-55 (SE of
ENID), take MS 32 NE for
4 miles (6.4 k). Turn Left (N)
at sign and drive 2 miles (3.2 k). (Also
see Point Pleasant.)
FREE so choose a chore. Open All Year.
13 scattered, tent sites.
Pit toilets, tables, fire rings, grills, boat
ramp, playground.
On Enid Lake in peaceful setting.
Swim, boat, waterski, and fish.
NO water. 14-day/35-ft limits. Hunting
in season. Crowded holidays.
290 ft (87 m)

MARATHON LAKE

Bienville NF (601) 782-4271
State map: I8
From FOREST, head S on
MS 35 for 11 miles (17.6 k).
Turn Left (E) on CR 506 and
go 9 miles (14.4 k) to sign.
$5. Open All Year.
35 close, screened sites.
Central faucet, flush toilets, showers,
tables, fire rings, grills, boat ramp.
In forest next to 50-acre lake.
Walk nature trail around lake. Fish or
boat (small motors only). Observe
wildlife. Swim ($2).
14-day limit.

MCLEOD WATER PARK

Pearl River Basin
(601) 467-1894
State map: N8
Find park in KILN off MS 603
at 8100 Texas Flat Rd.

$5; $8 electric; reservations accepted at (601) 354-6301.
Open All Year.
98 (50 tent-only) close, open sites.
Water at every site, flush toilets, showers, dump station, electric hookups, tables, grills, boat ramp, rentals, pay phone.
Under large live oak trees with Spanish Moss next to Jourdan River.
Swim, boat, or fish.
No generators.

MOODY'S LANDING

De Soto NF (601) 928-4423
State map: L9
From BROOKLYN, head E on CR 301 for 3.5 miles (5.4 k). (Also see Ashe Lake and Janice Landing.)
FREE so choose a chore.
Open All Year.
4 close, open, tent sites.
Central faucet, flush toilets, tables, fire rings, grills, boat ramp.
In scattered pine and hardwood on bank overlooking Black Creek Wild and Scenic River (nearby sandbar for float trip put-in and take-out).
Canoe or float creek. Fish. Hike Black Creek Trail. Birdwatch.
14-day limit.

NATCHEZ TRACE PARKWAY

(601) 680-4025
State map: E9–I5
FREE so choose a chore.
Open All Year.
14-day/35-ft limits. Crowded.

▲ Jeff Busby
Locate campground about 10 miles (16 k) S of MATHISTON at milepost 193.1 of Natchez Trace Parkway.
18 scattered, open sites. &
Central faucet, flush toilets, tables, grills, store, pay phone.
In pine-hardwood at base of Little Mountain.
Hike and bike beautiful, pastoral area. Walk nature trail. Take photos.
400 ft (120 m)

▲ Rocky Springs
Find campground about 17 miles (27.2 k) NW of PORT GIBSON at milepost 54.8 of Natchez Trace Parkway.
23 (2 tent-only) sites. &
Central faucet, flush toilets, tables, grills, pay phone.
In pine/hardwood forest.
Bike parkway. Walk section of original Trace. Explore 100-year-old Rocky Springs remains. Take photos.
200 ft (60 m)

NORTH ABUTMENT

COE (601) 226-1679
State map: D8
From GRENADA, head E on MS 8 about 3 miles (4.8 k). Turn left (N) on Scenic Route 333. Drive 6 miles (9.6 k), crossing dam. (Also see Old Fort. Nearby Hugh White SP costs $5.50–11.00.)
FREE so choose a chore. Open All Year.
21 scattered, open, tent sites. &
Central faucet, pit toilets, tables, fire rings, grills, boat ramp.
In semi-open area next to Grenada Lake dam.
Boat, ski, or fish. Walk nature trail. View wildlife. Use archery range.
14-day limit. Crowded summer weekends.
231 ft (69 m)

OAK GROVE

COE (601) 563-4531
State map: C7
From SARDIS, go E on MS 315 for 8 miles (12.8 k). (Also see Elmers Hill, Shady Cove, and Sleepy Bend.)
$3. Open All Year.
82 scattered, open sites.
Central faucet, flush toilets, tables, fire rings, grills, boat ramp, pay phone.
In oak and pine next to Lower Lake of Sardis Lake.
Swim, boat, and fish. Attend ranger programs.
14-day limit.
320 ft (96 m)

▲ ▲

OLD FORT

COE (601) 226-1679
State map: D8
From GRENADA, head E on
MS 8 for 3 miles (4.8 k). Turn
Left (N) on Scenic Route 333.
Drive 1 mile (800 m). Turn Right after
Civil War fort. (Also see Choctaw, Gums
Crossing, and North Abutment.)
FREE so choose a chore.
Open All Year.
20 scattered, open, tent sites.
Central faucet, pit toilets, tables, fire
rings, grills, boat ramp.
In convenient spot on Grenada Lake.
Swim, boat, or fish. Watch wildlife.
14-day limit. Crowded weekends and
holidays.
231 ft (69 m)

OUTLET CHANNEL

COE (601) 562-6261
State map: B7
From ARKABUTLA, drive N
on Scenic Loop 304 (Tate Rd)
for 4.5 miles (7.2 k). Turn Left
(W). (Also see Kelley's Crossing. Nearby
South Abutment costs $10.)
FREE so choose a chore. Open All Year.
Undesignated scattered, open sites.
Chemical toilets, tables, fire rings, grills,
boat ramp.
Below Arkabutla Lake dam in flat with
hardwood.
Boat or fish. Walk Big Oak Nature Trail
or hike farther. Watch wildlife.
NO water. 14-day limit. Hunting in
season. No generators. Crowded
weekends and holidays.
210 ft (63 m)

PATS BLUFF

COE (601) 563-4531
State map: C7
From BATESVILLE, take MS 6
NE for 11.3 miles (18 k). Turn
Left (N) at Sardis Dam Lake
sign and go 2.1 miles (3.4 k). Turn Right
(NE) at Pats Bluff sign and continue
4.6 miles (7.4 k). (Nearby Clear Creek
costs $10.)

FREE so choose a chore. Open All Year.
18 scattered, open sites.
Central faucet, flush toilets, tables, grills,
fire rings.
In pine and hardwood on point
overlooking Sardis Lake.
Fish. Observe wildlife.
14-day limit.
300 ft (90 m)

PINEY POINT

COE (601) 563-4531
State map: C7
From COMO, drive E on
MS 310 about 15 miles (24 k).
Turn Right (S) at sign on
gravel road. (Also see Wyatts Crossing.)
FREE so choose a chore.
Open All Year.
3 scattered, open, tent sites.
Tables, fire rings.
In woods near Sardis Lake.
Boat or fish. View wildlife.
NO water. No toilet facilities. 14-day
limit. Hunting in season.
300 ft (90 m)

PLEASANT HILL

COE (601) 562-6261
State map: B7
From HERNANDO, drive W
on MS 304 for 5 miles (8 k).
Turn Left (S) on Fogg Rd for
4 miles (6.4 k).
FREE so choose a chore.
Open All Year.
Undesignated scattered, open sites.
Chemical toilets, tables, fire rings, grills,
boat ramp.
Among open, rolling hills next to
Arkabutla Lake.
Swim, boat, or fish.
NO water. 14-day limit. Occasionally
noisy.

PLUM POINT

COE (601) 563-4571
State map: C7
From Exit 237 of I-55 (near
POPE), take US 51 S for 1 mile
(1.6 k). Turn Left (E) and drive

4 miles (6.4 k). Turn Right (SE) on gravel road and proceed 3.1 miles (5 k). Turn Right (S). (Also see Bynum Creek. Nearby Chickasaw Hill costs $10.)
FREE so choose a chore.
Open All Year.
9 scattered, open sites.
Central faucet, pit toilets, tables, fire rings, grills, boat ramp, playground.
Next to Enid Lake in peaceful setting.
Swim, boat, ski, or fish. Walk nature trail or hike farther.
14-day/35-ft limits. Hunting in season. Nearby horse trail. Crowded holidays.
290 ft (87 m)

POINT PLEASANT

COE (601) 563-4571
State map: C7
From Exit 227 of I-55 (SE of ENID), take MS 32 NE for 5.3 miles (8.5 k). Turn Left (N) at sign and drive 2 miles (3.2 k). (Also see Long Branch.)
FREE so choose a chore.
Open All Year.
5 scattered, open, tent sites.
Pit toilets, tables, fire rings, grills, boat ramp.
In peaceful setting by Enid Lake.
Swim, boat, waterski, and fish.
NO water. 14-day/35-ft limits. Hunting in season. Crowded holidays.
290 ft (87 m)

PUSKUS LAKE

Holly Springs NF
(601) 252-2633
State map: C9
From OXFORD, travel NE on MS 30 for 10 miles (16 k).
Turn Right (N) on gravel FR 838 and drive 3 miles (4.8 k).
FREE so choose a chore.
Open All Year.
22 close, open, tent sites.
Central faucet, pit toilets, tables, fire rings, grills, boat ramp.
In mixed pine trees next to 96-acre lake. Enjoy seclusion. Walk interpretive nature trail. Hike to see wildlife. Boat or fish.

14-day/22-ft limits. Hunting in season.
350 ft (105 m)

SHADY COVE

COE (601) 563-4531
State map: C7
From SARDIS, travel E on MS 315 for 10 miles (16 k). Take first Left after passing Engineers Point. (Also see Oak Grove.)
FREE so choose a chore.
Open All Year.
3 scattered, open, tent sites.
Pit toilets, tables, grills, fire rings.
On hardwood point overlooking small cove on Sardis Lake.
Boat or fish. Spot wildlife.
NO water. 14-day limit.
280 ft (84 m)

SHONGELO LAKE

Bienville NF (601) 782-4271
State map: I8
From RALEIGH, drive N on MS 35 for 5 miles (8 k).
$4. Open Apr 15–Oct 15.
4 close, screened sites.
Central faucet, chemical toilets, tables, grills, fire rings.
In forest on 5-acre lake near highway. Walk nature trail around lake. Fish. Watch wildlife. Swim ($2).
14-day limit.

SKUNA-TURKEY

COE (601) 226-1679
State map: D8
From GRENADA, take MS 8 E about 10 miles (16 k) to Gore Springs. Turn Left (N) and go about 8 miles (12.8 k). Turn Left (SW) and drive 1 mile (1.6 k). Turn Right (W) and continue 4 miles (6.4 k). (Also see Choctaw and Gums Crossing.)
FREE so choose a chore.
Open All Year.
5 scattered, open, tent sites.
Central faucet, pit toilets, tables, fire rings, grills, boat ramp.
In nice, wooded spot on Grenada Lake.
Boat, ski, or fish. Spot wildlife. Relax.

▲ ▲

14-day limit.
230 ft (69 m)

SLEEPY BEND

COE (601) 563-4531
State map: C7
From SARDIS, go E on MS 315
for 8 miles (12.8 k). (Also see
Beach Point, Elmers Hill, and
Oak Grove.)
FREE so choose a chore.
Open All Year.
50 scattered, open, tent sites.
Central faucet, chemical toilets, tables,
grills, fire rings.
In hardwood near Lower Lake of Sardis
Lake.
Swim, boat, and fish. View wildlife.
14-day limit.
220 ft (66 m)

TAILRACE

COE (601) 626-8431
State map: H10
From MERIDIAN, drive NW
on MS 19 for 8 miles (12.8 k).
Turn Right (E) on Okatibbee
Dam Rd. Go 1 mile (1.6 k). Turn Right
(S) on Tailrace Rd. (Also see Gin Creek.)
FREE so choose a chore.
Open All Year.
4 close, open, tent sites. Hand pump,
chemical toilets, tables, fire rings.
In heavy shade of hardwood canopy
below Okatibbee Lake dam.
Fish. Observe wildlife.
14-day limit.
358 ft (107 m)

TILLATOBA LAKE

Tombigbee NF
(601) 285-3264
State map: D7
From TILLATOBA, drive E on
CR 807 about 4 miles (6.4 k).
FREE so choose a chore. Open All Year.
Undesignated scattered, open sites.
Central faucet, pit toilets, tables, grills,
boat ramp.
Next to quiet, 40-acre lake.
Fish or boat. Hike.

14-day limit. Hunting in season.
550 ft (165 m)

TOWN CREEK WALK-IN

COE (601) 494-4885
State map: E10
From WEST POINT, take
MS 50 E about 10 miles (16)
to just before bridge. Turn Left
(N) and follow signs. Walk-in about
400 yds (400 m). (Also see Dewayne
Hayes Walk-In.)
$4. Open All Year.
10 close, screened, tent sites.
Tables, fire rings.
In secluded section near Tennessee-
Tombigbee Waterway.
Swim, boat, ski, or fish. Hike. Attend
ranger programs.
NO water. No trash arrangements (pack
it out). 14-day limit.

WALKIAH BLUFF WATER PARK

Pearl River Basin
(601) 798-0966
State map: M8
From PICAYUNE, head NW
on MS 43 for 4 miles (6.4 k).
Turn Left (W).
$3; $7 developed. Open All Year.
12 close, open sites.
Water at every site, flush toilets,
showers, tables.
In open area next to Pearl River.
Fish. Relax.

WYATTS CROSSING

COE (601) 563-4531
State map: C7
From COMO, drive E on
MS 310 about 18 miles (28.8 k).
Turn Right (S) at sign on
gravel road. (Also see Piney Point.)
$4; $10 electric. Open All Year.
10 scattered, open sites.
Water at every site, pit toilets, dump
station, electric hookups, tables, grills.
In woods overlooking Sardis Lake.
Boat or fish.
14-day limit. Crowded holidays.
300 ft (90 m)

▲ ▲

MISSOURI
CAMPGROUND LOCATIONS

► ► Find location on facing page map grid. ► ►
▼ ▼ Locate area campgrounds on these page numbers. ▼ ▼

Missouri

Grid conforms to official state map. For your copy, call (714) 751-4133
or write Division of Tourism, Truman Bldg, Box 1055, Jefferson City, MO 65102.

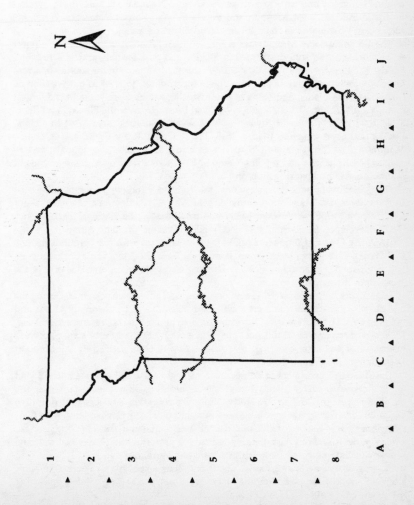

PUBLIC LANDS CAMPING

Missouri has tried to tame its wilds and its rivers. Now the Missouri River meets the Mississippi River with few mishaps. The state has become known for bubbling springs that feed gravel-bottomed streams and rivers perfect for canoeing and tubing. Flood-control lakes extend the range of water activities with swimming, boating, and waterskiing. Fish in intimate ponds, gentle creeks, sprawling lakes, or mighty rivers. Hike along many trails, including the 500-mile Ozark Trail starting near Saint Louis and extending to the Arkansas border. Study and photograph nature, birdwatch, bicycle, horseback ride, or auto-tour the state. Glade Top Trail, a National Scenic Byway in the Mark Twain National Forest (NF), is especially popular mid-to-late April for dogwoods and mid-to-late October for fall color. Also, you can drive parts of the famous emigrant trail now known as the Oregon National Historic Trail. The trail begins in Independence, Missouri and travels through Kansas, Nebraska, Wyoming, Idaho, and Washington in route to Oregon's Willamette Valley.

The 1.5 million-acre **Mark Twain NF** in southern Missouri is touted to be a forest that came back after suffering rapacious logging and poor farming practices, fires and floods. The forest stretches from the Saint Francois Mountains in the southeast, across Ozark foothills with granite and limestone outcroppings, to treeless but wildflower-thick limestone glades and balds of southwest Missouri. Here some of the largest springs in the country feed streams, rivers, and lakes. Discover the Eleven Point River, a National Wild and Scenic River or one of seven wilderness areas: Bell Mountain, Devil's Backbone, Hercules Glades, Irish, Paddy Creek, Piney Creek, and Rock Pile Mountain. The forest claims 175 species of birds, 30 species of mammals, and 70 species of amphibians and reptiles. Camp at 22 different developed campgrounds or at innumerable backpacking locations.

Ozark National Scenic Riverways offer floating and fishing opportunities along the Current River and Jacks Fork. Camp along the way as you float in a canoe, kayak, or raft. Be sure to follow all water safety tips provided by the **National Park Service** (NPS). Developed family sites cost $7.00 while gravel bar camping is free.

US Army Corps of Engineers (COE) lakes in Missouri with campgrounds include Bull Shoals, Clearwater, Mark Twain, Pomme de Terre, Stockton, Table Rock, Truman, and Wappapello. In addition, Fenway Landing Campground is on the shores of the Mississippi River. COE camping fees range from free to $12.00.

State Parks (SP) in Missouri use an on-season and off-season schedule. During the on-season (April–October at most parks), basic sites cost $6.00, electricity $10.00, and full hookups $11.00. Off-season (November–March at most parks), rates are $5.00 basic, $8.00 electricity, and $9.00 full hookups. There are more than thirty state parks and historic sites that offer camping in Missouri. All are administered by the Missouri Department of Natural Resources (DNR).

The Missouri Department of Conservation manages some 800 separate tracts of land for multiple uses such as forest conservation, wildlife habitat, fishing opportunities, outdoor recreation, and nature study. Many Conservation Areas permit primitive camping; some areas have free designated campgrounds. Any **Conservation Area** (CA) with either a water source, toilet, or table has been included in the following listings.

City parks round out the public lands camping opportunities. Places that welcome campers include Rothwell Park, Smith's Fork, and Versailles.

Flowing waters, regrowing forests, flood-controlling lakes…it's all a part of Missouri along with rolling farms, astounding Mark Twain lore, and reeling country music. Let the "Show Me" state show you a good time.

▲ ▲

ARROW ROCK SHS

(816) 837-3330
State map: E3
Locate site in ARROW ROCK off MO 41.

$5; $10 electric. Open Apr 1–Nov 1; dry camping allowed off-season.
46 close, open sites. &
Central faucet, flush toilets, showers, dump station, electric hookups, tables, grills, fire rings, pay phone.
Near restored 19th-century village.
Bike or hike. Explore buildings. Visit Sappington Cemetery.
15-day limit.

BAR K WRANGLER CAMP

Mark Twain NF
(417) 683-3410
State map: E7
From CHADWICK, take MO 125 SE for 6 miles (9.6 k). (Also see Camp Ridge and Cobb Ridge.)
FREE so choose a chore.
Open All Year.
Undesignated scattered, screened sites.
Pit toilets, tables, grills, fire rings.
In open meadow with some shade along Swan Creek next to 8500-acre nonmotorized area.
Hike or mountain bike trail system.
Swim or fish.
NO water. No trash arrangements.
Hunting in season. Horses in area.
800 ft (240 m)

BERRYMAN

Mark Twain NF
(314) 438-5427
State map: H5
From POTOSI, travel W on MO 8 about 16 miles (25.6 k). Turn Right (N) on gravel FR 2266. Go 1 mile (1.6 k). (Also see Brazil Creek and Hazel Creek.)
FREE so choose a chore.
Open All Year.
8 close, screened sites.
Pit toilets, tables, grills, fire rings, shelter.
In woods at start of 24-mile (38.4-k) Berryman Trail.
Hike. Mountain bike. View wildlife.

NO water. No trash arrangements (pack it out). 14-day limit. Hunting in season. Occasional ATVs and horses.
1500 ft (450 m)

BIG PINEY

Mark Twain NF
(417) 967-4194
State map: F6
From ROBY, take MO 17 N for 2 miles (3.2 k). Turn Right (E) on CR 2800 and go 7 miles (11.2 k). (Also see Paddy Creek.)
FREE so choose a chore. Open All Year.
6 close, screened sites.
Pit toilets, tables, fire rings.
On oak/hickory ridge at Big Piney Trailhead (to access Paddy Creek Wilderness).
Hike or mountain bike.
NO water. No trash arrangements.
14-day limit. Horses often present.
1200 ft (360 m)

BLUFF VIEW

COE (314) 223-7771
State map: H6
From PIEDMONT, drive NW on CR AA for 8 miles (12.8 k). (Also see River Road. Nearby Piedmont costs $7.)
$5; $10 electric. Open May 15–Sep 15.
59 scattered, open sites.
Central faucet, flush toilets, showers, dump station, electric hookups, tables, fire rings, grills, boat ramp, store, rentals, pay phone.
In open area on peninsula jutting into Clearwater Lake.
Swim, boat, ski, or fish. Walk nature trail. Bike. Attend ranger programs.
14-day limit.
570 ft (171 m)

BRAZIL CREEK

Mark Twain NF
(314) 438-5427
State map: G5
From BOURBON, head SE on CR N for 10.5 miles (16.8 k). Turn Right (S) on CR W and drive 6 miles

▲ ▲

(9.6 k). (Also see Berryman.)
FREE so choose a chore.
Open All Year.
8 close, open sites.
Pit toilets, tables, grills.
On Berryman Trail next to Brazil Creek.
Hike or bike. View wildlife. Swim. Fish.
NO water. No trash arrangements (pack it out). 14-day limit. Hunting in season.
Frequent ATVs and horses.
1500 ft (450 m)

BUFFALO CREEK

Mark Twain NF
(314) 996-2153
State map: H7
From DONIPHAN, take
MO 160 W for 17 miles (27.2 k). Turn Right (N) on gravel FR 3145. Go 1.5 miles (2.4 k). (See Fourche Lake.)
FREE so choose a chore.
Open All Year.
3 close, open sites.
Hand pump, pit toilets, tables, fire rings. Next to clear creek surrounded by hardwood.
Swim or fish. Observe wildlife.
14-day/22-ft limits. Hunting in season. Occasionally crowded.

CALUMET CREEK ACCESS

MO Dept of Conservation
(314) 248-2530
State map: H3
From LOUISIANA, drive
5 miles (8 k) SE on MO 79. (Also see DuPont Reservation CA.)
FREE so choose a chore.
Open All Year.
Undesignated close, open sites.
Pit toilets, boat ramp.
On grass slope next to parking lot.
Fish.
NO water. No trash arrangements (pack it out). 14-day limit.

CAMP FIVE POND TRAILHEAD

Mark Twain NF
(314) 996-2153
State map: H7
From DONIPHAN, take

MO 160 W for 20 miles (32 k). Turn Right (N) on CR J and go 7 miles (11.2 k). (Also see Fourche Lake.)
FREE so choose a chore.
Open All Year.
3 close, open, tent sites.
Pit toilets, tables, fire rings.
In woods at White's Creek Hiking Trail into Irish Wilderness.
Hike and explore.
NO water. 14-day limit.

CAMP RIDGE

Mark Twain NF
(417) 683-3410
State map: E7
From CHADWICK, take
MO 125 S for 1 mile (1.6 k). Turn Right (SW) on CR H and drive 1 mile (1.6 k). (Also see Cobb Ridge and Bar K Wrangler Camp.)
FREE so choose a chore.
Open All Year.
9 close, screened sites.
Pit toilets, tables, grills, fire rings.
On hardwood/pine ridge in Chadwick Motorcycle Use Area.
Hike. Relax, if possible.
NO water. No trash arrangements (pack it out). Heavy ATV use.
1100 ft (330 m)

COBB RIDGE

Mark Twain NF
(417) 683-3410
State map: E7
From CHADWICK, take
MO 125 S for 1 mile (1.6 k). Turn Right (SW) on CR H and proceed 2 miles (3.2 k). (Also see Camp Ridge and Bar K Wrangler Camp.)
FREE so choose a chore.
Open All Year.
18 close, open sites.
Pit toilets, tables, fire rings.
Along hardwood ridge in Chadwick Motorcycle Use Area.
Hike. Relax, when quiet.
NO water. No trash arrangements (pack it out). Heavy ATV use.
1100 ft (330 m)

▲ ▲

COUNCIL BLUFF LAKE

Mark Twain NF
(314) 438-5427
State map: H5
From POTOSI, drive S on CR P for 13 miles (20.8 k). Turn Right (W) on CR C and go .25 mile (400 m). Turn Left (S) on CR DD and continue 5.5 miles (8.8 k).
$5.
Open Apr 15–Nov 20.
59 (9 tent-only) close, screened sites.
Central faucet, pit toilets, tables, grills, fire rings, food storage, ball fields.
On wooded ridge above lake.
Swim, boat, or fish. Hike to view wildlife.
14-day limit.
1500 ft (450 m)

COW CREEK

COE (417) 334-4101
State map: E7
From BLUE EYE, take CR 86-10 N about 4 miles (6.4 k) to end. (Nearby Old Highway 86 costs $8.)
FREE so choose a chore. (Only under-$5 camp on lake; other 13 cost $8 and up.)
Open May 1–Sep 30.
33 close, open sites.
Central faucet, flush toilets, showers, dump station, tables, fire rings, grills, boat ramp, pay phone.
Next to Ozark's Table Rock Lake.
Swim, boat, ski, or fish.
14-day limit.
950 ft (285 m)

DANVILLE CA

MO Dept of Conservation
(314) 882-9880
State map: G4
From DANVILLE, head SE on CR RB. (Also see Loutre Lick Access.)
FREE so choose a chore.
Open All Year.
Undesignated close, open sites.
Pit toilets, fire rings.
In open area under tree canopy.
Hike. View wildlife.

NO water. No trash arrangements (pack it out). Hunting in season.
700 ft (210 m)

DEER LEAP

Mark Twain NF
(314) 996-2153
State map: H7
From DONIPHAN, go N on CR Y for 5 miles (8 k). Turn Left (W) on FR 4349 and continue 1.5 miles (2.4 k). (Also see Float Camp.)
$5. Open May 15–Sep 15.
11 close, open sites.
Central faucet, pit toilets, tables, fire rings, boat ramp, store.
In mixed hardwood/softwood next to Current River.
Swim, boat, or fish. Walk nature trail or hike farther to observe wildlife.
14-day limit. In flood plain. Occasionally crowded.

DEER RIDGE CA

MO Dept of Conservation
(314) 248-2530
State map: G2
From LEWISTOWN, drive N on CR H then CR Y for 5 miles (8 k).
FREE so choose a chore.
Open All Year.
Undesignated close, open sites.
Central faucet, pit toilets, tables, grills.
With access to North Fabius River.
Spot wildlife. Fish.
14-day limit. Hunting in season.

DIGGS ACCESS

MO Dept of Conservation
(314) 882-9880
State map: G3
From WELLSVILLE, take CR ZZ SW. Turn Right (W) on CR RA. Go 2 miles (3.2 k). (Also see Wellsville Lake CA and Whetstone Creek CA.)
FREE so choose a chore.
Open All Year.
6 close, open sites.
Pit toilets, boat ramp, shelter.
Under large oak trees next to lakes.
Fish. Observe wildlife.

▲ ▲

NO water. No trash arrangements (pack it out). Hunting in season.

DUPONT RESERVATION CA

MO Dept of Conservation
(314) 248-2530
State map: G3
From ASHBURN, head N for 1 mile (1.6 k). (Also see Calumet Creek Access and Ranacker.)
FREE so choose a chore. Open All Year.
16 close, screened sites.
Pit toilets, boat ramp.
Near Mississippi River.
Boat or fish. Observe wildlife.
NO water. No trash arrangements (pack it out). 14-day limit. Hunting in season.

ELEVEN POINT RIVER

Mark Twain NF
(314) 325-4233
State map: G7
From ALTON, head N on MO 19 for 2 miles (3.2 k). Turn Right (E) on CR AA. Drive 4.5 miles (7.2 k). Turn Left (N) on FR 3153. Go 4.5 miles (7.2 k) to put-in point. (Also see Greer.)
FREE so choose a chore.
Open All Year.
Pit toilets, tables, grills, fire rings.
NO water. Pack out trash.

▲ **Barn Hollow Boat-In**
Float downstream 5.5 miles (8.8 k).
4 scattered, open, tent sites.
In young pine trees near river.
Hike. Fish. Canoe.
470 ft (141 m)

▲ **Boze Mill Boat-In**
Float downstream 12 miles (19.2 k).
2 close, open, tent sites.
Next to large spring and river.
Fish. Canoe.
450 ft (135 m)

▲ **Greenbriar Boat-In**
Float downstream 9.4 miles (15 k).
2 close, open, tent sites.
On flat next to river.
Boat or fish.
400 ft (120 m)

▲ **Horseshoe Bend Boat-In**
Float downstream 4.6 miles (7.4 k).

6 close, screened, tent sites.
Within 15 ft (5 m) of river.
Canoe. Fish.
420 ft (126 m)

▲ **Stinking Pond Boat-In**
Float downstream .8 mile (1.3 k).
4 close, screened, tent sites.
In hollow next to river.
Fish. Canoe.
500 ft (150 m)

▲ **White's Creek Boat-In**
Float downstream 7 miles (11.2 k).
4 close, screened, tent sites.
On creek next to river and Irish Wilderness.
Hike into wilderness. Find caves.

▲ **Morgan Spring Boat-In**
Put in at RIVERTON. Float downstream 7.7 miles (12.3 k).
2 close, screened, tent sites.
On riverbank just N of large spring.
Canoe and fish.
400 ft (120 m)

▲ **Denny Hollow Boat-In**
Put in at THOMASVILLE. Float downstream 7 miles (11.2 k).
2 close, open, tent sites.
Next to river.
Canoe. Fish.
600 ft (180 m)

FENWAY LANDING

COE (217) 228-0890
State map: G2
Fron CANTON, head N on US 61. Turn Right (E) on gravel CR 464 and follow to park.
FREE so choose a chore.
Open All Year.
7 scattered, open sites. Hand pump, pit toilets, tables, fire rings, boat ramp.
On shores of Mississippi River.
Hike to view wildlife. Watch boat traffic on river. Boat or fish.
14-day limit. Occasional floods.

FLOAT CAMP

Mark Twain NF
(314) 996-2153
State map: H7
From DONIPHAN, go N

▲ ▲

on CR Y for 4.5 miles (7.2 k). Turn Left
(W) on FR 3210 and continue .5 mile
(800 m). (Also see Deer Leap.)
$5.
Open May 15–Sep 15; dry camping
allowed off-season.
16 close, open sites.
Central faucet, pit toilets, tables, fire
rings, store, pay phone.
In mixed hardwood/softwood next to
Current River.
Swim, boat, or fish. Walk nature trail.
Hike for photos or wildlife sightings.
14-day limit. In flood plain. Crowded at
times.

FOURCHE LAKE

Mark Twain NF
(314) 996-2153
State map: H7
From DONIPHAN, travel
W on US 160 for 18 miles (28.8 k). Turn
Left (S) on CR V. Drive 4 miles (6.4 k).
Turn Left (E) on gravel road. Continue
2 miles (3.2 k). (Also see Buffalo Creek
and Camp Five Pond Trailhead.)
FREE so choose a chore.
Open All Year.
4 scattered, open sites.
Pit toilets, tables, fire rings, boat ramp.
Among hardwood on bank of beautiful,
clear 50-acre lake.
Boat. View wildlife. Do nothing.
NO water. No trash arrangements (pack
it out). 14-day limit.

FRANK RUSSELL

COE (314) 735-4097
State map: G3
From MONROE CITY,
head E on CR W for
2 miles (3.2 k). Turn Right (S) on CR J
and proceed 10 miles (16 k). (Nearby
Ray Behrens and Indian Creek cost $8.)
$5; $6 weekends.
Open May 14–Sep 13.
60 scattered, screened sites. &
Central faucet, pit toilets, dump station,
electric hookups, tables, grills, fire rings,
playground, pay phone.
In medium-age hardwood trees

overlooking Mark Twain Lake.
Boat, ski, or fish. Observe wildlife. Swim
or hike at nearby John Spalding Day-Use
Area.
14-day limit. Hunting in season. No
generators in quiet hours. Crowded
weekends and holidays.
650 ft (195 m)

GLADE TOP TRAIL

Mark Twain NF
(417) 683-3410
State map: E7
From AVA, head S on
MO 5. Turn Right (SW) on MO A and
follow signs. Sites are scattered along
27 miles (43.2 k) of gravel scenic road.
(Also see Hercules Tower Trailhead.)
FREE so choose a chore.
Open All Year.
Undesignated scattered, screened sites.
Pit toilets, tables, grills, fire rings.
Along Missouri's only National Scenic
Byway, a CCC-built road with glades
and outcroppings, woods and grasses,
plus lots of wildlife.
Hike to spot wildlife. Take photos. Enjoy
ecology.
NO water. No trash arrangements (pack
it out). Hunting in season. Crowded
during spring and fall color times.
1200 ft (360 m)

GREENVILLE

COE (314) 222-8562
State map: H6
From GREENVILLE, drive
2 miles (3.2 k) S on US 67.
**$5; $6 electric; reservations accepted at
(314) 222-8562 for an additional $2.**
Open Apr 1–Nov 23.
111 (5 tent-only) close, open sites.
Central faucet, flush toilets, dump
station, electric hookups, tables, fire
rings, grills, boat ramp, pay phone.
With 25 heavily shaded and other
partially shaded sites next to
Wappapello Lake.
Boat or fish. Walk Old Greenville
historic trail. Explore and hike nearby
Johnson Natural Area or Ozark Trail.

View wildlife. Attend ranger programs.
14-day limit. Crowded holiday
weekends.
380 ft (114 m)

GREER

Mark Twain NF
(314) 325-4233
State map: G7
From ALTON, head N on
MO 19 for 9 miles (14.4 k). (Also see
Eleven Point River and McCormack
Lake.)
$5.
Open Apr 15–Oct 15; dry camping
allowed off-season.
19 scattered, screened sites.
Central faucet, pit toilets, tables, fire
rings, grills, boat ramp, pay phone.
Near Eleven Mile River with moderate
vegetation.
Hike McCormack–Greer Trail (part of
Ozark Trail). Canoe. Fish.
14-day limit. Small vehicles only.
Hunting in season.
550 ft (165 m)

HAWKER POINT SOUTH

COE (417) 276-3113
State map: D6
From STOCKTON, drive S
on MO 39 about 8 miles
(12.8 k). Turn Left (E) on CR H and
proceed 4 miles (6.4 k). (Nearby Hawker
Point costs $8.)
FREE so choose a chore. (Only under-$5
camp on lake; others are $8 and up.)
Open All Year.
28 close, open sites.
Pit toilets, tables, fire rings.
On timbered shore of Stockton Lake.
Swim, boat, ski, or fish.
NO water. 14-day limit. No generators
in quiet hours. Crowded weekends.
867 ft (260 m)

HAZEL CREEK

Mark Twain NF
(314) 438-5427
State map: G5
From POTOSI, drive S on

CR P for 13 miles (20.8 k). Turn Right
(W) on CR C and go 4 miles (6.4 k).
Turn Right (NW) on CR Z and continue
3 miles (4.8 k). (Also see Berryman.)
FREE so choose a chore.
Open All Year.
11 scattered, open sites.
Pit toilets, tables, grills.
In shade with creek next to Ozark Trail.
Hike or bike. View wildlife. Swim or
fish.
NO water. No trash arrangements (pack
it out). 14-day limit. Hunting in season.
Frequent ATVs and horses.
1500 ft (450 m)

HERCULES TOWER TRAILHEAD

Mark Twain NF
(417) 683-3410
State map: E7
From BRADLEYVILLE,
drive S for 6 miles (9.6 k) on MO 125.
(Also see Glade Top Trail.)
FREE so choose a chore.
Open All Year.
Undesignated scattered, screened sites.
Pit toilets, tables, grills, fire rings.
On hardwood ridge next to CCC-era
firetower aand 12000-acre Hercules
Glade Wilderness.
Hike into wilderness and savor solitude.
View wildlife.
NO water. No trash arrangements (pack
it out). Hunting in season.
1300 ft (390 m)

HIGHWAY K

COE (501) 425-2700
State map: E7
From FORSYTH, drive E
for 1 mile (1.6 k) on
US 160. Turn Right (S) on MO 76 and go
6.5 miles (10.4 k). Turn Left (E) on CR K
and travel 3.7 miles (5.9 k). (Nearby
River Run costs $10.)
$5. Open Mar 1–Nov 30; dry camping
allowed off-season.
19 close, open sites.
Central faucet, pit toilets, tables, fire
rings, boat ramp.
In quiet, shady spot next to Bull Shoals

▲ ▲ ▲ ▲ ▲ ▲ ▲ ▲ ▲ ▲ ▲ ▲ ▲ ▲ ▲ ▲ ▲ ▲ ● ▲ ● ▲ ● ▲ ▲ ▲ ▲ ▲ ▲ ▲ ▲

Lake.
Boat, ski, or fish. Watch wildlife. Do nothing.
14-day limit.
750 ft (225 m)

KISSEE MILLS

COE (501) 425-2700
State map: E7
From FORSYTH, drive 6.6 miles (10.6 k) E on US 160 to bridge. (Nearby Beaver Creek costs $7.)
$4. Open Mar 1–Nov 30; dry camping allowed off-season.
8 scattered, open sites.
Central faucet, pit toilets, tables, fire rings, boat ramp.
In mainly open area next to backwaters of Bull Shoals Lake.
Boat or fish. Walk nature trail.
14-day limit.
750 ft (225 m)

LANE SPRING

Mark Twain NF
(314) 364-4501
State map: F5
From ROLLA, drive S on MO 63 for 12 miles (19.2 k). Turn Right (W) on FR 1892 and continue 1 mile (1.6 k). (Also see Mill Creek.)
$5. Open All Year.
19 scattered, screened sites.
Hand pump, pit toilets, tables, fire rings.
Along Little Piney Creek in heavy forest. Walk Blossom Rock and Cedar Bluff trails. Fish.
14-day limit. Crowded on three-day weekends.
820 ft (246 m)

LITTLE SCOTIA POND

Mark Twain NF
(314) 729-6656
State map: G6
From BUNKER, travel NW on MO 72 for 9.2 miles (14.7 k). Turn Left (SW) on FR 2341 for final .5 mile (800 m).
$5. Open Apr 1–Nov 30; dry camping

allowed off-season.
14 close, open sites. Central faucet, pit toilets, tables, fire rings.
Next to pond.
Fish. Relax.
14-day limit.

LOGAN (WILLIAM R) CA

MO Dept of Conservation
(314) 248-2530
State map: G3
From TROY, head N on US 61 for 10 miles (16 k). Turn Left (W) on CR E. Turn Right (N) on CR RA.
FREE so choose a chore.
Open All Year.
Undesignated scattered, open sites.
Pit toilets.
In 1700-acre tract with small ponds.
Fish. Watch wildlife.
NO water. No trash arrangements (pack it out). 14-day limit. Hunting in season.

LOGGERS LAKE

Mark Twain NF
(314) 729-6656
State map: G6
From BUNKER, head W on MO A for .2 mile (320 m). Turn Left (SW) on FR 2221 and drive 6 miles (9.6 k). Turn Left (SE) on FR 2193 and go .5 mile (800 m). (Also see Oak Knoll.)
$5. Open Apr 1–Dec 1.
14 close, open sites. Central faucet, pit toilets, tables, fire rings.
Next to 25-acre lake.
Swim, fish, or boat (no gas motors). Walk Spring Creek Trail or loop trail around lake.
14-day limit.

LOUTRE LICK ACCESS

MO Dept of Conservation
(314) 882-9880
State map: G4
From MINEOLA, head W on CR N. Watch for sign. (Also see Danville CA.)
FREE so choose a chore.
Open All Year.
Undesignated close, open sites.

▲ ▲

Pit toilets.
Under open-feeling tree canopy on Loutre River.
Fish. View wildlife.
NO water. No trash arrangements (pack it out). Hunting in season.
700 ft (210 m)

MARBLE CREEK

Mark Twain NF
(314) 438-5427
State map: H6
Travel W on CR E from FREDERICKTOWN for 18 miles (28.8 k).
$5.
Open Apr 15–Nov 20.
27 close, screened sites.
Central faucet, pit toilets, tables, grills.
In heart of St Francois Mountains along scenic Marble Creek.
Enjoy seclusion. Walk nature trail. Swim or fish. View wildlife and take photos.
14-day limit. Hunting in season.
1500 ft (450 m)

MARI-OSA ACCESS

MO Dept of Conservation
(314) 882-9880
State map: F4
From JEFFERSON CITY, head E on US 50 about 6 miles (9.6 k).
FREE so choose a chore.
Open All Year.
Undesignated scattered, open sites.
Pit toilets, boat ramp.
Along Osage River bank.
Boat or fish.
NO water. 10-day limit.
750 ft (225 m)

MARION ACCESS

MO Dept of Conservation
(314) 882-9880
State map: F4
Locate site on E side of MARION.
FREE so choose a chore.
Open All Year.
Undesignated scattered, open sites.
Pit toilets, boat ramp.
On shore of Missouri River.

Fish and boat.
NO water. No trash arrangements (pack it out). 10-day limit.
750 ft (225 m)

MCCORMACK LAKE

Mark Twain NF
(314) 325-4233
State map: G7
From WINONA, head S on MO 19 for 13 miles (20.8 k). Turn Right (E) on FR 3155 and drive 2 miles (3.2 k). (Also see Greer.)
$5. Open All Year.
8 scattered, open sites. Central faucet, pit toilets, tables, grills, fire rings.
On grassy hill overlooking lake.
Hike McCormack–Greer Trail (part of Ozark Trail). Boat or fish.
14-day limit. Small vehicles only.
600 ft (180 m)

MILL CREEK

Mark Twain NF
(314) 364-4501
State map: F5
From NEWBURG, head S on CR T for .2 mile (320 m). Bear Right (SW) on CR P and drive 2.3 miles (3.7 k). Continue S on FR 1579 another 2.3 miles (3.7 k). (Also see Lane Spring.)
$5. Open May 1–Nov 30.
6 scattered, screened sites. Artestian well, pit toilets, tables, fire rings.
In woods along Mill Creek (trophy trout stream).
Walk nature trail. Find cave and natural bridge. Fish. Relax.
14-day limit. Crowded on three-day weekends.

MOORES MILL ACCESS

MO Dept of Conservation
(314) 882-9880
State map: G4
From CALWOOD, head SE on CR JJ. Watch for signs to E.
FREE so choose a chore.
Open All Year.
Undesignated close, open sites.
Pit toilets, boat ramp.

Under trees next to Auxvasse Creek.
Fish. Watch wildlife.
NO water. No trash arrangements (pack
it out). Hunting in season.
700 ft (210 m)

NOBLETT LAKE RA

Mark Twain NF
(417) 469-3155
State map: F7
From WILLOW SPRINGS,
take MO 76 W for 8 miles (12.8 k). Bear
Left (S) on MO 181 and continue
1.4 miles (2.2 k). Turn Left (SE) on
CR AP and proceed 2.9 miles (4.6 k).
Turn Right (SW) on FR 857 for final
2 miles (3.2 k). (Also see North Fork.)
$5; reservations accepted at
(417) 469-3155 for an additional $7.
Open May 15–Sep 15.
25 close, screened sites. Central faucet,
pit toilets, tables, grills, fire rings.
In hardwood forest with oak/pine
breaks next to 21-acre reservoir and
trailhead for 35-mile (56-k) Ridge Runner
Trail.
Hike to enjoy ecology and observe
wildlife. Boat or fish.
14-day limit. Hunting in season.
1000 ft (300 m)

NORTH FORK RA

Mark Twain NF
(417) 469-3155
State map: F7
From WEST PLAINS on
US 63 By-Pass, head W on CR CC for
15 miles (24 k). Turn Left (S) at sign.
(Also see Noblett Lake RA and
Tecumseh.)
$5. Open May 15–Oct 15; dry camping
allowed off-season.
20 close, open sites.
Central faucet, pit toilets, tables, fire
rings, grills, boat ramp.
In oak/pine hills next to North Fork
White River and Devil's Backbone
Wilderness.
Walk to beautiful Blue Spring. Hike
Ridge Runner Trail or into wilderness.
Fish or canoe. Take photos.

14-day limit. Hunting in season.
Occasionally crowded.
850 ft (255 m)

OAK KNOLL

Mark Twain NF
(314) 729-6656
State map: G6
From BUNKER, head W on
MO A for .2 mile (320 m). Turn Left
(SW) on FR 2221 and drive 6 miles
(9.6 k). Turn Left (SE) on FR 2193 and go
.5 mile (800 m). (Also see Loggers Lake.)
$5.
Open May 15–Oct 15.
27 close, open sites.
Central faucet, pit toilets, tables, fire
rings.
Above Loggers Lake.
Swim, fish, or boat (no gas motors).
Explore area.
14-day limit.

ONYX CAVE

Mark Twain NF
(417) 847-2144
State map: D7
From CASSVILLE, take
MO 112 S for 9 miles (14.4 k). Turn Left
(E) on gravel FR 197 (Sugar Camp Scenic
Drive) and go 4 miles (6.4 k).
FREE so choose a chore.
Open All Year.
2 close, open sites.
Tables, fire rings.
In hardwood area on scenic drive with
beautiful vista.
Explore area, including cave. Take
photos.
NO water. No toilet facilities. No trash
arrangements (pack it out). Hunting in
season. Occasional ATVs.
1500 ft (450 m)

OTTER SLOUGH CA

MO Dept of Conservation
(314) 624-5821
State map: I7
From DEXTER, take MO 25
S for 4 miles (6.4 k). Turn Left (W) on
CR H and drive to intersection with

▲ ▲

CR ZZ. Follow signs on gravel road for 4 miles (6.4 k).

FREE so choose a chore. reservations accepted at (314) 624-5821.

Open All Year.

Undesignated close, open sites.

Pit toilets, tables, boat ramp.

In open parking area near cypress-tupelo slough.

Fish or boat (small motors only). Walk nature trail and observe wildlife.

NO water. 14-day limit. Hunting in season. Mosquitos.

OUTLET

COE (417) 945-6411
State map: E5
From HERMITAGE, head SW on MO 254 for 4.5 miles (7.2 k) to W end of dam. (Also see Pittsburg Landing. Nearby Damsite costs $8.)

$4; $6 electric; reservations accepted at (417) 945-6411 for an additional $2.

Open Apr 16–Oct 15; dry camping allowed off-season.

28 close, open sites.

Central faucet, flush toilets, electric hookups, tables, fire rings, boat ramp, pay phone.

Among trees below dam on Pomme de Terre River.

Swim, boat, or fish. Float or canoe river. Hike to view wildlife.

14-day limit. Crowded holiday weekends.

800 ft (240 m)

OZARK RIVERWAYS
Gravel Bar Backcountry

NPS (314) 323-4236
State map: G7
Head N on MO 17 from MOUNTAIN VIEW for 6 miles (9.6 k) to Buck Hollow Put-In. Or, from SUMMERSVILLE, drive E on MO 106 for 10 miles (16 k). Turn Right (S) and go 5 miles (8 k). Turn Right again and continue 5 miles (8 k) to Bay Creek Put-In. Directions list only two of many put-ins; contact Headquarters for

map. (Nearby Alley Spring, Akers, and Big Spring cost $7.)

FREE so choose a chore.

Open All Year.

Undesignated scattered, open sites.

With numerous areas for canoeing/ tubing-camping along 134-miles (214-k) of Current and Jacks Fork Rivers.

Float rivers. Swim or fish. Explore. Tour caves. Find springs.

NO water. No toilet facilities. No trash arrangements (pack it out).

PADDY CREEK

Mark Twain NF
(417) 967-4194
State map: F6
From ROBY, take MO 17 N for 2 miles (3.2 k). Turn Right (E) on CR 2800 and go 6 miles (9.6 k). Turn Right (S) on FR 220 and proceed 2 miles (3.2 k). (Also see Big Piney.)

FREE so choose a chore.

Open Apr 1–Nov 30.

20 scattered, screened sites.

Pit toilets, tables, fire rings.

Along creek in forest about .25 mile (400 m) from Big Piney River.

Enjoy scenery. Walk Paddy Creek Trail to spectacular overlooks. Access Big Piney Trail for Paddy Creek Wilderness. Take photos.

NO water. 14-day limit.

900 ft (270 m)

PATRICK BRIDGE ACCESS

MO Dept of Conservation
(417) 256-7161
State map: F7
From GAINESVILLE, take US 160 E for 16 miles (25.6 k). Turn Left (NW) on CR H and drive 4 miles (6.4 k).

FREE so choose a chore. Open All Year.

12 close, open sites.

Pit toilets, tables, grills.

In open setting next to forest along North Fork River.

Canoe, swim, or fish. Watch wildlife.

NO water. 14-day limit. Hunting in season.

▲ ▲

PINE RIDGE

Mark Twain NF
(314) 642-6726
State map: F4
From GUTHRIE, drive W
on MO Y for 2.5 miles (4 k).
FREE so choose a chore.
Open Apr 15–Nov 30; dry camping
allowed off-season.
12 close, open sites.
Central faucet, pit toilets, tables.
In wooded picnic area next to 21-mile
(33.6 k) Cedar Creek Hiking Trail.
Hike to appreciate scenic area. Observe
wildlife.
14-day limit.

PINEWOODS LAKE

Mark Twain NF
(314) 785-1475
State map: H7
From ELLSINORE, travel
W on US 60 for 2 miles (3.2 k). (Nearby
Markham Spring costs $6.)
$5.
Open May 1–Sep 30; dry camping
allowed off-season.
15 scattered, screened sites. &
Central faucet, pit toilets, tables, fire
rings, grills, boat ramp, pier, shelter.
In oak/pine forest next to 31-acre lake.
Fish or boat (no gas motors). Walk
nature trail around lake or hike farther
to view wildlife.
14-day limit. No horses.

PITTSBURG LANDING

COE (417) 945-6411
State map: E5
From PITTSBURG, head S
on MO 64 for .75 mile
(1.2 k). Turn Left (E) on CR RA and
drive 2.5 miles (4 k). (Also see Outlet.
Nearby Nemo costs $8.)
FREE so choose a chore.
Open All Year.
Undesignated scattered, open sites.
Central faucet, pit toilets, tables, fire
rings, boat ramp.
In wooded hills next to Pomme de Terre
Lake.

Swim, boat, or fish. Hike to observe
wildlife.
14-day limit. Crowded holiday
weekends.
870 ft (261 m)

PRAIRIE HOME CA

MO Dept of Conservation
(314) 882-9880
State map: F4
From PRAIRIE HOME,
head W on CR J then S on CR W. (Also
see Wooldridge Access.)
FREE so choose a chore. Open All Year.
11 scattered, screened sites. &
Pit toilets.
With large trees close to streams and
lakes.
Fish. Hike to observe wildlife and take
photos.
NO water. No trash arrangements.
Hunting in season. Occasional horses.

RANACKER CA

MO Dept of Conservation
(314) 248-2530
State map: G3
From BOWLING GREEN,
drive N on US 61 for 9 miles (14.4 k).
Turn Right (SW) on CR RA. (Also see
DuPont Reservation CA.)
FREE so choose a chore. Open All Year.
Undesignated close, open sites. Pit toilet.
On 1600-acre tract.
Fish. View wildlife.
NO water. 14-day limit. Hunting in
season.

RED BLUFF

Mark Twain NF
(314) 438-5427
State map: G5
From POTOSI, drive W on
MO 8 for 17 miles (27.2 k). Turn Left (S)
on CR Y. Go 10 miles (16 k). Jog Right
(W) on CR C for .1 mile (160 m). Head
W on CR V for 4.5 miles (7.2 k).
$5. Open Apr 15–Oct 1.
49 close, screened sites.
Central faucet, pit toilets, tables, grills,
playing field.

In peaceful woods on Huzzah River.
Swim or fish. Walk nature trail or hike
farther to view wildlife.
14-day limit. Hunting in season.
1500 ft (450 m)

REDMAN CREEK

COE (314) 222-8562
State map: I7
From WAPPAPELLO, take
CR T SE across dam. (Also
see Snow Creek. Nearby Peoples Creek
costs $6.)
$5; $8 electric; reservations accepted at
(314) 222-8562 for an additional $2.
Open Apr 1–Nov 23.
108 (5 tent-only) screened sites. &
Central faucet, flush toilets, showers,
dump station, electric hookups, tables,
grills, fire rings, pay phone.
In very shady oak/hickory setting near
Wappapello Lake.
Walk nature trail and observe wildlife.
Attend ranger programs. Boat, swim, or
fish nearby.
14-day limit. Crowded holiday
weekends.
400 ft (120 m)

RIPPEE CA

MO Dept of Conservation
(417) 256-7161
State map: F7
From AVA, take MO 14 E
for 10 miles (16 k). Turn Left (NE) at
sign on gravel CR 328 and continue
2 miles (3.2 k).
FREE so choose a chore. Open All Year.
6 close, open, RV sites.
Pit toilets, tables, grills.
In forested corridor along Bryant Creek.
Swim, canoe, or fish. Observe wildlife
and take photos.
NO water. 14-day limit. Hunting in
season.

RIVER ROAD

COE (314) 223-7771
State map: H6
From PIEDMONT, head
SW on CR HH for 4.5 miles

(7.2 k). (Also see Bluff View and Webb
Creek Park. Nearby Piedmont costs $7.)
$4; $7 developed; $10 electric.
Open All Year.
108 scattered, open sites. &
Central faucet, flush toilets, showers,
dump station, electric hookups, tables,
fire rings, grills, boat ramp, pay phone.
In shade on Black River below
Clearwater Lake dam.
Fish. Canoe. Boat or ski nearby. Walk
Pines Bend Nature Trail. View wildlife.
14-day limit.
570 ft (171 m)

ROCKY FORKS LAKES CA

MO Dept of Conservation
(314) 882-9880
State map: F4
From COLUMBIA, drive N
on US 63 about 4 miles (6.4 k). Locate
sites on E side of road. (Also see Tri-City
Community Lake.)
FREE so choose a chore.
Open All Year.
Undesignated scattered, open sites.
Pit toilets, boat ramp.
In open, grassy fields at least 100 ft
(30 m) from any road.
Boat or fish. Hike. View wildlife.
NO water. 10-day limit. Hunting in
season.
775 ft (233 m)

ROTHWELL PARK

(816) 263-6757
State map: F3
In MOBERLY on Rothwell
Park Rd (S off US 24).
$3; $8 hookups.
Open All Year.
46 (10 tent-only) close, open sites.
Water at 36 sites, flush toilets, showers,
dump station, electric hookups, tables,
fire rings, shelter, pool, playground.
In city park with lake.
Swim. Fish. Hike. Cross-country ski in
winter.

▲ ▲

SILVERMINES

Mark Twain NF
(314) 438-5427
State map: H6
Take MO 72 W for 6 miles
(9.6 k) from FREDERICKTOWN. Turn
Left (S) on CR D and go 4 miles (6.4 k).
$5. Open All Year.
101 close, screened sites.
Central faucet, flush/pit toilets, tables,
grills, canoe launch.
Along beautiful, boulder-strewn St
Francis River at old mining location.
Walk nature trail. Hike and explore.
Take photos. Swim or fish. Canoe or
kayak.
14-day limit. Hunting in season.
1500 ft (450 m)

SMITH'S FORK CAMPGROUND

City of Smithville
(816) 532-1023
State map: C3
From SMITHVILLE, take
CR DD to Dam Rd.
**$4; $10 hookups; reservations accepted at
(816) 532-1023.**
Open All Year.
85 close, open sites.
Water at every site, flush toilets,
showers, dump station, electric hookups,
tables, grills, ball fields, pay phone.
With shady and open areas near lake.
Boat or fish. Enjoy sport activities.
Attend events in amphitheatre. Try
go-karts, golf driving range, archery (fees
charged).

SNOW CREEK

COE (314) 222-8562
State map: H7
From POPLAR BLUFF,
take US 67 N for 25 miles
(40 k). Turn Right (W) on MO 172. Go
about 6 miles (9.6 k). Bear Left (NW) on
CR W. Drive 4 miles (6.4 k) to Chaonia
Landing RA. (Also see Redman Creek.)
FREE so choose a chore.
Open All Year.
12 close, open sites.
Central faucet, flush toilets, tables, fire

rings, grills, boat ramp.
In shady, open setting on shore of Lake
Wappapello.
Boat or fish. Watch wildlife.
14-day limit. Hunting in season.
Crowded holiday weekends.
380 ft (114 m)

SPRING CREEK

COE (501) 425-2700
State map: F7
From ISABELLE, take
CR HH S for 4.2 miles
(6.7 k). (Also see Theodosia.)
FREE so choose a chore.
Open Mar 1–Nov 30; dry camping
allowed off-season.
12 close, open sites. Central faucet, pit
toilets, tables, fire rings, boat ramp.
In heavy shade on peninsula jutting into
Bull Shoals Lake.
Swim, boat, ski, or fish. Observe wildlife.
14-day limit.
750 ft (225 m)

SUTTON BLUFF

Mark Twain NF
(314) 729-6656
State map: H6
From CENTERVILLE, head
NE on MO 21 for 3 miles (4.8 k). Turn
Left (NW) on FR 2233 and go 7 miles
(11.2 k). Turn Left (S) on FR 2236 and
proceed 3 miles (4.8 k).
$5.
Open Apr 1–Dec 1.
35 close, open sites.
Central faucet, flush/pit toilets, tables,
fire rings.
Next to West Fork Black River.
Swim or fish. Walk Sutton Bluff Trail for
scenic valley views or hike farther along
Ozark National Recreation Trail.
14-day limit.

TAYLORS LANDING ACCESS

MO Dept of Conservation
(314) 882-9880
State map: F4
From MO 179 Exit off I-70
(near OVERTON), head N for 3 miles

(4.8 k) to gravel road with sign. (Also see Wooldridge Access.)
FREE so choose a chore. Open All Year.
1 screened site. Pit toilet, boat ramp.
With huge cottonwood trees beside Missouri River.
Fish and boat. Observe wildlife.
NO water. No trash arrangements (pack it out). Occasionally crowded.

TECUMSEH

COE (501) 425-2700
State map: F7
Locate site in TECUMSEH off US 160. (Also see North Fork RA and Udall.)
FREE so choose a chore. Open All Year.
7 close, open sites.
Hand pump, pit toilets, tables, fire rings, grills, boat ramp.
At junction of North Fork River and Norfolk Lake.
Boat or fish.
14-day limit. Deceptively swift current. Crowded holiday weekends and during white-bass spring spawn.

THEODOSIA

COE (501) 425-2700
State map: E7
Find site off US 160 in THEODOSIA just W of bridge. (Also see Spring Creek.)
$5; $8 electric; reservations accepted at (501) 425-2700 for an additional $2.
Open Mar 1–Nov 30; dry camping allowed off-season.
35 close, open sites. Central faucet, pit toilets, dump station, electric hookups, tables, fire rings, boat ramp, pay phone.
On Bull Shoals Lake shoreline with fair shade and views.
Swim, boat, ski, or fish. View wildlife.
14-day limit.
750 ft (225 m)

TRI-CITY COMMUNITY LAKE

MO Dept of Conservation
(314) 882-9880
State map: F3
From CENTRALIA, drive

W on CR CC. Turn Left (S) at sign on gravel road and proceed 2 miles (3.2 k). (Also see Rocky Ford Lakes CA.)
FREE so choose a chore.
Open All Year.
10 scattered, screened sites.
Pit toilets, fire rings, grills, boat ramp.
In semi-open setting with large trees ringing lake.
Fish. Watch wildlife.
NO water.

UDALL

COE (501) 425-2700
State map: F7
From BAKERSFIELD, drive W on CR O for 9 miles (14.4 k). (Also see Tecumseh and Red Bank, AR.)
$5. Open Apr 1–Oct 31; dry camping allowed off-season.
9 scattered, open sites. Central faucet, pit toilets, dump station, tables, fire rings, grills, boat ramp, rentals.
On bank of northern arm of Norfolk Lake.
Boat or fish.
14-day limit. Crowded weekends.

VANDALIA COMMUNITY LAKE

MO Dept of Conservation
(314) 882-9880
State map: G3
From LADDONIA, head E on CR K for 4 miles (6.4 k). At sign continue E on gravel CR 100 for 1.5 miles (2.4 k).
FREE so choose a chore.
Open All Year.
10 scattered, open sites.
Pit toilets, grills, fire rings.
In open setting near lake.
Fish. Relax.
NO water. No trash arrangements (pack it out). Occasionally crowded.

VERSAILLES CITY PARK

(314) 378-4634
State map: E4
Locate park in VERSAILLES at junction of

MO 52 and MO 5.
FREE so choose a chore.
Open Apr–Nov.
5 close, open, RV sites.
Central faucet, flush toilets, dump station, electric hookups, tables, grills, pay phone.
In city park.
Enjoy overnight stop.
3-day limit.

WEBB CREEK PARK
COE (314) 223-7771
State map: H6
From ELLINGTON, drive SE on CR H for 12 miles (19.2 k). (Also see River Road.)
$5; $10 electric.
Open May 15–Sep 15.
43 scattered, open sites.
Central faucet, flush toilets, showers, dump station, electric hookups, tables, fire rings, grills, boat ramp, store, rentals.
In natural Ozarks setting on hill overlooking Clearwater Lake.
Swim, boat, ski, or fish. View wildlife.
Attend ranger programs.
14-day limit.
570 ft (171 m)

WELLSVILLE LAKE CA
MO Dept of Conservation (314) 882-9880
State map: G3
From WELLSVILLE, drive S for 2 miles (3.2 k) on US 19. Turn Right (W). (Also see Diggs Access.)
FREE so choose a chore. Open All Year.
Undesignated close, open sites.
Pit toilets.
In open parking area near lake.
Fish. Observe wildlife.
NO water. No trash arrangements (pack it out). Hunting in season.
700 ft (210 m)

WHETSTONE CREEK CA
MO Dept of Conservation (314) 882-9880
State map: G3
From WILLIAMSBURG, go

N on gravel road for 2 miles (3.2 k). (Also see Diggs Access.)
FREE so choose a chore.
Open All Year.
Undesignated close, open sites.
Pit toilets, fire rings.
In creek setting with view of native woodlands.
Hike to see wildlife and take photos.
Fish.
NO water. No trash arrangements (pack it out). Hunting in season.
700 ft (210 m)

WINDSOR CROSSING
COE (816) 438-7317
State map: D5
Go N for 1 mile (1.6 k) on CR PP from TIGHTWAD.
FREE so choose a chore. (Only under-$5 camp on lake.)
Open All Year.
46 close, open sites.
Central faucet, pit toilets, tables, fire rings, grills, boat ramp.
In open, grassy setting (sapling trees) next to Truman Lake.
Swim, boat, or fish. View wildlife.
14-day limit. Hunting in season.
726 ft (218 m)

WOOLDRIDGE ACCESS
MO Dept of Conservation (314) 882-9880
State map: F4
On SW side of WOOLRIDGE, find gravel CR 179-3. Follow signs. (Also see Taylors Landing Access and Prairie Home CA.)
FREE so choose a chore. Open All Year.
1 open site. Pit toilet.
Next to wadable Petit-Saline Creek.
Fish. Watch wildlife.
NO water. No trash arrangements (pack it out).

NEBRASKA
CAMPGROUND LOCATIONS

▶ ▶ Find location on facing page map grid. ▶ ▶
▼ ▼ Locate area campgrounds on these page numbers. ▼ ▼

Nebraska

Grid conforms to official state map. For your copy, call (800) 228-4307
or write Travel & Tourism, PO Box 94666, Lincoln, NE 68509.

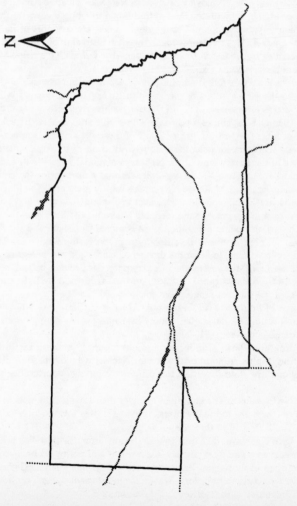

PUBLIC LANDS CAMPING

Nebraska is an Indian word meaning *land of flat water*. The Missouri River forms the state's eastern border. From it, a network of rivers fans across Nebraska's endless prairies, fertile farms, and uninterrupted ranches. The Platte River first served the Indians, then explorers, traders, and trappers. A way along this river became the Oregon and Mormon trails as well as the Overland Stage and Pony Express routes. Traveling northwest toward the headwaters of Nebraska's rivers, you encounter rolling hills, then buttes, plateaus, and canyons with fascinating geological features such as Chimney Rock, Scott's Bluff, Agate Fossil Beds, and Toadstool Park.

This "land of flat water" has enjoyed a rich past. Nebraska's Native Americans still celebrate their spiritual bond with the land at traditional tribal powwows on the Pine Ridge, Santee Sioux, Winnebago, and Omaha reservations. Descendants of European settlers celebrate Danish Days in Dannebrog, a Swedish festival in Stromsburg, and a kolache eating contest in the Czech town of Wilber. Two writers have helped record Nebraska's recent history: Willa Cather and Mari Sandoz.

The **National Park Service** (NPS) administers several areas in Nebraska, including one of the last free-flowing sections of the Missouri River. This designated Wild and Scenic River separates Nebraska and South Dakota. See the river's dynamic character exhibited in its islands, bars, chutes, and snags. Other NPS sites deal with geology or landmarks and events of American history. None of these sites offers camping.

National forests in Nebraska hold the unique distinction of having planted their trees: 25,000 acres in the Bessey Unit of the **Nebraska National Forest** (NF) and 2,500 acres of the Samuel R McKelvie NF. Bessey Unit serves as a nursery for the entire US Forest Service while Samuel R McKelvie NF remains mostly grassland. The Pine Ridge segments of the Nebraska NF contain native stands of ponderosa pine and parks of grasses (western wheatgrass, prairie sand reed, big bluestem, and little bluestem). Pine Ridge Ranger District also administers the Oglala National Grassland and the Soldier Creek Wilderness. Carved from old Fort Robinson property, the wilderness burned extensively in 1989. In wildlife, look for the threatened bald eagle and peregrine falcon plus the rare northern swift fox among the more common deer, coyote, bobcat, raccoon, wild turkey, red-tailed hawk, golden eagle, and great horned owl. To camp in Nebraska's national forests, cost ranges from free to $5.00.

US Army Corps of Engineers (COE) has built Lewis and Clark Lake which serves both Nebraska and South Dakota. Harlan County Lake offers seven campgrounds. COE camping fees extend from free to $10.00.

Nebraska Game and Parks Commission offers modern camping facilities for $5.00–$7.00 per night plus an additional $3.00 for electricity. Enjoy these facilities at 30 different locations. The state also offers free primitive camping opportunities at over 50 areas.

Too, friendly Nebraskans offer camping in many of their **towns**. Again, as in many midwestern states, there are too many places to name in this introduction to public lands camping. You'll find all of them in the listings.

While camping in Nebraska, take time to learn lessons from the past. Sea beds and volcanic dust preserved a variety of ancient life. Streams and pathways have exposed this diversity to open examination. Read the words of writers such as Cather and Sandoz who have recorded recent history. Retrace the footsteps of settlers, fur trappers, traders, Indians, mammoths, rhinoceroses, and dinosaurs.

▲ ▲

ALBION CAMPGROUND

(402) 395-2428
State map: H23
Find campground W of
Fuller Park in ALBION on Fairview St.
(Also see Ben Bowman Roadside Park.)
FREE; $3 electric.
Open All Year.
6 scattered, open, RV sites.
Central faucet, flush toilets, electric
hookups, tables, grills, playground, pool.
In shaded area.
Enjoy overnight stay.

ALEXANDRIA LAKES SRA

(402) 471-5566
State map: N25
Take gravel road E
from ALEXANDRIA for 4 miles (6.4 k).
(Also see Buning Dam RA.)
FREE; $3 electric; $2 entrance fee.
Open All Year.
40 scattered, open sites.
Hand pump, flush toilets, dump station,
electric hookups, tables, grills, fire rings,
playground, store.
Near lake.
Fish or boat (no gas motors). Hike.
14-day limit.
1390 ft (417 m)

ARCADIA GARDEN CLUB

(308) 789-6552
State map: I19
Find garden spot on W
edge of ARCADIA.
FREE; donations requested.
Open Apr–Oct.
2 close, open sites.
Central faucet, pit toilets, tables.
Near Loup River.
Fish. Enjoy overnight stop.

ARNOLD LAKE SRA

(402) 684-2921
State map: I15
From ARNOLD, head S
on NE 40 about 1 mile (1.6 k).
FREE; $2 entrance fee. Open All Year.
90 close, open sites. Central faucet, pit
toilets, electric hookups, tables, fire rings,

boat ramp, playground.
Near South Loup River with 22-acre
lake.
Fish or boat (no gas motors).
14-day limit.

ATKINSON LAKE SRA

(402) 684-2921
State map: D19
From ATKINSON,
drive W on NE 20 for 1 mile (1.6 k).
Turn Left (S) and go 1 mile (1.6 k).
FREE; $3 electric. Open All Year.
16 close, open sites.
Hand pump, pit toilets, electric hookups,
tables, grills, fire rings.
In shade surrounded by open fields next
to 14-acre lake.
Fish. Walk nature trail and view wildlife.
14-day limit.

BADER MEMORIAL PARK

Chapman City Parks
(308) 986-2420
State map: K22
From CHAPMAN, drive S for 3 miles
(4.8 k).
FREE; donations requested.
Open Apr 15–Oct 15.
25 close, open sites.
Central faucet, flush/pit toilets, electric
hookups, tables, fire rings.
Next to Platte River.
Swim or fish. Enjoy overnight stop.
3-day limit.

BANCROFT CAMPGROUND

State map: F27
Locate campground in
BANCROFT.
$4. Open Apr–Oct.
4 close, open sites. Central faucet, flush
toilets, electric hookups, tables, fire rings.
At W edge of town park.
Visit John Neihardt Historical Center.

BEN BOWMAN ROADSIDE PARK

State map: H23
From ALBION, go SE
1 mile (1.6 k) on NE 39.
(Also see Albion Campground.)

FREE so choose a chore. Open All Year.
Undesignated sites. Hand pump, tables.
In small area with trees.
Enjoy overnight stop.
No toilet facilities. 2-day limit.

BESSEY RA

Nebraska NF
(308) 533-2257
State map: G15

From HALSEY, travel W on NE 2 for
1 mile (1.6 k). Turn Left (S) on NE 86B
and go .5 mile (800 m).
$5; $8 electric; reservations accepted at
(308) 533-2257 for an additional $6.
Open May–Oct; dry camping allowed
off-season.
33 (1 tent-only) scattered, screened sites.
Water at every site, flush toilets,
showers, dump station, electric hookups,
tables, fire rings, pool, pay phone.
In island of trees within sea of rolling
sandhills prairie–largest hand-planted
forest (20000 acres) in Western
Hemisphere.
Hike to view wildlife (especially birds).
Take photos. Climb lookout tower.
Canoe, swim ($1.50), or fish. Bike.
Attend ranger programs. Cross-country
ski in winter.
14-day limit. Crowded hunting season
and major holidays.
2500 ft (750 m)

BLOOMFIELD FAIRGROUNDS

(402) 373-4396
State map: D24
Find fairgrounds on E
side of BLOOMFIELD.
$3; weekly/monthly rates.
Open Apr–Oct.
10 close, open, RV sites.
Central faucet, flush toilets, showers,
electric hookups.
Enjoy overnight stay.
Crowded during Aug county fair.

BLOOMFIELD MUNICIPAL PARK

(402) 373-4396
State map: D24
Locate park at

Washington & Denny streets in
BLOOMFIELD.
$5; weekly/monthly rates.
Open Apr–Oct.
6 close, open, RV sites.
Central faucet, flush toilets, electric
hookups, tables, playground.
In town park.
Relax at overnight stop.

BLUE RIVER CAMPGROUND

Hebron Parks
(402) 768-6322
State map: N24
Find campground in HEBRON.
$5. Open All Year.
70 close, open sites.
Central faucet, flush toilets, showers,
dump station, electric hookups, tables,
fire rings.
In municipal park on river.
Swim or fish.

BLUE RIVER SRA

(402) 471-5545
State map: L26
From DORCHESTER,
go 2 miles (3.2 k) N on NE 15. (Also see
Conestoga SRA and Pawnee Lake SRA.)
FREE; $2 entrance fee.
Open All Year.
25 scattered, open sites.
Hand pump, pit toilets, tables, fire rings.
Next to river.
Fish.
14-day limit.
1417 ft (425 m)

BLUESTEM LAKE SRA

(402) 471-5545
State map: L27
From SPRAGUE, drive
W on NE 33 for 3 miles (4.8 k). (Also see
Conestoga SRA, Olive Creek SRA,
Stagecoach Lake SRA, and Wagon Train
Lake SRA.)
FREE; $2 entrance fee. Open All Year.
219 (19 RV-only) scattered, open sites.
Hand pump, pit toilets, dump station,
tables, fire rings, grills, boat ramp,
playground.

▲ ▲

Next to 325-acre lake.
Swim, boat, and fish.
14-day limit. Hunting in season.
1330 ft (399 m)

BOWMAN LAKE SRA

(402) 684-2921
State map: J19
From LOUP CITY,
drive W on ME 92 for .5 mile (800 m).
FREE; $2 entrance fee.
Open All Year.
30 close, open sites.
Central faucet, pit toilets, tables, fire
rings, boat ramp, shelter, playground.
Next to 20-acre lake.
Fish or boat (no gas motors). Hike.
14-day limit.

BOX BUTTE RESERVOIR SRA

(308) 762-5605
State map: D6
From HEMINGFORD,
head N on CR for 9.5 miles (15.2 k).
FREE; $2 entrance fee. Open All Year.
60 close, open sites.
Central faucet, pit toilets, tables, fire
rings, boat ramp, shelter.
Next to 1600-acre lake on Niobrara River
S of Pine Ridge.
Swim, boat, and fish.
14-day limit.

BRIDGEPORT SRA

(308) 436-2383
State map: H6
Locate area on W edge
of BRIDGEPORT.
FREE so choose a chore. Open All Year.
Undesignated close, open sites.
Central faucet, pit toilets, dump station,
tables, fire rings, grills, boat ramp.
In river bottom land next to 5 water-
filled sand pits.
Swim, boat, ski, or fish. Canoe or bike.
14-day limit. Occasionally crowded.

BROWNVILLE SRA

(402) 883-2575
State map: M31
Find area on US 136 at

BROWNVILLE. (See Verdon Lake SRA.)
FREE; $2 entrance fee.
Open All Year.
14 close, open, RV sites. Central faucet,
pit toilets, grills, fire rings, boat ramp.
On Missouri River.
Boat or fish.
14-day limit.
890 ft (267 m)

BRUNING DAM RA

Little Blue Natural
Resources District
(402) 364-2145
State map: N24
From BRUNING, drive E for 2 miles
(3.2 k). Turn Left (N) and go 1 mile
(1.6 k). Turn Right (E) for final .75 mile
(1.2 k). (Also see Alexandria Lakes SRA.)
FREE so choose a chore. Open All Year.
Undesignated scattered, open sites.
Pit toilets, boat ramp.
Next to 250-acre lake.
Fish or boat (less than 5 hp). View
wildlife and take photos. Ice fish or skate
in winter.
NO water. Hunting in season.

BUCKLEY CREEK RA

Little Blue Natural
Resources District
(402) 364-2145
State map: O25
From REYNOLDS, head E on NE 8 for
1 mile (1.6 k). Turn Left (N) and go
.5 mile (800 m).
FREE so choose a chore. Open All Year.
Undesignated close, screened sites.
Central faucet, pit toilets, electric
hookups, tables, fire rings, grills, boat
ramp, shelter.
Near Clarke McNary Arboretum.
Fish and boat (less than 5 hp). Enjoy
flora and fauna. Take photos. Ice skate in
winter.
Snowmobiles in winter.

BUCKLEY PARK

Stromsburg Parks
(402) 764-8228
State map: J24

▲ ▲

Locate park on S edge of STROMSBURG on US 81.
FREE; donations requested.
Open May 1–Oct 15; dry camping allowed off-season.
75 close, open sites. Central faucet, flush toilets, dump station, tables, grills, pool.
In city park.
Swim. Enjoy overnight stop.
2-day limit (longer stays with permission).

BURWELL CITY PARK

(308) 346-4509
State map: G19
Find park on N 8th St in BURWELL.
$5. Open Apr–Oct; dry camping allowed off-season.
4 close, open sites.
Central faucet, pit toilets, electric hookups, tables, fire rings, shelter.
In city park.
Swim or fish. Relax.

BUSSELL PARK

Ord Parks
(308) 728-5791
State map: H19
Locate park in ORD at 24th & J streets.
$2. Open All Year.
16 (10 tent-only) close, open sites.
Central faucet, pit toilets, dump station, electric hookups, tables, fire rings.
In city park.
Swim or fish.
2-day limit (longer stays with permission).

BUTTE CITY PARK

State map: B20
Find park on E edge of BUTTE on NE 12.
FREE; $3 electric.
Open All Year.
Undesignated close, open sites.
Central faucet, pit toilets, electric hookups, tables, fire rings.
In town park.
Enjoy overnight stop.

CALAMUS SRA

(308) 346-5666
State map: G18
From BURWELL, head NW for 7 miles (11.2 k).
FREE; $2 entrance fee.
Open All Year.
14-day limit. Hunting in season.
▲ **Hannaman Bayou & Valleyview**
Undesignated scattered, open sites.
Hand pump, pit toilets, tables, fire rings, boat ramp.
In grassy area next to 5123-acre lake.
Boat and fish.
▲ **Nunda Shoals**
39 close, screened sites. &
Hand pump, pit toilets, tables, fire rings, grills, boat ramp, pay phone.
With asphalt pads separated by shrubs next to 5123-acre lake.
Swim, boat, or fish. Observe wildlife.

CAMBRIDGE CITY PARK

(308) 697-3711
State map: N15
Locate park on E edge of CAMBRIDGE, on N side of US 34.
FREE so choose a chore. Open All Year.
Undesignated scattered, open sites.
Central faucet, flush toilets, showers, electric hookups, tables.
On river.
Swim or fish.
5-day limit.

CARNEY PARK

O'Neill Parks
(402) 336-3640
State map: D20
Find park on S edge of O'NEILL on US 281.
FREE; donations requested.
Open All Year.
10 scattered, open sites. Water at every site, flush toilets, dump station, electric hookups, tables, grills, shelter, ball field.
In quiet area with trees and fishing pond.
Fish. Walk nature trail or hike farther.
Bike. View wildlife.
Crowded Jul–Aug.

CEDAR POINT

COE (308) 799-2105
State map: O18
From REPUBLICAN
CITY, go S for 3 miles (4.8 k) on NE A.
(Also see Gremlin Cove, Outlet North,
and Outlet South.)
FREE so choose a chore.
Open All Year.
106 scattered, open sites.
Hand pump, pit toilets, tables, fire rings.
In rolling hills with deep, forested draws
next to Harlan County Lake.
Swim, boat, or fish. Walk nature trail.
Observe wildlife.
30-day limit. Crowded in summer.
1950 ft (585 m)

CENTENNIAL PARK

Belvidere Parks
(402) 768-7313
State map: N24
From center of BELVIDERE, head 3
blocks N on Main St then 1 block E.
FREE so choose a chore.
Open All Year.
2 close, open sites. Central faucet, pit
toilets, tables, fire rings.
Relax in village park.
7-day limit.

CHAMPION LAKE SRA

(308) 535-8025
State map: M10
From CHAMPION,
head W for .5 mile (800 m).
FREE; $2 entrance fee.
Open All Year.
30 close, open sites. Central faucet, pit
toilets, tables, boat ramp.
Next to 50-acre lake.
Boat or fish. Visit state's last
water-powered grain mill.
14-day limit.

CHAUTAUQUA PARK

Beatrice Parks
(402) 228-3649
State map: N27
Locate park in BEATRICE, N of Grable
St on S bank of Big Blue River. (Also see

Riverside Park and Rockford Lake SRA.)
$3; reservations accepted at
(402) 228-3649.
Open Apr 1 – Nov 1; dry camping
allowed off-season.
25 close, open sites.
Central faucet, flush toilets, showers,
dump station, electric hookups, tables,
grills, fire rings, shelter, playground,
tennis court, ball field, pay phone.
In 66-acre state arboretum site along Big
Blue River.
Walk nature trail. Visit historic
tabernacle. Bike. Enjoy sports. Fish.

CHESTER CITY PARK

(402) 324-5755
State map: O24
Find park at NE 8 &
US 81 in CHESTER.
FREE so choose a chore. Open Apr–Oct.
12 (10 tent-only) close, open sites.
Central faucet, flush toilets, electric
hookups, tables, fire rings.
In town park.
Enjoy overnight stop.
1-day limit.

CHEYENNE SRA

(308) 384-4916
State map: L21
Take WOOD RIVER
Exit (#300) off I-80.
FREE; $2 entrance fee.
Open All Year.
15 scattered, open sites. Central faucet,
flush toilets, tables, grills, playground.
On 15-acre lake.
Fish or boat (no gas motors).
14-day limit.
1960 ft (588 m)

CHILVERS PARK

Plainview Parks
(402) 582-4928
State map: E23
Locate park in PLAINVIEW, 1 block N
of US 20.
FREE so choose a chore. Open All Year.
4 close, open sites. Central faucet, flush
toilets, tables, fire rings.

▲ ▲

In city park.
Swim. Enjoy overnight stop.
3-day limit.

CLARKSON CITY PARK

(402) 892-3100
State map: H25
Find park at 1st &
Bryan streets in CLARKSON.
$1; $2 electric; $4 electric & water; $5 full
hookups.
Open May 1–Oct 1; dry camping
allowed off-season.
25 close, open sites.
Central faucet, flush toilets, electric
hookups, tables, grills, pool, tennis court.
In beautiful park.
Swim. Play sports.
14-day limit.

CODY PARK

North Platte Parks
(308) 534-7611
State map: J13
Locate park in NORTH PLATTE at 1402
N Jeffers.
$4. Open May 1–Oct 15.
39 close, open sites.
Central faucet, flush toilets, tables.
In city park.
Relax at overnight stop.
7-day limit.

COLERIDGE VILLAGE PARK

(402) 283-4464
State map: D25
Find park in
COLERIDGE.
$5. Open All Year.
2 close, open, RV sites.
Central faucet, flush toilets, dump
station, tables, grills.
In village park.
Enjoy overnight stay.

CONESTOGA LAKE SRA

(402) 796-2362
State map: L26
From DENTON, drive
N on NE S55A for 2 miles (3.2 k). (Also
see Blue River SRA, Bluestem SRA, and

Pawnee Lake SRA.)
FREE; $2 entrance fee.
Open All Year.
30 scattered, open sites.
Hand pump, pit toilets, dump station,
tables, fire rings, grills, boat ramp.
Next to 175-acre lake.
Boat or fish.
14-day limit. Hunting in season.
Occasionally crowded.
1250 ft (375 m)

COTTONWOOD COVE

Dakota City Parks
(402) 987-3448
State map: D28
Locate campground in DAKOTA CITY
at 14th & Hickory.
$3; $4 electric. Open May 1–Oct 1.
6 close, open sites.
Central faucet, flush toilets, electric
hookups, tables, grills, boat ramp,
volleyball court.
In wooded area along Missouri River.
Walk nature trail. Fish or boat.

COTTONWOOD LAKE SRA

(402) 684-2921
State map: B10
From MERRIMAN,
drive E on US 20 for .5 mile (800 m).
Turn Right (S) and go .5 mile (800 m).
FREE; $2 entrance fee.
Open All Year.
25 close, open sites.
Central faucet, pit toilets, tables, fire
rings, boat ramp, shelter.
Next to 60-acre lake.
Visit nearby Bowring Ranch SHP. Boat
and fish.
14-day limit.

COTTONWOOD PARK

(308) 246-5278
State map: I21
Find park in
WOLBACH, just off NE 22.
FREE; $4 electric. Open All Year.
14 (10 tent-only) scattered, open sites.
Pit toilets, electric hookups, tables, grills,
pool.

Among cottonwood near two connected lakes with wildlife island.
Walk nature trail or hike farther. View wildlife. Bike. Boat or fish.
NO water. Hunting in season.

CRESTON PARK

(402) 285-0090
State map: H25
Locate park in
CRESTON, 2 blocks N of Baptist Church.
FREE so choose a chore.
Open May 1–Oct 31.
14 (10 tent-only) scattered, open sites.
Central faucet, flush toilets, showers, electric hookups, tables, fire rings.
In city park.
Swim. Enjoy overnight stay.

CRYSTAL LAKE SRA

(308) 535-8025
State map: M21
From AYR, head N for
1.5 miles (2.4 k).
FREE; $2 entrance fee. Open All Year.
70 close, open sites. Central faucet, pit toilets, dump station, electric hookups, tables, fire rings, boat ramp.
Next to 30-acre lake.
Swim, boat, or fish.
14-day limit.

CRYSTAL SPRINGS

Fairbury Parks
(402) 729-5155
State map: N25
From FAIRBURY, head S then W for
1.5 miles (2.4 k).
$4; $6 A/C.
Open May 1–Oct 31.
50 close, open sites.
Central faucet, flush toilets, showers, dump station, electric hookups, tables, fire rings.
In town park.
Fish. Enjoy overnight stop.

DANNEBROG MUNICIPAL PARK

(308) 226-2422
State map: J21
Locate park in

DANNEBROG.
FREE; $5 electric.
Open May 1–Sep 30; dry camping allowed off-season.
Undesignated close, open sites.
Central faucet, flush toilets, dump station, electric hookups, tables.
In shade along Oak Creek near Loup River.
Hike or bike. Relax.
Crowded 1st Jun weekend.

DAVID CITY CAMPGROUND

(402) 367-3914
State map: J25
Find campground in
DAVID CITY at 699 Kansas St.
$2.02. Open Mar 1–Oct 31.
Undesignated close, open sites.
Central faucet, flush toilets, showers, dump station, electric hookups, tables, fire rings, boat ramp.
In city park.
Swim, boat, and fish.

DEAD TIMBER SRA

(402) 664-3597
State map: H27
From SCRIBNER,
travel N on US 275 for 5 miles (8 k).
Turn Right (E) and go 1.5 miles (2.4 k).
Turn Right (S). Proceed .5 mile (800 m).
$5; $8 electric; $2 entrance fee.
Open All Year.
132 (100 tent-only) scattered, open sites.
Hand pump, pit toilets, electric hookups, tables, grills, fire rings, pay phone.
Along wooded Elkhorn River Valley.
Fish or boat (no gas motors). Canoe.
14-day limit. Hunting in season.

DESHLER CITY PARK

(402) 365-4260
State map: N24
Locate park in
DESHLER at 4th & Park.
FREE so choose a chore. Open All Year.
40 close, screened sites.
Central faucet, flush toilets, showers, dump station, electric hookups, tables, grills, pool, playground, ball field, tennis

▲ ▲

court, store, pay phone.
Among trees near small creek and business district.
Swim. Play sports. Bike. View wildlife.
3-day limit.

EAST CITY PARK

Ainsworth City Parks
(402) 387-2494
State map: D16
Find park in AINSWORTH.
FREE so choose a chore. Open Mar–Oct.
Undesignated close, open sites.
Central faucet, flush toilets, showers, dump station, electric hookups, tables.
In city park.
Swim. Relax.
14-day limit.

ELGIN PARK

(402) 843-5822
State map: F22
Locate park in ELGIN at North & Plantation streets.
FREE so choose a chore. Open May–Sep; dry camping allowed off-season.
6 scattered, open sites. Central faucet, flush toilets, showers, tables, grills, pool.
In town park.
Swim. Bike. Enjoy overnight stop.

ENDERS RESERVOIR SRA

(308) 394-5118
State map: M11
Find area just S of ENDERS.
FREE; $3 electric; $2 entrance fee.
Open All Year.
192 scattered, open sites. &
Central faucet, flush toilets, dump station, electric hookups, tables, fire rings, boat ramp, shelter.
Next to 1707-acre lake within waterfowl refuge.
Boat or fish. Observe wildlife.
14-day limit.

EUGENE T MAHONEY SP

(402) 944-2523
State map: J28
Take Exit 426 off I-80

and drive N (SE of ASHLAND). (Also see Memphis Lake SRA. Nearby Louisville SRA costs $6.)
$5; $13 RV w/hookups; reservations accepted at (402) 944-2523 for an additional $3.
Open All Year.
173 (24 tent-only) close, screened sites.
Central faucet, flush toilets, showers, dump station, electric hookups, tables, fire rings, pool, laundry, store, rentals, pay phone.
Among burr oak and red cedar near Platte River in two sections ($5 tent area SE of Little Creek section).
Walk nature trails or hike farther. Climb observation tower. View wildlife. Play sports. Swim or waterslide. Paddleboat. Fish. Sled, skate, or cross-country ski in winter.
14-day limit.

FEITS PARK

Blue Springs Parks
(402) 645-3539
State map: N27
Locate park in BLUE SPRINGS at Broad St & River Rd.
FREE so choose a chore.
Open Apr 1–Nov 1.
6 close, open sites.
Central faucet, pit toilets, electric hookups, tables, boat ramp, shelter.
In town park.
Boat or fish.
5-day limit.

GALLAGHER CANYON SRA

(308) 535-8025
State map: K16
From COZAD, drive S for 10 miles (16 k) on NE 21. Turn Left (E) and go 2 miles (3.2 k). Turn Left (N) for 1 mile (1.6 k) then Left (W) again for another 1 mile (1.6 k).
FREE; $2 entrance fee.
Open All Year.
20 scattered, open sites.
Central faucet, pit toilets, tables, fire rings, boat ramp.
Next to 400-acre lake.

▲ ▲

Fish or boat.
14-day limit.

GENOA CITY PARK

(402) 993-2330
State map: I23
Find park in GENOA,
4 blocks S of NE 22 & 39 intersection.
FREE; $10/week after 3 days.
Open All Year.
6 scattered, open sites. &
Central faucet, flush toilets, showers,
dump station, electric hookups, tables,
grills, fire rings, pool.
In natural setting near Beaver Creek.
Swim. Walk nature trail and observe
wildlife. Fish.
1600 ft (480 m)

GILMAN PARK CAMPING AREA

Pierce Parks
(402) 329-4535
State map: F24
Locate area in PIERCE on N Mill St.
$3. Open All Year.
14 (10 tent-only) close, open sites.
Central faucet, flush toilets, showers,
electric hookups, tables, grills, boat
ramp, shelter.
In city park.
Swim, boat, and fish.
7-day limit.

GLADSTONE PARK

Wausa Parks
(402) 586-2345
State map: D24
Find park in WAUSA at 203 E Clark.
FREE so choose a chore.
Open May 1–Sep 15.
5 close, open, RV sites.
Central faucet, flush toilets, electric
hookups, tables, grills, pool.
In town park.
Relax. Swim ($).
7-day limit.

GLENN CUNNINGHAM LAKE

(402) 444-4627
State map: I29
Locate lake at 8300

Rainwood Rd in OMAHA.
$4.50. Open May 15–Oct 15.
58 close, open sites.
Central faucet, flush toilets, showers,
dump station, tables, fire rings.
In city park.
Fish.
14-day limit.

GREMLIN COVE

COE (308) 799-2105
State map: O18
From REPUBLICAN
CITY, head S for 1.5 miles (2.4 k) on
NE A. (Also see Cedar Point and North
Cove.)
$4. Open All Year.
70 close, open sites.
Central faucet, flush toilets, tables, fire
rings, boat ramp.
On moderate slope next to Harlan
County Lake and dam.
Swim, boat, or fish.
14-day limit. Crowded in summer.
1990 ft (597 m)

HALL COUNTY PARK

(308) 381-5070
State map: K21
Find park in GRAND
ISLAND, .25 mile (400 m) E of US 281.
$3.88; $6.80 RV.
Open Apr–Sep.
37 (15 tent-only) close, open sites.
Central faucet, flush toilets, showers,
dump station, electric hookups, tables,
fire rings.
Enjoy overnight stop in county park.
3-day limit.

HAMILTON PARK

Gordon Parks
(308) 282-0837
State map: C9
Locate park in GORDON on E US 20.
FREE so choose a chore. Open All Year.
20 close, open sites.
Central faucet, pit toilets, dump station,
tables.
In town park.
Relax at overnight stop.

HARTINGTON CAMPGROUND

(402) 254-6353
State map: D25
Find campground in
HARTINGTON on N Broadway.
$5. Open Apr–Oct; dry camping allowed off-season.
6 close, open, RV sites.
Water at every site, dump station, electric hookups.
On edge of business district.
Enjoy overnight stay.
No toilet facilities.

HAWORTH PARK

(402) 293-3122
State map: J30
Locate park in
BELLEVUE at Payne Dr & NE 370.
$5; $9 hookups.
Open All Year.
116 (12 tent-only) close, open sites.
Water at 69 sites, flush toilets, showers, dump station, electric hookups, tables, fire rings, boat ramp, shelter.
In city park next to river.
Boat or fish.
14-day limit.

HEADWORKS PARK

Loup River Public
Power District
(402) 564-3171
State map: I23
From GENOA, drive SW for 6 miles (9.6 k) on NE 22. (Also see Lake North and Loup Park.)
FREE so choose a chore.
Open May 1–Nov 1.
25 scattered, open, RV sites. Hand pump, pit toilets, electric hookups, tables, grills.
Next to 2 small lakes and 35-mile (56-k) canal.
Swim or fish. Walk nature trail. Bike. View wildlife.
14-day limit. Occasional ATVs.

HICKMAN CITY PARK

(402) 792-2212
State map: L27
Find park just E of 2nd

& Main in HICKMAN.
$2. Open All Year.
8 close, open sites.
Central faucet, pit toilets, tables.
In city park.
Enjoy overnight or longer stay.
14-day limit.

HORD LAKE SRA

(308) 384-4916
State map: J23
From CENTRAL CITY,
head E on US 30 for 2 miles (3.2 k).
Continue E on 20th Ave.
FREE; $2 entrance fee.
Open All Year.
75 scattered, open sites.
Hand pump, pit toilets, tables, fire rings, grills, boat ramp, playground.
On flat, sandy spot next to 20-acre lake.
Swim, fish, or boat (no gas motors).
14-day limit.
1705 ft (512 m)

HUMBOLDT LAKE PARK

(402) 862-2590
State map: N30
Locate park at 1st &
Long Branch St in HUMBOLDT.
$5. Open All Year.
Undesignated scattered, open sites.
Central faucet, flush toilets, showers, electric hookups, tables.
Next to lake.
Swim. Relax.
2-day limit.

ISLAND PARK CAMPGROUND

Lyons Parks
(402) 687-4188
State map: G28
From LYONS at intersection of US 77 & Main, head W on Main for 1 mile (1.6 k).
$5; reservations accepted at (402) 687-4188.
Open Apr 1–Oct 31.
14 close, open, RV sites.
Water at every site, flush toilets, showers, dump station, electric hookups, tables, grills, fire rings, shelter, pool, tennis court, ball field.

On wooded, level terrain.
Swim. Fish. Play sports.
Occasional severe thunderstorms.
1300 ft (390 m)

KARRER PARK

McCook Parks
(308) 345-2022
State map: N14
Find park on E edge of MCCOOK.
FREE so choose a chore.
Open May 1–Nov 1.
Undesignated scattered, open sites.
Central faucet, flush toilets, showers,
dump station, electric hookups, tables,
grills, pay phone.
In town park.
Enjoy overnight stop.
3-day limit.
2550 ft (765 m)

KELLER PARK SRA

(402) 684-2921
State map: C17
From SPRINGVIEW,
drive S on US 183 for 8 miles (12.8 k).
(Also see Long Pine SRA.)
$3; $5 electric; **$2** entrance fee.
Open All Year.
24 close, open sites. Central faucet, flush
toilets, dump station, electric hookups,
tables, grills, fire rings.
Among scenic canyons and streams with
5 ponds, wildflowers, trees, and shrubs.
Hike to enjoy ecology and take photos.
Fish.
14-day limit. Hunting in season.

LAFAYETTE PARK

Gothenburg Parks
(308) 537-3459
State map: K15
Locate park in GOTHENBURG at NE 47
N and 27th St.
$2; $9 RV; reservations accepted at (308)
537-3459.
Open Apr 1–Nov 1; dry camping
allowed off-season.
55 scattered, open sites.
Central faucet, flush toilets, showers,
dump station, electric hookups, tables,

grills, playground, pay phone.
In quiet, shady spot only a covered
footbridge away from Lake Helen.
Hike to view wildlife. Fish.
14-day limit.

LAKE MAHONEY SRA

(308) 535-8025
State map: J13
Drive S on US 83 from
NORTH PLATTE for 6 miles (9.6 k).
FREE; $5 developed.
Open All Year.
156 scattered, open sites.
Central faucet, pit toilets, dump station,
electric hookups, tables, fire rings, grills,
boat ramp.
Next to 1000-acre lake.
Swim, boat, or fish.
14-day limit.

LAKE MCCONAUGHY SRA

(308) 284-3542
State map: J10
From OGALLALA,
take NE 61 N for 8 miles (12.8 k).
FREE; $2 entrance fee.
Open All Year.
Undesignated scattered, open sites.
Next to lake with white sandy beaches.
Swim, boat, waterski, and fish. View
wildlife.
14-day limit. No ATVs. Crowded
holiday weekends.
▲ **Arthur Bay**
Hand pump, pit toilets, tables, boat
ramp.
▲ **Lemoyne**
Hand pump, pit toilets, tables, grills,
boat ramp.
▲ **Martin Bay**
Hand pump, flush toilets, dump station,
tables, grills, boat ramp.
▲ **Omaha Beach**
Hand pump, pit toilets, tables, grills,
boat ramp.
▲ **Otter Creek**
Hand pump, pit toilets, tables, grills,
boat ramp, store.
▲ **Sandy Beach**
Hand pump, pit toilets, tables, boat

ramp.

▲ Eagle Canyon

From OGALLALA, take US 26 NW for 15 miles (24 k).
Hand pump, pit toilets, tables, boat ramp.

▲ Lakeview

From OGALLALA, take US 26 NW until sign for Gate 18.
Hand pump, pit toilets.

▲ Ogallala Beach

From OGALLALA, continue N through NE 61/US 26 intersection on gravel road.
Hand pump, pit toilets, tables.

LAKE MINATARE SRA

(308) 783-2911
State map: F4
Drive N on NE 71 from SCOTTSBLUFF about 3 miles (4.8 k). Turn Right (E) and continue about 11 miles (17.7 k).
FREE; $7 developed; $2 entrance fee.
Open Jan 15–Sep 30.
152 scattered, open sites. ⅋
Central faucet, flush toilets, showers, dump station, electric hookups, tables, fire rings, boat ramp, shelter, laundry, playground.
Next to 2158-acre lake in waterfowl refuge.
Swim, boat, or fish. Observe wildlife.
14-day limit.

LAKE NORTH

Loup River Public Power District
(402) 564-3171
State map: I25
From COLUMBUS at junction of US 30 and 18th Ave, drive N for 4 miles (6.4 k). (Also see Headworks Park, Loup Park, Powerhouse Park, and Tailrace Park.)
FREE so choose a chore.
Open May 1–Nov 1.
125 scattered, open sites.
Hand pump, pit toilets, tables, grills, boat ramp, shelter.
In narrow tree-lined stretch next to 200-acre lake.
Swim, boat, or fish. Hike to see wildlife.

Bike.
14-day limit. Occasional ATVs.

LAUREL CITY PARK

(402) 256-3112
State map: D25
Locate park at 3rd & Cedar in LAUREL.
FREE; donations requested.
Open Apr–Oct.
8 scattered, open sites. Central faucet, flush toilets, dump station, electric hookups, tables, grills, shelter.
Among old trees in grassy park.
Enjoy overnight stop. Bike.
1475 ft (443 m)

LAUREL LIONS PARK

(402) 256-3112
State map: D25
Find park in LAUREL at 6th & Wakefield.
FREE; donations requested.
Open May–Sep; dry camping allowed off-season.
6 scattered, open sites.
Central faucet, flush toilets, electric hookups, tables, grills, pool, tennis court.
With many trees next to city pool.
Swim. Play sports.
1475 ft (443 m)

LEWIS & CLARK LAKE SRA

(402) 373-2440
State map: C24
From CROFTON, head N on NE 121 for 9 miles (14.4 k). Turn Right (1 area) or Left (6 areas).
FREE; $2 entrance fee. Open All Year.
586 (300 tent-only) scattered sites. ⅋
Central faucet, flush toilets, showers, dump station, electric hookups, tables, fire rings, boat ramps, shelter.
Next to 32000-acre lake.
Swim, boat, ski, or fish.
14-day limit.

LIBERTY COVE RA

Little Blue Natural Resources District
(402) 364-2145

▲ ▲

State map: N22
From LAWRENCE, travel W on NE 4 for
2 miles (3.2 k). Turn Left (S) and go
2 miles (3.2 k). Turn Right (W) for final
.25 mile (400 m).
FREE so choose a chore. Open All Year.
Undesignated scattered, open sites.
Hand pump, pit toilets, tables, fire rings,
grills, boat ramp, shelter.
Near several springs feeding 36-acre
lake.
Walk nature trail to observe wildlife.
Swim, boat (less than 5 hp), or fish. Visit
arboretum. Sled or ice skate in winter.
Hunting in season. Snowmobiles in
winter.

LINCOLN PARK

(402) 879-4582
State map: O22
Locate park in
SUPERIOR on W 4th.
FREE; donations requested.
Open All Year.
20 scattered, open sites.
Water at every site, flush toilets, dump
station, electric hookups, tables, grills,
pay phone.
With grass and shade trees plus flower
garden and 1-acre pond.
Fish. Walk nature trail. Bike. Spot
wildlife.

LIONS CLUB CAMPER PARK

(402) 375-1781
State map: E26
From WAYNE, head E
on NE 35 for 1 mile (1.6 k) to airport.
(Also see Victor Park.)
$3; donations requested.
Open Mar 1 – Nov 1; dry camping
allowed off-season.
Undesignated scattered, open sites.
Central faucet, dump station, electric
hookups, tables, grills, shelter,
playground.
Among open fields.
Enjoy overnight stop.
No toilet facilities. 8-day limit. Crowded
holidays, county fair, and chicken show.
3500 ft (1050 m)

LONG LAKE SRA

(402) 684-2921
State map: D15
From JOHNSTOWN,
follow signed CR for 20 miles (32 k) SW.
FREE; $2 entrance fee.
Open All Year.
Undesignated scattered, open sites.
Hand pump, pit toilets, tables, fire rings.
Next to sandhill lake with few trees.
Fish.
Hunting in season.

LONG PINE SRA

(402) 684-2921
State map: D17
From LONG PINE,
drive W for 1 mile (1.6 k) on US 20.
(Also see Keller Park SRA and Rock
County Fairgrounds.)
FREE; $2 entrance fee. Open All Year.
30 scattered, open sites. Hand pump, pit
toilets, tables, grills, fire rings.
In dense forest with trout stream.
Swim or fish. Canoe. Observe wildlife.
Hunting in season.

LOUP PARK

Loup River Public
Power District
(402) 564-3171
State map: I25
From COLUMBUS at junction of US 30
& 18th Ave, drive N for 4 miles (6.4 k).
Turn Left (W) on Lakeview Dr. Go
1.5 miles (2.4 k). (See Headwaters Park,
Lake North, and Powerhouse Park.)
FREE so choose a chore.
Open May 1 – Nov 1.
170 scattered, open sites.
Hand pump, pit toilets, electric hookups,
tables, grills, shelter.
In small-park atmosphere.
Relax in quiet spot. Walk nature trail.
Bike. Fish.
14-day limit.

MEDICINE CREEK SRA

(308) 697-4667
State map: M15
From CAMBRIDGE,

travel W on US 34 about 2 miles (3.2 k).
Turn Right (N) and go 7 miles (11.2 k).
FREE; $7 developed; $2 entrance fee.
Open All Year.
323 scattered, open sites. &
Central faucet, flush toilets, showers,
dump station, electric hookups, tables,
fire rings, boat ramp, shelter.
Next to 1768-acre lake.
Swim, boat, ski, or fish.
14-day limit.

MEMORIAL PARK

Madison Parks
(402) 454-3214
State map: G24
Locate park in MADISON on N Main.
$4; $8 water & electric.
Open All Year.
12 (5 tent-only) scattered, open sites.
Central faucet, flush toilets, electric
hookups, tables, grills, fire rings.
In quiet, grassy spot.
Enjoy overnight stop. Bike.
3-day limit.

MEMPHIS LAKE SRA

(402) 471-5545
State map: J28
Find area in
MEMPHIS. (Also see Eugene T Mahoney
SP and Pioneer SRA.)
FREE; $2 entrance fee.
Open All Year.
100 (50 tent-only) scattered, open sites.
Hand pump, pit toilets, dump station,
tables, grills, fire rings, playground,
store, pay phone.
Next to 48-acre lake.
Fish or boat (no gas motors).
14-day limit. Hunting in season.
1100 ft (330 m)

MERRITT RESERVOIR SRA

(402) 684-2921
State map: D13
From VALENTINE,
drive SW on NE 97 for 25 miles (40 k).
FREE; $2 entrance fee.
Open All Year.
240 scattered, open sites.

Central faucet, pit toilets, dump station,
tables, fire rings, boat ramp, shelter.
Next to 2906-acre lake.
Boat or fish. View sandhills sunrise.
14-day limit.

MORGAN PARK

Callaway Parks
(308) 836-2262
State map: I16
Locate park in CALLAWAY at Morgan
& Pacific streets.
FREE; $5 electric. Open All Year.
10 close, open sites.
Central faucet, flush toilets, showers,
electric hookups, tables, fire rings.
In city park.
Swim. Relax at overnight stop.

MUNY PARK

Cozad Parks
(308) 784-3907
State map: K16
Find park in COZAD at 14th & O streets.
$5. Open All Year.
12 scattered, open, RV sites.
Central faucet, flush toilets, dump
station, electric hookups, tables, grills,
pool, playground.
With shade next to residential area and
airport.
Swim. Play sports.

N P DODGE MEMORIAL PARK

(402) 444-4673
State map: I29
Find park in OMAHA
at 11005 Pershing Dr. Take 30th St Exit
off I-680. Go E on Dick Collins Rd. Turn
Right (N) on Pershing for 2 miles (3.2 k).
$5; $6 RV; $7.50 electric.
Open Apr 15–Oct 1.
56 close, open sites. Central faucet, flush
toilets, showers, dump station, electric
hookups, tables, grills, boat ramp,
playground, pay phone.
In wood on banks of Missouri River.
Walk nature trail or hike farther. Boat or
fish.
14-day limit. Crowded summer holidays.

▲ ▲

NELIGH PARK

West Point Parks
(402) 372-2489
State map: G27
Locate park in WEST POINT off W
Bridge St.
FREE so choose a chore.
Open Apr–Oct 15.
Undesignated scattered, open sites.
Central faucet, flush toilets, electric
hookups, tables, fire rings, shelter.
In town park near Elkhorn River.
Swim or fish.
2-day limit.

NORTH COVE

COE (308) 799-2105
State map: O18
From REPUBLICAN
CITY, head W for 3 miles (4.8 k) on
US 136. Turn Left (S) on NE 21 and go
2 miles (3.2 k). (Also see Gremlin Cove.
Nearby Hunter Cove costs $8.)
FREE so choose a chore. Open All Year.
30 scattered, open sites. Hand pump, pit
toilets, tables, fire rings, shelter.
In grass-forest mix next to Harlan
County Lake.
Fish.
14-day limit. Crowded in summer.
1960 ft (588 m)

NORTH LOUP SRA

(402) 684-2921
State map: J21
From ST PAUL, drive
N on US 281 for 4 miles (6.4 k).
FREE; $2 entrance fee. Open All Year.
Undesignated scattered, open sites.
Central faucet, pit toilets, tables.
On North Loup River.
Fish a bunch.
14-day limit.

OAKLAND PARK

(402) 685-5822
State map: G28
Locate park on W edge
of OAKLAND on NE 32.
FREE; donations requested.
Open Apr–Oct.

12 close, open sites. Central faucet, flush
toilets, dump station, electric hookups,
tables, fire rings.
In city park.
Swim or fish.
3-day limit.

OBERT PARK

(402) 692-3216
State map: C26
Find park in OBERT at
NE 12 & Main St.
FREE; donations requested.
Open All Year.
3 close, open sites. Central faucet, pit
toilets, electric hookups, tables.
In town park.
Enjoy overnight stop.

OLIVE CREEK SRA

(402) 471-5545
State map: L26
From KRAMER, head
SE on gravel road for 1.5 miles (2.4 k).
(See Bluestem Lake SRA and Stagecoach
Lake SRA.)
FREE; $2 entrance fee. Open All Year.
50 scattered, open sites.
Hand pump, pit toilets, tables, fire rings,
grills, boat ramp.
Next to 175-acre lake.
Boat or fish.
14-day limit. Hunting in season.
1350 ft (405 m)

OLIVER SRA

(308) 235-4040
State map: I4
From KIMBALL, travel
W on US 30 for 10 miles (16 k).
FREE; $2 entrance fee.
Open All Year.
Undesignated scattered, open sites.
Central faucet, pit toilets, tables, fire
rings, grills, boat ramp.
Next to 270-acre prairie lake.
Swim, boat, canoe, or fish. Bike.
cross-country ski in winter.
14-day limit. Hunting in season.
Crowded summer weekends.
5200 ft (1560 m)

ORLEANS RV PARK

(308) 473-4185
State map: O18
Locate campground in ORLEANS on US 136.
FREE; $2 after 3 days.
Open All Year.
Undesignated scattered, open, RV sites.
Water at ever site, dump station, electric hookups, tables.
In small park with trees.
Enjoy overnight stop.
No toilet facilities. Crowded summers.

OSCEOLA CITY PARK

(402) 747-3411
State map: J24
Find park at 621 N State St in OSCEOLA.
FREE so choose a chore. Open All Year.
2 close, open, RV sites.
Central faucet, flush toilets, electric hookups, tables, fire rings, shelter, pool, pay phone.
In small area of park.
Swim. Enjoy overnight stop.

OUTLET NORTH

COE (308) 799-2105
State map: O18
From REPUBLICAN CITY, head S to Harlan County Lake Dam—on N side of spillway. (Also see Cedar Point.)
$4. Open All Year.
10 scattered, open sites.
Central faucet, pit toilets, tables, fire rings, shelter.
On flat with some trees next to Republican River.
Fish. Canoe or tube. Walk nature trail.
14-day limit. Hunting in season.
Crowded in summer.
1925 ft (578 m)

OUTLET SOUTH

COE (308) 799-2105
State map: O18
From REPUBLICAN CITY, head S to Harlan County Lake Dam—on S side of spillway. (Also see

Cedar Point.)
$4. Open All Year.
50 scattered, open sites.
Hand pump, pit toilets, tables, fire rings.
In mature cottonwood next to Republican River.
Canoe or tube. Fish. View wildlife.
14-day limit. Hunting in season.
Crowded in summer.
1920 ft (576 m)

PALISADE PARK

(308) 285-3320
State map: N12
In PALISADE, go E on County Ave to bottom of hill.
FREE so choose a chore. Open All Year.
Undesignated scattered, open sites.
Central faucet, pit toilets, dump station, tables, grills, shelter, pool, playground.
In large municipal park.
Swim ($1). Explore. Enjoy overnight stop.

PAWNEE LAKE SRA

(402) 796-2662
State map: K27
From LINCOLN, take Exit 401 off I-80 and head W on KS 34 for 9 miles (14.4 k). Turn Left (S) on signed road and go 1.5 miles (2.4 k). (Also see Blue River SRA, Conestoga SRA, and Pioneer SRA.)
FREE; $6 developed; $2 entrance fee.
Open All Year.
235 (35 tent-only) close, open sites.
Central faucet, flush toilets, showers, dump station, electric hookups, tables, fire rings, grills, boat ramp.
On wooded flatland next to 990-acre lake.
Swim, boat, ski, or fish. Bike. Walk nature trail. Hike farther to view wildlife.
14-day limit. Hunting in season.
Crowded weekends.

PELICAN POINT SRA

(402) 329-4053
State map: G26
From TEKAMAH, head

▲ ▲

E for 4 miles (6.4 k). Turn Left (N) and
travel 4 miles (6.4 k). Turn Right (E) and
go 1 mile (1.6 k).
FREE; $2 entrance fee.
Open All Year.
24 close, open sites.
Central faucet, pit toilets, tables, fire
rings, boat ramp, shelter.
Along Missouri River.
Boat or fish.
14-day limit.

PENN PARK

Neligh Parks
(402) 887-4443
State map: F22
Find park on W edge of NELIGH next to
NE 14. (Also see Riverside Park.)
FREE so choose a chore. Open All Year.
Undesignated scattered, open sites.
Central faucet, pit toilets, tables, fire
rings, grills, boat ramp.
Beside small fishing pond.
Boat or fish. Walk nature trail to view
wildlife.
7-day limit.

PIBEL LAKE SRA

(402) 684-2921
State map: G21
From BARTLETT, head
S on US 281 for 9 miles (14.4 k). Turn
Left (E) and drive 1 mile (1.6 k).
FREE; $2 entrance fee.
Open All Year.
30 scattered, screened sites.
Hand pump, pit toilets, tables, fire rings,
grills, boat ramp, playground.
Next to 24-acre lake.
Fish or boat (no gas motors).
14-day limit.
2000 ft (600 m)

PIONEER SRA

(402) 471-5545
State map: J27
From CERESCO, head
N for 3.5 miles (5.4 k) on US 77. (Also
see Memphis Lake SRA and Pawnee
Lake SRA.)
FREE; $2 entrance fee.

Open All Year.
Undesignated scattered, open sites.
Hand pump, pit toilets, tables, grills,
playground.
Next to highway.
Enjoy overnight spot.
14-day limit.
1219 ft (366 m)

POWERHOUSE PARK

Loup River Public
Power District
(402) 564-3171
State map: I25
From COLUMBUS at junction of US 30
and 3rd Ave, go N for 1.5 miles (2.4 k).
(Also see Lake North, Loup Park, and
Tailrace Park.)
FREE so choose a chore. Open All Year.
12 scattered, open sites.
Hand pump, pit toilets, tables, grills.
In small-park atmosphere near canal and
hydro-electric plant.
Fish. Walk nature trail and observe
wildlife. Take photos. Bike.
14-day limit.

PRAIRIE LAKE RA

Little Blue Natural
Resources District
(402) 364-2145
State map: M21
From JUNIATA, go S for 3 miles (4.8 k).
Turn Left (E) and proceed .25 mile
(400 m). (Also see Roseland Lake.)
FREE so choose a chore.
Open All Year.
Undesignated scattered, open sites.
Hand pump, pit toilets, grills, fire rings.
Near 36-acre lake among native grasses
and wildflowers with abundant wildlife.
Fish or boat (less than 5 hp). Enjoy
ecology. Ice skate in winter.
Hunting in season. Snowmobiles in
winter.

RAVENNA LAKE SRA

(402) 684-2921
State map: K20
From RAVENNA,
drive SE on NE 2 for 1 mile (1.6 k).

▲ ▲

FREE; $2 entrance fee.
Open All Year.
Undesignated scattered, open sites.
Central faucet, pit toilets, tables, fire
rings.
Next to 30-acre lake on South Loup
River.
Fish or boat (no gas motors).
14-day limit.

RED WILLOW SRA
(308) 345-5899
State map: N14
From MCCOOK, drive
N on US 83 for 11 miles (19.2 k).
FREE; $7 developed; $2 entrance fee.
Open All Year.
159 scattered, open sites. &
Central faucet, flush toilets, showers,
dump station, electric hookups, tables,
fire rings, boat ramp, shelter.
Beside 1628-acre lake.
Swim, boat, ski, or fish.
14-day limit.

RIVERSIDE PARK
Beatrice Parks
(402) 228-3649
State map: N27
Locate park in SW BEATRICE, N of
Rivers St. (Also see Chautauqua Park
and Rockford Lake SRA.)
$3; reservations accepted at
(402) 228-3649.
Open Apr 1–Nov 1; dry camping
allowed off-season.
20 close, open sites.
Central faucet, flush toilets, showers,
electric hookups, tables, grills, fire rings,
boat ramp, shelter, pool, playground,
ball field, tennis court, pay phone.
In partially wooded spot along Big Blue
River.
Swim or fish. Bike. Play sports.

RIVERSIDE PARK
Neligh Parks
(402) 887-4443
State map: F22
Find park on S edge of NELIGH at 2nd
& US 275. (Also see Penn Park.)

$5. Open Apr 1–Nov 1; dry camping
allowed off-season.
26 close, open sites.
Water at every site, flush toilets,
showers, dump station, electric hookups,
tables, grills, fire rings, pool.
Next to Elkhorn River.
Swim. Fish. Walk nature trail or hike
farther.
14-day limit.

RIVERVIEW MARINA SRA
(402) 471-5566
State map: L30
Locate area in
NEBRASKA CITY.
FREE; $2 entrance fee. Open All Year.
30 close, open sites. Central faucet, flush
toilets, showers, tables, boat ramp.
Along Missouri River.
Boat or fish.
14-day limit.

ROBERTS TRACT TRAILHEAD
Nebraska NF
(308) 432-4475
State map: C5
From CHADRON, take US 20 W for
8.5 miles (13.6 k). Turn Left (S) on gravel
CR 706 and drive 8 miles (12.8 k). Turn
Left (E) at small white church on CR 919
and go 2 miles (3.2 k).
FREE so choose a chore.
Open All Year.
6 scattered, open sites.
Hand pump, pit toilets, tables, fire rings.
On old homestead in grassland at base
of pine-forested buttes and hills.
Hike Rock Butte or Roberts trails to Pine
Ridge Trail. Spot wildlife. Take photos.
14-day limit. Hunting in season. Horses
in area.
3960 ft (1188 m)

ROCK COUNTY FAIRGROUNDS
(402) 684-3472
State map: D17
Locate fairgrounds in
BASSETT. (Also see Long Pine SRA.)
FREE; donations requested.
Open All Year.

▲ ▲

6 close, open, RV sites. &
Central faucet, flush toilets, showers,
dump station, electric hookups, tables,
grills, fire rings, pool.
On fairgrounds with historical buildings.
Swim. Enjoy overnight stop.

ROCKFORD LAKE SRA

(402) 471-5545
State map: N27
From BEATRICE, drive
E on NE 4 for 7 miles (11.2 k). Turn
Right (S) on gravel road and continue
2 miles (3.2 k). (Also see Chautauqua
Park and Riverside Park.)
FREE; $2 entrance fee. Open All Year.
100 scattered, open sites.
Hand pump, pit toilets, tables, fire rings,
grills, boat ramp, playground.
Next to 150-acre lake.
Swim, boat, or fish. Hike. Visit nearby
Homestead Monument.
14-day limit. Hunting in season.
1355 ft (407 m)

ROSELAND LAKE

Little Blue Natural
Resources District
(402) 364-2145
State map: M21
From JUNIATA, travel W for 4.5 miles
(7.2 k). Turn Right (S). Drive 2.25 miles
(3.6 k). (Also see Prairie Lake RA.)
FREE so choose a chore.
Open All Year.
Undesignated scattered, open sites.
Hand pump, pit toilets.
Beside 67-acre lake.
Fish. Spot wildlife.

SANDY CHANNEL SRA

(308) 535-8025
State map: L18
From ELM CREEK,
head S on US 183 for 3.5 miles (5.4 k).
FREE; $2 entrance fee. Open All Year.
35 close, open sites.
Central faucet, pit toilets, tables.
Next to 47-acre lake.
Swim, fish, or boat (no gas motors).
14-day limit.

SAUNDER COUNTY FAIRGROUNDS

(402) 443-5822
State map: J27
Find fairgrounds in
WAHOO at 635 E 1st.
$5; $25/week.
Open All Year.
40 sites. &
Water at every site, flush toilets,
showers, dump station, electric hookups.
In quiet, grassy area.
Enjoy overnight stop.
Full with exhibitors during fair–1st week
of Aug.

SCHUYLER CAMPGROUND

(402) 352-9972
State map: I26
Locate campground in
SCHUYLER at S edge.
FREE so choose a chore.
Open Apr 1–Sep 30.
30 close, open sites.
Water at every site, pit toilets, dump
station, electric hookups, tables, grills,
fire rings, pool.
On well-kept, grassy grounds.
Swim at pool or fish nearby.
5-day limit.
1200 ft (360 m)

SEWARD BLUE VALLEY
CAMPING AREA

(402) 643-3511
State map: K26
From SEWARD, head S
on NE 15 about .5 mile (800 m).
FREE; $5/day after 2 days.
Open Mar 1–Dec 1.
12 close, open sites.
Central faucet, pit toilets, dump station,
electric hookups, tables, fire rings.
Next to Big Blue River.
Fish.
7-day limit.

SHERMAN RESERVOIR SRA

(308) 745-0230
State map: J22
From LOUP CITY,
head E on NE 92 about 3 miles (4.8 k).

▲ ▲

Turn Left (N) and go 1.5+ miles (2.4+ k).
FREE; $2 entrance fee.
Open All Year.
360 scattered, open sites.
Central faucet, flush toilets, showers,
dump station, tables, fire rings, grills,
boat ramp.
In various areas among rolling hills
around 2845-acre lake.
Swim, boat, ski, or fish.
14-day limit.

SMITH FALLS SP

(402) 376-1306
State map: B15
From SPARKS, drive W
on NE 12 for 3 miles (4.8 k). Turn Left
(S) on gravel road. Go 4 miles (6.4 k).
$3 per person; reservations accepted at
(402) 376-1306.
Open Apr 1–Nov 30.
20 scattered, open, tent sites. &
Central faucet, pit toilets, tables, grills,
fire rings.
In unusual Ice-Age micro-ecology,
including spruce and birch next to
Niobrara River with Nebraska's tallest
waterfall.
Walk trails to view environment and
take photos. Canoe. Fish. Attend ranger
programs.
2000 ft (600 m)

SOLDIER CREEK TRAILHEAD

Nebraska NF
(308) 432-4475
State map: C4
From CRAWFORD, drive W on US 20
for 3.5 miles (5.4 k). Turn Right (N) on
Soldier Creek Rd and go about 6 miles
(9.6 k). (Also see Toadstool.)
FREE so choose a chore.
Open All Year.
Undesignated scattered, open sites.
Hand pump, pit toilets.
Next to 7794-acre Soldier Creek
Wilderness, former Fort Robinson
pasture and wood-gathering area, that
burned in 1989.
Hike to observe fire snags, recovery, and
wildlife. Fish.

14-day limit. Hunting in season. Horses
in area.
4130 ft (1239 m)

SOUTH PARK CAMPGROUND

Franklin Parks
(308) 425-6295
State map: O19
Find campground in FRANKLIN, off
Exit 279 at NE 10 & I St.
FREE; donations requested.
Open May 1–Oct 1.
4 close, open sites.
Central faucet, flush toilets, dump
station, electric hookups, tables.
In town park.
Enjoy overnight stop.
3-day limit.

SPALDING CITY PARK

(308) 497-2501
State map: H21
Locate park in
SPALDING.
FREE; donations requested.
Open All Year.
8 (4 RV-only) close, open sites. &
Water at every site, flush toilets, electric
hookups, tables, grills, pool.
In remote section of city park.
Swim. Walk to observe wildlife. Fish
nearby Cedar River.
2-day limit. Crowded Memorial Day.

SPENCER PARK-FAIRGROUNDS

(402) 589-1171
State map: C20
Find fairgrounds on W
side of SPENCER on Logan St.
FREE; $5 after 3 days.
Open May 1–Sep 30; dry camping
allowed off-season.
Undesignated close, open sites.
Central faucet, flush toilets, showers,
dump station, electric hookups, tables,
pool.
On flat terrain with some shade next to
fairground buildings.
Swim. Bike. Enjoy overnight stop.
3-day limit.
1684 ft (505 m)

▲ ▲

ST EDWARD PARK CAMP AREA

(402) 678-2855
State map: H23
Locate camp area in ST
EDWARD at 3rd & Clark streets.
FREE; donations requested.
Open Apr–Oct.
3 close, open sites.
Central faucet, flush toilets, dump
station, electric hookups, tables.
In town park.
Swim. Relax at overnight stop.
14-day limit.

STAGECOACH LAKE SRA

(402) 471-5545
State map: L27
From HICKMAN,
travel S for 1 mile (1.6 k) on gravel road.
Turn Right (W) and go .5 mile (800 m).
(See Bluestem Lake SRA, Olive Creek
SRA, and Wagon Train Lake SRA.)
FREE; $2 entrance fee.
Open All Year.
50 scattered, open sites.
Hand pump, pit toilets, tables, fire rings,
grills, boat ramp.
Beside 195-acre lake.
Boat or fish.
14-day limit. Hunting in season.
1300 ft (390 m)

STANTON LAKE

Falls City Parks
(402) 245-2613
State map: O31
Find lake in FALLS CITY on W 25th St.
$2.50; $5 electric; $7 electric & water.
Open Apr 1–Nov 1.
Undesignated close, open sites.
Central faucet, flush toilets, showers,
dump station, electric hookups, tables.
Next to lake.
Fish a bunch.
5-day limit.

STAPLETON CITY PARK

(308) 636-2960
State map: I14
Find park in
STAPLETON.

FREE; donations requested.
Open All Year.
Undesignated close, open sites.
Central faucet, flush toilets, electric
hookups, tables, fire rings.
In city park.
Enjoy overnight stop.

STEER CREEK

Nebraska NF
(308) 533-2257
State map: C12
From NENZEL, travel S on NE S16F for
19 miles (30.4 k).
FREE so choose a chore.
Open All Year.
23 scattered, screened sites.
Hand pump, pit toilets, tables, fire rings.
In secluded section of planted ponderosa
pine forest.
Hike to enjoy beautiful country. Observe
wildlife. Savor quiet. Bike.
14-day limit. Crowded in deer hunting
season.
3000 ft (900 m)

STERLING VILLAGE PARK

(402) 866-4681
State map: M28
Locate park at Iowa &
Lincoln streets in STERLING.
FREE; donations requested.
Open Apr–Oct.
Undesignated close, open sites.
Central faucet, flush toilets, electric
hookups, tables, fire rings.
In municipal park.
Enjoy overnight stop.

STREETER PARK

Aurora Parks
(402) 694-6922
State map: K23
Find park in AURORA at US 34 &
NE 14.
FREE; donations requested.
Open Mar–Nov; dry camping allowed
off-season.
12 close, open sites.
Central faucet, flush toilets, dump
station, electric hookups, tables, grills,

pool, pay phone.
In quiet park with creek and trees.
Swim. Walk nature trail.
3-day limit.
1802 ft (541 m)

STUART MUNICIPAL PARK

(402) 924-3223
State map: D19
Locate park on N side
of STUART.
$5. Open Apr–Oct; dry camping allowed
off-season.
12 close, open sites.
Water at every site, flush toilets,
showers, dump station, electric hookups,
tables, grills.
Under trees in grassy spot.
Hike to view wildlife. Bike.

SUMMIT LAKE SRA

(402) 374-1727
State map: G28
From CRAIG, head S
on signed gravel road for 2 miles (3.2 k).
Turn Left (E). Continue 4 miles (6.4 k).
FREE; $2.25 entrance fee.
Open All Year.
131 (30 tent-only) scattered, open sites.
Central faucet, pit toilets, tables, fire
rings, grills, boat ramp.
With shady and open camping areas
next to 190-acre lake.
Swim, canoe, boat (5 mph limit), or fish.
Walk nature trail or hike farther to
observe wildlife.
14-day limit. Hunting in season.
Crowded holiday weekends.

SUTHERLAND SRA

(308) 535-8025
State map: J12
Drive S on NE 25 for
2 miles (3.2 k) from SUTHERLAND.
FREE; $2 entrance fee. Open All Year.
85 scattered, open sites.
Central faucet, pit toilets, tables, fire
rings, boat ramp.
Next to 3020-acre lake.
Swim, boat, or fish.
14-day limit.

SWANSON LAKE SRA

(308) 276-2671
State map: N12
From TRENTON,
travel W on US 34 for 2 miles (3.2 k).
FREE; $7 developed; $2 entrance fee.
Open All Year.
212 scattered, open sites. &
Central faucet, flush toilets, showers,
dump station, electric hookups, tables,
fire rings, boat ramp, shelter.
Next to 4974-acre lake.
Swim, boat, ski, or fish.
14-day limit.

SYRACUSE CAMPGROUND

(402) 269-2601
State map: L29
Find campground in
SYRACUSE at 3rd & Midland.
$3. Open Apr–Nov.
Undesignated close, open sites.
Central faucet, flush toilets, dump
station, electric hookups, tables.
In city park.
Enjoy overnight stop.
14-day limit.

TAILRACE PARK

Loup River Public
Power District
(402) 564-3171
State map: I25
From COLUMBUS, travel E on 8th St for
3 miles (4.8 k). Turn Right (S) and go
1.5 miles (2.4 k). (Also see Powerhouse
Park and Lake North.)
FREE so choose a chore.
Open May 1–Nov 1.
36 scattered, open sites.
Hand pump, pit toilets, tables, grills.
At confluence of canal and Platte River.
Fish. Walk nature trail. Spot wildlife.
14-day limit.

TAYLOR TOURIST PARK

(308) 942-3149
State map: G18
Locate park on W edge
of TAYLOR.
$4; $7 full hookups.

Open Apr 15–Nov 20.
6 close, open, RV sites. Water at every site, electric hookups, tables.
In well-maintained spot just off highway.
Relax at overnight stop.
No toilet facilities.

TILDEN CITY CAMPGROUND

(402) 368-2232
State map: F23
Find campground in TILDEN on 2nd St between Walnut & East streets.
$2. Open May 1–Oct 1.
4 close, open sites.
Central faucet, flush toilets, electric hookups, tables, fire rings.
In municipal park.
Enjoy overnight stop.

TOADSTOOL

Nebraska NF
(308) 432-4475
State map: B4
From CRAWFORD, drive N on NE 71 for 4.5 miles (7.2 k). Turn Left (W) on gravel CR 904 and go 12 miles (19.2 k). Turn Left on CR 902, cross railroad tracks, and continue 1 mile (1.6 k). (Also see Soldier Creek Trailhead.)
FREE so choose a chore.
Open All Year.
6 scattered, open sites. Hand pump, pit toilets, tables, grills, fire rings.
In grasses with badlands-type geologic formations.
Walk loop trail to explore formations.
View "soddie" homestead.
14-day limit.
3780 ft (1134 m)

TOMAHAWK PARK

Broken Bow Parks
(308) 872-2139
State map: I17
Locate park in BROKEN BOW on 15th St, 1 block N of NE 2 W.
FREE so choose a chore. Open All Year.
7 close, open sites. Central faucet, flush toilets, showers, dump station, electric hookups, tables, fire rings.

In town park.
Enjoy overnight stop.
3-day limit.

TUXEDO PARK

Crete Parks
State map: L26
In CRETE, take NE 33 W to 13th. Follow 13th to Tuxedo Rd.
$3. Open Apr 15–Oct 15.
25 close, open sites. Central faucet, flush toilets, showers, dump station, electric hookups, tables, fire rings.
In city park.
Fish. Relax.
14-day limit.

UNION PACIFIC SRA

(308) 535-8025
State map: L18
Locate area at ODESSA
Exit 263 off I-80.
FREE; $2 entrance fee.
Open All Year.
20 close, open sites. ♿
Central faucet, flush toilets, tables.
Next to 12-acre lake.
Fish or boat (no gas motors).
14-day limit.

VALENTINE CITY PARK

(402) 376-2323
State map: C14
Find park on N Main St in VALENTINE.
FREE; donations requested.
Open May 1–Oct 1; dry camping allowed off-season.
Undesignated scattered, open sites.
Central faucet, flush toilets, showers, dump station, tables, grills, fire rings.
In woods with creek.
Fish. Canoe.

VERDON LAKE SRA

(402) 883-2575
State map: N30
From VERDON, drive W on US 73 for .5 mile (800 m). (Also see Brownville SRA.)
FREE; $2 entrance fee.

Open All Year.
20 scattered, open sites.
Hand pump, pit toilets, tables, grills, fire rings, playground.
Next to 45-acre lake.
Fish or boat (no gas motors).
14-day limit.
940 ft (282 m)

VICTOR PARK

Wayne Parks
(402) 375-1300
State map: E26
Find park in WAYNE at 316 S Main.
(Also see Lions Club Camper Park.)
$5. Open Apr 1–Nov 30; dry camping allowed off-season.
16 close, open sites.
Central faucet, flush toilets, dump station, electric hookups, tables, grills.
In small rural community.
Relax at overnight stop. Bike.
3-day limit. Crowded Jul 10.

VILLAGE PARK

Beaver Crossing Parks
(402) 532-3925
State map: L25
Locate park in BEAVER CROSSING on E Elk.
FREE; donations requested.
Open Apr–Oct.
Undesignated close, open sites.
Central faucet, flush toilets, electric hookups, tables, fire rings.
In town park.
Swim. Enjoy overnight stop.

WAGON TRAIN LAKE SRA

(402) 471-5545
State map: L27
From HICKMAN,
drive E for 2 miles (3.2 k) on gravel road. (Also see Bluestem Lake SRA and Stagecoach Lake SRA.)
FREE; $2 entrance fee.
Open All Year.
70 scattered, open sites.
Hand pump, pit toilets, dump station, tables, fire rings, grills, boat ramp, playground.

Next to 315-acre lake.
Swim, boat, or fish.
14-day limit. Hunting in season.
1300 ft (390 m)

WALGREN LAKE SRA

(308) 762-5605
State map: C7
From HAY SPRINGS,
head E on US 20. Turn Right (S) at sign for total distance of 5 miles (8 k).
FREE; $2 entrance fee.
Open All Year.
40 scattered, open sites.
Central faucet, pit toilets, tables, fire rings, boat ramp.
Beside 50-acre lake.
Fish or boat. Find lake monster!
14-day limit.

WAR AXE SRA

(308) 535-8025
State map: L20
Locate area at
SHELTON Exit 291 off I-80.
FREE; $2 entrance fee.
Open All Year.
10 scattered, open sites. &
Central faucet, flush toilets, tables, fire rings, shelter.
Next to 16-acre lake.
Fish and boat (no gas motors).
14-day limit.

WESTERN VILLAGE PARK

(402) 433-2882
State map: M25
Find park on Sumner
St in WESTERN.
FREE so choose a chore.
Open All Year.
3 scattered, open sites.
Central faucet, flush toilets, dump station, electric hookups, tables, grills.
In town park.
Bike. Relax at overnight stop.

WHITETAIL

Nebraska NF
(308) 533-2257
State map: G15

▲ ▲

From HALSEY, head S for 16 miles (25.6 k)–gravel for last 11 miles (17.6 k).
FREE so choose a chore.
Open All Year.
3 scattered, screened sites.
Hand pump, pit toilets, tables, fire rings.
Next to Dismal River under hardwoods.
Enjoy seclusion and beauty. Hike to view wildlife. Canoe.
No trash arrangements (pack it out).
14-day limit. Occasional horses and ATVs. Crowded major holidays and deer hunting season.
2500 ft (750 m)

WILDCAT HILLS SRA

(308) 436-2383
State map: G4
Drive S on NE 71 for 12 miles (19.2 k) from GERING. Turn Left (E).
FREE; $2.50 entrance fee.
Open All Year.
5 scattered, open sites.
Hand pump, pit toilets, tables, grills, fire rings.
Among pine and cedar-spotted hills with deep canyons and tall bluffs.
Hike to observe wildlife. Bike. Cross-country ski in winter.
14-day limit. Hunting in season.
4600 ft (1380 m)

WILDWOOD ACRES

Verdigre Parks
(402) 668-2621
State map: D22
Locate campground in VERDIGRE.
FREE so choose a chore.
Open All Year.
25 scattered, open sites.
Central faucet, flush toilets, showers, dump station, electric hookups, tables, grills, fire rings, pool.
In shady area next to stream.
Swim ($). Bike. Observe wildlife.
1500 ft (450 m)

WILLOW CREEK SRA

(402) 329-4053
State map: F24
From PIERCE, drive SW for 1 mile (1.6 k).
$4; $6 electric; $2.50 entrance fee.
Open All Year.
93 close, open sites; 10 private, hike-in, tent sites.
Central faucet, flush toilets, dump station, electric hookups, tables, grills, boat ramp, pay phone.
Among native grasses and young trees next to 700-acre lake.
Swim, boat, or fish. Hike. Watch upland birds and waterfowl. Cross-country ski in winter.
14-day limit. Hunting in season.

WISNER RIVER PARK

(402) 529-3383
State map: F26
Find park in WISNER.
FREE; $2 with pad; $5 electric.
Open Apr 15–Oct 31.
14 (10 tent-only) close, open sites.
Central faucet, flush toilets, dump station, electric hookups, tables, fire rings, boat ramp.
Next to Elkhorn River.
Boat or fish.

WYMORE ARBOR SP

(402) 645-3092
State map: N27
Locate state park in WYMORE at 9th & M streets.
FREE; $3 after 1 day; $4 with A/C.
Open Apr–Oct.
15 close, open sites.
Central faucet, flush toilets, showers, dump station, electric hookups, tables.
In municipal/state park.
Swim nearby. Relax.
14-day limit.

▲ ▲

NEW HAMPSHIRE
PUBLIC LANDS CAMPING

"It's Right in New Hampshire"—elevations from sea level to 6288-foot Mount Washington, tallest peak in the northeastern United States; 182 mountains over 3,000 feet; 18 miles of Atlantic Ocean coastline; 2,000 lakes and ponds; 4,000 miles of streams; 1,000,000 acres preserved for your outdoor enjoyment. In winter, skate, snowshoe, ski, sled, and sleigh. In summer, hike, cycle, horseback ride, swim, boat, and fish.

View the wildlife anytime. New Hampshire claims 300 species of vertebrates—fish, birds, mammals, reptiles and amphibians—and an additional 120 migratory species. Never feed the wildlife. Be especially careful cleaning up after meals and storing your food because of the proximity of black bears. Too, drive with greater caution at dusk and night because of the many moose on the roads throughout the state.

New Hampshire State Park (SP) camping costs from $12.00–$30.00, depending on location. Working from the north region to the southern part of the state, campgrounds can be found in the following state parks: Coleman, Crawford Notch, Franconia Notch, Lake Francis, Moose Brook, White Lake, Pillsbury, Greenfield, Monadnock, Bear Brook, and Pawtuckaway. In addition, New Hampshire offers RV parks at Franconia Notch, Ellacoya State Beach, and Hampton State Beach. The **Connecticut Lakes State Forest** (SF) offers primitive sites at Deer Mountain near the Canadian border. These drive-to $9.00 sites offer spring water, fireplaces, and wood.

Through New Hampshire meanders the Appalachian Trail. About half the trail falls within the **White Mountain National Forest** (NF). This forest offers other free backcountry camping opportunities too. Forest wilderness areas in New Hampshire include Great Gulf, Presidential Range/Dry River, Sandwich Range, and Pemigewasset. Dress sensibly and prepare for rapid weather changes. Remember to leave no trace of your camp on these public lands.

There are numerous hikes and scenic areas to enjoy within the White Mountains: Gibbs Brook, Snyder Brook, Rocky Gorge, Falls Pond, Greeley Ponds, Sawyer Pond. Wildcat Creek, a National Wild and Scenic River, is not canoeable, but the area bounds in hiking and cross-country skiing opportunities. Many areas can be enjoyed from the Kancamagus Highway, a 34.5-mile mountainous scenic byway from Pemigewasset River to Saco River.

The most popular time to visit the White Mountains is from Memorial Day through mid-October. Early September quietens as families return to homes and schools. Then in late-September through mid-October, a colorful blaze brings out all the leaf peepers.

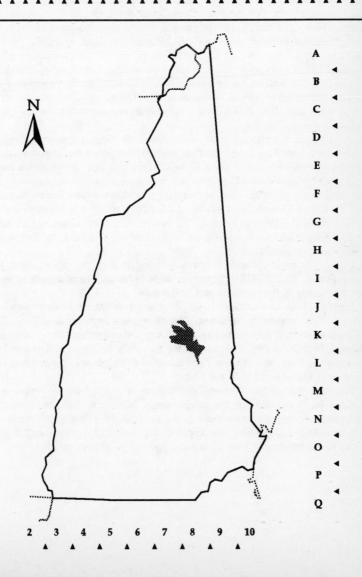

N

A ◄
B ◄
C ◄
D ◄
E ◄
F ◄
G ◄
H ◄
I ◄
J ◄
K ◄
L ◄
M ◄
N ◄
O ◄
P ◄
Q

2   3   4   5   6   7   8   9   10
▲   ▲   ▲   ▲   ▲   ▲   ▲   ▲   ▲

▲ ▲

NEW JERSEY
PUBLIC LANDS CAMPING

Complete with mountains, 127 miles of shoreline, and pristine wilderness, New Jersey offers such natural pleasures as hiking, biking, horseback riding, cross-country skiing, rock climbing, soaring, swimming, tubing, canoeing, boating, fishing, wildlife watching, berry-picking....

In the northernmost part of the state, backcountry camping is permitted along the Delaware River, a National Wild and Scenic River, and along the Appalachian Trail, a National Scenic Trail. For permits on the river, contact Delaware Water Gap National Recreation Area (NRA) Superintendent, Bushkill, PA 18324, (717) 588-2435. River sites are for boaters on trips of two or more days while trail sites are for backpackers on hikes of two or more days. Both areas have stay limits of one night and fill on a first-come, first-serve basis. The Appalachian Trail, of course, hits the high points of the state. The Delaware River, separating New Jersey and Pennsylvania, fills the low spots and creates one of New Jersey's most beautiful regions.

In the southern section of the state, the Pinelands National Preserve, also known as Wharton State Forest and the Pine Barrens, comprises the largest wilderness area east of the Mississippi River. Federal, state, and local governments plus the private sector have joined to protect over a million acres of swamp ecology along the Mullica River. At this time, all camping is within the **New Jersey State Parks** (SP) and **State Forests** (SF). Developed ("family") camping is available at Atsion for $10.00. Find primitive camping ("no modern facilities"–meaning pit toilets) at $8.00 sites throughout the preserve. Some sites are accessible by foot, 4-wheel drive, horse, or canoe.

Other state areas offering primitive camping at $8.00 per night include Jenny Jump Forest, Round Valley Recreation Area (RA), and Worthington Forest. All three areas are in the northern part of the state.

More modern camping, at $10.00 per site, can be found at these state areas: Allaire Park, Allamuchy Mountain Park (Stephen's Section). Bass River Forest, Belleplain Forest, Cheesequake Park, Delaware & Raritan Canal Park (Bull's Island Section), High Point Park, Lebanon Forest, Parvin Park, Spruce Run, Stokes Forest, Swartswood Park, and Vorhees Park. Some of these parks rent open and closed lean-tos at $12.00 and $15.00 per night.

The state of New Jersey offers 293,000 acres of public lands encompassing 35 state parks, 11 state forests, 5 recreation areas, 38 natural areas, 24 historic sites, and 4 state marinas. Combine these state areas with the federal public lands of the Delaware Water Gap NRA, the Appalachian Trail, and the Pinelands National Preserve. Discover why New Jersey and you can be perfect together.

New Jersey

Grid conforms to official state map. For your copy, call
or write Division of Travel & Tourism, CN 826, Trenton, NJ 08625-0826.

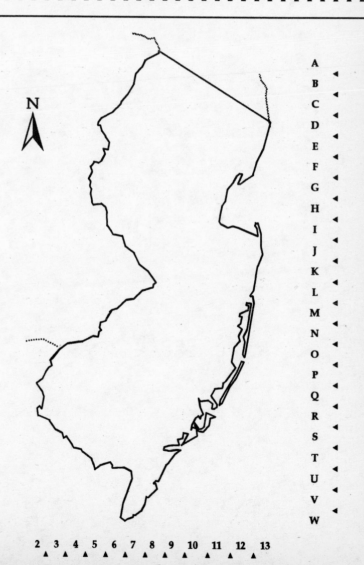

N

▲ ▲

NEW YORK
CAMPGROUND LOCATIONS

▸ ▸ Find location on facing page map grid. ▸ ▸
▾ ▾ Locate area campgrounds on these page numbers. ▾ ▾

New York

Grid conforms to official state map. For your copy, call (800) CALL-NYS
or write Department of Economic Development, Albany, NY 12245.

N

PUBLIC LANDS CAMPING

New York is more than a city. There's a whole state with a surprising amount of natural beauty upon its islands, in its valleys, on its mountains, along its rivers and streams, about its lakes. The eastern edge of New York is formed by Lake Champlain then the political lines of Vermont, Massachusetts, and Connecticut. Canada's boundary forms the northern edge along with the Saint Lawrence Seaway down to Lake Ontario. The Niagara River, its falls, and Lake Erie dominate New York's western tip. The Delaware River, then the state lines of Pennsylvania and New Jersey, form the southern boundary. Large parks in the Adirondack and Catskill mountains help protect these peaks and valleys filled with glacial streams and lakes plus deep, dark forests. Smaller preserves throughout the state protect a wide range of ecologies.

National Park Service (NPS) administers Fire Island National Seashore (NS). There's seasonal camping behind the sand dunes at ferry-accessible Watch Hill. The National Wild and Scenic River, the Upper Delaware, runs from Hancock to Sparrow Bush along the Pennsylvania border. Here, NPS provides public fishing and boating access. As part of the National Trail System, the Appalachian Trail passes through New York and the North Country begins at Crown Point, NY. Backcountry sites are available along these major trails.

Near Watkins Glen, discover the little **Finger Lakes National Forest** (NF) lying between Seneca and Cayuga lakes. Camp and enjoy the fruits of your labor at Blueberry Patch.

US Army Corps of Engineers (COE) has built lakes with recreation areas at Allegheny Reservoir, Almond Lake, and Whitney Point Lake. The campgrounds, however, are maintained by other administrators. Allegheny Reservoir is Allegheny National Forest; Almond Lake is Steuben County; Whitney Point is Broome County.

On the state level of public lands, **New York State Office of Parks** (SP) offers a variety of camping experiences: tent, tent platform, boat-in tent, recreational vehicle without electricity, and recreational vehicle with electricity and sewer hookups. Prices range from $9.00–$12.00 with additional charges for tent platforms and utilities at 66 different campgrounds.

The **New York Department of Environmental Conservation** (DEC) provides basic campgrounds at 52 forest preserves. Fees range from $9.00–$15.00, based on the site desirability rather than utilities. One location, Ausable Point, does offer electrical hookups for an additional $3.00.

A few **towns** and **counties** offer camping at their parks. Gaius M Cook Park in Chenango County qualifies for this book. If you consider weekly and biweekly rates, so do Steuben County's Kanakadea Park and Cattaraugus County's Onoville Marina. A few years ago, enterprising Greene County offered a jewel-encrusted kingpin to anyone who could follow the clues in a rewritten legend to find a rock inscribed with Rip Van Winkle's initials. It was one county's clever way to get more people acquainted with the many treasures of New York.

BLUEBERRY PATCH

Finger Lakes NF
(607) 594-2750
State map: N13
From BURDETT, head E
on NY 79 about 1 mile (1.6 k). Turn Left
on Logan Rd and drive 5 miles (8 k) to
Logan. Turn Right (E) on Picnic Rd and
go 2 miles (3.2 k).
$5. Open May–Dec.
9 close, open sites.
Hand pump, pit toilets, tables, grills, fire
rings.
In secluded forest setting.
Walk nature trail. Hike to view wildlife.
Fish nearby. Cross-country ski in winter.
14-day limit. Hunting in season.
Crowded major holidays.

FIRE ISLAND NS–Watch Hill
(516) 597-6633
State map: W27
From PATCHOGUE, take
ferry to Visitor Center.
Walk-in .25 mile (400 m).
$5; reservations accepted at
(516) 597-6633.
Open May 15–Oct 11.
25 close, open, tent sites. &
Central faucet, flush toilets, showers,
tables, grills, pay phone.
On beach behind dunes.
Play in ocean. Boat or fish. Walk nature
trail or farther into wilderness area.
Attend ranger programs.
5-day limit. Crowded Jul–Aug.
10 ft (3 m)

GAIUS M COOK
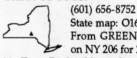
(601) 656-8752
State map: O16
From GREENE, drive E
on NY 206 for 2 miles (3.2
k). Turn Right (N) on Stine Rd then
Right on Park Rd. (Nearby Chenango
Valley SP costs $10.)
$5; $7 electric. Open May 20–Oct 1.
72 close, screened sites.

Central faucet, flush toilets, showers,
dump station, electric hookups, tables,
fire rings, pay phone.
On wooded hill next to 22-acre pond.
Hike. Fish. Relax.
14-day limit.

SANFORD LAKE DAY-USE AREA

NY DEC (607) 776-2165
State map: O11
From SAVONA, head NE
on NY 226 for 2 miles (3.2
k). Turn Left (W) on Round Lake Rd and
drive about 1 mile (1.6 k) to Sanford
Lake.
FREE so choose a chore; reservations
accepted at (607) 776-2165.
Open May 1–Sep 30; camping allowed
off-season.
7 (1 tent-only) close, open sites.
Pit toilets, grills.
In hardwood forest on lakeshore.
Canoe and fish. Hike to view wildlife.
NO water. No trash arrangements. 7-day
limit. Crowded weekends.

SUGAR HILL RA
NY DEC (607) 776-2165
State map: O12
From WATKINS GLEN,
take Mud Lake Rd W
about 6 miles (9.6 k). Turn Left (S) on
Spencer Rd. Go 1 mile (1.6 k). Turn Left
(W) on Tower Hill Rd to entrance.
FREE so choose a chore.
Open May 1–Sep 30; dry camping
allowed off-season.
Undesignated close, open sites. Hand
pump, chemical toilets, tables, grills.
At highest point in county among
natural hardwood.
Hike to observe wildlife. Practice
archery.
No trash arrangements (pack it out).
Horses and snowmobiles in area.
Crowded weekends.
2080 ft (624 m)

▲ ▲

NORTH CAROLINA
CAMPGROUND LOCATIONS

▸ ▸ Find location on facing page map grid. ▸ ▸
▾ ▾ Locate area campgrounds on these page numbers. ▾ ▾

GRID	PAGE
B3	298, 299, 300, 301
C2	300, 302
C3	297, 298, 302
D2	299, 302
E1	298, 301, 302
E2	298, 301
E3	299
G3	297, 303
H2	299, 300
K3	300
K4	300
L4	299

North Carolina

Grid conforms to official state map. For your copy, call (800) VISIT-NC
or write Travel & Tourism Division, 430 N Salisbury St, Raleigh, NC 27611.

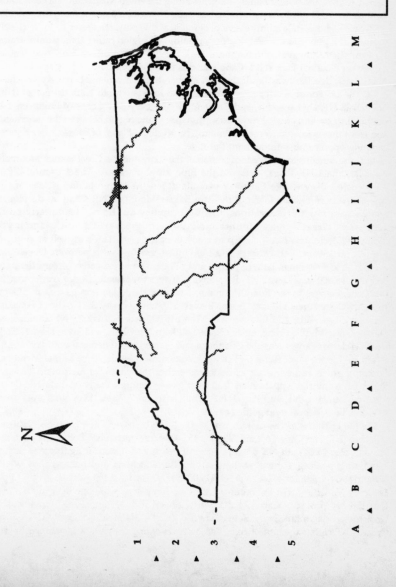

PUBLIC LANDS CAMPING

From the mountains to the coast, there are many natural beauties among the public lands of North Carolina. The mountains are called the Great Smoky Mountains and the Blue Ridge Mountains. As their names suggest, a blue-gray haze appears between you and the mountain ridges. As parts of the Appalachian Range, these mountains boast 43 peaks that approach 6,000 feet, including Mount Mitchell, highest point in the eastern United States. The coast, of course, is on the Atlantic Ocean. Here a chain of barrier islands, the "Outer Banks," stretches along the entire North Carolina coast. Most famous on the Outer Banks is treacherous Cape Hatteras, a place of many shipwrecks.

Because of this state's impressive geographical diversity, it's easier to more closely examine the public lands camping opportunities by region rather than administrator. In a nutshell, however, the National Park Service (NPS) offers the Great Smoky Mountain National Park (NP), Cape Hatteras National Seashore (NS), Cape Lookout NS, Blue Ridge Parkway, and, through cooperative management, the Appalachian Trail. The US Forest Service offers four national forests: Pisgah National Forest (NF), Nantahala NF, Uwharrie NF, and Croatan NF. The US Army Corps of Engineers has dammed rivers and created reservoirs, primarily in the region between the mountains and coast that is known as the piedmont. The NC State Parks, of course, offer diverse camping opportunities throughout the state.

In the mountains of the western section of the state, find the Great Smoky Mountain NP, Nantahala NF, Pisgah NF, and the Blue Ridge Parkway. The 470-mile, WPA-constructed **Blue Ridge Parkway** extends down the summits and ridges of the mountains from Shenandoah NP to Great Smoky Mountain NP. Camp at developed $8.00 sites or, with reservations, free backcountry locations. Headquartered in Tennessee, **Great Smoky Mountain NP** protects the world's best examples of temperate deciduous forest. Camp to enjoy the park's wildlands as well as restored pioneer structures. Backcountry sites, of course, are free with permits. Developed campground fees range between $6.00 and $11.00. The forest extends from the park into the 495,000-acre **Pisgah NF**. Pisgah NF manages the Linville Gorge Wilderness. In mid-June, be sure to see Roan Mountain, a natural rhododendron garden in bloom. Also, enjoy the Forest Heritage Scenic Byway, a 76-mile loop by the Cradle of Forestry, Looking Glass Falls, and Sliding Rock. The 516,000-acre **Nantahala NF** administers Shining Rock, Middle Prong, Ellicott Rock, Southern Nantahala, and Joyce Kilmer–Slick Rock wilderness areas plus the Chattooga and Horsepasture national wild and scenic rivers. Within the Joyce Kilmer–Slick Rock Wilderness, visit the Joyce Kilmer Memorial Forest, a green cathedral set aside to remember the poet and his poem, "Trees." Backpack along the Appalachian Trail as it passes through the Nantahala NF, Great Smoky Mountains NP, and Pisgah NF. While in the mountains, keep your eyes open for black bear, bobcat, and golden eagle.

On the coastline of the eastern part of the state, discover Cape Hatteras National Seashore (NS) and Cape Lookout NS plus 157,000-acre Croatan NF. Both **Cape Hatteras NS** and **Cape Lookout NS** provide miles of beach and historical lighthouses. Enjoy swimming, boating, fishing, shell collecting, birdwatching, and photography while camping. Cape Hatteras NS charges $11.00–$12.00 for its campgrounds while Cape Lookout NS offers free backcountry sites on ferry-accessible barrier islands. The **Croatan NF** provides Catfish Lake South, Sheep Ridge, Pond Pine, and Pocosin wilderness areas plus Cedar Point Tideland Trail, a National Recreation Trail. The Croatan NF claims the largest collection of insect-eating plants in any national forest,

▲ ▲

pocosins (raised bogs), a midwestern-type forest along Island Creek, plus great birdwatching and saltwater fishing.

Between the mountains and coast, there's the broad piedmont region in the center of the state. Here find the 46,000-acre **Uwharrie NF**. In this small forest, explore the Birkhead Mountain Wilderness and several forest ecologies ranging from bottomland to high mountain. These high mountains, however, have eroded down to 1000 feet. Also here, look for the red-cockaded woodpecker.

Together the national forests in North Carolina account for 800 campsites, 11 wilderness areas, and 1,300 miles of trails to view the wonders of nature. National forest camp fees range from free to $10.00.

US Army Corps of Engineers (COE) has created recreational facilities on B Everett Jordan Lake, Falls Lake, W Kerr Scott Reservoir, and, shared with Virginia, John H Kerr Reservoir. B Everett Jordan, Falls Lake, and John H Kerr campgrounds are maintained by the state at $9.00. COE camp fees at W Kerr Scott range from free to $12.00.

North Carolina State Parks (SP) such as Crowders Mountain, Eno River, Hammocks Beach, and South Mountains make this price-conscious guide. Other state park locations charge $9.00 per night or require a lengthy hike to campsites. Stone Mountain SP offers access to the South Fork of the New River, a National Wild and Scenic River. The **Clemmons Educational State Forest** (SF) offers tent camping and nature study. Be sure to call for reservations there.

From the mountains and foothills to the heartlands and coast, the state is full of sights, sounds, smells, feelings, faces, and memories that will never fade. North Carolina claims, "for a vacation you'll always remember, come to a state you'll never forget."

▲ ▲

AMMONS BRANCH

Nantahala NF
(704) 526-3765
State map: C3

From HIGHLANDS, head E on Horse Cove Rd for 8.5 miles (13.6 k). At pavement end, bear Right on Bull Pen Rd and continue 1.5 miles (2.4 k). (Also see Blue Valley and Burrell's Ford Walk-In, SC.)
FREE so choose a chore.
Open All Year.
3 close, screened sites.
Water needs treating, pit toilets, tables, fire rings.
Next to small creek (boil water) in mountainous treed area.
Hike into nearby Ellicott Rock Wilderness. Find waterfalls. Play in Chattooga River.
No trash arrangements. 14-day limit.
3600 ft (1080 m)

BADIN LAKE

Uwharrie NF
(919) 576-6391
State map: G3

From TROY, drive N on NC 109 for 15 miles (24 k). Turn Left (W) and follow signs on gravel FR 576 then FR 597 about 5 miles (8 k). (Also see Uwharrie Hunt Camp. Nearby Morrow Mountain SP costs $9.)
$5.
Open All Year.
37 close, screened sites.
Central faucet, chemical toilets, tables, fire rings, grills, boat ramp.
In mixed hardwood/pine next to lake.
Swim, boat, ski, or fish. Hike to view wildlife. Mountain bike.
14-day/32-ft limits. Hunting in season.
Crowded major holidays.
750 ft (225 m)

BLUE RIDGE PARKWAY
Basin Cove Walk-In

NPS (919) 372-8568
State map: E1

Find backcountry sites in Doughton Park at milepost 239. (Doughton Park Campground costs $8.) **FREE**; reservations accepted at (704) 298-0398.
Open May 1–Oct 31.
Undesignated screened, tent sites.
In forested southern Appalachian Mountains known for exquisite springs, green summers, and colorful autumns.
Hike to Bluff Mountain and Wildcat Rocks. Watch weaving demonstration at Brinegar Cabin.
NO water. No toilet facilities. No trash arrangements (pack it out). 14-day limit.
3600 ft (1080 m)

BLUE VALLEY

Nantahala NF
(704) 526-3765
State map: C3

From HIGHLANDS, head S on NC 28 for 6 miles (9.6 k). Turn Right (W) on gravel Blue Valley Rd and drive 2 miles (3.2 k). (Also see Ammons Branch. Nearby Cliffside Lake and Vanhook Glade cost $7.)
FREE so choose a chore.
Open All Year.
Undesignated scattered, screened sites.
Water needs treating, pit toilets.
In mountainous forest area.
Hike up to Glen Falls Scenic Area. Photograph waterfalls. Walk Bartram Trail.
No trash arrangements (pack it out). 14-day limit.

BOB ALLISON PICNIC AREA

Nantahala NF
(704) 837-5152
State map: B3

From ANDREWS, take US 19 E for 1 mile (1.6 k). Turn Right (SE) on NC 1505 (Junaluska) and go 5 miles (8 k). Turn Right (S) on FR 440 and continue 6 miles (9.6 k).

FREE so choose a chore.
Open All Year.
Undesignated scattered, open sites.
Hand pump, pit toilets, tables.
In woods.
Enjoy remote, mountainous area.
14-day limit.

BOONE FORK

Pisgah NF
(704) 652-2144
State map: E2

From LENOIR, head NW on NC 90 about 5 miles (8 k). Turn Right (N) on CR 1368 at Olivette Church and drive 4.75 miles (7.6 k). Turn Right (NE) on gravel FR 2055 and proceed 2 miles (3.2 k). (Also see Mortimer.)
FREE so choose a chore.
Open All Year.
16 close, open sites.
Hand pump, pit toilets, tables, grills.
In wooded area with small stream—only .5 mile (800 m) from fishing pond.
Hike to enjoy ecology. Fish. Relax.
14-day/22-ft limits.
1400 ft (420 m)

CABLE COVE

Nantahala NF
(704) 479-6431
State map: B3

From FONTANA VILLAGE, travel E on NC 28 for 5 miles (8 k). (Nearby Tsali costs $8.)
$5.
Open Apr 15–Oct 31.
26 scattered, screened sites. ♿
Central faucet, flush toilets, tables, grills, boat ramp.
In heavy wood with good underbrush screening next to Fontana Lake.
Walk nature trail and enjoy mountain environment. Boat or fish. Watch wildlife.
14-day/25-ft limits. No generators in quiet hours.
1600 ft (480 m)

▲ ▲

CAPE LOOKOUT NS-Backcountry

(919) 728-2250
State map: L4
From MOREHEAD
CITY, take US 70 E to NC 1335 and go
to end of road to Visitor Center. To
camp, take ferry ($12/person) or private
boat.
FREE so choose a chore.
Open All Year.
Undesignated scattered, open, tent sites.
Chemical toilets.
Along 55-miles (88-k) of undeveloped
barrier island in natural state.
Swim, boat, or fish. Collect shells. Canoe
or kayak. Observe wildlife. Explore. Visit
lighthouse.
NO water. No trash arrangements (pack
it out). Hunting in season. Occasional
ATVs.
10 ft (3 m)

CHEOAH POINT

Nantahala NF
(704) 479-6431
State map: B3
From ROBBINSVILLE, drive N on
US 129 about 6 miles (9.6 k) to sign.
Turn Left and follow signs. (Also see
Horse Cove.)
$5.
Open Apr 15–Oct 31.
26 scattered, screened sites. &
Central faucet, flush toilets, tables, grills,
boat ramp.
Overlooking Lake Santeetlah.
Hike to enjoy mountains. Explore nearby
Joyce Kilmer Wilderness. Boat or fish.
Swim at own risk.
14-day/22-ft limits. No generators in
quiet hours. Crowded weekends and
holidays.
2200 ft (660 m)

CLEMMONS EDUCATIONAL SF
WALK-IN

(919) 553-5651
State map: H2
From CLAYTON,
take US 70 W about 2.5 miles (4 k). Turn
Right (N) at sign on Old Gardner Rd.

Walk-in about 500 ft (152 m).
FREE so choose a chore; $25 refundable
deposit required; reservations accepted
at (919) 553-5651.
Open Mar 15–Nov 15.
Undesignated scattered, open sites.
Central faucet, pit toilets, tables, grills,
fire rings.
Among hardwood and longleaf pine.
Walk interpretive trail. Visit exhibit
center. Watch wildlife. Bike. Attend
ranger programs.
6-day limit. Closed Mondays.
359 ft (108 m)

CROWDERS MOUNTAIN SP

(704) 853-5375
State map: E3
From I-85 W of
GASTONIA, take Exit 13 (Edgewood Rd)
S to US 74. Turn Right at light and go
2 miles (3.2 k) to Sparrow Springs Rd.
Turn Left and continue 2.5 miles (4 k).
$5.
Open All Year.
16 close, open, tent sites.
Hand pump, pit toilets, grills, fire rings.
In hardwoods.
Hike ridge tops for views. Walk nature
trail. Rockclimb. Fish. Attend ranger
programs.
Crowded holiday weekends.
1620 ft (486 m)

CURTIS CREEK

Pisgah NF
(704) 652-2144
State map: D2
From OLD FORT, take US 70 E. Turn
Left (N) on NC 1227 then Right on
FR 482.
FREE so choose a chore.
Open All Year.
7 close, open, tent sites.
Hand pump, pit toilets, tables, fire rings.
In wood next to creek.
Enjoy mountain environment. Hike. Fish.
14-day limit.
2100 ft (630 m)

ENO RIVER SP WALK-IN

(919) 383-1686
State map: H2
Off I-85 at
DURHAM, take Exit 175. Drive N on Cole Mill Rd to end of road. Walk-in about 1 mile (1.6 k).
$5.
Open All Year.
6 scattered, screened tent sites.
Pit toilets.
In woods close to small river.
Enjoy seclusion. Canoe. Walk nature trail or hike farther. Fish. Attend ranger programs.
NO water. No trash arrangements (pack it out). 14-day limit.
460 ft (138 m)

FIRES CREEK

Nantahala NF
(704) 837-5152
State map: B3
From MURPHY, travel E on US 64 for 9 miles (14.4 k). Turn Left (N) at sign on NC 1302 and drive 4 miles (6.4 k). Continue N on NC 1344. (Also see Hanging Dog. Nearby Jackrabbit Mountain costs $8.)
FREE so choose a chore.
Open All Year.
15 scattered, open sites.
Pit toilets.
In primitive hunt-camp setting next to creek (near Bristol Horse Camp).
Hike to absorb mountain ecology. Fish. NO water. No trash arrangements (pack it out). Hunting in season.

FISHERS LANDING

Croatan NF
(919) 638-5628
State map: K3
From HAVELOCK, travel 6 miles (9.6 k) NW on US 70. (Nearby Flanners Beach costs over $5.)
FREE so choose a chore.
Open All Year.
Undesignated scattered, open sites.
Central faucet, chemical toilets, tables, grills, fire rings.

With mature pine and hardwood in open park next to Neuse River.
Swim or fish. Canoe or kayak. Watch wildlife.
14-day limit. Biting insects. Crowded summer and weekends.
25 ft (8 m)

GREAT SMOKY MOUNTAINS NP
Backcountry

(615) 436-1200
State map: C2
Find Oconaluftee
Visitor Center N of CHEROKEE on US 441. Obtain backcountry information and permit. Hike to selected site.
FREE; developed campgrounds cost from $6 to $9.
Open All Year.
Undesignated tent sites.
With over 800-miles (1280-k) of trails in spectacular mountain area.
Hike. Take photos. Commune with nature.
NO water. No trash arrangements (pack it out). Bear country. 3-day limit per site.

HAMMOCKS BEACH SP
WALK-IN/BOAT-IN

(919) 326-4881
State map: K4
Drive SW on Hammocks Rd (off NC 24) about 2 miles (3.2 k) from SWANSBORO. Take state ferry or private boat/canoe/kayak. Walk about .5 mile (800 m) from dock. (Nearby Cedar Point costs $10.)
$5.
Open All Year.
14 scattered, open, tent sites.
Central faucet, flush toilets, tables.
On undeveloped barrier island with 10 sites near beach and bathhouse and other 4 at either end of island (for private boaters) with 13 & 14 on bluff in maritime forest.
Swim and look for shells. Fish. Canoe or kayak. View wildlife. Enjoy natural wonders. Attend ranger programs.
No trash arrangements (pack it out). 14-day limit. Closed each full-moon

▲ ▲

period in summer (to protect loggerhead turtle nesting).

HANGING DOG

Nantahala NF
(704) 837-5152
State map: B3

From MURPHY, take NC 1326 (Joe Brown Hwy) N for 5 miles (8 k). (Also see Fires Creek. Nearby Jackrabbit Mountain costs $8.)
$4.
Open Apr 15–Oct 15; dry camping allowed off-season.
69 close, open sites.
Central faucet, flush toilets, tables, fire rings, grills, boat ramp, pay phone.
Next to Hiwassee Lake.
Boat, ski, or fish. Hike to enjoy mountain environment. Observe wildlife.
14-day/22-ft limits. Hunting in season.
No generators in quiet hours.

HORSE COVE

Nantahala NF
(704) 479-6431
State map: B3

From ROBBINSVILLE, drive N on US 129 about 8 miles (12.8 k). Turn Left (W) on gravel FR 305 and follow signs. (Also see Cheoah Point.)
$5.
Open Apr 15–Oct 31; dry camping allowed off-season.
17 scattered, screened sites. &
Central faucet, flush toilets, tables, grills.
In heavy wood on trout stream near Lake Santeetlah and Joyce Kilmer Wilderness.
Hike into wilderness to find only virgin forest left in eastern US. View wildlife. Fish.
14-day/25-ft limits. No generators in quiet hours. Crowded weekends.
2200 ft (660 m)

HURRICANE CREEK

Nantahala NF
(704) 524-6441
State map: B3

From FRANKLIN, head W on US 64 for 10 miles (16 k). Turn Left on Old 64 and go to Wallace Gap. Turn Right on FR 67 and drive 5 miles (8 k). (Nearby Standing Indian costs $8.)
FREE so choose a chore.
Open All Year.
Undesignated close, open sites.
Pit toilets.
In open, grass fields with stream.
Explore area. Fish.
NO water. 14-day limit.
3500 ft (1050 m)

MARLEY'S FORD

COE (919) 921-3390
State map: E1
Drive W on US 268

for 9 miles (14.4 k) from WILKESBORO. Turn Right. (Nearby Warrior Creek costs $8.)
FREE so choose a chore.
Open Mar 1–Nov 30.
23 scattered, screened tent sites.
Central faucet, pit toilets, tables, grills.
In wood on Yadkin River backwaters of W Kerr Scott Reservoir.
Enjoy quiet. Fish. View wildlife.
14-day/25-ft limits.
1250 ft (375 m)

MORTIMER

Pisgah NF
(704) 652-2144
State map: E2

From LENOIR, take NC 90 NW about 25 miles (40 k). (Also see Boone Fork.)
$4.
Open Apr 1–Oct 31; dry camping allowed off-season.
26 (5 tent-only) close, open sites.
Central faucet, pit toilets, tables, grills, fire rings.
On both sides of creek with large trees and rhododendron.
Enjoy peaceful setting. Hike. Fish.
14-day limit.
1500 ft (450 m)

NEW RIVER SP WALK-IN

(919) 982-2587
State map: E1
From JEFFERSON,
head E on NC 88 for 8 miles (12.8 k).
Turn Left (N) at Wagoner Baptist Church
on NC 1590 (Wagoner Access Rd) and
continue 2 miles (3.2 k). Walk-in about
300 yds (300 m).
$5.
Open All Year.
Undesignated scattered, open sites.
Central faucet, flush toilets, tables, fire
rings, canoe ramp.
In wooded to open area along New
National Wild and Scenic River.
Canoe or kayak. Swim. Walk nature trail.
Fish. Attend ranger programs.
14-day limit. Crowded holidays and
weekends.

NORTH MILLS RIVER

Pisgah NF
(704) 877-3265
State map: C3
From ASHEVILLE, head S on NC 191 for
13.3 miles (21.3 k) 'til just N of MILLS
RIVER. Turn Right (W) on FR 478.
Continue 5 miles (8 k).
$5.
Open Apr 20–Nov 1; dry camping
allowed off-season.
28 scattered, open sites.
Central faucet, flush toilets, dump
station, tables, fire rings.
On both sides of river under trees with
some screening.
Hike to enjoy mountain setting. Explore.
Fish.
14-day limit. Occasionally crowded.
Help clean-up area.

ROCKY BLUFF

Pisgah NF
(704) 622-3202
State map: C2
From HOT SPRINGS, drive NE on
NC 209 for 3 miles (4.8 k).
$5.

Open May 1–Oct 31.
30 close, open sites.
Central faucet, flush toilets, tables, grills.
Next to stream in southern Appalachian
forest.
Walk nature trail or hike farther to
explore ecology. Canoe. Fish.
14-day/18-ft limits. Small vehicles only.
1650 ft (495 m)

SOUTH MOUNTAINS SP

(704) 433-4772
State map: D2
Take NC 18 S from
MORGANTON to signed entrance road
and turn Right–total of 18 miles (28.8 k).
$5.
Open All Year.
11 scattered, screened sites.
Water needs treating, pit toilets, tables,
fire rings.
Along Jacob Creek. Also 14 walk-in sites
scattered about spots like High Shoals
Falls, Shinny Creek, and on Fox or
Sawtooth trails.
Hike to enjoy ecology. View falls.
Mountain bike. Observe wildlife. Look
for gold. Fish. Attend ranger programs.
14-day limit. Horses in area. Crowded
weekends.
1200 ft (360 m)

SUNBURST

Pisgah NF
(704) 877-3265
State map: C3
From WAYNESVILLE, drive E on
US 276 for 7 miles (11.2 k). Turn Right
(S) on NC 215. Proceed 6 miles (9.6 k).
$4.
Open Apr 20–Dec 12.
14 close, open sites.
Central faucet, flush toilets, tables, fire
rings.
Near Shining Rock Wilderness.
Hike to appreciate area. Drive nearby
Blue Ridge Parkway. Fish.
14-day/22-ft limits.
3000 ft (900 m)

▲ ▲

UWHARRIE HUNT CAMP

Uwharrie NF
(919) 576-6391
State map: G3

From TROY, drive N on NC 109 about
9 miles (14.4 k). Turn Left on NC 1153.
(Also see Badin Lake.)

$2.

Open All Year.

Undesignated scattered, open sites.

Chemical toilets, tables.

In woods.

Observe wildlife.

NO water. No trash arrangements (pack
it out). 14-day limit. Hunting in season.

NORTH DAKOTA
CAMPGROUND LOCATIONS

▶ ▶ Find location on facing page map grid. ▶ ▶
▼ ▼ Locate area campgrounds on these page numbers. ▼ ▼

North Dakota

Grid conforms to official state map. For your copy, call (800) HELLO-ND or write Parks & Tourism, 604 E Boulevard Ave, Bismarck, ND 58505.

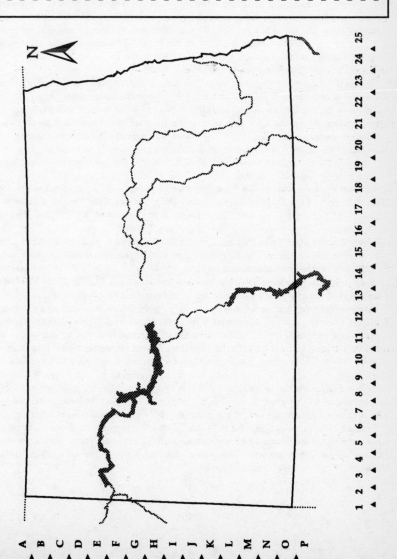

PUBLIC LANDS CAMPING

Discover the spirit of North Dakota. Feel the drum beats of Sioux, Chippewa, Mandan, and Hidatsa. Hear the wingbeats of ducks, geese, and other migratory fowl. See buffalo still roam; see deer and pronghorn antelope still play along with wild ponies, bighorn sheep, coyotes, prairie dogs, and 200 species of birds. Find all this among winding rivers, rich grasslands and badlands, birch and aspen forests, thousands of lakes, sloughs, and prairie potholes.

In addition to naturally occurring lakes in the state, **US Army Corps of Engineers** (COE) has created Homme Lake, Lake Ashtabula, Lake Oahe, Lake Sakakawea, and Pipestem Lake. The corps has established campgrounds and other recreational facilities around each lake. Walsh County administers the $5.00–$7.00 campground at Homme Lake. Stutsman County manages the free to $8.50 sites at Pipestem Lake. COE camp fees on the other three lakes range from free to $9.00.

National Park Service (NPS) presents Theodore Roosevelt National Park (NP). Here see samples of prairies, badlands, and wildlife. The park's two sections are 72 miles apart. Both units offer developed campgrounds at $7.00 as well as free backcountry opportunities. Along the Canadian border, the International Peace Garden provides developed camping from $6.00 to $10.00. Backpacking opportunities exist along the North Country Scenic Trail that ends at the Missouri River in North Dakota. Too, you can drive parts of the Lewis and Clark Trail. Eventually, this trail will provide hiking and boating opportunities as well.

Also on the federal level, **US Forest Service** provides free campgrounds in North Dakota as part of the Custer National Forest (NF): Burning Coal Vein in a badlands area plus CCC, Sather Lake, and Summit near Teddy Roosevelt NP. Too, the **Bureau of Reclamation** offers a free campground on Lake Tschida.

North Dakota State Parks (SP) boast over 1,100 campsites to pitch your tent or park your recreational vehicle. All developed state parks charge entrance and user fees year-round based on the level of available services. The entrance fee is $3.00. In-season tent-sites cost $9.00; in-season RV-sites with electricity go for $12.00. **State Wildlife Management Areas** (WMA), however, allow free camping for 10 days.

Counties offering campgrounds which qualify for this price-conscious guide include Burleigh, Carbury, Morton, Mountrail, Stutsman, Walsh, and Ward. Providing space for travelers, friendly North Dakota **towns** are so common that they're impossible to list here. To give you an idea, in the first three letters of the alphabet, find Aneta, Barney, Berthold, Binford, Bottineau, Carpio, Center, Cogswell, Cooperstown, Currington.... In the following pages, towns have confirmed campsites. Research indicates many more towns make space. If you find yourself traveling across the plains and in need of a campground, ask. Too, Sportsmans Clubs such as Baukol and Native American corporations such as White Earth Bay provide reasonable-cost camping.

Find a four-seasons playground in North Dakota. Enjoy great outdoors adventures while camping—hike, bike, ride horses, swim, waterski, boat, sail, canoe, fish, snow-ski, and snowshoe. From the wide Missouri to the Red River Valley—it's all in North Dakota.

▲ ▲

AMERICAN LEGION PARK

(701) 824-2779
State map: M7
Find park on SE edge of
MOTT.
FREE; donations requested.
Open May–Oct.
14 close, open sites.
Central faucet, flush toilets, dump
station, electric hookups, tables, grills.
Under trees beside river.
Enjoy overnight stop. View wildlife.
Fish.

ANETA CAMPGROUND

(701) 326-4568
State map: G20
Go 1 mile (1.6 k) W of
ANETA.
FREE so choose a chore.
Open May–Oct; camping allowed off-
season.
Undesignated scattered, open sites.
Pit toilets, tables, playground.
In rural setting.
Relax overnight.
NO water.

ASHTABULA CROSSING

COE (701) 845-2970
State map: K20
From VALLEY CITY, take
CR 21 N under Hi-Line railroad bridge
and continue for 15 miles (24 k). Watch
for signs. (Also see Eggert's Landing and
Old Highway 26.)
$5; $7 electric.
Open May 1–Sep 15; dry camping
allowed off-season.
82 close, screened sites.
Central faucet, flush toilets, showers,
dump station, electric hookups, tables,
fire rings, grills, boat ramp, store, rentals,
pay phone.
On west side and east side of Lake
Ashtabula in rolling prairie hills.
Watch white pelicans. Swim, boat, or
fish. Take photos. Attend ranger
programs.
14-day limit.
1300 ft (390 m)

BADGER BAY

COE (605) 845-2252
State map: M12
From BISMARCK, drive S
on ND 1804 for 32 miles (51.2 k). Turn
Right (W) at sign. (Also see Hazleton RA
and Beaver Creek.)
FREE so choose a chore. Open All Year.
Undesignated scattered, screened sites.
Pit toilets, tables, fire rings.
Along Badger Creek near confluence
with Missouri River.
Swim, fish, and boat. Observe wildlife.
NO water. Hunting in season.
1650 ft (495 m)

BALTA DAM RA

Balta Parks
(701) 542-9898
State map: E14
From BALTA, head S for .5 mile (800 m).
FREE so choose a chore.
Open All Year.
Undesignated scattered, open sites.
Central faucet, pit toilets, electric
hookups, tables, fire rings, boat ramp.
With some trees next to lake.
Swim, boat, ski, or fish.
No trash arrangements (pack it out).

BARNEY CITY PARK

(701) 439-2909
State map: N23
Locate park in BARNEY.
FREE so choose a chore.
Open All Year.
Undesignated close, open sites.
Central faucet, pit toilets, electric
hookups, tables, grills, fire rings,
playground, tennis court.
In quiet, clean, town park.
Enjoy overnight stop. Bike. Play sports.

BAUKOL-NOONAN DAM

Baukol Sportsman Club
(701) 925-5686
State map: B5
From NOONAN, drive 4 miles (6.4 k) E.
Turn Right (S). Continue 1 mile (1.6 k).
Turn Right (W) for final .5 mile (800 m).
FREE; donations requested.

Open All Year.
10 scattered, open sites.
Chemical toilets, electric hookups, tables, grills, boat ramp.
Next to lake.
Fish. Boat. Swim. Walk nature trail to see wildlife.
NO water. No trash arrangements (pack it out). Hunting in season.

BEAVER CREEK

COE (605) 845-2252
State map: N12
From LINTON, head W on ND 13 for 15 miles (24 k). (Also see Badger Bay, Cattail Bay, Hazelton RA, and Winona "Cattail Bay".)
FREE so choose a chore. Open All Year.
65 close, open sites.
Central faucet, flush toilets, showers, dump station, electric hookups, tables, fire rings, grills, boat ramp, pay phone.
In Missouri River "Breaks" with oak, ash, cedar, and spruce among rolling hills.
Swim, boat, ski, or fish. Walk nature trail or hike to view wildlife.
Hunting in season. Occasionally crowded.
1680 ft (504 m)

BERTHOLD CITY PARK

(701) 453-3641
State map: E9
Find park in BERTHOLD at 411 Tyler St NE.
FREE so choose a chore. Open All Year.
Undesignated scattered, open sites.
Central faucet, flush toilets, dump station, electric hookups, tables, grills.
In city park.
Enjoy overnight stay. Bike.

BEULAH BAY

Beulah Parks
(701) 873-5916
State map: J8
From BEULAH, head N on ND 49 (becomes ND 1806) for 19 miles (30.4 k). (Also see Hazen Bay RA.)
$4; $6 hookups; reservations accepted at (701) 873-5916.

Open May 15–Sep 15; dry camping allowed off-season.
10 close, screened sites.
Central faucet, pit toilets, dump station, electric hookups, tables, fire rings, grills, boat ramp, store, pay phone.
On open, rolling plains next to Lake Sakakawea.
Swim, boat, ski, or fish. Hike.
7-day limit.
1300 ft (390 m)

BINFORD CENTENNIAL PARK

(701) 676-2244
State map: H19
Locate park in BINFORD, 3 blocks W of Main St.
$4; $5 water; $6 electric; reservations accepted at (701) 676-2244.
Open May 25–Sep 5; dry camping allowed off-season.
Undesignated scattered, open sites.
Central faucet, flush toilets, dump station, electric hookups, tables, grills, rentals.
In town park.
Bike (cyclists camp free). Relax overnight.

BOTTINEAU CITY PARK

(701) 228-3030
State map: B13
Find park on E edge of BOTTINEAU, 1 block N of ND 5. (Also see Carbury RA.)
$4; +$1 for each hookup.
Open May 1–Oct 1; dry camping allowed off-season.
15 close, open sites.
Water at every site, flush toilets, showers, dump station, electric hookups, tables, grills, playground, tennis court, ball fields, pay phone.
Below foothills of Turtle Mountains.
Play sports. Bike. Enjoy overnight spot.
1200 ft (360 m)

BRADDOCK DAM

(701) 332-6632
State map: M14
From BRADDOCK, head S

for 1.5 miles (2.4 k). Turn Right (W) on gravel road and go .25 mile (400 m).
FREE so choose a chore.
Open All Year.
Undesignated close, open sites.
Chemical toilets, fire rings, grills, boat ramp.
In rolling grasslands surrounding lake.
Boat or fish.
NO water. No trash arrangements.

BUFFALO LAKE

Esmond Parks
(701) 249-3288
State map: F15
From ESMOND, head W on ND 19 for 4 miles (6.4 k). Turn Left (S). Go 1 mile (1.6 k) S. Turn Right (W) for last .25 mile (400 m). (Also see Esmond City Park.)
FREE so choose a chore.
Open All Year.
Undesignated scattered, open sites.
Hand pump, pit toilets, tables, grills, boat ramp.
In native prairie next to lake.
Boat. Watch wildlife.

BURNING COAL VEIN

Custer NF (701) 225-5151
State map: L3
Just W of AMIDON on US 85, take signed CR NW about 20 miles (32 k).
FREE so choose a chore.
Open All Year.
5 scattered, open sites.
Pit toilets, tables, grills.
In badlands next to century-old underground lignite fire.
Walk nature trail to investigate unusual ecology. Observe wildlife. Take photos.
NO water. No trash arrangements (pack it out). 14-day limit. Hunting in season.
2500 ft (750 m)

CARBURY RA

Bottineau County Parks
(701) 228-2225
State map: B12
From BOTTINEAU, head W on ND 5 for 4 miles (6.4 k). Turn Right (N) on ND 14

and travel 3.25 miles (5.2 k). Turn Left (W) and continue 1 mile (1.6 k). (Also see Bottineau City Park.)
FREE so choose a chore.
Open May 1–Sep 30.
10 close, open sites. &
Central faucet, pit toilets, electric hookups, tables, grills, boat ramp.
Next to 412-acre lake with some trees.
Swim, fish, or boat (10 hp limit). Observe wildlife.

CARPIO CITY PARK

(701) 468-5422
State map: D9
Locate park in CARPIO, 2 blocks N and 1 block E of US 52.
FREE; donations requested.
Open Apr 15–Nov 15.
15 close, open sites.
Central faucet, pit toilets, electric hookups, tables, grills, playground.
Surrounded by trees and bordered by DesLacs River on one side and old oxbow on other.
Watch wildlife, especially birds. Relax.
1698 ft (509 m)

CARRINGTON CITY PARK

(701) 652-3184
State map: I17
Find park on US 281 in CARRINGTON.
$5. Open Apr 15–Oct 15.
8 close, open sites.
Water at every site, flush toilets, dump station, electric hookups, tables, pool, playground, pay phone.
In town park with scattered trees.
Swim. Enjoy stop.

CCC

Custer NF (701) 842-2393
State map: H4
From WATFORD CITY, travel S on US 85 about 14 miles (22.4 k). Turn Right (W). (Also see Summit.)
FREE so choose a chore.
Open All Year.
4 close, open sites.
Pit toilets, tables.

In rolling hills.
Observe wildlife.
NO water. No trash arrangements (pack
it out). 14-day limit. Hunting in season.
Occasional horses in area.

CENTER PARK

(701) 794-3650
State map: J10
Locate park on S edge of
CENTER on ND 25
$3. Open May–Sep.
10 scattered, open sites.
Central faucet, flush toilets, dump
station, electric hookups, tables, grills,
fire rings, shelter, ball fields, pay phone.
Along Square Butte Creek with some
trees.
Play sports. Bike. Swim (indoor pool in
town).
2100 ft (630 m)

COGSWELL CAMPGROUND

(701) 724-3562
State map: O21
In COGSWELL, locate
park about .25 mile (400 m) off ND 11.
$5; $25/week.
Open May 25–Sep 5.
Undesignated scattered, open sites.
Central faucet, flush toilets, showers,
dump station, electric hookups, tables,
grills.
In peaceful setting with trees, bushes,
and flowers.
Relax. Enjoy overnight stay.

COOPERSTOWN CITY PARK

(701) 797-3613
State map: I20
In COOPERSTOWN, find
park at Foster & 10th.
$4; $5 RV; $6 hookups.
Open Apr–Oct.
6 RV plus undesignated, tent sites.
Water at every site, flush toilets,
showers, dump station, electric hookups,
tables, grills, pool, store.
In town park.
Bike. Enjoy overnight stop.

DEAD COLT CREEK RA

(701) 683-5555
State map: M21
From LISBON, head S on
ND 32 for 6 miles (9.6 k). Turn Left (E)
at sign and drive 1 mile (1.6 k).
FREE so choose a chore.
Open May 1–Sep 30.
Undesignated scattered, open sites.
Central faucet, flush toilets, electric
hookups, tables, fire rings, grills, boat
ramp.
Near Sheyenne River.
Swim, boat, or fish. Walk nature trail.
Watch wildlife.
7-day limit.

DEEPWATER

COE (701) 654-7411
State map: G7
From RAUB, drive W on
ND 37 about 5 miles (8 k).
FREE so choose a chore.
Open All Year.
Undesignated scattered, open sites.
Hand pump, pit toilets, tables, grills,
boat ramp, shelter.
On shore of Lake Sakakawea.
Boat. Fish a bunch.
14-day limit.
1900 ft (570 m)

DION LAKE

ND Game &Fish
(701) 662-3617
State map: B15
From ST JOHN, head W for 6.5 miles
(10.4 k). (Also see Grovel Lake, Hooker
Lake, and Lake Upsilon.)
FREE so choose a chore.
Open All Year.
Undesignated scattered, open sites.
Pit toilets, tables, boat ramp.
In opening within aspen-birch forest.
Walk nature trail or hike farther to see
wildlife. Boat or fish.
NO water. 14-day limit. Small vehicles
only. Hunting in season.
1700 ft (510 m)

▲ ▲

DOUGLAS CREEK

COE (701) 654-7411
State map: H9
Go W of EMMET about 2 miles (3.2 k). Travel S on CR about 6 miles (9.6 k).
FREE so choose a chore.
Open All Year.
Undesignated scattered, open sites.
Hand pump, pit toilets, tables, grills, boat ramp.
Next to Lake Sakakawea.
Fish and boat.
14-day limit.
1900 ft (570 m)

DRAKE CITY PARK

(701) 465-3788
State map: G13
Find park in DRAKE at N Lake & 6th Ave.
FREE; donations requested.
Open May 25–Sep 5.
20 (10 RV-only) scattered, open sites.
Central faucet, flush toilets, dump station, electric hookups, tables, grills, shelter, playground.
In grassy, city park.
Bike. Enjoy overnight stop.

DRAYTON DAM RA

Drayton Parks
(701) 454-3821
State map: C22
From DRAYTON, drive N for 2 miles (3.2 k). Turn Right (E). Go 1 mile (1.6 k).
$5.
Open May–Sep.
12 close, open sites.
Central faucet, pit toilets, boat ramp.
At dam on Red River of the North.
Fish.

EGGERT'S LANDING

COE (701) 845-2970
State map: K20
From VALLEY CITY, take CR 21 N under Hi-Line railroad bridge and continue 11 miles (19.2 k). Watch for signs. (Also see Ashtabula Crossing.)
$5; $7 electric.

Open May 1–Sep 15; dry camping allowed off-season.
23 (5 tent-only) screened sites. &
Central faucet, pit toilets, dump station, electric hookups, tables, fire rings, grills, boat ramp, store, pay phone.
On banks of Lake Ashtabula in mature windbreak.
Fish. Boat and waterski. Walk nature trail and view abundant wildlife. Attend ranger programs.
14-day limit.
1300 ft (390 m)

ESMOND CITY PARK

(701) 249-3288
State map: F15
Find park in ESMOND. (Also see Buffalo Lake.)
FREE so choose a chore.
Open May 1–Oct 15.
Undesignated scattered, open sites. &
Central faucet, flush toilets, showers, electric hookups, tables, grills, store.
In small park.
Bike. Enjoy overnight stop.
28-ft limit.

FORBES CITY PARK

(701) 357-7771
State map: O18
Locate park in FORBES at N 4th & Main.
FREE so choose a chore.
Open May 10–Oct 10.
Undesignated scattered, open sites.
Central faucet, flush toilets, electric hookups, tables, grills.
In area noted for ancient settlements (both native and European).
Walk nature trail. Observe wildlife. Explore White Stone Battlefield, Johnson Gulch Burial Grounds, Forbes Petroglyph Rock.
Hunting in season. No generators.

FORT BUFORD SHS

(701) 572-9034
State map: F2
From WILLISTON, take US 2 W for 5 miles (8 k). Turn Left (SW)

on ND 1804 for 16 miles (25.6 k). Turn at sign on gravel road for 1.5 miles (2.4 k).
FREE; donations requested.
Open May 15–Sep 15; dry camping allowed off-season.
Undesignated scattered, open sites.
Central faucet, flush toilets, tables, grills, fire rings.
In 5-acre, grassy spot with grove of cottonwood.
View wildlife. Visit museum ($). Bike. Canoe, boat, or fish nearby.
1900 ft (570 m)

FORT DAER

Pembina Parks
(701) 825-6205
State map: B22
In PEMBINA on Beaupre St.
$3; $5 RV.
Open May 1–Oct 1; dry camping allowed off-season.
38 scattered, open sites. &
Central faucet, flush toilets, showers, electric hookups, tables, grills, boat ramp, playground, ball courts.
Between Pembina and Red rivers.
Boat or fish. Play sports. Take photos.

FORT MANDAN HISTORIC SITE

McClean County
(701) 462-8129
State map: I11
From WASHBURN, drive W for 3 miles (4.8 k).
$5.
Open Apr 15–Oct 15; dry camping allowed off-season.
16 scattered, open sites.
Central faucet, flush toilets, electric hookups, tables, grills.
Along Missouri River.
Tour Visitor Center. Walk nature trail.
View wildlife. Fish and boat.
1200 ft (360 m)

FORT RICE

COE (605) 845-2252
State map: M12
From BISMARCK, travel S
on ND 1806 for 29 miles (46.4 k). Turn

Left (E) at sign.
FREE so choose a chore.
Open All Year.
Undesignated scattered, open sites.
Pit toilets, boat ramp.
In Missouri River hills with woody draws.
Boat or fish. View abundant wildlife.
NO water. Hunting in season.
1650 ft (495 m)

GATEWAY PARK RV CAMP

Wyndmere City Parks
(701) 439-2412
State map: N23
In WYNDMERE off 4th St N at Ash & RR Dr.
FREE so choose a chore.
Open All Year.
4 scattered, open sites.
Tables.
Under shade trees.
Enjoy overnight stay.
NO water. No toilet facilities.

GLEN ULLIN MEMORIAL PARK

(701) 348-3795
State map: L8
Find park in GLEN ULLIN
on old highway 10 W.
$3; $7 electric.
Open May–Oct.
30 close, open sites.
Central faucet, pit toilets, dump station, electric hookups, tables, playground.
In city park.
Enjoy overnight stop.
7-day limit.

GLENFIELD CITY PARK

(701) 785-2188
State map: I18
Find park in GLENFIELD.
FREE so choose a chore.
Open All Year.
16 (10 tent-only) close, open sites.
Central faucet, flush toilets, dump station, electric hookups, tables, grills, playground.
In town park.
Relax overnight.

▲ ▲

GRANER PARK
(SUGARLOAF BOTTOMS)
Morton County Parks
(701) 667-3360
State map: L12
From MANDAN, travel S on ND 1806
for 17 miles (27.2 k).
FREE; $5 for shelter and electric.
Open All Year.
110 scattered, open sites.
Hand pump, pit toilets, dump station,
tables, fire rings, grills, boat ramp.
On Missouri River bottomland at historic
Lewis & Clark campsite.
Boat or fish. Watch wildlife.
14-day limit. Crowded May 20–23 and
Jul 4.
1630 ft (489 m)

GRENORA CITY PARK
(701) 694-2462
State map: C2
Find park on NW side of
GRENORA.
FREE so choose a chore. Open Apr–Oct.
6 close, open sites.
Central faucet, flush toilets, dump
station, electric hookups, tables.
In town park.
Enjoy overnight stop.

GROVEL LAKE
ND Game & Fish
(701) 662-3617
State map: B15
From ST JOHN, head W for 6.5 miles
(10.4 k). (Also see Dion Lake, Hooker
Lake and Lake Upsilon.)
FREE so choose a chore. Open All Year.
Undesignated scattered, open sites.
Pit toilets, tables, boat ramp.
In aspen birch forest next to lake.
Walk nature trail. Hike. Boat or fish.
NO water. 14-day limit. Small vehicles
only. Hunting in season.
1700 ft (510 m)

HAHN'S BAY RA
Turtle Mountain SF
(701) 228-3700
State map: B13

From BOTTINEAU, head N on CR for
12 miles (19.2 k). Turn Right (E) on
ND 43 and go 6 miles (9.6 k). (Also see
Pelican Lake/Sandy Lake.)
$5. Open May–Oct; dry camping
allowed off-season.
35 (10 tent-only) close, open sites.
Hand pump, pit toilets, tables, fire rings,
boat ramp.
Next to large lake in aspen forest.
Swim, boat, or fish.
Small vehicles only.

HAVANA PARK
(701) 724-6449
State map: O21
Locate park in HAVANA
on E side at end of Main St.
FREE so choose a chore.
Open All Year.
Undesignated close, open sites.
Central faucet, pit toilets, electric
hookups, tables, grills, ball field.
In town park.
Bike. Enjoy overnight stop.
21-day limit.

HAZELTON PARK
(701) 782-4135
State map: M13
Find park at 400 Hazel
Ave in HAZELTON.
$2; $8 RV.
Open All Year.
12 close, open sites. &
Water at every site, flush toilets,
showers, dump station, electric hookups,
tables, grills, store.
In prairie setting.
Walk nature trail and spot wildlife. Bike.

HAZELTON RA
COE (605) 845-2252
State map: M12
From BISMARCK, head S
on ND 1804 for 30 miles (48 k). (Also see
Badger Bay and Beaver Creek.)
FREE so choose a chore.
Open All Year.
20 close, screened sites.
Pit toilets, tables, fire rings, grills, boat

▲ ▲

ramp, pay phone.
On Missouri River with trees planted in camping area.
Swim, boat, and fish. Watch wildlife.
NO water. Hunting in season.
1700 ft (510 m)

HAZEN BAY RA

Hazen Parks
(701) 748-6948
State map: I9
From HAZEN, head N on CR 27 for 15 miles (24 k). (Also see Beulah Bay.)
$4; $7.50 electric.
Open May 20–Oct 31.
27 close, open sites.
Central faucet, chemical toilets, electric hookups, tables, boat ramp.
On shore of Lake Sakakawea.
Swim, boat, ski, or fish.

HIAWATHA PARK

Sykeston City Parks
(701) 984-2380
State map: I16
Find park on N side of SYKESTON.
FREE so choose a chore.
Open All Year.
10 close, open sites.
Central faucet, flush toilets, electric hookups, tables, grills, playground.
In town park next to lake.
Swim. Relax.

HOMME DAM

Walsh County Parks
(701) 284-7841
State map: D21
From PARK RIVER, take ND 17 W and follow signs.
$5; $7 electric.
Open Apr–Nov.
19 scattered, open sites.
Central faucet, flush toilets, showers, dump station, electric hookups, tables, fire rings, grills, boat ramp, pay phone.
On Homme Lake in garden setting of trees and flowers.
Boat or fish. Take photos. Watch wildlife.
1279 ft (384 m)

HOOKER LAKE

ND Game & Fish
(701) 662-3617
State map: B15
From ST JOHN, head W for 6.5 miles (10.4 k). (Also see Dion Lake, Grovel Lake, and Lake Upsilon.)
FREE so choose a chore.
Open All Year.
Undesignated scattered, open sites.
Pit toilets, tables, boat ramp.
In aspen-birch.
Hike. Take photos. Fish.
NO water. 14-day limit. Small vehicles only. Hunting in season.
1700 ft (510 m)

JAYCEE CAMPGROUND

Wahpeton Parks
(701) 642-2811
State map: N25
Find campground in WAHPETON at 999 R J Hughes Dr.
$5. Open May 1–Oct 15; dry camping allowed off-season.
42 (30 tent-only) scattered, open sites.
Central faucet, flush toilets, showers, dump station, electric hookups, tables, fire rings, grills, boat ramp, zoo, pool, pay phone.
Next to Chahinkapa Zoo and Red River of the North.
Visit zoo. Walk nature trail. Swim. Boat and fish.
3-day limit.

JOHN MOSES MEMORIAL PARK

Hazen Parks
(701) 748-6948
State map: I9
Locate park in HAZEN, just E of high school. (Also see Riverside Park.)
$4; $7.50 electric.
Open May 25–Oct 31.
7 close, open sites.
Central faucet, chemical toilets, electric hookups, tables.
In town park.
Enjoy overnight stay.

▲▲▲▲▲▲▲▲▲▲▲▲▲▲▲▲▲▲▲▲▲▲▲▲▲▲▲▲▲▲▲▲▲

KENMARE CAMPGROUND

(701) 385-4232
State map: C8
On NE side of KENMARE,
locate campground off US 52.
$5; $95/month. Open May 1–Sep 30; dry
camping allowed off-season.
25 close, open sites.
Water at every site, flush toilets,
showers, dump station, electric hookups,
tables.
Next to highway and De Lac Lake.
Swim. Walk nature trail or hike farther
to view wildlife. Take photos.
Hunting in season.

KIMBALL BOTTOMS

COE (605) 845-2252
State map: L12
From BISMARCK, go S on
ND 1804 for 7.5 miles (12 k).
FREE so choose a chore.
Open All Year.
Undesignated scattered, open sites.
Pit toilets, boat ramp.
Along Missouri River bottomland with
numerous trees.
Swim, boat, or fish. Watch abundant
wildlife.
NO water. Hunting in season.
Occasionally crowded.
1630 ft (489 m)

KIWANIS PARK

New Rockford City Parks
(701) 947-2403
State map: H17
Locate park on N edge of NEW
ROCKFORD at ND 15 & US 281.
$5; $25/week. Open May 1–Sep 30.
28 close, open sites.
Central faucet, chemical toilets, electric
hookups, tables, grills, pool, tennis court.
With footbridge across James River.
Fish. Boat. Swim.
1520 ft (456 m)

LAKE BREKKEN

Turtle Lake Parks
(701) 448-2596
State map: H11

Head N on CR for 2 miles (3.2 k) from
TURTLE LAKE.
FREE; $7 electric. Open Apr–Oct; dry
camping allowed off-season.
30 close, open sites.
Central faucet, flush toilets, dump
station, electric hookups, tables, fire
rings, grills, boat ramp, playground, ball
field, pay phone.
On east side of lake.
Play sports. Fish. Spot wildlife.
Hunting in season.
1835 ft (551 m)

LAKE PARK

Powers Lake Parks
(701) 464-5434
State map: D6
Find park in POWERS LAKE. (Also see
Lonetree and Smishek Dam.)
FREE; donations requested.
Open May 1–Oct 1; dry camping
allowed off-season.
6 close, open sites.
Hand pump, pit toilets, electric hookups,
tables.
Next to lake.
Swim or fish.

LAKE TSCHIDA
(HEART BUTTE DAM)

Bureau of Reclamation
(701) 584-3588
State map: M8
From ELGIN, drive N on ND 49 for
14 miles (22.4 k).
FREE so choose a chore.
Open May 25–Sep 5; dry camping
allowed off-season.
Undesignated scattered, open sites.
Hand pump, pit toilets, dump station,
tables, fire rings, grills, boat ramp, store,
pay phone.
On lakeshore.
Swim, boat, ski, or fish. View wildlife.
2070 ft (621 m)

LAKE UPSILON

ND Game & Fish
(701) 662-3617
State map: B15

From ST JOHN, head W for 6.5 miles
(10.4 k). (Also see Dion Lake, Grovel
Lake, and Hooker Lake.)
FREE so choose a chore.
Open All Year.
Undesignated scattered, open sites.
Pit toilets, tables, grills, fire rings, boat
ramp.
With aspen-birch forest.
Walk nature trail. Hike. Fish.
NO water. 14-day limit. Small vehicles
only. Hunting in season.
1700 ft (510 m)

LANGDON CITY PARK
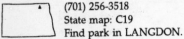
(701) 256-3518
State map: C19
Find park in LANGDON.
FREE so choose a chore.
Open All Year.
10 close, open sites.
Central faucet, flush toilets, showers,
dump station, electric hookups, tables,
playground.
In town park.
Enjoy overnight stop.

LEHR CITY PARK
(701) 378-2526
State map: N16
In LEHR, locate park at
201 S Main.
FREE so choose a chore.
Open All Year.
10 (4 tent-only) close, screened sites.
Central faucet, flush toilets, electric
hookups, tables, grills, shelter,
playground.
On mowed grass area with trees.
Relax overnight.

LIGNITE PARK
(701) 933-2572
State map: B6
Locate park in LIGNITE.
FREE so choose a chore.
Open All Year.
2 close, open sites. Central faucet, flush
toilets, showers, tables, playground.
In small park with trees.
Enjoy overnight stay.

LONETREE
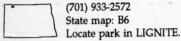
Powers Lake Parks
(701) 464-5434
State map: D6
From POWERS LAKE, drive 1 mile
(1.6 k) E on ND 50. Turn Right (S) and
go 1 mile (1.6 k). (Also see Lake Park
and Smishek Dam.)
FREE; donations requested.
Open May 1–Oct 1; dry camping
allowed off-season.
38 (30 tent-only) scattered, open sites.
Hand pump, chemical toilets, electric
hookups, tables.
Next to lake.
Swim, boat, or fish.

MARION CITY PARK
(701) 669-2379
State map: L19
Find park on E side of
MARION.
FREE so choose a chore. Open All Year.
Undesignated scattered, open sites. &
Central faucet, flush toilets, electric
hookups, tables, shelter, playground.
Among trees and flowers.
Enjoy overnight stop.

MEDINA CITY PARK
(701) 486-3548
State map: K16
Locate park on S edge of
MEDINA.
FREE so choose a chore.
Open May 1–Oct 30.
22 close, open sites. &
Central faucet, flush toilets, showers,
dump station, electric hookups, tables,
grills, shelter.
In clean, quiet park.
Walk nature trail. Spot wildlife. Bike.

MEL RIEMAN RA
COE (701) 845-2970
State map: K20
From VALLEY CITY, take
CR 21 N under Hi-Line railroad bridge.
Turn Left (W) at grain elevator on River
Road and drive 11 miles (17.6 k). Watch
for signs.

$5; $7 electric.
Open May 1–Sep 15; dry camping allowed off-season.
28 (10 tent-only) close, open sites.
Hand pump, flush toilets, showers, dump station, electric hookups, tables, fire rings, grills, boat ramp, store, rentals, pay phone.
On Lake Ashtabula, close to Baldwin Dam, with sunset views.
Swim, boat, ski, or fish. Walk nature trail and see wildlife.
14-day limit.
1300 ft (390 m)

MILNOR CITY PARK
(701) 427-5203
State map: N22
In MILNOR, find park on ND 13.
FREE; donations requested; $20/week.
Open Jun–Aug.
Undesignated scattered, open sites.
Hand pump, flush toilets, showers, electric hookups, tables, grills, pool, tennis and volleyball courts, track.
In nice park right in town.
Swim. Play sports.
Often used by work crews.

MIRROR LAKE PARK
Hettinger Parks
(701) 567-4592
State map: O8
From HETTINGER, drive S on ND 8.
Pass railroad tracks and take first Left.
$3; $6 RV. Open May 1–Oct 31; dry camping allowed off-season.
24 close, open sites. Water at every site, flush toilets, showers, dump station, electric hookups, tables, grills, boat ramp, rentals, pay phone.
In prairie setting next to small lake.
Swim, boat, or fish. Walk nature trail or hike farther to observe wildlife.
32-ft limit. Crowded Jul 4.

MOHALL CAMPGROUND
(701) 756-7277
State map: C9
Locate campground on E

edge of MOHALL on ND 5.
FREE; $4 after 3 days.
Open May 1–Oct 31; dry camping allowed off-season.
23 (5 tent-only) close, open sites.
Water at every site, dump station, electric hookups, tables, grills, store, pay phone.
Within city limits.
Swim and fish. Observe wildlife.
No toilet facilities. Hunting in season.
1650 ft (495 m)

MONANGO CITY PARK
(701) 349-5318
State map: N18
In MONANGO, find park.
FREE; donations requested.
Open May 15–Sep 15; dry camping allowed off-season.
3 close, open sites.
Central faucet, flush toilets, electric hookups, tables, grills, playground, volleyball court.
In small park.
Bike. Enjoy overnight stop.

NELSON MEMORIAL PARK
Arnegard City Park
(701) 586-3565
State map: G3
In ARNEGARD, locate park on Main St.
$5.
Open May–Sep.
4 close, open, RV sites.
Central faucet, flush toilets, showers, dump station, electric hookups, tables, grills, fire rings, shelter, playground, tennis court.
Among beautiful trees and flowers.
Play sports. Enjoy overnight stay.

NEWBURG CITY PARK
(701) 272-6158
State map: C11
Find park in NEWBURG.
FREE so choose a chore.
Open May–Sep; dry camping allowed off-season.
Undesignated close, open sites.
Central faucet, flush toilets, electric

hookups, tables, grills, shelter, tennis court, pay phone.
In open area with windbreaks.
Relax overnight.

NORTH PARK

New Salem Parks
(701) 843-7704
State map: K10
In NEW SALEM, find park.
FREE so choose a chore.
Open All Year.
14 close, open sites.
Central faucet, flush toilets, electric hookups, tables, playground, tennis court, golf course.
In park setting.
Enjoy overnight stop.
3-day limit.

OLD HIGHWAY 26

COE (701) 845-2970
State map: K20
From VALLEY CITY, take CR 21 N under Hi-Line railroad bridge and continue 18 miles (28.8 k). Turn Right (E) on signed gravel road. (Also see Ashtabula Crossing.)
FREE so choose a chore.
Open May 1–Sep 15; dry camping allowed off-season.
7 scattered, open sites.
Hand pump, pit toilets, tables, fire rings, grills, boat ramp.
With rows of lilacs to campground in remote setting adjacent to wildlife area on Ashtabula Lake.
Fish. Observe wildlife.
14-day limit.
1300 ft (390 m)

OLD SETTLER'S PARK

Ward County Highway Department (701) 838-2810
State map: C9
In BURLINGTON, go E on Park Rd. Pass 3-way stop and cross over bridge. Turn Left on N Project Rd.
$3; $5 electric.
Open May–Oct.
28 scattered, open sites.

Central faucet, flush toilets, showers, electric hookups, tables, grills, fire rings, playground, ball field, pay phone.
On level, wooded area with river running through it.
Swim or fish. Play sports. Bike. View wildlife.
Crowded last week of Jul.
1600 ft (480 m)

PARKHURST

Stutsman County Parks
(701) 252-6002
State map: K18
From JAMESTOWN, drive NW on US 52/281 for 6 miles (9.6 k).
FREE so choose a chore.
Open All Year.
16 scattered, open sites.
Central faucet, pit toilets, tables, grills, boat ramp.
Overlooking Pipestem Reservoir.
Boat and fish. Spot wildlife.
14-day limit. Hunting in season.
1490 ft (447 m)

PATTERSON LAKE

Dickinson Parks
(701) 225-2074
State map: K5
From DICKINSON, head W for 3 miles (4.8 k). Turn Left (S) on old Hwy 10 for 1 mile (1.6 k).
$5; $9 modern; **$1** entrance fee.
Open Apr 1–Sep 30; dry camping allowed off-season.
60 (40 tent-only) close, open sites.
Central faucet, flush toilets, showers, dump station, electric hookups, tables, grills, boat ramp, pay phone.
Among trees near lake.
Swim, boat, ski, or fish. Walk nature trail or hike farther. Bike.
Hunting in season. No generators in quiet hours.

PELICAN LAKE/SANDY LAKE

Turtle Mountain SF
(701) 228-3700
State map: B13
From BOTTINEAU, head N on CR for

12 miles (19.2 k). Turn Right (E) on
ND 43 and go 12 miles (19.2 k). (Also see
Hahn's Bay RA.)
$5.
Open May–Oct; dry camping allowed
off-season.
13 close, open sites.
Hand pump, pit toilets, tables, fire rings,
boat ramp.
Next to 50-acre lake.
Swim, boat, or fish.
Small vehicles only.

PIONEER PARK
Pekin City Park
(701) 296-4533
State map: G19
Locate park in NE corner of PEKIN.
$1. Open All Year.
14 scattered, open sites.
Central faucet, chemical toilets, electric
hookups, tables, grills.
In peaceful spot.
Enjoy overnight stop.

RIVERSIDE PARK
Hazen Parks
(701) 748-6948
State map: I9
From HAZEN, head S on CR 27 for
1 mile (1.6 k). (Also see John Moses
Memorial Park.)
$4. Open May 25–Oct 31.
Undesignated scattered, open sites.
Central faucet, chemical toilets, tables.
Next to Knife River.
Swim or fish.
No trash arrangements (pack it out).

RIVERSIDE RA
Beulah Parks
(701) 873-5852
State map: J8
On S edge of BEULAH, find area off
ND 49.
$3; reservations accepted at
(701) 873-5916.
Open Apr 1–Nov 1.
Undesignated scattered, open sites.
Hand pump, pit toilets, electric hookups,
tables, grills, fire rings.

In woods next to scenic Knife River.
Canoe or fish. Hike to spot wildlife.
7-day limit.
1100 ft (330 m)

ROLLA CITY PARK
(701) 477-3782
State map: B15
Find park on W end of
ROLLA off ND 5.
FREE so choose a chore.
Open All Year.
12 close, open sites.
Central faucet, flush toilets, showers,
dump station, electric hookups, tables,
grills, pool.
In city park.
Swim. Enjoy overnight stay.

SANDAGER PARK
Lisbon City Parks
(701) 683-4166
State map: M21
In LISBON, locate park on 2nd Ave W.
$3; $6 RV.
Open May 15–Oct 15.
20 close, open sites.
Water at every site, flush toilets,
showers, dump station, electric hookups,
tables, grills, fire rings, pool.
On scenic banks of Sheyenne River.
Swim. Fish. Walk nature trail.

SATHER LAKE
Custer NF (701) 842-2393
State map: G3
From ALEXANDER, travel
S for 10 miles (16 k) on ND 68.
FREE so choose a chore.
Open All Year.
8 close, open sites.
Pit toilets, tables, fire rings.
Next to small lake among gentle hills.
Observe wildlife.
NO water. No trash arrangements (pack
it out). 14-day limit. Hunting in season.

SEEMAN PARK

Linton Parks
(701) 254-4717
State map: N13

Follow signs on gravel road 1 mile
(1.6 k) S of LINTON.
$5.
Open All Year.
52 (12 RV-only) close, open sites.
Central faucet, flush toilets, showers,
electric hookups, tables.
In woods.
Fish. Bike.

SILVER LAKE RA

Sargent County Parks
(701) 724-6241
State map: O21
From FORMAN, head S on ND 32 about
5 miles (8 k). Turn left (E) on CR and go
3 miles (4.8 k). Turn Right (S) at sign.
FREE so choose a chore.
Open May 1 – Sep 1; dry camping
allowed off-season.
20 close, open sites.
Central faucet, pit toilets, dump station,
electric hookups, tables, boat ramp,
playground.
Next to lake.
Swim, boat, or fish.

SMISHEK DAM

Powers Lake Parks
(701) 464-5434
State map: D6
From POWERS LAKE, drive W on
ND 50 for 1 mile (1.6 k). Turn Right (N)
and go 2 miles (3.2 k). (Also see Lake
Park and Lonetree.)
FREE; donations requested.
Open May 1 – Oct 1; dry camping
allowed off-season.
60 (52 tent-only) scattered, open sites.
Hand pump, pit toilets, electric hookups,
tables, fire rings, boat ramp.
Next to lake.
Fish. Boat. Swim.

STANLEY CAMPGROUND

(701) 628-2225
State map: E7
Find park in STANLEY on
ND 8.
FREE so choose a chore.
Open Apr – Oct.

15 close, open sites.
Central faucet, flush toilets, showers,
dump station, electric hookups, tables,
grills, playground.
In city park.
Relax at overnight stop.
5-day limit.

STOKES MEMORIAL PARK

Streeter Parks
(701) 424-3317
State map: L16
Locate park on SW side of STREETER.
FREE so choose a chore.
Open May – Oct.
4 scattered, open sites. &
Central faucet, flush toilets, tables, grills.
On hill with lots of trees.
Enjoy overnight stay.

STRAWBERRY LAKE

Turtle Mountain SF
(701) 228-3700
State map: B13
From BOTTINEAU, head N on CR for
12 miles (19.2 k). Turn Left (W) on
ND 43 and go 8 miles (12.8 k).
$5.
Open May – Oct; dry camping allowed
off-season.
25 close, open sites.
Hand pump, pit toilets, tables, fire rings,
boat ramp.
Among aspen next to 40-acre lake.
Swim, fish, or boat (no gas motors).
Small vehicles only.

SUMMIT

Custer NF (701) 842-2393
State map: H4
From WATFORD CITY,
travel S on US 85 about 20 miles (32 k).
(Also see CCC.)
FREE so choose a chore.
Open All Year.
5 close, open sites.
Pit toilets, tables, fire rings.
In rolling hills next to badlands.
Hike to explore and take photos.
NO water. No trash arrangements (pack
it out). 14-day limit.

▲ ▲

SWEETBRIAR LAKE

Morton County Parks
(701) 667-3360
State map: K10
From MANDAN, drive 20 miles (32 k)
W on I-94.
FREE so choose a chore.
Open All Year.
Undesignated scattered, open sites.
Hand pump, pit toilets, tables, fire rings,
grills, boat ramp.
On natural prairie next to man-made
lake.
Boat or fish. View wildlife.
14-day limit. Hunting in season.
1780 ft (534 m)

THEODORE ROOSEVELT NP
Backcountry

(701) 623-4466
State map: K3
Access North Unit 15 miles
(24 k) S of WATFORD CITY on US 85.
Access South Unit near MEDORA.
Obtain permit and map. Hike at least
.5 mile (800 m). (Developed Cottonwood
and Squaw Creek cost $7.)
FREE; $4 entrance fee.
Open All Year.
Undesignated scattered, open sites.
In Little Missouri Badlands (river
bottomland, broken topography, and
prairie).
Hike to observe wildlife, especially
buffalo. (All trails are buffalo-made and
maintained.)
NO water. No toilet facilities. No trash
arrangements (pack it out). 14-day limit.
2000 ft (600 m)

TIOGA CITY PARK

(701) 664-2563
State map: D5
Locate park in TIOGA.
FREE so choose a chore.
Open May–Sep.
12 close, open sites.
Central faucet, flush toilets, showers,
dump station, electric hookups, tables,
grills, playground.
In town park.

Enjoy overnight stop. Swim or fish
nearby.

TOTTEN TRAIL

COE (701) 654-7411
State map: H10
Go N on US 83 from
COLEHARBOR, crossing lake. (Also see
Wolf Creek.)
FREE so choose a chore.
Open All Year.
Undesignated scattered, open sites.
Central faucet, pit toilets, tables, grills,
boat ramp.
Next to Lake Sakakawea.
Boat or fish.
14-day limit.
1900 ft (570 m)

VALLEY CITY MUNICIPAL
CAMPGROUND

(701) 845-3294
State map: K20
Find campground on Main
St in VALLEY CITY.
$5; $9 full hookups.
Open May–Sep.
18 close, open sites.
Water at 16 sites, flush toilets, showers,
dump station, electric hookups, tables,
playground.
In small woods next to gas station.
Enjoy overnight stop. Swim or boat
nearby.

VAN HOOK-TRAYNOR PARK

Mountrail County Parks
(701) 627-3811
State map: F6
From NEW TOWN, drive E on ND 23
for 7 miles (11.2 k). Turn Left (S) and
travel 2 miles (3.2 k).
$5; $7 electric.
Open May 1–Sep 15; dry camping
allowed off-season.
165 (100 tent-only) scattered, open sites.
Central faucet, flush toilets, showers,
dump station, electric hookups, tables,
grills, boat ramp, food storage, store, pay
phone.
On the Van Hook arm of Lake

Sakakawea at old townsite.
Swim, boat, or fish. Bike.
Occasionally crowded.
1852 ft (556 m)

WALES CITY PARK

(701) 283-5151
State map: B18
Locate park in WALES.
FREE so choose a chore.
Open Jun–Oct; camping allowed off-season.
1 open site. Chemical toilets, electric hookup, table, grill.
In small, town park.
Enjoy overnight stay.
NO water.

WATFORD CITY TOURIST PARK

(701) 842-2234
State map: G4
On E side of WATFORD CITY, find park off ND 23.
$5. Open May 1–Nov 30; dry camping allowed off-season.
30 close, open sites.
Central faucet, flush toilets, showers, dump station, electric hookups, tables, grills, fire rings, pay phone.
Under trees along Cherry Creek.
Explore area. Bike. Enjoy stop.
7-day limit.

WESTHOPE TRAILER COURT

(701) 245-6316
State map: B11
On E side of WESTHOPE, locate area.
$5; $25/week; reservations accepted at (701) 245-6316.
Open All Year.
8 close, open, RV sites.
Water at every site, electric hookups.
Enjoy stay in farmland 2 miles (3.2 k) from Mouse River.
No toilet facilities.

WESTSIDE PARK

Harvey Parks
(701) 324-4744
State map: G14

Find park on W side of HARVEY, next to ND 3 and US 52 Bypass.
$5; $7 electric.
Open May 15–Oct 15; dry camping allowed off-season.
19 (2 tent-only) scattered, open sites.
Central faucet, flush toilets, showers, dump station, electric hookups, tables, grills, shelter, pool, playground, tennis court.
In grassy section of city park.
Swim, boat, or fish.
Occasionally crowded with construction workers.

WHITE EARTH BAY

(701) 755-3277
State map: E6
From TIOGA, head S on ND 40 about 10 miles (16 k). Turn Left (E) on ND 1804 and travel about 11 miles (17.6 k). At sign turn on gravel road and continue 9 miles (14.4 k).
FREE so choose a chore.
Open All Year.
12 scattered, open sites. &
Pit toilets, tables, grills, boat ramp.
On point in Lake Sakakawea.
Swim, boat, canoe, or fish. Observe wildlife. Ice fish in winter.
NO water. No trash arrangements (pack it out). 14-day limit. Occasionally crowded weekends.
1860 ft (558 m)

WILLOW CITY PARK

(701) 366-4445
State map: C13
In WILLOW CITY, find park.
FREE so choose a chore.
Open All Year.
2 sites.
Central faucet, flush toilets, tables, grills.
In small, town park.
Bike. Relax overnight.

WING CITY PARK

(701) 943-2375
State map: J13
In WING, locate park at

▲ ▲

junction of ND 14 & 38.
FREE; donations requested.
Open Apr 30–Nov 1; dry camping allowed off-season.
Undesignated scattered, open sites.
Central faucet, flush toilets, dump station, electric hookups, tables, grills, fire rings, tennis court, ball field, store, pay phone.
In rolling hills of rural North Dakota.
Fish. Play sports. Bike. Spot wildlife.
Crowded Jul 4 and Jul 17-18.

WINONA "CATTAIL BAY"
COE (605) 845-2252
State map: O12
From LINTON, head W on ND 13 for 15 miles (24 k). Turn Left (S) on ND 1804 and go about 10 miles (16 k). (Also see Beaver Creek.)
FREE so choose a chore.
Open All Year.
10 close, screened sites.
Pit toilets, tables, fire rings, boat ramp.
Along Missouri River with scattered trees.
Boat or fish. Watch wildlife.
NO water. Hunting in season.
Occasionally crowded.
1630 ft (489 m)

WOLF CREEK
COE (701) 654-7411
State map: H10
From RIVERDALE, head N on CR about 3 miles (4.8 k). (Also see Totten Trail.)
FREE so choose a chore.
Open All Year.
Undesignated scattered, open sites.
Pit toilets, tables, grills, boat ramp.
On peninsula in Lake Sakakawea.
Fish and boat.
NO water. 14-day limit.

ZAP CITY PARK
(701) 948-2257
State map: I8
In ZAP, locate park on 3rd Ave N.
$5; $25/week.
Open All Year.
9 close, open sites.
Water at every site, pit toilets, dump station, electric hookups, tables, grills, tennis court.
Across from main park in wooded, grassy area next to Spring Creek.
Enjoy stay. Play sports.

▲ ▲

OHIO
CAMPGROUND LOCATIONS

▶ ▶ Find location on facing page map grid. ▶ ▶
▼ ▼ Locate area campgrounds on these page numbers. ▼ ▼

Ohio

Grid conforms to official state map. For your copy, call (800) BUCKEYE or write Division of Tourism, PO Box 1001, Columbus, OH 43266-0001.

N

2
3
4
5
6
7
8
9
10
11
12
13
14
15
16
17
18

A B C D E F G H I J K L M N O P

▲ ▲

PUBLIC LANDS CAMPING

Ohio considers itself in "the heart of it all!" Indeed, Ohio is an interesting mix of urban and rural environments. Being along a great river and a great lake has put Ohio in the middle of much change as well as history. As you travel across the Buckeye State from its rolling hills overlooking the Ohio River Valley to its sandy shores of Lake Erie, you'll find yourself surrounded by a surprising amount of natural beauty. It's tucked among the farms and around the industries of big cities. It coexists with Ohio history at its mysterious Indian earthworks, sites of battles, and homes of past presidents. See it beside the hiking trails of the Wayne-Hoosier National Forest (NF). View it on the water.

You'll find yourself around a lot of water in Ohio. In the north, there's Lake Erie. Ohio's southern border and a sizable portion of its eastern boundary are created by the Ohio River. Too, in Ohio, you'll find one of the largest manmade lakes in the world—Grand Lake Saint Marys. Canoe on the Mohican and Tuscarawas rivers; ride a canal boat on the Erie Canal, powerboat on Lake Erie, and sail on many lakes in the Muskingum Watershed Conservancy.

The 178,000-acre Wayne portion of the **Wayne-Hoosier NF** lies in three sections in the foothills of the Appalachian Mountains in southeastern Ohio. Here find hardwood forests, picturesque "runs" or creeks, and remains of the once-important iron industry around Ironton. Camp at developed (free to $10.00) or dispersed (free) sites. Picnic, hike, ride horses, canoe, swim, or fish. View wildlife such as deer, wild turkey, grouse, and many types of songbird.

US Army Corps of Engineers (COE) maintains campgrounds on the lake projects they have constructed: Berlin, C J Brown Reservoir, Caesar Creek, West Fork of Mill Creek, William H Harsha, Mohawk Dam, and North Branch of Kokosing River. The Ohio Department of Natural Resources manages Buck Creek State Park (SP) on C J Brown Reservoir, Mound Ridge Campground on Caesar Creek Lake, and East Fork SP on William H Harsha Lake. The Hamilton County Park District operates the recreational facilities at Mill Creek Lake. COE administers camping sites at Mohawk Dam and North Branch of Kokosing projects for $5.00 per night.

Also, on the federal public lands level, the North Country National Scenic Trail passes through Ohio as it makes its way from New York to North Dakota. Backcountry camping is permitted along this long trail.

Ohio State Parks (SP) manage 207,000 acres of natural places. Here you can study the coming and going of oceans, glaciers, prairies, forests, and many plants and animals. The state has developed 9,285 campsites with a range of settings and facilities, including a Rent-A-Camp program, in 56 of its parks. A basic site ranges from $6.00–$8.00. Using electrical hookups and bringing pets cost more. There are free primitive camps at Blue Rock, Pymatuning, Scioto Trail, and Tar Hollow state parks. Some of these sites require a short walk with your own water supply. Too, Ohio offers camping at the following **State Forests (SF)**: Fernwood ($3.00), Harrison ($3.00), and Zaleski (free).

Come get in the middle of it all. Ohio promises a warmhearted welcome.

▲ ▲

BURR OAK COVE

Wayne-Hoosier NF
(614) 592-6644
State map: K13
From GLOUSTER, travel N
on OH 13 for 4 miles (6.4 k). Turn Right
(E) on CR 107 and drive .5 mile (800 m).
(Nearby Burr Oak SP costs over $5.)
$4.
Open May 15–Sep 30.
19 (5 tent-only) scattered, screened sites.
Central faucet, pit toilets, tables, grills,
fire rings.
In dense woods on NW tip of Burr Oak
Reservoir.
Fish. Hike and observe wildlife.
14-day/22-ft limits. Hunting in season.
800 ft (240 m)

GERMAN CHURCH

COE (216) 547-3781
State map: N6
From ALLIANCE, head N on
OH 225 about 2.5 miles
(4 k)–pass lake. Turn Right (E) on
German Church Rd and continue .5 mile
(800 m).
FREE so choose a chore.
Open Apr–Oct.
Undesignated close, open sites. &
Central faucet, flush toilets, tables, fire
rings, boat ramp.
Next to 5000-acre Berlin Lake.
Swim, boat, or fish.
14-day limit.
1030 ft (309 m)

HAUGHT RUN

Wayne-Hoosier NF
(614) 373-9055
State map: M13
From MARIETTA, travel NE
on OH 26 about 17 miles (27.2 k). At
camping sign and covered bridge, take
next Right and after 50 yds (50 m),
another Right. (Also see Hune Bridge
and Ring Mills.)
FREE so choose a chore.
Open All Year.
5 scattered, open sites.
Pit toilets, tables, grills, fire rings.

Under trees along Little Muskingum
River.
Enjoy quiet. Canoe or fish. Hike to see
wildlife.
NO water. 14-day limit.
630 ft (189 m)

HIDDEN HOLLOW

Fernwood SF (614) 264-5671
State map: O9
From WINTERSVILLE off
CR 22A, take signed Bantam
Road Rd S to forest. (Also see
Ronsheim.)
$3.
Open All Year.
22 scattered, screened sites.
Hand pump, pit toilets, tables, fire rings.
In shade of forest.
Walk nature trail and view wildlife. Fish.
14-day limit. Hunting in season. Gun
range nearby. No alcohol.
1200 ft (360 m)

HUNE BRIDGE

Wayne-Hoosier NF
(614) 373-9055
State map: M13
From MARIETTA, travel NE
on OH 26 about 14 miles (22.4 k). At
covered bridge, take Right (maximum
vehicle height of 6′ 8″). (Also see Haught
Run and Lane Farm.)
FREE so choose a chore.
Open All Year.
2 scattered, open sites.
Pit toilets, tables, fire rings.
Along Little Muskingum River.
Canoe. Fish. Hike and observe wildlife.
NO water. 14-day limit.
660 ft (198 m)

LANE FARM

Wayne-Hoosier NF
(614) 373-9055
State map: M13
From MARIETTA, travel NE
on OH 26 about 5 miles (8 k) to NF
entrance sign. (Also see Hune Bridge.)
FREE so choose a chore.
Open All Year.

▲ ▲

4 scattered, open, tent sites.
Pit toilets, tables, grills, fire rings.
In pleasant setting on Little Muskingum
River.
Fish. Canoe. Hike to spot wildlife.
NO water. 14-day limit.
620 ft (186 m)

MOHAWK DAM

COE (614) 824-4343
State map: K9
From COSHOCTON, head W
on US 36 for 13 miles
(20.8 k). Turn Right (NW) on OH 715
and travel 1 mile (1.6 k).
$5.
Open May 28 – Sep 7; dry camping
allowed off-season.
39 close, open sites.
Central faucet, flush toilets, tables, fire
rings, boat ramp.
Next to lake and within walking distance
of historic canal lock.
Walk nature trail. Tour dam. Canoe.
Fish.
14-day limit.
800 ft (240 m)

NORTH BRANCH OF
KOKOSING LAKE

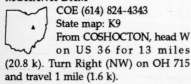

COE (614) 824-4343
State map: I8
From FREDERICKTOWN,
take Waterford Rd NW (off
OH 13) for 2 miles (3.2 k).
$5; reservations accepted at
(614) 824-4343 for an additional $2.
Open May 28 – Sep 7.
36 close, open sites.
Central faucet, pit toilets, tables, fire
rings, boat ramp.
Next to 154-acre lake.
Boat or fish.
14-day limit.
1150 ft (345 m)

RING MILLS

Wayne-Hoosier NF
(614) 373-9055
State map: M13
From MARIETTA, travel NE

on OH 26 about 22 miles (35.2 k). At
sign, take Right on gravel road and drive
3 miles (4.8 k). (Also see Haught Run.)
FREE so choose a chore.
Open All Year.
Undesignated scattered, open sites.
Pit toilets, tables, grills, fire rings, shelter.
In quiet, wooded setting along Little
Muskingum River.
Canoe or fish. Hike.
NO water. 14-day limit.

RONSHEIM

Fernwood SF (614) 264-5671
State map: O9
From CADIZ, head E on
US 22. Turn Left (N) on
CR 13 and follow signs. (Also see
Hidden Hollow.)
$3.
Open All Year.
7 scattered, open sites.
Hand pump, pit toilets, tables, fire rings.
In forest shade.
Hike to spot wildlife. Fish.
14-day limit. Hunting in season. Nearby
gun range. Occasional horses. No
alcohol.
1200 ft (360 m)

SCIOTO TRAIL SP WALK-IN

(614) 663-2125
State map: G14
From CHILLICOTHE, drive S
on US 23. Turn Left (E) on
OH 372. Walk-in from 100 ft (31 m) to
2600 ft (790 m).
FREE; $6 drive-in; $11 electric.
Open All Year; dry camping allowed off-
season.
82 (25 tent-only) scattered, open sites.
Central faucet, pit toilets, dump station,
electric hookups, tables, fire rings, grills,
boat ramp, pay phone.
In hardwood forest with streams and
two lakes.
Walk nature trail or hike farther.
Mountain bike. Canoe, boat, or fish.
Attend ranger programs.
Hunting in season.

▲ ▲

ZALESKI SF WALK-IN

(614) 596-5781
State map: I14
From ZALESKI, head N on
OH 278 for 4 miles (6.4 k).
Walk-in to 1 of 3 backpack camps.
(Nearby Lake Hope SP costs over $5.)
FREE so choose a chore.
Open All Year.
Undesignated close, open sites.
Hand pump, pit toilets, fire rings.
Among steep hills covered with
hardwood.
Observe wildlife. Take photos.
No trash arrangements (pack it out).
14-day limit. Hunting in season.
Occasionally crowded.
1000 ft (300 m)

▲ ▲

OKLAHOMA
CAMPGROUND LOCATIONS

▶ ▶ Find location on facing page map grid. ▶ ▶
▼ ▼ Locate area campgrounds on these page numbers. ▼ ▼

Oklahoma

Grid conforms to official state map. For your copy, call (800) 652-6552
or write Tourism, Box 60789, Oklahoma City, OK 73146.

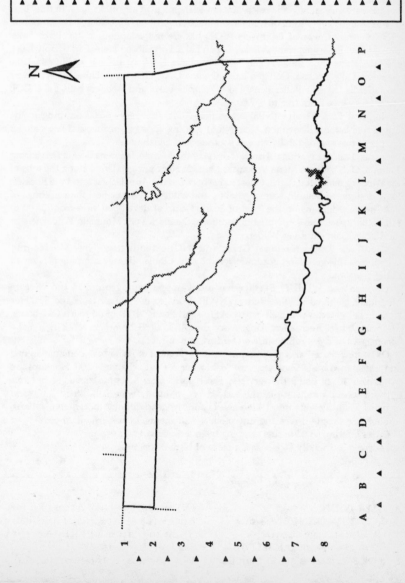

▲▲▲▲▲▲▲▲▲▲▲▲▲▲▲▲▲▲▲▲▲▲▲▲▲▲▲▲▲▲▲▲

PUBLIC LANDS CAMPING

Oklahoma claims to be America in its native state: pure, natural, and unspoiled. The state is diverse with eroded mountains, buffalo-spotted prairies, deep forests, immense waters, and vast skies. The public lands recreational opportunities seem endless, whether camping in the woods, having fun on one of many lakes, or simply basking in the frequent sunshine. Hike, mountain bike, or horseback ride along the trails. Climb ancient peaks in the Wichita Mountains. Raft a swift river or canoe a still stream.

There are more manmade reservoirs in Oklahoma than any other state. In this "blue heaven," enjoy every kind of water sport, including fishing for catfish, bass, and trout. The **US Army Corps of Engineers** (COE) has created campgrounds on Birch Lake, Broken Bow Reservoir, Canton Lake, Copan Lake, Fort Gibson Lake, Fort Supply Lake, Heyburn Lake, Hugo Lake, Hulah Lake, Kaw Lake, Keystone Lake, Lake Eufaula, Lake Skiatook, Lake Texoma, Oologah Lake, Optima Lake, Pine Creek Lake, Robert S Kerr Lake, Sardis Lake, Tenkiller Ferry Lake, Waurika Lake, and Webbers Falls Lake. COE camp fees range from free to $12.00.

National Park Service (NPS) offers first-come, first-serve $6.00 camping in the Chicasaw National Recreation Area (NRA). Mineral springs, streams, and lakes attract people to this wooded, hilly area in south-central Oklahoma.

In the **Ouachita National Forest** (NF), take the 54-mile Talimena Scenic Drive from Talihina, Oklahoma to Mena, Arkansas (outside Hot Springs). Drive along the tops of the Winding Stair Mountains, tallest range between the Appalachians and the Rockies. View designated botanic, scenic, wildlife, and wilderness areas. Feel the sufferings of the Cherokee Indians on the Trail of Tears. Camp at developed sites from $4.00 to $10.00. Backpack into more pristine locations, the Black Fork Mountain Wilderness or the Upper Kiamichi River Wilderness.

The **Black Kettle National Grassland** (NG) extends from New Mexico into Oklahoma. This grassland is administered by the Cibola NF. Free camping is allowed in the grassland's picnic areas.

US Fish and Wildlife Service has a developed campground in the Wichita Mountains National Wildlife Refuge (NWR). Doris costs $6.00 for tents and $9.00 for recreational vehicles using electricity. At the Salt Plains NWR in northern Oklahoma, camp free at Jet Recreation Area. Also, camp free at Tishomingo NWR near Lake Texoma. All of these refuges are on bird migration routes.

Oklahoma State Parks (SP) permit camping at most of its 56 parks on an assigned and unassigned basis. Tent sites cost $6.00 while RV sites charge $10.00. Hookups are extra, even if not using the services. These parks offer access to alabaster caverns, gypsum sand dunes, salt plains, shady rivers, plunging waterfalls, steep cliffs, and canyons. Gain insights into Oklahoma history from traditional Indian civilizations, through great cattle drives and tiny pioneer settlements, to modern oil empires.

Cities offering $5.00-or-less camping include Eufaula and Lawton.

Welcome to friendly Oklahoma, a piece of Native America.

▲ ▲

ANGLER POINT
COE (405) 888-4226
State map: D2
From HARDESTY, head
E on OK 3 for 2 miles (3.2 k). Turn Left

(N) on Optima Lake Access Rd for 3 miles (4.8 k). At S end of dam, bear Right to bottom of hill. (Nearby Hardesty Park costs $7.)
FREE so choose a chore. Open All Year.

▲ ▲

21 scattered, open sites. Central faucet, pit toilets, tables, grills, fire rings.
In woods near stream below Optima Lake Dam.
Fish. Walk nature trail or hike farther. Hunting in winter. No generators in quiet hours.
2750 ft (825 m)

APPACHIA BAY

COE (918) 865-2621
State map: M3
Head W on US 64/412 from SAND SPRINGS for 9 miles (14.4 k). Take Bear's Glen Exit, cross overpass, turn Right, take first Left (SW) at sign. Continue 1 mile (1.6 k). (Also see Cowskin Bay South. Nearby Washington Irving South costs $7.)
$4. Open May 21–Sep 10.
18 close, open sites.
Central faucet, pit toilets, tables, fire rings, grills, boat ramp.
Under lots of trees by Keystone Lake. Swim, boat, or fish. Watch wildlife. Bike.
14-day limit. Crowded summer holidays.
750 ft (225 m)

BIG CREEK

COE (918) 443-2250
State map: N1
From NOWATA, head E on US 60 for 5.1 miles (8.2 k). Turn Left (N) on access road and go 2 miles (3.2 k). (Also see Double Creek Cove.)
$4. Open Mar 1–Nov 30; dry camping allowed off-season.
16 close, open sites. Central faucet, pit toilets, tables, fire rings.
Next to Oologah Lake.
Fish. Boat and waterski.
14-day limit.
680 ft (204 m)

BILLY CREEK

Ouachita NF
(918) 653-2991
State map: P6
From BIG CEDAR, head W on OK 63 about 6 miles (9.6 k). Turn Right (N) on CR 22 (changes to dirt) and drive 3 miles

(4.8 k). (Also see Winding Stair.)
$4. Open All Year.
12 scattered, open,, tent sites.
Hand pump, pit toilets, fire rings.
Along south slope of Winding Stair Mountain in remote locale near stream.
Hike to spot wildlife (Billy Creek Trail heads up mountain). Fish.
No trash arrangements (pack it out). 14-day/22-ft limits. Hunting in season.
850 ft (255 m)

BLAINE PARK

COE (405) 886-2989
State map: I3
From CANTON, head N on OK 58A for 1.7 miles (2.7 k)–cross spillway. (Also see Sandy Cove. Nearby Big Bend and Canadian cost $7.)
FREE so choose a chore. Open All Year.
Undesignated scattered, open sites.
Central faucet, pit toilets, tables.
Below Canton Lake dam along North Canadian River.
Boat or fish. Walk Frank Raab Nature Trail.
14-day limit.
1640 ft (492 m)

BLUE CREEK COVE

COE (918) 443-2250
State map: N2
From FOYIL, drive W on CR for 2.3 miles (3.7 k). Turn Right (N). Go 1.2 miles (1.9 k). Turn Left (W) Continue 1.5 miles (2.4 k). (Also see Clermont and Verdigris River Park.)
$5; $10 electric. Open Apr 1–Sep 30; dry camping allowed off-season.
50 close, open sites. Central faucet, flush toilets, showers, dump station, electric hookups, tables, fire rings, boat ramp.
On shores of Oologah Lake.
Boat, ski, or fish.
14-day limit.
680 ft (204 m)

BULL CREEK PENINSULA

COE (918) 396-3170
State map: M2
From SKIATOOK,

▲ ▲

travel W on OK 20 for 15 miles 924 k).
Turn Right (N) and drive 4 miles (6.4 k).
Turn Right (E) for final 1 mile (1.6 k).
(Nearby Tall Chief costs $10.)
FREE so choose a chore.
Open All Year.
26 close, open sites. Pit toilets, tables, fire
rings, grills, boat ramp.
On steep, picturesque bluffs above blue
Skiatook Lake.
Fish. Boat. Take photos.
NO water. 14-day limit. No generators
in quiet hours. Crowded weekends.

BUTCHER PEN

COE (903) 465-4990
State map: L7
Just NE of BROWN,
locate area off OK 78 on Washita River.
(Also see Tishomingo NWR.)
FREE so choose a chore. Open All Year.
10 scattered, open sites. Central faucet,
pit toilets, tables, boat ramp.
Next to Washita River acess point.
Fish.
14-day limit.

CARTERS LANDING

COE (918) 487-5252
State map: O3
From TAHLEQUAH,
travel S on OK 82 for 13 miles (20.8 k).
Turn Left (NE) at sign. (Nearby Elk
Creek and Pettit Bay cost $7.)
$5. Open All Year.
35 scattered, open sites.
Central faucet, pit toilets, tables, fire
rings, grills, boat ramp.
In Blue Mountains on Tenkiller Lake.
Boat. Fish. View wildlife. Take photos.
14-day limit. Hunting in season. No
generators in quiet hours.
632 ft (190 m)

CATO LANDING

COE (918) 487-5252
State map: O4
From VIAN, travel N
on OK 82 for 10 miles (16 k). Turn Left
(W) at sign. (Also see Damsite and
Sixshooter. Nearby Chicken Creek and

Snake Creek cost $7.)
FREE so choose a chore. Open All Year.
6 scattered, open sites.
Central faucet, pit toilets, tables, fire
rings, grills, boat ramp.
In beautiful Snake Creek area of
Tenkiller Lake.
Swim, boat, ski, or fish. Walk nature trail
or hike farther. Spot wildlife.
14-day limit. Hunting in season. No
generators in quiet hours.
632 ft (190 m)

CITY OF EUFAULA CAMPING

(918) 689-2534
State map: N4
Take Lakeshore Dr off
Main St in EUFAULA. (Also see
Highway 9 East.)
FREE so choose a chore. Open All Year.
6 scattered, open,, tent sites.
Central faucet, flush toilets, showers,
tables, grills, boat ramp, store, rentals,
pay phone.
In woods on shore of Lake Eufaula.
Swim, boat, waterski, and fish. Take
photos.

CLERMONT

COE (918) 443-2250
State map: N2
From FOYIL, drive W
on CR for 2.3 miles (3.7 k). Turn Right
(N) and go 3.2 miles (5.1 k). Turn Left
(W). Continue 2.7 miles (4.4 k). (Also see
Blue Creek and Spencer Creek Cove.)
$4. Open Mar 1–Sep 30; dry camping
allowed off-season.
8 close, open sites. Central faucet, flush
toilets, tables, fire rings, boat ramp.
On peninsula in Oologah Lake.
Boat and ski. Fish.
14-day limit.
680 ft (204 m)

COWLINGTON POINT

COE (918) 775-4474
State map: P4
From SALLISAW, head
S on US 59 for 10 miles (16 k). Turn
Right (W) at sign and go 3 miles (4.8 k).

▲ ▲

(Also see Short Mountain Cove and Keota Landing.)
$5; $8 electric. Open All Year.
58 (28 RV-only) scattered, open sites.
Hand pump, pit toilets, dump station, electric hookups, tables, fire rings, grills, boat ramp.
Among rolling hills with mature timber next to Robert S Kerr Lake.
Swim, boat, ski, or fish. Hike and view wildlife.
14-day limit. Hunting in season.
480 ft (144 m)

COWSKIN BAY SOUTH

COE (918) 865-2621
State map: M3
From SAND SPRINGS, take US 64/412 W for 13.5 miles (21.6 k). Drive 1 mile (1.6 k) N on CR. (Also see Appachia Bay.)
$4. Open All Year.
30 close, open sites.
Central faucet, pit toilets, tables, fire rings, grills, boat ramp.
Under big shade trees with good view of Keystone Lake.
Swim. Boat. Fish.
14-day limit.
750 ft (225 m)

CROWDER POINT

COE (918) 484-5135
State map: N5
From EUFAULA, head S on US 69 about 10 miles (16 k). Turn Left. (Also, 5 sites on W side of highway.) (Also see Oak Ridge.)
FREE so choose a chore. Open All Year.
23 close, open sites.
Central faucet, flush toilets, showers, dump station, tables, grills, boat ramp.
Beside Lake Eufaula.
Swim, boat, ski, or fish. Hike loop trail.
14-day limit.
600 ft (180 m)

DAMSITE

COE (918) 487-5252
State map: O4
From GORE, drive N

on OK 100 for 6 miles (9.6 k). (Also see Cato Landing.)
FREE so choose a chore.
Open All Year.
8 close, open, tent sites. Pit toilets, tables, fire rings, grills, boat ramp.
At Tenkiller Lake dam.
Boat, waterski, and swim. Fish. Walk overlook trail. Watch wildlife.
NO water. 14-day limit.
632 ft (190 m)

DAMSITE

COE (918) 247-6391
State map: M3
From KELLYVILLE, travel W on OK 66 for 5 miles (8 k). Turn Right (N) and go 1.5 miles (2.4 k). (Also see Sunset Bay. Nearby Heyburn Park costs $10.)
FREE so choose a chore.
Open All Year.
11 close, open sites. Central faucet, pit toilets, tables, grills, fire rings.
Next to Heyburn Lake dam.
Swim, boat, ski, or fish. View wildlife.
Attend ranger programs.
14-day limit.

DEAD INDIAN LAKE

Black Kettle NG
(405) 497-2143
State map: G4
From CHEYENNE, travel N on OK 47 for 11 miles (17.6 k). (Also see Spring Creek Lake.)
FREE so choose a chore. Open All Year.
12 close, open sites.
Central faucet, pit toilets, tables.
Beside lake.
Fish. Observe wildlife.
14-day limit.
2100 ft (630 m)

DOUBLE CREEK COVE

COE (918) 443-2250
State map: N1
From NOWATA, head S on US 169 about 1 mile (1.6 k). Turn Left (E) on CR before bridge and go 3 miles (4.8 k). (Also see Big Creek.)

▲ ▲

FREE so choose a chore. Open All Year.
Undesignated scattered, open sites.
Central faucet, pit toilets, dump station,
tables, fire rings, boat ramp.
On Oologah Lake.
Boat, ski, or fish.
14-day limit.
680 ft (204 m)

FORT GIBSON PARK

COE (918) 489-5541
State map: O3
From FORT GIBSON,
drive NW across river.
FREE so choose a chore. Open All Year.
7 close, open sites. Central faucet, pit
toilets, dump station, tables, fire rings.
Next to Grand (Neosho) River at end of
Chouteau National Recreation Trail.
Fish. Hike.
No trash arrangements. 14-day limit.

GENTRY CREEK

COE (918) 484-5135
State map: N4
From CHECOTAH,
head W on US 266 about 8 miles (12.8 k).
Turn Left (S).
$4; $7 electric. Open Apr 1–Oct 31.
40 close, open sites. Central faucet, flush
toilets, showers, dump station, electric
hookups, tables, grills, boat ramp.
Next to Lake Eufaula.
Boat or fish.
14-day limit. Hunting in season.
Crowded holidays.
600 ft (180 m)

GORE LANDING

COE (918) 775-4474
State map: O4
From GORE, drive E on
US 64 for 2 miles (3.2 k). (Also see
Sallisaw Creek.)
$5. Open All Year.
24 scattered, open sites.
Central faucet, pit toilets, dump station,
tables, fire rings, grills, boat ramp.
On shaded Illinois River bank with trout
stream.
Fish or boat.

14-day limit.
480 ft (144 m)

HICKORY POINT

COE (918) 484-5135
State map: N5
From MCALESTER,
drive E on OK 31 for 4 miles (6.4 k).
Bear Right (E) on signed CR and travel
6 miles (9.6 k).
FREE so choose a chore.
Open All Year.
10 close, open sites. Central faucet, pit
toilets, tables, boat ramp.
Beside Lake Eufaula.
Boat and fish.
14-day limit.
600 ft (180 m)

HIGHWAY 9 EAST

COE (918) 484-5135
State map: N5
From EUFAULA, take
OK 9 SE about 6 miles (9.6 k)–cross lake.
Turn Right (S). (Larger camp across
highway costs $7. Also see City of
Eufaula and Oak Ridge.)
$4; $7 electric. Open Apr 1–Oct 31; dry
camping allowed off-season.
12 close, open sites. Central faucet, flush
toilets, showers, dump station, electric
hookups, tables, grills, boat ramp.
Next to Lake Eufaula so swim, boat, ski,
or fish. Walk nature trail.
14-day limit.
600 ft (180 m)

HOLIDAY COVE

COE (918) 484-5135
State map: N4
Take EXIT 250 off I-40
(W of CHECOTAH). Go S on OK 150 for
2 miles (3.2 k). Turn Left (E).
FREE so choose a chore.
Open Apr 1–Oct 31.
15 scattered, open sites. Central faucet,
pit toilets, tables, boat ramp.
On Lake Eufaula.
Boat and fish.
14-day limit. Hunting in season.
600 ft (180 m)

▲ ▲

JACKSON BAY

COE (918) 682-1602
State map: O3
From WAGONER,
drive S on OK 16 for 7 miles (11.2 k).
Turn Left (E) on CR and go 4 miles
(6.4 k) toward Sequoah Bay SP. Turn
Left (N) and continue 2 miles (3.2 k).
(Nearby Sequoah Bay costs $9.)
FREE so choose a chore. Open All Year.
Undesignated scattered, open sites.
Pit toilets, tables, fire rings, boat ramp.
Next to Fort Gibson Lake.
Fish or boat.
NO water. No trash arrangements (pack
it out). 14-day limit.
585 ft (176 m)

KEOTA LANDING

COE (918) 775-4474
State map: O4
From KEOTA, go N for
2 miles (3.2 k). (See Cowlington Point.)
$5. Open All Year.
32 scattered, open sites.
Central faucet, pit toilets, dump station,
tables, fire rings, grills, boat ramp.
Under native oak beside Robert S Kerr
Lake.
Swim, boat, ski, or fish. Observe wildlife.
14-day limit. Hunting in season.
480 ft (144 m)

KEYSTONE RAMP

COE (918) 865-2621
State map: M3
From MANNFORD,
take OK 51 E for 4 miles (6.4 k). Turn
Left (N) on access road and proceed
1.5 miles (2.4 k). (Also see Old Mannford
Ramp. Nearby New Mannford Ramp
and Salt Creek North cost $7.)
FREE so choose a chore. Open All Year.
10 close, open sites.
Central faucet, pit toilets, tables, fire
rings, grills, boat ramp.
With some trees along beautiful rocky
bluffs of Keystone Lake.
Boat and fish. Swim.
14-day limit.
750 ft (225 m)

KIAMICHI PARK

COE (405) 326-3345
State map: N7
From HUGO, head E on
US 70 for 5 miles (8 k). Turn Left (N) on
CR. Follow signs. (Also see Salt Creek.)
$5 at 10 sites; others $7-10.
Open Mar 1–Nov 30.
108 close, open sites.
Central faucet, flush toilets, showers,
dump station, electric hookups, tables,
grills, fire rings, pay phone.
Next to Hugo Lake in dense woods of
maple, ash, sycamore, elm, oak, and
hickory plus flowering shrubs and
wildflowers.
Swim, boat, ski, or fish. Walk nature
trail. Take photos. Spot wildlife.
14-day limit.

LAKE LAWTONKA EAST

Lawton City Parks
(405) 529-2663
State map: I6
From LAWTON, take I-44 N about
7 miles (11.2 k). Exit W on OK 49 and go
5 miles (8 k). Turn Right (N) on OK 58
and continue 3 miles (4.8 k). (Nearby
Lake Ellsworth costs $8.)
$5 primitive; $8 in campground.
Open All Year.
30 scattered, open sites.
Central faucet, flush toilets, showers,
dump station, electric hookups, tables,
fire rings, grills, boat ramp.
Next to lake with western view of Mt
Scott in Wichita Mountains.
Swim, boat, and waterski. Fish. View
wildlife.
14-day limit. Hunting in season.
Occasionally crowded.

LEBANON

COE (903) 465-4990
State map: L7
From LEBANON, head
1 mile (1.6 k) S.
$5; $8 electric. Open All Year.
20 close, screened sites.
Water at every site, pit toilets, dump
station, electric hookups, tables, fire

rings, grills, boat ramp.
Next to Lake Texoma so boat or fish.
14-day limit.

LEFLORE LANDING

COE (918) 775-4474
State map: P4
From SPIRO, go E on
OK 9 for 2 miles (3.2 k). Turn Left (N)
and travel 6 miles (9.6 k).
FREE so choose a chore. Open All Year.
14 scattered, open sites.
Central faucet, pit toilets, dump station,
tables, fire rings, grills, boat ramp.
In shade along Arkansas River.
Fish. Boat. Visit nearby Spiro Mounds to
appreciate rich, mystical native culture.
14-day limit. High water possible.
460 ft (138 m)

LONGDALE

COE (405) 886-2989
State map: I3
From LONGDALE,
drive W on CR for 2 miles (3.2 k). (Also
see Sandy Cove.)
$4. Open Apr 25–Sep 10; dry camping
allowed off-season.
42 close, open sites.
Central faucet, pit toilets, tables, fire
rings, boat ramp, shelter.
Beside Canton Lake.
Swim, boat, ski, or fish.
14-day limit.
1640 ft (492 m)

LOST RAPIDS

COE (918) 933-4239
State map: O7
Locate area near NEW
RINGOLD, off OK 3. (Also see Turkey
Creek. Nearby Little River costs $8.)
$5; $8 electric. Open Mar 1–Nov 30.
Undesignated close, open sites.
Central faucet, flush toilets, dump
station, electric hookups, tables, fire
rings, grills, boat ramp.
Next to Pine Creek Lake.
Boat and fish.
14-day limit. Occasionally crowded.
Hunting in season.

MILL CREEK BAY

COE (918) 484-5135
State map: N4
From EUFAULA, drive
W on OK 9 for 6 miles (9.6 k). Turn Left
(S) and go 2 miles (3.2 k).
FREE so choose a chore. Open All Year.
12 close, open sites. Central faucet, pit
toilets, tables, grills, boat ramp.
On Lake Eufaula.
Boat or fish.
14-day limit.
600 ft (180 m)

MONEKA PARK

COE (405) 963-2111
State map: J7
From WAURIKA, drive
NW for 5 miles (8 k) on OK 5. (Also see
Wichita Ridge. Nearby Chisholm Trail
Ridge and Kiowa I cost $10.)
FREE so choose a chore. Open All Year.
38 scattered, open sites. Central faucet,
pit toilets, tables, grills, fire rings.
Next to creek in woods off Waurika
Lake.
Fish. Walk nature trail and view wildlife.
14-day limit.

MOUNTAIN FORK PARK

COE (405) 494-6374
State map: P7
From BROKEN BOW,
travel E on US 70 for 5 miles (8 k). Turn
Left (N) on CR. Proceed 3 miles (4.8 k).
$5. Open All Year.
12 close, screened sites. Water at every
site, pit toilets, tables, grills.
On Mountain Fork River below Broken
Bow Lake dam.
Canoe, boat, or fish. Watch wildlife.
14-day limit.
410 ft (123 m)

OAK RIDGE

COE (918) 484-5135
State map: N5
From EUFAULA, go S
on US 69 for 4 miles (6.4 k). Turn Left
(E) on OK 9A. (Also see Highway 9 East
and Crowder Point.)

▲ ▲

$4; $7 electric. Open Apr 1–Oct 31; dry
camping allowed off-season.
13 close, open sites.
Central faucet, pit toilets, electric
hookups, tables, grills, boat ramp.
Next to Lake Eufaula.
Swim, boat, ski, or fish.
14-day limit.
600 ft (180 m)

OLD MANNFORD RAMP

COE (918) 865-2621
State map: M3
From MANNFORD,
head W on OK 51 for 2 miles (3.2 k).
Turn Right (N) on OK 48 and drive
4 miles (6.4 k). Turn at sign. (Also see
Keystone Ramp. Nearby New Mannford
Ramp costs $7.)
FREE so choose a chore. Open All Year.
29 close, screened sites.
Central faucet, pit toilets, tables, fire
rings, grills, boat ramp.
Among large, old shade trees next to
Keystone Lake.
Boat and fish. Swim. Relax.
14-day limit.
750 ft (225 m)

OSAGE PLAINS

COE (918) 532-4334
State map: M1
From COPAN, go W on
OK 10 for 4 miles (6.4 k). Turn Right (N)
on gravel road and continue 2 miles
(3.2 k). (Nearby Post Oak and
Washington Cove cost $10.)
FREE so choose a chore. Open All Year.
24 close, screened sites. Pit toilets, tables,
fire rings, grills, boat ramp.
Among bottomland hardwood
overlooking Copan Lake.
Swim, boat, ski, or fish. View wildlife.
NO water. 14-day limit. Hunting in
season.

OSAGE POINT

COE (918) 865-2621
State map: M2
From CLEVELAND,
drive NE on OK 99 for 2 miles (3.2 k).

Turn Right (E) on twisting CR and travel
4 miles (6.4 k).
FREE so choose a chore. Open All Year.
19 scattered, open sites. Central faucet,
flush toilets, showers, dump station,
tables, fire rings, grills, boat ramp.
Under big shade trees along shores of
Keystone Lake.
Fish and boat. Enjoy seclusion.
14-day limit.

PECAN PARK

COE (918) 489-5541
State map: N3
From WAGONER, head
S on US 69 about 9 miles (14.4 k),
passing river. Turn Left (E) toward
Chouteau Dam.
FREE so choose a chore. Open All Year.
10 close, open sites. Central faucet, pit
toilets, tables, fire rings.
In two units (North and South) next to
Verdigris River dam at mile 46.5 of
Chouteau National Recreation Trail.
Fish. Hike.
No trash arrangements. 14-day limit.

POTATO HILLS SOUTH

COE (918) 569-4131
State map: O6
From CLAYTON, drive
N on OK 2 for 6 miles (9.6 k). (Nearby
Potato Hills Central costs $10.)
FREE so choose a chore. Open All Year.
18 close, open sites.
Central faucet, pit toilets, dump station,
tables, fire rings, grills, boat ramp.
Among hardwood and pine next to
Sardis Lake.
Swim, boat, or fish. Walk nature trail.
View wildlife.
14-day limit. Occasionally crowded.

RATTAN LANDING

COE (405) 326-3345
State map: N7
From RATTAN, travel
W on OK 3 about 4 miles (6.4 k).
FREE so choose a chore.
Open All Year.
10 close, open sites.

Central faucet, pit toilets, tables, fire rings, grills, boat ramp.
On Kiamichi River.
Boat or fish. Observe wildlife.
14-day limit. Hunting in season.

ROADS END

COE (903) 465-4990
State map: L7
From KINGSTON, drive S on OK 70A about 7 miles (11.2 k).
FREE so choose a chore.
Open All Year.
18 scattered, open sites.
Pit toilets, tables, fire rings, boat ramp.
On Lake Texoma.
Fish or boat.
NO water. No trash arrangements (pack it out). 14-day limit.

ROCKY POINT

COE (918) 489-5541
State map: N3
From INOLA, drive SW on OK 33 for 4 miles (6.4 k). Turn Left.
FREE so choose a chore. Open All Year.
20 close, open sites.
Central faucet, pit toilets, tables, fire rings, boat ramp, shelter.
Next to confluence of Commodore Creek and Verdigris River at mile 16.5 of Chouteau National Recreation Trail.
Boat. Fish. Hike.
14-day limit.

SALLISAW CREEK

COE (918) 775-4474
State map: O4
W of SALLISAW, exit I-40 at 303 milemarker. Drive S for 2.5 miles (4 k). (Also see Gore Landing.)
FREE so choose a chore.
Open All Year.
11 close, screened sites.
Hand pump, pit toilets, dump station, tables, fire rings, grills, boat ramp.
In shade with scenic view of Robert S Kerr Lake.
Swim, boat, ski, or fish. Spot wildlife.
14-day limit.
490 ft (147 m)

SALT CREEK

COE (405) 326-3345
State map: N7
On E side of HUGO, take OK 93 N for 3 miles (4.8 k). Turn Right (E) on CR and go 1 mile (1.6 k). (Also see Kiamichi Park.)
$5 at 12 sites; others $7.
Open Mar 1 – Nov 30; dry camping allowed off-season.
25 close, open sites. Central faucet, flush toilets, showers, dump station, tables, fire rings, grills, boat ramp.
In woods next to Hugo Lake.
Boat or fish. View wildlife.
14-day limit. Hunting in season.

SALT PLAINS NWR-Jet RA

(405) 626-4794
State map: I2
From JET, drive N for 3 miles (4.8 k) on OK 38.
FREE so choose a chore.
Open Apr 1–Oct 15.
15 scattered, open sites. Central faucet, pit toilets, tables, fire rings, boat ramp.
Along .75 mile (1.2 k) strip of grass and trees next to Great Salt Plains Lake.
Swim, boat, or fish. View wildlife.
14-day limit. Crowded holidays.
1125 ft (338 m)

SANDY COVE

COE (405) 886-2989
State map: I3
From CANTON, head N on OK 58A for 5.2 miles (8.3 k) – cross dam. (Also see Blaine Park or Longdale.)
$5; $8 electric. Open All Year.
37 close, open sites. Central faucet, flush toilets, showers, electric hookups, tables, fire rings, boat ramp, shelter.
On shores of Canton Lake.
Swim, boat, waterski, and fish.
14-day limit.
1680 ft (504 m)

SARDIS COVE

COE (918) 569-4131
State map: O6
From CLAYTON, go W

▲ ▲

on OK 43 for 10 miles (16 k).
$5; $8 electric. Open All Year.
45 close, open sites. Central faucet, pit toilets, dump station, electric hookups, tables, fire rings, grills, boat ramp.
In hardwood/pine next to Sardis Lake.
Boat or fish.
14-day limit. Occasionally crowded.

SHORT MOUNTAIN COVE

COE (918) 775-4474
State map: P4
From SALLISAW, head S on US 59 for 9 miles (16 k). Turn Right (W) at sign and go 2 miles (3.2 k). (Also see Cowlington Point. Nearby Applegate Cove costs $10.)
$5; $8 electric. Open All Year.
48 scattered, open sites. Hand pump, pit toilets, dump station, electric hookups, tables, fire rings, grills, boat ramp.
In scenic, shaded setting on Robert S Kerr Lake.
Swim, boat, ski, or fish. Walk nature trail. Hike for photos and wildlife.
14-day limit. Hunting in season.
480 ft (144 m)

SIXSHOOTER

COE (918) 487-5252
State map: O4
From VIAN, travel N on OK 82 for 14 miles (22.4 k). Turn Left (W) at sign and go 2 miles (3.2 k). (Also see Cato Landing.)
FREE so choose a chore. Open All Year.
25 close, open sites. Central faucet, pit toilets, tables, fire rings, boat ramp.
On Tenkiller Lake.
Boat and fish. Swim.
14-day limit.
670 ft (201 m)

SIZEMORE

COE (918) 487-5252
State map: O3
From TAHLEQUAH, travel S on OK 82 about 8 miles (12.8 k). Continue S through Pettit (W side of lake) for 4 miles (6.4 k). Turn Left (SE) for final 2 miles (3.2 k). (Nearby Pettit

Bay and Strayhorn Landing cost $7.)
$5. Open All Year.
32 close, open sites.
Central faucet, pit toilets, tables, fire rings, grills, boat ramp.
On wooded, gentle slope next to Tenkiller Lake.
Swim, boat, ski, or fish. Observe wildlife.
14-day limit. Hunting in season. No generators in quiet hours.
632 ft (190 m)

SKIPOUT LAKE

Black Kettle NG
(405) 497-2143
State map: G4
From CHEYENNE, travel W on OK 47 for 10 miles (16 k). (Also see Spring Creek Lake.)
FREE so choose a chore. Open All Year.
12 close, open sites.
Central faucet, pit toilets, tables.
Next to lake.
Fish. Relax. Spot wildlife.
14-day limit.
2100 ft (630 m)

SPENCER CREEK COVE

COE (918) 443-2250
State map: N2
From FOYIL, go W on CR for 2.3 miles (3.7 k). Turn Right (N). Drive 5 miles (8 k). (Also see Clermont.)
$5; $10 electric. Open Apr 1–Sep 30; dry camping allowed off-season.
85 close, open sites.
Central faucet, flush toilets, showers, dump station, electric hookups, tables, fire rings, boat ramp, shelter.
Next to Oologah Lake.
Boat, ski, or fish.
14-day limit.
680 ft (204 m)

SPRING CREEK LAKE

Black Kettle NG
(405) 497-2143
State map: G4
From CHEYENNE, travel N on OK 47 for 10 miles (16 k). Turn Left (W) on CR and go about 8 miles (12.8 k). (Also

see Dead Indian Lake and Skipout Lake.)
FREE so choose a chore. Open All Year.
9 close, open sites.
Central faucet, pit toilets, tables.
In band of trees next to lake.
Fish. Observe wildlife.
14-day limit.
2300 ft (690 m)

STANDING ROCK

COE (918) 487-5252
State map: O3
From TAHLEQUAH,
travel S on OK 82 for 19 miles (30.4 k).
Turn Right (E) at sign. (Nearby Cookson
Bend and Elk Creek cost $7.)
$5. Open All Year.
10 close, open sites.
Central faucet, pit toilets, tables, fire
rings, grills, boat ramp.
On gentle, wooded slope next to
Tenkiller Lake.
Swim, boat, ski, or fish. Walk nature
trail. Hike for photos and wildlife.
14-day limit. Hunting in season. No
generators in quiet hours.
632 ft (190 m)

SUNNYSIDE RAMP

COE (918) 443-2250
State map: N2
From TALALA, travel E
on CR for 4 miles (6.4 k).
FREE so choose a chore. Open All Year.
8 close, open sites. Central faucet, pit
toilets, tables, fire rings, boat ramp.
Next to Oologah Lake.
Boat and waterski. Fish.
14-day limit.
680 ft (204 m)

SUNSET BAY

COE (918) 247-6391
State map: M3
From KELLYVILLE,
travel W on OK 66 for 5 miles (8 k).
Turn Right (N) and drive 1.5 miles
(2.4 k). (Also see Damsite. Nearby
Heyburn Park costs $10.)
$4. Open May 1–Oct 31; dry camping
allowed off-season.

14 close, open sites.
Central faucet, pit toilets, tables, fire
rings, grills, boat ramp.
Next to Heyburn Lake.
Swim, boat, ski, or fish. Take photos.
14-day limit.

TISHOMINGO NWR

(405) 371-2402
State map: L7
From TISHOMINGO,
drive E on OK 78 for .5 mile (800 m).
Turn Right (S) at sign and go 3 miles
(4.8 k). (Also see Butcher Pen.)
FREE so choose a chore. Open All Year.
10 scattered, open sites. Central faucet,
flush toilets, tables, fire rings.
In hardwood-covered bottomland among
rolling savannah.
Climb observation tower. View wildlife,
including incredible array of birds. Fish.

TRADERS BEND

COE (405) 762-5611
State map: K1
From NEWKIRK, travel
E on CR for 6 miles (9.6 k). Turn Left (N)
on gravel road and drive 1 mile (1.6 k).
Turn Right (E) and go 1 mile (1.6 k).
Turn Left (N) for last 1 mile (1.6 k).
(Nearby Bear Creek Cove costs $11.)
FREE so choose a chore. Open All Year.
10 close, open sites.
Central faucet, pit toilets, tables, fire
rings, grills, boat ramp.
On river floodplain at backwaters of
Kaw Lake.
Boat or fish. Observe wildlife.
14-day limit. Hunting in season.
1050 ft (315 m)

TULLAHASSEE LOOP

COE (918) 489-5541
State map: N3
From MUSKOGEE,
drive N on US 69 for 6 miles (9.6 k).
Head W on OK 51B for 3 miles (4.8 k).
Turn Right (N) and go 2 miles (3.2 k).
$5. Open All Year.
9 close, open sites.
Central faucet, flush toilets, dump

▲ ▲

station, tables, fire rings, boat ramp.
On bend in Verdigris River at mile 41.5
on Chouteau National Recreation Trail.
Boat and fish. Hike. Observe wildlife.
14-day limit.

TURKEY CREEK

COE (918) 933-4239
State map: O7
Find area between
RINGOLD and NEW RINGOLD, off
OK 3. (Also see Lost Rapids.)
FREE so choose a chore. Open All Year.
Undesignated scattered, open sites.
Central faucet, dump station, tables, fire
rings, grills, boat ramp.
In two sections with good views of Pine
Creek Lake.
Fish and boat.
14-day limit. Hunting in season.
Occasionally crowded and noisy.

TWIN COVE POINT

COE (918) 847-2001
State map: M2
From BARNSDALL,
head S for 1 mile (1.6 k). (Nearby Birch
Cove costs $10.)
FREE so choose a chore. Open All Year.
12 close, open sites.
Central faucet, pit toilets, tables, fire
rings, boat ramp, shelter, playground.
Among rolling hills with oak/hickory
stands next to Birch Lake.
Swim, boat, or fish. Observe wildlife.
14-day limit. Hunting in season.

VERDIGRIS RIVER PARK

COE (918) 443-2250
State map: N2
From OOLOGAH, drive
E on OK 88 about 5 miles (8 k). Cross
dam. (Also see Blue Creek Cove. Nearby
Hawthorne Bluff costs $10.)
FREE so choose a chore. Open All Year.
9 close, open sites.
Central faucet, pit toilets, dump station,
tables, fire rings.
Near Oologah Lake.
Boat or fish nearby. Walk Skull Hollow
Nature Trail at Hawthorn Bluff.

14-day limit.
680 ft (204 m)

WICHITA RIDGE

COE (405) 963-2111
State map: J7
From HASTINGS, head
N on CR for 4.5 miles (7.2 k). (Also see
Moneka Park. Nearby Chisholm Trail
Ridge and Kiowa I cost $10.)
$4; $7 electric. Open All Year.
27 scattered, open sites. Central faucet,
pit toilets, electric hookups, tables, fire
rings, grills, boat ramp, shelter.
On flat prairie next to Waurika Lake.
Swim, boat, or fish.
14-day limit.

WILLAFA WOODS

COE (903) 465-4990
State map: L7
From CARTWRIGHT,
drive N for 4 miles (6.4 k).
$4. Open All Year.
14 close, open sites.
Central faucet, pit toilets, dump station,
tables, fire rings, boat ramp.
On shady banks of Lake Texoma.
Fish and boat.
14-day limit.

WINDING STAIR

Ouachita NF
(918) 653-2991
State map: P6
From BIG CEDAR, drive N on US 259
for 5 miles (8 k). Turn Left (W) on OK 1
(Talimena Scenic Drive) for 2.5 miles
(4 k). (Also see Billy Creek.)
$5. Open Apr 15–Nov 30.
26 scattered, screened sites.
Hand pump, flush toilets, tables, grills,
fire rings.
On mountain top in secluded
pine/hardwood setting with good views.
Enjoy Emerald Vista overlook. Walk
nature trail or hike farther along
Ouachita National Recreation Trail or
Billy Creek Trail.
14-day limit. Hunting in season.
2300 ft (690 m)

▲ ▲

PENNSYLVANIA
CAMPGROUND LOCATIONS

▶ ▶ Find location on facing page map grid. ▶ ▶
▼ ▼ Locate area campgrounds on these page numbers. ▼ ▼

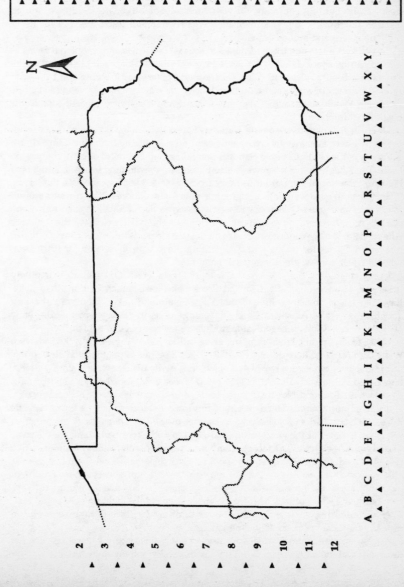

Pennsylvania

Grid conforms to official state map. For your copy, call (800) VISIT-PA or write Travel Marketing, 453 Forum Building, Harrisburg, PA 17120.

PUBLIC LANDS CAMPING

Pennsylvania boasts "America starts here." American liberty began here three centuries ago when a Quaker, William Penn, founded the colony, Penn's Woods, as a haven for the oppressed. Later, Philadelphia hosted the meeting for the signers of the Declaration of Independence. Then, General George Washington turned revolutionaries into soldiers at a place now called Valley Forge. Other firsts include newspaper, cookbook, lending library, university, savings bank, stock exchange, independent hospital, firefighting company, oil well, steam locomotive, steamship, computer, electron microscope, robotics institute. Pennsylvania still leads the way for its 12 million citizens and millions of visitors.

Too, there's a treasure trove of things to see–vibrant cities and traditional farms as well as natural spaces filled with trees, lakes, and streams. Blaze a trail and explore all the natural beauty–view fall color; ski through winter; watch spring paint the wild rhododendron, dogwood, and mountain laurel; while away summer sailing Lake Erie or fishing Pymatuning (one of the largest manmade lakes) or Conneaut (one of the deepest natural lakes).

Discover the rugged **Allegheny National Forest** (NF), 500,000 acres of dense forest in northwestern Pennsylvania, with miles and miles of hiking trails (including almost 100 miles of the North Country National Scenic Trail) and 44 miles of cross-country ski trails. The Allegheny NF operates 17 campgrounds, 4 swimming beaches, and 8 boat launches. Developed campgrounds range from $5.00–$11.00. For canoeists, the service offers 6 boat-in (also walk-in) campgrounds plus 4 conventional campgrounds around the 91-mile shoreline of Allegheny Reservoir. Between Buckaloons Recreation Area and the town of Tionesta, seven islands in the Allegheny River create the 400-acre Allegheny Islands Wilderness. Nearby Hickory Creek Wilderness provides 8,570 forever-wild acres for hiking and backpacking. Keep your eyes open for black bear, whitetail deer, turkey, grouse, pheasant, and more.

Lakes created by the **US Army Corps of Engineers** (COE) include Allegheny Reservoir, Cowanesque Lake, Crooked Creek Lake, East Branch Clarion River Lake, Raystown Lake, Shenango River Lake, Tioga-Hammond Lakes, Tionesta Lake, and Youghiogheny Lake. Allegheny Reservoir campgrounds are managed by the Allegheny National Forest. COE-managed campgrounds range from free to $11.00.

Other federal public lands camping areas include canoe-camping on the Delaware Water Gap National Recreation Area (NRA). For a permit to paddle and camp in this scenic area between Pennsylvania and New Jersey, write the Delaware Water Gap NRA Superintendent in Bushkill, PA 18234 or call (717) 588-2435. Too, the major hiking trails, Appalachian Trail and North Country Trail, wind their ways through Pennsylvania.

The commonwealth's Department of Environmental Resources administers the Bureau of **State Parks** (SP). 55 state parks offer over 7,000 campsites. Some are open year-round; some, for the long season (mid-April to mid-December); some, for the short season (mid-April to mid-October). Camping rates vary with facilities from primitive ($7.00) to modern ($9.00) plus electric hookup. Backpack the 70-mile Laurel Highlands Hiking Trail that also serves cross-country skiers and snowshoers. There are 8 free overnight areas. Each area contains 5 shelters, space for 30 tents, 2 comfort stations, and a drinking water source. Make reservations to spend the night on this special trail.

A few **counties**, such as Venango, offer camping facilities though fees are too expensive to qualify for the following listings.

As you explore Pennsylvania from first to last, experience the sense of personal discovery that makes travel so fulfilling. There's really nothing quite like it.

▲ ▲

BEAVER MEADOWS

Allegheny NF
(814) 927-6628
State map: G4

From MARIENVILLE, drive N on N Forest St for 5 miles (8 k)–becomes gravel FR 128.
$5; reservations accepted at (814) 927-6628 for an additional $6.
Open Apr–Dec; dry camping allowed off-season.
38 close, screened sites.
Hand pump, pit toilets, tables, fire rings, boat ramp, pay phone.
In peaceful, red pine forest near small lake.
Hike. Fish or boat (no motors). Observe wildlife.
14-day limit. Hunting in season. Crowded holiday weekends.
1760 ft (528 m)

HEARTS CONTENT

Allegheny NF
(814) 968-3232
State map: F4

S of WARREN, take Pleasant Dr (Mohawk Exit off US 6) S for 11 miles (17.6 k). Turn Left (SE) and continue 4 miles (6.4 k).
$5.
Open May 12–Sep 30; dry camping allowed off-season.
26 scattered, screened sites.
Central faucet, pit toilets, dump station, tables, grills, fire rings.
In remote, scenic setting.
Hike several trails and view wildlife or take photos. Fish.
14-day limit. Hunting in season.
2000 ft (600 m)

KELLETTVILLE

COE (814) 755-3512
State map: F4

From TIONESTA, head N on US 62 for 7 miles (11.2 k). Turn Right (E) on PA 666 for 11 miles (17.6 k) to KELLETTVILLE. Look for bridge on Right.
$4.

Open May–Sep; dry camping allowed off-season.
20 close, open sites.
Central faucet, flush toilets, dump station, tables, fire rings.
Along sparkling waters of Tionesta Creek in secluded valley of mountainous region.
Canoe. Swim or fish. Walk nature trail. Hike nearby North Country National Scenic Trail. Mountain bike. Attend ranger programs.
14-day limit. Hunting in season. No generators in quiet hours.
1100 ft (330 m)

MERCER RA

COE (412) 962-7746
State map: B5

Head S on PA 18 about 15 miles (24 k) from GREENVILLE to East Lake Rd. Follow signs. (Nearby Shenango RA costs $8.)
FREE for 10 sites; $4 for 20 sites.
Open May 15–Sep 15.
30 close, open sites.
Hand pump, pit toilets, tables, fire rings, pay phone.
Next to Shenango River Lake.
Boat and ski. Canoe. Swim or fish. Hike. Observe wildlife.
14-day limit.
900 ft (270 m)

MINISTER CREEK

Allegheny NF
(814) 968-3232
State map: G4

From SHEFFIELD, take PA 666 SW for 14.7 miles (23.5 k).
$5.
Open May 12–Sep 30; dry camping allowed off-season.
6 scattered, screened sites.
Hand pump, pit toilets, tables, fire rings.
Next to creek.
Fish. Hike to view wildlife (North Country Scenic Trail passes through).
14-day limit. Hunting in season.
1200 ft (360 m)

▲ ▲

OLD STATE ROAD
WALK-IN/BOAT-IN

Allegheny NF
(814) 362-4613
State map: H3

From MARSHBURG, drive W on PA 59 about 9 miles (14.4 k). Bear Right (NW) on FR 147 and go about 1.5 miles (2.4 k). Walk-in about .5 mile (800 m). To boat, put in at PA 59 bridge and go N for 1 mile (1.6 k). (Also see Pine Grove Boat-In.)
FREE so choose a chore.
Open Apr 15–Sep 30; dry camping allowed off-season.
28 close, screened, tent sites.
Hand pump, pit toilets.
On Allegheny Reservoir.
Enjoy seclusion. Fish.
No trash arrangements (pack it out).
14-day limit.
1350 ft (405 m)

PINE GROVE BOAT-IN

Allegheny NF
(814) 362-4613
State map: H3

From MARSHBURG, drive W on PA 59 about 11 miles (17.6 k). Put in at PA 59 bridge and go N for 1.5 miles (2.4 k). (See Old State Road Walk-In/Boat-In.)
FREE so choose a chore.
Open Apr 15–Sep 30; dry camping allowed off-season.
28 close, screened, tent sites.
Hand pump, pit toilets.
Next to Allegheny Reservoir.
Fish. Enjoy quiet.
No trash arrangements (pack it out).
14-day limit.

SUSQUEHANNOCK

COE (814) 658-3405
State map: L9
From HUNTINGDON, drive S on PA 26 for 7 miles (11.2 k). Turn Left (SW) at road to Hesston and travel 3 miles (4.8 k). At "Y" in road, bear Left and go 1 mile (1.6 k). At first road on Right, turn into entrance. (Nearby Seven Points costs $11.)

FREE at 16 sites; $5 for 53 sites.
Open Apr 1–Dec 15.
69 (8 tent-only) close, open sites.
Central faucet, pit toilets, tables, grills.
In wooded location on Raystown Lake.
Canoe, boat, or fish. Hike. Watch birds.
Take photos.
30-day limit.

TIONESTA LAKESHORE BOAT-IN

COE (814) 755-3512
State map: F5
From TIONESTA, go S on PA 36 for 1 mile (1.6 k). Turn Left (E) at sign and drive to boat launch. Boat-in sites range from 1–2 miles (1.6–3.2 k).
FREE so choose a chore.
Open All Year.
30 close, open, tent sites.
Fire rings, boat ramp.
In two locations on shores of beautiful Tionesta Lake in rugged hill country.
Swim, boat, ski, or fish. Observe wildlife.
NO water. No toilet facilities. No trash arrangements (pack it out). 14-day limit.
1100 ft (330 m)

TIONESTA OUTFLOW

COE (814) 755-3512
State map: F5
Head S out of TIONESTA on PA 36. Turn Left (E) before Tionesta Creek Bridge and drive 1 mile (1.6 k).
FREE at 7 sites; $7 at sites 1–32.
Open All Year.
39 close, open sites.
Central faucet, pit toilets, dump station, tables, fire rings, grills, boat ramp, playground, pay phone.
Along pristine waters of Tionesta Creek in forested valley below dam.
Swim, boat, or fish. Canoe too. Walk nature trail or hike farther to view wildlife. Mountain bike. Attend ranger programs.
14-day limit.
1100 ft (330 m)

▲ ▲

TOMPKINS WALK-IN

COE (717) 827-2166

State map: P3

Head E on Bliss Rd for 5 miles (8 k) from LAWRENCEVILLE. Register at main campground then drive E on Bliss Rd for .25 mile (400 m). Walk-in about 500 ft (150 m).

FREE so choose a chore.

Open May 15 – Sep 5; dry camping allowed off-season.

16 close, open, tent sites.

Hand pump, pit toilets, tables, fire rings.

In woods next to Cowanesque Lake.

Swim, boat, and fish. Enjoy seclusion.

14-day limit.

1090 ft (327 m)

▲ ▲

RHODE ISLAND
PUBLIC LANDS CAMPING

The tiny state of Rhode Island offers surprising variety in its natural settings. Camp in the woods covering over 50 percent of the state, along the 400-mile coast, or on the islands of Narragansett Bay.

Unfortunately, to qualify for this price-conscious guide, the only developed public lands camping area requires a horse. Around Exeter, find the state's $3.00 per night Legrand G Reynolds Horsemen's Camping Area.

Rhode Island State Parks (SP) charge residents $8.00 and non-residents $12.00 to camp at its developed sites. There is an additional $2.00 charge for utilities where available. Near Charlestown, camp at Burlingame SP, Charleston Breachway, or Ninigret Conservation Area (CA). At Chepache, try the George Washington Management Area. Last, but not least, find the Fishermen's Memorial SP near Narragansett.

Municipalities such as Jamestown, Middletown, and Portsmouth provide camping too. The prices, however, range from $13.00 for tents to $22.00 for recreational vehicles requiring hookups.

Under Rhode Island law, overnight camping is prohibited in rest/picnic areas, on public highways, and on noncamping state and municipal beaches and their parking lots. By town ordinance, there is no camping on Block Island. So, before setting up your camp in a questionable undeveloped location, check with police or conservation officers.

Rhode Island

Rhode Island sends an information packet. Call (800) 556-2484
or write Tourism Division, 7 Jackson Waterway, Providence, RI 02903.

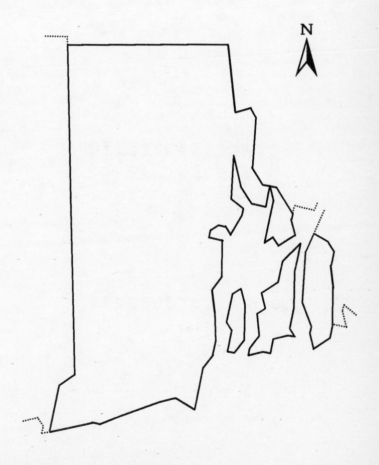

N

SOUTH CAROLINA
CAMPGROUND LOCATIONS

▶ ▶ Find location on facing page map grid. ▶ ▶
▼ ▼ Locate area campgrounds on these page numbers. ▼ ▼

GRID	PAGE
A2	355, 358
B1	355, 356, 361
B2	356, 358
C1	358
C2	357, 360
C4	355, 356, 359, 360
C5	361
C9	359
D3	356, 359
E3	357, 358, 359
E4	358
G8	357, 360
G9	356

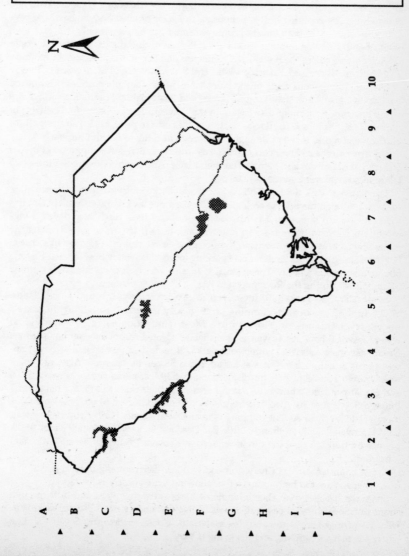

South Carolina

Grid conforms to official state map. For your copy, call (803) 734-0122
or write Division of Tourism, PO Box 71, Columbia, SC 29201.

▲ ▲

PUBLIC LANDS CAMPING

In South Carolina, look for smiling faces and beautiful places. This southeastern state claims to have friendly people stretching from its shell-studded sands to its mist-crowned peaks. Between the coast and the mountains, find sparkling lakes, quiet rivers, and frolicking streams among patchwork of forest, farm, and town.

On the federal level of public lands, the **US Forest Service** manages the Sumter and Francis Marion national forests. Sumter National Forest (NF) contains 265,000 acres while the Francis Marion NF encompasses 250,000 acres. The two forests claim 450 developed campsites, 1 wilderness (Ellicott Rock), the Chattooga National Wild and Scenic River, 2 swimming beaches, thousands of acres of lakes and streams, and over 200 miles of trails. In both forests, primitive camping is by permit only–for your own safety. South Carolina hunting season is the longest in the country. Sumter NF lies in three sections - one in the Blue Ridge Mountains and two in the piedmont or foothills. Ellicott Rock Wilderness, Chattooga Wild and Scenic River, and SC 107 Scenic Byway are in the mountainous areas of the Sumter NF. In the foothills portions, find mixed hardwoods, giant cane stands, broad rivers, and lots of lakes. Francis Marion NF lies in the lowcountry north of Charleston. In this "Swamp Fox" country, find remains of plantations, churches, Civil War earthworks, and tar pits. Also, see the path of Hurricane Hugo as it swept through pine forests in route to North Carolina.

US Army Corps of Engineers (COE) lakes with recreation and campground facilities include Lake Hartwell and J Strom Thurmond Lake. At campgrounds around these two lakes, fees range from none to $12.00.

The **National Park Service** (NPS) offers several backcountry camping opportunities. Backpack through the diverse ecologies of the Congaree Swamp near Columbia. In this tract of southern bottomland hardwood forest, many trees reach record size. Kings Mountain National Military Park allows camping off its trails, crisscrossing the mountainous area where American frontiersmen defeated British soldiers in a crucial battle for independence. Another backpacking location is Ninety Six National Historic Site in Greenwood County. The colonial village of Ninety Six was held and fortified by the British during the Revolutionary War.

South Carolina Parks (SP) invite you to explore their year-round wonderlands. You'll find 35 parks with camping strategically located throughout the state's upcountry, midlands, and lowcountry. Most family campsites offer individual water/electrical hookups as well as picnic tables. Heated restrooms offer hot showers. Dump stations are situated within each park. All campsites rent on a first-come, first-serve basis although some sites at Edisto Beach SP can be reserved. Also, each park reserves two accessible sites for disabled campers. Most parks charge between $9.00 and $11.00 per family campsite. Beach parks raise their rates to $15.00 from April 1 through September 30. Also, lakefront sites cost an additional $1.00 in season. On a more rustic level, $5.00 tent camping is available at Devils Fork, Keowee-Toxaway, Lake Hartwell, Hamilton Branch, Little Pee Dee, and Sadlers Creek state parks. $1.00-per-person trailside camping can be enjoyed at Keowee-Toxaway, Caesars Head, and Jones Gap.

A few **counties** such as Charleston and Oconee offer camping in local parks. The fees, however, are too high to make the following price-conscious listings.

Share the beaches with shorebirds. Float blackwater riverways and drift through strands of Spanish moss covering stands of live oak and cypress. Bicycle backroads. Hike fern-fringed trails to cascading waterfalls. Come on down to South Carolina where the fish are jumping and the living is easy.

▲ ▲

ANDREW PICKENS RANGER DISTRICT-Dispersed

Sumter NF (803) 638-9568
State map: B1
Drive NW on SC 28
about 5 miles (8 k) from
WALHALLA to Ranger Station and get
map and permit. Find 30 different
named camps in district; dispersed
camps not allowed without permit.
FREE so choose a chore.
Open All Year.
Undesignated scattered, screened sites.
Water needs treating, fire rings.
In variety of forest settings, such as Big
Bend, Crane Creek, Double Branch, Hell
Hole, Lands Bridge, Long Mountain,
Norton Field, Owl Branch, Pine
Mountain, Riley Moore Ford....
Hike to explore scenic area. View
waterfalls. Swim in rivers. Whitewater
kayak or raft. Fish.
No toilet facilities. No trash
arrangements (pack it out). 14-day limit.
Hunting in season.

BRICKHOUSE

Sumter NF (803) 276-4810
State map: C4
From WHITMIRE, take
SC 66 SW for 7 miles
(11.2 k). Turn at entrance sign.
FREE so choose a chore.
Open All Year.
23 scattered, open sites.
Central faucet, pit toilets, tables, grills,
fire rings.
Among large pine in remote setting.
Walk nature trail. Hike.
14-day limit. Crowded hunting season.
Occasional horses.
500 ft (150 m)

BURRELL'S FORD WALK-IN

Sumter NF (803) 638-9568
State map: B1
Drive NW on SC 28 for
8 miles (12.8 k) from
WALHALLA. Bear Right (N) on SC 107
and travel 12 miles (19.2 k). Turn Left on
gravel Burrell's Ford Rd and continue

3 miles (4.8 k). Walk-in about 300 yds
(274 m). (Also see Cherry Hill and
Ammons Branch, NC.)
FREE so choose a chore.
Open All Year.
9 scattered, screened, tent sites.
Hand pump-treat water, pit toilets,
tables, grills, fire rings.
Under tree canopy on level,
rhododendron-covered area next to
Chattooga Wild and Scenic River.
Play in water. Walk to King Creek and
Spoonauger waterfalls. Hike into Ellicott
Rock Wilderness. Fish.
14-day limit. Hunting in season.
Crowded summer weekends.

CAESARS HEAD SP WALK-IN

(803) 836-6115
State map: A2
At CAESARS HEAD, off
US 276, obtain permit and
camp spot before walking from
.15–3 miles (220 m–4.8 k). (Also see
Jones Gap SP Walk-In.)
$1 per person.
Open All Year.
17 scattered, open, tent sites.
Fire rings.
Along Scenic Middle Saluda River in
fragile, diverse ecology among huge
trees (part of Mountain Bridge
Wilderness and Recreation Area).
Hike to appreciate natural beauty of
area. View wildlife. Mountain bike. Fish.
Attend ranger programs.
NO water. No toilet facilities. No trash
arrangements (pack it out). Limited sites.
No-trace camping a must.
3266 ft (980 m)

CASSIDY BRIDGE HUNT CAMP

Sumter NF (803) 638-9568
State map: B1
Drive NW on SC 28 from
WALHALLA to .25 mile
(400 m) beyond Ranger Station. Turn
Left (W) on Whetstone Rd. Take next
Left on Cassidy Bridge Rd. (Also see
Cherry Hill.)
FREE so choose a chore; reservations

▲ ▲

accepted at (803) 638-9568.
Open Oct 1–Dec 31; dry camping allowed off-season.
Undesignated close, open sites.
Hand pump, chemical toilets, fire rings. In open field surrounded by forest close to Chauga River (site used for groups except in hunting season).
Fish.
14-day limit. Hunting in season.

CHERRY HILL

Sumter NF (803) 638-9568
State map: B1
From WALHALLA, drive NW on SC 28 for 8 miles (12.8 k). Bear Right (N) on SC 107 and proceed 8 miles (12.8 k). (Also see Burrell's Ford Walk-In and Cassidy Bridge Hunt Camp.)
$5.
Open All Year.
29 close, screened sites.
Central faucet, flush toilets, showers, dump station, tables, grills, fire rings.
In mountain forest with stream.
Walk nature trail. Hike to explore scenic area. Attend ranger programs.
14-day limit. Crowded weekends in summer and fall.
2200 ft (660 m)

COLLINS CREEK HUNT CAMP

Sumter NF (803) 276-4810
State map: C4
Travel NE on SC 72 from WHITMIRE, for 3 miles (4.8 k). Turn Right (SE) on SC 45 for 5 miles (8 k). Turn Right (SW) at "Hunt Camp" sign on FR 393. (Also see Scenic Area Hunt Camp.)
FREE so choose a chore.
Open All Year.
40 scattered, open sites.
Hand pump, pit toilets.
In remote, large pine setting.
Observe wildlife. Hike.
14-day limit. Hunting in season.
500 ft (150 m)

DEVILS FORK SP

(803) 944-2639
State map: B2
From SALEM, head N to SC 11 (Cherokee Foothills Scenic Hwy). Turn Right (NE) and go about 2 miles (3.2 k) to signed entrance road. (Also see Keowee-Toxaway SP.)
$5; $12 electric.
Open All Year.
79 (20 tent-only) screened sites. ♿
Central faucet, flush toilets, showers, dump station, electric hookups, tables, fire rings, grills, boat ramp.
Nestled along tree-lined shore of beautiful Lake Jocassee in Appalachian foothills.
Swim and fish. Canoe, boat, and ski. Walk nature trail. Hike farther to explore area. Attend ranger programs.
14-day limit. Crowded summer and holidays.
2000 ft (600 m)

ELMWOOD HUNT CAMP

Francis Marion NF
(803) 887-3257
State map: G9
Take US 17 N from MCCLELLANVILLE for 6 miles (9.6 k). Turn Left (W) on SC 857S (Rutledge Rd). Drive 4 miles (6.4 k)–last .5 mile (800 m) unpaved. Turn Left on FR 211 (Mill Branch). Go .25 mile (400 m) to stop sign. Turn Right. (Also see Honey Hill.)
FREE so choose a chore.
Open All Year.
25 scattered, open sites.
Central faucet, pit toilets.
Under Spanish moss-covered live oak trees with open grassy areas.
Observe wildlife. Fish or boat nearby.
14-day limit. Crowded hunting season. Occasional ATV use. Summer mosquitos.
40 ft (12 m)

FELL HUNT CAMP

Sumter NF (803) 229-2406
State map: D3
Just N of BRADLEY on SC 10, turn Left (SW) on

SC 47 and go about 1.5 miles (2.4 k).
FREE so choose a chore.
Open All Year.
24 scattered, open sites.
Central faucet, chemical toilets.
In open, pine forest.
Hike. Mountain bike. Observe wildlife.
14-day limit. Hunting in season.
Occasional ATV use.
500 ft (150 m)

GUILLARD LAKE

Francis Marion NF
(803) 887-3257
State map: G8
From JAMESTOWN,
travel E on SC 45 for 3.5 miles (5.4 k).
Turn Left on gravel FR 150 (Guillard
Lake Rd) and drive 1.5 miles (2.4 k).
Turn on FR 150-G and continue 1 mile
(1.6 k). (Also see Honey Hill.)
FREE so choose a chore.
Open All Year.
6 close, open sites.
Pit toilets, tables, primitive boat ramp.
On bluff next to 5-acre oxbow lake
formed by adjacent Santee River.
Boat or fish. View wildlife. Explore
scenic area with ancient cypress.
NO water. 14-day limit. Occasional river
flooding. Hunting in season. Summer
mosquitos.
40 ft (12 m)

HALFWAY CREEK TRAIL CAMP

Francis Marion NF
(803) 887-3257
State map: G8
Drive S on US 17 from
MCCLELLANVILLE for 9 miles (14.4 k).
Turn Right (W) on SC 133-S (Steed
Creek) and travel 5 miles (8 k). Turn Left
on SC 98-S (Halfway Creek) and go
.5 mile (800 m).
FREE so choose a chore.
Open All Year.
15 scattered, open, tent sites.
Hand pump.
In grassy clearing with some oak shade
next to 22-mile (35.2-k) Swamp Fox
National Recreation Trail.

Hike to spot wildlife and explore
lowcountry ecology. Bike.
No toilet facilities. 14-day limit. Hunting
in season. Summer mosquitos.
40 ft (12 m)

HAMILTON BRANCH SP

(803) 333-2115
State map: E3
From MCCORMICK,
head SE for 12 miles
(19.2 k) on US 221.
$5; $10 electric.
Open All Year.
200 close, open sites. &
Water in every site, flush toilets,
showers, dump station, electric hookups,
tables, grills, boat ramp.
On J Strom Thurmond Lake.
Swim, boat, ski, or fish.
14-day limit.

HONEY HILL

Francis Marion NF
(803) 887-3257
State map: G8
Take SC 45 W from
MCCLELLANVILLE for 8.5 miles
(13.6 k) to fire tower on Left. (Also see
Elmwood Hunt Camp, Guillard Lake,
and Round Pond ATV Trailhead.)
FREE so choose a chore.
Open All Year.
9 scattered, open sites.
Hand pump, pit toilets, tables.
Under live oak and pine.
Enjoy overnight stop. Explore nearby
historical structures.
14-day limit. Mosquitos in summer.
40 ft (12 m)

ISLAND POINT

COE (404) 376-4788
State map: C2
From ANDERSON, drive
SW on US 29 for 14 miles
(22.4 k). (Also see Sadlers Creek SP.)
FREE so choose a chore.
Open May 1–Sep 9.
37 close, screened sites.
Central faucet, flush toilets, dump

station, tables, fire rings, grills, boat ramp.

On gentle slope with scattered pine and hardwood next to Lake Hartwell.

Swim, boat, ski, or fish. Observe wildlife. 30-day limit.

670 ft (201 m)

JONES GAP SP WALK-IN

(803) 836-3647
State map: A2
From MARIETTA, head NW on US 276 about 6 miles (9.6 k) following signs. Walk-in from 100 yds (100 m) to 5 miles (8 k). (Also see Caesars Head SP Walk-In.)

$1 per person.

Open All Year.

17 scattered, open, tent sites.

Flush toilets, showers, fire rings, pay phone.

In wilderness setting along a 5.3-mile (8.5-k) trail (part of Mountain Bridge Wilderness and Recreation Area).

Hike to view scenery. Take photos. Swim or fish. Attend naturalist interpretive program.

NO water. No trash arrangements (pack it out). 14-day limit.

2000 ft (600 m)

KEOWEE-TOXAWAY SP

(803) 868-2605
State map: B2
From PICKENS, take SC 183 SW to edge of town. Turn Right (W) on Shady Grove Rd. Drive about 8 miles (12.8 k) to stop sign. Turn Right (W) on SC 133. Go to intersection with SC 11 and signed park entrance. (Also see Devils Fork SP.)

$5; $9 electric.

Open All Year.

24 (14 tent-only) screened sites. &

Water in every site, flush toilets, showers, dump station, electric hookups, tables, fire rings.

In mountainous terrain on shores of Lake Keowee.

Walk nature trail and examine exhibits on native Cherokee culture. Hike farther

to explore area. View wildlife. Fish and boat nearby.

1000 ft (300 m)

LAKE HARTWELL SP

(803) 972-3352
State map: C1
Near LAVONIA, GA, exit off I-85 onto SC 11 (Cherokee Foothills Scenic Hwy). Drive N for 6 miles (9.6 k).

$5; $10 RV.

Open All Year.

150 (31 tent-only) screened sites. &

Water in every site, flush toilets, showers, dump station, electric hookups, tables, grills, boat ramp, laundry, store, pay phone.

Next to Lake Hartwell.

Boat, ski, or fish. Walk nature trail. Attend ranger programs.

14-day limit. Crowded holidays.

LEROY'S FERRY

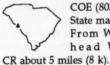

COE (803) 333-2476
State map: E3
From WILLINGTON, head W then S on CR about 5 miles (8 k).

$5.

Open All Year.

10 close, open sites.

Central faucet, pit toilets, tables, fire rings, boat ramp.

Next to J Strom Thurmond Lake.

Swim, boat, ski, or fish.

14-day limit.

LICK FORK LAKE

Sumter NF (803) 637-5396
State map: E4
From EDGEFIELD, travel W on SC 23 for 7 miles (11.2 k). Turn Left (S) on SC 230 and go .25 mile (400 m). Turn Left (SE) on SC 263 and continue 3 miles (4.8 k).

$5.

Open All Year.

11 (1 tent-only) scattered, screened sites. Central faucet, flush toilets, showers, tables, fire rings, grills, boat ramp.

In moderate hills covered with mature pine/hardwood next to 11-acre lake. Swim, fish, canoe, or boat (no motors). Walk nature trail or hike farther. Bike. 14-day limit. Hunting in season.

LITTLE PEE DEE SP

(803) 774-8872
State map: C9
On E side of DILLON on SC 9, turn Right (S) on SC 57 and drive about 10 miles (16 k). Turn Left (NE) at sign.
$5; $9 full hookups.
Open All Year.
50 (18 tent-only) close, open sites. &
Water in every site, flush toilets, showers, dump station, electric hookups, tables, fire rings.
In mature woods next to 55-acre lake. Swim, boat, or fish. Walk nature trail. Hike. Take photos. Attend ranger programs.
150 ft (45 m)

LONG LANE HUNT CAMP

Sumter NF (803) 276-4810
State map: C4
From NEWBERRY, drive N on SC 121 about 6 miles (9.6 k). Turn Left (W) on Old Whitmire Hwy and go .5 mile (800 m) to entrance sign. (Also see Willow Oak Hunt Camp.)
FREE so choose a chore.
Open All Year.
30 scattered, open sites.
Pit toilets.
With large pine and dogwood in remote setting.
Observe wildlife.
NO water. 14-day limit. Hunting in season.
500 ft (150 m)

MIDWAY HUNT CAMP

Sumter NF (803) 229-2406
State map: D3
From GREENWOOD, go W on SC 72 for 6 miles (9.6 k). Turn Left (S) at Beulah Church.

FREE so choose a chore.
Open Sep 15–Jan 5.
10 scattered, open sites.
Hand pump, chemical toilets.
In quiet spot.
Relax. Observe wildlife.
14-day limit. Hunting in season.

MORROW BRIDGE HUNT CAMP

Sumter NF (803) 229-2406
State map: E3
From MCCORMICK, travel NW on SC 28 about 10 miles (16 k). Turn Left (W) on SC 37 and go .5 mile (800 m). Turn Left (SW) on SC 39. Continue 1 mile (1.6 k).
FREE so choose a chore.
Open Sep 5–Jan 5.
11 scattered, open sites.
Hand pump, chemical toilets.
In remote setting.
Spot wildlife.
14-day limit. Hunting in season.
400 ft (120 m)

PARSONS MOUNTAIN LAKE

Sumter NF (803) 229-2406
State map: D3
From ABBEVILLE, take SC 72 SW for 2.2 miles (3.5 k). Turn Left (S) on SC 28 and drive 2 miles (3.2 k). Turn Left (SE) on SC 251 and go 2 miles (3.2 k). Turn Right (S) on FR 343 for final 1 mile (1.6 k).
$5. Open Apr 1–Nov 15.
23 scattered, screened sites.
Central faucet, flush toilets, showers, dump station, tables, grills, fire rings.
On forested shore of 32-acre, mountain lake.
Swim or boat (no motors). Walk nature trail. Hike (lookout tower on mountain). 14-day limit. Hunting in season. Occasional ATV use.
500 ft (150 m)

ROCKY BRANCH HUNT CAMP

Sumter NF (803) 276-4810
State map: C4
From NEWBERRY, head NE on SC 34 for 18 miles

▲ ▲

(28.8 k). Turn Left (N) on gravel FR 412
and drive 2.5 miles (4 k).
FREE so choose a chore.
Open All Year.
15 scattered, open sites.
Hand pump, pit toilets.
Under large pine in remote setting.
Observe wildlife.
No trash arrangements (pack it out).
14-day limit. Hunting in season.
500 ft (150 m)

ROUND POND ATV TRAILHEAD

Francis Marion NF
(803) 887-3257
State map: G8
Take SC 45 W from
MCCLELLANVILLE for 9 miles (14.4 k).
Turn Left (SW) on SC 98-S (Halfway
Creek) and go 5 miles (8 k). (Also see
Honey Hill.)
FREE so choose a chore.
Open All Year.
25 scattered, open sites.
Pit toilets.
At busy trailhead.
Fish nearby.
NO water. 14-day limit. Heavy ATV use
on weekends. Noisy. Mosquitos in
summer.
40 ft (12 m)

SADLERS CREEK SP

(803) 226-8950
State map: C2
From ANDERSON, travel
SE on US 29 for 10 miles
(16 k). Turn Right (N) on SC 187 and
drive 1 mile (1.6 k). Turn Left (W) on
access road and go 1 mile (1.6 k). (Also
see Island Point.)
$5; $10 electric.
Open All Year.
100 close, open sites. &
Water in every site, flush toilets,
showers, dump station, electric hookups,
tables, grills, boat ramp.
On Lake Hartwell.
Swim, boat, ski, or fish.
14-day limit.

SCENIC AREA HUNT CAMP

Sumter NF (803) 276-4810
State map: C4
From WHITMIRE, travel
NE on SC 72 for 3 miles
(4.8 k). Turn Right (SE) on SC 45 and
drive 6 miles (9.6 k). Turn Left (N) on
SC 54. Turn Right at stop sign then Right
again at "Hunt Camp" sign. (Also see
Collins Creek Hunt Camp.)
FREE so choose a chore.
Open All Year.
20 scattered, open sites.
Pit toilets.
Among large pine in remote locale.
Observe wildlife.
NO water. No trash arrangements (pack
it out). 14-day limit. Hunting in season.
500 ft (150 m)

TIP TOP HUNT CAMP

Sumter NF (803) 276-4810
State map: C4
From WHITMIRE, drive
W on SC 72 for 9 miles
(14.4 k).
FREE so choose a chore.
Open All Year.
20 scattered, open sites.
Pit toilets.
On old fire tower site.
Relax. View wildlife.
NO water. No trash arrangements (pack
it out). 14-day limit. Hunting in season.
Occasional ATV use.
500 ft (150 m)

WILLOW OAK HUNT CAMP

Sumter NF (803) 276-4810
State map: C4
From NEWBERRY, drive
N on SC 121 about
6 miles (9.6 k). Turn Right (SE) on
US 176 and go 3 miles (4.8 k) to Molly's
Rock Picnic Area sign. Turn Left and
follow "Hunt Camp" signs. (Also see
Long Lane Hunt Camp.)
FREE so choose a chore.
Open All Year.
20 scattered, open sites.
Pit toilets.

▲ ▲

Under large willow oak in remote location.

Relax. Spot wildlife.

NO water. No trash arrangements (pack it out). 14-day limit. Hunting in season. 500 ft (150 m)

WOODALL SHOALS

Sumter NF (803) 638-9568
State map: B1
From WESTMINSTER, take US 76 NW for 18 miles (28.8 k) to Long Creek. Turn Left (W) on Orchard Rd. Take first Right on gravel Woodall Shoals Rd.

FREE so choose a chore.

Open All Year.

Undesignated scattered, open sites.

Pit toilets, fire rings.

In clearing of old road bed about .1 mile (200 m) from Class VI rapid on Chattooga River.

Whitewater kayak or raft. Swim or fish. NO water. 14-day limit. Crowded summer weekends.

WOODS FERRY

Sumter NF (803) 427-9858
State map: C5
From CHESTER, travel SW on SC 72 for 12.1 miles (19.4 k). Turn Right (N) on SC 25 and drive 2.1 miles (3.4 k). Continue N on SC 49 for 3.6 miles (5.8 k). Turn Left (NW) on SC 574 and go 3.6 miles (5.8 k).

FREE so choose a chore.

Open May 1 – Sep 30; dry camping allowed off-season.

36 close, open sites.

Central faucet, flush toilets, tables, fire rings, boat ramp.

On Neal Shoals Reservoir with many historical antebellum ruins and cemeteries nearby.

Swim, boat, ski, or fish. Walk nature trail. Explore area.

14-day/22-ft limits.

SOUTH DAKOTA
CAMPGROUND LOCATIONS

▶ ▶ Find location on facing page map grid. ▶ ▶
▼ ▼ Locate area campgrounds on these page numbers. ▼ ▼

South Dakota

Grid conforms to official state map. For your copy, call (800) 843-1930
or write Tourism, 711 E Wells Ave, Pierre, SD 57501-3369.

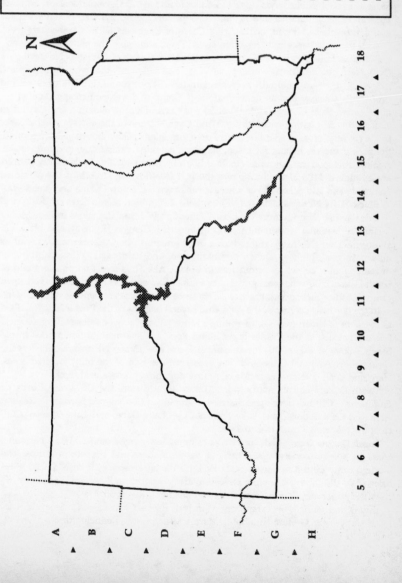

▲ ▲

PUBLIC LANDS CAMPING

When you camp in South Dakota, you're following an age-old tradition. Over 12,000 years ago, hunters wandered the great plains in search of bison and mammoth. It was only 800 years ago that the Mandan and Arikara brought agriculture to the area. About 200 years ago, the Sioux then the French and British traders arrived, heralding rapid lifestyle changes. You can still see the world's largest publicly owned buffalo herd in South Dakota and you can still locate remote-feeling places to set your camp. On the federal level of public lands, look to Badlands and Wind Cave national parks; Black Hills and Custer national forests; Buffalo Gap, Fort Pierre, and Grand River national grasslands; plus a handful of US Army Corps of Engineers lakes. On the state level, look in the state parks and recreation areas. Then, remember the many town parks.

National Park Service (NPS) preserves the 244,000 acres of Badlands National Park (NP). Here find erosion at work on soft clays and sediments that create pastel spires, ridges, and, even, "melted ice cream sundaes." Spot roaming buffalo, deer, and pronghorn antelope and an occasional fossil. Camp in developed campgrounds (free at primitive Sage Creek and $8.00 at 98-site Cedar Pass) or obtain a free permit to explore this fascinating backcountry. Wind Cave NP, one of the oldest national parks in the country, protects 68-miles of rare cave formations below ground. Above ground, the park preserves habitat for bison, elk, deer, antelope, prairie dog, and rattlesnake. Again, developed campgrounds ($8.00 at Elk Mountain) and free backcountry permits are available. NPS also administers the last free-flowing stretch of the Missouri National Wild and Scenic River where it runs between South Dakota and Nebraska.

Black Hills National Forest (NF) contains 1.3 million scenic acres of peaks and woods that rise abruptly from the Great Plains. Special forest attractions include Mount Rushmore National Monument (NM), the Spearfish Canyon Highway, and Black Elk Wilderness. In this high, rugged area, find unusual plant occurrences as well as mountain goat, bighorn sheep, mountain lion, and bald eagle. While camping at developed sites expect fees from free to $14.00. Also, this forest administers two of South Dakota's three national grasslands: Buffalo Gap and Fort Pierre. Set up your own camp to fish or rockhound. Practice safety since these areas are popular with hunters.

In the northwest corner of the state, find several sections of the **Custer NF**, described as "islands of green in a sea of rolling prairie." Too, discover interesting geological formations such as the Castles and Capitol Rock, national natural landmarks. In the South Dakota section of this forest, campsites are free. Custer NF also administers the Grand River National Grassland. The grassland lies east of the hilly, forested areas. Here find deer, antelope, coyote, fox, prairie dog, turkey, geese, and duck.

South Dakota counts many glacial lakes. In addition, the **US Army Corps of Engineers** (COE) has developed places for camping at Cottonwood Springs Recreation Area and Cold Brook Lake, Lake Francis Case, Lake Oahe, and Lake Sharpe. COE camping fees range from free to $9.00.

South Dakota Game, Fish, and Parks camping fees range from $5.00 for a basic site, $6.00 for a semi-modern space, to $7.00 for all modern and equestrian camps. The modern campground at Custer State Park (SP) is an exception; it costs $10.00. Find basic $5.00 sites at the following recreation areas: Angostura Reservoir, Bear Butte SP, Deerfield Reservoir, Fort Sisseton SHP, and Shadehill Reservoir.

Towns promoting their campgrounds include Burke, Clear Lake, De Smet, Eureka, Faith, Gettysburg, Groton, Humboldt, Martin, Miller, Pierre, Redfield, Roscoe, Tyndall, and White River.

▲ ▲

Enjoy the same scenery and magic that shaped the Lakota peoples and, in turn, permeated the Oscar-winning movie, *Dances With Wolves.* "Hau Kola!" say the Sioux or "Hello, Friend," greet South Dakotans.

▲ ▲

AMSDEN DAM

SD Game & Fish
(605) 225-5325
State map: B15
From GROTON, drive E on US 12 for 6 miles (9.6 k). Turn Right (S). Go 5 miles (8 k). Turn Left (E). Travel 1 mile (1.6 k), then Right (S) for 1 mile (1.6 k).
FREE so choose a chore.
Open All Year.
Undesignated scattered, open sites.
Central faucet, pit toilets, tables, boat ramp.
Next to lake.
Swim, boat, or fish.
No trash arrangements (pack it out). 14-day limit.

BADLANDS NP-Sage Creek

(605) 433-5361
State map: F8
From CEDAR PASS Visitor Center, head NW on SD 240 about 15 miles (24 k). Continue NW on rough gravel road another 10 miles (16 k). Turn Left (SE). (Nearby Cedar Pass costs $8.)
FREE. Also, free backcountry permits available from Visitor Center.
Open All Year.
Undesignated scattered, open sites.
Pit toilets.
In remote grassland at edge of badlands.
Hike. Take photos.
NO water. No trash arrangements (pack it out). 14-day limit.

BEAR BUTTE SP

(605) 374-5240
State map: D6
From STURGIS, travel E for 4 miles (6.4 k) on SD 34. Turn Left (N) on SD 79 and go 2 miles (3.2 k).
$5; $2 entrance fee.
Open All Year.

15 scattered, open sites. Hand pump, pit toilets, tables, grills, fire rings.
Near Black Hills in open prairie next to Bear Butte Lake and sacred mountain.
Swim, boat, and fish. Walk nature trail or hike to spot wildlife. Mountain bike.
Attend ranger programs.
Occasionally crowded.
3400 ft (1020 m)

BIG SIOUX SRA

(605) 594-3824
State map: F18
From BRANDON, head S on SD 11 about 1.5 miles (2.4 k).
$5; $2 entrance fee.
Open All Year.
10 close, open sites.
Central faucet, pit toilets, tables, fire rings, shelter, playground.
In 430-acre park.
Enjoy overnight stop.
14-day limit.

BLACK FOX

Black Hills NF
(605) 574-2534
State map: E5
From HILL CITY, take FH 17 NW about 4 miles (6.4 k). Bear Right on gravel FR 231 and continue 27 miles (43.2 k). (Also see Castle Peak.)
FREE so choose a chore.
Open Mar 31–Dec 15.
9 close, open sites.
Hand pump, pit toilets, tables, grills, fire rings.
In pine/spruce forest next to Rhoads Fork Creek near Cook's Tower.
Fish. Observe wildlife. Enjoy seclusion.
Cross-country ski in winter.
No trash arrangements. 10-day limit.
Hunting in season. Crowded weekends.
5900 ft (1770 m)

▲ ▲

BLUE BLANKET

COE (605) 845-2252
State map: B11
From MOBRIDGE, head E on US 12 about 1 mile (1.6 k). Turn Right (S). (Also see Thomas Bay.)
FREE so choose a chore.
Open All Year.
Undesignated scattered, open sites.
Hand pump, pit toilets, boat ramp.
Next to Lake Oahe.
Fish and boat. Observe wildlife.
No trash arrangements (pack it out).
Hunting in season.

BLUE DOG SOUTH

SD Game & Fish
(605) 886-4769
State map: B16
From WAUBAY, drive N for .5 mile (800 m). (Also see Enemy Swim.)
FREE so choose a chore.
Open All Year.
Undesignated scattered, open sites.
Central faucet, pit toilets, tables, fire rings, boat ramp, shelter, playground.
On Blue Dog Lake next to Waubay NWR.
Swim, boat, or fish. View wildlife.
No trash arrangements. 14-day limit.

BOWDLE BEACH

COE (605) 845-2252
State map: B11
From AKASKA, head N on CR about 2 miles (3.2 k). Turn Left (W) Drive to end of road. (See Swan Creek and Walth Bay.)
FREE so choose a chore.
Open All Year.
Undesignated scattered, open sites.
Hand pump, pit toilets, boat ramp.
Next to Lake Oahe.
Swim, boat, or fish. Spot wildlife.
No trash arrangements (pack it out).

BROOKS MEMORIAL PARK

Martin Municipal Parks
(605) 685-6525
State map: G9
Find park in MARTIN at 602 1st Ave.

FREE; donations requested.
Open Apr–Nov; camping allowed off-season.
Undesignated scattered, open sites.
Flush toilets, electric hookups, tables, indoor pool.
Among trees and grass in city park.
Swim. Bike. Enjoy overnight stop.
NO water.
3331 ft (999 m)

BUFFALO SOUTH

SD Game & Fish
(605) 448-5701
State map: B16
From EDEN, drive E on CR for 4 miles (6.4 k). Turn Right (SE) and go .5 mile (800 m). (Also see Clear Lake.)
FREE so choose a chore.
Open All Year.
Undesignated scattered, open sites.
Pit toilets, tables, boat ramp.
Next to lake.
Boat or fish.
NO water. No trash arrangements (pack it out). 14-day limit.

BURKE CITY PARK

(605) 775-2913
State map: G13
Locate park on 7th in BURKE.
FREE so choose a chore.
Open All Year.
Undesignated close, open sites.
Central faucet, flush toilets, electric hookups, tables, grills, playground, tennis court, ball fields.
In quiet, peaceful city park.
Play sports. Enjoy overnight stop.

BURKE LAKE SRA

(605) 775-2968
State map: G13
From BURKE, head SE on US 18 about 2 miles (3.2 k).
$5; $2 entrance fee.
Open All Year.
15 close, open sites.
Central faucet, flush/pit toilets, tables, fire rings, boat ramp, playground.

Next to lake.
Swim, boat, or fish. Hike to observe wildlife.
14-day limit.

BURYANEK

COE (605) 487-7847
State map: F13
From PLATTE, drive W on SD 50 about 18 miles (28.8 k)–cross bridge. Turn Right (N) at sign and go 2.5 miles (4 k). (Also see West Bridge. Nearby Snake Creek costs $7.)
FREE so choose a chore.
Open All Year.
6 close, open sites.
Pit toilets, tables, fire rings, boat ramp, shelter.
On Lake Francis Case.
Swim, boat, waterski, and fish.
NO water. No trash arrangements (pack it out). 14-day limit.

BUSH'S LANDING

COE (605) 845-2252
State map: D11
From ONIDA, drive W for 18 miles (28.8 k). Turn Right (N) on CR, then Left (W). (Also see Little Bend and Sutton Bay.)
FREE so choose a chore.
Open All Year.
Undesignated scattered, open sites.
Pit toilets, tables, boat ramp.
Next to Lake Oahe.
Boat, ski, or fish.
NO water. No trash arrangements (pack it out). 14-day limit.

CASTLE PEAK

Black Hills NF
(605) 574-2534
State map: E5
From HILL CITY, take FH 17 N to FR 187 (almost to ROCHFORD). Turn Right (SE) and proceed 3 miles (4.8 k). (Also see Black Fox.)
FREE so choose a chore.
Open All Year.
9 close, screened sites.
Hand pump, pit toilets, tables, grills, fire

rings.
Along Castle Creek in deep canyon with pine and spruce.
Fish. Watch wildlife. Cross-country ski in winter.
No trash arrangements (pack it out). 10-day limit. Hunting in season.
Crowded weekends.
5300 ft (1590 m)

CLEAR LAKE

SD Game & Fish
(605) 448-5701
State map: A16
From LAKE CITY, drive SE on SD 10 for 4 miles (6.4 k). (Also see Buffalo South.)
FREE so choose a chore.
Open All Year.
Undesignated scattered, open sites.
Pit toilets, tables, boat ramp.
Next to lake.
Boat or fish.
NO water. No trash arrangements (pack it out). 14-day limit.

CLEAR LAKE CITY PARK

(605) 874-2121
State map: C17
Find park on SD 15 N in CLEAR LAKE. (Also see Ulven Park.)
$3.
Open May 1 – Oct 1; dry camping allowed off-season.
12 close, open sites.
Hand pump, chemical toilets, dump station, electric hookups, tables, grills.
Within city park in shady, green area.
Enjoy overnight stay.

COLD BROOK

COE (605) 745-5476
State map: F6
Drive N on US 385 from HOT SPRINGS for 1 mile (1.6 k). Turn Left (W). (Also see Cottonwood Springs.)
FREE so choose a chore.
Open All Year.
Undesignated scattered, open sites.
Central faucet, pit toilets, tables, fire rings, boat ramp, playground.
In ponderosa pine-filled canyon next to

30-acre lake.
Swim, fish, or boat (no gas motors).
Enjoy autumn color. Cross-country ski or
ice skate in winter.
14-day limit.
3585 ft (1076 m)

COLLEGE MEMORIAL PARK

Springfield City Parks
(602) 369-2309
State map: G16
Find park in SPRINGFIELD on W 10th
St. (Also see Tyndall City Park.)
FREE so choose a chore.
Open All Year.
Undesignated open sites. Central faucet,
flush toilets, tables, pool, ball field.
In town park.
Swim. Explore area (Lewis & Clark Lake
nearby).

COTTONWOOD SPRINGS

COE (605) 745-5476
State map: F5
Drive W on US 18 from
HOT SPRINGS about 5 miles (8 k). Turn
Right (N). (Also see Cold Brook.)
FREE so choose a chore.
Open All Year.
18 close, open sites.
Central faucet, flush toilets, tables, fire
rings, playground.
In wooded canyon next to normally dry
lakebed.
Hike to canyon top for overlook. Relax.
14-day/32-ft limits.
3970 ft (1191 m)

COW/SPRING CREEK

COE (605) 845-2252
State map: D11
From PIERRE, drive N on
SD 1804 about 19 miles (30.4 k). Turn
Left (W). (Also see Okobojo Point and
Peoria Flats.)
FREE so choose a chore.
Open All Year.
31 close, open sites.
Central faucet, pit toilets, tables, fire
rings, boat ramp, shelter.
Next to Lake Oahe.

Swim, boat, ski, or fish.
No trash arrangements (pack it out).
14-day/30-ft limits.

CRYSTAL PARK

Miller City Parks
(605) 853-2431
State map: D14
Locate park in MILLER.
FREE so choose a chore.
Open Apr–Oct.
Undesignated close, open sites.
Central faucet, flush toilets, electric
hookups, tables, grills, playground.
In park with lighted fountains and lake.
Enjoy overnight stay.
3-day limit.

CUSTER TRAIL

Black Hills NF
(605) 574-2534
State map: E5
From HILL CITY, take FH 17 N past
DEERFIELD to FR 417. Turn Right (SE).
(Nearby Dutchman costs $7.50.)
$5.
Open All Year.
16 (6 tent-only) close, open sites.
Hand pump, pit toilets, tables, fire rings,
grills, boat ramp.
On shore of 414-acre Deerfield Lake.
Swim, fish, or boat (5 mph limit). Walk
all or part of Loop Trail. Mountain bike.
Take photos.
10-day limit. Hunting in season. No
generators in quiet hours.
5900 ft (1770 m)

DODGE DRAW

SD Game & Fish
(605) 765-9410
State map: B11
From AKASKA, drive S on CR 1804 for
13 miles (20.8 k). Turn Right (W) and go
8 miles (12.8 k).
FREE so choose a chore.
Open All Year.
Undesignated scattered, open sites.
Pit toilets, tables, fire rings, boat ramp.
Next to Lake Oahe.
Boat. Fish.

▲ ▲

NO water. No trash arrangements (pack it out). 14-day limit.

DUDE RANCH

COE (605) 487-7847
State map: F13
From CHAMBERLAIN, drive W on US 16, crossing bridge. Turn Left (S) at sign. (Nearby American Creek costs $9.)
FREE so choose a chore.
Open All Year.
Undesignated scattered, open sites.
Pit toilets, tables, boat ramp.
On Lake Francis Case.
Boat, waterski, swim, or fish.
NO water. No trash arrangements (pack it out). 14-day limit.

DURKEE LAKE

Faith City Parks
(605) 967-2261
State map: C8
From FAITH, drive 3 miles (4.8 k) S on SD 73. (Also see Faith City Park.)
FREE so choose a chore.
Open All Year.
Undesignated scattered, open sites.
Pit toilets, electric hookups, tables, grills, boat ramp.
Next to small lake.
Swim, boat, or fish. Golf nearby. Bike. Spot wildlife.
NO water.

ELM CREEK

COE (605) 487-7847
State map: F13
From PUKWANA, drive S on SD 50 for 12.5 miles (20 k). Turn Right (W) and go 7 miles (11.2 k).
FREE so choose a chore.
Open All Year.
Undesignated open sites.
Pit toilets, tables, fire rings, boat ramp, shelter.
Boat or fish Lake Francis Case.
NO water. No trash arrangements (pack it out). 14-day limit.

ENEMY SWIM

SD Game & Fish
(605) 886-4769
State map: B16
From WAUBAY, drive N for 6 miles (9.6 k). (Also see Blue Dog South.)
FREE so choose a chore.
Open All Year.
Undesignated scattered, open sites.
Pit toilets, boat ramp.
Next to lake.
Fish and boat.
NO water. No trash arrangements (pack it out). 14-day limit.

FAITH CITY PARK

(605) 967-2261
State map: C8
In FAITH, go S on Main St for .5 mile (800 m). (See Durkee Lake.)
$5.
Open All Year.
10 scattered, open sites.
Central faucet, flush toilets, electric hookups, tables, grills.
In town park.
Bike. Enjoy overnight stop.

FOREST CITY

SD Game & Fish
(605) 765-9410
State map: C11
From GETTYSBURG, travel W on US 212 for 19 miles (30.4 k)–cross over bridge. (Also see Whitlocks East.)
FREE so choose a chore.
Open All Year.
Undesignated scattered, open sites.
Pit toilets, tables, boat ramp.
Next to Lake Oahe.
Boat or fish.
NO water. No trash arrangements (pack it out). 14-day limit.

FORT SISSETON SHP

(605) 448-5701
State map: A16
From LAKE CITY, travel NE on SD 10 for 6 miles (9.6 k). Turn Left (S) on CR and go 6 miles (9.6 k). (Also see Four Mile/Bullhead.)

▲ ▲

$5; $2 entrance fee.
Open All Year.
12 close, open sites.
Central faucet, pit toilets, tables.
At historical site.
Explore area. Examine exhibits.
14-day limit.

FOSTER BAY

COE (605) 845-2252
State map: D10
From HAYES, drive W on
US 14 for 5 miles (8 k). Turn Right (N)
on SD 63 and go about 21 miles (33.6 k).
Turn Right (NW) on CR and continue
about 5 miles (8 k).
FREE so choose a chore.
Open All Year.
20 close, open sites.
Central faucet, pit toilets, tables, fire
rings, boat ramp.
On Cheyenne River Arm of Lake Oahe.
Fish or boat.
No trash arrangements (pack it out).
14-day/30-ft limits.

FOUR MILE/BULLHEAD

SD Game & Fish
(605) 448-5701
State map: A16
From LAKE CITY, go NW on SD 10 on
2.5 miles (4 k). Turn Left (S) and drive
1 mile (1.6 k). Turn Left (W). Go .5 mile
(800 m). (Also see Fort Sisseton SHP.)
FREE so choose a chore.
Open All Year.
Undesignated scattered, open sites.
Pit toilets, tables, boat ramp.
On Roy Lake.
Boat or fish.
NO water. No trash arrangements (pack
it out). 14-day limit.

FRENCH CREEK

Black Hills NF
(605) 745-4107
State map: F6
From FAIRBURN, head E for 11 miles
(17.6 k) on gravel roads.
FREE so choose a chore.
Open All Year.

Undesignated scattered, open sites.
Hand pump, pit toilets, tables, fire rings.
In wooded draw among native grassland
with Black Hills in distance.
Observe wildlife. Relax. Rockhound.

GETTYSBURG CITY PARK

(605) 765-2264
State map: C12
Find park 5 blocks S of
US 212 & Main St in GETTYSBURG at
200 W King.
FREE so choose a chore.
Open May 1–Sep 30.
20 (6 RV-only) scattered, open sites.
Central faucet, flush toilets, showers,
dump station, electric hookups, tables,
grills, pool, playground, tennis court.
On prairie with some shade.
Swim. Play. Enjoy stop.
3-day limit. Noisy on Wed night
(softball). Crowded holidays and
celebrations.
2061 ft (618 m)

GOOD SOLDIER

COE (605) 245-2255
State map: E13
Head S on SD 47 from
FORT THOMPSON, crossing dam. (Also
see Old Fort Thompson.)
FREE so choose a chore.
Open All Year.
Undesignated open sites. Pit toilets,
tables, fire rings, grills, boat ramp.
Next to Lake Sharpe.
Swim, boat, or fish.
NO water. 14-day limit.
1420 ft (426 m)

GRAND RIVER

COE (605) 845-2252
State map: B11
From MOBRIDGE, travel
W on US 12 about 26 miles (41.6 k).
FREE so choose a chore.
Open All Year.
Undesignated scattered, open sites.
Hand pump, pit toilets, boat ramp.
On Grand River arm of Lake Oahe.
Boat and fish. Spot wildlife.

No trash arrangements (pack it out).
14-day limit. Hunting in season.

GRIFFIN MUNICIPAL PARK

(605) 224-5921
State map: D11
Find park in PIERRE, S of
SD 34.
FREE so choose a chore.
Open May–Oct.
50 close, open sites.
Central faucet, flush toilets, dump
station, electric hookups, tables, fire
rings, boat ramp, playground, tennis
court.
In city park next to Missouri River.
Swim or boat. Walk or bike.
3-day limit.

GROTON CITY PARK

(605) 397-8422
State map: B15
Locate park in GROTON
on S Main.
FREE so choose a chore.
Open Apr 15–Oct 15; dry camping
allowed off-season.
16 scattered, open sites.
Central faucet, flush toilets, electric
hookups, tables, grills, playground.
In quiet, residential park.
Walk. Bike. Swim (1 block away). Enjoy
overnight stop.
3-day limit.

HAV-A-REST CAMPGROUND

Redfield City Parks
(605) 472-0667
State map: C14
Find campground on W edge of
REDFIELD on US 212.
FREE so choose a chore.
Open All Year.
10 scattered, open sites.
Central faucet, pit toilets, electric
hookups, tables, fire rings.
Next to Redfield Lake.
Fish. Bike. Enjoy overnight stop.

IRON NATION

COE (605) 245-2255
State map: E13
Drive W for 5 miles (8 k)
from LOWER BURLE.
FREE so choose a chore.
Open All Year.
Undesignated scattered, open sites.
Central faucet, pit toilets, tables, fire
rings, boat ramp, shelter, playground.
Next to Lake Sharpe.
Boat or fish.
No trash arrangements. 14-day limit.
1430 ft (429 m)

JAMES RIVER UNIT 2

SD Game & Fish
(605) 225-5325
State map: D15
From HURON, drive N on ND 37 for
15 miles (24 k). Turn Left (W). Go 1 mile
(1.6 k). Turn Left (S). Go .5 mile (800 m).
Find more primitive Unit 1 about 1 mile
(1.6 k) S. (Also see Lake Byron.)
FREE so choose a chore.
Open All Year.
4 scattered, open sites.
Central faucet, pit toilets, tables, boat
ramp.
Along James River.
Fish and boat.
No trash arrangements. 14-day limit.

JOE DAY BAY

COE (605) 487-7847
State map: G14
From PICKSTOWN drive
W on SD 46 about 10 miles (16 k). Turn
Left (N) and go about 2 miles (3.2 k).
(Also see South Scalp Creek.)
FREE so choose a chore.
Open All Year.
Undesignated scattered, open sites.
Pit toilets, tables, boat ramp, shelter.
On Lake Francis Case.
Boat. Fish.
NO water. No trash arrangements (pack
it out). 14-day limit.

▲ ▲

LAKE BYRON

SD Game & Fish
(605) 225-5325
State map: D15

From HURON, drive N on ND 37 for
12 miles (19.2 k). Turn Right (E) and go
3 miles (4.8 k). (See James River Unit 2.)
FREE so choose a chore.
Open All Year.
Undesignated open sites.
Central faucet, pit toilets, tables, boat
ramp.
Along lakeshore.
Swim, boat, or fish.
No trash arrangements (pack it out).
14-day limit.

LAKE COCHRANE SRA

(605) 886-4769
State map: C18
From CLEAR LAKE, drive
E on SD 22 for 10 miles (16 k). (Also see
Ulven Park.)
$5; $8 electric; $2 entrance fee.
Open All Year.
15 close, open sites.
Central faucet, flush/pit toilets, electric
hookups, tables, grills, boat ramp,
shelter, playground.
Next to lake.
Fish. Swim. Boat.
14-day limit.

LAKE FAULKTON

SD Game & Fish
(605) 853-2533
State map: C13

From FAULKTON, head W for 2.5 miles
(4 k). Turn Left (S). Go .5 mile (800 m).
FREE so choose a chore.
Open All Year.
Undesignated scattered, open sites.
Hand pump, pit toilets, electric hookups,
tables, fire rings, grills, boat ramp.
In open prairie surrounded by trees next
to lake and 9-hole golf course.
Boat or fish. Play golf.
1600 ft (480 m)

LAKE HIDDENWOOD SP

(605) 649-7876
State map: B12
From SELBY, drive NE on
US 12 for 3 miles (4.8 k). Turn Right (N)
on US 83 and proceed 2 miles (3.2 k).
$5; $8 electric; $2 entrance fee.
Open All Year.
14 close, open sites.
Central faucet, pit toilets, electric
hookups, tables, fire rings, boat ramp,
shelter, playground.
Next to lake.
Swim, boat, or fish. Hike. View wildlife.
14-day limit.

LAKE VERMILLION SRA

(605) 296-3643
State map: F17
Travel E for 5 miles (8 k)
from CANISTOTA. Turn Right (S). Go
past main entrance to "T" intersection.
Turn Left (E). Go to East Unit entrance.
(Also see Larry Pressler City Park.)
$5; $7 West; $10 electric; $2 entrance fee;
reservations accepted at (605) 296-3643
for an additional $5.
Open Apr 15 – Oct 15; dry camping
allowed off-season.
74 close, open sites. ♿
Central faucet, flush toilets, showers,
dump station, electric hookups, tables,
fire rings, grills, boat ramp.
On grassy breakwater for Lake
Vermillion.
Boat, ski, or fish. Canoe or bike.
7-day limit. Crowded weekends and
holidays.
1500 ft (450 m)

LAKESIDE PARK

Eureka Municipal Parks
(605) 284-2441
State map: A12
Locate park in EUREKA.
FREE so choose a chore.
Open All Year.
20 close, open sites.
Hand pump, flush toilets, dump station,
electric hookups, tables, grills, boat
ramp, shelter, laundry, store, pay phone.

In nice park surrounded by 3 lakes.
Boat. Swim. Fish.
Hunting in season.

LARRY PRESSLER CITY PARK

Humboldt City Parks
(605) 363-3440
State map: F17

Find park on S end of HUMBOLDT at
6th & Washington. (Also see Lake
Vermillion SRA.)
FREE so choose a chore.
Open All Year.
Undesignated close, open sites.
Central faucet, flush toilets, tables, grills,
shelter, playground, tennis court, ball
courts.
In farm country with nice-sized trees.
Bike. Play sports. Enjoy overnight stop.
Noise from town.

LITTLE BEND

COE (605) 845-2252
State map: D11
From ONIDA, drive W for
26 miles (41.6 k). (Also see Bush's
Landing.)
FREE so choose a chore.
Open All Year.
30 close, open sites.
Central faucet, pit toilets, tables, fire
rings, boat ramp.
On peninsula in Lake Oahe within Fort
Sully Game Refuge.
Boat or fish. Observe wildlife.
No trash arrangements (pack it out).
14-day limit.

LITTLE MOREAU SRA

(605) 765-9410
State map: B10
Drive S for 6 miles (9.6 k)
from TIMBER LAKE.
$5; $2 entrance fee. Open All Year.
14 scattered, open sites.
Central faucet, pit toilets, tables, fire
rings, boat ramp, shelter, playground.
Along Little Moreau River.
Swim, boat, or fish.
14-day limit.

LLEWELLYN JOHN'S MEMORIAL SRA

(605) 374-5114
State map: A8
From SHADEHILL, head N
on SD 73 to signed turnoff (on Left).
(Nearby Shadehill SRA costs $7.)
FREE; $2 entrance fee; reservations
accepted at (605) 374-5114 for an
additional $6.
Open All Year.
10 close, open sites.
Hand pump, pit toilets, electric hookups,
tables, grills.
On shore of Flat Creek.
Fish. Observe wildlife.

MINNECONJOU

COE (605) 845-2252
State map: C10
Head NW on CR from
MISSION RIDGE about 4 miles (6.4 k).
FREE so choose a chore.
Open All Year.
Undesignated scattered, open sites.
Pit toilets, tables, fire rings, boat ramp.
In remote setting on Lake Oahe.
Boat or fish.
NO water. No trash arrangements (pack
it out). 14-day limit.

MOON

Black Hills NF
(307) 746-2783
State map: E5
From NEWCASTLE, WY, drive E on
US 16 for 8 miles (12.8 k). Turn Left (N)
on gravel FR 117 and go 16 miles
(25.6 k). (Also see Redbank Spring.)
FREE so choose a chore.
Open May–Oct; dry camping allowed
off-season.
3 close, open sites.
Hand pump, pit toilets, tables, grills, fire
rings.
In isolated spot with ponderosa pine.
Enjoy quiet. View wildlife.
Hunting in season.
6400 ft (1920 m)

▲ ▲

NEWELL LAKE

SD Game & Fish
(605) 374-5240
State map: C6

From NEWELL, drive N on SD 79 for 8 miles (12.8 k). Turn Right (E) and continue 2 miles (3.2 k).
FREE so choose a chore.
Open All Year.
Undesignated scattered, open sites.
Pit toilets, boat ramp.
Next to lake.
Swim, boat, and fish.
NO water. No trash arrangements (pack it out). 14-day limit.

NORTH BEND

COE (605) 245-2255
State map: D12

From PIERRE, travel SE on SD 34 about 31 miles (49.6 k). Turn Left (S) at sign and go 4 miles (6.4 k).
FREE so choose a chore. Open All Year.
10 close, open sites.
Pit toilets, tables, fire rings, boat ramp.
On Lake Sharpe at Chaney Rush Creek.
Boat or fish. Observe waterfowl.
NO water. No trash arrangements (pack it out). 14-day limit.
1430 ft (429 m)

NORTH SHORE

COE (605) 245-2255
State map: E13

Head SW from FORT THOMPSON on SD 47. Turn Right (NW) before dam and pass Visitor Center. (Also see Old Fort Thompson.)
FREE so choose a chore. Open All Year.
Undesignated scattered, open sites.
Central faucet, pit toilets, tables, fire rings, boat ramp.
Along Lake Sharpe.
Swim, boat, or fish.
No trash arrangements. 14-day limit.
1430 ft (429 m)

NORTH WHEELER

COE (605) 487-7847
State map: G14

From PLATTE, travel S on SD 45 for 10 miles (16 k). Continue S on CR another 7 miles (11.2 k). (Also see Pease Creek.)
FREE so choose a chore.
Open All Year.
Undesignated scattered, open sites.
Hand pump, pit toilets, tables, fire rings, boat ramp.
On Lake Francis Case.
Boat. Fish.
No trash arrangements (pack it out). 14-day limit.

OKOBOJO POINT

COE (605) 845-2252
State map: D11

From PIERRE, drive N on SD 1804 about 20 miles (32 k). Turn Left (W). (Also see Cow/Spring Creek.)
FREE so choose a chore.
Open All Year.
Undesignated scattered, open sites.
Pit toilets, tables, fire rings, boat ramp.
On Lake Oahe.
Fish and boat.
NO water. No trash arrangements (pack it out). 14-day limit.

OLD FORT THOMPSON

COE (605) 245-2255
State map: E13

Locate area on SW side of FORT THOMPSON. (Also see Good Soldier and North Shore.)
FREE so choose a chore.
Open All Year.
Undesignated close, open sites.
Central faucet, flush toilets, tables, fire rings, boat ramp.
Next to Lake Sharpe spillway.
Boat or fish. Observe wildlife.
14-day limit. Hunting in season.
1348 ft (404 m)

PEASE CREEK

COE (605) 487-7847
State map: G14

From GEDDES, head S on SD 50 for 8 miles (12.8 k). Turn Left (SW) at sign. (Also see North Wheeler.)
FREE so choose a chore.

▲ ▲

Open All Year.
25 close, open sites.
Central faucet, pit toilets, tables, fire
rings, boat ramp, shelter.
On Lake Francis Case.
Swim, boat, waterski, or fish.
No trash arrangements (pack it out).
14-day limit.

PELICAN LAKE SRA

(605) 886-4769
State map: C17
From WATERTOWN, drive
W on US 212 about 4 miles (8 k). Turn
Left (S). Continue 3 miles (4.8 k). (Also
see Pelican North West SRA.)
$5; $2 entrance fee.
Open All Year.
20 close, open sites.
Central faucet, pit toilets, tables, fire
rings, boat ramp, shelter, playground.
Next to lake.
Swim, boat, and fish. Hike to observe
wildlife.
14-day limit.

PELICAN NORTH WEST SRA

(605) 886-4769
State map: C17
From WATERTOWN, drive
W on US 212 from about 4 miles (8 k).
Turn Left (S) and go 2 miles (3.2 k).
(Also see Pelican Lake SRA.)
$5; $2 entrance fee.
Open All Year.
15 close, open sites. Central faucet, pit
toilets, tables, fire rings, boat ramp.
Next to Pelican Lake.
Boat or fish.
No trash arrangements (pack it out).
14-day limit.

PEORIA FLATS

COE (605) 845-2252
State map: D11
From PIERRE, drive N on
SD 1804 about 15 miles (24 k). Turn Left
(W). (Also see Cow/Spring Creek.)
FREE so choose a chore.
Open All Year.
Undesignated scattered, open sites.

Pit toilets, tables, fire rings, boat ramp.
On Lake Oahe.
Boat or fish.
NO water. No trash arrangements (pack
it out). 14-day limit.

PICNIC SPRINGS

Custer NF (605) 797-4432
State map: A6
From LUDLOW, travel N
on US 85 for 2 miles (3.2 k). Turn Left
(W) on gravel CR and drive 4 miles
(6.4 k). Turn Right (N) and go 1 mile
(1.6 k). Turn Right (W) on FR 114 and
continue 1 mile (1.6 k). Turn Left for
final .5 mile (800 m).
FREE so choose a chore.
Open May–Sep; dry camping allowed
off-season.
7 scattered, open sites.
Central faucet, pit toilets, tables, grills,
fire rings.
On bench with scattered ponderosa pine,
natural spring, and caves in area.
Hike to explore ecology. View wildlife.
Take photos. Mountain bike.
No trash arrangements (pack it out).
14-day limit. Occasional ATVs. Crowded
fall hunting season.
3600 ft (1080 m)

REARING PONDS

SD Game & Fish
(605) 886-4769
State map: B18
From BIG STONE CITY, drive N on
SD 109 for 4 miles (6.4 k).
FREE so choose a chore.
Open All Year.
Undesignated scattered, open sites.
Pit toilets, tables, boat ramp.
Near Big Stone Lake.
Boat or fish.
NO water. No trash arrangements (pack
it out). 14-day limit.

REDBANK SPRING

Black Hills NF
(307) 746-2783
State map: E5
From NEWCASTLE, WY, drive E on

▲ ▲

US 16 for 8 miles (12.8 k). Turn Left (N) on gravel FR 117. Go 19 miles (30.4 k). Turn Right (E) on FR 384 for additional 2 miles (3.2 k). (Also see Moon.)
FREE so choose a chore.
Open May–Oct; dry camping allowed off-season.
5 close, open sites.
Central faucet, pit toilets, tables, grills, fire rings.
In ponderosa pine/aspen with meadow (cattle-graze) and spring-fed pond.
Fish. Relax. Spot wildlife.
Hunting in season.
6600 ft (1980 m)

REVA GAP

Custer NF (605) 797-4432
State map: B6
From REVA, drive W on SD 20 for 4 miles (6.4 k).
FREE so choose a chore.
Open May–Sep; dry camping allowed off-season.
Undesignated scattered, screened sites.
Hand pump, pit toilets, tables, grills, fire rings.
In badlands topography with hardwood and ponderosa pine.
Visit The Castles National Natural Landmark. Hike to take photos and spot wildlife. Mountain bike.
No trash arrangements (pack it out). 14-day limit. Occasional ATVs. Crowded fall hunting season.
3600 ft (1080 m)

RIFLE PIT

Black Hills NF
(605) 673-4853
State map: F6
From PRINGLE, drive E on US 385 for 4 miles (6.4 k). (Also see Wind Cave NP-Backcountry.)
FREE so choose a chore.
Open May 25–Sep 5.
14 scattered, open sites.
Pit toilets, tables, fire rings.
In peaceful Black Hills setting shaded by pine trees.
Explore nearby Jewel Cave NM, Custer

SP, and Wind Cave NP. Hike. View wildlife.
NO water. 10-day limit.
4700 ft (1410 m)

ROSCOE CITY PARK

State map: B13
Locate park on 3rd Ave N in ROSCOE.
FREE; donations requested.
Open May 15–Oct 1.
6 sites.
Central faucet, flush toilets, dump station, electric hookups, tables, grills, shelter, playground.
In small, town park.
Bike. Enjoy overnight stop.
3-day limit.

ROSE HILL

SD Game & Fish
(605) 853-2533
State map: D14
Head S for 9 miles (14.4 k) from WESSINGTON. Turn Right (W) at lake access sign on gravel road and go 3 miles (4.8 k).
FREE so choose a chore.
Open All Year.
Undesignated scattered, open sites.
Hand pump, pit toilets, tables, fire rings, boat ramp.
Next to lake in open prairie surrounded by trees.
Swim, boat, or fish. View wildlife.
Hunting in season.
1600 ft (480 m)

SAND CREEK

SD Game & Fish
(605) 668-3435
State map: G16
From SPRINGFIELD, drive N on SD 37 for 1 mile (1.6 k). Turn Right (E) on CR and go 3 miles (4.8 k). (Also see Springfield SRA.)
$5; $2 entrance fee.
Open All Year.
12 close, open sites.
Central faucet, pit toilets, tables, fire rings, boat ramp, shelter, playground.

On Lewis & Clark Lake.
Fish. Boat and waterski.
14-day limit.
1200 ft (360 m)

SHAW CREEK

COE (605) 845-2252
State map: A11
From POLLOCK, head S
on SD 1804 about 6 miles (9.6 k). Turn
Right (W) on access road. (Also see West
Pollock.)
FREE so choose a chore.
Open All Year.
Undesignated scattered, open sites.
Hand pump, pit toilets.
Next to Lake Oahe.
Boat or fish. View wildlife.
No trash arrangements (pack it out).
Hunting in season.

SICA HOLLOW SP

(605) 448-5701
State map: A17
From CLAIRE CITY, head
S for 10 miles (16 k). Turn Right (W) and
drive 7 miles (11.2 k).
$5; $2 entrance fee.
Open All Year.
Undesignated scattered, screened sites.
Pit toilets, tables.
Near legendary bog with trees and
stream.
Walk Trail of the Spirits and watch for
monster.
NO water. No trash arrangements (pack
it out). 14-day limit.

SOUTH SCALP CREEK

COE (605) 487-7847
State map: G14
From FAIRFAX, head E on
US 18 for 9 miles (14.4 k). Turn Left (N)
and drive 5 miles (8 k). (Also see Joe
Day Bay.)
FREE so choose a chore.
Open All Year.
Undesignated scattered, open sites.
Central faucet, pit toilets, tables, fire
rings, boat ramp, shelter.
On shore of Lake Francis Case.

Swim, boat, ski, or fish.
No trash arrangements. 14-day limit.

SOUTH SHORE

COE (605) 487-7847
State map: G14
From PICKSTOWN, drive
W on US 18 and cross dam. Turn Right
(N). (Also see Spillway.)
FREE so choose a chore.
Open All Year.
Undesignated open sites.
Pit toilets, tables, fire rings, boat ramp,
shelter.
Along shore of Lake Francis Case.
Swim, boat, ski, or fish.
NO water. No trash arrangements (pack
it out). 14-day limit.

SOUTH WHEELER

COE (605) 487-7847
State map: G14
From BONESTEEL, head
SE on US 18 about 1 mile (1.6 k). Bear
Left (NE) on CR. Drive 10 miles (16 k).
FREE so choose a chore.
Open All Year.
Undesignated scattered, open sites.
Pit toilets, tables, fire rings, boat ramp,
shelter.
On Lake Francis Case.
Fish and boat.
NO water. No trash arrangements (pack
it out). 14-day limit.

SPILLWAY

COE (605) 487-7847
State map: G14
On SD 46 just W of
PICKSTOWN, turn Left (S) before dam.
(Also see South Shore. Nearby Randall
Creek and North Point cost $9.)
FREE so choose a chore.
Open All Year.
Undesignated open sites.
Pit toilets, tables, fire rings, boat ramp,
shelter.
On Missouri River.
Boat or fish.
NO water. No trash arrangements (pack
it out). 14-day limit.

SPRINGFIELD SRA

(605) 668-3435
State map: G16
From SPRINGFIELD, go E
for 1 mile (1.6 k). (Also see Sand Creek.)
$5; $2 entrance fee.
Open All Year.
12 close, open sites.
Central faucet, flush/pit toilets, dump
station, electric hookups, tables, fire
rings, boat ramp, shelter, playground.
Next to Lewis & Clark Lake.
Boat and waterski. Swim. Fish.
14-day limit.
1200 ft (360 m)

SUTTON BAY

SD Game & Fish
(605) 765-9410
State map: C11
From AGAR, drive W for 12 miles
(19.2 k). Turn Right (N) on CR 1804. Go
4 miles (6.4 k). (See Bush's Landing.)
FREE so choose a chore.
Open All Year.
Undesignated open sites. Pit toilets,
dump station, tables, boat ramp.
Next to Lake Oahe.
Boat or fish.
NO water. No trash arrangements (pack
it out). 14-day limit.

SWAN CREEK

SD Game & Fish
(605) 765-9410
State map: B11
From AKASKA, proceed W on CR for
9 miles (14.4 k). (Also see Bowdle Beach.)
$5; $2 entrance fee.
Open All Year.
25 scattered, open sites.
Central faucet, flush/pit toilets, tables,
fire rings, boat ramp, shelter.
On Lake Oahe.
Fish and boat.
14-day limit.

TABOR

SD Game & Fish
(605) 668-3435
State map: G16

From TABOR, travel S for 6 miles (9.6 k)
following signs.
FREE so choose a chore.
Open All Year.
10 close, open sites.
Pit toilets, boat ramp.
Next to Lewis & Clark Lake.
Boat or fish.
NO water. No trash arrangements (pack
it out). 14-day limit.
1200 ft (360 m)

THOMAS BAY

COE (605) 845-2252
State map: B11
From GLENHAM, head S
on SD 1804 about 5 miles (8 k). (Also see
Blue Blanket and Walth Bay.)
FREE so choose a chore.
Open All Year.
Undesignated scattered, open sites.
Hand pump, pit toilets, boat ramp.
On Lake Oahe.
Boat. Fish. Watch wildlife.
No trash arrangements (pack it out).
Hunting in season.

TWIN LAKES

SD Game & Fish
(605) 256-3613
State map: E15
Drive S for 6 miles (9.6 k) from
WOONSOCKET. Turn Right (W) and
continue 3 miles (4.8 k).
FREE so choose a chore.
Open All Year.
7 close, screened sites.
Hand pump, pit toilets, tables, fire rings.
Next to small lake.
Fish and boat.
Occasionally crowded.
1564 ft (469 m)

TYNDALL CITY PARK

(605) 589-3481
State map: G16
Find park in TYNDALL.
(Also see College Memorial Park.)
FREE so choose a chore.
Open May 1 – Oct 15; dry camping
allowed off-season.

2 close, open sites.
Central faucet, flush toilets, showers, dump station, electric hookups, tables, grills, pool, pay phone.
In city park.
Swim.
7-day limit. Occasionally crowded and noisy.

ULVEN PARK

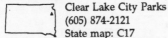

Clear Lake City Parks
(605) 874-2121
State map: C17

Just E of CLEAR LAKE, find park on SD 22. (Also see Clear Lake City Park and Lake Cochrane SRA.)
$3.
Open May–Oct.
22 close, open sites.
Water at 5 sites, pit toilets, dump station, electric hookups, tables.
In municipal park next to lake and golf course.
Fish. Enjoy overnight stop.

VANDER VORSTE BAY

COE (605) 845-2252
State map: A11
From POLLOCK, drive NW on SD 1406 about 5 miles (8 k). (Also see West Pollock.)
FREE so choose a chore.
Open All Year.
Undesignated scattered, open sites.
Hand pump, pit toilets, boat ramp.
On Lake Oahe.
Boat or fish. Watch wildlife.
No trash arrangements (pack it out).
Hunting in season.

WALTH BAY

COE (605) 845-2252
State map: B11
From GLENHAM, head S on SD 1804 about 7 miles (11.2 k). (Also see Bowdle Beach and Thomas Bay.)
FREE so choose a chore.
Open All Year.
Undesignated scattered, open sites.
Hand pump, pit toilets, boat ramp.

Next to Lake Oahe.
Boat. Fish. See wildlife.
No trash arrangements (pack it out).
Hunting in season.

WASHINGTON PARK

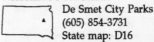

De Smet City Parks
(605) 854-3731
State map: D16

Find park at 3rd St & Harvey Dunn Ave in DE SMET.
$5; $7 electric; reservations accepted at (605) 854-3731.
Open May 1–Oct 31.
40 (30 tent-only) close, open sites.
Central faucet, flush toilets, showers, electric hookups, tables, grills.
Among trees and flowers in town park.
Bike. Enjoy overnight stop.
1753 ft (526 m)

WEST BRIDGE

COE (605) 487-7847
State map: F13
From PLATTE, drive W on SD 50 for 18 miles (28.8 k)–cross bridge.
Turn Left (S). (Also see Buryanek.)
FREE so choose a chore.
Open All Year.
Undesignated scattered, open sites.
Pit toilets, boat ramp.
Next to Lake Francis Case.
Boat or fish.
NO water. No trash arrangements (pack it out). 14-day limit.

WEST POLLOCK

COE (605) 845-2252
State map: A11
Locate area on W edge of POLLOCK. (Also see Shaw Creek and Vander Vorste Bay.)
FREE so choose a chore.
Open All Year.
Undesignated scattered, open sites.
Hand pump, pit toilets, boat ramp.
On arm of Lake Oahe.
Fish and boat.
No trash arrangements (pack it out).

WEST SHORE

COE (605) 845-2252
State map: D11
From PIERRE, head N on ND 1804 to dam road. Turn Left (W) and cross dam. Turn Right (N).
FREE so choose a chore.
Open All Year.
Undesignated scattered, open sites.
Pit toilets, tables, fire rings, boat ramp.
On Lake Oahe.
Boat. Fish.
NO water. No trash arrangements (pack it out). 14-day limit.

WHETSTONE BAY

COE (605) 487-7847
State map: G14
From BONESTEEL, drive N on SD 1806 for 10 miles (16 k).
FREE so choose a chore.
Open All Year.
10 close, open sites.
Central faucet, pit toilets, tables, fire rings, boat ramp, shelter.
Next to Lake Francis Case.
Boat or fish.
No trash arrangements. 14-day limit.

WHITE RIVER CITY PARK

(605) 259-3242
State map: F10
Find in WHITE RIVER.
FREE so choose a chore.
Open All Year.
8 scattered, open sites.
Hand pump, pit toilets, tables, tennis court, ball fields.
In municipal park with shade trees.
Explore scenic area. Bike.
Crowded 3rd weekend in Aug (Frontier Days).

WHITE SWAN

COE (605) 487-7847
State map: G14
From LAKE ANDES, travel W on SD 50 about 10 miles (16 k). Turn Left (SW) at sign and go 2 miles (3.2 k).

FREE so choose a chore.
Open All Year.
Undesignated open sites.
Pit toilets, tables, fire rings, boat ramp, shelter.
Next to Lake Francis Case.
Boat or fish.
NO water. No trash arrangements (pack it out). 14-day limit.

WHITLOCKS EAST

SD Game & Fish
(605) 765-9410
State map: C11
From GETTYSBURG, head W on US 212 for 13 miles (20.8 k). Turn Right (NW). Go 3 miles (4.8 k). (Also see Forest City.)
$5; $2 entrance fee.
Open All Year.
10 close, open sites.
Central faucet, pit toilets, tables, fire rings, boat ramp, shelter.
On Lake Oahe.
Fish and boat.
14-day limit.

WICKHAM GULCH

Custer NF (605) 797-4432
State map: B5
Head W on SD 20 from CAMP CROOK for 3 miles (4.8 k). Turn Right on CR 3049 (Capitol Rock Rd). Go 3 miles (4.8 k). Turn on CR 3060. Drive 1.5 miles (2.4 k) to Wickham Gulch.
FREE so choose a chore.
Open May–Sep; dry camping allowed off-season.
Undesignated open sites.
Central faucet, pit toilets, tables, grills, fire rings.
Close to Capitol Rock National Natural Landmark in hardwood draw with intermittent stream and natural spring.
Hike to explore area. Mountain bike. Take photos.
No trash arrangements (pack it out). 14-day limit. Crowded fall hunting season.
3600 ft (1080 m)

▲ ▲

WIND CAVE NP-Backcountry
(605) 745-4600
State Map: F6
From HOT SPRINGS, drive
N on US 385 for 13 miles (20.8 k). Obtain
permit and regulations at Visitor Center.
(Also see Rifle Pit. Elk Mountain
campground costs $8.)
FREE.
Open All Year
Undesignated scattered tent sites.
Along edge of Black Hills with wooded
slopes and stream-cut grasslands.
Hike. Observe wildife (especially bison).
Take lots of photos.
NO water. No toilet facilities. No trash
arrangements (pack it out).

TENNESSEE
CAMPGROUND LOCATIONS

▶ ▶ Find location on facing page map grid. ▶ ▶
▼ ▼ Locate area campgrounds on these page numbers. ▼ ▼

GRID	PAGE
A10	388
A11	385
A12	385
A16	387
A17	385
B8	386
B9	386
B15	387, 388
B16	385, 386, 387, 388
C7	386
C15	387, 388
D6	388
D12	385, 387, 389
E12	389

Tennessee

Grid conforms to official state map. For your copy, call (615) 741-2158
or write Dept of Tourist Development, PO Box 23170, Nashville, TN 37202.

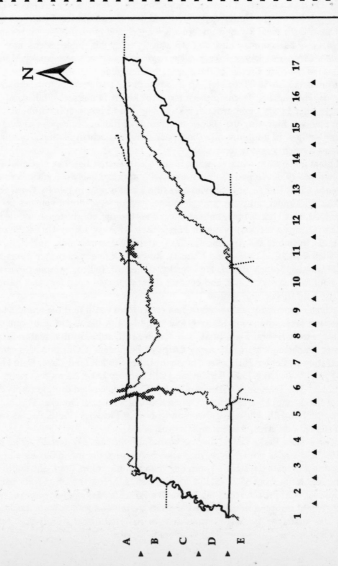

PUBLIC LANDS CAMPING

A wide state, Tennessee stretches from the Mississippi Delta, to mountain plateaus and valleys, then up the Great Smoky Mountains. Traveling across the state, see lots of natural and rural beauty, hear the country music, and experience genuine southern hospitality.

The **National Park Service** (NPS) manages Big South Fork National River and Recreation Area (RA), Great Smoky Mountains National Park (NP), and Natchez Trace Parkway. On the Cumberland Plateau, Big South Fork National River RA has reclaimed the Big South Fork of the Cumberland River and its main tributaries (Clear Fork, North White Oak and the New River) from farmers, loggers, and miners. Now while camping at developed or backcountry sites, you can actively enjoy this rugged scenic area - fish, whitewater canoe, raft, kayak, hike, bicycle, or ride horseback. Great Smoky Mountain NP preserves the climax forest of the Appalachian highlands. Camp in ten developed campgrounds ($6.00–$8.00) or sign up in advance for free permits to backpack into park wilds. The Natchez Trace northern terminus lies in Tennessee. While camping at free Meriwether Lewis Campground, hike to view and photograph nature along the tranquil pathway following the historic trade route of Indians, European traders, then American settlers. In addition, hike/backpack the Appalachian National Scenic Trail that passes through eastern Tennessee.

Find great inspiration while camping in the 625,000-acre **Cherokee National Forest** (NF). There are 29 developed camping areas with approximately 685 sites. Fees range from free to $8.00. In this Appalachian area (the forest is split in two by Great Smoky Mountains NP), most campsites accommodate tents or recreational vehicles up to 22 feet. Campers may choose other splendid locations throughout the forest. While in the Cherokee NF, drive the first National Forest Scenic Byway, Ocoee-US 64. Enjoy 105 hiking trails, including the Appalachian Trail. Access wilderness areas, including Joyce Kilmer-Slick Rock, Gee Creek, and Cohutta. Run one of five whitewater rivers in the forest: Hiwassee, French Broad, Nolichucky, Ocoee, or Tellico. Sample other water sports: trout fishing, swimming, and boating. Keep your eyes open for black bear, wild boar, deer, wild turkey, and grouse.

Enjoy water recreation year-round in Tennessee. Here you'll find the world's largest underground lakes, the second-largest manmade lake in the world, plus one of the world's greatest rivers. Fish, boat, sail, canoe, raft, tube, scuba, waterski, even houseboat Tennessee waters. **US Army Corps of Engineers** (COE) provides camping and recreation at Center Hill Lake, Cheatham Lake, Cordell Hull Lake, Dale Hollow Lake, J Percy Priest Lake, Lake Barkley, and Old Hickory Lake. Camp fees range from free to $24.00. The **Tennessee Valley Authority** (TVA) has created campgrounds on the following flood-control lakes: Chatuge, Cherokee, Chickamauga, Douglas, Fort Loudon, Kentucky, Melton Hill, Nickajack, Normandy, Norris, Pickwick, Watts Bar, as well as Foster Falls Natural Area. Basic campsites cost $8.00.

Tennessee State Parks (SP) showcase beautiful mountains, waterfalls, animal and plant life. Bald eagles winter here; rhododendrons paint the mountainsides in June; water sports dominate the stage all summer; then autumn colors drape the entire state. Camping fees range from $5.25–$11.00 for rustic sites. Access the Obed National Wild and Scenic River at Frozen Head SP. **Tennessee Wildlife Management Areas** (WMA) allow overnight camping in designated areas by permission from area manager, park ranger, lake manager, park superintendent or national forest supervisor. Among **counties** and **towns**, Anderson County offers $7.00 sites.

▲ ▲

When you drive Tennessee's highways, look for the mockingbird signs indicating a scenic parkway. While you camp Tennessee's public lands, you may find Tennessee is playing your song.

▲ ▲

BACKBONE ROCK

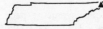

Cherokee NF
(615) 542-2942
State map: A17
From SHADY VALLEY, head N on TN 133 for 9 miles (14.4 k).
$5.
Open May–Nov.
13 close, screened sites.
Central faucet, flush toilets, tables, grills, fire rings.
Along a stream in mountain cove.
Fish. Hike to explore area.
14-day limit. Hunting in season.
2000 ft (600 m)

BIG SOUTH FORK NRA
Backcountry

(615) 569-9778
State map: A12
Head W on TN 297 from ONEIDA for 12 miles (19.2 k) to Visitor Center. Obtain backcountry information and hike to selected site.
FREE; developed sites at Bandy Creek cost $10.
Open All Year.
Undesignated sites.
Chemical toilets, boat ramp.
Along Big South Fork of Cumberland River in rugged scenic area.
Whitewater raft or kayak. Fish. Swim (tricky currents). Hike to find scenic beauty, flora and fauna, abandoned structures. Ride scenic railway ($).
NO water. No trash arrangements (pack it out). Hunting in season (check on dates).
1700 ft (510 m)

CARDENS BLUFF

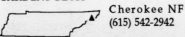

Cherokee NF
(615) 542-2942

State map: B16
From HAMPTON, head NE on US 321 for 3 miles (4.8 k). (Also see Dennis Cove.)
$5.
Open May 1–Oct 5.
43 scattered, screened sites.
Central faucet, flush toilets, tables, fire rings, grills, boat ramp.
On wooded hillside-peninsula on south side of Watauga Lake.
Fish or boat. Explore nearby scenic area. Hike.
14-day/16-ft limits.
2000 ft (600 m)

COVE CREEK

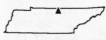

COE
(615) 243-3136
State map: A11
From BYRDSTOWN, head SW on CR for 3 miles (4.8 k). (Nearby Obey River costs $8.)
FREE so choose a chore.
Open All Year.
10 scattered, open sites.
Pit toilets, tables, grills, boat ramp.
On shore of Dale Hollow Lake.
Swim, boat, ski, or fish. View wildlife.
NO water. 14-day limit.
675 ft (203 m)

DAVIS BRANCH

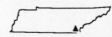

Cherokee NF
(615) 253-2520
State map: D12
From TELLICO PLAINS, take TN 165 E about 4 miles (6.4 k). Bear Right (SE) on FR 210 (see sign to Bald River Falls) and go about 14 miles (22.4 k). (Also see Holly Flats, Spivey Cove, and Stateline. Nearby Big Oak Cove costs $6.)
$5.
Open All Year.

4 close, open sites.
Hand pump, pit toilets, tables, grills, fire rings.
Next to Tellico River.
Fish. Explore area.
14-day limit. Hunting in season. Occasionally crowded.

DENNIS COVE

Cherokee NF
(615) 743-4452
State map: B16
From HAMPTON, take FR 50 E for 5 miles (8 k). (Also see Cardens Bluff.)
FREE so choose a chore.
Open May 7–Dec 15.
18 close, open, tent sites.
Central faucet, flush toilets, tables, grills.
In upland hardwood with stream.
Hike along Laurel Fork. Fish.
No trash arrangements. 14-day limit.
2600 ft (780 m)

FALL CREEK

COE
(615) 889-1975
State map: B8
On I-24 SE of NASHVILLE, exit onto Sam Ridley Pkwy. Drive N to TN 266. Turn Left and go to Mona Rd. Turn Left and follow signs–total of 14 miles (22.4 k) from I-24.
FREE so choose a chore.
Open Apr 1–Oct 31.
37 scattered, screened sites. ♿
Tables, boat ramp.
In isolated, forest setting on J Percy Priest Lake (only free choice in area).
Swim, boat, ski, or fish. Mountain bike. Spot wildlife.
NO water. No toilet facilities. 14-day limit.
500 ft (150 m)

GREAT SMOKY MOUNTAINS NP
Backcountry

(615) 436-1200
State map: C14
Find Visitor
Center in GATLINBURG. Obtain backcountry information and permit.

Hike to selected site.
FREE; developed campgrounds cost from $6 to $9.
Open All Year.
Undesignated sites.
With over 800-miles (1280-k) of trails in spectacular mountain area.
Hike. Take photos. Commune with nature.
NO water. No trash arrangements (pack it out). Bear country. 3-day limit per site.

HARPETH RIVER BRIDGE

COE
(615) 792-5697
State map: C7
From ASHLAND CITY, travel W on TN 49 for 7 miles (11.2 k).
FREE so choose a chore.
Open All Year.
15 scattered, open sites.
Chemical toilets, tables, fire rings, boat ramp.
Next to Harpeth River in medium shade.
Boat or fish.
NO water. 14-day limit. Crowded weekends.
395 ft (119 m)

HOLLOMAN'S BEND

COE
(615) 735-1034
State map: B9
From GRANVILLE, drive E on TN 53 for .5 mile (800 m). Turn Left (N) on Holloman's Bend Rd and go 3 miles (4.8 k) to end.
FREE so choose a chore.
Open All Year.
6 close, open sites.
Central faucet, chemical toilets, tables, fire rings, boat ramp.
In grassy area next to Cordell Hull Lake.
Boat or fish.
No trash arrangements (pack it out). 14-day limit. Occasionally crowded with horses.

HOLLY FLATS

Cherokee NF
(615) 253-2520

▲ ▲

State map: D12
From COKER CREEK, take gravel
FR 126 E about 7 miles (11.2 k). (Also see
Davis Branch and Spivey Cove.)
FREE so choose a chore.
Open All Year.
17 close, screened sites.
Hand pump, pit toilets, tables, grills, fire
rings.
On Bald River.
Walk nature trail. Hike to explore Bald
River Gorge. Mountain bike. Swim. Fish.
No trash arrangements (pack it out).
14-day limit. Hunting in season.

HORSE CREEK

Cherokee NF
(615) 638-4109
State map: B15

From GREENEVILLE, drive NE on
TN 107 for 6 miles (9.6 k). Turn Right
(SE) on signed FR 94 for 2 miles (3.2 k).
(Also see Old Forge.)
$5. Open Apr 10–Oct 15.
18 (6 tent-only) screened sites. &
Central faucet, flush/pit toilets, tables,
grills, fire rings.
Along creek in wooded setting.
Swim. Fish (special regulations). Walk
nature trail or hike farther for photo
opportunities.
14-day limit.
1720 ft (516 m)

HOUSTON VALLEY

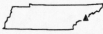

Cherokee NF
(615) 638-4109
State map: C15

From NEWPORT, go E on US 25 for
12 miles (19.2 k). Turn Left (N) on
TN 107 and drive 4 miles (6.4 k). (Also
see Paint Creek.)
$5. Open Apr–Nov.
10 scattered, screened sites.
Central faucet, flush toilets, tables, grills,
fire rings.
At base of hill in oak-hickory forest.
Hike scenic area and spot wildlife. Take
photos.
14-day limit.
1800 ft (540 m)

JAKE BEST

Cherokee NF
(615) 253-2520
State map: D12

From TELLICO PLAINS, drive E on
TN 165 about 9 miles (14.4 k). At
switchback, turn Left (NE) on gravel
FR 345 (changes to 35-1) and go another
7 miles (11.2 k). Pass Indian Boundary
($7) and Double Camp ($6).
FREE so choose a chore.
Open All Year.
11 close, open sites.
Pit toilets, tables, grills, fire rings.
Along Citico Creek.
Fish. Explore area.
NO water. No trash arrangements (pack
it out). 14-day limit. Hunting in season.
Occasionally crowded.

LIMESTONE COVE

Cherokee NF
(615) 743-4452
State map: B16

From UNICOI, drive E on TN 107 for
4 miles (6.4 k).
FREE so choose a chore.
Open May 1–Oct 1.
18 close, open sites.
Hand pump, pit toilets, tables, grills.
In mountainous area next to stream.
Fish. Hike.
14-day/22-ft limits.

LOW GAP

Cherokee NF
(615) 542-2942
State map: A16

From ELIZABETHTON, drive NE on
TN 91 for 12 miles (19.2 k). Turn Left
(W) on gravel FR 56 (Holston Mountain)
and continue 6.5 miles (10.4 k), bearing
Left at fork.
FREE so choose a chore. Open All Year.
8 scattered, screened sites.
Pit toilets, tables, fire rings.
At gap on top of mountain.
Relax. Enjoy mountains.
NO water. No trash arrangements (pack
it out). 14-day/16-ft limits.
4000 ft (1200 m)

▲ ▲

NATCHEZ TRACE PARKWAY
Meriwether Lewis

(601) 535-7142
State map: D6
Find camp on
Natchez Trace Parkway at milepost
385.9, about 7 miles (11.2 k) SE of
HOHENWALD.
FREE. Open All Year.
32 scattered, open sites. &
Central faucet, flush toilets, tables, grills.
In hardwood forest at site of Grinder's
Inn (where Meriwether Lewis died).
Walk nature trail. Hike or bike to
explore historic area (Steele's Iron Works
and Napier Ore Pit nearby).
14-day/35-ft limits. Occasionally
crowded.
900 ft (270 m)

OLD FORGE

Cherokee NF
(615) 638-4109
State map: B15
From GREENEVILLE, drive NE on
TN 107 for 6 miles (9.6 k). Turn Right
(SE) on signed FR 94. Travel 2 miles
(3.2 k). Bear Right (S) on FR 331. Go
3 miles (4.8 k). (Also see Horse Creek.)
$5. Open Apr 3–Oct 15.
9 scattered, screened tent sites. &
Hand pump, pit toilets, tables, grills, fire
rings.
In woods set back from creek.
Walk nature trail or hike. Swim or fish.
14-day limit. Occasional horses in area.
2000 ft (600 m)

PAINT CREEK

Cherokee NF
(615) 638-4109
State map: C15
From NEWPORT, go E on US 25 for
12 miles (19.2 k). Turn Left (N) on
TN 107 and drive 10 miles (16 k). Turn
Right (SE) on FR 31 and continue 2 miles
(3.2 k). (Also see Houston Valley.)
$5. Open Apr–Oct.
21 (3 tent-only) screened sites. &
Hand pump, pit toilets, tables, grills, fire
rings.

In mountain cove along Paint Creek.
Hike to take photos. Fish.
14-day limit. Occasionally crowded.
1800 ft (540 m)

PLEASANT GROVE

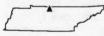

COE
(615) 243-3555
State map: A10
From CELINA, travel N on TN 53 for
3 miles (4.8 k). Turn Right (E) and follow
signs. (Nearby Dam RA costs $12.)
FREE so choose a chore.
Open Apr 1–Oct 31.
20 scattered, open, tent sites.
Central faucet, flush toilets, tables, fire
rings, grills, boat ramp, pay phone.
On peninsula in Dale Hollow Lake with
swinging bridge to island.
Scuba dive. Swim, boat, ski, or fish. Hike
to observe wildlife and take photos.
14-day limit. Crowded holidays.
675 ft (203 m)

ROCK CREEK

Cherokee NF
(615) 743-4452
State map: B16
From ERWIN, take Rock Creek Rd E for
3 miles (4.8 k).
$5. Open May 7–Oct 7.
36 scattered, open sites.
Central faucet, flush toilets, showers,
dump station, tables, grills, fire rings.
In mountain cove with hardwood next to
creek.
Swim. Walk nature trail. Hike and
explore scenic area.
14-day limit. Occasionally crowded.
2200 ft (660 m)

ROUND MOUNTAIN

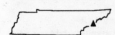

Cherokee NF
(615) 638-4109
State map: C15
From NEWPORT, go E on US 25 for
10 miles (16 k). Turn Right (S) at Del Rio
on TN 107 and drive 12 miles (19.2 k).
$5. Open Apr–Oct.
16 scattered, screened sites. Hand pump,
pit toilets, tables, grills, fire rings.

▲ ▲

Near top of Round Mountain.
Hike (Appalachian Trail nearby). Take
photos from viewpoints. Relax.
14-day limit. Small vehicles only.
3000 ft (900 m)

SPIVEY COVE

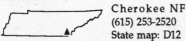

Cherokee NF
(615) 253-2520
State map: D12

From TELLICO PLAINS, take TN 165 E
about 4 miles (6.4 k). Bear Right (SE) on
FR 210 (see sign to Bald River Falls) and
go 12 miles (19.2 k). (Also see Davis
Branch and Holly Flats. Nearby North
River costs $6.)
$5. Open Apr–Dec.
17 scattered, open sites.
Hand pump, pit toilets, tables, grills, fire
rings.
In beautiful mountain cove near Tellico
River.
Hike to spot wildlife and take photos.
Mountain bike. Fish.
14-day limit. Hunting in season.

STATELINE

Cherokee NF
(615) 253-2520
State map: D12

From TELLICO PLAINS, take TN 165 E
about 4 miles (6.4 k). Bear Right (SE) on
FR 210 (see sign to Bald River Falls) and
go about 16 miles (25.6 k). (Also see
Davis Branch.)
$5. Open All Year.
7 close, open sites. Hand pump, pit
toilets, tables, grills, fire rings.
Near Tellico River.
Canoe. Fish. Explore.
14-day limit. Hunting in season. ATVs
in area.

SYLCO

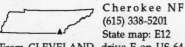

Cherokee NF
(615) 338-5201
State map: E12

From CLEVELAND, drive E on US 64
for 11 miles (17.6 k) to Cherokee
Corners. Turn Right on Baker's Creek Rd
(becomes FR 55) and go 10 miles (16 k).

FREE so choose a chore.
Open All Year.
12 close, screened sites.
Pit toilets, tables, grills.
In isolated, mountainous area.
Relax. Hike to explore.
NO water. No trash arrangements (pack
it out). 14-day/22-ft limits. No trailers.

THUNDER ROCK

Cherokee NF
(615) 338-5201
State map: E12

From CLEVELAND, travel W on US 64
for 25 miles (40 k). At Ocoee #3
Powerhouse, cross bridge. Turn Right.
Follow around powerhouse and take
next Right. (Also see Tumbling Creek.)
$4. Open Apr–Oct; dry camping allowed
off-season.
29 close, open sites.
Hand pump, pit toilets, tables, grills.
Next to Ocoee River at put-in spot for
whitewater rafting.
Raft or kayak. Walk nature trail.
14-day limit.

TUMBLING CREEK

Cherokee NF
(615) 338-5201
State map: E12

From CLEVELAND, travel W on US 64
for 25 miles (40 k). At Ocoee #3
Powerhouse, cross bridge and turn
Right. Follow road around powerhouse
and go 2 miles (3.2 k). Bear Left at fork
on FR 221 and drive 6 miles (9.6 k).
(Also see Thunder Rock.)
FREE so choose a chore.
Open Apr–Oct; dry camping allowed
off-season.
8 close, open sites.
Hand pump, pit toilets, tables, grills.
In isolated area near stream.
Enjoy quiet. Fish. Explore.
No trash arrangements (pack it out).
14-day limit. No trailers.

TEXAS
CAMPGROUND LOCATIONS

▶ ▶ Find location on facing page map grid. ▶ ▶
▼ ▼ Locate area campgrounds on these page numbers. ▼ ▼

GRID	PAGE	GRID	PAGE	GRID	PAGE
A11	420	J18	409, 410, 411, 417	N12	410
B10	418	J20	405	N14	419
B12	406	J21	407	N15	398
C10	402, 406	J22	397, 402, 411	N17	397, 403, 412, 420, 421
C11	402	K8	394	N18	400
D9	396	K11	400, 405, 416	N22	396, 416
F12	397	K12	405	N23	402, 421
G8	410	K13	404, 416	N24	417
G9	396, 408, 420	K18	408	O15	395, 415
G10	398	K22	409	O16	418
G16	395, 404, 420	L4	401	O17	401
G18	395, 410, 413	L10	398	O20	404, 418
G19	398, 405	L13	414	O23	396, 399
G20	408, 416	L15	402	P16	399
H9	398	L17	397, 404, 411, 413, 417, 419	P19	412, 415
H11	398	L18	413, 421	P23	397
H15	401	L23	414	Q16	403, 410
H16	416, 421	M12	408, 415	Q21	393
H17	395	M13	394, 412	Q22	399, 400, 404, 409, 421
H18	399, 411, 418	M14	401	R7	394
H19	407	M16	400	R11	393
H21	399, 412, 419	M17	410	R22	404
H22	402, 403, 408, 411, 413	M19	405, 414	S6-S7	394
H23	419	M21	414	T16	418
J9	400	M22	399	T17	401
J12	401, 417	M23	403, 408, 415, 419	U19	409
J15	405	N8	416	V17	413
J17	415, 420	N10	414	V18	412, 413

Texas

Grid conforms to official state map. For your copy, call (800) 8888-TEX
or write Dept of Transportation, PO Box 5064, Austin, TX 78763-5064.

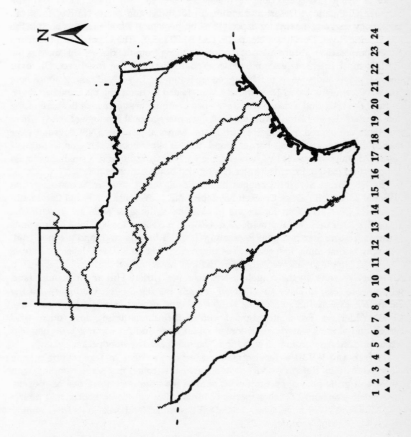

PUBLIC LANDS CAMPING

The great state of Texas offers several ecologies for your outdoor pleasure: mountains in the west, plains in the panhandle, pine forests in the east, granite hills in the center, 600 sun-swept miles of beach along the gulf, and subtropics in its tip.

Amistad National Recreation Area (NRA), Big Bend National Park (NP) including the Rio Grande Wild and Scenic River, Guadalupe Mountains NP, and Lake Meredith NRA offer developed **National Park Service** (NPS) campgrounds as well as free backcountry opportunities. At Amistad NRA at the confluence of the Rio Grande, Devil's, and Pecos rivers, an international reservoir has been created. Enjoy all water sports as well as hiking and camping (developed sites are free). In Big Bend NP, choose between Chihuahuan Desert and mountain locations and more. Native American mythology suggests the Creator deposited all his geological leftovers at this bend in the Rio Grande River. Developed campsites cost $4.00–$5.00. The Guadalupe Mountains NP encompasses an abrupt mass of mountains rising from the desert. This mass is the world's most extensive example of an exposed Permian Era fossil reef. Discover unusual plants and animals in this rugged environment. Developed campgrounds here cost $6.00 per night. Lake Meredith NRA was created by damming the Canadian River. Around the lake, find a dozen free developed camping areas. The south shore of the lake borders the prehistoric Alibates Flint Quarries National Monument (NM) where free tours are offered. Although Padre Island National Seashore (NS) does not offer backcountry permits on this barrier island, it does allow boondocking on 65 miles of beach (7.5 miles accessible by 2-wheel-drive vehicle) in addition to a small developed campground ($4.00). Enjoy saltwater fishing and beach activities here.

The **US Forest Service** manages five national forest areas in Texas: Angelina National Forest (NF), Davy Crockett NF, Sabine NF, Sam Houston NF, and Caddo–LBJ Grassland (NG). The four forests are in east Texas; the grasslands are in northeast Texas. Together these areas provide 25 developed recreation areas, 3 long hiking trails (including Lone Star National Recreation Trail), a bicycle trail, and a canoe trail. Camping is first-come, first-serve. Fees range from free to $8.00 in developed areas. Dispersed camping is allowed anywhere in forest areas—except during hunting season for safety reasons. In the Angelina NF, discover Turkey Hill and Upland Island wilderness areas. In Davy Crockett NF, there's the Big Slough Wilderness. In the Sabine NF, explore Indian Mounds Wilderness, and in Sam Houston NF, Little Lake Creek Wilderness. Frequently sighted wildlife include mourning dove, quail, wild turkey, and various waterfowl, cottontail rabbit, gray and fox squirrel, wild hog and whitetail deer. An uncommon sighting is the red-cockaded woodpecker.

US Fish and Wildlife Service manages several refuges in Texas. Buffalo Lake National Wildlife Refuge (NWR) provides free first-come, first-serve camping with tables and grills plus opportunities to admire the migratory fowl. See bald eagle, peregrine falcon, and 272 other species of birds. Also, view deer, bobcat, and prairie dog. Muleshoe NWR offers water, toilet facilities, tables, and grills at its free camping area while viewing wildlife.

Rounding out federal public lands opportunities, **US Army Corps of Engineers** (COE) provides camping at B A Steinhagen Lake, Bardwell Lake, Benbrook Lake, Canyon Lake, Georgetown Lake, Granger Lake, Grapevine Lake, Hords Creek Lake, Lake O' The Pines, Lake Somerville, Lake Texoma, Lake Waco, Lavon Lake, Lewisville Lake, Navarro Mills, O C Fisher Lake, Pat Mayse Lake, Proctor Lake, Sam Rayburn Reservoir, Somerville Lake, Stillhouse Hollow Lake, Whitney Lake, and Wright Patman Lake. Basic COE camping fees range from free to $12.00.

▲ ▲

Out of 125 **Texas State Park** (SP) facilities, 71 parks offer developed campsites, 30 provide primitive sites, and 20 have backpacking opportunities. The fee structure is complex, varying with the availability of facilities, the popularity of the park, as well as the season of the year or day of the week. In-season or weekend camping costs $2.00 more than out-of-season or weekday fees that range from $4.00–$15.00.

Texas has created **public utilities** that allow camping along power-generating waterways. The Lower Colorado River Authority offers free primitive camping around Lake Travis and $3.00 developed camping around Lake Buchanan. Look at the primitive areas provided by the Brazos River Authority and Guadalupe-Blanco River Authority, too.

In addition, Texas allows 24-hour stops at its **state highway picnic and rest areas**. Erect no tents or other structures in these places. Too, do not confuse state areas with federal highway rest stops.

Numerous **towns** and **counties** provide camping: Abilene, Andrews, Ballinger, Chambers County, Coleman, Colorado City, Franklin County, Gatesville, Harris County, Limestone County, Littlefield, McCamey, Montague County, Nueces County, Orange County, Pampa, Perryton, and Quitman.

Thanks to the untiring efforts of Lady Bird Johnson, Mother Nature puts on a spectacular wildflower show in Texas each spring. The Texas state flower, the blue bonnet or blue lupine, is particularly eye-catching along highways and byways.

▲ ▲

ALEXANDER DEUSSEN COUNTY PARK

(713) 454-7057
State map: Q21
On E side of HOUSTON at I-10 and Beltway 8, take Beltway 8 N about 15 miles (24 k). Exit on C E King Parkway. Drive NE for 4 miles (6.4 k).
FREE; $4 RV.
Open All Year.
14 scattered, open sites.
Water at every site, flush toilets, dump station, electric hookups, tables, grills, boat ramp, playground, pay phone.
In wooded area next to Houston Lake.
View wildlife exhibit. Walk nature trail.
Bike. Swim, boat, ski, or fish.
14-day limit.

AMISTAD NRA

(512) 775-7491
State map: R11
FREE. Also, free backcountry permits available.
Open All Year.

▲ **277 North**
From DEL RIO, take US 277/377 N to just past bridge.
8 scattered, open sites.
Chemical toilets, tables, grills.
On gentle slope next to Lake Amistad with typical plants and shrubs of Chihuahuan Desert.
Swim, boat, and fish. Ski nearby.
Observe wildlife. Attend occasional ranger programs.
NO water. 14-day limit. Crowded Dec–Apr.

▲ **Governor's Landing**
From DEL RIO, drive W on US 90 about 4 miles (6.4 k). Turn Left (S) on Spur 349 (road to dam). Take first Right.
17 close, open sites. Chemical toilets, dump station, tables, grills.
On rocky shoreline with low shrubs and trees.
Swim. Fish. View wildlife.
NO water. 14-day limit. Crowded Dec–Apr and holidays.

▲ **San Pedro Flats**
From DEL RIO, head W on US 90 to dirt Spur 454. Turn Right (N) and go .5 mile

▲▲▲▲▲▲▲▲▲▲▲▲▲▲▲▲▲▲▲▲▲▲▲▲

(800 m).
17 scattered, open sites.
Chemical toilets, tables, grills, boat ramp.
In open flat with low trees and shrubs next to lake.
Boat or fish. Spot wildlife. Take photos.
NO water. 14-day limit. Crowded Feb–Apr.

▲ **Spur 406**
From DEL RIO, take US 90 W about 20 miles (32 k). Turn Right (SE) on Spur 406 and continue 4.5 miles (7.2 k).
6 scattered, open sites.
Chemical toilets, tables, grills, boat ramp.
On gentle slope with typical West Texas shrubs and trees.
Boat. Fish. Watch birds.
NO water. 14-day limit. Crowded Dec–Apr and holiday weekends.

ANDREWS RV PARK

(915) 523-2695
State map: K8
Locate RV park in ANDREWS at 700 W Broadway, behind Chamber of Commerce.
FREE so choose a chore.
Open All Year.
12 close, open, RV sites. Water at every site, dump station, electric hookups, tables, grills, pay phone.
In town.
Enjoy overnight stop.
No toilet facilities. 3-day limit.

BALLINGER CITY PARK

(915) 365-3511
State map: M13
Find park on N side of BALLINGER off 3rd St.
$5. Open All Year.
4 close, open sites. &
Water at every site, flush toilets, showers, dump station, electric hookups, tables, grills, playground, pool.
In renovated city park next to Elm Creek with native pecan and mesquite.
Swim and fish.
3-day limit.
1668 ft (500 m)

BALLINGER MUNICIPAL LAKE

(915) 365-3511
State map: M13
From BALLINGER, head NW on TX 158. Watch for signs. Drive total of 5 miles (8 k).
$5; $7 electric. Open All Year.
22 close, open sites. &
Water at every site, flush toilets, dump station, electric hookups, tables, grills, boat ramp.
In rolling plains valley next to lake.
Swim, boat, ski, or fish.
1658 ft (497 m)

BIG BEND NP

(915) 477-2251
State map: R7–S6–S7
Also, **free** backcountry permits available at any ranger station.

▲ **Chisos Basin**
From MARATHON, go S on US 385 for 70 miles (112 k) to Park Headquarters. Turn Right (W). Go 3 miles (4.8 k) to Basin Junction. Turn Left (S) on steep, winding road for another 6 miles (9.6 k).
$5. Open All Year.
63 close, open sites.
Central faucet, flush toilets, dump station, tables, grills.
In high mountain basin with pinyon pine and juniper.
Hike to fully appreciate spectacular area. Windows and South Rim trails rate fantastic. Birdwatch. View other wildlife. Attend ranger programs.
14-day/24-ft limits. Crowded Thanksgiving and spring–early summer.
5400 ft (1620 m)

▲ **Cottonwood**
From MARATHON, go S on US 385 for 70 miles (112 k) to Park Headquarters. Turn Right (W) and go 13 miles (20.8 k) to Santa Elena Junction. Turn Left (S) and continue 23 miles (36.8 k).
$3. Open All Year.
35 close, open sites.
Central faucet, pit toilets, tables, grills.
Under large cottonwood trees next to

▲ ▲

Rio Grande River.
Hike to explore Chihuahuan Desert ecology. Watch wide variety of birds. Raft river.
14-day/24-ft limits. Crowded Thanksgiving and spring.
2000 ft (600 m)

▲ Rio Grande Village
From MARATHON, go S on US 385 for 70 miles (112 k) to Park Headquarters. Continue SE for 21 miles (33.6 k).
$5. Open All Year.
100 close, open sites. Central faucet, flush toilets, dump station, tables, grills, boat ramp, store, pay phone.
In shade of large cottonwoods next to Rio Grande River.
Walk nature trail to spot birds. Hike to explore geologic wonders. Boat or fish. Attend ranger programs.
14-day limit. Hot much of year. Crowded Thanksgiving and Mar.
1800 ft (540 m)

BIG MINERAL RA

COE (903) 786-2227
State map: G18
From SADLER, head N on TX 901 for 8 miles (12.8 k). Turn Right (E) on Big Mineral Rd. Drive 2 miles (3.2 k).
FREE so choose a chore; reservations accepted at (903) 465-4990.
Open All Year.
20 scattered, open sites.
Pit toilets, tables, fire rings, boat ramp.
In large area next to Lake Texoma.
Swim, boat, ski, or fish. Hike. View wildlife.
NO water. No trash arrangements (pack it out). 14-day limit. Occasional horses.
617 ft (185 m)

BLACK CREEK LAKE RA

Caddo-LBJ NG
(817) 627-5475
State map: H17
From DECATUR, head NE on FM 730 for 4 miles (6.4 k). Turn Left (N) on Red Door Rd and drive 3.2 miles (5.1 k).

Turn Left (W) on Clayburn Rd and go .25 mile (400 m), then Right (N) on Portwood Rd for .5 mile (800 m). Turn Left (W) on FR 902.
FREE so choose a chore.
Open All Year.
Undesignated scattered, open sites.
Central faucet, pit toilets, tables, fire rings, boat ramp.
Next to 30-acre lake.
Boat and fish. Hike to Cottonwood Lake. Observe wildlife.
14-day limit.

BLACK ROCK PARK

Lower Colorado River Authority (512) 473-4083
State map: O15
From BUCHANAN DAM, head N on TX 261 for 4 miles (6.4 k). (Free primitive camping available along river.)
$3; $2 entrance fee. Open All Year.
20 close, open sites. Central faucet, flush toilets, dump station, tables, grills, fire rings, pay phone.
Among oak and cedar next to Lake Buchanan.
Swim, boat, or fish. Take photos.
Fluctuating lake level.
1020 ft (306 m)

BOONE PARK

North Montague Water District (817) 825-3282
State map: G16
From NOCONA, head N on FM 103 for 6 miles (9.6 k). Turn Right (E) on FM 2634 and drive 3 miles (4.8 k). Turn Left (NE) on FM 2953 and go 3 miles (4.8 k). Turn Right (S) on gravel road for 1.5 miles (2.4 k), then W for .5 mile (800 m). (Also see Joe Benton Park and Weldon Robb Memorial Park.)
FREE so choose a chore.
Open All Year.
Undesignated scattered, open sites.
Pit toilets, tables, grills, boat ramp.
With shade trees next to Lake Nocona.
Boat and waterski. Swim. Fish.

NO water. 21-day limit. Occasional ATVs.

BOUTON LAKE

Angelina NF
(409) 639-8620
State map: N22
From ZAVALLA, travel E on TX 63 for 7 miles (11.2 k). Turn Right (S) on dirt FR 303 and continue 8 miles (12.8 k). (Also see Boykin Springs and Caney Creek RA.)
FREE so choose a chore.
Open All Year.
7 close, open, tent sites.
Central faucet, pit toilets, fire rings.
Around 15-acre oxbow lake.
Fish. Hike to spot wildlife (try Sawmill Trail along Neches River).
14-day limit.

BOYKIN SPRINGS

Angelina NF
(409) 639-8620
State map: N22
From ZAVALLA, drive E on TX 63 for 10.6 miles (17 k). Turn Right (S) at sign on FR 313 and proceed 2.7 miles (4.3 k). (Also see Bouton Lake, Caney Creek RA, and Sandy Creek RA.)
$4. Open All Year.
36 (4 tent-only) close, open sites.
Water at every site, flush toilets, tables, fire rings.
With CCC-built structures under longleaf pine near natural springs and 10-acre lake.
Swim or fish. Hike Sawmill Trail along Neches River. Attend ranger programs.
14-day/22-ft limits.

BUFFALO LAKE NWR

(806) 499-3382
State map: D9
Go S for 1.5 miles (2.4 k) from UMBARGER.
FREE; $2 entrance fee.
Open All Year.
27 scattered, open sites. Central faucet, flush/pit toilets, tables, grills.

Among large tract of shortgrass prairie, croplands, marsh, and water ("lake" dry except during heavy rain).
Watch birds migrating along Lower Central Flyway. Walk Prairie Dog Interpretive Trail and Cottonwood Birding Trail. Explore.

BULL LAKE

Littlefield Parks
(806) 385-5161
State map: G9
From LITTLEFIELD, drive W on TX 54 for 8 miles (12.8 k). (Also see Waylon Jennings RV Park.)
$3. Open All Year.
Undesignated scattered, open sites.
Tables, grills, boat ramp.
Next to lake.
Swim, boat, or ski. Walk nature trail or hike farther.
NO water. No toilet facilities.
3553 ft (1066 m)

CAMPERS COVE PARK

COE (409) 429-3491
State map: O23
From WOODVILLE, drive E on US 190 for 15 miles (24 k). Turn Right (S) on FM 92 and travel 3 miles (4.8 k). Turn Left (E) on dirt road for final .5 mile (800 m). (Also see East End Park. Nearby Magnolia Ridge costs $8.)
FREE so choose a chore.
Open All Year.
25 scattered, open sites.
Central faucet, pit toilets, tables, fire rings, grills, boat ramp.
In medium to heavy woods next to Steinhagen Lake.
Swim, boat, and fish. Observe wildlife. 14-day limit. Hunting in season.

CANEY CREEK RA

Angelina NF
(409) 639-8620
State map: N22
From ZAVALLA, travel E on TX 63 for 5 miles

▲ ▲

(8 k). Turn Left (N) on FM 2743. (Also
see Bouton Lake and Boykin Springs.)
$5. Open All Year.
128 close, open sites.
Water at every site, flush toilets,
showers, dump station, electric hookups,
tables, fire rings, boat ramp, pay phone.
In five forested loops next to Sam
Rayburn Reservoir.
Swim, boat, or fish. Walk nature trail.
14-day limit.

CEDAR CREEK PARK

COE (817) 622-3332
State map: L17
From WHITNEY, drive
NW on FM 933 to
second blinking light.
Turn Left (SW) on FM 2604. (Also see
Old Fort Park. Nearby Cedron Creek
and McCown Valley cost $8.)
FREE so choose a chore.
Open All Year.
20 scattered, open sites.
Central faucet, pit toilets, tables, fire
rings, boat ramp.
On flat with scattered trees next to Lake
Whitney.
Boat. Swim. Fish.
14-day limit. Crowded weekends and
holidays.
550 ft (165 m)

CEDAR RIDGE PARK

COE (817) 939-1829
State map: N17
From BELTON, travel N
on TX 317 for 9 miles
(14.4 k). Turn Left (NW)
on TX 36 and drive about 2 miles (3.2 k)
to Moffat. Turn Left (S) on Cedar Ridge
Park Rd. (Also see White Flint Park.)
FREE; $10 electric (1/2 of sites);
reservations accepted at (817) 939-1829
for an additional $6.50.
Open All Year.
65 scattered, screened sites. &
Water at 40 sites, flush toilets, showers,
dump station, electric hookups, tables,
fire rings, grills, boat ramp.
In two beautiful areas next to Belton

Lake under live oak and ash.
Swim, boat, ski, or fish. Spot wildlife.
Take photos.
14-day limit.

CEDAR SPRINGS CREEK

COE (903) 665-2336
State map: J22
From ORE CITY, head N
on US 259 for 2 miles
(3.2 k). Turn Right (E) on
TX 155 and drive about 1 mile (1.6 k).
Turn Right (S). (Also see Oak Valley.)
FREE so choose a chore.
Open All Year.
15 close, open, tent sites. Central faucet,
pit toilets, tables, grills, boat ramp.
In woods next to Lake O' The Pines.
Swim, boat, or fish. Take photos and
watch wildlife.
14-day limit. Hunting in season.

CHILDRESS CITY PARK

(817) 937-3684
State map: F12
Find park on N Main St
in CHILDRESS.
FREE so choose a chore.
Open All Year.
Undesignated scattered, open sites.
Central faucet, flush toilets, electric
hookups, tables, fire rings, pool, tennis
court, playground.
In town park next to creek.
Swim. Enjoy overnight stop.
4-day limit.

CLAIBORNE WEST COUNTY PARK

(409) 745-2255
State map: P23
Near VIDOR, take Exit
869 off I-10 and go W on
access road for 3 miles
(4.8 k). OR, take Exit 864, cross I-10, and
go E on access road for 2 miles (3.2 k).
$3; reservations accepted at
(409) 745-2255.
Open All Year.
20 scattered, open, tent sites.
Central faucet, flush toilets, tables, grills,
pay phone.

▲ ▲

In beautiful woods near duck pond. Walk nature trail. Hike to spot wildlife. Take photos.
7-day limit.
16 ft (5 m)

COFFEE MILL LAKE

Caddo-LBJ NG
(817) 627-5475
State map: G19
From HONEY GROVE, drive N on FM 100 for 12 miles (19.2 k). Turn Left (W) on FM 409 and go 4.4 miles (7 k). (Also see Lake Davy Crockett.)
FREE so choose a chore.
Open All Year.
Undesignated open sites. Central faucet, pit toilets, tables, boat ramp.
Next to 750-acre lake.
Boat, ski, or fish. Hike to spot wildlife.
14-day limit.

COLEMAN PARK

(806) 637-6421
State map: H9
Find park on 1st St S in BROWNFIELD.
FREE so choose a chore.
Open All Year.
12 close, open sites. Water at every site, flush toilets, electric hookups, tables, pool, playground, tennis court.
In 44-acre town park.
Swim. Enjoy overnight stay.
4-day limit.

COLORADO BEND SP

(915) 628-3240
State map: N15
From BEND, drive S on gravel road for 6 miles (9.6 k).
$3. Open All Year.
Undesignated scattered, open sites.
Central faucet, chemical toilets, tables, fire rings, boat ramp, pay phone.
Along picturesque 3-mile (4.8 k) section of Colorado River.
Find private spot. Swim, canoe, boat, or fish. Walk nature trail or hike series of

trails. Mountain bike. View wildlife. Take photos. Attend ranger programs.
14-day limit. No open fires.

COMANCHE TRAIL PARK

Big Spring City Parks
(915) 263-8311
State map: L10
Locate park on S edge of BIG SPRING. (Nearby Moss Lake costs $10.)
$5. Open All Year.
19 (10 tent-only) close, open sites.
Water at 9 sites, flush toilets, dump station, electric hookups, tables, grills, boat ramp, pool, golf course, playground.
In city park.
Swim in pool. Fish or boat (no motors). Walk nature trail. Play golf.
3-day limit.

CROSBYTON 1, 2, 3, 4

White River Water Authority (806) 263-4240
State map: H11
From CROSBYTON, drive S on TX 651 for 14 miles (22.4 k). Turn Left (E) on FM 2794 and go 8 miles (12.8 k). (Also see Crosbyton City Park.)
$2; $2 entrance fee. Open All Year.
70 scattered, open sites. Central faucet, flush toilets, electric hookups, tables, grills, boat ramp, shelters.
In four locations around White River Lake with few trees (#4 offers remoteness but only tables and shelters).
Swim, boat, ski, or fish.
14-day/25-ft limits.

CROSBYTON CITY PARK

(806) 675-2301
State map: G10
Find park on US 82 at E edge of CROSBYTON.
(See Crosbyton 1, 2, 3, 4.)
FREE so choose a chore. Open All Year.
5 close, open sites.
Central faucet, pit toilets, dump station, tables, grills, pool, playground.

In town park.
Swim ($). Enjoy overnight stop. Visit nearby Silver Falls Rest Area.
3-day limit.

DINK PEARSON

Travis County Parks
(512) 473-9437
State map: P16
From CEDAR PARK,
take FM 1431 SW about
12 miles (19.2 k). Turn Left (S) on Lohman's Ford Rd and go to end. (Nearby Arkansas Bend costs $10.)
FREE so choose a chore. Open All Year.
Undesignated scattered, open sites.
Chemical toilets, tables, fire rings, grills, boat ramp.
In beautiful, secluded Hill Country setting on Lake Travis.
Swim, boat, or fish. View wildlife and take photos.
NO water. 7-day limit. No ATVs. No generators in quiet hours.

DOGWOOD PARK

Franklin County Water
District (903) 588-2352
State map: H21
Go S on TX 37 from
MOUNT VERNON for
1 mile (1.6 k). Turn Left (SE) on FM 21 for 7.8 miles (12.5 k). Turn Right (S) on FM 3007. Drive 2.5 miles (4 k). (See Mary King Park or W D "Jack" Guthrie Park.)
$5. Open All Year.
Undesignated close, open sites. Flush toilets, dump station, tables, boat ramp.
In woods next to water on south side of Lake Cypress Springs dam.
Swim, boat, and fish.
NO water. 14-day limit. Crowded holiday weekends.

DOUBLE BAYOU PARK

Chambers County Parks
(409) 267-8381
State map: Q22
From ANAHUAC, head
S on Eagle Ferry Rd for
12 miles (19.2 k). (Also see Fort Anahuac Park, James H Robbins Memorial Park, and Job Beason Park.)
FREE so choose a chore. Open All Year.
Undesignated scattered, open sites.
Flush toilets, tables.
In wooded spot along East Fork of Double Bayou.
Fish. Observe wildlife.
NO water. 10-day limit.

EAST END PARK

COE (409) 429-3491
State map: O23
From JASPER, head W
on US 190 for 15 miles
(24 k). Turn Left (S) on
FM 777 and drive 2 miles (3.2 k). Turn Right (W) on dirt road and continue 2 miles (3.2 k). (Also see Campers Cove Park. Nearby Sandy Creek costs $6.)
FREE so choose a chore. Open All Year.
6 close, open sites.
Central faucet, pit toilets, tables, fire rings, grills, boat ramp.
In medium to heavy wood next to Steinhagen Lake.
Boat or fish. Spot wildlife.
14-day limit. Hunting in season.

EASTVALE PARK

COE (214) 434-1666
State map: H18
From THE COLONY,
drive N on TX 423 for
.5 mile (800 m). Just past
bridge, turn Left.
FREE so choose a chore. Open All Year.
Undesignated open sites. Central faucet, pit toilets, tables, boat ramp.
In open, grassy setting with little shade (only free area on Lewisville Lake).
Boat. Swim. Fish. Watch wildlife.
14-day limit. Crowded weekends.
522 ft (157 m)

ETOILE PARK

COE (409) 384-5716
State map: M22
From ETOILE, drive W
on TX 103 for 2 miles
(3.2 k).

▲ ▲

FREE so choose a chore. Open All Year.
9 close, screened sites.
Central faucet, pit toilets, tables, fire rings, boat ramp.
On pine/hardwood ridge next to Sam Rayburn Reservoir.
Swim, boat, or fish. View wildlife and take photos.
14-day limit. Crowded weekends and holidays.
200 ft (60 m)

FALLS ON THE BRAZOS PARK

(817) 883-3203
State map: N18
From MARLIN, head W on TX 7 for 3 miles.
$4; $9.50 water & electric; $50/week; $180/month.
Open All Year.
14 (8 tent-only) close, open sites. Water at 6 sites, flush toilets, dump station, electric hookups, tables, grills, store.
Next to Brazos River under cottonwood trees near old fording spot.
Fish. Relax.

FAUNT LEROY PARK

(817) 865-2226
State map: M16
In GATESVILLE, locate park on S 7th St.
FREE; $5 after 2 days; reservations accepted at (817) 865-2226.
Open All Year.
13 scattered, open sites. &
Water at every site, flush toilets, showers, dump station, electric hookups, tables, grills, pay phone.
On banks of Leon River.
Swim or fish. Walk nature trail. Observe wildlife.
14-day limit.
680 ft (204 m)

FISHER PARK

(915) 728-8100
State map: K11
From COLORADO CITY, drive S on TX 208 for 10 miles (16 k). Turn

Right (W) on CR 123 and go 2 miles (3.2 k). (Also see Ruddick Park.)
$4 bank; $7 with shed; $2 entrance fee.
Open All Year.
24 scattered, open sites.
Central faucet, flush toilets, showers, electric hookups, tables, fire rings, grills, boat ramp, store, pay phone.
With mesquite, cacti, and rock ledges next to clear, 100-acre Champion Creek Reservoir.
Swim, boat, or fish. View wildlife.
14-day limit. Crowded major holidays.
2152 ft (646 m)

FORREST PARK

(806) 872-2124
State map: J9
Find park in LAMESA at Bryan Ave & 9th St.
FREE so choose a chore.
Open All Year.
10 close, open sites.
Water at every site, flush toilets, dump station, electric hookups, tables, grills, playground.
In "High Plains" town park.
Enjoy overnight stop.
3-day limit.

FORT ANAHUAC PARK

Chambers County Parks
(409) 267-8381
State map: Q22
Locate park in ANAHUAC. (Also see Double Bayou Park and Whites Memorial Park.)
$1.50; reservations accepted at (409) 267-8381.
Open All Year.
Undesignated close, open sites.
Water at every site, flush toilets, electric hookups, tables, boat ramp.
Next to Trinity River at site of start of Texas Revolution.
Boat or fish. Take photos.
4-day limit. Occasionally crowded.
20 ft (6 m)

FORT BELKNAP COUNTY PARK

(817) 846-3222
State map: H15
From NEWCASTLE,
travel S on TX 251 for
1.9 miles (3 k).

FREE; donations requested.
Open All Year.
8 close, open sites. Water at every site,
flush toilets, electric hookups, tables,
playground, tennis court, ball field.
At 1850 Army post along Brazos River.
Visit museum and 6 original buildings.
Relax.
3-day limit.

FRIENDSHIP PARK

COE (915) 625-2322
State map: M14
From COLEMAN, drive
W on TX 153 for 8 miles
(12.8 k). Turn Left (S)
and go .5 mile (800 m). (Nearby Flatrock
and Lakeside cost $10.)
FREE; $10 at 23 sites; reservations
accepted at (915) 625-2322 for an
additional $6.
Open All Year.
38 close, open sites.
Water at every site, flush toilets,
showers, dump station, electric hookups,
tables, fire rings, grills, boat ramp,
laundry, store, pay phone.
Under oaks next to Horde Creek Lake.
Swim. Boat and waterski. Fish. Take
photos. View wildlife.
14-day limit. Hunting in season.

FRIENDSHIP PARK

COE (512) 859-2668
State map: O17
From GRANGER, take
FM 971 E for 7 miles
(11.2 k). (Nearby Willis
Creek costs $6.)
FREE so choose a chore. Open All Year.
13 close, open, tent sites. Central faucet,
flush toilets, tables, grills, boat ramp.
Next to Granger Lake.
Swim, boat, ski, or fish. Observe wildlife.
14-day limit.

GOLIAD SHP

(512) 645-3405
State map: T17
Locate park at edge of
GOLIAD on US 183 S.
$4; $6 developed; $9
electric; $10 full hookups; $3 entrance
fee; reservations accepted at
(512) 645-3405.
Open All Year.
76 (10 tent-only) close, open sites.
Water at every site, flush toilets,
showers, electric hookups, tables, grills,
fire rings, pay phone.
Along San Antonio River under mature
live oak.
Explore Mission Espiritu Santo de
Zuniga plus other historical buildings
and ruins. Walk nature trail. View
wildlife. Fish. Attend ranger programs.
14-day limit.
300 ft (90 m)

GUADALUPE MOUNTAINS NP
Backcountry

(915) 828-3251
State map: L4
Obtain backcountry
permit at Vistor Center
in PINE SPRINGS or at
any ranger station and hike to
designated sites. (Pine Springs and Dog
Canyon cost $6.)
FREE. Open All Year.
10 scattered, tent sites.
Explore most extensive exposed fossil
reef in world. View highest peak in
Texas. Hike over 80-miles (128-k) of
trails in forests, canyons, and desert.
Enjoy nature study and photography.
NO water. No toilet facilities. No trash
arrangements (pack it out). No open
fires.

HAMLIN CITY PARK

(915) 576-2711
State map: J12
Find park in SW part of
HAMLIN, off 5th St on
Ave E. (See South Park.)
FREE so choose a chore.

▲ ▲

Open All Year.
Undesignated scattered, open sites.
Central faucet, flush toilets, tables, grills,
pool, playground.
In town park.
Swim. Enjoy overnight stop.
7-day limit.

HARVEY CREEK RA

Angelina NF
(409) 639-8620
State map: N23
From BROADDUS, take
TX 83 E for 4 miles
(6.4 k). Turn Right (S) on FM 2390. (Also
see Townsend Park RA.)
$4. Open All Year.
22 close, open sites.
Central faucet, chemical toilets, tables,
fire rings, boat ramp.
Next to Sam Rayburn Reservoir.
Boat or fish.
14-day limit.

HERRON CREEK PARK

COE (903) 838-8781
State map: H22
From MAUD, travel S on
TX 8 for 2 miles (3.2 k).
Turn Left (E) on CR 1234
and go .5 mile (800 m). Turn Right (S) on
CR 1205 and continue about 1.5 miles
(2.4 k). (Also see Jackson Creek Park and
Malden Lake Park.)
FREE so choose a chore.
Open All Year.
15 scattered, open sites. Central faucet,
pit toilets, tables, grills, boat ramp.
On upper section of Wright Patman
Lake.
Boat. Enjoy good fishing spot.
14-day limit. Hunting in season.

HIGH POINT PARK

COE (817) 879-2498
State map: L15
From PROCTOR, drive
NW on FM 1476 for
3 miles (4.8 k). Turn Left
(S) on FM 1496 and go 1 mile (1.6 k).
(Nearby Copperas Creek and Sowell

Creek cost $12.)
FREE so choose a chore. Open All Year.
21 (14 tent-only) scattered, open sites.
Central faucet, pit toilets, dump station,
tables, fire rings, grills, boat ramp.
In slightly hilly terrain with few trees
next to Proctor Lake (only area below
$10 on lake).
Swim, boat, or fish.
14-day limit.
1180 ft (354 m)

HOBART STREET PARK

City of Pampa Parks
(806) 669-5770
State map: C11
In PAMPA, find park 1
block N of US 60 on
TX 70. (Nearby Pampa Recreation Park
costs $8.)
FREE so choose a chore.
Open All Year.
35 close, open sites. Water at 15 sites,
flush toilets, dump station, electric
hookups, tables, grills, pay phone.
Under trees in town park.
Enjoy overnight stay.
3-day limit.
3400 ft (1020 m)

HUBER PARK

Borger Parks
(806) 273-2883
State map: C10
Find park in BORGER at
1300 Main St. (Also see
Lake Meredith NRA.)
FREE so choose a chore. Open All Year.
10 close, open sites.
Water at every site, pit toilets, dump
station, electric hookups, tables.
In town park.
Take scenic drive to Lake Meredith area.
3-day limit.

HURRICANE CREEK

COE (903) 665-2336
State map: J22
From JEFFERSON, head
N on TX 49 about
4 miles (6.4 k). Bear Left

▲ ▲

(NW) on FM 729. Drive 6 miles (9.6 k).
Turn Left (W). (Also see Oak Valley.)
FREE so choose a chore. Open All Year.
21 close, open, tent sites.
Central faucet, flush toilets, tables, fire
rings, grills, boat ramp.
In trees next to Lake O' The Pines.
Swim, boat, or fish. Watch wildlife.
14-day limit. Hunting in season.

INDIAN MOUNDS RA

Sabine NF
(409) 344-6205
State map: M23
From HEMPHILL, take
TX 83 E for 11 miles
(17.6 k). Turn Right (S) on FR 3382 and
drive 4 miles (6.4 k). Turn Left (E) on
FR 130 and go 1 mile (1.6 k). (Also see
Lakeview RA and Red Hills Lake RA.)
$4. Open Mar 1–Oct 1.
56 close, open sites. Central faucet,
chemical toilets, tables, grills, boat ramp.
Next to Toledo Bend Reservoir.
Boat and fish.
14-day limit.

INTAKE HILL

COE (903) 838-8781
State map: H22
From TEXARKANA,
drive S on US 59 for
9 miles (14.4 k). Turn
Right (W) on FM 2148 to Lake Rd.
Follow park road past dam to first road
on Left. (Also see Oak Park and Piney
Point Park.)
FREE so choose a chore. Open All Year.
20 scattered, open sites. Central faucet,
pit toilets, tables, grills, fire rings.
Along main portion of Wright Patman
Lake near marina.
Boat or fish. Hike.
14-day limit. Crowded holidays.

IRON BRIDGE PARK

COE (817) 939-1829
State map: N17
From BELTON, travel N
on TX 317 for 9 miles
(14.4 k). Turn Left (NW)

on TX 36 and drive about 10 miles
(16 k). Turn Right (N) on Iron Bridge
Park Rd and go about 2 miles (3.2 k).
(Also see Owl Creek Park.)
FREE so choose a chore. Open All Year.
5 scattered, open sites. Pit toilets, tables,
fire rings, grills, boat ramp.
In shady spot on Leon River (backwaters
of Belton Lake).
Swim, boat, ski, or fish.
NO water. 14-day limit.

JACKSON CREEK PARK

COE (903) 838-8781
State map: H22
From ATLANTA, head
W on TX 77 about
5 miles (8 k). Turn Right
(N) on FM 96 and travel 2.7 miles (4.3 k).
Turn Left (W) on CR 2791 and drive
1.6 miles (2.6 k). Turn Right (N) on
CR 2116 and go 1 mile (1.6 k). Turn Left
(W) on CR 2118. (Also see Herron Creek
Park and Malden Lake Park.)
FREE so choose a chore.
Open All Year.
16 scattered, screened sites.
Central faucet, pit toilets, tables, fire
rings, grills, boat ramp.
In mixed pine/hardwood forest next to
Wright Patman Lake.
Boat or fish.
14-day/25-ft limits. Hunting in season.

JACOBS CREEK PARK

COE (512) 964-3341
State map: Q16
Drive NW on FM 306
from NEW BRAUNFELS
for 15 miles (24 k). Turn
Left (W) on Jacobs Creek Park Rd–just
past North Park Rd. (Also see North
Park. Nearby Canyon Park costs $6.)
FREE so choose a chore.
Open All Year.
65 scattered, open sites.
Central faucet, flush toilets, showers,
dump station, tables, fire rings, grills,
boat ramp, pay phone.
In typical hill country vegetation of oak
and juniper next to Canyon Lake.

Swim, sail, boat, ski, or fish. Hike to observe wildlife. Take photos.
14-day limit. Crowded holidays.
940 ft (282 m)

JAMES H ROBBINS MEMORIAL PARK

Chambers County Parks
(409) 267-8381
State map: R22
Drive S on FM 562 for 25 miles (40 k) from ANAHUAC. (See Double Bayou Park.)
FREE so choose a chore.
Open All Year.
Undesignated close, open sites.
Flush toilets, boat ramp.
With birdwatching tower next to saltwater.
View wildlife. Boat or fish.
NO water. 14-day limit.
5 ft (2 m)

JOB BEASON PARK

Chambers County Parks
(409) 267-8381
State map: Q22
From ANAHUAC, drive S for 12 miles (19.2 k) to Oak Island. (See Double Bayou Park.)
FREE so choose a chore.
Open All Year.
Undesignated close, open sites.
Flush toilets, tables, boat ramp.
Fish nad boat on Trinity Bay.
NO water. 14-day limit.
5 ft (2 m)

JOE BENTON PARK

North Montague Water District (817) 825-3282
State map: G16
From NOCONA, head N on FM 103 for 6 miles (9.6 k). Turn Right (E) on FM 2634 and travel 3 miles (4.8 k). Turn Left (NE) on FM 2953. Proceed 1.2 miles (1.9 k). (Also see Boone Park and Weldon Robb Memorial Park.)
FREE so choose a chore. Open All Year.
Undesignated scattered, open sites.

Pit toilets, tables, grills, boat ramp.
Under shade trees next to Lake Nocona.
Swim, boat, waterski, or fish.
NO water. 21-day limit. Occasional ATVs.

JOHNSON PARK

Abilene City Parks
(915) 676-6218
State map: K13
From ABILENE off I-20, take FM 600 N for 6.6 miles (10.6 k). Turn Right (E) on FM 1082 and go .6 mile (1 k). (Also see Seabee Park.)
FREE so choose a chore. Open All Year.
Undesignated scattered, open sites.
Central faucet, flush toilets, fire rings, boat ramp.
With few scattered trees on Lake Fort Phantom Hill.
Boat or fish.
2-day limit.

KELLEY'S PONDS

Sam Houston NF
(409) 344-6205
State map: O20
Head W on FM 1375 from NEW WAVERLY about 9 miles (14.4 k). Turn Left (S) on FR 204 and drive .7 mile (1.1 k). Turn Right (W) on FR 271 and go to end of road. (Also see Stubblefield Lake RA.)
FREE so choose a chore. Open All Year.
8 close, open sites.
Pit toilets, tables, grills.
In quiet forest setting.
View wildlife. Hike (Lone Star Trail nearby). Mountain bike.
NO water. 14-day limit. Hunting in season.

KIMBALL BEND PARK

COE (817) 622-3332
State map: L17
From KOPPERL, take FM 56 W for 2 miles (3.2 k). Turn Right (NE) on TX 174 and drive 3 miles (4.8 k)—just before Brazos River. (Also see Plowman

Creek Park.)
FREE so choose a chore. Open All Year.
12 scattered, open sites.
Water at every site, pit toilets, tables, fire rings, boat ramp.
On low flat with large pecan trees next to Brazos River.
Swim, boat, or fish. Canoe or kayak scenic river.
14-day limit. Crowded weekends.
550 ft (165 m)

KINDLEY PARK

Graham City Parks
(817) 549-3324
State map: J15
From GRAHAM, head NW on US 380 for 7 miles (11.2 k) to E end of bridge. (Nearby Firemen's and Lake Eddleman cost $8.)
$5. Open All Year.
26 close, open sites.
Central faucet, flush toilets, electric hookups, tables, boat ramp.
On shores of Lake Graham.
Boat and fish.

LAKE DAVY CROCKETT

Caddo-LBJ NG
(817) 627-5475
State map: G19
From HONEY GROVE, drive N on FM 100 for 12 miles (19.2 k). Turn Left (W) on FM 409 and go .5 mile (800 m). (Also see Coffee Mill Lake.)
$5. Open All Year.
Undesignated open sites. Central faucet, pit toilets, tables, boat ramp.
On W side of 450-acre lake.
Fish or boat. Hike to view wildlife. Enjoy spring wildflowers.
14-day limit.

LAKE HOLBROOK PARK

(903) 763-2716
State map: J20
From MINEOLA, drive W on US 80 for 3.6 miles (5.8 k). Bear Right on

CR and go 1 mile (1.6 k). Turn Right (N) and continue .3 mile (480 m).
FREE so choose a chore.
Open All Year.
10 close, open sites.
Pit toilets, dump station, electric hookups, tables, boat ramp, playground.
Next to 653-acre Holbrook Lake.
Boat. Swim. Fish.
NO water. No trash arrangements (pack it out). 15-day limit.

LAKE J B THOMAS

Colorado River Municipal Water District
(915) 267-6341
State map: K11–K12
FREE so choose a chore.
Open All Year.
Undesignated scattered, open sites.
Swim, boat, or fish.
NO water. 7-day limit.
2270 ft (681 m)
Next to lake (other areas scattered around lake).

▲ **Sandy Beach**
From SNYDER, take TX 350 SW about 10 miles (16 k). Turn Right (W) on FM 2085 and go 8 miles (12.8 k). Continue W to N end of dam.
Flush toilets, tables, grills, boat ramp.

▲ **White Island**
From SNYDER, take TX 350 SW about 10 miles (16 k). Turn Right (W) on FM 2085 and go 8 miles (12.8 k). Turn Left (S) on FM 1298. Drive 3 miles (4.8 k). Turn Left (W) South Side Rd. Go 2 miles (3.2 k).
Pit toilets, tables, grills, boat ramp, shelter.

LAKE LIMESTONE
Area 2 West & 3 East

Limestone County Parks
(817) 729-3810
State map: M19
From GROESBECK, head SE on FM 937 about 11 miles (17.6 k). Turn Left (NE) at old Union store on FM 3371 and go 2 miles (3.2 k). Find sites at either end of bridge.

(Also see Public Use Area 5.)
FREE so choose a chore.
Open All Year.
Undesignated scattered, open sites.
Chemical toilets, tables, grills, boat ramp.
Next to Lake Limestone.
Swim, boat, ski, and fish. Hike to observe wildlife.
NO water. 14-day limit.

LAKE MARVIN

Black Kettle NG
(405) 497-2143
State map: B12
From CANADIAN, head
N on US 83 for .5 mile
(800 m) across river. Turn Right (E) on
FM 2266 and go 11 miles (17.6 k).
FREE so choose a chore.
Open All Year.
27 close, open sites.
Central faucet, pit toilets, tables, grills.
Among trees next to 63-acre lake.
Walk Jackson Wildlife Trail or Big Tree
Trail. Observe birds, including bald
eagles in winter. Fish.
14-day limit. No hunting.
2000 ft (600 m)

LAKE MEREDITH NRA

(806) 857-3151
State map: C10
(Also see Huber Park
and Stinnett City Park.)
FREE. Backcountry
permits also available.
Open All Year.
3000 ft (900 m)
▲ **Blue Creek Bridge**
From SANFORD, head NW on CR 1319
about 2 miles (3.2 k). Turn Left (W) on
CR 3395. Go about 6 miles (9.6 k). Turn
Left (SW) on CR 1915. Go 2 miles (3.2 k).
20 scattered, open sites.
Chemical toilets, tables, grills.
In canyon.
Relax.
NO water. 14-day limit. ATVs in creek
beds.
▲ **Blue West**
From SANFORD, head NW on CR 1319

about 2 miles (3.2 k). Turn Left (W) on
CR 3395 and travel about 6 miles (9.6 k).
Turn Left (SW) on CR 1915 and continue
5 miles (8 k). Turn Left (E) on CR 1913
and drive almost to end. Turn Left (N).
40 scattered, open sites.
Chemical toilets, dump station, tables,
grills, boat ramp, sun shelters.
On caprock bluff overlooking lake.
Boat or fish (difficult access).
NO water. 14-day limit.
▲ **Bugbee**
From SANFORD, head NW on CR 1319
about 2 miles (3.2 k). Turn Left (W) on
CR 3395. Drive about 1.5 miles (2.4 k).
Turn Left (S) for final 1 mile (1.6 k).
25 scattered, open sites.
Chemical toilets, tables.
On lakeshore.
Fish and boat.
NO water. 14-day limit. Crowded
weekends and holidays.
▲ **Cedar Canyon**
From SANFORD, drive SW following
signs about 3 miles (4.8 k).
Undesignated close, open sites.
Central faucet, flush toilets, dump
station, tables, boat ramp.
In sandy cove off Sanford-Yake access
road.
Swim, boat, or fish.
14-day limit. No alcohol. Crowded
summer weekends.
▲ **Chimney Hollow**
From SANFORD, head NW on CR 1319
about 2 miles (3.2 k). Turn left (W) on
CR 3395 and travel about 6 miles (9.6 k).
Turn Left (SW) on CR 1915 and proceed
5 miles (8 k). Turn Left (E) on CR 1913
and drive to end of road.
Undesignated scattered, open sites.
Chemical toilets, tables, grills.
Near Blue West boat ramp with
protection from southern winds.
Boat. Fish. Swim.
NO water. 14-day limit. Crowded
summer weekends.
▲ **Fritch Fortress**
From E side of FRITCH, drive N about
5 miles (8 k).
10 scattered, open sites.

▲ ▲

Central faucet, flush toilets, dump station, tables, grills, boat ramp.
On high bluff near amphitheater overlooking lake.
Boat or fish.
14-day limit.

▲ **Harbor Bay**
From FRITCH, go W for 2 miles (3.2 k).
19 scattered, open sites.
Chemical toilets, dump station, tables, grills, boat ramp.
In large, open area next to lake.
Swim, boat, and fish.
NO water. 14-day limit. Crowded summer weekends.

▲ **McBride Canyon/Mullinaw Creek**
From FRITCH, drive S on TX 136 about 6 miles (9.6 k). Turn Left (W) on road to Alibates Flint Quarries NM and go 3 miles (4.8 k). Turn Left (SW) and continue 3 miles (4.8 k). Another area (Mullinaw Creek) is 3 more miles (4.8 k)–always bearing Left.
Undesignated close, open sites.
Chemical toilets, tables, grills.
In canyon under large cottonwood.
Spot wildlife.
NO water. 14-day limit. Hunting in season. Crowded summer weekends.

▲ **Plum Creek**
From SANFORD, head NW on CR 1319 about 2 miles (3.2 k). Turn Left (W) on CR 3395 and drive 6 miles (9.6 k). Turn Left (SW) on CR 1915 and go 5 miles (8 k). Turn Right (W) on CR 1913 and continue 3 miles (4.8 k). Turn Left (S) and drive almost to end.
15 scattered, open sites. Chemical toilets, dump station, tables, grills.
In canyon under large shade trees.
Observe wildlife.
NO water. 14-day limit. Hunting in season. Crowded summer weekends.

▲ **Rosita Cycle Area**
From AMARILLO, drive N on US 87 for 12 miles–almost to Canadian River. Turn Right (E). Continue 5 miles (8 k).
25 scattered, open sites.
Chemical toilets, tables, grills.
On Canadian River.
NO water. 14-day limit. Hunting in

season. ATVs. Noisy. Crowded summer weekends.

▲ **Sanford-Yake**
From SANFORD, drive SW following signs about 3 miles (4.8 k).
50 close, open sites.
Central faucet, flush toilets, dump station, tables, grills, boat ramp, shelters, store, pay phone.
On high bluff overlooking lake.
Boat or fish.
14-day limit. Crowded summer weekends.

▲ **Spring Canyon**
From SANFORD, head NW on CR 1319 about .5 mile (800 m). Bear Right and drive below dam about 1 mile (1.6 k).
6 scattered, open sites. ♿
Chemical toilets, tables, grills, shelters.
Next to Stilling Basin.
Swim or fish.
NO water. 14-day limit. No alcohol.
Crowded summer weekends.

LAKE WINNSBORO NORTH PARK

(903) 629-7317
State map: J21
From WINNSBORO, drive S on TX 37 for 5 miles (8 k). Turn Right (W) on CR 4890. Continue 1 mile (1.6 k).
FREE so choose a chore.
Open All Year.
15 close, open sites.
Central faucet, flush toilets, showers, electric hookups, tables, grills, store.
Next to Lake Winnsboro.
Swim, boat, waterski, and fish.
15-day limit.

LAKELAND PARK

COE (214) 442-3141
State map: H19
From FARMERSVILLE, head S on TX 78 about 4 miles (6.4 k). Turn Right (W) on FM 550 and go 2 miles (3.2 k). (Nearby East Fork costs $10 and Lavonia costs $6.)
FREE so choose a chore.
Open All Year.

▲ ▲

32 close, open, tent sites.
Central faucet, flush toilets, tables, fire rings, grills, boat ramp.
With large trees and good view of northern section of Lake Lavon.
Swim, boat, ski, or fish. Take photos.
14-day limit. No generators in quiet hours.

LAKEVIEW PARK

COE (915) 949-4757
State map: M12
On NW side of SAN ANGELO, locate park on Mercedes St (off Glenna).
(Also see Riverbend Park.)
FREE so choose a chore. Open All Year.
28 (4 tent-only) close, open sites.
Pit toilets, tables, grills, boat ramp.
Below O C Fisher Lake Dam in flat with mesquite and willow.
Boat, ski, and swim. Fish. Watch wildlife.
NO water. 14-day limit.
1938 ft (581 m)

LAKEVIEW RA

Sabine NF
(409) 344-6205
State map: M23
Drive S on TX 87 for 9 miles (14.4 k) from HEMPHILL. Turn Left (E) on FR 2928.
Go 3 miles (4.8 k). Continue E on gravel road for 2.5 miles (4 k). (Also see Indian Mounds RA and Willow Oak RA.)
$3. Open Mar 1–Oct 1.
10 close, open sites. Central faucet, chemical toilets, tables, grills, boat ramp.
On peninsula in Toledo Bend Reservoir.
Boat or fish.
14-day/16-ft limits.

LAMAR POINT

COE (903) 732-3020
State map: G20
From PARIS, drive N on US 271 for 3.6 miles (5.8 k). Turn Left (W) on FM 1499. Travel 5.3 miles (8.5 k). Turn Right (N) on FM 1500 and go 4.5 miles (7.2 k). (Also see Sanders Cove Park.)

FREE so choose a chore. Open All Year.
26 close, open sites.
Central faucet, pit toilets, dump station, tables, fire rings, grills, boat ramp.
Among oak/hickory stands and native grasses next to Pat Mayse Lake.
Swim, boat, or fish.
14-day limit. Crowded weekends and holidays.
451 ft (135 m)

LEVELLAND CITY-COUNTY CAMP

(806) 894-0113
State map: G9
From LEVELLAND, head S on US 385 for 3.3 miles (5.3 k). Register with city police.
FREE so choose a chore. Open All Year.
12 close, open, RV sites. Water at every site, flush toilets, dump station, electric hookups, tables, fire rings.
In town park.
Enjoy overnight stay.
3-day limit.

LOVE PARK

COE (214) 875-5711
State map: K18
From ENNIS, take TX 34 SW for 3.5 miles (5.4 k). Turn Left (S) and drive 2.5 miles (4 k).
FREE so choose a chore.
Open Mar 1–Oct 31.
20 scattered, open, tent sites.
Central faucet, pit toilets, tables, grills, boat ramp.
Next to Bardwell Lake (only choice under $6).
Swim, boat, or fish.
14-day limit.

MALDEN LAKE PARK

COE (903) 838-8781
State map: H22
From MAUD, travel S on TX 8 for 4 miles (6.4 k). (Also see Herron Creek Park and Jackson Creek Park.)
FREE so choose a chore. Open All Year.

12 close, open sites. Pit toilets, tables, fire rings, grills, boat ramp.
At confluence of Sulphur River and Wright Patman Lake.
Fish and boat in river and lake.
NO water. 14-day limit.

MARTIN CREEK LAKE SP

(903) 836-4336
State map: K22
From TATUM, head SW on TX 43 for 3.5 miles (5.6 k). Turn Left (SE) on CR 2181 and follow signs. If desire primitive island site, walk-in about .5 mile (800 m).
$4; $9 developed; $3 entrance fee; reservations accepted at (903) 836-4336.
Open All Year.
72 (12 tent-only) close, screened sites.
Water at every site, flush toilets, showers, dump station, electric hookups, tables, fire rings, boat ramp.
Next to 5000-acre Martin Lake among pine and hardwood with primitive sites on island (pit toilet nearby).
Swim, boat, ski, or fish. Walk nature trail. Hike and spot wildlife. Attend ranger programs.
14-day limit. Crowded in summer.

MARY KING PARK

Franklin County Water District (903) 588-2352
State map: H21
Drive S on TX 37 from MOUNT VERNON for 1 mile (1.6 k). Turn Left (SE) on FM 21 and travel 7.8 miles (12.5 k). Turn Right (S) on FM 3007 and go 6.9 miles (11 k). (Also see Dogwood Park.)
$5; $9 electric; reservations accepted at (903) 588-2352.
Open Mar–Oct 31.
9 close, open sites.
Water at every site, flush toilets, electric hookups, tables, grills, boat ramp.
In woods next to Lake Cypress Springs.
Swim, boat, and fish.
14-day limit. Crowded holiday weekends.

MATAGORDA ISLAND SP BOAT-IN

(512) 983-2215
State map: U19
In PORT O'CONNOR, find ferry at Maple & 16th or use private boat.
$4; $2 shuttle; $12 ferry; reservations accepted at (512) 983-2215.
Open All Year.
Undesignated open sites.
Pit toilets, tables, fire rings, grills, shelters.
On 38-mile (60.8-k) long barrier island.
Canoe or kayak. Swim. Fish. Watch abundant birdlife. Hike. Attend ranger programs.
NO water. No trash arrangements (pack it out). 14-day limit. Hunting in season.

MCCOLLUM PARK

Chambers County Parks (409) 267-8381
State map: Q22
From BAYTOWN, head E for 10 miles (16 k) on FM 2354. (See Whites Memorial Park.)
FREE so choose a chore.
Open All Year.
Undesignated close, open sites. Tables.
Overlooking Upper Trinity Bay.
Fish.
NO water. No toilet facilities. 14-day limit.
20 ft (6 m)

MCPHERSON SLOUGH

COE (817) 481-4541
State map: J18
From GRAPEVINE off Business 114, head N on Dove Rd to sign on Left.
(Also see Oak Grove Park and Silver Lake Park.)
$3. Open All Year.
8 close, open, tent sites.
Central faucet, pit toilets, tables, fire rings, boat ramp.
In small, wooded flat near Grapevine Lake.
Swim or boat. Take photos.
14-day limit. No glass bottles or alcohol.

Crowded summer holidays.
550 ft (165 m)

MIDDLE CONCHO

San Angelo City Parks
(915) 944-3850
State map: N12
From SAN ANGELO,
head S on US 87. Turn
Right (SW) on FM 584 and go toward
airport. Follow signs to Spring Creek
Marina–buy permit. (See Twin Buttes
Park. Nearby Red Arroyo costs $6.)
$3. Open All Year.
Undesignated scattered, open sites.
Central faucet, flush toilets, tables, fire
rings, boat ramp.
Under mesquite trees around Lake
Nasworthy.
Swim, boat, ski, or fish.
14-day limit.

MIDWAY PARK

COE (817) 756-5359
State map: M17
From WACO, travel W
on TX 6 about 6 miles
(9.6 k). Take Midway
Park Exit.
FREE so choose a chore.
Open All Year.
22 scattered, open, tent sites.
Central faucet, flush toilets, showers,
tables, boat ramp, store, pay phone.
In rolling terrain with large oak and
scattered cedar next to Lake Waco (other
choices on lake are at least $6).
Swim, boat, and fish.
14-day limit. Occasionally crowded.
465 ft (140 m)

MILL CREEK RESORT

COE (903) 786-2227
State map: G18
From POTTSBORO,
travel W on FM 996 for
6 miles (9.6 k). Turn
Right (N) on Locust & Mill Creek Rd. Go
3 miles (4.8 k). Stay in COE section.
$5; more for concession sites;
reservations accepted at (903) 465-4990.

Open All Year.
11 scattered, open sites. Central faucet,
flush toilets, showers, tables, fire rings,
grills, boat ramp, store, rentals.
Next to Lake Texoma.
Swim, boat, or fish.
14-day limit.
617 ft (185 m)

MULESHOE NWR

(806) 946-3341
State map: G8
From MULESHOE, drive
S on TX 214 for 20 miles
(32 k). Turn Right (W)
on unpaved road and continue
2.25 miles (3.6 k).
FREE so choose a chore.
Open All Year.
Undesignated scattered, open sites.
Central faucet, pit toilets, tables, grills.
Among recently-planted, small trees.
Walk nature trail. Observe wildlife.

MURRELL PARK

COE (817) 481-4541
State map: J18
From DALLAS, take
I-35E NW to Exit for
FM 3040. Head SW to
Simmons Rd. Turn Left. Watch for signs.
$3.
Open Mar 1–Oct 31.
36 close, open, tent sites.
Central faucet, pit toilets, tables, fire
rings, boat ramp.
In wooded, rolling terrain next to
Grapevine Lake.
Swim, boat, or fish. Walk nature trail or
hike farther. Take photos.
14-day limit. No glass containers or
alcohol. Crowded summer holidays.
550 ft (165 m)

NORTH PARK

COE (512) 964-3341
State map: Q16
Travel NW on FM 306
for 15 miles (24 k) from
NEW BRAUNFELS. Turn
Left (W) on signed North Park Rd. (Also

see Jacobs Creek Park. Nearby Canyon costs $6.)
FREE so choose a chore.
Open All Year.
20 scattered, open sites.
Central faucet, pit toilets, tables, grills, fire rings.
Under oak/juniper next to Canyon Lake.
Boat or fish. Scuba dive or swim. Watch wildlife.
14-day limit. Crowded holidays.
940 ft (282 m)

OAK GROVE PARK

COE (817) 481-4541
State map: J18
From GRAPEVINE off Business 114, head N on Dove Rd to sign on Right. (Also see McPherson Slough and Silver Lake Park.)
$3.
Open All Year.
10 close, open sites.
Central faucet, pit toilets, tables, fire rings, grills, boat ramp.
Under trees close to Grapevine Lake.
Swim, boat, or fish. Take photos.
14-day limit. No glass bottles or alcohol.
Crowded summer holidays.
550 ft (165 m)

OAK PARK

COE (903) 838-8781
State map: H22
From TEXARKANA, drive S on US 59 for 10 miles (16 k). Turn Right (W) on Park Road at first lake entrance. Follow signs. (Also see Intake Hill and Piney Point Park.)
FREE so choose a chore.
Open All Year.
30 scattered, open sites.
Central faucet, flush toilets, dump station, tables, grills.
In hardwood forest below dam for Wright Patman Lake.
Fish.
14-day limit.

OAK VALLEY

COE (903) 665-2336
State map: J22
From ORE CITY, head N on US 259 for 2 miles (3.2 k). Turn Right (E) on TX 155 and drive 4 miles (6.4 k). Turn Right (S) on FM 729 and go 2 miles (3.2 k). Turn Right (SW). (Also see Cedar Springs Creek and Hurricane Creek.)
FREE so choose a chore.
Open All Year.
10 close, open, tent sites.
Central faucet, pit toilets, tables, grills, boat ramp.
In woods next to Lake O' The Pines.
Swim, boat, and fish. Observe wildlife.
14-day limit. Hunting in season.

OAKLAND PARK

COE (214) 434-1666
State map: H18
From LEWISVILLE, take I-35E N to Exit 457A. Veer Right toward Lake Dallas. Turn Right on Carlisle St. At stop sign, turn Right on Main St and drive past Westlake Park.
$4; $8 developed; $12 electric.
Open All Year.
83 (27 tent-only) scattered, open sites.
Water at 66 sites, flush toilets, showers, dump station, electric hookups, tables, fire rings, grills, boat ramp, pay phone.
Next to lake under oak, cottonwood, and willow.
Swim, boat, ski, or fish. Spot wildlife.
14-day/25-ft limits. Crowded weekends.
522 ft (157 m)

OLD FORT PARK

(817) 694-2540
State map: L17
From WHITNEY, drive NW on FM 933 to second blinking light. Turn Left (SW) on FM 2604 and follow to end. (Also see Cedar Creek Park.)
FREE so choose a chore.
Open All Year.
5 close, open sites.

Central faucet, pit toilets, tables, grills, boat ramp.
In former CCC camp on Lake Whitney.
Boat, waterski, and fish.
No trash arrangements. 14-day limit.

OVERLOOK PARK

Franklin County Water District (903) 588-2352
State map: H21
Drive S on TX 37 from MOUNT VERNON for
1 mile (1.6 k). Turn Left (SE) on FM 21 and proceed 3.2 miles (5.1 k). Turn Right (S) on FM 2723 and continue 4.6 miles (7.4 k). (Also see Walleye Park.)
$5. Open All Year.
Undesignated close, open sites.
Flush toilets, boat ramp.
In woods next to Lake Cypress Springs.
Swim, boat, or fish.
NO water. 14-day limit.

OVERLOOK PARK

COE (409) 596-1622
State map: P19
From SOMERVILLE, travel S on TX 36 for 4 miles (6.4 k). Turn
Right (W) on FM 1948 then Right (N) on first road past railroad tracks. (Also see Rocky Creek Park.)
FREE; $10 developed; $12 electric.
Open All Year.
55 close, open sites.
Central faucet, flush toilets, showers, dump station, electric hookups, tables, fire rings, grills, boat ramp, pay phone.
In several natural settings next to Somerville Lake (free primitive camp has 6 sites).
Swim, boat, and ski. Fish. Observe wildlife. Attend ranger programs.
14-day limit. Crowded 3-day weekends.

OWL CREEK PARK

COE (817) 939-1829
State map: N17
From BELTON, travel N on TX 317 for 9 miles (14.4 k). Turn Left (NW)
on TX 36 and drive about 6.7 miles (10.7 k). Turn Left (S) on Owl Creek Rd and go about 3 miles (4.8 k). (Also see Iron Bridge Park and White Flint Park.)
FREE so choose a chore. Open All Year.
10 scattered, open sites.
Central faucet, pit toilets, tables, fire rings, grills, boat ramp.
Under live oak next to Lake Belton.
Swim, boat, ski, or fish.
14-day limit.
670 ft (201 m)

PADGITT PARK

Colorado River Municipal Water District (915) 267-6341
State map: M13
From VOSS, head S on FM 503 for 1 mile (1.6 k). Turn Left (W) on FM 2134 and go 6 miles (9.6 k). Turn Left into park.
FREE so choose a chore.
Open All Year.
Undesignated scattered, open sites.
Pit toilets, tables, fire rings, boat ramp.
Next to O H Ivie Reservoir.
Swim, boat, and fish.
NO water. 7-day limit.
1560 ft (468 m)

PADRE BALLI PARK

Nueces County Parks (512) 949-8121
State map: V18
Head SE on Park Rd 22 about 5 miles (8 k) from
CORPUS CHRISTI. (Also see Port Aransas County Park.)
$4 on beach; $10 water & electric.
Open All Year.
126 (60 tent-only) close, open sites.
Water at 66 sites, flush toilets, showers, dump station, electric hookups, tables, grills, laundry, pay phone.
On beach at southern end of Mustang Island.
Enjoy beach. Swim. Fish.
3-day limit. Beach bathhouse only open in summer.
5 ft (2 m)

▲▲▲▲▲▲▲▲▲▲▲▲▲▲▲▲▲▲▲▲▲▲▲▲▲▲

PADRE ISLAND NS

(512) 937-2621
State map: V17
Travel SE on Park Rd 22
for 14.1 miles (22.6 k)
from CORPUS CHRISTI.
Free camping allowed along 65-mile
(104-k) beach S of Visitor Center.
$4. Open All Year.
40 close, open sites.
Central faucet, flush toilets, showers,
dump station, tables, grills, sun shelters.
On Gulf of Mexico barrier island.
Swim. Walk beach. Fish.
14-day limit.
5 ft (2 m)

PAW PAW CREEK RESORT

(903) 523-4414
State map: G18
Just N of SADLER on
FM 901, turn Right (E)
on Rock Creek Rd and
drive 2.9 miles (4.6 k). Turn Right and
follow signs.
$5; $9.50 RV water & electric.
Open All Year.
108 close, open sites.
Water at every site, pit toilets, electric
hookups, tables, boat ramp, playground,
store, rentals, pay phone.
In concession-run facility in wooded
cove on Lake Texoma.
Swim, boat, ski, or fish. Walk nature
trail. Hike to take photos. View wildlife.
14-day limit. Crowded major holidays.

PECAN POINT

COE (817) 578-1431
State map: L18
From FROST, head SE
on FM 667 for 8 miles
(12.8 k). Turn Right (SW)
on FM 744 and drive 2.5 miles (4 k).
Turn Left (S) on FM 1578 and proceed
2 miles (3.2 k). Go W for .25 mile
(400 m). (Also see Wolf Creek Park 2.)
FREE so choose a chore. Open Mar–Oct.
33 close, open sites.
Central faucet, pit toilets, tables, fire
rings, boat ramp.

On Navarro Mills Lake.
Fish. Boat. Swim.
14-day limit.
440 ft (132 m)

PINEY POINT PARK

COE (903) 838-8781
State map: H22
From TEXARKANA,
drive S on US 59 for
12 miles (19.2 k). Turn
Right (W) on first lake entrance after
passing Sulphur River. Follow signs.
(Also see Intake Hill and Oak Park.)
FREE so choose a chore.
Open Mar 1–Oct 31.
73 close, open sites.
Central faucet, flush toilets, tables, fire
rings, grills, boat ramp.
In pine along Wright Patman Lake with
good views.
Boat or fish. Take photos.
14-day limit. Crowded holidays.

PLOWMAN CREEK PARK

COE (817) 622-3332
State map: L17
Locate park on E side of
KOPPERL. (Also see
Kimball Bend Park.)
FREE so choose a chore.
Open Mar 15–Nov 15; dry camping
allowed off-season.
15 close, open sites.
Water at every site, flush toilets,
showers, tables, fire rings, boat ramp.
On low, rolling land covered with brush
and some trees next to Lake Whitney.
Swim, boat, or fish.
14-day limit. Hunting in season.
Crowded holidays.
550 ft (165 m)

PORT ARANSAS COUNTY PARK

Nueces County Parks
(512) 749-6117
State map: V18
Find park in PORT
ARANSAS. (Also see
Padre Balli Park.)
$4 on beach; $10 water & electric.

▲ ▲

Open All Year.
75 close, open sites. &
Water at every site, flush toilets,
showers, dump station, electric hookups,
tables.
On beach at north tip of Mustang Island.
Swim. Enjoy beach. Fish.
Beach bathhouse only open in summer.

PRESS MORRIS PARK

(915) 382-4635
State map: L13
From COLEMAN, drive
N on US 283 for 15 miles
(24 k). Turn Left (W) at
sign and continue 2.5 miles (4 k).
FREE; $5 electric.
Open All Year.
27 (15 tent-only) scattered, open sites.
Flush/pit toilets, electric hookups, tables,
fire rings, grills, boat ramp, store.
Next to clear Lake Coleman with
scattered mesquite and mulberry for
shade.
Swim, boat, waterski, and fish.
NO water. 12-day limit. Crowded
holidays.
1718 ft (515 m)

PUBLIC USE AREA 5

Brazos River Authority
(903) 529-2141
State map: M19
From MARQUEZ, take
FM 1146 N for 6.7 miles
(10.7 k). Turn Left (W) and go 1.8 miles
(2.9 k) to E end of dam. (Also see Lake
Limestone.)
FREE so choose a chore. Open All Year.
Undesignated scattered, open sites.
Pit toilets, boat ramp.
Near Lake Limestone.
Swim, boat, or fish.
NO water. 14-day limit.

RAGTOWN RA

Sabine NF
(409) 275-2632
State map: L23
From SHELBYVILLE,
take TX 87 SE for

6.5 miles (10.4 k). Turn Left (E) on
FM 139 and drive 6.5 miles (10.4 k). Bear
Right (E) on FM 3184 and go 4 miles
(6.4 k). Continue on FR 132.
$4. Open Mar 1–Dec 15.
36 close, screened sites.
Central faucet, flush toilets, showers,
dump station, tables, grills, boat ramp.
On high pine bluff overlooking Toledo
Bend Reservoir with spectacular
sunrises.
Take photos. Walk nature trail and spot
wildlife. Fish and boat.
14-day limit. No generators after dark.
No ATVs.
260 ft (78 m)

RATCLIFF LAKE RA

Davy Crockett NF
(409) 544-2046
State map: M21
Head E on TX 7 for
20 miles (32 k) from
CROCKETT.
$5. Open All Year.
75 (25 RV-only) close, open sites.
Central faucet, flush toilets, dump
station, electric hookups, tables, fire
rings, grills, boat ramp, rentals.
In piney wood next to 50-acre lake.
Swim, fish, or boat (no gas motors).
Walk nature trail or hike farther on Tall
Pine or 4C trails. View wildlife. Take
photos. Attend ranger programs.
14-day/26-ft limits. Crowded holidays.
300 ft (90 m)

REAGAN COUNTY PARK

(915) 884-2014
State map: N10
Locate park in BIG
LAKE on Utah Ave N.
FREE; donations
requested.
Open All Year.
18 (6 tent-only) close, open sites.
Water at 5 sites, flush toilets, electric
hookups, tables, grills, pool, tennis court,
playground.
In large park with replica of Santa Rita
No 1 (big oil pool).

Swim. Bike. Enjoy overnight stop.
3-day limit.

RED HILLS LAKE RA

Sabine NF
(409) 344-6205
State map: M23
From HEMPHILL, travel
N on TX 87 for
10.5 miles (16.8 k). Turn Right (E). (Also
see Indian Mounds RA.)
$5.
Open Mar 1–Oct 1.
30 (16 tent-only) close, open sites.
Central faucet, flush toilets, showers,
dump station, electric hookups, tables,
grills, boat ramp.
Next to lake.
Swim, fish, or boat (no motors). Walk
nature trail.
14-day/22-ft limits.

RIVERBEND PARK

COE (915) 949-4757
State map: M12
From SAN ANGELO,
head NW on US 87
about 5 miles (8 k). Exit
S on FM 2288. Go about 3 miles (4.8 k).
Turn Left. (Also see Lakeview Park.)
FREE so choose a chore.
Open All Year.
20 scattered, open sites.
Central faucet, pit toilets, tables, grills.
Among mesquite, cacti, and broken rock
ledges overlooking Concho River above
Lake O C Fisher.
Canoe, kayak, or boat. Fish. Take photos.
Observe wildlife.
14-day limit.
1938 ft (581 m)

ROBINSON CITY PARK

(915) 247-4158
State map: O15
From LLANO, travel W
on FM 152 for 2 miles
(3.2 k).
FREE so choose a chore.
Open All Year.
Undesignated scattered, open sites.

Central faucet, flush toilets, showers,
tables, boat ramp, pool, playground.
In scenic spot on Llano River.
Swim, fish, or boat (5 hp limit). Hike to
take photos. Play golf nearby.
14-day limit.

ROCKY CREEK PARK

COE (817) 292-2400
State map: J17
In FORT WORTH on
I-20, take Old Granbury
Rd Exit. Head SW for
3.9 miles (6.2 k). Turn Right at "T"
intersection. Drive 2 miles (3.2 k), then
turn Right on Rocky Creek Park Rd for
last 1.3 miles (2.1 k). (Nearby Bear Creek
costs $8 and Mustang Point costs $6.)
FREE so choose a chore.
Open All Year.
18 (1 tent-only) close, open sites.
Central faucet, pit toilets, dump station,
tables, fire rings, boat ramp.
Among grassy, rolling hills with some
oak and cottonwood near Benbrook
Lake.
Swim, boat, and fish. Watch wildlife.
14-day limit.

ROCKY CREEK PARK

COE (409) 596-1622
State map: P19
From SOMERVILLE,
travel S on TX 36 for
4 miles (6.4 k). Turn
Right (W) on FM 1948 and drive 4 miles
(6.4 k). (Also see Overlook Park. Nearby
Yequa Creek costs $6.)
FREE; $10 developed; $12 electric.
Open All Year.
148 close, open sites.
Water at every site, flush toilets,
showers, dump station, electric hookups,
tables, fire rings, grills, boat ramp, pay
phone.
Among trees next to Somerville Lake
(one free area of 31 sites).
Swim, boat, and ski. Fish. Take photos.
Bike.
14-day limit. Crowded 3-day weekends.

▲ ▲

RUDDICK PARK

Colorado City Parks
(915) 728-3463
State map: K11
In COLORADO CITY,
take 7th St off TX 208.
(Also see Fisher Park.)
FREE so choose a chore.
Open All Year.
Undesignated scattered, open, RV sites.
Central faucet, electric hookups, tables,
pool.
In city park with grass, trees, and nearby
Lone Wolf Creek.
Swim. Watch ducks and geese. Enjoy
overnight stop.
No toilet facilities. 14-day/28-ft limits.
2152 ft (646 m)

SANDERS COVE PARK

COE (903) 732-3020
State map: G20
From PARIS, drive N on
US 271 for 11.2 miles
(17.9 k). Turn Left (W)
on FM 906 and travel 1 mile (1.6 k). Turn
Left (S) at sign and continue 1 mile
(1.6 k). (Also see Lamar Point.)
$5; $8 electric. Open All Year.
85 close, open sites. Central faucet, pit
toilets, dump station, electric hookups,
tables, fire rings, grills, boat ramp.
Among shrubs and grasses under oak,
hickory, and pine trees next to Lake Pat
Mayse.
Swim, boat, or fish.
14-day limit. Crowded weekends and
holidays.
451 ft (135 m)

SANDY CREEK RA

Angelina NF
(409) 639-8620
State map: N22
From ZAVALLA, head E
on TX 63 for 18 miles
(28.8 k). Turn Left (N) on FM 2743. (Also
see Boykin Springs.)
$4. Open All Year.
16 close, open sites.
Water at every site, flush toilets,

showers, tables, fire rings, boat ramp.
Next to Sam Rayburn Reservoir.
Boat and fish. Spot wildlife.
14-day limit.

SANTA FE PARK

McCamey City Parks
(915) 652-3333
State map: N8
Locate park on US 67 at
E edge of MCCAMEY.
FREE so choose a chore; reservations
accepted at (915) 652-3333.
Open All Year.
19 (7 RV-only) scattered, open sites.
Central faucet, flush toilets, dump
station, electric hookups, tables, grills,
playground, pay phone.
With shade and scenic mountain view.
Visit museum. Observe wildlife. Find
Castle Gap dinosaur tracks. Take photos.
Bike.
2-day limit.
2433 ft (730 m)

SEABEE PARK

Abilene City Parks
(915) 676-6218
State map: K13
From ABILENE off I-20,
take FM 600 N for
3.2 miles (5.1 k). Turn Right (E). (Also
see Johnson Park.)
FREE so choose a chore. Open All Year.
Undesignated scattered, open sites.
Central faucet, flush toilets, fire rings.
In clearings of mesquite forest near Lake
Fort Phantom Hill.
Fish. Boat and waterski.
2-day limit.

SELMA PARK

Bowie City Parks
(817) 872-1114
State map: H16
From BOWIE, head SW
on TX 59 for 3.5 miles
(5.4 k). Turn Left (S) on FM 2583 and go
3.6 miles (5.8 k).
FREE so choose a chore. Open All Year.
Undesignated scattered, open sites.

Flush toilets, dump station, tables, boat ramp, shelter.
Next to Lake Amon Carter.
Swim, boat, ski, or fish.
NO water.

SILVER LAKE PARK

COE (817) 481-4541
State map: J18
From GRAPEVINE off Business 114, head N on Dooley Rd to sign on Left. (Also see McPherson Slough and Oak Grove Park.)
FREE for 1 day; $8 water; $10 electric; reservations accepted at (817) 481-4541 for an additional $6.50.
Open All Year.
79 (23 tent-only) close, open sites.
Central faucet, flush toilets, showers, dump station, electric hookups, tables, boat ramp.
In two sections with free one near dam and other in wooded flat next to Grapevine Lake.
Swim, boat, and fish. Spot wildlife. Attend ranger programs.
14-day limit. No glass containers or alcohol. Crowded summer holidays.
550 ft (165 m)

SITE 7

Sabine River Authority (409) 746-2192
State map: N24
From BURKEVILLE, drive NE on TX 662 about 15 miles (24 k) to E end of dam.
FREE so choose a chore. Open All Year.
Undesignated scattered, open sites.
Pit toilets, tables, boat ramp.
On shores of Toledo Bend Reservoir.
Swim, boat, ski, or fish.
NO water. 14-day limit.

SOLDIERS BLUFF

COE (817) 622-3332
State map: L17
From WHITNEY, take TX 22 S across dam. Turn Right. (Also see

Walling Bend Park.)
FREE so choose a chore.
Open All Year.
14 (6 tent-only) close, open sites.
Central faucet, flush toilets, tables, fire rings.
On gentle slope to Lake Whitney with some large trees.
Boat and fish. Swim.
14-day limit. Crowded major holidays.
550 ft (165 m)

SOUTH PARK

Hamlin City Parks
(915) 576-2711
State map: J12
From HAMLIN, drive S on FM 126 for 3.5 miles (5.4 k). Turn Left (E) and go .5 mile (800 m). (Also see Hamlin City Park.)
FREE so choose a chore.
Open All Year.
Undesignated scattered, open, RV sites.
Central faucet, tables, grills, boat ramp.
Next to South Lake.
Boat or fish.
No toilet facilities. No trash arrangements (pack it out).

STEELES CREEK PARK

COE (817) 622-3332
State map: L17
From LAGUNA PARK, head W on TX 22 about 2 miles (3.2 k). Turn Right (NW) on FM 56 and travel 18 miles (28.8 k) to Mooney Village. Turn Right on first paved road then Right again. Drive 2 miles (3.2 k).
FREE so choose a chore.
Open Mar 15–Nov 15; dry camping allowed off-season.
14 scattered, open sites.
Central faucet, pit toilets, tables, fire rings, boat ramp.
On low, rolling land with scrubby trees next to Lake Whitney.
Swim, boat, ski, and fish.
14-day limit. Hunting in season. Crowded holidays.
550 ft (165 m)

STINNETT CITY PARK

(806) 878-2422
State map: B10
Find park in STINNETT
1 block SW of
courthouse. (Also see
Lake Meredith NRA.)
FREE so choose a chore.
Open All Year.
8 close, open sites.
Central faucet, flush toilets, tables, grills,
pool, playground.
In town park.
Swim. Enjoy overnight stay.
3-day limit.

STUBBLEFIELD LAKE RA

Sam Houston NF
(409) 344-6205
State map: O20
Head W on FM 1375
about 9 miles (14.4 k)
from NEW WAVERLY. Turn Right (N)
on FR 215 and proceed 2 miles (3.2 k).
(Also see Kelley's Ponds.)
$4. Open All Year.
30 scattered, open, tent sites.
Central faucet, flush toilets, showers,
tables, grills, fire rings.
In forest next to lake.
Walk nature trail. Hike to spot wildlife
and take photos. Fish.
14-day limit. Hunting in season.

SYCAMORE BEND PARK

COE (214) 434-1666
State map: H18
From LEWISVILLE, take
I-35E N about 7 miles
(11.2 k) to Exit 457B.
Drive 1.5 miles (2.4 k) on Turbeville Rd
W. Turn S on local road for final 1 mile
(1.6 k). (Nearby Hickory Park costs $12.)
FREE so choose a chore.
Open Mar–Oct.
Undesignated scattered, open sites.
Pit toilets, tables, grills, boat ramp.
Next to Lake Lewisville.
Swim, boat, ski, or fish.
NO water. 14-day limit.

TEJAS CAMP

COE (512) 863-3016
State map: O16
From GEORGETOWN,
head NW on FM 2338
for 7 miles (11.2 k). Turn
Left (W) on FM 3405 and drive 6 miles
(9.6 k). Turn Left (S) on CR 258 and
continue 3 miles (4.8 k).
FREE so choose a chore.
Open All Year.
12 scattered, open, tent sites.
Central faucet, pit toilets, tables, fire
rings.
In thick grove of hardwood on N San
Gabriel River above Lake Georgetown.
Fish. Swim (life jacket advised). Canoe or
kayak. Hike Good Water Trail.
14-day limit. Occasionally crowded.
820 ft (246 m)

TICKY CREEK

COE (214) 442-3141
State map: H18
From PRINCETON,
travel S on FM 982 for
3.3 miles (5.3 k). Turn
Left (E) on FM 3364 for 1 mile (1.6 k),
then S for 2 miles (3.2 k). (Nearby
Clearlake costs $6.)
FREE so choose a chore.
Open All Year.
17 close, open, tent sites.
Central faucet, pit toilets, tables, grills,
boat ramp.
Next to Lake Lavon.
Swim, boat, ski, or fish.
14-day limit. No generators in quiet
hours.

TIPS PARK

Three Rivers City Parks
(512) 786-2528
State map: T16
From THREE RIVERS,
take TX 72W about
1 mile–just past Frio River bridge. Look
for park on S side of highway.
$4; $9 electric & water; reservations
accepted at (512) 786-2528.
Open All Year.

26 (10 tent-only) scattered, open sites.
Central faucet, flush toilets, showers,
dump station, electric hookups, tables,
grills.
Near Frio River in grass and dense trees
with Spanish moss.
Walk nature trail. View wildlife.
14-day limit. Occasionally noisy and
crowded.

TOWNSEND PARK RA

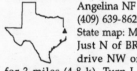

Angelina NF
(409) 639-8620
State map: M23
Just N of BROADDUS,
drive NW on FM 1277
for 3 miles (4.8 k). Turn Left (W) on
FM 2923 and travel 2 miles (3.2 k). (Also
see Harvey Creek RA.)
$4. Open All Year.
22 close, open sites.
Water at every site, pit toilets, tables,
grills, fire rings.
On Sam Rayburn Reservoir near
Bannister WMA.
Fish or boat. Observe wildlife. Take
photos.
14-day limit.

TWIN BUTTES PARK

San Angelo City Parks
(915) 944-3850
State map: N14
From SAN ANGELO,
drive SW on US 67 about
3.5 miles (5.4 k). Turn Left (SE). (Also see
Middle Concho.)
$3. Open All Year.
45 close, open sites. Central faucet, flush
toilets, dump station, electric hookups,
tables, grills, boat ramp.
In open spot on Twin Buttes Reservoir.
Swim, boat, waterski, and fish.
14-day limit.

W D "JACK" GUTHRIE PARK

Franklin County Water
District (903) 588-2352
State map: H21
Travel S on TX 37 from
MOUNT VERNON for
1 mile (1.6 k). Turn Left (SE) on FM 21
and proceed 7.8 miles (12.5 k). Turn
Right (S) on FM 3007. Continue 1.4 miles
(2.2 k). (Also see Dogwood Park.)
$5; **$9** electric; reservations accepted at
(903) 588-2352.
Open Nov 1–Oct 31.
39 close, open sites. Water at every site,
flush toilets, showers, dump station,
electric hookups, tables, grills, boat
ramp, ball courts, pay phone.
In wooded area on north side of dam for
Lake Cypress Springs.
Swim, boat, or fish. Play sports.
14-day limit.

WALLEYE PARK

Franklin County Water
District (903) 588-2352
State map: H23
From MT VERNON,
drive S on TX 37 for
1 mile (1.6 k). Turn Left (SE) on FM 21
and proceed 3.2 miles (5.1 k). Turn Right
(S) on FM 2723 and go 2 miles (3.2 k).
Turn Right on local road for last 2 miles
(3.2 k). (Also see Overlook.)
$5; **$9** electric; reservations accepted at
(903) 588-2352.
Open All Year.
86 (34 tent-only) close, open sites.
Central faucet, flush toilets, showers,
dump station, electric hookups, tables,
grills, boat ramp, shelter, volleyball
court, pay phone.
Next to Lake Cypress Springs in wooded
setting.
Fish. Swim. Boat.
14-day limit. Crowded holiday
weekends.

WALLING BEND PARK

COE (817) 622-3332
State map: L17
From LAGUNA PARK,
head W on TX 22 about
2 miles (3.2 k). Turn
Right (NW) on FM 56. Go 2 miles (3.2 k).
Turn Right (NE) on FM 2841. Go 4 miles
(6.4 k) to end. (Also see Soldiers Bluff.)
FREE so choose a chore.

Open All Year.
10 scattered, open sites.
Pit toilets, tables, fire rings, boat ramp.
On gently rolling terrain with sparse trees next to Lake Whitney.
Swim, boat, and fish.
NO water. 14-day limit. Crowded summer weekends.
550 ft (165 m)

WAYLON JENNINGS RV PARK

Littlefield Parks
(806) 385-5161
State map: G9
From LITTLEFIELD, head N for 1 mile (1.6 k) on US 385. (Also see Bull Lake.)
FREE so choose a chore.
Open All Year.
48 scattered, open, RV sites.
Tables, grills.
In roadside park.
Enjoy overnight stop.
NO water. No toilet facilities. 4-day limit.
3553 ft (1066 m)

WELDON ROBB MEMORIAL PARK

North Montague Water District (817) 825-3282
State map: G16
From NOCONA, head N on FM 103 for 6 miles (9.6 k). Turn Right (E) on FM 2634 and drive 4 miles (6.4 k). (Also see Boone Park and Joe Benton Park.)
FREE so choose a chore.
Open All Year.
Undesignated scattered, open sites.
Pit toilets, tables, grills, boat ramp.
In shade next to Lake Nocona.
Swim, boat, ski, or fish.
NO water. 21-day limit. Occasional ATVs.

WESTCREEK CIRCLE

COE (817) 292-2400
State map: J17
From BENBROOK, head SW on US 377 for 6.4 miles (10.2 k). Turn

Left (E) on FM 1187 and drive 1.4 miles (2.2 k). Turn Left on CR 1125 and go .6 mile (1 k), bearing Left at "Y." (Nearby Bear Creek costs $8 and South Holiday costs $6.)
FREE so choose a chore.
Open All Year.
4 close, open, tent sites.
Pit toilets, tables, fire rings.
On open floodplain with some oak and cottonwood at Bear Creek near Benbrook Lake.
Fish. View wildlife.
NO water. 14-day limit.

WHIGHAM PARK

Perryton City Parks
(806) 435-4014
State map: A11
In PERRYTON, find park at 900 S Main (US 83).
FREE so choose a chore.
Open All Year.
5 close, open sites.
Water at every site, flush toilets, dump station, electric hookups, tables, grills, fire rings, playground, store, laundry, pay phone.
In city park.
Relax overnight.
2-day limit. Occasionally crowded.
2900 ft (870 m)

WHITE FLINT PARK

COE (817) 939-1829
State map: N17
From BELTON, travel N on TX 317 for 9 miles (14.4 k). Turn Left (NW) on TX 36. Go about 6 miles (9.6 k)–cross Belton Lake. Turn Right (N) on Winkler Park Rd. (Also see Cedar Ridge Park, Owl Creek Park, and Winkler Park.)
FREE so choose a chore.
Open All Year.
14 scattered, screened sites. Pit toilets, tables, fire rings, grills, boat ramp.
Next to Belton Lake with shade for tables.
Swim, boat, or fish.
NO water. 14-day limit.

WHITES MEMORIAL PARK

Chambers County Parks
(409) 267-8381
State map: Q22
Just S of HANKAMER
on I-10, take TX 61 Exit S
for .2 mile (320 m). (Also see Fort
Anahuac Park, McCollum Park, and
Winnie Stowell Park.)
FREE so choose a chore; reservations
accepted at (409) 267-8381.
Open All Year.
Undesignated close, open sites.
Central faucet, flush toilets, electric
hookups, tables, boat ramp.
In wooded area near Turtle Bayou and
Lake Anahuac.
View birdlife. Take photos. Boat. Fish.
14-day limit.
25 ft (8 m)

WILLOW OAK RA

Sabine NF
(409) 344-6205
State map: N23
From HEMPHILL, drive
S on TX 87 for 15 miles
(24 k). (Also see Lakeview RA.)
$4. Open All Year.
10 close, open sites.
Central faucet, chemical toilets, dump
station, tables, grills, boat ramp.
Next to Toledo Bend Reservoir.
Boat and waterski. Fish.
14-day limit.

WINKLER PARK

COE (817) 939-1829
State map: N17
From BELTON, travel N
on TX 317 for 9 miles
(14.4 k). Turn Left (NW)
on TX 36. Drive 6 miles (9.6 k)−cross
Belton Lake. Turn Right (N) on Winkler
Park Rd. Go about 2 miles (3.2 k). (Also
see White Flint Park.)
$4. Open Apr 1−Sep 30.
10 scattered, open sites.
Water at every site, pit toilets, tables, fire
rings, grills, boat ramp.
With some shade on slope to Belton

Lake.
Swim, boat, or fish.
14-day limit.

WINNIE STOWELL PARK

Chambers County Parks
(409) 267-8381
State map: Q22
Find park in WINNIE on
LeBlanc Rd (1 block E of
TX 124). (See Whites Memorial Park.)
FREE so choose a chore. Open All Year.
Undesignated close, open sites.
Central faucet, flush toilets, showers,
electric hookups, tables, grills.
At home of Texas Rice Festival.
Enjoy overnight stop.
14-day limit.
25 ft (8 m)

WISE COUNTY PARK

Wise County Parks
(817) 627-6655
State map: H16
From CHICO, head W
on FM 1810 for 1.2 miles
(1.9 k). Turn Left (S) on FM 2952 and go
2.5 miles (4 k).
$3. Open All Year.
25 close, open sites. Central faucet, flush
toilets, tables, grills, boat ramp.
Next to Lake Bridgeport.
Swim, boat, ski, and fish. Bike.

WOLF CREEK PARK 2

COE (817) 578-1431
State map: L18
From FROST, head SE
on FM 667 for 8 miles
(12.8 k). Turn Right (SW)
on FM 744 and proceed 2.5 miles (4 k).
Turn Left (S) on FM 1578 and go 2 miles
(3.2 k). (Also see Pecan Point.)
FREE so choose a chore. Open Mar−Oct.
45 close, open sites. Central faucet, pit
toilets, tables, grills, boat ramp.
In rolling, wooded land next to Navarro
Mills Lake.
Swim, boat, or fish.
14-day limit.
440 ft (132 m)

▲ ▲

VERMONT
CAMPGROUND LOCATIONS

▶ ▶ Find location on facing page map grid. ▶ ▶
▼ ▼ Locate area campgrounds on these page numbers. ▼ ▼

Vermont

Grid conforms to official state map. For your copy, call (802) 828-3236
or write Vermont Dept of Travel & Tourism, 134 State St, Montpelier, VT 05602.

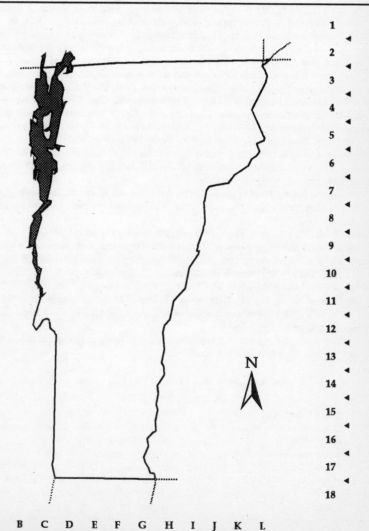

N

▲ ▲

PUBLIC LANDS CAMPING

Vermont calls itself the Green Mountain State. Indeed, you'll love the quiet, scenic beauty of the lush Green Mountains. And, you'll love that no billboards intrude on this state's landscape. Banning billboards is only one example of how Vermont has set an example in land use policy for the rest of the United States.

As you enjoy recreational opportunities here, you'll find Vermont's history and art integrate with the natural beauty located in the public lands of the national forests, state parks, and forests. You can cycle the roads. You can hike the Appalachian Trail, Long Trail, or others. Views range from glacial lakes with thick woods to agrarian scenes of dairying, maple-syruping, and wine-making. Summit panoramas offer colorful vistas, particularly during autumn. Especially rewarding forest walks include Texas Falls and, in White Rocks National Recreation Area (NRA), the Ice Beds. Also, in Vermont, you can find trails designated for cross-country skiing and snowshoeing. You can enjoy lakes set aside for peace and quiet as well as others for motorboating and waterskiing. Too, discover ideal canoe trips along the following waterways: Battenkill, Connecticut, Lamoille, Lemon Fair, Missisquoi, Otter Creek, and Winooski.

Besides the developed campsites available in the **Green Mountain National Forest** (NF), primitive camping can be enjoyed too—particularly in the six wilderness areas: Bristol Cliffs, Breadloaf, Big Branch, Peru Peak, Lye Brook, and George D Aiken. Primitive camping is free; developed campgrounds range from free to $10.00. If you want to try winter camping, keep in mind Grout Pond, Silver Lake, and Chittenden Brook campgrounds with their fireplaces.

Also on the federal level of public lands, the **US Army Corps of Engineers** (COE) offers a campground at Ball Mountain Lake. Walk-in sites are free; drive-in sites cost $10.00.

State Park (SP) and **State Forest** (SF) camping fees cost $8.00–$12.00 for developed sites and $14.00–$16.00 for lean-tos. Vermont offers free primitive camping for groups of ten or less in the following areas: Aitkin SF, Ascutney SP, Camel's Hump SF and SP, Coolidge SF, Darling SF, Dorand SF, Elmore SP, Grafton SF, Groton SF, L R Jones SF, Mathewson SF, Mount Mansfield SF, Okemo SF, Proctor–Piper SF, Putnam SF, Roxbury SF, Townshend SF, Victory SF, Washington SF, West Rutland SF, and Willoughby SF. Be sure to pick up a *Vermont Guide to Primitive Camping on State Lands* to know about restricted areas and other rules.

Whether hiking, biking, boating, skiing, or camping, Vermont recognizes the various needs of people. Vermont makes it special.

▲ ▲

CHITTENDEN BROOK

Green Mountain NF
(802) 767-4261
State map: E10
From ROCHESTER, drive W on VT 73 for 5.2 miles (8.32 k). Turn Left on unpaved, steep FR 45 at campground sign. Go another 2.5 miles (4 k). (Also see Moosalamoo and Silver Lake Walk-In. Nearby Gifford Woods SP costs $7.50)

$5.
Open May 25–Oct 12; dry camping allowed off-season.
17 close, screened sites. ♿
Hand pump, pit toilets, tables, fire rings. In secluded woods next to scenic brook. Hike (trails lead from site #7). View wildlife or fish.
14-day/18-ft limits. Crowded on long weekends and during fall foliage season. 1760 ft (528 m)

▲ ▲

GROUT POND

Green Mountain NF
(802) 362-2307
State map: E16
From STRATTON, go about 3 miles (4.8 k) W. Turn Left (S) on signed Grout Pond access road. (Also see Red Mill.)
FREE so choose a chore.
Open All Year.
12 scattered, open, tent sites. &
Hand pump, pit toilets, tables, fire rings, grills, boat ramp.
Near 79-acre pond.
Explore 1600 acres by hiking and canoeing. Swim or relax.
No trash arrangements (pack it out).
14-day limit. Pesty mosquitos. Crowded all summer.
1960 ft (588 m)

MOOSALAMOO

Green Mountain NF
(802) 388-4362
State map: D10
From RIPTON, drive SE on VT 125 about .5 mile (800 m). Turn Right (S) on FR 32 and go 3.5 miles (5.6 k) to FR 24. (Also see Chittenden Brook and Silver Lake Walk-In.)
$5.
Open May–Sep 15.
19 scattered, open sites. &
Hand pump, pit toilets, tables, grills, fire rings.
In beautiful natural setting.
Hike, explore, mountain bike, view wildlife, or fish.
14-day/34-ft limits. Hunting in season. No ATVs. Often buggy May–Jun. Crowded summers.
1600 ft (480 m)

RED MILL

Green Mountain NF
(802) 362-2307
State map: D17
From BENNINGTON, drive E on VT 9 for 10 miles (16 k). Turn Left (N) on FR 274 and go 1 mile (1.6 k). (Also see Grout Pond. Nearby Woodford SP

costs $9.)
FREE; donations requested.
Open May–Oct; dry camping allowed off-season.
20 close, screened sites.
Hand pump, pit toilets, tables, fire rings.
In dense forest of mixed hard- and softwoods.
Take photographs or view wildlife.
No trash arrangements (pack it out).
14-day limit. Pesty mosquitos.

SILVER LAKE WALK-IN

Green Mountain NF
(802) 388-4362
State map: D10
From GOSHEN, drive FR 32 N for 2.3 miles (3.68 k). Turn Left (NW) on FR 27 and go to end of road. Walk Goshen Trail about .6 mile (1 k). (Also see Moosalamoo and Chittenden Brook.)
FREE so choose a chore.
Open All Year.
16 close, open, tent sites.
Water in every site, pit toilets, tables, grills, fire rings.
On lake with large, private sites.
Enjoy trail network and observe wildlife.
Swim, canoe, or fish.
No trash arrangements (pack it out).
14-day limit. Bugs in Jun.

WINDHALL BROOK WALK-IN

COE (802) 874-4881
State map: E15
From RAWSONVILLE, drive N on VT 100 for 2 miles (3.2 k). Turn Right (SE) on signed road. Walk to free sites.
FREE at 3 sites; $10 for 110 drive-in sites.
Open May 15–Sep 15.
113 (3 tent-only) close, open sites. &
Central faucet, flush toilets, showers, dump station, tables, grills, fire rings.
In Green Mountains near Ball Mountain Lake.
Hike trail system to view wildlife and take photos. Swim, canoe, or fish. Mountain bike. Attend ranger programs.
14-day limit.

VIRGINIA
CAMPGROUND LOCATIONS

▸ ▸ Find location on facing page map grid. ▸ ▸
▾ ▾ Locate area campgrounds on these page numbers. ▾ ▾

GRID	PAGE
D6	430, 434
D7	429
E6	430, 432
G7	430, 434
H6	435
I5	434
I6	429, 430
I7	434
J4	432
J5	429, 430, 431, 432, 433
K4	431, 433
L3	431, 435
M3	432, 434
M7	432
O3	434
O6	433
Q6	431

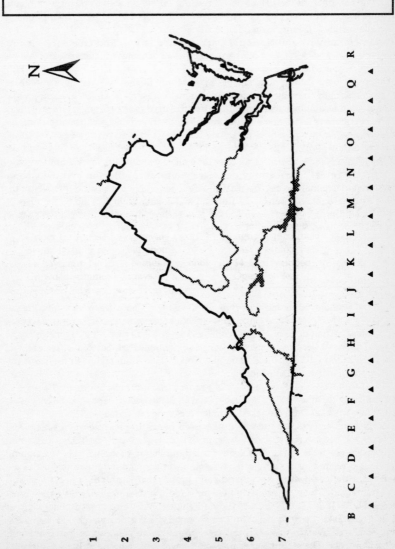

Virginia

Grid conforms to official state map. For your copy, call (800) VISIT-VA
or write Tourism Development, 1021 E Cary St, Richmond, VA 23219.

▲ ▲

PUBLIC LANDS CAMPING

For over 200 years, Virginia has attracted lovers of history and of natural beauty. This mid-Atlantic state claims the first permanent English settlement in the New World. It boasts the birthplaces of 8 American presidents. It commands the position of more Civil War battles than any other state. Stretching from the Atlantic Ocean to the Blue Ridge and Allegheny mountains, discover sandy beaches on barrier islands, bountiful seafood from the ocean and Chesapeake Bay, peaceful countryside filled with charming colonial homes, and wide-spreading forests on awe-inspiring mountains. Excellent opportunities exist on Virginia's public lands for camping, hiking, biking, horseback riding, fishing, swimming, boating....

Associated with the **National Park Service** (NPS), find free backpacking opportunities and developed campgrounds. Developed sites in Shenandoah National Park (NP) cost $9.00–$12.00. In Cumberland Gap National Historical Park (NHP), Wilderness Road Campground charges $8.00. Mount Rogers National Recreation Area (NRA) is administered by the Jefferson National Forest (NF). Listed by campground name, camp fees in this area range from free to $10.00 for single sites. Prince William Forest Park offers a free and a $7.00 campground. There is no backpacking along the Blue Ridge Parkway or Skyline Drive, but you'll find an array of $8.00–$12.00 campgrounds along the way. Assateague Island National Seashore (NS) and the Appalachian National Scenic Trail offer dramatically contrasting backcountries.

The **US Forest Service** provides recreation in the Jefferson and the George Washington national forests. The 690,000-acre Jefferson NF follows the contours of the Blue Ridge Mountains. In mixed hardwood and conifer ecologies, the forest offers 16 developed campgrounds (free to $10.00) plus backpacking into special areas such as James River Face Wilderness. Hike along the Cascades and Mount Rogers national recreation trails as well as the Appalachian National Scenic Trail. Ride horses along the Virginia Highlands Horse Trail. Drive the Big Walker Mountain and Mount Rogers scenic byways. One-million-acre George Washington NF adjoins the Jefferson NF and lies in sections south and east of Shenandoah NP. As in the Jefferson NF, all developed camping areas in the George Washington NF open by mid-spring. Some locations are open but without water facilities through the winter. Camp fees range from free to $22.00 for a double site. Most single sites without hookups cost $10.00 or less. Backpack into Ramseys Draft or Saint Mary's wilderness areas. Motor along the Highlands Scenic Tour. The forest service cooperates with the National Park Service in recreational offerings at Mount Rogers and along the Appalachian Trail, and with the US Army Corps of Engineers on Lake Moomaw.

US Army Corps of Engineers (COE) projects with campgrounds in the state of Virginia include John H Kerr Reservoir, John W Flannagan Reservoir, Lake Moomaw, and Philpott Lake. On these lakes, camping fees range from free to $12.00.

In November 1992, Virginia citizens passed bonds to preserve open spaces and habitats for endangered species as well as to update state park facilities. This action helps **Virginia State Parks** (SP) protect a natural legacy of scenic beauty. Camping facilities exist in 20 parks across the coastal, piedmont, and mountain regions of the state. On the coast, find developed campgrounds at Kiptopeke, Seashore, and Westmoreland. There's primitive, hike-in/bike-in/boat-in camping at False Cape, accessible via Back Bay National Wildlife Refuge (NWR). In the piedmont, camp at Bear Creek Lake, Fairy Stone, Twin Lakes, Holliday Lake, Occoneechee, Pocahontas, and Staunton River. In this heartland area, primitive camping can be found at Smith Mountain Lake. The mountainous areas offer developed camping at Breaks Interstate

▲ ▲

(shared with Kentucky), Claytor Lake, Douthat, Grayson Highlands, Hungry Mother, and Natural Tunnel. More primitive opportunities exist at Clinch Mountain Wildlife Management Area (WMA) and Sky Meadows. Generally, camping fees cost $6.00 for primitive spots, $8.50 for developed sites, and $12.00 for sites with hookups. Rates are higher at coastal Seashore and Kiptopeke. Pet fees ($3.00 per day) are added as is tax.

At the **New Kent Forestry Center** in Providence Forge (between Richmond and Williamsburg), six RV campsites are available in exchange for volunteer work. If interested in this well-organized volunteer program, call (804) 966-2201.

Cities, regions, and **counties** also offer camping while visiting Virginia historical and recreational areas. Find camping around the municipalities of Bristol, Buena Vista, Hampton, Lexington, Newport News, and Portsmouth. Also find camping in the parks of Fairfax and Wythe counties. Look for Bull Run and Pohick Bay regional parks within driving distance of Washington, DC. Find Natural Chimney Regional Park near Mount Solon between Shenandoah NP and George Washington NF.

While you camp on Virginia public lands, get in touch with her natural beauty. Too, Virginia offers ample opportunities to revisit her past and get in touch with the present and future.

▲ ▲

ASSATEAGUE NS
Backcountry (See MD)

BARK CAMP

Jefferson NF
(703) 328-2931
State map: D7

From NORTON, head SE on US 58A for 6.3 miles (10.1 k). Turn Right (S) on VA 706 and drive 4.1 miles (6.6 k). Jog Left (E) on VA 699 and go .3 mile (480 m). Turn Right (SE) on VA 822 and continue 1.7 miles (2.7 k). (Nearby High Knob costs $8.)
$5. Open May 15–Oct 15.
23 close, screened sites.
Central faucet, flush toilets, dump station, tables, grills, boat ramp.
In Appalachian hardwood next to 40-acre lake.
Boat or fish. Hike to appreciate mountainous area.
14-day limit. No horses.
2700 ft (810 m)

BLOWING SPRINGS

Geo Washington NF
(703) 839-2521
State map: J5

From WARM SPRINGS, drive W on

VA 39 over mountain. Turn left. (Also see Hidden Valley. Nearby Bolar Mountain costs $10.)
$4. Open Apr–Nov.
22 (9 tent-only) close, screened sites.
Hand pump, pit toilets, tables, grills, fire rings.
In level, wooded setting on Black Creek.
Swim or fish. Watch wildlife.
14-day limit. Hunting in season.

BOLEY FIELDS

Jefferson NF
(703) 552-4641
State map: I6

From BLACKSBURG, head W on US 460 about 4 miles (6.4 k). Turn Left (SW) on gravel FR 708 and go 4.5 miles (7.2 k). (Also see Caldwell Fields.)
FREE so choose a chore.
Open All Year.
Undesignated scattered, open sites.
Pit toilets, fire rings.
In 2-acres of grassy meadow next to stocked Poverty Creek.
View wildlife (rabbit, turkey, grouse, deer, raccoon). Fish. Watch butterflies.
NO water. No trash arrangements (pack it out). 14-day limit.
1800 ft (540 m)

BUBBLING SPRINGS

Geo Washington NF
(703) 839-2521
State map: J5

From MILLBORO SPRINGS, head SE on VA 633 to MILLBORO. Continue following signs.
FREE so choose a chore.
Open All Year.
Undesignated sites.
Hand pump, pit toilets, tables, grills.
In open area surrounded by forest plus stream.
Enjoy seclusion and quiet. Hike to spot wildlife and take photos. Fish.
No trash arrangements (pack it out).
14-day limit. Hunting in season.

CALDWELL FIELDS

Jefferson NF
(703) 552-4641
State map: I6

From BLACKSBURG, head W on US 460 about 5 miles (8 k). Turn Right (NE) on VA 621 and proceed 8 miles (12.8 k)–becomes gravel. (Also see Boley Fields.)
FREE so choose a chore.
Open All Year.
Undesignated scattered, open sites.
Pit toilets, fire rings.
Among several open, grassy fields along Craigs Creek surrounded by forest.
Hike to explore area. Fish.
NO water. No trash arrangements (pack it out). 14-day limit. Hunting in season.
Occasionally crowded weekends when college in session.
1760 ft (528 m)

CANE PATCH

Jefferson NF
(703) 328-2931
State map: D6

From POUND, take VA 671 W for 6.5 miles (10.4 k).
$5. Open May 15–Oct 15.
30 close, open sites.
Central faucet, flush toilets, showers, tables, fire rings, playground.
In open field along stream course.

Fish. Enjoy peaceful setting.
14-day/32-ft limits. No horses.
1600 ft (480 m)

COMERS ROCK

Jefferson NF
(703) 783-5196
State map: G7

From SPEEDWELL, head S on US 21 about 5 miles (8 k). Turn Right (W) on gravel FR 57. Drive about 2 miles (3.2 k). (Nearby Raccoon Branch costs $6.)
FREE so choose a chore.
Open All Year.
10 close, open, tent sites.
Central faucet, pit toilets, tables, fire rings.
In remote, forest setting.
Hike Iron Mountain Trail. Explore scenic area and take photos. Watch wildlife.
14-day limit. Hunting in season.
3800 ft (1140 m)

CRAIG CREEK

Jefferson NF
(703) 864-5195
State map: J5

From ORISKANY, take VA 704 E for .5 mile (800 m). Turn Right on FR 5058 and go about 1.5 miles (2.4 k). (Also see Pines.)
FREE so choose a chore.
Open All Year.
Undesignated close, open sites.
Hand pump, flush toilets, tables.
In rural, farm-like setting with fields and some trees next to large creek.
Swim, fish, or boat (no motors). Hike. Spot wildlife. Relax.
14-day limit. Crowded holiday weekends.
1200 ft (360 m)

CRANESNEST AREAS 1, 2, 3

COE (703) 835-9544
State map: E6
From CLINTWOOD,

drive E for 2.5 miles (4 k) on VA 83. Turn Left (N) on dirt entrance road and travel 2 miles (3.2 k). (Also see Lower Twin RA and Pound River RA.)

$5.
Open May 25–Sep 30; dry camping allowed off-season.
37 close, open sites. &
Central faucet, flush toilets, dump station, tables, fire rings, boat ramp.
In open and wooded spots along Cranesnest River.
Fish or boat. Hike to appreciate area.
14-day limit. No alcohol.
1425 ft (428 m)

CUMBERLAND GAP NHP
Backcountry (See KY)

GOSNOLD'S HOPE PARK

Hampton City Parks
(804) 850-5116
State map: Q6
In HAMPTON on I-64, take W Mercury Blvd Exit. Head E for 3 miles (4.8 k). Turn Left (N) on King St. Drive 1 mile (1.6 k). Turn Right on Little Back River Rd. Continue 2.5 miles (4 k). Turn Left.
$4.70; $5.70 electric.
Open All Year.
60 close, open sites.
Central faucet, flush toilets, showers, dump station, electric hookups, tables, boat ramp.
In city park within forested area.
Boat or fish. Enjoy park facilities.
14-day limit.
15 ft (5 m)

GREENWOOD POINT
BOAT-IN/WALK-IN

Geo Washington NF
(703) 839-2521
State map: J5
From WARM SPRINGS, drive W on VA 39 for 13 miles (20.8 k). Turn Left (SW) on VA 600 and travel 6 miles (9.6 k). Watch for Bolar Mountain signs. Ask for further directions—boat about 2 miles (3.2 k) S of Bolar Mountain. (Also see McClintic Point.)
FREE so choose a chore.
Open All Year.
5 scattered, open, tent sites.
Chemical toilets, tables, grills, fire rings.

On wooded knoll overlooking Lake Moomaw.
Enjoy seclusion. Canoe or boat. Swim or fish. Hike. View wildlife.
NO water. No trash arrangements (pack it out). 14-day limit. Hunting in season.

HIDDEN VALLEY

Geo Washington NF
(703) 839-2521
State map: J5
From WARM SPRINGS, drive W on VA 39 for 3 miles (4.8 k). Turn Right (N) on VA 621 and follow signs. (Also see Blowing Springs.)
$4. Open Apr–Nov.
30 close, screened sites.
Hand pump, pit toilets, tables, fire rings.
In wooded area surrounded by fields near Jackson River.
Fish. Hike to observe wildlife and take photos.
14-day limit. Hunting in season.

HIGH CLIFF CANOE CAMP

Geo Washington NF
(703) 984-4101
State map: L3
From COLUMBIA FURNACE, take VA 675 W to WRAY; then continue W for 4 miles (6.4 k). Turn Right (N) on VA 684 and drive 9 miles (14.4 k) to Goods Landing. Canoe N for 1 mile (1.6 k). (Also see Wolf Gap. Nearby Camp Roosevelt costs $6.)
FREE so choose a chore.
Open All Year.
5 close, screened, tent sites.
Pit toilets, tables.
In forest setting next to South Fork of Shenandoah River.
Enjoy seclusion. Observe nature. Fish.
NO water. No trash arrangements (pack it out). 14-day limit. Hunting in season.
700 ft (210 m)

HONE QUARRY

Geo Washington NF
(703) 828-2591
State map: K4
From DAYTON, head W on VA 257 for

11.3 miles (18.1 k). Turn Right (N) at sign on FR 62 and drive 1.7 miles (2.7 k).
FREE so choose a chore.
Open All Year.
10 close, open sites.
Hand pump, pit toilets, dump station, tables, grills, fire rings.
In forest and bottomland setting next to river.
Swim or fish. Hike to take photos and spot wildlife.
14-day/22-ft limits.
2500 ft (750 m)

IVY HILL PARK

COE (804) 738-6144
State map: M7
From BULLOCK, NC, drive N on US 15 about 2 miles (3.2 k). Turn Right (NE) on CR 1501/VA 825. Go to end of road—about 8 miles (12.8 k).
FREE so choose a chore.
Open Apr–Oct.
25 scattered, screened sites.
Central faucet, pit toilets, tables, fire rings, boat ramp.
In mixed woodland on peninsula in Kerr Lake.
Swim, boat, or fish. Windsurf.
14-day limit. Hunting in season. No generators in quiet hours.
400 ft (120 m)

LITTLE FORT

Geo Washington NF
(703) 984-4101
State map: M3
From WOODSTOCK, travel E on VA 758 for 6 miles (9.6 k).
FREE so choose a chore.
Open All Year.
10 scattered, screened sites.
Spring, pit toilets, tables, fire rings.
In secluded mountain forest next to small stream.
Hike to enjoy area—Woodstock Observation Tower only 1 mile (1.6 k). Mountain bike. Fish.
14-day limit. Hunting in season. Occasional ATVs.
1500 ft (450 m)

LOCUST SPRINGS

Geo Washington NF
(703) 839-2521
State map: J4
From BARTOW, WV, head E on WV 28 about 8 miles (12.8 k). Turn Right (E). Cross into VA. (Also see Island, WV.)
FREE so choose a chore.
Open All Year.
Undesignated scattered, open sites.
Hand pump, pit toilets, tables.
In open area surrounded by woods, streams, and bogs.
Hike into Laurel Fork Area to study ecology. Spot wildlife. Take photos. Fish.
No trash arrangements (pack it out).
14-day limit. Crowded hunting season.

LOWER TWIN RA

COE (703) 835-9544
State map: E6
From HAYSI, head NW on VA 63 for 5 miles (8 k). Continue Straight onto VA 614 then bear Right (N) on VA 739—go 5 miles (8 k), crossing dam. Turn Left (SW) on VA 611 and continue 3 miles (4.8 k). Turn Left (S) at sign. (Also see Cranesnest Areas 1, 2, 3.)
$5; $6 electric.
Open May 25–Sep 30.
32 (5 tent-only) close, open sites. ⅙
Central faucet, flush toilets, showers, dump station, electric hookups, tables, fire rings, boat ramp.
In wooded hollow leading to John Flannagan Reservoir.
Boat, ski, or fish. Walk nature trail. Hike to explore scenic area. Attend ranger programs.
14-day limit. No alcohol.
1420 ft (426 m)

MCCLINTIC POINT

Geo Washington NF
(703) 839-2521
State map: J5
From WARM SPRINGS, drive W on VA 39 for 13 miles (20.8 k). Turn Left (SW) on VA 600 and travel 6 miles (9.6 k). Watch for Bolar Mountain signs. Turn Left (NE) on VA 603 and continue

▲ ▲

about 3 miles (4.8 k). (Also see Greenwood Point Boat-In/Walk-In. Nearby Bolar Mountain costs $10.)
FREE Dec–Mar; $4 May–Sep.
18 close, open sites.
Hand pump, chemical toilets, tables, grills, fire rings.
On old farmsite with wood and thick undergrowth next to Lake Moomaw.
Swim, boat, or fish. Hike to enjoy mountain setting and take photos. Attend ranger programs.
14-day limit.

NEW KENT FORESTRY CENTER VOLUNTEERS CAMP

(804) 966-2201
State map: O6
Locate center off US 60 at PROVIDENCE FORGE.
FREE; reservations required at (804) 966-2201.
Open All Year.
6 close, open, RV sites.
Water at every site, electric hookups, tables.
In wooded area next to pristine Chickahominy River.
Camp free for a few hours volunteer work per day (various tasks available). Take nature walks. Watch birds. Take photos. Bike.
No toilet facilities.

NORTH CREEK

Jefferson NF
(703) 291-2189
State map: J5
From BUCHANAN, drive NE on US 11 for 2.1 miles (3.4 k). Take I-81 N for .5 mile (800 m). Exit E on VA 614 and go 2.9 miles (4.6 k). Turn Left (NE) on FR 59 and drive 2.4 miles (3.8 k).
$5.
Open All Year.
15 close, open sites.
Central faucet, pit toilets, dump station, tables, fire rings.
In forest setting near stream (several free walk-in shelters nearby for tenting with more privacy).

Fish. Hike to explore area.
14-day limit.

NORTH RIVER

Geo Washington NF
(703) 828-2591
State map: K4
From CHURCHVILLE, drive W for 10 miles (16 k) on US 250. Turn Right (NE) on VA 715/FR 96 and go 8.5 miles (13.6 k). Turn Right on FR 95 and proceed 2.1 miles (3.4 k). Turn Right on FR 95B for final 1 mile (1.6 k). (Nearby Todd Lake costs $7.)
$3.
Open All Year.
Undesignated scattered, open sites.
Hand pump, pit toilets, tables, grills, fire rings.
In grassy field with some pine next to North River.
Swim or fish. Hike to spot wildlife and take photos. Mountain bike.
14-day limit.
2000 ft (600 m)

PINES

Jefferson NF
(703) 864-5195
State map: J5
From NEW CASTLE, head NE on VA 615 about 3 miles (4.8 k). Continue on VA 609 another 2 miles (3.2 k). Turn Left (W) on VA 611 and travel 4 miles (6.4 k). Turn Right (NE) on VA 617 and go 5 miles (8 k). (Also see Craig Creek and Steel Bridge.)
FREE so choose a chore.
Open All Year.
18 close, open sites.
Hand pump, pit toilets, tables, grills.
In mixed hardwood/pine next to stocked trout stream.
Fish. Hike to observe wildlife and take photos. Mountain bike.
14-day limit. Crowded in Nov deer-hunting season.
1800 ft (540 m)

POUND RIVER RA

COE (703) 835-9544
State map: D6
From CLINTWOOD,
go N on VA 631 for 2.5 miles (4 k). Turn
Right (E) on dirt VA 754. Drive 1.5 miles
(2.4 k). (See Cranesnest Areas 1, 2, 3.)
FREE so choose a chore.
Open May 25–Sep 30; dry camping
allowed off-season.
18 close, open sites.
Central faucet, pit toilets, tables, fire
rings, boat ramp.
With wooded and open sites next to
Pound River on backwaters of John
Flannagan Reservoir.
Boat or fish.
14-day limit. No alcohol. Occasionally
crowded.
1415 ft (425 m)

PRINCE WILLIAM FOREST PARK
Chopawamsic

NPS (703) 221-7181
State map: O3
From TRIANGLE, take
VA 619 W to .25 mile (400 m) beyond
I-95 (or take Exit 150 off I-95). Obtain
permit and map from Visitor Center and
find walk-in sites about .5–3 miles (800
m–4.8 k) from parking area. (Nearby
Oak Ridge costs $7 and Pohick Bay
Regional Park costs $11.)
FREE; $4 entrance fee; reservations
accepted at (703) 221-7181.
Open Feb 1–Oct 15.
10 scattered, screened, tent sites.
Tables, fire rings.
In forested 400-acre tract.
Hike. Canoe or kayak. Relax.
NO water. No toilet facilities. No trash
arrangements (pack it out). 3-day limit.

RAVEN CLIFF

Jefferson NF
(703) 783-5196
State map: G7
From SPEEDWELL, drive E on VA 619
about 10 miles (16 k).
$4; $2 off-season.
Open All Year.

20 close, open sites.
Hand pump, chemical toilets, tables, fire
rings.
In woods next to Cripple Creek.
Swim or fish. Hike to take photos and
spot wildlife.
14-day limit.
2200 ft (660 m)

RYANS BRANCH

COE (703) 629-2703
State map: I7
From FERRUM, take
VA 623 SW about 10 miles (16 k).
(Nearby Jamison Mill costs $8.)
FREE so choose a chore.
Open May 1–Sep 5.
13 close, screened sites.
Hand pump, pit toilets, tables, fire rings,
grills, boat ramp.
In mixed forest next to Philpott
Reservoir (only under-$8 choice on lake).
Boat, ski, or fish. Enjoy remote spot.
14-day limit. No generators.
1200 ft (360 m)

SHENANDOAH NP-Backcountry

(703) 999-2266
State Map: M3
Find headquarters on
US 211 E of LURAY. Obtain permit here
or at any Visitor Center, entrance station,
or ranger station. (Drive-In camps along
Skyline Drive cost from $9 to $12.)
FREE. Open All Year.
Undesignated scattered, tent sites.
Explore on over 500-miles (800-k) of
trails through mountainous regions and
along swift-flowing rivers.
NO water. No toilet facilities. No trash
arrangements (pack it out).

STEEL BRIDGE

Jefferson NF
(703) 864-5195
State map: I5
From just E of PAINT BANK, take
VA 18 NE for 3 miles (4.8 k). (Also see
Pines.)
FREE so choose a chore.
Open All Year.

▲ ▲

20 scattered, screened sites.
Hand pump, pit toilets, tables, grills.
In mixed pine/hardwood next to stocked trout stream.
Fish. Hike to view wildlife.
14-day limit. Crowded holiday weekends and Nov deer-hunting season.
1800 ft (540 m)

WALNUT FLATS

Jefferson NF
(703) 552-4641
State map: H6

From POPLAR HILL, drive SW on VA 42 for 10 miles (16 k). Turn Right (N) on VA 606 and go 1 mile (1.6 k). Turn Right just past small store on gravel VA 201 and continue 2.5 miles (4 k), passing White Pines Horse Camp.
FREE so choose a chore.
Open All Year.
6 scattered, open sites.
Hand pump, chemical toilets, tables, grills, fire rings.
In grassy area with walnut and white pine next to small pond.
Hike one of several area trails including Appalachian. Visit nearby Falls of Dismal. Fish. Take photos.
14-day limit. No horses. Crowded hunting season.
2400 ft (720 m)

WHITE ROCKS

Jefferson NF
(703) 552-4641
State map: H6

From PEMBROKE, head NW on US 460 to VA 635. Turn Right (NE) and drive 17 miles (27.2 k). Turn Right (SE) on gravel FR 613 and go .8 mile (1.3 k).
$4; $2 in Apr, Oct–Nov.
Open Apr–Dec 1.
49 scattered, open sites.
Central faucet, flush toilets, dump station, tables, grills, fire rings.
In wooded spot with several open grassy fields nearby.
Take Virginia's Walk to view wetlands and beaver activity. Hike scenic section of Appalachian Trail. Explore area

including Cascades RA with 66-ft waterfall, Mountain Lake, and Minie Ball Hill historical site. Fish streams.
14-day limit. No horses. Crowded hunting season.
2300 ft (690 m)

WOLF GAP

Geo Washington NF
(703) 984-4101
State map: L3

From EDINBURG, travel W on VA 675 for 10 miles (16 k). (Also see High Cliff Canoe Camp. Nearby Elizabeth Furnace costs $9.)
FREE so choose a chore.
Open All Year.
10 close, screened sites.
Hand pump, pit toilets, tables, fire rings.
In forest setting.
Hike to appreciate mountain ecology like Big Schloss Geological Area.
No trash arrangements (pack it out).
14-day limit. Hunting in season.
2000 ft (600 m)

▲ ▲

WEST VIRGINIA
CAMPGROUND LOCATIONS

▸ ▸ Find location on facing page map grid. ▸ ▸
▾ ▾ Locate area campgrounds on these page numbers. ▾ ▾

GRID	PAGE
B7	442, 443
B9	442
C7	440
C9	441
C10	439
C11	441
F4	443
F5	440
F7	439, 443
P9	444
G9	439, 440, 444
G10	440
H9	439, 441, 443, 445
I6	439, 441
I7	442, 444
I8	442
J7	440, 443
K5	443
K6	444
L6	441
M5	444

West Virginia

Grid conforms to official state map. For your copy, call (800) CALL-WVA
or write Division of Tourism, 2101 Washington St E, Charleston, WV 25305.

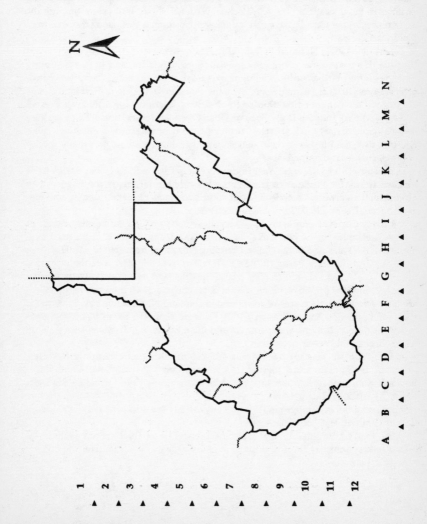

▲ ▲

PUBLIC LANDS CAMPING

Find yourself in West Virginia. There's spectacular scenery with outdoor adventure and fun for all. That includes exciting whitewater; unsurpassed fishing; great downhill and cross-country skiing; miles of hiking, biking, and horseback riding; thrilling rock climbing and caving; and, of course, relaxing camping. Too, time-honored family traditions make West Virginia a refreshing change from a fast-paced world.

Three rivers of national distinction flow through West Virginia: Bluestone National Scenic River, Gauley River National Recreation Area (NRA), and New River Gorge National River. At this time, however, there are no federal camping or recreation facilities in these locations. The Appalachian National Scenic Trail passes through the eastern neck of the state. Backcountry camping opportunities exist along this trail from Maine to Georgia.

The **Monongahela National Forest** (NF) contains over 900,000 acres in eastern West Virginia. It's a vast area containing majestic forests, glades, and bogs resembling ecologies found farther north. Campgrounds exist at 20 locations. Camp fees range from free to $10.00 for a single site. Tour the forest via the 45-mile Highland Scenic Highway. Take delight in the Spruce Knob-Seneca Rocks National Recreation Area (NRA). Backpack into the Dolly Sods or Otter Creek wilderness areas. Enjoy picking berries–cranberries, huckleberries, teaberries, and blueberries. Sight black bear, whitetail deer, wild turkey, grouse, snowshoe hare, cottontail rabbit, plus many species of birds, snakes, and amphibians.

Jefferson NF and **George Washington NF** leap over political boundaries from Virginia into West Virginia. In the George Washington NF, enjoy the Shenandoah Mountain, Brandywine, Camp Run, Trout Pond, and Hawk recreation areas. Camp fees extend from free to $19.00 for a single electric site.

US Army Corps of Engineers (COE) has developed projects with campgrounds at Burnsville Lake, East Lynn Lake, Jennings Randolph Lake, R D Bailey Lake, Summersville Lake, and Sutton Lake. Camping fees range from free to $12.00.

West Virginia State Parks (SP) and **State Forests** (SF) offer a range of parks: historical parks, natural areas, forests, vacation parks, and resort parks. There's also a range in campsites: primitive, rustic, standard, and deluxe. $6.00 primitive designations are undeveloped; some places have water and sanitation facilities nearby. $8.00 rustic spots offer pit toilets and well water. $10.00 standard sites offer picnic tables and grills as well as nearby drinking water sources and flush toilets. $11.00 deluxe sites provide water, electric, and sewer hookups.

A few **Wildlife Management Areas** (WMA) provide rustic camping facilities, primarily for hunters and fishermen. Check out Lewis Wetzel, Teter Creek Lake, Edwards Run, Nathaniel Mountain, Short Mountain, Sleepy Creek, Handley, Big Ugly, Chief Cornstalk, and Laurel Lake.

Administrators of campgrounds on the **city-county** level include Beckley/Raleigh County, Grafton, and Point Pleasant.

Come to West Virginia for that welcome change. Savor the natural beauty of its public lands. Adjust to its slower pace. When you leave, you may feel the biggest change in yourself.

▲ ▲

BEAR HAVEN RA

Monongahela NF
(304) 478-3251
State map: I6
From ELKINS, drive E on
US 33 for 8 miles (12.8 k). Bear Left (NE)
on FR 91 (Stuart Memorial Dr) and go
2 miles (3.2 k). (Nearby Stuart costs $7.)
FREE so choose a chore.
Open All Year.
8 close, screened sites.
Hand pump, pit toilets, tables, fire rings.
Next to Otter Creek Wilderness.
Hike over 50-miles (80-k) of trails in
wilderness (free permit required). Enjoy
nearby Bickle Knob Overlook.
14-day limit.
3600 ft (1080 m)

BEE RUN

COE (304) 765-2816
State map: F7
From SUTTON, drive NE
on US 19 about 4 miles
(6.4 k). Turn Right (SE) on WV 15 and
go 1 mile (1.6 k). Turn Right (S) at sign
on access road. (Nearby Gerald Freeman
costs $9.)
FREE so choose a chore.
Open All Year.
12 scattered, open sites.
Central faucet, pit toilets, fire rings,
grills, boat ramp.
In shady spot on Sutton Lake (only
choice under $9).
Swim, boat, ski, or fish. Walk nature
trail. View wildlife.
14-day limit. Hunting in season.
1000 ft (300 m)

BIG ROCK

Monongahela NF
(304) 846-2695
State map: G9
Just E of RICHWOOD, take
gravel FR 76 N about 6 miles (9.6 k).
(Also see Bishop Knob, Cranberry, and
Summit Lake.)
$4.
Open Mar 15–Dec 1.
5 close, screened sites.

Hand pump, pit toilets, tables, fire rings.
In forest.
Fish. Observe wildlife. Explore
mountains.
14-day limit. Hunting in season.
2500 ft (750 m)

BIG UGLY WMA

WVDNR (304) 675-0871
State map: C10
Find area E of LEET.
$3.50.
Open All Year.
11 close, open sites.
Central faucet, pit toilets, tables, fire
rings.
In mature upland forest.
Relax. Spot wildlife.
No trash arrangements (pack it out).
14-day limit. Hunting in season.
1000 ft (300 m)

BIRD RUN

Monongahela NF
(304) 799-4334
State map: H9
From FROST, drive E for
1 mile (1.6 k) on WV 84. (Also see
Pocahontas.)
FREE so choose a chore.
Open Mar 15–Dec 15; dry camping
allowed off-season.
12 scattered, screened sites.
Hand pump, pit toilets, tables, fire rings.
In woods next to Bird Run Creek.
Hike to enjoy area. Relax.
14-day limit. Hunting in season.
2700 ft (810 m)

BISHOP KNOB

Monongahela NF
(304) 846-2695
State map: G9
Just E of RICHWOOD, take
gravel FR 76 N about 7 miles (11.2 k).
Bear Left (N) on FR 81 and continue
about 11 miles (17.6 k). (Also see Big
Rock and Cranberry.)
$2.
Open Apr 15–Dec 1.
33 close, screened sites.

Hand pump, pit toilets, tables, fire rings.
In wooded setting.
Hike for photos and wildlife observation.
Fish.
14-day limit. Hunting in season.
3100 ft (930 m)

BLUE BEND RA-Blue Meadow

Monongahela NF
(304) 536-2144
State map: G10
From WHITE SULPHUR
SPRINGS, travel N on WV 92 for 6 miles
(9.6 k). Turn Left (W) on WV 16/2 and
drive 4 miles (6.4 k). (Nearby Lake
Sherwood RA costs $8.)
$3 in Blue Meadow; $6 in Blue Bend.
Open All Year.
40 (4 tent-only) scattered, screened sites.
Hand pump (at Blue Bend), flush toilets,
tables, fire rings.
Along two loops under large hemlock
and pine next to Anthony Creek.
Swim or fish. Walk Blue Bend Loop Trail
for panoramic views or Anthony Creek
Trail for streamside experience. Explore
scenic area.
14-day limit.
2500 ft (750 m)

CAMP RUN

George Washington NF
(703) 828-2591
State map: J7
From OAK FLAT, head NE
on WV 3 for 10 miles (16 k). Turn Right
(SE) on rough, gravel WV 3/1 and travel
1.5 miles (2.4 k). Turn Right on FR 526
and go to end of road.
FREE so choose a chore.
Open All Year.
9 close, open, tent sites.
Pit toilets, tables, grills, fire rings.
In forest setting along drainage off
Shenandoah Mountain.
Enjoy seclusion. Explore mountainous
area. Watch wildlife.
NO water. 14-day limit. Occasional
ATVs.
2000 ft (600 m)

CHIEF CORNSTALK WMA

WVDNR(304) 675-0871
State map: C7
From SOUTHSIDE, travel
W on Nine-Mile Rd to sign
for area.
$3.50.
Open All Year.
25 close, open sites.
Central faucet, pit toilets, tables, fire
rings.
In hardwood forest with one 5-acre lake
and two 1-acre lakes.
Fish. View wildlife.
No trash arrangements (pack it out).
14-day limit. Hunting in season.

CONAWAY RUN LAKE

(304) 758-2681
State map: F5
From MIDDLEBOURNE,
drive E on WV 18 for
10 miles (16 k). Turn at sign.
$3.50.
Open All Year.
10 scattered, open sites.
Central faucet, pit toilets, tables, fire
rings.
At upper end of 30-acre lake.
Boat or fish. Walk nature trail. Observe
wildlife.
Hunting in season.
1000 ft (300 m)

CRANBERRY

Monongahela NF
(304) 846-2695
State map: G9
Just E of RICHWOOD, take
gravel FR 76 N about 15 miles (24 k).
(Also see Big Rock and Bishop Knob.)
$5; $8 on sites 1–9.
Open Mar 15–Dec 1.
30 (6 tent-only) close, open sites.
Hand pump, pit toilets, tables, fire rings.
In open and wooded areas next to
Cranberry River.
Fish. Hike to spot wildlife. Take photos.
14-day/22-ft limits. Hunting in season.
Crowded Apr-Jun.
2600 ft (780 m)

▲ ▲

DAY RUN

Monongahela NF
(304) 799-4334
State map: H9
From MARLINTON, head
N on US 219 for 7 miles (11.2 k). Turn
Left (W) on WV 150 and drive 8 miles
(12.8 k). Turn Left (SE) on gravel
FR 86/216 and continue 4 miles (6.4 k).
(Also see Tea Creek.)
$4.
Open Mar 15–Dec 15; dry camping
allowed off-season.
12 scattered, screened sites.
Hand pump, pit toilets, tables, fire rings.
In forest next to Williams River.
Enjoy mountains. Fish.
14-day/30-ft limits. Hunting in season.
2900 ft (870 m)

FORK CREEK WMA

WVDNR (304) 675-0871
State map: C9
From NELLIS, head NW on
CR 2 for 1 mile (1.6 k).
$3.50.
Open All Year.
20 close, open sites.
Central faucet, pit toilets, tables, fire
rings.
Among steep, hardwood-covered slopes
with small stream and pond.
Relax. Fish. View wildlife.
No trash arrangements (pack it out).
14-day limit. Hunting in season.

GUYANDOTTE

COE (304) 664-8494
State map: C11
From JUSTICE, head SE on
US 52 to WV 97. Bear Left
(E) and go 5 miles (8 k). Turn Left on
tunneled entrance road.
FREE at 8 sites; $7 developed; $8 electric.
Open May 15–Sep 15.
179 close, open sites. &
Central faucet, flush toilets, showers,
dump station, electric hookups, tables,
fire rings, grills, boat ramp, playground,
pay phone.
In 4 sections along 6-mile (9.6-k) scenic

stretch of Guyandotte River at upper end
of R D Bailey Lake.
Boat or fish. Spot wildlife. Bike. Relax.
14-day limit.

HANDLEY WMA

WVDNR (304) 637-0245
State map: H9
Just S of EDRAY, turn
Right (W) on WV 17 and
drive to sign.
$4.
Open All Year.
13 close, open sites.
Central faucet, pit toilets, tables, fire
rings.
In hardwood-covered hills with 2 small
ponds and 5-acre lake.
Fish. Observe wildlife.
No trash arrangements (pack it out).
14-day limit. Hunting in season.
3200 ft (960 m)

HAWK

George Washington NF
(703) 984-4101
State map: L6
From STRASBURG, VA,
head W on VA 55 for 17 miles (27.2 k).
Turn Right (N) on gravel FR 502 and
continue 3 miles (4.8 k). Turn Left (W)
on FR 347 for final 1 mile (1.6 k).
FREE so choose a chore.
Open Apr 1–Dec 31.
15 scattered, screened sites.
Hand pump, pit toilets, tables, fire rings.
In remote, forest location.
Hike. Watch wildlife. Relax.
No trash arrangements (pack it out).
14-day limit. Hunting in season.
Crowded holidays.
1200 ft (360 m)

HORSESHOE RA

Monongahela NF
(304) 478-3251
State map: I6
From ST GEORGE, travel E
on WV 1 for 3 miles (4.8 k). Bear Left
(NE) on WV 7 and go 4 miles (6.4 k).
$5.

Open May 14–Oct 12.
13 close, open sites.
Central faucet, flush toilets, tables, fire rings.
In woods near stream.
Fish. Hike to explore area.
14-day/22-ft limits.
1700 ft (510 m)

ISLAND

Monongahela NF
(304) 456-3335
State map: I8
From BARTOW, drive NE on WV 28 for 5 miles (8 k). Turn left at signed entrance. (Also see Lake Buffalo and Locust Springs, VA.)
FREE so choose a chore.
Open All Year.
6 close, screened sites. &
Pit toilets, tables, grills, fire rings.
Nestled among yellow birch and maple along East Fork Greenbrier River.
Fish. Hike. Enjoy peaceful spot.
NO water. 14-day limit. Bear country (keep site clean). Crowded Nov-Dec hunting season.

KRODEL PARK

Point Pleasant City Parks
(304) 675-1068
State map: B7
Locate park in POINT PLEASANT at WV 2 & 62.
$5; $9 hookups.
Open Apr 15–Nov 1.
75 close, open sites.
Water in every site, flush toilets, showers, electric hookups, tables, fire rings, laundry, store, rentals, pay phone.
Under trees next to Krodel Park Lake.
Swim, fish, or boat (no motors).

LAKE BUFFALO

Monongahela NF
(304) 456-3335
State map: I8
From BARTOW, travel NE on WV 54 for 2 miles (3.2 k). Turn Right (SE) on WV 54 and go 4 miles (6.4 k). (Also see Island.)

FREE so choose a chore.
Open All Year.
5 (1 tent-only) close, screened sites.
Hand pump, pit toilets, tables, fire rings.
In peaceful, wooded setting spread along SE edge of Lake Buffalo.
Fish or boat (small only). Hike to find wildlife. Take photos.
14-day limit. Bear country (keep site clean). Crowded Nov–Dec hunting season.

LAUREL CREEK

COE (304) 849-5000
State map: B9
From EAST LYNN, take WV 37 SE for 3 miles (4.8 k) to area below dam. (Nearby East Fork costs $9.)
FREE so choose a chore.
Open All Year.
15 scattered, open sites.
Pit toilets, tables, grills, fire rings.
In woods below East Lynn Lake.
Boat or fish nearby.
NO water. 14-day limit.

LAUREL FORK

Monongahela NF
(304) 456-3335
State map: I7
From BARTOW, drive NE on WV 28 for 4.5 miles (7.2 k). Turn Left (N) on FR 14 and proceed 17 miles (27.2 k).
FREE so choose a chore.
Open All Year.
14 close, open sites.
Hand pump, pit toilets, tables, grills, fire rings.
Between Laurel Fork North and Laurel Forth South wilderness areas along Laurel Fork River.
Relish peaceful, remote setting. Hike to appreciate ecology. Take photos. Fish.
14-day/22-ft limits. Bear country (keep site clean). Crowded Nov-Dec hunting season.
3200 ft (960 m)

▲ ▲

LEWIS WETZEL WMA

WVDNR (304) 367-2720
State map: F4
From JACKSONBURG,
drive S on Buffalo Run Rd
for .75 mile (1.2 k).
$3.
Open All Year.
20 close, open sites.
Central faucet, pit toilets, tables, grills.
Among oak, hickory, and beech trees.
Observe wildlife. Relax.
No trash arrangements (pack it out).
14-day limit. Hunting in season.
1000 ft (300 m)

MCCLINTIC WMA

WVDNR (304) 675-0871
State map: B7
From POINT PLEASANT,
drive N for 5 miles (8 k).
$3.50.
Open All Year.
9 close, open sites. &
Central faucet, pit toilets, tables, fire
rings.
Among farmland, brushland, wetland,
and woodland with 39 ponds.
Observe wide variety of wildlife. Fish.
No trash arrangements (pack it out).
14-day limit. Hunting in season.
750 ft (225 m)

NATHANIEL MOUNTAIN WMA

WVDNR (304) 822-3551
State map: K5
Just E of ROMNEY, take
WV 50 (Grassy Lick Rd) S
to entrance road. Turn Left (SE).
$3.50.
Open All Year.
75 scattered, open sites.
Central faucet, pit toilets, tables, fire
rings.
In 8 areas among oak, hickory, and pine
near Mill Run.
Fish for trout. Hike. Watch wildlife.
No trash arrangements (pack it out).
14-day/18-ft limits. Hunting in season.
1500 ft (450 m)

POCAHONTAS

Monongahela NF
(304) 799-4334
State map: H9
From MINNEHAHA
SPRINGS, drive S on WV 92 for 6 miles
(9.6 k). (Also see Bird Run.)
$4.
Open Mar 15 – Dec 15; dry camping
allowed off-season.
10 scattered, screened sites.
Hand pump, pit toilets, tables, fire rings.
In forest.
Hike to enjoy mountains.
14-day/30-ft limits. Hunting in season.
2400 ft (720 m)

RIFFLE RUN PRIMITIVE

COE (304) 853-2583
State map: F7
From BURNSVILLE, head E
on WV 5 for 3.5 miles
(5.4 k). Register. Find site N of day-use
area. (Nearby Riffle Run costs $10.)
FREE so choose a chore.
Open Apr 15 – Nov 30.
6 close, open sites.
Nearby flush toilets, fire rings.
In mountain valley close to Burnsville
Lake (lake sites are $10).
Boat or fish. Hike to spot wildlife.
NO water. No trash arrangements (pack
it out). 14-day limit. Hunting in season.
Crowded holiday weekends.
789 ft (237 m)

SENECA SHADOWS WALK-IN

Monongahela NF
(304) 257-4488
State map: J7
From SENECA ROCKS,
drive SW on WV 55 for 1 mile (1.6 k).
$5; $10 drive-in; $12 electric; reservations
accepted at (304) 257-4488 for an
additional $6.
Open Apr 15 – Oct 31.
80 (40 tent-only) close, open sites.
Central faucet, flush toilets, showers,
dump station, electric hookups, tables,
grills.
Within Spruce Knob-Seneca Rocks NRA.

▲ ▲

Canoe or kayak. Fish. Mountain bike. Walk nature trail or hike farther. Attend ranger programs.
14-day limit.

SHORT MOUNTAIN WMA

WVDNR (304) 822-3551
State map: K6
From AUGUSTA, travel S on WV 29 for 8 miles (12.8 k). Turn Left (SE) at sign.
$3.50.
Open All Year.
30 scattered, open sites.
Central faucet, pit toilets, tables.
In 6 areas in horseshoe-shaped basin along North River.
Fish. Spot wildlife.
No trash arrangements (pack it out).
14-day/18-ft limits. Hunting in season.

SLEEPY CREEK WMA

WVDNR (304) 822-3551
State map: M5
From JONES SPRING, head W on CR.
$3.50.
Open All Year.
75 scattered, open sites.
Central faucet, pit toilets, tables, fire rings, boat ramp.
In pine/oak forest with 205-acre lake.
Boat or fish. Watch wildlife.
No trash arrangements (pack it out).
14-day/17-ft limits. Hunting in season.

SPRUCE KNOB LAKE WALK-IN

Monongahela NF
(304) 257-4488
State map: I7
From RIVERTON, travel S on US 33 for 2 miles (3.2 k). Turn Right (W) on CR 33/4 (Briery Gap) and drive 2.5 miles (4 k). Turn on signed narrow, gravel FR 112 and continue 14 miles (22.4 k).
$5; $7 drive-in.
Open Apr 1–Dec 1; dry camping allowed off-season.
42 (12 tent-only) close, open sites.
Hand pump, pit toilets, tables, fire rings,

boat ramp.
In remote setting near highest point in West Virginia.
Fish. Walk nature trail or hike to appreciate mountains. Spot wildlife. Mountain bike.
14-day limit.
4000 ft (1200 m)

SUMMIT LAKE

Monongahela NF
(304) 846-2695
State map: G9
From RICHWOOD, drive E on WV 39 for 6 miles (9.6 k). Turn left (N) on WV 77 and go 2 miles (3.2 k). (Also see Big Rock.)
$5.
Open Mar 15–Dec 1.
33 (3 tent-only) close, screened sites.
Hand pump, pit toilets, tables, fire rings, boat ramp.
In woods next to lake.
Fish. Walk nature trail or hike farther. Take photos.
14-day limit. Hunting in season. No generators in quiet hours. Crowded Apr–May.
3400 ft (1020 m)

TAILWATERS

COE (304) 872-3459
State map: F9
From SUMMERSVILLE, head S on US 19 for 5 miles (8 k). Turn Right (NW) on WV 129 and go 2.5 miles (4 k). Cross dam and turn Left at Visitor Center. (Nearby Battle Run costs $12.)
FREE so choose a chore.
Open All Year.
Undesignated scattered, open sites.
Pit toilets, tables, fire rings.
Below Summersville Lake dam in fishermen access and camping area on Gauley River.
Fish. View Visitor Center and Observation Tower. Boat on lake.
NO water. 14-day limit.
1350 ft (405 m)

▲ ▲

TEA CREEK

Monongahela NF
(304) 799-4334
State map: H9
From MARLINTON, head
N on US 219 for 7 miles (11.2 k). Turn
Left (W) on WV 150 and drive 8 miles
(12.8 k). Turn Right (NW) on gravel
FR 86 for final 1 mile (1.6 k). (Also see
Day Run.)

$4.

Open Mar 15–Dec 15; dry camping
allowed off-season.

29 scattered, screened sites.

Hand pump, pit toilets, tables, fire rings.

In forest next to Tea Creek and Williams
River.

Fish. Walk nature trail or hike farther to
view wildlife. Mountain bike. Explore
adjacent Cranberry Wilderness.

14-day limit. Hunting in season.

2800 ft (840 m)

▲ ▲

WISCONSIN
CAMPGROUND LOCATIONS

► ► Find location on facing page map grid. ► ►
▼ ▼ Locate area campgrounds on these page numbers. ▼ ▼

Wisconsin

Grid conforms to official state map. For your copy, call (800) 432-TRIP
or write Tourism Development, Box 7606, Madison, WI 53707.

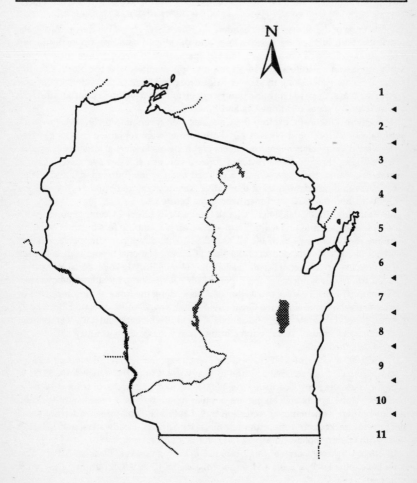

▲ ▲

PUBLIC LANDS CAMPING

Wisconsin considers itself a paradise and a playground. Varying with the seasons, you can discover peaceful places to escape and great spots for adventure on Wisconsin public lands.

National Park Service (NPS) offers backpacking and developed camping opportunities at Apostle Islands National Lakeshore (NL). Camping is free in the Apostle Islands, whether at developed Presque Isle or permitted backcountry sites on the 21 islands in Lake Superior. Boat there yourself or take a concessionaire shuttle during the summer. Units of Ice Age National Scientific Reserve showcase glacial remains such as kettle lakes, eskers, and moraines. The Ice Age National Scenic Trail connects units of the reserve and meanders up, down, and across Wisconsin. Along the in-process trail, NPS offers backpacking and developed camping opportunities in conjunction with the national forests and state parks. Another cooperative effort among public lands administrators provides camping opportunities near the North Country National Scenic Trail. Along the Lower Saint Croix and Saint Croix national wild and scenic riverways, there are no backcountry opportunities; developed campgrounds are provided by the states of Minnesota and Wisconsin.

In northern Wisconsin, explore the Chequamegon (pronounced "Sho-wa-me-gon") National Forest (NF) and Nicolet NF. Both forests were replanted by the Civilian Conservation Corps after relentless loggers and hopeless farmers abandoned the areas. When walking through these restored forests, you can still see symmetrical earth formations, abandoned narrow-gauge railroad beds, stone foundations, and rusted tools. These findings remind us of the Native American mound builders, the loggers, the farmers, and the CCC workmen who came before us.

For camping, the 850,000-acre **Chequamegon NF** offers 24 campgrounds with varying fees depending on facilities and site location. Camping fees begin at $4.00 for primitive sites and range to $5.00, $7.00 and $10.00 at developed Chippewa. Hike or backpack along a 60-mile section of the North Country National Scenic Trail, a 40-mile piece of the Ice Age National Scenic Trail, or the 14-mile Rock Lake National Recreation Trail. North Woods wilderness areas, perfect for backpacking, include Rainbow Lake and Porcupine Lake. Fish for muskellunge. Canoe along the forks of the Chippewa or Flambeau rivers. Drive along the Great Divide Highway, 29 miles of State Highway 77 through forest, lakes, streams, and marshes. Sight black bear, whitetail deer, bobcat, bald eagle, and grouse. When winter brings heavy snow, cross-country ski over 50 miles of groomed trails.

The 650,000-acre **Nicolet NF**, named for French explorer Jean Nicolet, offers a range of campgrounds from relative solitude to heavy use. Camp fees range from $5.00 to $8.00 for lakeshore sites. There are over 1,200 lakes and 1,100 miles of trout streams in the forest. Water sports and hiking are popular in summer as is cross-country skiing in winter. There's one national recreation trail, Lauterman, and three wilderness areas that provide backcountry opportunities: Blackjack Springs, Headwaters, and Whisker Lake. With sugar maples and aspen, fall color is a vision here.

Discover **US Army Corps of Engineers** (COE) campgrounds at Blackhawk Park, Eau Galle Lake, plus Lock & Dam # 11 on the Mississippi River. COE camping fees range from free to $9.00.

While camping Wisconsin, explore 125,000 acres of state lands: forests, lakes, rivers, beaches, marshes, and prairies. Campgrounds can be found at 44 of the 65 **Wisconsin State Parks** (SP). The state extends a preferred rate to its camping citizens of $6.00–$8.00 per site. Non-residents pay $8.00–$10.00 per site. Parks with more services

▲ ▲

charge the higher amount. Electricity hookups and admission stickers are additional fees.

Villages and **counties** extending hospitality and offering camping facilities to travelers include Ashland, Blair, Bruce, Dunn County, Gilman, Harstad County, Jackson County, Juneau County, La Farge, Lafayette County, Marshfield, Pepin, Price County, Readstown, Taylor County, Viola, and Washburn County.

Find Wisconsin a state for many reasons and all seasons.

▲ ▲

APOSTLE ISLANDS NL-Boat-In

(715) 779-3397
State map: 1D
Take ferry or private boat from BAYFIELD.
FREE.
Open May 25–Sep; dry camping allowed off-season.
19 scattered, screened sites.
Central faucet, pit toilets, tables, grills, fire rings.
On pine bluff overlooking Lake Superior on Stockton Island (Presque Isle Campground) or in backcountry locations on 18 other islands.
Swim, boat, canoe, or kayak. Hike to view wildlife and appreciate ecology. Attend ranger programs.
610 ft (183 m)

BANKER PARK

Viola Parks (608) 627-1831
State map: 9D
Locate park in VIOLA.
$3; $5 electric.
Open May–Oct; dry camping allowed off-season.
45 scattered, screened sites.
Central faucet, flush toilets, showers, dump station, electric hookups, tables, grills, fire rings, laundry, store, rentals.
On banks of Kickapoo River.
Boat or fish. Watch wildlife. Bike.

BEAVER LAKE

Chequamegon NF
(715) 264-2511
State map: 2D
From MELLEN, head SW on CR GG for 8 miles (12.8 k). Turn Right

(W) on gravel FR 187 and drive 3 miles (6.4 k). Continue W on FR 198 another 2 miles (3.2 k). (Also see Lake Three.)
$4.
Open May 25–Sep 5; dry camping allowed off-season.
10 close, screened sites.
Hand pump, pit toilets, tables, fire rings, boat ramp.
In hardwood/large red pine next to lake. Boat or fish. Hike along North Country Trail.
14-day limit. Hunting in season.

BIG FALLS

Price County Forestry
(715) 339-4505
State map: 4E
From KENNAN, head S for 12 miles (19.2 k).
FREE so choose a chore.
Open Apr 15–Nov 15; dry camping allowed off-season.
4 scattered, screened sites.
Hand pump, pit toilets, tables, grills, shelter.
In wooded, wilderness setting next to South Fork Jump River.
Canoe. Walk nature trail. Hike for photo-taking and wildlife-viewing. Fish.
Hunting in season.
1500 ft (450 m)

BIRCH GROVE

Chequamegon NF
(715) 373-2667
State map: 2D
From WASHBURN, travel W on CR C (Wannebo Rd) for 7 miles (11.2 k). Turn Left (S) on gravel FR 435

▲ ▲

and proceed 3 miles (4.8 k).
$5.
Open May 1–Oct 15.
16 close, screened sites.
Hand pump, pit toilets, tables, fire rings, boat ramp.
In forest between two lakes.
Boat or fish. Walk Valhalla Trail. Explore nearby Moquah Natural Area.
1400 ft (420 m)

BLACKHAWK MEMORIAL

Lafayette County Parks
(608) 776-4830
State map: 11F
Find area just N of WOODFORD at 2995 CR Y.
$5; $1 entrance fee.
Open All Year.
Undesignated scattered, screened sites.
Central faucet, chemical toilets, electric hookups, tables, boat ramp.
In rolling dairy country among oak and maple along river and lake.
Boat and fish. Walk nature trail and hike. Take photos.
700 ft (210 m)

BRUCE VILLAGE PARK

(715) 868-2185
State map: 4D
Locate park on W side of BRUCE on US 8.
FREE; donations requested.
Open All Year.
25 scattered, open sites.
Central faucet, flush toilets, electric hookups, tables, ball fields.
Among tall pine trees.
Enjoy overnight stop.
2-day limit.

BRULE RIVER

Nicolet NF (715) 528-4464
State map: 3G
From ALVIN, head N on WI 55 for 4.5 miles (7.2 k)– just before MI stateline. (Also see Lake Ottawa, MI.)
$5.
Open May–Nov.

11 close, screened sites.
Hand pump, pit toilets, tables, fire rings.
Under red pines along Brule River.
Canoe. Fish. View wildlife. Take photos.
14-day limit.

CHIPMUNK RAPIDS

Nicolet NF (715) 528-4464
State map: 3H
From TIPLER, drive SE on FR 2450. Bear Left (E) on FR 2156 and go 2.5 miles (4 k), crossing Pine River. (Also see Lauterman Lake Walk-In and Perch Lake Walk-In. Nearby Lost Lake costs $6.)
$5. Open May–Nov.
6 scattered, screened sites.
Artesian well, pit toilets, tables, fire rings.
Near road in forest along Pine River.
Canoe or fish. Hike Ridge Trail or Lauterman National Recreation Trail. Spot wildlife and take photos.
14-day limit.

CHIPPEWA

Chequamegon NF
(715) 748-4875
State map: 5D
Just S of HANNIBAL, head E on CR M about 5 miles (8 k). Turn Right (S) on FR 1417 and proceed 1 mile (1.6 k). (Also see Gilman Village Campground and Kathryn Lake.)
$5; $7 & $10 also; reservations accepted at (715) 748-4875 for an additional $6.
Open May 17–Nov 30; dry camping allowed off-season.
90 scattered, screened sites. &
Central faucet, flush toilets, showers, dump station, tables, fire rings, boat ramp, pay phone.
In northern hardwood on Chequamegon Waters Flowage.
Swim, boat, or fish. Hike to spot wildlife. Take photos. Attend ranger programs.
14-day limit. Occasional ATVs.
1500 ft (450 m)

CRAWFORD HILLS ATV

Jackson County Parks
(715) 333-5832
State map: 7D
From BLACK RIVER FALLS,
take WI 54 for 15 miles (24 k). (Also see
Merlin Lambert Park.)
$5.
Open Apr–Dec.
18 close, screened sites.
Hand pump, flush toilets, tables, grills,
fire rings.
With access to 100 miles of trails and
intensive use area.
21-day limit. Noisy.

DAY LAKE

Chequamegon NF
(715) 264-2511
State map: 3D
From CLAM LAKE, drive N
on CR GG for 1 mile (1.6 k). Turn Left.
(Also see East Twin Lake.)
$5; reservations accepted at
(715) 264-2511 for an additional $6.
Open All Year.
66 close, screened sites. &
Hand pump, pit toilets, tables, fire rings,
boat ramp.
Next to lake in northern hardwood and
red/jack pine stand.
Swim, boat, or fish. Walk nature trail.
14-day limit.

DELTA LAKE COUNTY
CAMPGROUND

Bayfield County Parks
(715) 372-8610
State map: 2C
From IRON RIVER, drive SE
on CR H for 7 miles (11.2 k) to Scenic
Dr. Continue 4 miles (6.4 k). (Also see
Perch Lake.)
$5.
Open May 1–Oct 31; dry camping
allowed off-season.
25 scattered, open sites.
Hand pump, pit toilets, tables, fire rings,
boat ramp.
In woods on small, spring-fed lake.

Swim, boat, or fish. Walk nature trail
and observe wildlife. Enjoy quiet.

EAST TWIN LAKE

Chequamegon NF
(715) 264-2511
State map: 3D
From CLAM LAKE, drive N
on CR GG for 4 miles (6.4 k). Turn
Right. (Also see Day Lake.)
$5.
Open May 25–Sep 5; dry camping
allowed off-season.
12 (2 tent-only) close, screened sites.
Hand pump, pit toilets, tables, fire rings,
boat ramp.
In northern hardwood, aspen, and
hemlock next to lake.
Boat or fish.
14-day limit.

EASTWOOD

Chequamegon NF
(715) 748-4875
State map: 5E
From WESTBORO, travel W
on CR D for 6.4 miles (10.2 k). Turn Left
(S) on FR 104 for final .5 mile (800 m).
(Also see Spearhead Point and
Westpoint.)
$5; reservations accepted at
(715) 748-4875 for an additional $6.
Open May 20–Nov 30; dry camping
allowed off-season.
22 scattered, screened sites.
Hand pump, pit toilets, dump station,
tables, fire rings, grills, boat ramp, store,
rentals, pay phone.
In northern hardwood forest along
Mondeaux Flowage.
Swim, boat, ski, or fish. Hike part of Ice
Age Trail. Attend ranger programs.
14-day limit.
1500 ft (450 m)

EMILY LAKE

Chequamegon NF
(715) 762-2461
State map: 3E
Head NW on WI 47 from
LAC DU FLAMBEAU for 2 miles (3.2 k).

Turn Left (SW) and go 2 miles (3.2 k). Turn Right (W) on FR 142 and continue 4 miles (6.4 k). (Also see Twin Lake and Wabasso Lake.)

$5.

Open May 28–Oct 25; dry camping allowed off-season.

10 scattered, screened sites.

Hand pump, pit toilets, tables, fire rings, grills, boat ramp.

Next to lake surrounded by forest in secluded spot.

Swim, canoe, or fish. Enjoy quiet. Observe wildlife.

14-day limit. Crowded holidays.

1576 ft (473 m)

FANNY LAKE WALK-IN

Nicolet NF (715) 276-6333
State map: 5H
From TOWNSEND, drive SW on CR T about 5 miles (8 k) to Jones Spring Area. Walk in about .5 mile (800 m).

FREE so choose a chore.

Open All Year.

5 scattered, screened, tent sites.

Tables, fire rings.

In isolated setting next to 19-acre lake.

Hike area trails. Observe wildlife. Pick berries. Fish. Relax. Cross-country ski in winter.

NO water. No toilet facilities. No trash arrangements (pack it out). 14-day limit.

GILMAN VILLAGE CAMPGROUND

(715) 447-5764
State map: 5D
In GILMAN, head S on CR B to Riverside Dr. Turn Right (W). (Also see Chippewa.)

FREE so choose a chore.

Open Apr–Nov; dry camping allowed off-season.

10 close, open sites.

Hand pump, pit toilets, tables, grills, fire rings.

In wooded setting along Yellow River. Swim, canoe, or fish. Spot wildlife. Bike. Cross-country ski in winter.

HARSTAD COUNTY PARK

Eau Claire County Parks
(715) 839-4738
State map: 6D
From AUGUSTA, travel NW on US 12 for 3 miles (4.8 k). Turn Right (N) on CR HH and proceed another 3 miles (4.8 k). (Nearby Coon Fork Lake costs $7.)

$5; $25/week.

Open May 15–Sep 15; dry camping allowed off-season.

27 scattered, screened sites.

Hand pump, pit toilets, tables, grills, fire rings.

Under oak in rural region next to river.

Canoe. Fish. Mountain bike. Watch wildlife.

14-day limit.

HIGHLAND RIDGE

COE (715) 778-5562
State map: 6B
From SPRING VALLEY, head E on WI 29 for 3 miles (4.8 k). Turn Left (N) on WI 128, then turn again on 10th Ave. Follow 10th to CR NN, then turn Right.

FREE at 2 sites; $6 others; $7 electric; reservations accepted at (715) 778-5562 for an additional $2.

Open May 1–Oct 31; dry camping allowed off-season.

34 (7 tent-only) close, screened sites.

Central faucet, pit toilets, dump station, electric hookups, tables, fire rings, grills, boat ramp, pay phone.

In mature stand of hardwood with screening next to Eau Galle Lake.

Walk Lousy Creek Trail. Swim, fish, and boat (no gas motors). View wildlife. Attend ranger programs.

14-day limit.

1050 ft (315 m)

KATHRYN LAKE

Chequamegon NF
(715) 748-4875
State map: 5E
From PERKINSTOWN, head S on FR 121 for .5 mile (800 m). (Also see

Chippewa.)

$5.

Open May 15–Nov 30; dry camping allowed off-season.

10 scattered, screened sites.

Hand pump, pit toilets, tables, fire rings, boat ramp.

In hardwood forest next to lake.

Swim, boat, or fish. View wildlife.

14-day limit.

1500 ft (450 m)

KENNEDY PARK

Juneau County Parks
(608) 843-4352
State map: 8E
On W side of NEW LISBON, head N on CR M. Turn Right.

FREE so choose a chore.

Open May 1–Sep 30.

Undesignated scattered, open sites.

Hand pump, pit toilets, tables, grills, shelter, playground.

In wooded setting on grass and sand.

Walk trails. View wildlife. Canoe. Fish.

30-day limit. Hunting in season.

LA FARGE VILLAGE PARK

(608) 625-4422
State map: 9D
Locate park in LA FARGE on Adams St.

$3; $7 RV; +$1 electric.

Open May 31–Sep 6; dry camping allowed off-season.

15 close, open sites.

Hand pump, pit toilets, electric hookups, tables, fire rings.

In heavy wood with lots of shade.

Canoe. Relax. Enjoy overnight stop.

LAKE THREE

Chequamegon NF
(715) 264-2511
State map: 2D
From MELLEN, head SW on CR GG for 8 miles (12.8 k). Turn Right (W) on gravel FR 187. Drive 4 miles (6.4 k). (Also see Beaver Lake and Mineral Lake.)

$4.

Open May 25–Nov 30.

8 close, screened sites. Hand pump, pit toilets, tables, fire rings, boat ramp.

In northern hardwood next to lake.

Boat or fish. Hike along North Country Trail. Visit nearby Morgan Falls.

14-day limit. Hunting in season.

LAUTERMAN LAKE WALK-IN

Nicolet NF (715) 528-4464
State map: 3H
From TIPLER, drive E on WI 70 for 5 miles (8 k). Turn Right (S) on FR 2154 and go .1 mile (160 m) to parking area. Walk in from .75–1.5 miles (1.2–2.4 k). (Also see Perch Lake Walk-In and Chipmunk Rapids.)

FREE so choose a chore.

Open All Year.

5 scattered, screened, tent sites.

Tables, fire rings.

In hardwood, cedar, and balsam fir forest next to lake.

Hike along national recreation trail. Fish. Relax. Spot wildlife.

NO water. No toilet facilities. No trash arrangements (pack it out). 14-day limit.

MERLIN LAMBERT PARK

Jackson County Parks
(715) 333-5832
State map: 7D
From BLACK RIVER FALLS, drive E on WI 54 for 20 miles (32 k). (Also see Crawford Hills ATV and Spaulding Pond.)

$5.

Open Apr–Dec; dry camping allowed off-season.

40 close, screened sites.

Hand pump, pit toilets, tables, fire rings, grills, boat ramp.

In woods next to Potters Flowage.

Canoe. Fish. Observe wildlife.

21-day limit. Crowded hunting season.

MINERAL LAKE

Chequamegon NF
(715) 264-2511
State map: 2D
From MELLEN, head SW on

CR GG for 9 miles (14.4 k). (Also see Lake Three.)

$4.

Open May 25–Sep 5; dry camping allowed off-season.

10 close, screened sites.

Hand pump, pit toilets, tables, fire rings, boat ramp.

Next to lake in sugar maple stand.

Boat or fish.

14-day limit. Hunting in season.

MORGAN LAKE

Nicolet NF (715) 528-4464
State map: 4H
From FENCE, drive W on gravel FR 2169 for 8 miles (12.8 k). Turn Right (NW) on FR 2161 and continue 2 miles (3.2 k).

$5.

Open May–Oct.

18 close, screened sites.

Hand pump, pit toilets, tables, fire rings, boat ramp.

Overlooking 45-acre lake in pine or aspen/paper birch.

Swim. Canoe. Observe wildlife. Take photos.

14-day limit.

MYRON PARK

Dunn County Parks
(715) 232-1651
State map: 5C
From SAND CREEK, head N on CR I for 3 miles (4.8 k).

$5; $8 electric.

Open May 1–Sep 30.

50 scattered, open sites. Hand pump, pit toilets, electric hookups, tables, fire rings, grills, boat ramp, pay phone.

In tall pines along Red Cedar River.

Canoe or kayak. Swim. Fish. Hike trails to see wildlife or take photos.

17-day limit. Crowded holidays.

NORTH TWIN LAKE

Chequamegon NF
(715) 748-4875
State map: 5E
Just S of WHITTLESEY, drive

W on CR M for 7 miles (11.2 k). Turn Right (N) on CR E and travel 6 miles (9.6 k). Turn Right (E) on FR 102 and proceed 2 miles (3.2 k). (Also see Spearhead Point and Westpoint.)

$5.

Open May 15–Sep 20.

6 scattered, screened sites.

Hand pump, pit toilets, tables, fire rings, boat ramp.

On lake in northern hardwood/paper birch forest.

Swim, boat, or fish. View wildlife.

14-day limit.

1500 ft (450 m)

PEPIN CITY PARK

(715) 442-2461
State map: 7B
Find park in PEPIN at WI 35 & Locust.

FREE so choose a chore.

Open May 1–Oct 15.

10 close, open sites.

Central faucet, flush toilets, tables, grills.

In grassy area with some shade 2 blocks N of Lake Pepin.

Enjoy overnight stop. Bike.

3-day limit.

PERCH LAKE

Chequamegon NF
(715) 373-2667
State map: 2D
From DRUMMOND, drive N on FR 35 for 5 miles (8 k). (Also see Delta Lake County Campground.)

$5.

Open May 1–Oct 15.

16 close, screened sites.

Hand pump, pit toilets, tables, fire rings, boat ramp.

In forest next to 72-acre lake with Rainbow Lake Wilderness nearby.

Boat or fish. Walk Virgin Pine Interpretive Trail. Hike on North Country Trail.

1200 ft (360 m)

PERCH LAKE WALK-IN

Nicolet NF (715) 528-4464
State map: 3H
From TIPLER, drive E on
WI 70 for 5 miles (8 k). Turn
Left (N) on FR 2150 and go .5 mile
(800 m) to parking area. Walk in from
.25-1 mile (400 m-1.6 k). (Also see
Chipmunk Rapids and Lauterman Lake
Walk-In.)
FREE so choose a chore.
Open All Year.
5 scattered, screened, tent sites.
Tables, fire rings.
In hardwood forest next to 51-acre lake.
Enjoy solitude. Fish. Hike (trail connects
with Lauterman National Recreation
Trail). Observe wildlife. Listen to loons.
NO water. No toilet facilities. No trash
arrangements (pack it out). 14-day limit.

PICNIC POINT

Chequamegon NF
(715) 748-4875
State map: 5E
Just S of WHITTLESEY, drive
W on CR M for 7 miles (11.2 k). Turn
Right (N) on CR E and travel 8.5 miles
(13.6 k). Turn Right (E) on FR 1563. (Also
see Westpoint and Spearhead Point.)
$5.
Open May 15-Nov 30; dry camping
allowed off-season.
3 scattered, open sites.
Hand pump, pit toilets, tables, fire rings,
boat ramp.
In northern hardwood along Mondeaux
Flowage.
Boat or fish. Hike. Watch wildlife.
14-day limit.
1500 ft (450 m)

PRASCHAK WAYSIDE

Marshfield City Parks
(715) 384-4642
State map: 6E
Locate on S side of
MARSHFIELD on WI 13 (S Roddis Ave).
$3; $4 electric.

Open May-Sep.
8 close, open sites.
Central faucet, flush toilets, electric
hookups, tables.
In small wayside area.
Enjoy overnight stop.

PRENTICE PARK

Ashland City Parks
(715) 682-7071
State map: 2D
From ASHLAND, drive W
for 1 mile (1.6 k) on US 2.
$5.
Open May 15-Oct 15.
14 scattered, open sites.
Central faucet, flush toilets, electric
hookups, tables, fire rings, boat ramp.
With artesian water, deer yard, nature
trail, and watefowl habitat.
Walk. Take photos. Fish.
650 ft (195 m)

READSTOWN TOURIST PARK

(608) 629-5672
State map: 9D
Find park at WI 131 N &
US 14 in READSTOWN.
FREE; donations requested.
Open All Year.
100 scattered, open sites.
Central faucet, flush toilets, electric
hookups, tables, grills, fire rings,
playground, ball field, pay phone.
Next to Kickapoo River.
Canoe. Bike. Walk nature trail.

RIVERSIDE MEMORIAL PARK

Blair Parks (608) 989-2517
State map: 7D
Find park in BLAIR on Park
Rd.
$4; $5 electric.
Open All Year.
24 close, open sites.
Central faucet, chemical toilets, electric
hookups, tables, boat ramp, pool.
In park next to Trempeadeau River.
Swim, boat, or fish.

SAILOR LAKE

Chequamegon NF
(715) 762-2461
State map: 3E
From FIFIELD, drive W on WI 70 for 8 miles (12.8 k). Turn Right (S) on gravel FR 139 and go 3 miles (4.8 k). (Also see Smith Rapids.)

$5.

Open May 28–Oct 25; dry camping allowed off-season.

20 scattered, screened sites.

Hand pump, pit toilets, tables, fire rings, boat ramp, shelter.

In forest next to 171-acre lake.

Swim, canoe, and fish. Hike to spot wildlife.

14-day limit. Hunting in season. ATVs in area. Crowded holidays.

1500 ft (450 m)

SAWMILL PARK

Washburn County Forests
(715) 466-2922
State map: 4C
From BIRCHWOOD, head N on CR T for 5 miles (8 k). Continue N on dirt Birchwood Fire Lane for 2.5 miles (4 k) to sign. Turn Right.

$5.

Open All Year.

26 scattered, screened, tent sites.

Hand pump, pit toilets, tables, fire rings. Next to canoe portage area within county forest among several small lakes. Canoe. Swim and fish. Hike to view wildlife. Take photos.

No vehicles allowed in forest except in park area.

SMITH RAPIDS

Chequamegon NF
(715) 762-2461
State map: 3E
From FIFIELD, drive W on WI 70 for 13 miles (20.8 k). Turn Left (N) on gravel FR 148 and continue 2 miles (3.2 k). (Also see Sailor Lake.)

$5.

Open May 28–Oct 25; dry camping allowed off-season.

13 (3 tent-only) scattered, screened sites. Hand pump, pit toilets, tables, fire rings, grills, boat ramp, shelter.

Near covered bridge on South Fork Flambeau River.

Canoe. Walk nature trail or hike farther to appreciate area. Take photos. Mountain bike.

14-day limit. Occasional horses.

SPAULDING POND

Jackson County Parks
(715) 333-5832
State map: 7D
From BLACK RIVER FALLS, drive E on WI 54 for 24 miles (38.4 k). Turn Left (S). (Also see Merlin Lambert Park.)

$5.

Open Apr–Dec; dry camping allowed off-season.

20 close, screened sites. Hand pump, pit toilets, tables, grills, fire rings.

In private setting next to pond.

Swim or fish. Walk nature trail. Spot wildlife.

21-day limit. Hunting in season.

SPEARHEAD POINT

Chequamegon NF
(715) 748-4875
State map: 5E
Just S of WHITTLESEY, head W on CR M for 7 miles (11.2 k). Turn Right (N) on CR E. Go 8.5 miles (13.6 k). Turn Right (E) on FR 1563. (Also see Eastwood, Picnic Point, Westpoint, and North Twin Lake.)

$5; $7 premium.

Open May 20–Sep 15.

27 scattered, screened sites. &

Hand pump, pit toilets, dump station, tables, fire rings, grills, boat ramp, store, rentals, pay phone.

In hardwood on Mondeaux Flowage.

Swim, boat, or fish. Hike along part of Ice Age Trail. Take photos. Attend ranger programs.

14-day limit. Occasionally crowded.

1500 ft (450 m)

▲ ▲

TWIN LAKE

Chequamegon NF
(715) 762-2461
State map: 3E
Head NW on WI 47 from
LAC DU FLAMBEAU for 2 miles (3.2 k).
Turn Left (SW) and go 2 miles (3.2 k).
Turn Right (W) on FR 142 and continue
8 miles (12.8 k). (Also see Emily Lake
and Wabasso Lake.)
$5.
Open May 28–Oct 25; dry camping
allowed off-season.
17 scattered, screened sites. &
Hand pump, pit toilets, tables, fire rings,
grills, boat ramp.
In quiet forest setting next to lake.
Swim, canoe, or fish. Walk nature trail.
Take photos. Relax.
14-day limit. Crowded holidays.

WABASSO LAKE

Chequamegon NF
(715) 762-2461
State map: 3E
Head NW on WI 47 from
LAC DU FLAMBEAU for 2 miles (3.2 k).
Turn Left (SW) and proceed 2 miles
(3.2 k). Turn Right (W) on FR 142 and
travel 3.5 miles (5.6 k). (Also see Emily
Lake and Twin Lake.)
$5.
Open May 28–Oct 25.
13 (1 tent-only) scattered, screened sites.
Hand pump, pit toilets, tables, fire rings,
grills, boat ramp.
In isolated setting on lake.
Swim, canoe, or fish. Spot wildlife.
14-day limit. Crowded holidays.
1580 ft (474 m)

WANOKA

Chequamegon NF
(715) 373-2667
State map: 2D
From IRON RIVER, drive E
on US 2 for 7 miles (11.2 k). Turn Right
(S) on FR 234.
$5.
Open May 1–Oct 15.

20 close, screened sites.
Hand pump, pit toilets, tables, fire rings.
In forest next to 15-acre lake.
Boat or fish. Explore nearby Moquah
Natural Area.
1300 ft (390 m)

WESTPOINT

Chequamegon NF
(715) 748-4875
State map: 5E
Just S of WHITTLESEY, drive
W on CR M for 7 miles (11.2 k). Turn
Right (N) on CR E and go 8.5 miles
(13.6 k). Turn Right (E) on FR 1563. (Also
see Eastwood, North Twin Lake,
Spearhead Point, and Picnic Point.)
$5.
Open May 20–Sep 15.
15 scattered, screened sites.
Hand pump, pit toilets, tables, fire rings.
Along Mondeaux Flowage in northern
hardwood.
Fish. Hike to observe wildlife. Take
photos.
14-day limit.
1500 ft (450 m)

WINDSOR DAM

Nicolet NF (715) 479-2827
State map: 3G
From EAGLE RIVER, travel E
on WI 70 for 20 miles (32 k).
Turn Right (S) on FR 2174 and proceed
3 miles (4.8 k).
FREE so choose a chore.
Open May 1–Dec 8.
8 close, open sites.
Hand pump, pit toilets, tables, fire rings.
Next to North Branch Pine River.
Canoe. Fish. Observe wildlife.
14-day limit. Hunting in season.

WOOD LAKE

Taylor County Parks
State map: 5E
From RIB LAKE, go NE on
WI 102 for 2 miles (3.2 k).
Turn Right (E) on gravel Wood Lake Rd.
Drive 3 miles (4.8 k).

▲ ▲

FREE so choose a chore.
Open May 25–Sep 5.
5 close, open sites. Hand pump, pit
toilets, tables, fire rings, boat ramp.
In undisturbed wood next to lake.
Swim, fish, or boat (no motors). Hike to
explore ecology. Spot wildlife. Take
photos.
Hunting in season.

Index

▲ ▲ ▲ ▲ ▲ ▲ ▲ ▲ ▲ ▲ ▲ ▲ ▲ ▲ ▲ ▲ ▲ ▲ ▲

Listing of all towns mentioned in directions.

▲ ▲

▲ ▲

▲ ▲

▲ ▲

▲ ▲

▲ ▲

▲ ▲